An Introduction to the Gothic Language

Ancient Language Resources

K. C. Hanson, Series Editor

A. H. Sayce
Assyrian Grammar

Samuel A. B. Mercer
Introduction to Assyrian Grammar

The Student's Concise Hebrew-English Lexicon of the Bible

Heinrich Ewald
Syntax of the Hebrew Language of the Old Testament

S. R. Driver
A Treatise on the Use of the Tenses in Hebrew

M. H. Segal
A Grammar of Mishnaic Hebrew

William B. Stevenson
Grammar of Palestinian Jewish Aramaic

Carl Brockelmann
Lexicon Syriacum

J. Payne Smith
A Compendious Syriac Dictionary

Theodor William Jennings
Lexicon to the Syriac New Testament

Eberhard Nestle
Syriac Grammar

Theodor Nöldeke
Compendius Syriac Grammar

Theodor Nöldeke
Mandaean Grammar / Mandäische Grammatik

August Dillman, Carl Bezold, and James A. Crichton
Ethiopic Grammar

William W. Goodwin
A Greek Grammar

William W. Goodwin
Syntax of the Moods and Tenses of the Greek Verb

Ernest D. Burton
Syntax of the Moods and Tenses of New Testament Greek

J. B. Smith
Greek-English Concordanc to the New Testament

W. E. Crum
A Coptic Dictionary

Thomas O. Lambdin
An Introduction to the Gothic Language

An Introduction to the Gothic Language

Thomas O. Lambdin

Wipf & Stock Publishers
Eugene, Oregon

AN INTRODUCTION TO THE GOTHIC LANGUAGE
Ancient Language Resources

Copyright © 2006 Wipf & Stock Publishers. All rights reserved. Except for brief quotations in critical publications or reviews, no part of this book may be reproduced in any manner without prior written permission from the publisher. Write: Permissions, Wipf & Stock, 199 W. 8th Ave., Suite 3, Eugene, OR 97401.

The Laser Greek, Laser Transliterator, and Laser IPA fonts used in printing this work are available from Linguists Software, Inc., PO Box 580, Edmonds, WA, 98020-0580, USA, tel (425) 775-1130

ISBN: 1-59752-394-1

Cataloging-in-Publication data:

Lambdin, Thomas Oden.
An introduction to the Gothic language / by Thomas O. Lambdin.

p. ; cm.

Ancient Language Resources

ISBN: 1-59752-394-1 (alk. paper)

1. Gothic language—Grammar. I. Title. II. Series.

PD1123 L3 2006

Manufactured in the U.S.A.

Series Foreword

The study of languages forms the foundation of any study of ancient societies. While we are dependent upon archaeology to unearth pottery, tools, buildings, and graves, it is through reading the documentary evidence that we learn the nuances of each culture—from receipts and letters to myths and legends. And the access to those documents comes only through the basic work of deciphering scripts, conjugating verbs, untangling syntax, and mastering vocabulary.

Ancient Language Resources brings together some of the most significant reference works for the study of ancient languages, including grammars, dictionaries, and related materials. While most of the volumes will be reprints of classic works, we also intend to include new publications. The linguistic circle is widely drawn, encompassing Egyptian, Sumerian, Akkadian, Ugaritic, Phoenician, Hattic, Hittite (Nesite), Hurrian, Hebrew, Aramaic, Syriac, Ethiopic, Arabic, Greek, Coptic, Latin, Mandaean, Armenian, and Gothic. It is the hope of the publishers that this will continue to encourage study of the ancient languages and keep the work of groundbreaking scholars accessible.

—K. C. Hanson
Series Editor

Preface

The present work is designed to provide a carefully graded introduction to the grammar and vocabulary of the Gothic language. The material is presented in a way that I have found very effective in my teaching of other languages over the years, with enough examples and exercise material to lead the student to a rapid and intelligent reading of the extant texts.

In addition to this purely practical goal, I have also tried to clarify, to the extent possible, the aspectual nature of the Gothic verb, a subject somewhat neglected in the textbooks currently available in English. In order to do so, it was necessary to enter into more detail than usual on the corresponding grammatical features of the underlying Greek text in regard both to the basic structure of New Testament Greek narrative and discourse and to verbal usage, especially in various participial constructions. A knowledge of Greek on the part of the student, while helpful, is not essential since all the examples are translated and adequately explained. One cannot, in my opinion, overemphasize the importance of the underlying Greek for appreciating the style of Wulfila's translation.

Because the study of Gothic is usually undertaken by students of Germanic or Indo-European philology, I have included a discussion of the historical phonology and morphology in a supplementary series of lessons whose contents parallel that of the corresponding lessons in the Grammar. My approach here has been conservative, and the few instances where I have ventured to make suggestions of my own are clearly noted as such. A brief etymology for each of the words introduced in the lesson vocabularies is also included.

The texts given include all extant portions of the four gospels together with the extant portions of Romans and First Timothy. The Gospel According to Luke has been fully glossed at the foot of each page to spare the student the loss of time in looking up words, a task on which many of us have wasted a measurable portion of our lives. The end Glossary contains the complete vocabulary of the Gothic bible with the exception of proper names and a few transliterated Greek words.

I have tried to write the kind of textbook I wish I had had at my disposal when I first studied Gothic more than fifty years ago. I hope that it will encourage others to explore this interesting and linguistically important language, especially those who wish to do so without the aid of a teacher.

Thomas O. Lambdin
Manchester, New Hampshire
October 2005

Table of Contents

Table of Contents

Abbreviations and Conventions

A	accusative
Abl	ablative
adj	adjective
adv	adverb, adverbial
Aram	Aramaic
AS	Anglo-Saxon
Av	Avestan
BSl	Balto-Slavic
cpd	compound
D	dative
d	dual
encl	enclitic
Eng	English
f	feminine
G	genitive
Ger	German
Gk	Greek
Heb	Hebrew
Hit	Hittite
IE	Proto-Indo-European
imperf	imperfective
impers	impersonal
Instr	instrumental
interrog	interrogative
irreg	irregular
Lat	Latin
Lith	Lithuanian
Loc	locative
m	masculine
MHG	Middle High German
Mk	Mark
mss	manuscripts
Mt	Matthew
N	nominative
n	neuter
neg	negative
OCSl	Old Church Slavonic
OE	Old English
OHG	Old High German
OIr	Old Irish
ON	Old Norse
OSax	Old Saxon
P	preterite
partic	participle
pass	passive
PBSl	Proto-Balto-Slavonic
perf	perfective
pers	person
PG	Proto-Germanic
pl	plural
PP	preterite-present
pp	past (passive) participle
pred	predicate
prep	preposition
pres	present
pret	preterite
pron	pronoun, pronominal
PWG	Proto-West Germanic
Russ	Russian
s	singular
sf	strong feminine
sing	singular
Skr	Sanskrit
sm	strong masculine
smn	someone
sn	strong neuter
sthg	something
subj	subjunctive
suff	suffix
sv I	strong verb, Class I etc.
V	vocative
vn	verbal noun
wv I	weak verb, Class I etc.

<	is derived from, developed from
>	became, developed into
Ø	(zero ending)
«	resulted from a merger with
»	was replaced by or merged with
→	became by replacement
[ ]	(encloses phonetic symbols)
<>	(indicates an added emendation to the text)
*	(indicates an unattested or reconstructed form)

Hirt (see Selected Bibliography)
LIV (see Selected Bibliography)
Pokorny (see Selected Bibliography)
Wright (see Selected Bibliography)
Smythe H. W. Smyth, *Greek Grammar*, revised by G. M. Messing, Cambridge, Mass., 1956.
Streitberg (see Selected Bibliography)

Introduction

I. The Goths

The Goths, or, as they called themselves, Gutþiuda,[1] were a Germanic tribe which according to their own tradition[2] originated in Scandinavia.[3] Through a series of migrations they finally settled in the area to the north and west of the Black Sea, where a substantial Gothic empire was established, with the Visigoths to the west of the Dnieper and the Ostrogoths to the east.

The Visigoths were in constant friction with the East Roman Empire during most of the fourth century. After the invasion of the Huns c. 375 they were forced to migrate into East Roman territory, where continued hostilities with the government culminated in the Visigothic invasion and conquest of Italy and the sacking of Rome under their chieftain Alaric in 410. After Alaric's death the Visigoths left Italy and moved westward into Gaul and Spain. By 480 an extensive Visigothic empire had been established embracing all of Spain and Aquitaine with the capital at Toulouse, but subsequent conflict with the Franks under Clovis I in 510 forced them to yield the Gallic territories and move the capital to Toledo. With varying degrees of success the Visigoths ruled most of Spain during the next two centuries until defeated by the Muslim Moors under Tarik ibn Ziyad in 711, when they ceased to be a viable political or military entity.

The Ostrogoths were subdued by the Huns c. 375 and remained under their rule until the death of Attila in 453. After migrating westward into the province of Pannonia, which comprised parts of modern Hungary, Austria, and Yugoslavia, they allied themselves with the East Roman Empire and chose Theodoric the Great as their king in 471. The East Roman emperor Zeno commissioned Theodoric to reconquer Italy from the Germanic usurper Odoacer.[4] This he did and set up his own Ostrogothic hegemony in Italy with its capital at Ravenna. Subsequent civil strife led the East Roman emperor Justinian I to free Italy from Ostrogothic domination. The Ostrogothic capitulation to these forces in 555 marked the end of their political power, though the cultural achievements of Theodoric's reign were not insignificant.

II. Sources of the Gothic Language

Apart from a few brief runic inscriptions, the fourth century translation of the New Testament and portions of the Old Testament into Gothic by Ulfilas (Wulfila) (c. 311-383), Bishop of the Goths in the Danube region, is the earliest known text in a Germanic language. Because of the size of the corpus and its careful transmission it provides us with a fairly comprehensive knowledge of the grammar and lexicon of the Gothic language as spoken by the Goths who at that time inhabited the provinces of Dacia and Moesia, bordering the Lower Danube to the north

[1] Attested in the fragment of a Gothic Calendar found in Codex Ambrosianus A (see below).

[2] This tradition, together with much other valuable information on the Goths, is reported in *De origine actibusque Getarum* of the 6th century historian Jordanes, himself an Ostrogoth resident in Ravenna. His work is actually an abridgement of a history of the Goths written by Flavius Magnus Aurelius Cassiodorus (485-585!), a high official under Theodoric the Great and several succeeding Gothic rulers.

[3] A Scandinavian origin for the Goths is thought by many scholars to be supported by the occurrence of their name in Gotland, an island in the Baltic Sea, and Östergötland, a district in Sweden. It must be kept in mind, however, that in speaking of the origin of the Goths we are referring to a secondary point of dispersion in the vast millennia-long migrations of the Indo-Europeans from their original homeland, a logical fiction which may never have existed as such.

[4] Odoacer was the chieftain of the Heruli, Germanic tribesmen serving as mercenaries under the West Roman emperor Romulus Augustus. The Heruli rebelled and proclaimed Odoacer their king in 476.

and south respectively in what is now Rumania and Bulgaria. The precise birthplace of Ulfilas is unknown. He was consecrated bishop in 341 and devoted the remainder of his life to the conversion and instruction of his fellow Goths, including his translation of the Scriptures into Gothic. His converts in Dacia were so persecuted by the heathen remnant under the Visigothic chieftain Athanaric that he was forced, with the permission of the East Roman emperor Constantinus, to lead them across the Danube to Moesia, a province more securely under East Roman rule. He died on a visit to Constantinople in 383.

The surviving fragments of the Gothic Bible are found in the following manuscripts, all of which originated in northern Italy during the fifth and sixth centuries. Most important of all is the

Codex Argenteus (sigillum: CA), now in the library of Upsala University after passing through many hands. This striking manuscript, written with silver and gold ink on purple parchment, originally contained all four gospels on 330 leaves, but only 187 leaves survive. Next in importance are the

Codices Ambrosiani (Ambr) in the Ambrosian Library in Milan. These include five codices:

Codex A: 95 leaves containing fragments of the Pauline epistles and of a Gothic Calendar
Codex B: 77 leaves containing fragments of the Pauline epistles
Codex C: 2 leaves containing fragments of the Gospel according to Matthew XXV-XXVII
Codex D: 3 leaves containing fragments of Nehemiah
Codex E: 8 leaves, 3 of which are in the Vatican. This codex contains the fragments of a commentary on the Gospel according to John, published by Massman in 1834 under the title *Skeireins aiwaggeljons þairh Iohannen* (A Clarification of the Gospel according to John), henceforth referred to simply as the Skeireins (Sk). Of less importance are

Codex Carolinus (Car), a palimpsest now in the library of Wolfenbüttel. Under four leaves of a copy of Isidore's *Etymologiae* it contains fragments of Romans XI-XV;

Codex Taurinensis (Taur) in Turin, 4 leaves containing fragments of Galatians and Colossians;

Codex Gissensis (Giss), originally discovered near Antinoë in Egypt, taken to Giessen but now destroyed, consisting of a single double sheet containing fragments of the Gospel according to Luke in Latin and Gothic.

As the earliest surviving Germanic language, Gothic has proven invaluable for the reconstruction not only of Proto-Germanic, but also of Proto-Indo-European. Nearly two centuries of intensive scholarship have produced a very large bibliography, which the reader may pursue through the works cited in the Selected Bibliography on p. 356 of this work. It is recommended that the reader begin with the standard reference grammars of Streitberg, Wright, and Mossé, where extensive further bibliography may be found on all aspects of the Goths and their history, on Ulfilas and the Gothic Bible, and on the Gothic language and its relevance for Germanic and Indo-European comparative philology.

III. The Germanic Languages

The languages belonging to the Germanic subfamily of Indo-European are usually divided into three distinct subgroups: (1) East Germanic, (2) North Germanic (Scandinavian), and (3) West Germanic. East Germanic is represented only by Gothic, the date and sources of which are discussed above.

The earliest form of North Germanic is called Old Norse and is attested in runic inscriptions as early as the third century; the principle source of Old Norse, however, is in the Old Icelandic literature of the period c.850-c.1250. The differentiation of Old Norse into the early phases of the modern Scandinavian languages was already well marked by c.1000. A distinction is usually made between West Norse (Norwegian and Icelandic) and East Norse (Swedish and Danish).

The West Germanic languages include the old (until c.1200), middle (c.1200-c.1500), and modern (after c.1500) stages of High German (Hochdeutsch), Low German (Plattdeutsch), English, Frisian, and Dutch. The earliest records in this group are the literary works in Anglo-Saxon dating from the end of the seventh century; the next oldest are those in Old High German from the eighth century. Old Low German is generally called Old Saxon, and Old Dutch is called Old Franconian. Frisian is the language of Friesland, a province of the Netherlands.

The division of language families and subfamilies into smaller subgroups is based on the occurrence or non-occurrence of certain distinguishing phonological and morphological features. Because the degree of importance attached to a particular feature is often a matter of subjective judgement, there is always room for scholarly disagreement on such subdivisions. A substantial group of scholars, for example, favors a bipartite division of Germanic into North Germanic, subsequently branching into Gothic and Scandinavian, and South Germanic, as given above under West Germanic. The interested reader may refer to Wright pp. 375-7 and the bibliography cited there.

IV. The Gothic alphabet

According to reliable tradition the Gothic alphabet used in the extant monuments was invented by Bishop Wulfila himself. Formally it is mostly an adaptation of the contemporary fourth century Greek uncial script represented, for example, by the famous Codex Sinaiticus, but with the necessary adjustments to the sounds of Gothic. As noted in the remarks below, there is a strong possibility that Wulfila was influenced both by the Runic *fuþark* alphabet and by the contemporary Latin alphabet, though there is little agreement on the extent of this influence. The Gothic alphabet, together with the transliteration of each letter as used in this book and the numerical value of each letter, is as follows. Note that the order of the letters is determined by their numerical value.

𐌰	𐌱	𐌲	𐌳	𐌴	𐌵	𐌶	𐌷	𐌸
a	**b**	**g**	**d**	**e**	**q**	**z**	**h**	**þ**
1	2	3	4	5	6	7	8	9
𐌹̈ 𐌹	𐌺	𐌻	𐌼	𐌽	𐌾	𐌿	𐍀	𐍁
i	**k**	**l**	**m**	**n**	**j**	**u**	**p**	--
10	20	30	40	50	60	70	80	90
𐍂	𐍃	𐍄	𐍅	𐍆	𐍇	𐍈	𐍉	𐍊
r	**s**	**t**	**w(y)**	**f**	**x**	**hw**	**o**	---
100	200	300	400	500	600	700	800	900

The sounds represented by these letters are discussed in section V below. These correspond to the sounds of the underlying Greek with the following exceptions:

(1) **q** occupies the place filled by digamma (Ϝ), phonetically [w], in the oldest Greek alphabet. Subsequent to the Attic standardization of the alphabet in the late 5th century B.C., digamma was used only to represent the number 6. The assignment of Gothic **q** to this slot seems completely arbitrary. The Gothic letter itself is formally a direct borrowing from a contemporary cursive form of Latin *q*.

(2) The use of Greek *eta* (η), phonetically [e:] or [æ:], later [i:], for Gothic **h** follows the Latin usage of this letter.

(3) **j** is arbitrarily assigned to the position of Greek ξ [ks]; the origin of the form is obscure.

(4) The symbol for 90 is *koppa* (ϙ) of the old Greek alphabet; it survived in standard Attic only as a symbol for the number 90, as in Gothic.

(5) **u** is directly borrowed from Runic, where it has the same value. Its placement in the position of Greek omicron (o) [ɔ] is arbitrary.

(6) Greek υ, phonetically [ü], later [i], represents Gothic **w** [w]. It retains its Greek value as a vowel in Greek loanwords and the transcriptions of biblical proper names, in which case we have used the transliteration y.

(7) The symbol for 900 stands in the place of the early Greek letter *sanpi* (ϡ), which had only a numerical value in the standard Greek alphabet, as in Gothic.

(8) **f** is a direct borrowing from Latin *f.* It is interesting to note that Latin *f* is formally a descendent, via Etruscan, of Greek digamma mentioned in (1) above.

(9) **hw** occupies the position of Greek ψ [ps]. Formal correspondents are unknown, and its placement in this slot seems arbitrary.

(10) **r** is closer in form to the Runic *r* than to the Greek uncial *r*. Perhaps a significant difference in pronunciation (e.g. guttural versus trilled) prompted the substitution.

When the letters are employed to designate numbers, they are so marked in the mss by a point before and after or by a stroke over the letter.

When **i** begins a syllable it is marked with a diaeresis. This is normally omitted in the transliterations of the texts when it occurs in word-initial position; thus **imma** (to him) and not **ïmma.** Its very rare occurrence elsewhere is sometimes indicated by a hyphen, as in **fra-itan** (to devour), to avoid possible misinterpretation.

V. The Sounds of Gothic

The conventional pronunciation of Gothic is inferred from three sources: (1) the way the alphabet is used in transcribing the proper names in the Greek biblical text, (2) a comparison with the phonetic inventory of other old Germanic languages, especially Old High German, Old Norse, and Old English, and (3) spelling variations within Gothic itself.

A. The consonants

The letters transcribed as **p, t, k, f, l, m, n, s, w,** and **z** represent those sounds as pronounced in English. Note that **s** is always voiceless, as in *sit, sing.*

The letter **q** represents [k^w], the initial sound of English *quick, queen.*

The letter **þ** represents [θ], the initial sound of English *thick, thin.* The transliteration symbol **þ** is taken from the Icelandic alphabet and is ultimately of Runic origin.

h was probably pronounced like the *ch* of German *Bach*, phonetically [x] or [χ], but may have been like English *h* [h] in some positions, especially initially before vowels, as in **haban** (to have), **her** (here).

hw, usually transcribed as **ƕ**, a symbol not in the fonts at our disposal, was pronounced as [hʷ] or [xʷ], that is, as [h] or [x] with simultaneous lip rounding. The possibility of confusion with **h** + **w** is minimal, since the latter occurs only at obvious morpheme boundaries, especially with the verbal prefix **þairh**-, as in **þairhwisan**.

r was probably trilled or flapped, rather than being the retroflex continuant of American English.

j represents [y] as in English *yet, year.*

The letter **g** is used in the sequences –**gg**- and –**gk**- to represent the velar nasal [ŋ]; thus **bringan** [brɪŋgɑn] (to bring), **drigkan** [drɪŋkɑn] (to drink). This is an imitation of the same convention in Greek spelling; note, for example, συγγενής [syŋgɛne:s] (kinsman) for *συν- + -γενης. Occasionally [ŋg] and [ŋk] are spelled –**ng**- and –**nk**- respectively; this spelling alternative dispels any doubt about the pronunciation of –**gg**- and –**gk**-.

The sequence **ggw** had two values: (a) [ŋgw], where –**gg**- represents [ŋg] as above; (b) [ggw], presumably a long [g] plus [w]. The second value occurs only in four word stems: **bliggw**- (to strike), **triggw**- (trustworthy), **glaggw**- (accurate) and **skuggw**- (mirror). For this second value see below, p. 231, §III(4).

The letters **b, d**, and **g** (apart from the combinations just discussed) each had three different sounds:

(1) Initially and medially when preceded by a consonant they represent the voiced stops [b], [d], and [g] of English *boy, dog,* and *go.*

(2) Medially when preceded by a vowel they represent the voiced spirants [v], [ð], and [ɣ]. [v] and [ð] are like the medial sounds in English *heaven* and *heathen* respectively. [ɣ] is the voiced counterpart of [x]; it is represented by ȝ in older linguistic works.

(3) In final position following a vowel they represent [f], [θ], and [x]. **b** and **d** is this position are usually, but by no means always, replaced with **f** and **þ** in the spelling. See Lesson I, §1.2, for a discussion of the Devoicing Rule.

(4) The letter **x** occurs frequently in the abbreviated writing **Xs** etc. for **Xristus** etc. Christ, Gk Χριστός. There are only two other occurrences of the letter, both in transcribed proper names; it was presumably pronounced as [k] or [x].

B. The vowels

I. The vowel system of Gothic is represented in spelling by the simple vowel symbols **a, e, i, o,** and **u**, from which are formed also the digraphs **ei, ai, iu,** and **au**. The conventional pronunciation of the vowels is approximately as follows:

a	[ɑ] as in *father*
ai	[ɛ] as in *let, met*
e	[e] as in French *été* or Eng *sate, bait, late* without the off-glide
i	[ɪ] as in *it, pit*
ei	[i] as in *beat, seat*
o	[o] as in French *faut,* or Eng *foe, toe* without the off-glide
au	[ɔ] as in *bought, fought*
u	[ʊ] as in *put, soot,* or [u] as in *boot, boon*

iu [iu, iw] as in *few, new, cute,* but with emphasis on the [i] element

There is no indication of vowel length in Gothic and there is no compelling reason to suppose that vowel length was structurally significant. The attribution of length to certain vowels found in most grammars of Gothic is based solely on the historical antecedents of the vowels in Proto-Germanic and Proto-Indo-European, the details of which are given in the Historical Grammar section of this textbook.

2. The vowels **e, o,** and **ei** are regularly referred to as long vowels since they can usually be traced etymologically to long vowels or diphthongs in PG or IE. The fact that **e** sometimes varies with **ei** in spelling, and **o** sometimes with **u,** suggests that both of these vowels were higher and certainly tenser than the English counterparts suggested above. Most Gothic grammars also make a distinction between short **a** [ɑ] and long **ā** [ɑ:] and between short **u** [ʊ] and long **ū** [u:] on the basis of similar etymological considerations.

3. Since the early years of Indo-European studies it has been a convention in Gothic grammars to indicate the historical distinctions between **ái** = PG **ay,* the diphthong [ɑy] as in *nice,* and **aí** = PG **i.* A third **ai,** printed with no diacritic, is allegedly found prevocalically in a few words, i.e. **saian** (to sow), **faian** (to find fault), **waian** (to blow), where it corresponds to PG **ǣ,* the [æ] of *at, sat,* but longer. And likewise for **áu** = PG **aw,* the diphthong [ɑw] as in *house,* **aú** = PG **u,* and **au** = ?PG **ō* [ō] or [ū]. We see no need to follow this convention since it implies that each of these digraphs actually had these three different pronunciations in Gothic, for which there is no evidence whatsoever.

4. The Gothic vowel system may be interpreted thus:

	Front		Central	Back	
	Tense	Lax		Tense	Lax
High	**ei**	**i**		**u**	
Mid	**e**	**ai**		**o**	**au**
Low			**a**		

5. In IE and PG, however, vowel length did have morphological significance as is evidenced by the divergent development of words containing the suffix IE **-y-/-ey-* > PG **-y-/-iy-.* In Gothic the slight differences in the resulting inflections of j-stem nouns and adjectives (see Lesson 3) and of verb with infinitives in **–jan** (see Lessons 5 and 18) are described in terms of the length of the final stem syllable before the suffix and inflectional endings. Long stem syllables include (a) all stems ending in two consonants, e.g. **hairdeis** (herdsman), **wasti** (garment); **laistjan** (to follow), **wandjan** (to turn); (b) all stems ending in a single consonant preceded by a long vowel, as defined above, or the diphthong **iu,** e.g.

e: **lekeis** (physician); **meljan** (to write), **merjan** (to preach)
ei: **sildaleikjan** (to be amazed)
o: **siponeis** (disciple); **sokjan** (to seek), **rodjan** (to speak)
iu: **þiuþjan** (to bless),

or by **au** or **ai** when these are descended from true diphthongs in PG, e.g.

au: **hauhjan** (to elevate), **gaumjan** (to notice)
ai: **hwaiteis** (wheat), **haiþi** (field); **laisjan** (to teach), **urraisjan** (to raise).

(c) polysyllabic stems (discounting prefixes), although there are very few certain examples, either verbal or nominal.[5] Words with final short stem syllables are less frequent. Short stem syllables end in a single consonant preceded by a short vowel, i.e. descended from a short vowel in PG. These include **a**, **i**, and **u**:[6]

a:	**harjis** (army), **halja** (hell); **lagjan** (to lay), **taujan** (=***tawjan**, to do)
i:	**niþjis** (kinsman), **sibja** (relationship); **bidjan** (to ask), **siujan** (=***siwjan**, to sew)
u:	**sunja** (truth); **bugjan** (to buy)

C. Spelling variations

1. (**i**, **e**, **ei**): The interchange of **e** and **ei** occurs fairly frequently, e.g. **leikeis** (physician) for **lekeis**, **ize** (relative pronoun) for **izei**. Less frequent are the interchange of **i** and **e**, e.g. **birusjos** (parents) for **berusjos**, **hweleik-** (of what sort?) for **hwileik-**, and of **ei** and **i**, as in **usdreibeina** (they drive out) for **usdribeina**, **laisaris** (teacher) for **laisareis**.

2. (**u**, **o**, **au**): The interchange of **u** and **o** is very infrequent, e.g. **supuda** (he seasoned) for **supoda**, **lauhmoni** (lightning) for **lauhmuni**. The interchange of **au** and **u**, however, is quite frequent, especially in the inflection of u-stem nouns in the singular, e.g. **sunaus** for **sunus** (son, nominative), **sunus** for **sunaus** (son; genitive), etc.

3. (**b**, **d**, **z**) and (**f**, **þ**, **s**): The interchange of **b**, **d**, **z** with **f**, **þ**, **s** respectively occurs primarily in word-final position, where the Devoicing Rule should result in **f**, **þ**, **s**. These exceptions occur frequently in Luke, and sporadically, but not rarely, elsewhere; they may be, in part, conditioned by the initial sound of the following word, i.e. **f**, **þ**, and **s** were *revoiced* before a vowel or voiced consonant.

4. There are over 70 instances in the first seven chapters of Luke, as well as numerous instances elsewhere, where the verbal ending **-þ** (3rd pers. sing. and 2nd pers. pl.) is written **-d**. About two-thirds of these are followed by an initial vowel or voiced consonant in the following word, and they may, like the preceding fluctuations, be due to this conditioning factor. It is also possible, and to the present writer more likely, that with the neutralization of the phonemic contrast between /b, d, z/ and /f, þ, s/ in final position by the application of the Devoicing Rule, the scribe was at liberty to employ either set of letters for these sounds in that position.

5. There is often an interchange of **w** and **u** within a paradigm, e.g. N **þius**, G **þiwos** (servant). This represents a contrast between the consonantal and vocalic allophones of the phoneme /w/. In general /w/ is written as **u** after **a** and **i** when it is not followed by a vowel; thus, N **þius**, G **þiwos**, D **þiwa**, A **þiu**. /w/ is otherwise written as **w**.

---

[5] The nominal suffix **–areis** is a good example of the analytical ambiguity sometimes encountered. The **–a-** of this suffix is generally assumed to be long on the basis both of its alleged origin in Latin *-ārius* and of the nominative/genitive ending **–eis** rather than **–jis**. But since all of the words in Gothic with this compound suffix are polysyllabic, **-eis** could just as well be attributed to this feature (likewise with **siponeis** above) rather than to vowel length in the preceding syllable. It is quite possible, therefore, that the **–a-** of **–areis** is a short vowel and that the suffix could be a direct descendant from IE **-or(e)y-* > PG **-ar(i)y*. The remarks on this suffix in the Historical Grammar section (pages 264 and 309) are based on the accepted view that the **–a-** is long, but the alternate view suggested here should be noted. OHG shows evidence of a long or a short vowel in this suffix: *-āri*, *-ari*, or *-eri*.

[6] All of the **–jan** verbs introduced in the lesson vocabularies belong to one of the groups enumerated here, and there is therefore no ambiguity about their inflection. Since **au** and **ai** in Gothic may also have developed from the PG short vowels **u* and **i* before **r*, **h*, and **hw*, verb stems ending in **-(u, i)(r, h, hw)-* [Gothic (**au**, **ai**)(**r**, **h**, **hw**)] would be reckoned as short, but I am not aware of any such verbs.

D. Assimilations

The final **-h** of the conjunctions **-uh** (and), **nih** (and not, nor), and **jah** (and) is frequently assimilated to a following **þ** or **s**, e.g.

wasuþþan for **wasuh þan** (there was, by the way...)
nissijai for **nih sijai** (Let it not be! God forbid!)

Assimilation of **-h** to other consonants is less frequent except for

janni for **jah ni** (and ... not)

Of the remaining sporadic assimilations and elisions of sounds, only the loss, probably in spelling only, of the **j** between **i** and a following vowel deserves special comment. This occurs in the forms of the verb *to be* which have the stem form **sij-**, e.g. **sium** for **sijum** (we are), **siai** for **sijai** (that he be), etc., and in a few other lexical items, especially the derivatives of the stems **frij-** (love) and **fij-** (hate). Other changes will be noted as required *passim.*

Lesson I

I.1 Nouns: number, case, gender, declension.

1. The Gothic noun is inflected in two numbers (singular and plural) and five cases (nominative, genitive, dative, accusative, and vocative).

2. A given noun belongs to one of three gender categories: masculine, feminine, or neuter. The gender of a noun is determined primarily from its inflectional type and only secondarily from its meaning, but nouns denoting animate beings usually have a correspondence between grammatical and natural gender.

3. Gothic nouns are subdivided into three declensions according to their stems:

(a) The **strong declension** includes those nouns whose stems originally, i.e. in Proto-Germanic (PG) and Proto-Indo-European (IE), ended in a vowel;

(b) The **weak declension** contains those nouns whose stems originally ended in *-n-*;

(c) There are several small groups of nouns whose stems originally ended in consonants other than *-n-*, usually referred to as the **consonant declension.**

For a full discussion of the historical antecedents of these types see the lessons in the Historical Grammar section corresponding to the lessons where the individual inflections are introduced.

I.2 Strong masculine nouns of the type *dags* (day).

This very large class contains nouns whose stems in PG ended in **-a-*, from IE **-o-*, and which are variously referred to as a-stem nouns or o-stem nouns. Their inflection is as follows:

	Singular	Plural
Nominative	**dags**	**dagos**
Genitive	**dagis**	**dage**
Dative	**daga**	**dagam**
Accusative	**dag**	**dagans**
Vocative	**dag**	---

As noted in the introduction, intervocalic -**b**-, -**d**-, -**g**-, and -**z**- were pronounced as voiced spirants. When these sounds come to stand after a vowel in word-final position or before word-final -**s**, they are regularly devoiced; in spelling, **b** is replaced by **f, d** by **þ**, and **z** by **s**. Devoiced **g** (phonetically χ) continues to be written as **g.**

Applications of this important rule, which we shall refer to as the Devoicing Rule, will appear frequently in our study of the nominal and adjectival paradigms. Note that the stem of a noun or adjective must be defined from a form in the paradigm where the consonants in question occur as intervocalic. For example, the nominative singular forms of **aiþs** (oath) and **hundafaþs** (centurion) do not permit a determination of the stem-final consonant, but we see from the dative singular forms **aiþa** and **hundafada** that the underlying stems are **aiþ**- and **hundafad**- respectively.

Two examples of this rule from nouns of the type **dags** are **hlaib**- (bread) and **laub**- (leaf):

N	**hlaifs**	**laufs**	The plural forms show no variation:
G	**hlaibis**	**laubis**	**hlaibos** etc., **laubos** etc.
D	**hlaiba**	**lauba**	
A	**hlaif**	**lauf**	
V	**hlaif**	**lauf**	

When the stem ends in a vowel + **-r-** or **-s-**, the final **-s** of the nominative singular is dropped. All other forms are regular:

N	**wair** (man)	**frehals** (freedom)
G	**wairis...**	**frehalsis ...**

Nouns of the type **dags** are labeled simply *sm* (strong masculine) in the vocabularies and Glossary.

I.3 The demonstrative adjective[1] *sa* (masculine).

Singular	N	**sa**	*Plural*	**þai**
	G	**þis**		**þize**
	D	**þamma**		**þaim**
	A	**þana**		**þans**

The various uses of **sa** will be dealt with as required in the following lessons. For the present lesson note that when used before an otherwise unmodified noun, **sa** has two possible functions:

(I) specifying: indicating that the noun refers to someone or something that has already been introduced into the discourse;
(2) deictic: corresponding to a true demonstrative adjective *this* or *that.*

Thus **sa þiudans** may be translated, depending on the context, as *this king, that king, the aforementioned king,* or simply *the king.* Generally the choice is between *the* and *that.*

The following examples may be considered paradigmatic when two otherwise unmodified nouns are concerned:

laubos bagmis	a tree's leaves, the[2] leaves of a tree, tree leaves
laubos þis bagmis	the leaves[2] of the (already mentioned) tree
þai laubos þis bagmis	the (already mentioned) leaves of the (already mentioned) tree

Apart from this use of **sa** there is in Gothic no overt correspondent to the English definite or indefinite article before an unmodified noun. The reader must use his common sense in translating, taking his cues from the context. The absence of the definite article is perhaps most noticeable with self-defined or one-of-a-kind nouns such as **himins** *the* sky, **winds** *the* wind, **sauil** *the* sun, and **airþa** *the* earth, and with nouns governed by the genitive of such nouns, such as **fuglos himinis** *the* birds of the sky, **liuhaþ sauilis** *the* light of the sun, **sunus Gudis** *the* son of God, or the genitive of a **sa**-determined noun, as in **laubos þis bagmis** in the above example.

---

[1]Because ***sa*** also has pronominal uses, it is generally referred to as a pronoun. This can be misleading.

[2]The English definite article with "leaves" has a generic rather than specifying function; thus there is no correspondent in Gothic.

I.4 Prepositions. Some Gothic prepositions govern a following noun in one case only; thus, for example, **du** (to), **fram** (from), and **us** (out of) are always followed by the dative case; **and** (throughout) and **undar** (under) by the accusative case. Other prepositions may govern the accusative or dative, e.g. **ana** (on, upon), **hindar** (behind, beyond). The preposition **in** is unique in that a following noun may be in the genitive, dative, or accusative case.

The meaning of a preposition is intimately bound up with the verbal context in which it is employed. These nuances in meaning will be indicated when a verb is first presented in the lesson vocabularies. For the present lesson learn the basic meanings of the following prepositions:

(a) **in** + G: (1) about, concerning; (2) on account of, because of
in + D: (1) in, on (static location); (2) in (a state or position); (3) in, at, during (a time period); (4) (motion) into, onto[3]
in + A: (motion) into, onto

(b) **du** + D: to (a person or place; after verbs of motion, speaking, giving, praying, etc.)

(c) **fram** + D: (1) by, through the agency of (often after a passive verb); (2) (motion) from (a place or person); (3) from, since (a point in time); (4) partitive after numbers, e.g. (three) of

(d) **ana** + D: (static location) on (a surface or object), in (a circumscribed area, e.g. a field)
ana + A: (motion or placing) onto (a surface), into (an area)

(e) **us** + D: (1) out of, from (place, source, origin); (2) from, since (a period of time)

There are a number of instances where prepositions are used without an object, i.e. adverbially. Attested are **du** *thereto*, **fram** *therefrom, on ahead*, and **ana** *thereon*. Note also **nehwa** (p. 7) and **faur(a)** (p. 26).

I.5 Adverbial predication. Prepositional phrases may function as the predicate in sentences with the verb *to be* (copula), the 3rd person present and preterite forms of which are

ist	(he, she, it) is, there is	**was**	(he etc.) was, there was
sind	(they) are, there are	**wesun**	(they) were, there were.

The position of these verbs in the predication (sentence or clause) is largely dependent on the syntax of the underlying Greek: the present tense forms tend to stand after the predicate, whereas the past tense forms tend to be initial or to stand between subject and predicate. For example,

Ana wiga sind.	They are on the road.
In himina ist.	He (she, it) is in the sky (or, in heaven).
Sa skalks ana akra ist.	The servant is in the field. (no particular field)
Sa skalks was ana akra.	The servant was in the field. "
Was ana þamma akra wulfs.	There was a wolf in that field.

---

[3] Contrary to the normal usage in the underlying Greek, "(motion) into, onto" may be expressed with *either* the dative *or* the accusative with prepositions like *in* and *ana*.

Lesson 1

Vocabulary I

akrs *sm* cultivated field.
þiudans *sm* king.
stains *sm* stone.
sitls *sm* nest; seat, stall.
himins *sm* heaven, the sky.
winds *sm* wind; cardinal point.
wair *sm* man, person.
bagms *sm* tree.
wigs *sm* road, path, way (lit. or fig.).
hlaifs *sm* (*G* **-bis**) bread, loaf.
fugls *sm* bird, fowl.
fisks *sm* fish.
jah *conj* and.
skalks *sm* slave, servant (= Gk δοῦλος).
asts *sm* branch.
hunds *sm* dog.
laufs *sm* (*G* **-bis**) leaf, foliage.
ligrs *sm* bed.
wulfs *sm* wolf.
hwar *interrog adv* where?

And the words introduced in the lesson: **sa** (§I.3); **in, ana, du, fram, us** (§I.4); **ist, sind, was, wesun** (§I.5).

Exercises

Translate:

A. 1. þai hlaibos
2. sa wulfs
3. sa wair
4. þai skalkos
5. þai astos
6. sa hunds
7. sa wigs
8. þai wairos
9. sa þiudans
10. sa bagms
11. þai fiskos jah þai hlaibos
12. sa þiudans jah sa skalks

B. 1. akros þiudanis
2. astos bagmis
3. fuglos himine
4. asts bagmis
5. skalks þiudanis
6. hunds þis skalkis
7. stainos þis akris
8. skalks þis wairis
9. laufs þis bagmis
10. sitls þize fugle
11. ligrs þis skalkis
12. hundos jah wulfos

C. 1. in fugle himinis
2. in þamma sitla
3. ana þamma akra
4. ana þaim bagmam
5. fram þaim wigam
6. us himina
7. du þamma þiudana
8. ana asta þis bagmis
9. ana þana akr
10. in himinans
11. in hunde jah wulfe
12. in hlaibis jah fiskis
13. du þaim wairam
14. du himinam
15. ana þamma staina
16. fram þaim bagmam
17. in wigans jah akrans
18. ana sitla þis fuglis
19. us wigam jah akram
20. us þaim stainam
21. fram þamma hunda

D. 1. Sa þiudans ana wiga ist.
2. Þai fuglos ana þaim bagmam sind.
3. Was ana þamma akra skalks.
4. Hunds þis skalkis was ana ligra.
5. Was winds us himina.
6. Sa fugls ist in þamma sitla.
7. Þai wairos sind ana þamma akra.
8. Was fugls in himina.
9. Hwar sind þai fiskos?
10. Hwar sind sa wair jah sa hunds?
11. Wesun ana þamma asta fuglos.
12. Wesun in þamma wiga stainos.

Lesson 2

2.I Neuter nouns of the type ***waurd*** (word) differ from **dags** in their inflection only in the nominative singular and accusative singular and plural. **haubid-** (head) and **diuz-** (wild beast) illustrate the Devoicing Law:

	singular	plural	singular	plural	singular	plural
N	**waurd**	**waurda**	**haubiþ**	**haubida**	**dius**	**diuza**
G	**waurdis**	**waurde**	**haubidis**	**haubide**	**diuzis**	**diuze**
D	**waurda**	**waurdam**	**haubida**	**haubidam**	**diuza**	**diuzam**
A	**waurd**	**waurda**	**haubiþ**	**haubida**	**dius**	**diuza**

2.2 The neuter inflection of the demonstrative adjective ***sa.***

	singular	plural
N	**þata**	**þo**
G	**þis**	**þize**
D	**þamma**	**þaim**
A	**þata**	**þo**

2.3 Predicate adjectives. Adjectives standing in predicate position with the verb "to be" and its equivalents (e.g. become, seem, be considered as) are in the nominative case and generally agree in number and gender with the subject of the predication. The masculine and neuter forms for the majority of adjectives are as follows:

	masculine		neuter	
stem	singular	plural	singular	plural
mikil- (large)	**mikils**	**mikilai**	**mikil**	**mikila**
leitil- (little, small)	**leitils**	**leitilai**	**leitil**	**leitila**
god- (good)	**goþs**	**godai**	**goþ**	**goda**

The remarks concerning the position of the verb "to be" given in §I.6 apply here as well. E.g.

Sa stains mikils ist.	The stone is large.
Þo waurda ubila sind.	The words are evil.
Jah þata dius was mikil.	And that beast was large.

As pointed out in §I.6, word order depends largely on the underlying Greek. Since the copula may be omitted in Greek in present general statements with adjectival predicates, we occasionally find the construction imitated in the Gothic text. E.g.

Luke I4:34 **God salt.** Salt is good. Καλὸν οὖν τὸ ἅλας.
Luke I0:2 **Asans managa iþ waurstwjans fawai.** The harvest is bountiful, but workers are few.
ὁ μὲν θερισμὸς πολύς, οἱ δὲ ἐργάται ὀλίγοι.

2.4 Further remarks on the Devoicing Rule. Although the forms obtained by the application of the Devoicing Rule are taken as the standard in Gothic grammar, the texts themselves contain innumerable exceptions. These occur especially in the Gospel of Luke, where such forms as *N* **hlaibs** (not **hlaifs**) and *A* **hlaib** (not **hlaif**) occur frequently. The standard forms will generally be used in the exercises, but when actual quotations are used there or as illustrations the spelling of the manuscripts will be followed. The adjective **god** in the above quotation is a case in point; the standard spelling is **goþ**.

2.5 Negation. The adverb **ni** is used to negate verbal and non-verbal predicates as well as other individual phrases of a sentence. **Ni ist** always combines into **nist** unless other words intervene.

2.6 Cardinal numbers. The cardinal numbers above *three* are usually undeclined, standing before or after the noun modified:

fidwor skalkos *or* **skalkos fidwor** four servants

There are insufficient attestations of numbers for complete certainty about their usage. The inflected numbers, *one* to *three*, will be dealt with later on. A few of the numbers above *three*, namely *four, nine, eleven*, and *twelve*, occur both inflected and uninflected. If inflected, the dative ending is **-im** and the Genitive is **-e**. These are, of course, plural endings. Learn the numbers given below in the vocabulary.

2.7 *Guþ*. The word **Guþ** (God) is formally a neuter noun of the type **waurd**. When referring to God, the word is always abbreviated in the manuscripts (*N* **gþ**, *G* **gþs**, *D* **gþa**); the plural **guda** is spelled out twice (John 10:34,35), where the word is used in a generic sense; the same form with the same meaning is written **gþa** in Gal 4:8. For a brief discussion of the controversy over the reading of these abbreviation see Wright, pp. 372-3. In the opinion of the present writer, the forms cited above and all related linguistic evidence point to the readings used in this textbook (*N* **Guþ**, *G* **Gudis**, *D* **Guda**, *A* **Guþ**). When referring to God, adjectival modifiers and pronominal reference are masculine singular.

Vocabulary 2

Nouns:

dags *sm* day.
dius (*G* **diuzis**) *sn* wild animal, beast.
land *sn* land, country.
Guþ *sn* God.
skip *sn* ship, boat.
jer *sn* year.
witoþ (*G* **witodis**) *sn* law; The Law of Moses.
waurd *sn* word, utterance, saying; thing, action, topic.
agis (*G* **agisis**) *sn* fear.
barn *sn* child.
akran *sn* fruit (lit. and fig.).

Adjectives:

mikil- *adj* large, great, important.
leitil- *adj* little, small, unimportant.
god- *adj* good.
hail- *adj* healthy, whole, sound.
inwind- *adj* unjust, unrighteous.
garaiht- *adj* just, righteous.
ubil- *adj* bad; evil; also used a neuter noun: evil.
siuk- *adj* sick, ill.

Other:

and *prep A* throughout, out along.
inuh, inu *prep A* without.
nehwa *prep D* near; *adv* near, nearby, nigh.
jainar *adv* there, in that place.
her *adv* here, in this place.
ni *neg adv* not; **nist** = **ni ist** (there, he) is not.

The cardinal numbers: **fidwor** (four), **fimf** (five), **saihs** (six), **sibun** (seven), **ahtau** (eight), **niun** (nine), **taihun** (ten)

Exercises

A. 1. witoþ þis landis
2. sibun wulfos
3. þata skip þis wairis
4. fidwor windos
5. agis fram himina
6. witoþ þize þiudane
7. sitlos þize waire
8. saihs jera
9. akrana þize akre
10. hlaifs þize barne
11. taihun astos
12. þo sibun waurda
13. ahtau wigos
14. dagos þis þiudanis
15. þai fimf dagos
16. niun jera jah fidwor dagos

B. 1. and þata land
2. and wigans þis landis
3. inuh witoþ
4. inuh akrana
5. in þize skipe
6. du þaim waurdam
7. in þamma jera
8. fram waurdam þis witodis
9. nehwa þamma skipa
10. us þaim landam
11. fram Guda
12. in diuze þis landis
13. ana ligra barnis
14. inuh agis
15. inuh lauf
16. us þamma daga

C. 1. Sa þiudans garaihts ist.
2. Sa akrs was mikils.
3. Þo waurda wesun ubila.
4. Þai fuglos leitilai sind.
5. Þata witoþ ubil ist.
6. Þai stainos mikilai sind.
7. Barn þis skalkis was siuk.
8. Sa fisks leitils ist.
9. Ni was jainar agis.
10. Akran þis bagmis goþ ist.
11. Þata skip mikil ist.
12. Þiudans þis landis ubils jah inwinds ist.
13. Sa hunds nist hails; siuks ist.
14. Jainar wesun diuza jah fuglos
15. Her sind fidwor skipa.
16. Guþ goþs jah garaihts ist.
17. Ni inwindai sind.
18. Þo barna haila sind; ni siuka sind.

Lesson 3

3.1 Strong feminine nouns of the type ***giba*** (gift), derived from PG ō-stems < IE ā-stems, are inflected as follows:

	Singular	Plural
N	**giba**	**gibos**
G	**gibos**	**gibo**
D	**gibai**	**gibom**
A	**giba**	**gibos**

3.2 The feminine predicate adjective has the nominative forms of **giba**: **mikila** (sing.), **mikilos** (pl.).

3.3 The feminine forms of the demonstrative adjective ***sa***:

N	**so**	**þos**
G	**þizos**	**þizo**
D	**þizai**	**þaim**
A	**þo**	**þos**

3.4 j-stem nouns. Nouns belonging to the general types **dags, waurd,** and **giba** have slight differences in their inflections if their stems end in **-j-**. It is further necessary to distinguish between nouns whose stem-final syllables are short (*CvC-j-*) and those with long stem-final syllables (*CvCC-j-* or *Cv̄C-j-*)[1]. Corresponding to the type **dags** we have **harjis** (army; *CvC-j-*) and **siponeis** (disciple; *Cv̄C-j-*):

N	sing.	**harjis**	plural	**harjos**	sing.	**siponeis**	plural	**siponjos**
G		**harjis**		**harje**		**siponeis**		**siponje**
D		**harja**		**harjam**		**siponja**		**siponjam**
A,V		**hari**		**harjans**		**siponi**		**siponjans**

The distinction between the two types of stem syllables is usually not maintained in neuter nouns. Compare the inflection of **fairguni** (mountain) with that of **waurd**:

N	**fairguni**	**fairgunja**	**gawi**	**gauja**
G	**fairgunjis**	**fairgunje**	**gaujis**	**gauje**
D	**fairgunja**	**fairgunjam**	**gauja**	**gaujam**
A	**fairguni**	**fairgunja**	**gawi**	**gauja**

Occasionally, *Gs* forms in **-eis** are found with long stem-final syllables, e.g. **andbahteis** (*G* of **andbahti,** service), beside the more common **andbahtjis.**

Feminine j-stem nouns are represented by **sunja** (truth; *CvC-j-*) and **wasti** (garment; *CvCC-j-*). **Sunja** is exactly like **giba** in its inflection (**sunja, sunjos** etc.); **wasti** differs only in the *Ns* (**wasti, wastjos** etc.). The stems

---

[1] In these formulas *C* = any consonant, *v* = any short vowel, and *v̄* = any long vowel or historically real diphthong.

of the two nouns **mawi** (young woman; *G* **maujos** etc.) and **þiwi** (female servant; *G* **þiujos**) are apparently reckoned as having long stem-final syllables; otherwise we would expect Ns ***mauja** and ***þiuja**, like **sunja** above and **niuja** below.

3.5 j-stem adjectives.

Parallel to the -**j**- stem nouns there are -**j**- stem adjectives. The distinction between short and long stem-final syllables is maintained, as can be seen from the following predicate adjective (i.e. nominative) forms (cf. **mikils, mikilai; mikil, mikila; mikila, mikilos**):

	masculine		neuter		feminine	
Stem	singular	plural	singular	plural	singular	plural
niu-j- (new)	**niujis**	**niujai**	**niwi**	**niuja**	**niuja**	**niujos**
wilþ-j- (wild)	**wilþeis**	**wilþjai**	**wilþi**	**wilþja**	**wilþi**	**wilþjos**

The short syllable forms are poorly attested. For the spelling interchange of **u** and **w** in **niujis** see Intro. §V.C.5.

3.6 Syntactic notes.

(1) Predicate adjectives modifying a subject including both natural genders are put in the neuter plural, e.g.

Wesun sa wair jah so mawi gredaga. The man and girl were hungry.

(2) As grammatical equivalents of the verb *to be*, **warþ** and **waurþun** are followed by predicate adjectives, e.g.

Sa wair warþ gaurs. The man became sad.

Vocabulary 3

Nouns:

harjis *sm* army, host.
siponeis *sm* disciple.
gawi *sn* district, region.
waldufni *sn* power, dominion, authority (over: *G*, **ana** *A*, **ufar** *D*).
sunja *sf* truth, the truth.
þiudangardi *sf* kingdom; the royal court .
þiwi *sf* (*G* **þiujos**) female servant.
laisareis *sm* teacher.
fairguni *sn* mountain.
mawi *sf* (*G* **maujos**) young woman, girl.
airþa *sf* earth, the earth, the ground.
stibna *sf* voice.
wasti *sf* garment, cloak, robe; clothes, clothing.
giba *sf* gift.

Adjectives:

gaur- *adj* sad.
hauh- *adj* high, lofty, elevated.
jugg- *adj* young.
niuj- *adj* new.
gredag- *adj* hungry.
sineig- *adj* old (not young).
fairnj- *adj* old (not new), ancient.
wilþj- *adj* wild; not cultivated.

Other:

warþ *verb* (he, she, it) became.
waurþun *verb* (they) became.
hindar *prep* (*A* if motion is implied; *D* otherwise) beyond, across, behind.
miþ *prep D* together with, accompanied by.
ufar *prep* (*A* if motion is implied; *D* otherwise) over, above.
filu *adv* very (before or after a predicate adjective); much, a lot, a great deal.

Exercises

A. 1. harjis himinis
2. waurda þis laisareis
3. gibos þize þiudane
4. diuza þize fairgunje
5. waldufni þiudanis
6. sunja þize waurde
7. siponjos þize laisarje
8. stibna laisareis
9. wasti þis barnis
10. wastjos þizos þiujos
11. þiudangardjos airþos
12. skalkos jah þiujos
13. harjos þize fidwor þiudane
14. agis þizos maujos

B. 1. hindar þaim fairgunjam
2. waldufni ufar þiudangardjom airþos
3. in sunjai
4. in sunjos þize waurde
5. miþ siponjam þis laisareis
6. and gauja þis landis
7. inuh gibos; fram þaim gibom
8. du stibnai þizos þiujos
9. fram himina ana airþa
10. hindar þaim skipam
11. in wastjo jah gibo
12. ufar þizai maujai
13. us þamma harja
14. in þiudangardjai himinis

C. 1. Jah þata agis warþ mikil filu ufar þamma landa.
2. Þai hundos wilþjai sind.
3. So mawi warþ gaura.
4. Þo fairgunja hauha sind.
5. Sa skalks was filu gredags.
6. So þiwi ni was gredaga.
7. Hwar sind skipa þis harjis?
8. Akran þize bagme filu goþ ist.
9. Wastjos þis laisareis ni niujos wesun.
10. Þos maujos juggos sind.
11. Þiudangardi Gudis ana airþai jah in himina ist.
12. Sa þiudans warþ sineigs jah siuks.
13. Sa skalks jah so þiwi waurþun gaura.
14. Þata gawi hindar þaim fairgunjam ist.
15. Þai siponjos waurþun gredagai.
16. Ni was giba fram þamma waira.
17. Þos wastjos niujos sind; fairnjos ni sind.
18. Jainar in þamma gauja was fairguni, jah þata fairguni was hauh filu.
19. Her ist harjis þis þiudanis, jah sa harjis mikils ist.
20. Jainar sind diuza, jah þo diuza mikila jah wilþja sind.
21. Wesun sa skalks jah so þiwi sineiga filu.

Lesson 4

4.1 Attributive adjectives agree in case, number, and gender with the noun they modify. There are two distinct inflections: strong and weak. In general, if a noun is determined by the demonstrative adjective **sa**, an attributive adjective has the weak inflection. Otherwise the adjective has the strong inflection. There are some exceptions to this general rule and they will be noted as required. The strong inflection of adjectives whose stems end in a consonant, e.g. **mikil-** (large, great) is as follows:

	masculine		neuter		feminine	
	singular	plural	singular	plural	singular	plural
N	**mikils**	**mikilai**	**mikil, mikilata**	**mikila**	**mikila**	**mikilos**
G	**mikilis**	**mikilaize**	**mikilis**	**mikilaize**	**mikilaizos**	**mikilaizo**
D	**mikilamma**	**mikilaim**	**mikilamma**	**mikilaim**	**mikilai**	**mikilaim**
A	**mikilana**	**mikilans**	**mikil, mikilata**	**mikila**	**mikila**	**mikilos**

The **-j-** stem adjectives require no special comment:

N	**niujis**	**niujai**	**niwi, niujata**	**niuja**	**niuja**	**niujos**
G	**niujis**	**niujaize**, etc.	**niujis**	**niujaize**, etc.	**niujaizos**	**niujaizo**, etc.
N	**wilþeis**	**wilþjai**	**wilþi, wilþjata**	**wilþja**	**wilþi**	**wilþjos**
G	**wilþeis**	**wilþjaize**, etc.	**wilþeis**	**wilþjaize**, etc.	**wilþjaizos**	**wilþjaizo**, etc.

The origin of the strong inflection, a mixture of nominal and pronominal forms, is discussed in the historical comments for the lesson. As a rule-of-thumb, the *Ns* follows the strong nouns **dags, waurd,** and **giba** (or, for **-j-** stems, **harjis, siponeis, fairguni, sunja**, and **wasti**), but the rest of the forms follow the demonstrative **sa, þata, so,** except that **þo** = **-a**, and demonstrative **-iz-** corresponds to adjectival **-aiz-** except for **þizai** = **-ai.**

The Nominative neuter forms in **-ata** are not used as predicate adjectives. When the stem ends in **-d-**, **-b-**, or **-z-**, the Devoicing Rule is applied, e.g. **frod-** (wise), masc. *N* **froþs,** *G* **frodis**; neuter *NA* **froþ**; **liub-** (beloved), masc. *N* **liufs,** *G* **liubis** etc. A few adjectives ending in **-r** preceded by a long vowel or **au** (< PG **aw*) retain the **-s** of the masc. sing. *N*, unlike the noun **wair**; thus: **gaurs** (sad), **swers** (honored), and **skeirs** (clear).

4.2 Uses of the strong inflection:

a. We have already treated the strong adjectives used as predicate adjectives. The very few exceptions to this usage will be discussed in later lessons.

b. As noted above, the strong inflection is used for attributive adjectives modifying an otherwise undetermined noun; the adjective normally follows the modified noun:

stains mikils	a large stone
skalkos managai	many servants
ana asta hauhamma	on a high branch
barna haila	healthy children
in akranis ubilis	concerning evil fruit

þiudangardi mikila	a great kingdom
wasti niuja	a new garment

c. A small but important group of determinant adjectives always occur in the strong form. These include the pronominal possessive adjectives of the first and second person (**mein-** my, **þein-** thy, **unsar-** our, **izwar-** your), the ordinal **anþar-** (second, other), the demonstrative adjective **jain-** (that, that over there), and a residual group of quantifiers (**ain-** one, **all-** all, **full-** full, **halb-** half, **ganoh-** enough, and **midj-** middle), which will be taken up individually in later lessons. Typical constructions are

laisareis unsar	our teacher
waurda laisareis unsaris	the words of our teacher
du siponjam þeinaim	to your (s.) disciples
us razna meinamma	out of my house
fram skalkam izwaraim	from your servants
ana fairgunja jainamma	on that mountain
us þiudangardjai jainai	from that kingdom

The adjective may be placed before the noun for emphasis or contrast, e.g.

Luke 14:26	**...ni mag meins siponeis wisan.**	(he) cannot be my disciple.

The demonstrative adjective **sa** may be placed before nouns determined by adjectives from this group, as in

Luke 15:24	**sa sunus meins**	that son of mine,

where a father is speaking to his other son, or

Mk 13:19	**þai dagos jainai**	those (particular) days,

in reference to the final days of the world. In Luke 5:33 Jesus is asked, "Why is it that the disciples of John (**siponjos Iohannes**) fast often... but these disciples of yours (**þai þeinai siponjos**) eat and drink?" This example combines the emphatic preposing of **þeinai** and the deictic use of **þai.**[1] But the contrast between **anþar** and **sa anþar** is simply "another" as opposed to "the other," as in

	John 18:15	**Paitrus ... jah anþar siponeis**	Peter ... and another disciple
but	John 18:61	**sa siponeis anþar**	the other disciple.

Note finally that the adjectives **unsar-**, **izwar-**, and **anþar-** do not occur with the neuter ending **-ata.**

d. The substantival use of adjectives to express collectives, e.g. *the poor, the rich, the living, the dead,* is frequent in Gothic. One may employ either **sa** plus a weak adjective (see Lesson 8) or the plain strong plural, as in Mt. 11:5, where we have a reference to **dauþai, blindai, haltai,** and **þrutsfillai** (the dead, the blind, the lame, the leprous), or

[1] These constructions employing **sa** are probably not exceptions to the rule stating that **sa**-determined nouns require weak modifying adjectives. The **sa** of **sa sunus meins,** for example, modifies the whole noun-phrase **sunus meins** and not just the noun **sunus: (sa) + (sunus meins) = sa +** N. An even more complex example is provided by Luke 1:70: **swaswe rodida þairh munþ weihaize þize fram anastodeinai aiwis praufete seinaize** (as he said through the mouth of his holy prophets from the beginning of the world), where the prepositional phrase introduced with **þize** seems to modify the whole noun-phrase **weihaize praufete seinaize,** as can be seen from the Greek original: καθὼς ἐλάλησεν διὰ στόματος τῶν ἁγίων ἀπ' αἰῶνος προφητῶν αὐτοῦ.

Mk 12:27 **Nist Guþ dauþaize, ak qiwaize.** He is not God of the dead, but of the living.

e. Strong adjectives in the singular are occasionally used as indefinite nouns, e.g. **blinds** a blind man, **frawaurts** a sinner.

4.3 Pronominal possession in the third person is expressed with the Genitive case of the corresponding personal pronoun: **is** (referring to a masc. or neuter noun: *his, its*), **izos** (referring to a fem. noun: *her, its*), **ize** (referring to a masc. or neuter noun: *their*), **izo** (referring to a fem. noun: *their*). E.g.

siponjos is	his disciples
fram barnam izos	from her children
waurda ize	their words
ahwos is	its rivers (referring, e.g., to **land**)

A preposed **sa** has the same force as with **mein-** etc. When *his, her,* or *their* refers to the subject of the sentence, the possessive adjective **sein-** is used; this belongs to group (c) above and is always inflected strong. Contrast

	Insandida siponjans seinans...	He sent his (own) disciples...
with	**Ik gasahw siponjans is...**	I saw his disciples...

Vocabulary 4

Nouns:

ahwa *sf* river; flood.
saiwala *sf* soul.
haiþi *sf* meadow, field.
asneis *sm* hired worker.
motareis *sm* tax-collector, publican.
weihs *sn* (*G* **weihsis**) village.
hrot *sn* roof.
andeis *sm* (*irreg Apl* **andins**) end.
andbahts *sm* servant (= Gk διάκονος ; cf. **skalks**, Lesson 1).

Adjectives:

frod- *adj* wise, understanding.
lagg- *adj* long.
manag- *adj* many, numerous, much.
blind- *adj* blind.
mein- *adj* my.
sein- *adj* his, her, its, their (when referring to the subject of the sentence).
anþar- *adj* other, second.
liub- *adj* dear, beloved.
diup- *adj* deep.
faw- *adj* few, a few.
halt- *adj* lame, halt.
þein- *adj* thy, your (s.).
unsar- *adj* our.
izwar- *adj* your (pl.).
jain- *adj* that (over there).

Pronouns: **is** (of him, his), **ize** (of them masc. , their), **izos** (of her, her), **izo** (of them fem., their).

Preposition: **und** *prep A* (motion) to, up to (person, place, time); **und hita, und hina dag** until now, until this day; *prep D*: for, in exchange for.

Lesson 4

Exercises

A. Translate and pluralize (e.g. I. **anþara fairgunja**):

I. anþar fairguni
2. wulfs gredags
3. ahwa diupa
4. wigs laggs
5. skalks liufs
6. siponeis froþs
7. laisareis garaihts
8. saiwala liuba
9. sa asneis
10. andbahts halts
11. hrot hauhata
12. anþar weihs
13. wair blinds
14. giba mikila
15. stains leitils
16. haiþi jaina
17. anþara wasti
18. sitls leitils
19. sa andbahts anþar
20. bagms hauhs
21. asts laggs
22. hunds wilþeis
23. so anþara giba
24. motareis sineigs

B. Translate:

I. stibna laisareis unsaris
2. saiwala þiudanis jainis
3. stainos haiþjos jainaizos
4. wigos weihsis ize
5. astos jainaize bagme
6. skalks þis motareis
7. andjos airþos
8. fiskos þizos ahwos
9. hlaifs asnje seinaize
10. waurda siponje meinaize
11. sunja witodis ize
12. diuza gaujis jainis
13. stibna þiujos þeinaizos
14. wastjos þiujos izos
15. stibnos haltaize jah blindaize
16. waurda þiudanis izwaris
17. waldufni ufar garaihtaim jah inwindaim
18. andeis þis wigis

C. Translate:

I. in saiwalai seinai
2. ana hrota meinamma
3. hindar jaina fairgunja
4. miþ siponjam þeinaim
5. fram weihsa unsaramma
6. us andbahtam is
7. und þata gawi
8. us haiþjai jainai
9. and wigans landis izwaris
10. miþ þamma motarja
11. nehwa ahwai diupai
12. hindar akr þeinana
13. inuh laisari meinana
14. fram andjam airþos
15. und andins þiudangardjos is
16. ana þo haiþja
17. in saiwalo garaihtaize
18. inuh þiujos izos
19. and fidwor windans
20. miþ laisarja ize
21. und andi himinis

D. Translate

I. Wesun ana þamma hrota managai fuglos.
2. Warþ gaurs filu in saiwalai seinai.
3. Her in þizai ahwai sind fawai fiskos.
4. Ana þamma fairgunja was weihs leitil.
5. Waurþun siponjos is filu gredagai.
6. Ahwos þis landis ni sind diupos.
7. Jainar nist hlaifs gredagaim.
8. Was wulfs mikils ana þizai haiþjai.
9. So þiwi was miþ þizai maujai und hina dag.
10. Þai asnjos wesun ana þamma skipa.
11. Laisareis ize was froþs jah garaihts.
12. Ana þamma wiga wesun blindai.
13. Hwar ist sa laisareis þeins?
14. Fairgunja is ni sind hauha.

Lesson 5

5.1 Types of verbs. Gothic verbs are divided into two large groups:

a. the seven classes of strong verbs that form their preterites by ablaut, i.e. a change in the stem vowel (as in **giba** *I give*, **gaf** *I gave*) or by reduplication with or without ablaut (as in **haita** *I call*, **haihait** *I called*; **teka** *I touch*, **taitok** *I touched*);

b. the four classes of weak verbs that form their preterites by suffixing **-d-** or **-t-** (as in **matja** *I eat*, **matida** *I ate*; **haba** *I have*, **habaida** *I had*; **bugja** *I buy*, **bauhta** *I bought*).

There are also several very small groups of irregular verbs that will require special attention as we proceed.

Verbs may be simple or compounded with prefixes, e.g. **giban, atgiban; gaggan, usgaggan.**

The basic lexical form of the verb is the infinitive, which ends in **-an** in all classes of verbs except weak verbs of class 2, where the ending is **-on.** E.g. **giban** *to give*, **arjan** *to plow*, but **laþon** *to invite*.

5.2 Verbs: inflectional categories. Verbs are inflected in two tenses (present, preterite), three moods (indicative, subjunctive or optative, imperative), two voices (active, passive), three numbers (singular, dual, plural), and three persons (first, second, third). There is one infinitive, which serves both active and passive functions, a present active participle, and a past passive (or stative) participle. A large number of verbs are also marked for aspect (perfective, imperfective).

5.3 Aspect. It is regrettable that the most controversial feature of the Gothic verb must be dealt with at the very outset of our study of the verb, but the problem of aspect is of such fundamental importance that it cannot be ignored or deferred. Aspectual distinctions in the verbal system of a given language, usually spoken of as perfective-imperfective oppositions, can be associated with several contrasting factors. The most frequent, perhaps, is the punctual-durative contrast: a punctual verb describes the occurrence of a single event as completed within a closed time period and capable of being placed in temporal sequence with events described by other perfective verbs. For example, in *He sat down, opened the book, and began to read*, the verbs *sat down, opened*, and *began* are perfective (punctual) verbs. Imperfective (durative) verbs, on the other hand, describe an action or situation as in progress, as in *I am presently studying Gothic*, where *am studying* describes an ongoing activity. Another contrast sometimes associated with the perfective-imperfective distinction is that of real *versus* habitual. Compare *The bird flew away* with *Some birds fly south in the winter*. The first sentence describes a real one-time event; the second expresses a general truth. A third possible aspectual contrast, at least with some verbs, is that of directed *versus* undirected activity. This is possibly relevant to the Gothic verb: the verbal prefixes in Gothic add directional specification to many verbs, much like the adverbs in English ***fall down, sit up, turn over***, etc., and to judge from a comparison with the underlying Greek, where aspect is clearly marked in many instances, the majority of compound verbs in Gothic tend to be used perfectively.

Many Gothic verbs, regardless of class, occur both with and without the prefix **ga-**, with little difference in their lexical meaning. There is general agreement among scholars that **ga-** marks these verbs as perfective, but there is little agreement on the extent to which a mark of aspect (or lack thereof) was a mandatory, as opposed to expressive or optional, feature of the verb. It would take us too far afield to enter into the details of this debate. In view of the extremely limited nature of the text material at our disposal, the issue cannot be resolved with any certainty. The aspectual situation in Gothic is formally closely parallelled by that of Old and Middle High German and, in part, is very similar to that of the Slavic languages.

The distinction between perfective and imperfective verbs is perhaps clearest when dealing with the preterite forms and the participles active and passive. In these forms it is possible to make positive correlations between the Gothic forms and the underlying Greek, where the aorist-imperfect contrast usually corresponds to the Gothic perfective-imperfective contrast in the past tense, e.g.

Luke 8:42	**so swalt** (imperfective)	ἀπέθνησκεν	she was dying (or: on the point of death)
Luke 8:53	(**so**) **gaswalt** (perfective)	ἀπέθανεν	she died

and similarly with the active participles, where, e.g., the present (imperfective) participles βλέπων and θεωρῶν are translated by **saihwands** (seeing, viewing, watching), and the aorist (perfective) ἰδών by **gasaihwands** (having seen).

Most simple (uncompounded) verbs in Gothic are either imperfective or aspectually neutral. There is a group of simple verbs, however, that are sometimes referred to as *lexically perfective* because of what we may call the *passive participle test*. The reasoning is as follows. With verbs that have clearly contrasting aspectual forms with **ga-** or some other prefix, the past passive participle is generally formed on the perfective verb, corresponding to the Greek aorist passive or perfect passive participle, and, much less frequently, on the imperfective verb when the meaning is clearly habitual or general. Some simple verbs, however, never have a prefixed **ga-** on the past passive participle, regardless of the real aspect of the form. These verbs, designated as lexically perfective, include **giban** (to give), **niman** (to take), **letan** (to leave, abandon), **finþan** (to learn of), **qiþan** (to say). But since there are many examples of these same verbs in clearly imperfective uses, it is better to classify these verbs as aspectually neutral or aspectually unmarked.

Anyone who wishes to insist on a rigorous aspectual system in Gothic is faced with the numerous contradictions that occur in the corpus itself. A good example is in Luke 16:6-7, where the wayward steward says to the first debtor, **Nim þus bokos jah gasitands sprauto gamelei fim tiguns** (Get your account book and, having sat down, write quickly 'fifty.'), and to the second debtor, **Nim þus bokos jah melei ahtautehund** (Get your account book and write 'eighty.'). The situational context of the imperatives **gamelei** and **melei** is obviously the same and it is well-nigh impossible to explain why one is marked as perfective with **ga-** and the other is not, except as an arbitrary stylistic feature. The Greek original has the perfective (aorist) imperative γράψον in both places.

When verbs are introduced in the lesson vocabularies, every effort will be made to point out imperfective-perfective pairs when they can be unambiguously isolated in the corpus. The numerous verbal prefixes will be taken up individually in the following lessons since they all (including **ga-**) have lexical significance in addition to their tendency to perfectivize the simple verb to which they are attached. The following guidelines should suffice for the translation, in non-subordinate clauses, of indicative verbs exhibiting formal aspectual distinctions.

Gothic:	Imperfective present (**melja**)	English: general present (I write)[1]
		present progressive (I am writing)
		habitual future (I shall write [e.g. regularly])
		future progressive (I shall be writing)
	Perfective present (**gamelja**)	simple future (I shall write)
		present perfect (I have written)

[1] Remember that the general present of a few English verbs of perception (e.g. hear, know, understand, see) is equivalent to the present progressive, which is not used with these verbs in their normal lexical meanings. Otherwise, the English general present has a habitual or gnomic force.

Imperfective preterite (**melida**)	past progressive (I was writing) past habitual (I used to write, I would regularly write I wrote [regularly]) present perfect progressive (I have been writing)
Perfective preterite (**gamelida**)	simple past (I wrote) present perfect (I have written)

The English active present perfect, past perfect (pluperfect), and future perfect have no explicit counterparts in Gothic and depend very much on the interpretation of the translator; they would ordinarily correspond to perfective verbs. There are, however, more explicit ways to express various passive perfect forms as well as the active progressive forms using the verbs **wisan** (to be) and **wairþan** (to become, get [in this sense]) with active and passive participles. This will be dealt with in a later lesson.

The imperative is used mainly for commands meant to be carried out immediately and generally corresponds to the Greek aorist imperative. Admonitions concerning general future conduct require the use of the subjunctive (optative), which will be introduced later on. Finite verbal forms other than the imperative are negated with **ni**. **Ni** appears with the imperative very rarely, usually with the sense of requesting cessation of an activity already in progress. Prohibitions otherwise are expressed by the negative of the subjunctive.

5.4 Weak verbs, Class I.

This is the largest single class of verbs in Gothic. Verbs of this class are clearly distinguished by infinitives ending in **-jan**, where **-j-** belongs to the stem,[2] and **-an** is the infinitival ending. As in the case of **j**-stem nouns and adjectives (e.g. **harjis, siponeis**), it is necessary to distinguish between verbs having short stem-final syllables (e.g. **nasjan** to save) and long stem-final syllables (e.g. **sōkjan** to seek). The paradigms of these two types differ only in four forms, where the type **nasjan** has **-ji-** and the type **sokjan** has **-ei-**. The indicative active present, preterite, and imperative are as follows:[3]

		singular	plural	singular	plural
Present	1	**nasja**	**nasjam**	**sokja**	**sokjam**
	2	**nasjis**	**nasjiþ**	**sokeis**	**sokeiþ**
	3	**nasjiþ**	**nasjand**	**sokeiþ**	**sokjand**
Imperative	2	**nasei**	**nasjiþ**	**sokei**	**sokeiþ**
Preterite	1	**nasida**	**nasidedum**	**sokida**	**sokidedum**
	2	**nasides**	**nasideduþ**	**sokides**	**sokideduþ**
	3	**nasida**	**nasidedun**	**sokida**	**sokidedun**

5.5 Subject pronouns.

Pronominal subjects of verbs are generally understood from the verb form alone, but subject pronouns may be added for emphasis or contrast. The subject pronouns are

ik	I	**weis**	we
þu	thou, you (s.)	**jus**	you (pl.)
is	he	**eis**	they (m.)
si	she	***ijos**	they (f.)
ita	it	**ija**	they (n.)

2 There is a very small group of strong verbs also having infinitives in *-jan*; these will be dealt with in good time.

3 Dual forms will be treated separately in a later lesson. We will restrict the term imperative to the imperative proper of the 2nd person; first person (cohortative) and third person (jussive) forms will be taken up later on.

The neuter plural **ija** is also used when referring back to a plural or dual subject including both natural genders. For example, in Luke 2:50, in reference to Joseph and Mary, we find **Iþ *ija* ni froþun**... but *they* did not understand.

5.6 The verb ***mag-*** (to be able, can) belongs to a special class of verbs known as preterite-present verbs, having present meaning with inherited preterite, or more accurately, perfect forms. Learn the following:

ik mag	I can	**weis magum**	we can
þu magt	you (s.) can	**jus *maguþ**	you (pl.) can
is mag	he can	**eis magun**	they (m.) can

The forms may be used absolutely or with a following infinitive.

Vocabulary 5

Verbs:

hausjan (*imperf.* and *perf.*), **gahausjan** (*perf.*) *wv 1* to hear, listen to (smn: *D*; sthg :*A*); to hear about (smn: **bi** *A*, **fram** *D*); to heed (sthg: *G*). **gahausjan** often has the added nuance of (hearing and) *understanding*.
sokjan *wv 1* to seek, look for (smn or sthg: *A*); to look for an excuse (to do sthg: inf.); to engage in a disputation (with smn: **miþ** *D*).
gairnjan *wv 1* to desire (sthg: *G*; to do sthg: inf.).
matjan (*imperf.*), **gamatjan** (*perf.*) *wv 1* to eat (sthg: *A*).
hailjan (*imperf.*), **gahailjan** (*perf.*) *wv 1* to heal, cure (smn or sthg:*A*).
fraqistjan *wv 1* to destroy (smn or sthg: *D* or, less commonly, *A*).
laisjan[4] *wv 1* to teach (smn: *A*; sthg: *A*; smn to do sthg: *A* + inf.).
merjan *wv 1* to preach, proclaim, make known (sthg: *A*).
sandjan (*imperf.* and *perf.*), **insandjan** (*perf.*) *wv 1* to send (smn: *A*; to a person or place: **du** *D*; to do sthg: inf.).
mag- *PP* (see §5.6) can, be able to (+ inf.).

Nouns:

huzd *sn* treasure.
lamb *sn* lamb.
swein *sn* pig, swine.
mel *sn* time (extent or instant)
mela *sn pl* writings, scripture, the scriptures.
haimos *sf in pl* villages, rural areas.
stols *sm* throne.
razn *sn* house.
munþs *sm* mouth.
unhaili *sn* illness, disease.

Adjectives:

unhail- *adj* ill, sick.
unled- *adj* poor, destitute.

Other:

duhwe *interrog adv* why? for what reason?
bi *prep A* about, concerning; according to; around, surrounding; at approximately (a time point), within (a time period); **bi** is also followed much less commonly by the dative in the relational and temporal meanings as well as in a number of idiomatic uses with certain verbs (e.g. take *by* the hand, strike foot *against*).

---

[4] **laisjan** is used in both aspects; there is a verb **galaisjan**, which is used in somewhat specialized contexts and does not seem to be limited to the perfective aspect.

ni ... waiht *pron phrase* nothing at all.
(ni) goþ ist ... *impers pred* it is (not) good to (+ inf.).
bi sunjai *adv phrase* in truth, in reality; really, truly, indeed.
mela lagga *adv phrase* for a long time.
manag mel *adv phrase* many a time.
us þamma mela *adv phrase* from that time on.

Exercises

A. 1. stols Gudis
2. barn liubata
3. huzda mikila
4. fimf lamba
5. sweina managa
6. munþs þis laisareis
7. razna þize motarje
8. mela ubila
9. sunja mele izwaraize
10. unhaili saiwalos þeinaizos
11. sweina jainis gaujis
12. þos haimos ize
13. unledai jah unhailai
14. mel þis þiudanis
15. sitlos þize motarje
16. haimos unsaris landis
17. bagmos haiþjos jainaizos
18. hrot raznis is
19. þo weihsa ize
20. razn þis laisareis

B. 1. nehwa razna meinamma
2. in ahwai diupai
3. bi mel jainata
4. and haimos ja weihsa unsaris gaujis
5. ana akrans jah haiþjos
6. bi witoþ ize
7. bi waurda þis laisareis
8. us munþam barne
9. hindar haimos jainos
10. bi skalk inwindana
11. du unledaim þizo haimo
12. bi mauja unhaila
13. und þos anþaros haimos
14. in þaim anþaraim raznam

C. Translate.

1. Goþ ist sokjan sunja.
2. Ni gahausidedum waiht bi þans siponjans.
3. Ni magun gahailjan þata barn.
4. Sokjand fraqistjan laisarja unsaramma.
5. Stols Gudis bi sunjai himins ist.
6. Wesun her fram dagam þiudanis jainis und hita.
7. Þu bi sunjai wig Gudis laiseis.
8. Is gairnida matjan.
9. Ni goþ ist fraqistjan witoda.
10. Hausjam waurde witodis.
11. Mela lagga is sokida þata lamb.
12. Gahausei waurda meina.
13. Jah is insandida þans siponjans seinans and wigans þis landis merjan þiudangardja Gudis.
14. Duhwe miþ motarjam matjiþ laisareis izwar?
15. Ik ni mag matjan miþ skalkam jah þiujom.
16. Jus sokideduþ filu miþ þamma laisarja jah siponjam is.
17. Weis gairnidedum hailjan siukans jah sandjan hlaif du gredagaim jah du unledaim.
18. Gamatei þana hlaif.
19. Ni magum hailjan unhailja izos.
20. In þamma gauja wesun sweina managa.
21. Ni merjam in þaim haimom.
22. Ni goþ ist razn inuh hrot.
23. Goþ ist hausjan meinaizos stibnos.
24. Is gairnida manag mel fraqistjan þamma razna.
25. Ni sokida waiht in jainamma weihsa.
26. Ni gahausja laisarja ubilamma.
27. Duhwe gairneis fraqistjan jainamma þiudana?
28. Ni wesun unledai in unsaramma weihsa.
29. Insandeiþ skalk seinana hindar þo ahwa sokjan hlaif.
30. Duhwe sokeis huzda þeina her ana airþai?
31. Merei waurda is und andins airþos.
32. Duhwe þu insandides skalk þeinana du þamma motarja?
33. Ik gairnja hlaibis.

Lesson 6

6.1 Weak nouns. As noted in Lesson 1, nouns designated as belonging to the weak declension originally had stems ending in **-n.** The **n** appears everywhere in the inflection of these nouns in Gothic except in the *Ns* and *Dpl* forms. Given below are the inflections of masculine **atta** (father), neuter **hairto** (heart), feminine **qino** (woman) and feminine **managei** (multitude):

	Masculine		Neuter	
	singular	plural	singular	plural
N	**atta**	**attans**	**hairto**	**hairtona**
G	**attins**	**attane**	**hairtins**	**hairtane**
D	**attin**	**attam**	**hairtin**	**hairtam**
A	**attan**	**attans**	**hairto**	**hairtona**

	Feminine			
	singular	plural	singular	plural
N	**qino**	**qinons**	**managei**	**manageins**
G	**qinons**	**qinono**	**manageins**	**manageino**
D	**qinon**	**qinom**	**managein**	**manageim**
A	**qinon**	**qinons**	**managein**	**manageins**

A few masculine and neuter nouns are irregular in the plural. The following irregular plural forms are attested:[1]

aba (husband)	*Gpl* **abne**, *Dpl* **abnam**
auhsa* (ox)	*Gpl* **auhsne**
wato (water)	*Dpl* **watnam**
namo (name)	*NApl* **namna**

The singular forms of **aba, wato,** and **namo** are regular; **auhsa*** is not attested in the singular.

The noun **manna** (man) is irregular:

N	**manna**	**mans, mannans**
G	**mans**	**manne**
D	**mann**	**mannam**
A	**mannan**	**mans, mannans**

6.2 Weak verbs, class I, with preterites in -t-. A small group of Class I weak verbs have irregular preterite forms in **-t-** instead of **-id-**:

---

[1] For purposes of reference all well attested members of various grammatical subgroups will be listed in the lessons that follow. Only those resumed in the lesson vocabularies will be used in the exercises.

brukjan	**bruhta**	to use
bugjan	**bauhta**	to buy
kaupatjan	**kaupasta**	to smack
þagkjan	**þahta**	to think
þugkjan	**þuhta**	to seem
waurkjan	**waurhta**	to do, work

The inflection of these preterites is exactly like that of **nasida**:

ik bauhta	**weis bauhtedum**
þu bauhtes	**jus bauhteduþ**
is bauhta	**eis bauhtedun**

6.3 The interrogative pronouns ***hwas*** (who? masc.), ***hwa*** (what? neut.), and ***hwo*** (who? fem.) are inflected as follows:

	Masculine	Neuter	Feminine
N	**hwas**	**hwa**	**hwo**
G	**hwis**	**hwis**	***hwizos**
D	**hwamma**	**hwamma**	**hwizai**
A	**hwana**	**hwa**	**hwo**

No plural forms are attested. The use of these forms as indefinite pronouns will be taken up in a later lesson; their use as interrogative pronouns is uncomplicated. E.g.

Hwana sokeiþ?	Whom do you seek?
Hwis ist þata skip?	Whose ship is that?

6.4 ***Wisan*** and ***ist***. The verb **wisan** (to be) is replaced in the present indicative by the copula (IE root *es-*); the preterite is normal:

Present:	**ik im**	**weis sijum**
	þu is	**jus sijuþ**
	is... ist	**eis... sind**
Preterite:	**ik was**	**weis wesum**
	þu wast	**jus wesuþ**
	is... was	**eis... wesun**

6.5 Some uses of the dative. In addition to the use of the dative case with certain prepositions, the following further uses should be noted:

a. Many verbs require an object in the dative corresponding to a direct object in the English translation. We have already encountered **hausjan** and **fraqistjan**; others will be met in nearly every lesson. With some verbs the dative and accusative alternate with no difference in meaning.

b. The dative of indirect object, with or without the preposition **du**, depending on the particular verb, is common with verbs of *speaking, giving, likening, seeming,* etc. Most such verbs also take a direct object in the accusative.

c. The dative case also serves as an instrumental case with a wide range of meanings. E.g.

slahan lofam	to strike (**slahan**) with the palms of the hand (**lofa**)
galukan haurdai	to close in with a door (**haurds**)
knussjan kniwam	to kneel with the knees
wopjan stibnai mikilai	to cry out in a loud voice
gawasjan wastjai	to clothe in a garment

These are the three principal adverbal uses of the dative. Other uses will be introduced later.

Vocabulary 6

Verbs:

waurkjan (*imperf.*), **gawaurkjan** (*perf.*) *wv 1* (*P* **waurhta**) do, perform (*A*); make, prepare (*A*); produce (*A*); earn as interest (*A*); to cause (smn: *A*) to do (Inf.); to make (sthg: *A*) + predicate complement (*A*).
bugjan (*imperf.* and *perf.*), **usbugjan** (*perf.*) *wv 1* (*P* **bauhta**) to buy (sthg: *A*; for a price: *D* or **us** *D*; for smn: *D*); to buy (smn: *A*) free, redeem (*A*).
frabugjan *wv 1* (*P* **frabauhta**) to sell (sthg: *A* or *D*; for a price: **in** *A*).
anakumbjan *wv 1* to recline at a meal, to dine.
daupjan (*imperf.* and *perf.*), **ufdaupjan** (*perf.*) *wv 1* to baptize, submerge, wash (smn or sthg: *A*; with: *D* or **in** *D*).
gaumjan *wv 1* to notice, see, perceive (smn or sthg: *D*).
timrjan (*imperf.* and *perf.*), **gatimrjan** (*perf.*) *wv 1* to build, construct (sthg: *A*); often used in figurative sense.

Nouns:

managei *wf* crowd, throng; the people, the masses; less commonly: a people, a nation. **managei filu** a lot (of); **manageins filu** dense crowds, many people.[2]
kas *sn* (G **kasis**) vessel, pot.
kasja *wm* potter; **Akrs Kasjins** Potter's Field.
atta *wm* father; pl. forefathers.
aiþei *wf* mother.
aba *wm* husband.
namo *sn* name; **namin** by name, named; **bi namin** (call smn) by name.
frauja *wm* lord, master; the Lord (God or Jesus).
manna *wm irreg* man, person.
skatts *sm* coin, money; usually a denarius.
waurstw *sn* work, deed, act.
wato *wn* water.
hairto *wn* heart (lit. and fig.).
qino *wf* woman, wife.
ahma *wm* spirit; **ahma weihs** the Holy Spirit; **ahmin seinamma** to himself, in his mind.

Other:

kald- *adj* cold; **kald ist** it is cold (i.e. the weather).
weih- *adj* holy.
frawaurht- *adj* sinning, sinful, wicked.
unte *conj* because.
iþ *conj* but (weak contrast).
The pronouns introduced in the lesson.

---

[2] Both **managei** and **manageins filu** may govern either singular or plural verbs and predicate adjectives.

Lesson 6

Exercises

A. Translate and convert to the genitive. E.g. (1) **attane unsaraize**, (2) **kasis niujis...**

1. attans unsarai
2. kas niwi
3. wato kald
4. jains kasja
5. qino sineiga
6. waurstwa ubila
7. hairto frawaurht
8. namo weih
9. ahma weihs
10. qino frawaurhta
11. skatts leitils
12. skatts fairneis
13. kasja unleþs
14. aba gaurs
15. manna wilþeis
16. frauja mikils
17. managei gredaga
18. aiþei meina
19. aba þeins
20. namo mikil
21. abans izo
22. aiþeins ize
23. fraujans izwarai
24. namna izwara

B. Translate and convert to past tense:

1. Ik im laisareis is.
2. Þu is aba þizos qinons.
3. Jus sijuþ siponjos þis mans.
4. Weis sijum skalkos jainis fraujins.
5. Weis sijum qinons frawaurhtos.
6. Eis sind mannans unledai jah gredagai.
7. Hwa ist namo fraujins þeinis?
8. Hwa ist namo abins izos?
9. Þiudans im landis jainis.
10. Gredags im jah gaurs.
11. Duhwe sijuþ siponjos þis laisareis?
12. Duhwe sijum in razna is?

C. Translate and pluralize as the sense permits. E.g. **miþ aiþeim unsaraim...**

1. miþ aiþein unsarai
2. und þata anþar weihs
3. ufar þata wato
4. in hairtin þis mans
5. du mann þis raznis
6. du barna þis mans
7. fram namin þis fraujins
8. miþ managein jainai
9. und þata gawi
10. du þizai qinon
11. ufar fairgunja hauhamma
12. miþ sweina wilþjamma
13. und andi airþos
14. du namin þis siponeis
15. ana abin þizos qinons

D. Translate:

1. Magt bugjan kasa in razna þis kasjins.
2. Þai skalkos jah andbahtos waurhtedun haurja (charcoal fire) unte was kald.
3. Ik bauhta fimf kasa skattam sibun.
4. Was jainar managei motarje mikila jah anþaraize, jah anakumbidedun miþ þamma laisarja jah siponjam is.
5. Sa skalks bauhta lamba jah sweina fraujin seinamma.
6. Duhwe anakumbeiþ sa laisareis izwar miþ motarjam jah frawaurhtaim?
7. Hwamma gaumideduþ in þamma weihsa? Gaumidedum razna leitilamma inuh hrot.
8. Ni mag matjan in þizos manageins.
9. Usbugei þaim barnam hlaif.
10. Jah waurhta þo managein anakumbjan du matjan þans fiskans jah þans hlaibans.
11. Wesum gredagai jah gairnidedum anakumbjan jah matjan.
12. Frabugja þata razn þeinamma abin in niun skattans.
13. Bagms goþs waurkeiþ akran goþ, iþ ubils bagms akran ubil waurkeiþ.
14. Sa skatts þeins gawaurhta sibun skattans anþarans.
15. Ni magum frabugjan þo kasa; ni unsara sind.
16. Duhwe bauhtedun jainana akr?
17. Hwa sokjand siponjos godai? Sunja sokjand.
18. Merei waurd Fraujins fram andjam airþos und andi himinis.
19. Ik daupja þo managein watin þizos ahwos, iþ is daupeiþ þo managein in ahmin weihamma.

20. Gaumida waurstwam frawaurhtaize jah warþ gaurs filu.
21. Hwa mag ik bugjan þamma skatta? Ni magt waiht bugjan.
22. Hwar gairneis timrjan razn niwi? Gatimrja razn niwi nehwa razna þis motareis.
23. Insandida siponi seinana und þos haimos du merjan þiudangardja Gudis.
24. Hwas bauhta razn þein? Sa laisareis bauhta razn mein.
25. Hwis sind þos gibos?
26. Hwo ist meina aiþei, jah hwas ist meins atta?
27. Bauhtedum fidwor fuglans jah fimf fiskans.
28. Hwamma gaumideduþ ana wiga?
29. Hwas gairneiþ fraqistjan witoda Gudis?
30. Hwamma bauhtes þans fuglans?
31. Jah eis usbauhtedun us þaim skattam þana Akr Kasjins.
32. Hwar gatimrides razn þein?
33. Hwa bauhtedun atta þeins jah aiþei þeina in weihsa jainamma? Ija bauhtedun kasa niuja ahtau.

Lesson 7

7.1 i-stem nouns. Strong nouns of the types masc. **gasts** (guest) and fem. **taikns** (sign) originally had stems ending in **-i-** in PG and IE. The singular forms of the masculine noun were assimilated to those of **dags**, but the plural forms retain some features of the PG inflection. The feminine nouns continue the PG i-stem inflection in both the singular and plural:

	masculine				feminine			
N	sing.:	**gasts**	plural:	**gasteis**	sing.:	**taikns**	plural:	**taikneis**
G		**gastis**		**gaste**		**taiknais**		**taikne**
D		**gasta**		**gastim**		**taiknai**		**taiknim**
A,V		**gast**		**gastins**		**taikn**		**taiknins**

These nouns will be labeled *sm(i)* and *sf* respectively in the lesson vocabularies and final glossary. There are no neuter nouns of this type.

7.2 The five nouns of relationship, English *father, mother, brother, sister, daughter,* constituted a special group known as **r**-stem nouns in PG. Only three of these survive in Gothic; **fadar** (father) was replaced by **atta**, and ***modar** was replaced by **aiþei**. **broþar** (brother), **swistar** (sister) and **dauhtar** (daughter) are all inflected as follows:

N	sing.:	**broþar**	plural:	**broþrjus**
G		**broþrs**		**broþre**
D		**broþr**		**broþrum**
A,V		**broþar**		**broþruns**

7.3 Third person pronouns. The full inflection of the personal pronouns of the third person, the *N* and *G* of which we have already introduced, is as follows (the third person reflexive pronoun is the same for all genders and numbers):

	he	it	she	they(m.)	they(n.)	they(f.)	reflexive
N	**is**	**ita**	**si**	**eis**	**ija**	***ijos**	---
G	**is**	**is**	**izos**	**ize**	***ize**	**izo**	**seina**
D	**imma**	**imma**	**izai**	**im**	**im**	**im**	**sis**
A	**ina**	**ita**	**ija**	**ins**	***ija**	**ijos**	**sik**

7.4 Some verb forms:

a. The past tense of the Preterite-present verb **mag-** (to be able) has the stem **maht-** and follows the weak inflection of **bauht-**:

ik	***mahta**	**weis**	**mahtedum**
þu	***mahtes**	**jus**	***mahteduþ**
is	**mahta**	**eis**	**mahtedun**

b. The preterite of the strong verb **gaggan** (to go) is irregular, based on the stem **iddj-** and inflected like a weak verb:

ik	**iddja**	**weis**	**iddjedum**
þu	**iddjes**	**jus**	**iddjeduþ**
is	**iddja**	**eis**	**iddjedun**

This preterite replaces **gaggan** in all compounds as well; e.g. **usgaggan** (to go out), preterite **usiddja.**

c. Although all of the classes of verbs will be taken up individually in subsequent lessons, it is convenient to introduce at this point a number of strong verbs to be used in the infinitive and in the present indicative. The inflexion of the present indicative of all strong verbs is the same as that of **nasjan** in Lesson 5. For example, **niman** (to take) is inflected as follow:

ik	**nima**	**weis**	**nimam**
þu	**nimis**	**jus**	**nimiþ**
is	**nimiþ**	**eis**	**nimand**

The imperative has no ending in the singular and **-iþ** in the plural: **nim, nimiþ.**

Vocabulary 7

Verbs:

andhafjan *sv 6* to answer (smn: *D* or **wiþra** *A*), say (sthg: *A*) in reply.
usgaggan *sv 7* (*P* **usiddja**) to go forth, go out (of a place: **ut us** *D*).
galeiþan *sv 1* to go, walk.
gawandjan *wv 1* intrans.: to return, go or come back; trans.: to bring (*A*) back, give (*A*) back (to: *D*); reflexive (+ **sik**) = intrans.
niman *sv 4* to take, accept, take hold of (*A*).
bigitan *sv 5* to find (*A*).
wairpan *sv 3* to throw (sthg: *D* or *A*); **stainam wairpan** to stone (smn: *A*).
saihwan; **gasaihwan** (*perf.*) *sv 5* to see; **gasaihwan** also: to see and *understand.*
sitan (*imperf.*), **gasitan** (*perf.*) *sv 5* to sit, be sitting; *perf.*: to sit down, take a seat.

Nouns:

gards *sm(i)* house; in cpds: an enclosed area, e.g. **weinagards** vineyard.
staþs *sm(i)* (*G* **stadis**) place.
taikns *sf* sign, omen.
qens *sf* wife, woman.
fiskja *wm* fisherman.
nati *sn* net.
broþar *m(r)* brother (lit. and fig.).
swistar *f(r)* sister.
dauhtar *f(r)* daughter.
marei *wf* sea, lake.
auþida *sf* wilderness, desert.
unhulþo *wf* demon, evil spirit.
haims *sf* (*G* **haimais**) village (but see Voc. 5).

Other:

dalaþ *adv* downward (motion implied); **dalaþa** *adv* down below (static position).
faur *prep A* (spatial) along; to, at or along the front or side of; (temporal) before; (general) for, on behalf of, for the benefit of; **faura** *prep D* same range of spatial and temporal meanings, but with less implication of motion in some spatial uses; because of; also used idiomatically with certain verbs, e.g. *to flee from, hide from, beware of.* **faur, faura** *adv* on ahead, in front; previously.
ut *adv* out, outward (motion implied); **uta** *adv* outside (static position).

Lesson 7

skuld ist (*impers pred*) it is right, proper, lawful (for smn: *D*; to do sthg: Inf.).
wiþra *prep A* against; opposite, on the opposite side of; (go out) to meet; (respond) to.
goþ ist (*impers pred*) it is good (to do sthg: Inf).

Exercises

A. Translate and pluralize. E.g. (1) **fraujans þize garde**

1. frauja þis gardis
2. namo meinis broþrs
3. wato þizos mareins
4. dius auþidos
5. gards þis motareis
6. taikns jainis melis
7. swistar meinaizos aiþeins
8. namo jainis stadis
9. skip þis fiskjins
10. þiwi qenais þeinaizos
11. broþar þis þiudanis
12. unhulþo jainis stadis
13. aba qinons jainaizos
14. nati þis fiskjins
15. skatts þis mans
16. qens þis fraujins
17. hairto wairis godis
18. namo þis akris
19. wasti þeinaizos dauhtrs
20. staþs þis fairgunjis
21. waurstw þizos unhulþons

B. Translate and singularize. E.g. (1) **ana asta hauhamma**

1. ana astam hauhaim
2. du mannam seinaize garde
3. wiþra þans anþarans broþruns
4. miþ kasam þize kasjane
5. faur fiskjans þize stade
6. us natjam þize fiskjane
7. wiþra waurda dauhtre þeinaizo
8. und andins þizo mareino
9. fram taiknim himine
10. du dauhtrum þize asnje
11. faur swistruns unsaros
12. bi mela jaina
13. wiþra harjans mikilans
14. faur þans attans jah þos aiþeins
15. ut us seinaim gardim
16. faur manageins gredagos
17. bi taiknins jainos
18. in wulfe þizos auþidos
19. wiþra gardins þize manne
20. faur þo mela
21. bi *watna þizo ahwo

C. Replace the nominal phrases in B with the appropriate third person pronoun. E.g. (1) **ana im**

D. Give the singular of the phrases in Exercise C. E.g. (1) **ana imma**

E. Translate the following and replace the direct object of the verbs with the appropriate pronoun. E.g. (1) **Sa laisareis nimiþ ina miþ sis.**

1. Sa laisareis nimiþ þana siponi miþ sis.
2. Ni mahtedun bigitan barn sein.
3. Sa fiskja usbauhta natja niun.
4. Ni mahta bigitan qen meina.
5. Hwas nimiþ jainos wastjos?
6. Frabauhtedum gard unsarana.
7. Hwas gatimrida þans gardins?
8. Hwas ufdaupida swistar þeina?
9. Þo barna wairpand stainans.
10. Weis gasaihwam taiknins managos.
11. Ni goþ ist niman þana hlaif.
12. Duhwe ni gaumides þamma skipa?
13. Ni magum andhafjan laisarja unsaramma.
14. Ik gawaurhta þo barna gasitan faur marein.
15. Ik gawandja þans skattans þamma motarja.
16. Sa fiskja ni mahta wairpan sein nati.
17. Ni mahteduþ bigitan wato jah hlaif.
18. Hwas waurhta kasa in jainamma weihsa?
19. Ni skuld ist im matjan þana fisk.
20. Hwar usbauhteduþ þos wastjos?

F. Translate:

1. Ni goþ ist galeiþan and jainans wigans.
2. Þai motarjos nimand skattans unsarans.
3. Ni mahtedun bigitan barna seina jah gawandidedun sik du garda seinamma inuh ija.
4. Duhwe usiddjeduþ ut us jainamma stada?

5. Is gawandida sik gaurs du garda seinamma.
6. Ni mahtedun stainam wairpan jaina qinon.
7. Jah is ni mahta galeiþan faur marein in þizos manageins.
8. So unhulþo usiddja us þamma waira.
9. Wesum ana hauhamma fairgunja jah mahtedum gasaihwan ahwa lagga dalaþa.
10. Weis sijum in garda jah so managei ist uta.
11. Ni was laisareis froþs jah siponjos is ni wesun mannans garaihtai.
12. Ni skuld ist im galeiþan in gardins manne ubilaize.
13. Ni goþ ist niman hlaif barne jah wairpan hundam.
14. Is usiddja ana auþida jah jainar gadaupida manageins in namin Gudis.
15. Sitam her mela lagga jah wairpam stainans leitilans in ahwa.
16. Gaumida swistr þis fiskjins ana þamma wiga.
17. Is mag niman siponjans seinans miþ sis.
18. Weis magum galeiþan jainar jah anakumbjan miþ im.
19. Goþ ist sitan faur marein jah saihwan þo skipa.
20. Frabauhtedun imma fidwor natja in skattans auhtau.
21. Gawaurhta broþar seinana galeiþan in haiþi sokjan þata lamb.
22. Sa þiudans usiddja miþ harja seinamma wiþra þana anþarana þiudan.
23. Is gawaurhta waurstwa goda manageim þis landis.

Lesson 8

8.1 The weak inflection of adjectives follows exactly that of the weak nouns of the corresponding gender, thus like masculine **atta**, feminine **qino**, neuter **hairto**.

	Masculine		Neuter		Feminine	
	Singular	Plural	Singular	Plural	Singular	Plural
N	**mikila**	**mikilans**	**mikilo**	**mikilona**	**mikilo**	**mikilons**
G	**mikilins**	**mikilane**	**mikilins**	**mikilane**	**mikilons**	**mikilono**
D	**mikilin**	**mikilam**	**mikilin**	**mikilam**	**mikilon**	**mikilom**
A	**mikilan**	**mikilans**	**mikilo**	**mikilona**	**mikilon**	**mikilons**

And likewise **niuja, niujins** etc.; **wilþja, wilþjins** etc.

8.2 The uses of the weak inflection of adjectives:

a. When a noun is determined with **sa**, any attributive modifiers follow the weak inflection, e.g.

	þiudans sa mikila	the great king
Lk 2:26	**fram ahmin þamma weihin**	by the Holy Spirit
Mk 2:22	**wein þata niujo**	the new wine
Mk 5:7	**Gudis þis hauhistins**	of the Highest God

Less commonly, **sa** and the adjective may precede the noun:

Eph 6:21	**sa liuba broþar**	the beloved brother

It should be noted that occurrences of both of these constructions are relatively rare with simple adjectives (as opposed to participles). Our exercises constructed on these models are to be viewed primarily as drill on the forms of the weak inflection, although there is no doubt about the authenticity of these constructions.

The evidence, again sparse, for attributive modifiers added to nouns determined by one of the determinant adjectives in §4.2c is ambiguous. Contrast

	Mt 27:60	**in niujamma seinamma hlaiwa**	in his own new tomb
	Lk I:72	**triggwos weihaizos seinaizos**	(of) his holy covenant
with	Mk I:11	**þu is sunus meins sa liuba**	you are my beloved son

Sa with an adjective alone functions as a nominal phrase: *the one who is..., that which is...*, or similarly.

þai gredagans	the hungry, those who are hungry
þo niujona	the new ones
so siuko	the sick person (f.)
sa frawaurhta	the sinner, the sinful one

b. There is a special group of restrictive adjectives which are always inflected weak. These include **sama** (same), **silba** (self), ordinal numerical adjectives (except **anþar**), a few adjectives ending in **-um-** (an old superlative ending), and all adjectives in the comparative degree. All of these will be dealt with individually in later lessons.

c. The active participle of the verb always follows the weak inflection. See details below.

d. In the few attested instances of adjectives in the vocative the weak inflection seems to be preferred, as in

John 17:11 **atta weiha** O Holy Father

but contrast the strong form **bauþs** in

Mk 9:25 **þu ahma, þu unrodjands jah bauþs** you deaf and dumb spirit

e. On the occasional use of the weak inflection on predicate adjectives, e.g.

Lk 1:42 **þiuþido þu in qinom jah þiuþido akran qiþaus þeinis**
blessed are you among women and blessed is the fruit of your womb

see the discussion on the weak adjective in Historical Grammar Lesson 8.

8.3 The active participle of verbs of all types is formed by adding **-d-** to the **-an** or **-on** of the infinitive, e.g.

merjan	to preach	**merjand-**	preaching
qiman	to come	**qimand-**	coming
saihwan	to see	**saihwand-**	seeing

The active participle is always inflected like a weak adjective, regardless of its syntactic function. There are two divergences, however, from the inflection of ordinary adjectives:

(1) In the masculine *Ns*, **-s** alternates with **-a** with no distinction in meaning: **sa qimands** or **sa qimanda** (the one who is coming).

(2) The weak feminine inflection of the participle follows that of **managei**, not that of **qino**: thus **merjandei, merjandeins,** etc.

As a reflection of the underlying Greek constructions, the active participle is ubiquitous in the narrative style of the Gothic gospels and corresponds to the Greek present (imperfective) and aorist (perfective) active, middle, or middle deponent participles. Two of the most frequent uses of the active participles are as subject and object complements.

(1) As a subject complement, the participle agrees in number, gender, and case with the subject of the clause. Study the following examples from the many in the first few chapters of Luke.

(a) Lk 1:35 **jah andhafjands** (ἀποκριθείς) **sa aggilus qaþ du izai**
and the angel, answering, said to her

(b) Lk 1:22 **usgaggands** (ἐξελθών) **þan ni mahta du im rodjan**
but having emerged, he was not able to speak to them

(c) Lk 1:28 **jah galeiþands** (εἰσελθών) **inn sa aggilus du izai qaþ**
and having entered, the angel said to her

(d) Lk 1:39 **usstandandei** (ἀναστᾶσα) **þan Mariam in þaim dagam iddja...**
having arisen then in those days, Mary went

(e) Lk 1:63 **iþ is sokjands** (αἰτήσας) **spilda nam...**
but he, having requested a writing tablet, took (it)...

(f) Lk 2:16 **qemun sniumjandans** (σπεύσαντες) they came hastening

(g) Lk 2:45 **jah ni bigitandona** (μὴ εὑρόντες) **ina gawandidedun sik... sokjandona** (ἀναζητοῦντες) **ina**
and not having found him, they returned... looking for him

(h) Lk 2:48 **jah gasaihwandans** (ἰδόντες) **ina sildaleikidedun**
and having seen him, they were astonished

(i) Lk 3:3 **jah qam ... merjands** (κηρύσσων) **daupein idreigos**
and he came ... preaching the baptism of repentance

These translations are literal, preserving the participles in English. In actual practice, however, other translation models are preferable:

(1) When the participle stands before the main verb, translate it and the main verb as two coordinated verbs. Thus, e.g. (a) the angel answered and said, (c) the angel entered and said to her, (d) Mary arose and went.

(2) Or, if the sense requires it, translate the participle as a temporal clause; e.g. (b) but when he came out, he was unable to speak to them, (g) and when they could not find him, they returned ...

Both of these models preserve the essential feature of the Greek construction: a perfective (i.e. aorist) participle indicating a completed punctual act prior to the act expressed by the main verb. Strict accuracy requires us to note that certain verbs of speaking and of manner are used idiomatically in this construction, where logically, as in (a), the answering and the speaking are essentially the same thing, or as in (f) below, the hastening describes the manner of coming. For this reason this participial usage is sometimes classified as adverbial, e.g. *by-way-of-answering* he said. In the great majority of cases, however, two consecutive punctual acts are described and the translation models given above are adequate.

When the participle follows the main verb, like **sokjandona** in (g) or **merjands** in (i), it usually translates a Greek imperfective (present) participle and indicates a continuous action or state concomitant with the action of the main verb. The participle **sniumjandans** in (f) corresponds to a Greek aorist participle and is best taken as adverbial, as mentioned just above.

(2) As an object complement, agreeing in number, gender, and case with the direct object of a verb. E.g.

Lk 2:46 **bigetun ina in alh sitandan** (καθεζόμενον) **in midjaim laisarjam jah hausjandan** (ἀκούοντα) **im jah fraihnandan** (ἐπερωτῶντα) **ins**
they found him in the temple sitting in the midst of the teachers and listening to them and questioning them

Lk 5:27 **gasahw motari, namin Laiwwi, sitandan** (καθήμενον) **ana motastada**
he saw a tax-collector by the name of Levi sitting at (his) customs house

Mk 1:16	**gasahw Seimonu jah Andraian ... wairpandans** (ἀμφιβάλλοντας) **nati in marein** he saw Simon and Andreas ... casting a net into the sea

The participles in this construction generally translate Greek imperfective participles and describe the state or the activity being engaged in by the direct object. As the examples show, translation with the English active participle is quite adequate.

8.4 *all- (all):* pronoun and adjective.

(a) As an adjective, **all-** is always inflected strong and agrees in case, number, and gender with the noun modified. With a singular noun **all-** usually corresponds to *all of the, the whole;* with a plural noun, to *all, all the, all those.* Note that the demonstrative **sa** is used only when the noun refers to something already mentioned in the discourse. The corresponding Greek construction always has the definite article. E.g.

Lk 1:10	**alls hiuhma**	the whole crowd	πᾶν τὸ πλῆθος
Lk 1:75	**allans dagans unsarans**	all our days	πάσαις ταῖς ἡμέραις ἡμῶν
Lk 2:10	**allai managein**	to all the people	παντὶ τῷ λαῷ
Lk 2:1	**allana midjungard**	the whole world	πᾶσαν τὴν οἰκουμένην
Lk 7:1	**alla þo waurda seina**	all those words of his	πάντα τὰ ῥήματα αὐτοῦ

(b) Used as a neuter singular pronoun, **all** (or **allata**) has the meaning *everything;* the masculine plural **allai** as a pronoun signifies *everybody:*

Lk 4:7	**wairþiþ þein all**	everything will be yours	πᾶσα
Lk 2:3	**iddjedun allai**	everybody came	πάντες
Lk 2:39	**ustauhun allata**	they completed everything	πάντα

(c) Used as a neuter singular pronoun, **all** followed by a noun in the genitive plural generally corresponds to English *each, every.* Note the corresponding Greek: πᾶς + singular noun, with agreement in case.

Lk 3:5	**all fairgunje**	every mountain	πᾶν ὄρος
Lk 3:6	**all leike**	every living person (lit. body, flesh)	πᾶσα σάρξ
Lk 5:17	**us allamma haimo**	from every village	ἐκ πάσης κώμης
Lk 4:4	**all waurde Gudis**	every word of God	παντὶ ῥήματι θεοῦ
Lk 4:13	**all fraistubnjo**	every temptation	πάντα πειρασμόν

Vocabulary 8

Verbs:

afletan *sv 7* to leave, abandon, forsake, divorce (all with *A* direct object); to forgive (smn: *D;* a sin or debt: *A*).
laistjan *wv 1* to follow (smn: *A*, **afar** *D*); to pursue, seek after (sthg: *A*).
rodjan *wv 1* to speak, talk; to say (sthg: *A;* to smn: *D*, **du** *D*).
sildaleikjan *wv 1* to be amazed, astonished (at: **ana** *D*, **bi** *A*, **in** *G;* rarely *A* alone).
wairþan *sv 3* to become, take place, happen; used with most adjectives to describe the attainment of a state, thus functioning as the perfective counterpart to **wisan** to be: e.g. **sad- wairþan** to get full, **swikunþ- wairþan** to become known. **warþ** and **waurþun** (Lesson 2) are the 3rd person preterite forms of this verb.

Lesson 8

Nouns:

frawaurhts *sf* sin.
mahts *sf* might, power; usually in pl.: mighty deed(s).
mizdo *wf* reward, compensation, pay.
waurstwja *wm* worker, laborer.
bloma *wm* flower.
gahugds *sf* thoughts, thinking, the mind.
ansts *sf* favor, grace.
andwairþi *sn* presence.

Adjectives:

triggw- *adj* trustworthy, reliable, faithful.
untriggw- *adj* untrustworthy etc.
swikunþ- *adj* known, manifest, revealed.
swinþ- *adj* strong, healthy.
mahteig- *adj* mighty, powerful; capable, able, strong enough (to do: inf.); possible.
dauþ- *adj* dead.
sad- *adj* full, sated.
fulgin- *adj* hidden, secret.
hweit- *adj* white.
wairþ- *adj* worthy (to do: inf.; of: *G*).

Other:

all- *adj* and *pron* See §8.4 above.
afar *prep A* after (temporal); *prep D* following, behind

Exercises

A. Translate and convert to the genitive case. E.g. (1) the great reward; **mizdons þizos mikilons**

1. mizdo so mikilo
2. þiudans sa mahteiga
3. gahugds so ubilo
4. sa triggwa waurstwja
5. wastjos þos hweitons
6. mahteis þos managons
7. siponeis sa wairþa
8. akran þata godo
9. bloma sa hweita
10. dagos þai kaldans
11. ansts so mikilo
12. land þata godo
13. andbahts sa untriggwa
14. þos fulginons mizdons
15. jera þo ubilona
16. asnjos þai triggwans
17. skalkos þai wairþans
18. witoþ þata swikunþo
19. skip þata hweito
20. waurstwja sa swinþa
21. blomans þai leitilans
22. frawaurhteis þos swikunþons
23. razna þo fairnjona
24. ansteis þo swikunþons

B. Convert the expressions in A to the indeterminate or indefinite form by omitting the demonstrative adjective. Give the genitive form as well. E.g. (1) **mizdo mikila**, a great reward; *G* **mizdons mikilaizos.**

C. Translate the following and convert to the determined form. E.g. (1)concerning a hidden treasure, **bi huzd þata fulgino.**

1. bi huzd fulgin
2. nehwa stola mikilamma
3. afar laisarja godamma
4. inuh mizdon swikunþa
5. faur mauja siuka
6. fram managein sadai
7. ana staþ fulginana
8. and wigans laggans
9. du sweinam seinaim managaim
10. wiþra þiudan mahteigana
11. und haimos anþaros
12. afar mannam frawaurhtaim
13. bi lamb dauþ
14. nehwa razna leitilamma
15. in taiknim swikunþaim
16. du qenai seinai gaurai
17. fram fiskjam managaim
18. faur waurstwjan triggwana
19. us natja mikilamma
20. wiþra waurda ubila
21. in auþidai mikilai
22. afar mel ubil
23. ana skipa niujamma
24. bi agis swikunþ

D. Translate.

1. allos frawaurhteis unsaros
2. allai blomans seinai
3. allos ansteis Gudis unsaris
4. alla gahugds þize manne
5. allai waurstwjans þis stadis
6. alla diuza þizos auþidos
7. alla waurda witodis
8. allai þai inwindans
9. allai þai siukans
10. all mizdono
11. all blomane
12. alla airþa
13. all ahwo jah all fairgunje
14. alla jera jainis þiudanis
15. alla razna weihsis ize
16. all mareino
17. allos unhulþons
18. alla jaina sweina

E. Prefix the preposition **du** to each of the expressions in Ex. D. E.g. (1) **du allaim frawaurhtim unsaraim.**

F. Translate.

1. Hwas mag afletan allos frawaurhtins unsaros?
2. Sokjand anstins þos mikilons fram þamma þiudana.
3. Hwa rodides du managein þizai gredagon?
4. Allai þai mannans sildaleikidedun in waurde þis laisareis.
5. Hwas afletiþ barna seina jah qen seina jah laisteiþ afar laisarja þamma garaihtin?
6. Þai gredagans sadai wairþand.
7. Mizdo þize garaihtane mikila wairþiþ.
8. Ana hwamma sildaleikeis? Sildaleikja ana þaim taiknim.
9. Is rodida im bi waurda witodis.
10. Goþ ist afletan gahugd þo ubilon jah laistjan sunja.
11. Afar hwamma laistjam? Laisteiþ afar þamma godin laisarja.
12. Alla þo fulginona wairþand swikunþa.
13. Gawaurkeiþ mahteins managos in þaim dagam.
14. Rodida im in þize fulginane jah þize swikunþane.
15. Ni skuld ist imma afletan qen seina.
16. Du hwamma rodeis? Rodja du siponja is þamma frodin.
17. Ni mahtedum hailjan þans siukans.
18. Ik rodida du im bi skalk þana untriggwan.
19. Ni mahtedun afletan allata.
20. Gaumidedun taiknai þizai niujon jah sildaleikidedun.

G. Translate.

1. Gahausjandans alla þo waurda sildaleikidedun jah ni mahtedun rodjan waiht.
2. Þu bigitis ina sitandan in þamma garda.
3. Anakumbjandans weis matidedum jah rodidedum mela lagga bi mahtins laisareis unsaris.
4. Usiddja und allos haimos þis landis merjands þiudangardja Gudis.
5. Galeiþam and allans wigans merjandans jah hailjandans þans siukans.
6. Gaumidedum izai sitandein miþ þaim anþaraim qinom.
7. Was in auþidai daupjands þans frawaurhtans ahmin weihamma.
8. Fraqistjam raznam þaim fairnjam jah gatimrjam niuja.
9. Bigitam þans fiskjans sitandans in skipa ize faur marein.
10. So siuko insandida þiuja seina sokjan aban seinana.
11. Nimands þans skattans usiddja us þamma stada jah gawandida sik in weihs sein.
12. Gahausjandans waurda is þai fiskjans afletand allata jah laistjand afar imma.
13. Gasitandei laisida barna seina bi fuglans himinis jah blomans haiþjos.
14. Ni bigitandei aban seinana gawandida sik du swistr seinai.
15. Andhafjands im rodida du im bi witoþ Gudis jah þiudangardja himinis.

Lesson 9

9.1 u-stem nouns. Strong nouns of the types masc. **sunus** (son) and fem. **handus** (hand) preserve much of the IE u-stem inflection from which they are derived. There is no difference between the inflection of the masculine noun and that of the feminine:

	masculine				feminine			
N	sing.	**sunus**	pl.	**sunjus**	sing.	**handus**	pl.	**handjus**
G		**sunaus**		**suniwe**		**handaus**		**handiwe**
D		**sunau**		**sunum**		**handau**		**handum**
A, V		**sunu**		**sununs**		**handu**		**handuns**

Nouns of this type constitute a relatively small group. There was also a still smaller group of neuter u-stem nouns in IE and PG, but only a few isolated forms survive in our Gothic corpus. Note in particular **faihu** (property, wealth), the attested forms of which are *NA sing.* **faihu,** *Ds* **faihau. Faihu** also appears as the first element of several compounds, e.g. **faihufrik-** (greedy for property or wealth).

9.2 The numbers *ain-* (one), *twai* (two), and **þreis* (three) are fully inflected, agreeing in number, gender, and case with the counted noun. **ain-** is always inflected as a strong adjective; **twai** is like the plural of the strong adjective except for the *Gpl* **twaddje**; and ***þreis** resembles the plural of i-stem nouns like **gasteis** and **ansteis**, again excepting the *Gpl* **þrije**. The neuter forms of ***þreis** have no nominal counterpart. The attested forms are as follows:

	m.	n.	f.	m.	n.	f.	m.	n.	f.
N	**ains**	**ain**	**aina**	**twai**	**twa**	**twos**	***þreis**	**þrija**	***þreis**
G	**ainis**	**ainis**	**ainaizos**	**twaddje**	**twaddje**	--	**þrije**	**þrije**	--
D	**ainamma**	**ainamma**	**ainai**	**twaim**	**twaim**	**twaim**	**þrim**	**þrim**	--
A	**ainana**	**ain**	**aina**	**twans**	**twa**	**twos**	**þrins**	**þrija**	**þrins**

In addition to their normal adjectival use, the numbers may be construed as substantives and followed by the genitive plural in a partitive sense:

twans siponje seinaize	two of his disciples
ains ize	one of them

The number **ain-** has two special uses:

a. With a singular noun, in the sense *some, a certain*:

Mt 26:69	**aina þiwi**	a certain maidservant
Mt 9:18	**reiks ains**	a certain leading citizen

b. With a singular or plural noun, in the sense *only, alone,* often after **niba** (except):

Mk 2:26	**niba ainaim gudjam**	except for the priests alone

Lk 18:19	**niba ains Guþ**	except God alone
Mt 5:46	**þans frijondans izwis ainans**	only those who love you
Jn 6:22	**ainai siponjos is**	only his disciples

9.3 *sums* (some): adjective and pronoun.

(1) **sum-** may be used as a strong adjective in the sense *some, a certain.* E.g.

Lk 14:16	**manna sums**	a certain man
Lk 15:8	**suma qino**	a certain woman
Lk 7:41	**dulgahaitjin sumamma**	to a certain creditor

(2) The noun may be omitted, forcing a pronominal interpretation on **sum-**. E.g.

Mk 4:7	**sum gadraus**	some (seed: **fraiw**, n.) fell
Lk 9:57	**qaþ sums du imma**	a certain person said to him

(3) Quite frequently **sum-** is used as a pronoun with the partitive genitive plural:

Lk 8:49	**sums manne**	a certain one of the men, a certain man
Lk 6:2	**sumai Fareisaie**	certain (ones of the) Pharisees
Lk 7:2	**hundafade sumis skalks**	the servant of a certain (one of the) centurion(s)

9.4 The past (passive) participle (abbreviated p.p.) is an adjective describing the state resulting from the action of the verb. The past participle of transitive verbs is passive in voice, e.g. **giban-** *given,* **numan-** *taken,* **gahausid-** *heard.* For intransitive verbs the participle is a stative (resultative) adjective, e.g. **usgaggan-** *(having) gone out,* **gaquman-** *(having) assembled.* With those verbs exhibiting imperfective-perfective pairs, a distinction in meaning can be made, e.g. ***hausid-** *being heard* versus **gahausid-** *having been heard,* but there are too few contrasting examples to allow a determination on the consistency of this distinction. Most attested past participles are formed from perfective verbs or from verbs where the lexical distinction between the two aspects is not present. The form of the past participle depends on the verbal class of the verb and will be dealt in the appropriate lesson; for weak verbs, class I, the stem of the past participle is the same as that of the preterite, including the verbs with preterites in **-t-**; thus **merida** *he preached,* **merid-** *having been preached,* **insandida** *he sent,* **insandid-** *having been sent;* **frabauhta** *he sold,* **frabauht-** *having been sold.* Keep the devoicing rule in mind.

The past participle may be used as an attributive or complementary adjective following the general rules for strong and weak inflection. E.g.

Lk 7:29	**ufdaupidai daupeinai Johannis**	having been baptized with the baptism of John
Lk 10:23	**gawandiþs du siponjam seinaim ... qaþ**	having turned to his disciples, he said

When used predicatively with **wisan** or **wairþan,** the past participle expresses various tenses of the passive. Study the following examples:

Lk 1:19	**insandiþs im** (ἀπεστάλην) **rodjan du þus**	I have been sent to speak to you
Lk 1:13	**andhausida ist** (εἰσηκούσθη) **bida þeina**	your prayer has been heard
Lk 4:16	**þarei was fodiþs** (ἦν τεθραμμένος)	where he had been reared (**fodjan**: to rear)
Lk 8:29	**bundans was** (πολλοῖς γὰρ χρόνοις... ἐδεσμεῖτο) **eisarnabandjom**	for many times ... he had been bound (**bindan**: to bind) in iron fetters

	draibiþs was (ἠλαύνετο) **fram þamma unhulþin ana auþidos** he had been driven (**draibjan**: to drive) by that evil spirit into the wild lands
Lk 9:32	**Paitrus jah þai miþ imma wesun kauridai** (ἦσαν βεβαρημένοι) **slepa** Peter and those with him had been (or: were) weighed down (**kaurjan**: to weigh down) with sleep
Lk 8:37	**agisa mikilamma dishabaidai wesun** (συνείχοντο) they had been (or: were) seized (**dishaban**: to seize) with a great fear
Lk 16:1	**sa frawrohiþs warþ** (διεβλήθη) **du imma** charges were brought (**frawrohjan**: to bring charges) against him (the steward) before him (the master) [lit., he was charged to him]
Lk 17:14	**gahrainidai waurþun** (ἐκαθαρίσθησαν) they were cleansed, became cleansed (**gahrainjan**: to cleanse).

In general the past participle with the present tense of **wisan** corresponds to the English present perfect passive, and with the past tense to the preterite passive or past perfect (pluperfect) passive. The used of **wairþan** instead of **wisan** seems to place an emphasis on the process (fientic) rather than the achieved state. Note that the agent with a passive verb is introduced with the preposition **fram.**

9.5 Substantivized participles.

Both present and past participles may be used substantively with the demonstrative **sa-**:

Lk 3:11	**sa habands twos paidos**	he who has two tunics
Lk 2:18	**allai þai gahausjandans**	all those who heard
Lk 9:27	**sumai þize her standandane**	some of those standing here
Lk 4:18	**þans gamalwidans hairtin**	those oppressed of heart
Lk 2:18	**bi þo rodidona fram þaim hairdjam du im**	about those things said to them by the herdsmen
Lk 8:34	**þata waurþano**	that which had happened

When phrases of this type are added to a noun as a modifier, we have the equivalent of a relative clause:

Lk 1:19	**ik im Gabriel sa standands in andwairþja Gudis** I am Gabriel who stands in the presence of God
Lk 19:38	**sa qimanda þiudans in namin Fraujins** the king who is coming in the name of the Lord
Lk 9:32	**þans twans wairans þans miþstandandans imma** the two men who were standing with him
Lk 2:15	**waurd þata waurþano** the thing that has taken place

Occasionally one encounters substantivized expressions like

Lk 8:13	**þai ana þamma staina**	the ones on the rock
Lk 8:45	**þai miþ imma**	those with him

where a prepositional phrase or other adverbial element occurs without the expected participle of **wisan** or the like.

9.6 Final remarks on *sa*.

The use of **sa** as a simple demonstrative pronoun offers no particular problems. When referring to persons or things already mentioned in a given context, **sa** is virtually equivalent to a personal pronoun, only occasionally requiring a more emphatic translation such as *that person, that one.* The neuter form is especially frequent in its use as a general referent, like English *this* and *that* in *when he heard **that**..., I have done **this**....*

Vocabulary 9

Verbs:

manwjan (*imperf.* and *perf.*), **gamanwjan** (*perf.*) *wv 1* to prepare, make ready.
taujan (*imperf.*), **gataujan** (*perf.*) *wv 1* intrans.: to do, act, behave (toward: *D*); trans.: to do, perform, produce (*A*).
þiuþjan (*imperf.* and *perf.*), **gaþiuþjan** (*perf.* [rare]) to bless (smn: *A* or *D*).
lagjan (*imperf.* and *perf.*), **galagjan** (*perf.*) *wv 1* to put, place, lay (*A*; on: **ana** *A*; in: **in** *A*).
meljan (*imperf.*), **gameljan** (*perf.*) *wv 1* to write, set forth in writing; **þata gamelido** Scripture.

Nouns:

hairdeis *sm* herdsman, shepherd.
sunus *sm* son.
magus *sm* boy, servant.
faihu *sn* property, wealth.
taihswo *wf* right hand, right side; **af** or **in** **taihswon** on the right (of: *G*).
hleidumei *wf* left hand, left side; **af** or **in** **hleidumein** on the left (of: *G*).
boka *sf sing.:* letter of the alphabet; *pl.:* writing, a written document, letter.
þiuþ *sn* good, goodness, blessing; **unþiuþ** *sn* evil.
dauþus *sm* death.
wulþus *sm* glory, splendor.
handus *sf* hand.
bida *sf* prayer.
sabbatus *sm* (*Gpl* **-e**, *Dpl* **-im**) the sabbath; pl. also used in singular sense.
sabbato *m* (uninflected)the sabbath; **sabbato dags** idem.
Sunus Mans The Son of Man, a contemporary Messianic term used frequently by Jesus in reference to himself.

Other:

af *prep D* from, from out of, away from.
uf *prep A* (motion implied, e.g. to put, lay, set sthg) under, into subjection under; *D* (static, e.g. situated) under, subject to, during reign of.
ufta *adv* often.
samaleiko *adv* likewise, in the same way.
ains, twai, þreis, sums as given above in the lesson.

Exercises

A. Translate and convert to the accusative. E. g. (1) two potters; **twans kasjans**

1. twai kasjans
2. twa kasa niuja
3. all meinata faihu
4. þreis sunjus
5. seinos twos handjus
6. aina seinaizo handiwe
7. twai þize hairdje
8. allos saiwalos unsaros
9. twai magjus juggai
10. ains laisareis sineigs
11. þrija skipa leitila
12. twai þize blomane
13. dauþus allis manne
14. wulþus Fraujins unsaris
15. all þiuþe jah all unþiuþe

B. Translate and use after the preposition **fram**. E. g. (1) a certain laborer; **fram sumamma waurstwjin**

1. sums waurstwja
2. sums kasjane
3. suma mawi
4. sum fairgunje
5. suma hairtona
6. sumos ansteis
7. suma stibna
8. sums siponje
9. suma qinono
10. suma þiujo

C. Translate and convert to the corresponding plural form of the pluperfect. E. g. (1) the vessel has been fashioned; **gawaurhta wesun þo kasa** (the vessels had been fashioned).

1. gawaurht ist þata kas
2. rodiþ ist þata waurd
3. ufdaupida ist so qino
4. gatimriþs ist sa gards
5. insandiþs im
6. gahausida ist þeina bida
7. frabauht ist þata skip
8. gawandiþs ist sa skalks
9. fraqistiþ ist razn is
10. gahailiþs im
11. þiuþida is þu
12. galagida ist ansts is ana ins
13. gameliþ ist þein namo
14. gatawida ist so mahts

D. Translate.

1. þo rodidona bi þata fram jainaim hairdjam
2. saiwala so fraqistido fram frawaurhtim
3. sunja so laistido fram allaim frodaim mannam
4. gards sa gatimrida ana fairgunja hauhamma
5. þai afletandans qenins seinos jah barna seina jah laistjandans afar þamma laisarja
6. þo gatawidona in sabbato daga
7. þai daupidans watin jah þai daupidans ahmin weihamma
8. þai siukans þai galagidans ana wiga
9. siponjos þai gamanwidans fram laisarja þamma frodin
10. sa hausjands waurda meina jah taujands þo
11. sa insandida us himina fram Guda
12. wigs sa gamanwida Fraujin unsaramma
13. magus sa insandida fram fraujin is
14. þai anakumbjandans miþ imma in garda þis motareis
15. þai usdaupidans fram þamma weihin
16. þo bauhtona jah frabauhtona in stada jainamma
17. þai sildaleikjandans bi alla seina waurda
18. natja þo manwidona fram þaim fiskjam
19. þai taujandans þiuþ anþaraim mannam
20. mahteis þos gatawidons fram þamma garaihtin laisarja

E. Translate

1. Jus bigitiþ in þamma stada twa skipa gamanwida faur mannans izwarans.
2. Wesun þai fiskjans in skipa seinamma manwjandans natja seina.
3. Gamelida sind alla þo rodidona bi ina fram siponjam is in bokom mikilaim.
4. Hwas gasitiþ in taihswon þeinai jah hwas in hleidumein?
5. Nimands sa skalks þos bokos gawandida þos du fraujin seinamma.
6. Þu bigitis magu þana siukan galagidana ana ligra in razna jainamma.
7. In daga jainamma weis gasaihwam Fraujan unsarana sitandan wulþau in taihswon Gudis Attins.
8. Þiuþidai þai waurkjandans waurstwa goda jah taujandans waurda witodis Gudis.
9. Gahausjandeins waurda is usiddjedun unhulþons managos af þamma siukin jah is warþ gahailiþs.
10. Samaleiko þai taujandans ubil fraqistjand saiwalos seinos.
11. Gahausjands bi dauþu attins seinis warþ gaurs filu jah ni mahta matjan waiht.
12. Insandja im bokos þos weihons þairh sunu meinana þana galeiþandan in weihs sein in sabbato daga.
13. Ni magum galeiþan af þamma weihsa in sabbato dagam.
14. Is waurhta þans mannans meljan namna seina ana bokom jainaim.
15. Ik gaumida þrim wastjom hweitaim galagidaim ana airþai faur razna jainamma.

Lesson 10

10.1 Weak verbs, Class 3. Verbs of this type, represented by **haban** (to have), are inflected as follows in the indicative active:

	Singular	Plural		Singular	Plural
Present:	**haba**	**habam**	Preterite:	**habaida**	**habaidedum**
	habais	**habaiþ**		**habaides**	**habaideduþ**
	habaiþ	**haband**		**habaida**	**habaidedun**

Imperative: sing. **habai**, pl. **habaiþ**
Present (active) participle: **haband-**
Past (passive, stative) participle: **habaid-**

There are two verbs, **bauan** (to dwell) and **trauan** (to trust), whose stems end in the vowel **-au-**, which is uniformly spelled **-au-** and does not alternate with **-aw-** as we have seen in the noun inflections, e.g. **mawi, maujos. bauan** is further irregular in having the 3rd pers. sing. present **bauiþ** instead of ***bauaiþ**; the remaining forms of the active present are not attested except for the 1st pers. sing. **baua** (I dwell). Following is a list of all verbs belonging to this class:[1]

(ga)ainan	isolate	**jiukan**	contend	**slawan**	bec. still
aistan	honor	**(ga)kunnan**	recognize	**(and)staurran**	murmur against
arman	pity	**leikan**	please	**sweran**	honor
bauan	dwell	**liban**	live	**þahan**	bec. silent
faian (?)	find fault	**liugan**	marry	**(ga)þarban**	be in want of
fastan	fast; keep	**maurnan**	mourn	**(ga)þiwan**	enslave
fijan	hate	**munan**	think, intend	**þulan**	bear, endure
(ga)geigan	gain	**reiran**	tremble	**trauan**	trust
haban	have	**saurgan**	grieve	**weihan**	consecrate
hahan	hang	**sifan**	rejoice	**witan**	observe
hatan	hate	**(ana)silan**	bec. silent		
hweilan	rest, cease	**skaman**	shame		

10.2 The remaining nominal inflections. Various remnants, so to speak, of the IE consonantal inflections, corresponding generally to the Third Declensions of Latin and Greek, have survived in Gothic and are best taken up as a single group. The inflections of **frijonds** (masc., friend) and **baurgs** (fem., city) should be learned since they represent groups of fairly frequent nouns.

N	sing.	**frijonds**	pl.	**frijonds**	sing.	**baurgs**	pl. **baurgs**
G		**frijondis**		**frijonde**		**baurgs**	**baurge**
D		**frijond**		**frijondam**		**baurg**	**baurgim**
A,V		**frijond**		**frijonds**		**baurg**	**baurgs**

These two types are designated simply as *m* and *f* in the glossaries. Nouns of the type **frijonds** should not be confused with the substantivized participles (e.g. **sa frijonda** the one who loves, from the verb **frijon** *wv 2* to love). The stems of the two forms were originally identical, but the split into nominal versus adjectival inflection had already taken place in PG.

---

[1] The lists of verbs given here and in subsequent lessons do not include compound verbs unless the simple verb is not attested. These lists are for reference only; the more frequent verbs and their compounds will be introduced in the lesson vocabularies.

The forms given below for the nouns **reiks** (masc., leader), **menoþs** (masc. month), ***weitwoþs** (masc. witness) and **fon** (neuter, singular only, fire) are the only attested forms for these words and are given here for reference.

N	sing.	**reiks**	pl. **reiks**	sing.	**menoþs**	pl.	**menoþs**
G		**reikis**	**reike**		--		--
D		**reik**	**reikam**		**menoþ**		**menoþum**
A		--	--		--		**menoþs**

N	sing.	**fon**	sing.	***weitwoþs**	pl. **-weitwoþs**
G		**funins**		--	**weitwode**
D		**funin**		--	--
A		**fon**		**weitwod**	--

10.3 Verbal nouns.

Several of the verbal classes have a particular nominal form associated with them which we shall refer to simply as the verbal noun, usually abstract but sometimes also concrete in meaning. Because of our limited corpus not all of these are well documented. Weak verbs, class I, quite consistently have a related verbal noun ending in **-eins**, inflected like **taikns** *sf* but with *Npl* **-os**, *Gpl* **-o**. Note the following:

hausjan, gahausjan to hear	**hauseins** *sf* sense of hearing; report, word, teaching **gahauseins** *sf* idem
sokjan to seek	**sokeins** *sf* inquiry; the point under inquiry
fraqistjan to destroy	**fraqisteins** *sf* waste, destruction
laisjan to teach	**laiseins** *sf* teaching; doctrine
daupjan to baptize	**daupeins** *sf* baptism
timrjan to build	**timreins** *sf* building, construction; discipline, training
gatimrjan to build (*perf.*)	**gatimreins** *sf* construction, edification (fig.)
þiuþjan to bless	**þiuþeins** *sf* goodness, blessing
gameljan to write (*perf.*)	**gameleins** *sf* writing
nasjan to save, redeem	**naseins** *sf* salvation

The verb **gairnjan** has the verbal noun **gairnei** *wf* (desire, longing), inflected like **managei**.

Weak verbs, class 3, introduced in the present lesson, have an associated verbal noun ending in **-ains** inflected throughout like **taikns** *sf.* Attested are

liban to live	**libains** *sf* life
bauan to dwell	**bauains** *sf* abode, habitation
leikan to please	**leikains** *sf* liking, pleasure
trauan to trust	**trauains** *sf* trust
þahan to be silent	**þahains** *sf* silence

For the verbs **fijan** (to hate) and **fastan** (to keep, to fast) we have **fiaþwa** *sf* (hatred, enmity) and **fastubni** *sn* (fasting, observance) respectively. For the noun-forming suffix **-ubni** see §22.3.

10.4 Verbal prefixes.

As noted in §5.3, many of the verbal prefixes in Gothic add a directional specification to the basic meaning of the verb and by so doing tend to produce a perfective verb. The verbal prefixes themselves are mostly identical in form with corresponding prepositions and bear approximately the same primary meanings. Although the development of secondary extended meanings makes predictions of meanings only approximate, it is nevertheless helpful to examine the more important of these prefixes individually.[2] We begin with the prefix **at-** and its corresponding preposition:

> **at** *prep D* (static) at, by, with, near; with verbs of acquisition: from, of (e.g. **finþan at** to find out from); *D* (motion) to, up to; *D* or *A* (temporal) at the time of.

As a verbal prefix **at-** specifies that the action of the verb is directed toward or reaches a specific goal. This is clearest with verbs of movement and conveyance:

satjan to set, place	**atsatjan** to present (sthg) to, to offer to
tekan to touch, be in contact with	**attekan** to (reach out and) touch
walwjan to roll	**atwalwjan** to roll (sthg) up to

Noteworthy is the added nuance of *downward, down toward (the speaker or point of reference)*, as in

wairpan to throw	**atwairpan** to throw down (into)
gaggan to go, walk	**atgaggan** to approach, approach and enter; to come down to
steigan to go, step, mount	**atsteigan** to descend, come down to

When the simple verb describes a state rather than an action, **at-** adds the notion of proximity or contiguity, as in

standan to stand	**atstandan** to stand near(by)
wisan to be	**atwisan** to be at hand

For extended meanings of **at-** verbs note especially

saihwan to see	**atsaihwan** to occupy oneself with; to beware of
giban to give	**atgiban** to hand to, hand over to, > (*sensu malo*) to betray.

10.5 The personal pronouns of the first and second person, singular and plural, are inflected as follows:

	singular	plural	singular	plural
N	**ik**	**weis**	**þu**	**jus**
G	**meina**	**unsara**	**þeina**	**izwara**
D	**mis**	**uns, unsis**	**þus**	**izwis**
A	**mik**	**uns, unsis**	**þuk**	**izwis.**

Vocabulary 10

Verbs:

haban *wv 3* to have, own, possess (*A*); + inf.: to intend (to do), be destined (to do); **ubil haban** to be ill; **unhulþon haban** to be possessed by an evil spirit.

fijan *wv 3* to hate (*A*).

þahan *wv 3* (*imperf.*) to be or remain silent; **gaþahan** *wv 3* (*perf.*) to fall silent.

[2] The reader should keep in mind the limited nature of our corpus. Many of the verbs discussed in this and similar paragraphs later on occur only a few times each, making a completely clear contrast between the simplex and compound verb impossible.

witan *wv 3* to guard, keep an eye on (*D*); **sabbate daga witan** to keep (observe) the sabbath.
fastan *wv 3* intrans.: to fast; trans.: (1) to keep, observe (laws, rules, etc.: *A*); (2) to bind, make secure (e.g. with fetters); (3) to guard, preserve. **gafastan** *wv 3* (*perf.*) transitive meanings of **fastan** only.
liban *wv 3* to live, be alive; **liban taujan** to make live, give life to; **liban bi** to live on (sthg: *A*)
nasjan *wv 1* (*imperf.* and *perf.*) to save, rescue, redeem (*A*). **ganasjan** *wv 1* (*perf.*) idem; also: to heal.
atgaggan *sv 7* (P **atiddja**) to approach, come or go up (to: **du** *D*); to enter (a place: **in** *A*); ± **dalaþ**: to descend, go or come down (to, onto: **ana** *A*; from, off of: **af** *D*).
nehwjan *wv 1* (*imperf.*), **atnehwjan** *wv 1* (*perf.*) ± **sik** to come near (to smn: *D*), be nigh, be at hand (unto: **und** *A*, **ana** *A*); the preterite often has present meaning, e.g. **atnehwida sik** is at hand.
atsaihwan *sv 5* to beware (of: **faura** *D*); to take care (not to do sthg: **ni** + inf.); to busy oneself with, give one's attention to (*G*, **du** *D*).
giban *sv 5* (*imperf.* and *perf.*) to give (sthg: *A*; to: *D*); **giban** *D* **matjan** to feed, give food to; **giban wulþu** to glorify, praise (*D*).
atgiban *sv 5* (*perf.*) to give or hand (sthg: *A*; to: *D*), to give (*A*) back to (*D*); to hand over to, deliver up (for punishment or imprisonment). **atgiban-** (*p.p.*) **ist** (**mis**) (I) have been given the ability to, (I) have been entrusted with.

Nouns:

frijonds *m* friend.
nasjands *m* saviour, redeemer.
baurgs *f* city.
bokareis *sm* scribe, scholar.
kunþi *sn* knowledge.
laun *sn* reward, compensation, pay.
fijands *m* enemy, detractor.
alhs *f* temple; the Temple in Jerusalem.
fon *n* fire.
armaio *wf* mercy, pity; alms-giving, charity.
idreiga *sf* repentance.
bandi *sf* bond, fetter.

And the verbal nouns as given in §10.3: **naseins, daupeins, laiseins, fraqisteins, libains,** and **þahains.**

Other:

aiþþau *conj* or, or otherwise
þatei *conj* that, the fact that, the statement that (e.g. **gameliþ ist þatei**... it has been written that...)
at *prep* see §10.4.

Exercises

A. Translate. Pluralize the expression and use it with the preposition **du**. E.g. (1) the death of my enemy; **du dauþau fijande meinaize.**

1. dauþus fijandis meinis
2. alhs gudis ize
3. bida qinons jainaizos
4. namo þis bokareis
5. hrot alhs jainaizos
6. armaio fraujins unsaris
7. laun þis frawaurhtins
8. kunþi þis bokareis
9. þahains þis laisareis
10. armaions is þos mikilons
11. laiseins laisareis þis niujins
12. daupeins broþrs þeinis
13. fraqisteins þizos alhs
14. managei þizos baurgs
15. kunþi þis frodins
16. frijonds þis þiudanis
17. idreiga skalkis þis frawaurhtins
18. þahains þizos manageins
19. fraqisteins þizos baurgs
20. kunþi laiseinais anþaraizos
21. libains andbahtis þis garaihtins
22. laiseins siponeis þis anþaris

B. Translate

1. faur gardins baurgs ize
2. wiþra maht þizo unhulþono
3. afar dag dauþaus is
4. fram frawaurhtai du idreigai
5. du naseinai saiwalo unsaraizo
6. at stola Gudis in himina
7. af þizai ubilon baurg
8. afar laiseinim ubilaim
9. and allans wigans þizos baurgs
10. uf hrota meinis gardis
11. du allaim þaim taiknim
12. af taihswon nasjandis unsaris
13. at þamma ubilin þiudana
14. und allos haimos jah baurgs þis gaujis
15. fram dauþau du libainai
16. faur dauhtruns broþrs is
17. uf wulþau himinis
18. at alh þizai mikilon
19. bi waurda þize hairdje
20. ana stada þizos auþidos

C. Translate

1. sa fijanda þuk
2. sa habands unhulþon
3. þo fastaidona fram unsis
4. þai ganasidans fram armaion Gudis
5. þai gaþahandans
6. sa habands atgiban laisari unsarana
7. sa witands siponjam is
8. sa gafastaida bandjom
9. þai libandans libain ubila
10. sa habands ubil
11. sa gibands skattans þaim magum
12. sa atgagganda in alh
13. sa fijaida fram broþrum is
14. þai atnehwjandans sik ana baurg unsarai
15. þai witandans sabbate daga
16. þai libandans in frawaurhtai
17. sa atgaggands dalaþ af fairgunja
18. þai fastandans witoþ
19. sa atsaihwands du bokom jah gamelein
20. sa gibanda wulþu Guda

D. Translate.

1. Manweiþ izwis, unte atnehwida sik ana izwis þiudangardi Gudis.
2. Atgiban ist imma waldufni haban ufar unhulþom.
3. Jah is merida in allaim þaim baurgim bi daupein jah idreiga.
4. Atsaihwiþ armaion izwara ni taujan in andwairþja manne du saihwan im,[3] aiþþau laun ni habaiþ fram attin izwaramma.
5. Gahausjands is stibnos ize atiddja ut du im jah rodida du im.
6. Duhwe siponjos is fastand ufta jah bidos taujand, iþ þai þeinai siponjos matjand jah ni fastand?
7. Ahma ist sa taujands unsis liban.
8. Sa atgibands mik atnehwida.
9. Atiddja fon mikil us himina jah fraqistida þos twos baurgs frawaurhtons.
10. Atgiban ist mis hailjan þans siukans jah þans habandans unhulþons.
11. Duhwe atsaihwis laiseino þizo ubilono?
12. Atgaggandei in alh Fraujins gatawida bidos managos in sunaus seinis þis siukins.
13. Aiþei is gafastida alla þo waurda in hairtin seinamma.
14. Þus giba þata waldufni þizo þiudangardjo allata jah wulþu izo.
15. Insandida mik atta meins du sokjan jah ganasjan þans unhailans jah þans frawaurhtans.
16. Gameliþ ist þatei ni bi hlaib ainana libaiþ manna, ak (but) bi all waurde Gudis.
17. Goþ ist atsaihwan du waurda Gudis jah laiseinai nasjandis unsaris.
18. Jah alla managei sokidedun atgaggan du imma, unte mahts usiddja ut us imma jah ganasida allans.
19. Guþ insandida ina du giban kunþi naseinais managein seinai.
20. Ni magum atgiban þus þos bokos unte ni sind unsaros du atgiban.

---

[3] There is no passive infinitive in Gothic. The ordinary infinitive may be used passively with a dative agent: *to be seen by them.*

Lesson 11

11.1 Relative pronouns and relative clauses. The relative pronouns are formed by adding the particle **-ei** to the demonstrative pronoun **sa:**

	masculine		feminine		neuter	
	sing.	plural	sing.	plural	sing.	plural
N	**saei**	**þaiei**	**soei**	**þozei**	**þatei**	**þoei**
G	**þizei**	**þizeei**	**þizozei**	***þizoei**	**þizei**	**þizeei**
D	**þammei**	**þaimei**	**þizaiei**	**þaimei**	**þammei**	**þaimei**
A	**þanei**	**þanzei**	**þoei**	**þozei**	**þatei**	**þoei**

Note the loss of **-a** on **þammei, þanei, þatei** and the (re)voicing of final **-s** to medial **-z-**.

Relative clauses headed by **saei** etc. are used to modify both nouns and pronouns. Ideally the case of the relative pronoun is determined by its function within the relative clause, while its number and gender are determined by its antecedent in the main clause. Exceptions to the general rule occur and will be dealt with in Lesson 12. Study the following examples:

N Lk 2:11 **nasjands, saei ist Xristus Frauja** a saviour, who is Christ the Lord
Lk 8:2 **qinons þozei wesun galeikinodos** women who had been healed

G Lk 1:27 **abin** (Dat.), **þizei namo Iosef** to a husband whose name was Joseph
Lk 3:16 **swinþoza** (Nom.) **mis, þizei ik ni im wairþs andbindan skaudaraip skohis is** one mightier than I whose shoelace I am not worthy to untie
Ro 9:4 **broþruns meinans** (Acc.) ... **þaiei sind Israeleitai, þizeei ist frastisibja** my brothers ... who are Israelites, of whom is [i.e. who possess] the (divine) adoption

D Lk 4:29 **und auhmisto þis fairgunjis ana þammei so baurgs ize gatimrida was** to the highest point of the mountain on which their city had been built
Lk 15:9 **unte bigat drakman þammei fralaus** because she found the drachma which she lost [the verb **fraliusan** *to lose* takes a dative object]
Lk 19:15 **þans skalkans þaimei atgaf þata silubr** the servants to whom he had handed over the money

A Lk 1:73 **aiþis** (Gen.) **þanei swor wiþra Abraham** of the oath which he swore to Abraham
Lk 9:9 **hwas ist sa bi þanei ik hausja swaleik?** Who is this concerning whom I hear such things?

11.2 *Sama* (same) and *silba* (self). Both of these words always follow the weak adjectival inflection. **Sama** is used as an adjective with or without the demonstrative **sa.** E.g.

Lk 2:8 **in þamma samin landa** in that same land
Lk 17:34 **ana ligra samin** in the same bed, in one and the same bed

Note that the word covers the two attributive meanings of English *same:* (1) identical to the one already mentioned; (2) one and the same, a single. For the predicate use of *same,* as in *They are not the same,* Gothic employs the adjective **samaleik-** (of the same sort), as in

Mk 14:56 **Samaleikos þos weitwodiþos ni wesun.** The testimonies were not the same (i.e. were inconsistent).

Sa sama and **þata samo** are used pronominally as *the same one, the same thing* (or *matter*), as in

Rom 10:12 **Sa sama auk Frauja allaize...** For the same One is Lord of all (peoples)...
Lk 6:33 **þai frawaurhtans þata samo taujand** the sinners do the same thing

Silba, more an appositional complement to a personal pronoun than an adjective, is nevertheless inflected like a weak adjective. Like English *self,* **silba** may have intensive or reflexive meaning. It regularly co-occurs with an overt personal pronoun except for a few nominative uses where the personal pronoun is implicit in the verbal ending, as in

Lk 1:22 **jah silba was bandwjands im** and he himself was making signs to them

Typical collocations include **is silba, si silbo; mis silbin, mik silban; þuk silban; sis silbin** (sing.), **sis silbam** (pl.). In expressions like **seina silbins saiwala** (his own soul, *A*), **seina** is the strong *pron. adj.* **sein-** (his own), agreeing in number, gender, and case with the modified noun (here **saiwala**); **silbins** is the genitive of **silba** (masc. sing. self), which takes its gender from the noun to which it refers; if, for example, the reference were to a woman's soul, the expression would be **seina silbons saiwala** (her own soul).

11.3 The verb ***wiljan*** (want, will, wish) has no proper indicative present, the forms in use being those of the subjunctive with indicative meaning:

ik wiljau	**weis wileima**
þu wileis	**jus wileiþ**
is wili	**eis wileina**

The present (active) participle is normal, **wiljand-**, and the preterite stem is **wild-**, inflected like a weak preterite. The use of **wiljan** with a following infinitive is similar to English usage and poses no translation problems. E.g.

Mk 15:15 **Peilatus, wiljands þizai managein fullafahjan...** Pilate, wanting to satisfy the crowd, ...
Mk 7;24 **ni wilda witan mannan** he did not want anyone to know
Lk 19:14 **ni wileima þana þiudanon ufar unsis** we do not want him (*A*) to rule over us
Jn 9:27 **ibai jah jus wileiþ þamma siponjos wairþan?** Do you too want to become his disciples?

wiljan may also be used with a nominal direct object in the accusative, as in

Mt 9:13 **armahairtiþa wiljau jah ni hunsl** I desire mercy, and not sacrifice

or be used alone with no complement, as in

Lk 5:13 **Wiljau. Wairþ hrains!** I (so) wish. Become cleansed!

11.4 The present (active) participle is used as a predicate with the verb **wisan** to express progressive (durative) action in present and past time. E. g.

Lk 1:21 **jah was managei beidandans Zakariins** and the crowd was waiting for Zakarias
Lk 2:51 **jah was ufhausjands im** and he was obeying them
Lk 6:43 **Ni auk ist bagms gods taujands akran ubil...** For a good tree does not produce evil fruit...

Past tense occurrences are relatively frequent, but present tense occurrences are few and far between. Note that the imperfective present and preterite indicative of the verb cover this same range of meaning.

When used with **wairþan**, the active participle expresses the intended or immediate future of English *is going to,* as in

Lk 6: 16 **Iudan Iskarioten** (Acc.), **saei warþ galewjands ina** Judas Iskariot, who was going to betray him
Jn 16:20 **jus saurgandans wairþiþ** you are going to mourn

This is not a frequent construction.

11.5 Reflexive verbs are of two kinds: direct and indirect. Direct reflexives are simply transitive verbs with an accusative reflexive pronominal direct object: **sik** in all numbers and genders of the 3rd person, and the ordinary accusative form of the personal pronoun in the 1st and 2nd persons. E.g.

Lk 1:56 **Mariam ... gawandida sik du garda seinamma** Mary ... returned to her home
Lk 2:45 **gawandidedun sik in Iairusalem** they returned to Jerusalem
Lk 17.4 **idreigo mik** I repent

Indirect reflexives contain a dative reflexive pronoun: **sis** in all genders and numbers of the 3rd person, and the regular dative form of the personal pronoun in the 1st and 2nd persons. The verb itself may be transitive or intransitive. Contrast the following:

Lk 19:21 **ohta mis auk þuk** for I was afraid of you
Lk 1:30 **ni ogs þus** don't be afraid!

With some verbs the use of the reflexive pronoun, either accusative or dative, appears to be optional. Compare the following with the examples above:

Lk 20:19 **jah ohtedun þo managein** but they feared the masses
Lk 10:6 **iþ jabai ni, du izwis gawandjai** but if not, let it return to you
Mk 1:15 **idreigoþ jah galaubeiþ in aiwaggeljon** repent and believe in the gospel!

11.6 Loanwords and proper names from the Greek original abound in our corpus, often mediated through Latin. The principal inflected forms will be indicated in the vocabularies, but they need not be memorized in every detail since the forms are usually identifiable from their context; the inflection of proper names is somewhat quixotic.

Lesson 11

There is some consistency in the treatment of words taken over with the nominative singular form in **-us**, e.g. **praufetus** (Gk προφητής), **aggilus** (Gk ἄγγελος). These nouns generally follow the inflection of **sunus** except for the *Npl*, where **-jus** alternates with **-eis**, and the *Gpl*, where only **-e** (not **-iwe**) is attested. Cf. **sabbatus** in Voc. 9.

The name of Jesus (Gk 'Ιησοῦς) is always abbreviated in the texts and follows the inflection of **dags**, taking the stem as **Iesu-**: *N* **is** = **Iesus**, *G* **iuis** = **Iesuis**, *D* **iua** = **Iesua** (or **iu** = **Iesu**), *A* **iu** = **Iesu**.

Vocabulary 11

Verbs:

arman (*imperf.* and *perf.*), **gaarman** (*perf.*) *wv 3* to take pity on (*A*), show mercy to (*A*).
bauan *wv 3 irreg* (see §10.1) (*imperf.*) to dwell, reside (in: **in** *D*); nearly all occurrences refer to spiritual rather than physical indwelling. **gabauan** *wv 3 irreg* to take up residence.
leikan (*imperf.*), **galeikan** (*perf.*) *wv 3* to please, be pleasing to (*D*); used impersonally: it is pleasing (to smn: *D;* to do: inf.); very rarely: to take pleasure in (*D*), be pleased with (*D*).
liugan *wv 3* (*imperf.* and *perf.*) to marry, take a wife (*A*).
trauan (*imperf.*) *wv 3* to trust, place one's trust in (smn: *D*, **du**, **in** *D*; in sthg: **in** *D*; that ...: **þatei...**). **gatrauan** (*perf.*) *wv 3 idem;* to have been convinced, to believe.
þulan (*imperf.*), **gaþulan**, **usþulan** (*imperf.*, *perf.*) *wv 3* to endure, tolerate, put up with (*A*); suffer, undergo (*A*; at the hands of: **fram** *D*). **usþuland-** *part adj* patient.
weihan (*imperf.*), **gaweihan** (*perf.*) *wv 3* to consecrate, sanctify.
winnan (*imperf.*), **gawinnan** (*perf.*) *sv 3* to suffer pain or sorrow.
wasjan (*imperf.*), **gawasjan** (*perf.*) *wv 1* to clothe (smn: *A*; in: *D*); intrans. or reflex. with **sik**: to dress oneself.
gamotjan *wv 1* to meet, encounter (smn: *D*).
wailamerjan *wv 1* to preach (sthg: *A*, **bi** *A*) as good news (to: *D;* among: **in** *D*), speak well of (*A*).
wajamerjan *wv 1* to blaspheme, to speak ill of (*A*).

Nouns:

leik *sn* body, corpse; often body as opposed to spirit.
lekeis, leikeis *sm* physician.
fairhwus *sm* world, usually with **sa**.
unhulþa *wm* a demon; the Devil (do not confuse with **unhulþo** *wf*).
daupjands *m* baptizer.
wraka *sf* or **wrakja** *sf* persecution.
skadus *sm* shade, shadow.
widuwo *wf* widow.

Other:

waila *adv* well, in a pleasing manner; **waila taujan** to do good, act well (toward: *D*). Cf. **wailamerjan** above.

Loanwords (see §11.4):

aggilus *sm* angel, messenger.
Zakarias, *Zaxarias Zakarias (*G* **-iins**; *A* **-ian**).
Iohannes John (*N* **-es, is**; *G* **-es, -is**; *D* **-e, -en**; *A* **-e, -en**); **Iohannes sa daupjands** (*G* **þis -dins**, *D* **þamma -din**, *A* **þana -d**) John the Baptist.
praufetus *sm* prophet.
Iesus Jesus.
Fareisaius *sm* a Pharisee (Jewish sectarian).

Lesson 11

Exercises

A. Translate.

1. kunþi þatei atgiban ist unsis fram Guda
2. sa blinda þanei Iesus gaarmaida
3. manns þanzei fijam jah sokjam fraqistjan
4. bagms sa mikila in þammei fuglos himinis gabauaidedun
5. mahteis in þizoei rodidedun jah bi þozei sildaleikidedun
6. so stibna soei galeikaida unsis waila
7. manna saei afletiþ qen seina
8. managei ana þoei atnehwida sik þiudangardi Gudis
9. so widuwo þizozei sunus siuks warþ
10. daupeins idreigos þoei Iohannes sa daupjands was merjands in auþidai
11. so qino þoei ik wiljau liugan
12. mahteis þozei waurþun in andwairþja unsaramma
13. þai gredagans jah þai unledans þanzei weis armaidedum
14. laisareis þammei witand skalkos þiudanis
15. þai skalkos þaiei waurkjand inuh mizdon
16. þai gredagans þaiei sadai wairþand
17. sa weiha in þammei bauiþ ahma Gudis
18. waurda þis praufetaus þoei ni galeikaidedun þamma þiudana
19. praufetus þizei waurda laistidedun
20. wair þammei gamotidedum atgaggandin dalaþ af fairgunja
21. daupeinos þozei gawaurhtedun Iohannes sa daupjands jah siponjos is
22. waurda þoei rodida sa unhulþa Fraujin unsaramma
23. sa wair saei liugaida twos qenins
24. baurgs þoei gatimridedun in þamma stada
25. sunja soei warþ swikunþa in þamma daga
26. wrakos þozei winniþ nasjands unsar
27. þai weihans þaiei atsaihwand du witoda jah praufetum
28. waurda þoei nasjands unsar habaiþ rodjan þamma unhulþin jah aggilum is

B. Translate and convert to past tense.

1. Duhwe þu ni wileis bauan in þizai baurg?
2. Weis ni wileima gamotjan im.
3. Hwamma wileis gawasjan þuk?
4. Ni wili gawasjan sik þaim wastjom.
5. Wileima trauan du imma, iþ ni magum.
6. Ik ni wiljau winnan manag.
7. Ik wiljau gaweihan þana gard jah þans bauandans is.
8. Weis ni wileima gaþulan þata fram þus.
9. Wileina hausjan waurda Iohannis þis daupjandins, iþ ni magun galeiþan in auþida.
10. Wiljau sitan in skadau þis bagmis.

C. Translate and convert into predications with **ist** or **sind**. E.g. (1) the reliable physician; **Sa leikeis triggws ist.**

1. leikeis sa triggwa
2. waurstwa þis fijandis þo ubilona
3. mahteis þos mikilons
4. skadus sa diupa
5. laun þata mikilo
6. sunus sa dauþa þizos widuwons
7. waurstwja sa swinþa
8. wrakos þos ubilons
9. armaio so mikilo
10. hrot þata hauho þizos alhs
11. blomans þai dauþans
12. aggileis þai weihans
13. gahugds so fulgino
14. praufeteis þai untriggwans
15. leik þata dauþo
16. wato þata kaldo
17. waurda þo swikunþona þis praufetaus

D. Translate.

1. Is silba gawasjiþ sik silban wulþau.
2. Þata usbauhta ik mis silbin.
3. Þu bigitis ins in þamma samin stada.
4. Twai motarjos bauaidedun in samon baurg.
5. Jah weis silbans wileima gataujan þata samo.
6. Ni mahta ganasjan seina silbins saiwala.
7. Wesun fiskjans in þamma samin skipa.
8. Jains frauja habaiþ skalkans managans uf sis silbin.
9. Þai ubilans þis fairhwaus fraqistjand sis silbam.
10. Is galeiþiþ in baurg, iþ silba gawandja mik in fairguni.
11. Sa magus galeikaida im filu.
12. Iesus gaarmaida þana haltan jah gahailida ina.
13. Atsaihwiþ faura frawaurhtim þaim bauandeim in leikam izwaraim.
14. Goþ ist taujan waurstw þatei leikaiþ Guda.
15. Gawandida sik in sein land jah liugaida qen jainar.
16. Hwas mag gaweihan unsara niuja alh?
17. Galeikaida mis þus meljan bi þos mahtins þozei gatawida nasjands unsar.
18. So siuko gaþulaida fram managaim leikjam þaiei ni mahtedun gahailjan ija.
19. Skuld ist uns usþulandans wisan in þamma mela.
20. Broþar is liugaida swistar Zakariins.
21. Ni skuld ist wajamerjan witoþ jah laisein attane unsaraize.
22. Weis usþulaidedum wrakos managos in laiseinais unsaraizos.
23. Sa atta þeins jah ik winnandona sokidedum þuk jah ni mahtedum bigitan þuk. Hwar wast?
24. Is winniþ manag fram Faireisaium.
25. Atsaihwiþ faura praufetum þaim ubilam þaiei qimand at izwis in wastjom lambe, iþ bi sunja sind wulfos wilþjai.

Lesson 12

12.1 Strong verbs: classes 4 and 5. The full conjugation of a strong verb requires a knowledge of four principal parts: the infinitive, the 1st pers. sing. and plural of the preterite, and the past participle. The principal parts of these two classes of strong verbs are as follows:

Class 4	**niman**	**nam**	**nemum**	**numan-**	to take
	bairan	**bar**	**berum**	**bauran-**	to bear
Class 5	**giban**	**gaf**	**gebum**	**giban-**	to give
	qiþan	**qaþ**	**qeþum**	**qiþan-**	to say
	saihwan	**sahw**	**sehwum**	**saihwan-**	to see

Historically these constituted a single class, but the presence of a liquid or nasal consonant (*l, m, n, r*) in stem-final position led to a divergence in the development of the past participle: verbs of class 4 have the stem vowel -*u*- in the participle, while those of class 5 have -*i*-. A secondary change, characteristic of Gothic but not of Proto- Germanic, is the lowering of -*i*- to -[*ɛ*]- before *r* and *h*, thus **bairan** (for ***biran**) and **saihwan** (for ***sihwan**), and the lowering of -*u*- to -[*ɔ*]- before *r*, as in **bauran-** (for ***buran-**).

The full conjugation of the present indicative active was given in §7.4. The preterite of strong verbs in general is conjugated as follows:

ik nam	**weis nemum**	**ik gaf**	**ik qaþ**
þu namt	**jus nemuþ**	**þu gaft**	**þu qast**
is nam	**eis nemun**	**is gaf**	**is qaþ**

Two phonological rules must be observed. The first is the Devoicing Rule, whereby, e.g. **ik *gab > ik gaf.** The second is specific to the 2nd pers. sing.: stem final -*b*- becomes -*f*- before -*t*, e.g. **þu *gabt > þu gaft**; all dentals (*t, d, þ*) become -*s*- before -*t*, e.g. **þu *qaþt > þu qast, þu *bigatt > þu bigast.** The following verbs belong to these two classes:

Class 4:	**niman**	to take	**bairan**	to bear	**brikan**	to break
	qiman	to come	**stilan**	to steal	**(ga)tairan**	to tear
	(ga)timan	to suit	**trudan**	to tread		
Class 5:	**bidjan**	to pray	**diwan**	to die	**fitan**	to be in labor
	fraihnan	to ask	**(bi)gitan**	to find	**hlifan**	to steal
	itan	to eat	**ligan**	to lie	**lisan**	to gather
	(ga)nisan	to be saved	**niþan**	to help	**rikan**	to heap up
	sitan	to sit	**qiþan**	to say	**giban**	to give
	saihwan	to see	**sniwan**	to hasten	**(in)widan**	to reject
	(ga)wigan	to shake	**wisan**	to be	**(ga)widan**	to unite
	wrikan	to persecute				

The -*j*- of **bidjan** and the -*n*- of **fraihnan** belong only to the infinitive and present stems; the preterites and passive participles are normal: **bidjan, baþ, bedum, bidan-; fraihnan, frah, frehum, fraihan-. brikan** is included under class 4 because of the attested participle **-brukan-**; otherwise one would expect it to be a member of class 5. **trudan** likewise has an attested participle **-trudan**; the infinitive **trudan** is completely anomalous in class 4, however, as is **wulan** (to rage), usually also classified here; English *tread* and German *treten* represent the normal form of the infinitive and present stem from PG **tritan*, but this form is itself considered a neologism in PG since Old Icelandic, like Gothic, preserves the anomalous form in *troða* (to tread).

Verbal nouns of the verbs belonging to these two classes are formed by suffixing *-t-* or *-þ-* to the stem of the past participle; they are inflected like **taikns** *sf.* The following are attested:

From	**giban**	**-gifts**	in	**fragifts** *sf* betrothal (pl. only)
	niman	**-numts**		**andanumts** *sf* acceptance
	bairan	**-baurþs**		**gabaurþs** *sf* birth, generation, birth-place
	qiman	**-qumþs**		**gaqumþs** *sf* assembly
	qiþan	**-qiss < *-qiþts**		**gaqiss** (*G* **-ssais**) *sf* consent
	-nisan	**-nists**		**ganists** *sf* salvation
	-widan	**-wiss < *-widts**		**gawiss** *sf* ligament, connection

12.2 The verbal prefixes *fra-* and *us-*.

The verbal prefix **fra-** has no corresponding preposition in Gothic and is related historically to the IE forerunner of the Latin and Greek prefixes *pro-* and προ-, both with the general meaning of *forward away from (a reference point)*, but with many secondary nuances. This same sense is found sometimes in Gothic with verbs of separation, where **fra-** reinforces the notion of removal or exchange, as in

letan to leave, abandon; to let, allow	**fraletan** to liberate, set free from
***liusan** to lose	**fraliusan** to lose
bugjan to buy	**frabugjan** to sell
***gildan** to pay	**fragildan** to pay back

More frequently, however, **fra-** adds or emphasizes the notion of ruin, corruption, or total consumption, as in

wairþan to become	**frawairþan** to go bad, become corrupt
waurkjan to do, act	**frawaurkjan** to sin
itan to eat	**fra-itan** to devour

as well as **fraqistjan** (to destroy) and **frawardjan** (to destroy).

Related to this sense is the **fra-** of the two verbs **fraqiman** and **frawisan,** where the base verbs are intransitive and both compounds require a dative direct object. The original construction probably meant something like *to go too far with, be excessive with,* plus an instrumental (> dative in Gothic), eventually having the meanings

fraqiman + *D*	to spend, use up, destroy
frawisan + *D*	to spend, use up, waste.

The "bad" sense of **fra-** is also found with **fraqiþan** (to disparage, reject) and **frakunnan** (to despise; **kunnan** to know, recognize). With other verbs it reinforces but does not materially alter the "bad" meaning of the base verb, as in **frahinþan** (to imprison), **frawrohjan** (to denounce), **fralewjan** (to betray), **frawilwan** (to rob, plunder).

The prefix **us-**, like its corresponding preposition, denotes primarily that an action is directed outward or upward from within. E.g.:

wairpan to throw	**uswairpan** to throw away, cast out
standan to stand	**usstandan** to stand up, arise, come out of

steigan to step, climb — **ussteigan** to go up, ascend
sitan to be seated — **ussitan** to sit up

us- also denotes that an activity is carried out thoroughly or to completion, as in

fulljan to fill — **usfulljan** to fulfill, carry out to completion

and often seems to form an alternate perfective counterpart along with **ga**-, as in **þulan, gaþulan, usþulan** (to bear, endure, tolerate).

Similar to **fraqiman** and **frawisan** above, we have **usqiman** (to destroy, kill), with the direct object in the dative or accusative, the former probably being the more original construction.

12.3 More on relative pronouns and relative clauses.

a. The relative pronouns **saei, soei, þatei** may be used absolutely, without an antecedent, in the sense *he who, the one who, that which.* Concerning case, two possibilities arise:

(1) The case required by the principal clause is the same as that required by the relative clause. E.g.

N,N	Rom 13:8	**saei frijoþ nehwundjan witoþ usfillida** he who loves his neighbor has fulfilled the law
G,G	ICor 10:30	**duhwe anaqiþaidau in þizeei ik awiliudo**? Why should I be denounced on account of that for which I give thanks? [**awiliudon in** *G*: to give thanks for]
D,D	Rom 10:14	**Hwaiwa nu bidjand du þammei ni galaubidedun**? How then will they pray to him in whom they have not believed? [**galaubjan** to believe (smn: *D*)]
A,A	Rom 9:15	**Gaarma þanei arma, jah gableiþja þanei bleiþja** I will have mercy on him on whom I have mercy, and I will show compassion to him to whom I show compassion.

(2) The cases required by the principal and relative clauses differ. Many of the examples that could be cited here involve neuter **þatei** and **þoei**, where the formal identity of nominative and accusative conceals the syntactic ambiguity. E.g.

A,N	Mk 11:23	**þatei qiþiþ gagaggiþ** what he says will come to pass

But there are quite a few instances of unresolved grammatical conflict. E.g.

G,A	Lk 9:36	**mann ni gataihun ... ni waiht þizei gasehwun** they told no one anything of what they had seen [**gasaihwan** normally requires an accusative object]
N,D	Jn 13:26	**Sa ist þammei ik ufdaupjands þana hlaif giba**. It is he to whom I give the bread after dipping it [the main clause requires the nominative]
D,A	Jn 6:29	**ei galaubjaiþ þammei insandida jains** that you believe in him whom that one

sent [the relative clause requires the accusative]

b. Occasionally the relative pronoun precedes its antecedent in imitation of the underlying Greek construction known as incorporation (cf. Smythe, p. 570). E.g.

Lk 9:4 **jah in þanei gard gaggaiþ, þar saljiþ**
καὶ εἰς ἣν ἂν οἰκίαν εἰσέλθητε, ἐκεῖ μένετε
and remain in the house which you chance to enter

Lk 17:27 **und þanei dag galaiþ Nauel in arka**
ἄχρι ἧς ἡμέρας εἰσῆλθεν Νῶε εἰς τὴν κιβωτόν
until the day that Noah entered the ark

c. Relative pronouns of the first and second person are formed by suffixing **-ei** to the appropriate form of the personal pronoun. E.g.

Gal 5:4 **juzei in witoda garaihtans qiþiþ izwis** you who justify yourselves in the law

Lk 3:22 **þu is sunus meins sa liuba, in þuzei waila galeikaida** You are my beloved son, in whom I have been well pleased.

Attested forms are *N* **ikei**; *N* **þuei**, *D* **þuzei**; *N* **juzei**, *D* **izwizei.** Because occurrences are few and sometimes syntactically ambiguous, these forms will not be imitated in the exercises.

Vocabulary 12

Verbs:

qiman, qam *sv 4*[1] to come (used with a full range of prepositions; may also be followed by an infinitive of purpose).
fraqiman, fraqam *sv 4* to squander, spend (sthg: *D*; on: **in** *A*); to destroy (*D*).
usqiman, usqam *sv 4* to kill, destroy (smn: *A* or *D*).
gabrikan, gabrak *sv 4* to break (*A*).
fulljan (*imperf.*), **gafulljan** (*perf.*) *wv 1* to fill (smn, sthg: *A*; with: *G*).
usfulljan *wv 1* to fulfill, complete, bring to intended end; to finish (doing sthg: participle).
bidjan, baþ *sv 5 irreg* to pray; to ask (smn: *A*; to do sthg: inf.; on behalf of: **bi** *A*).
fraihnan, frah *sv 5 irreg* to ask, question (smn: *A*; for: *G*; about: *G*, **bi** *A*).
gatairan, gatar *sv 4* to relax (trans.), fail to maintain (*A*); to destroy (*A*).
qiþan, qaþ *sv 5* to say (sthg: *A*; to smn: *D*, **du** *D*); to name, designate (smn as smn: *A A*).
fraqiþan, fraqaþ *sv 5* to disparage (*A*), reject (*A*) as unsuitable (for: **ana** *A*); to curse (*A*).
itan, et *sv 5 irreg* to eat (*A*); **saþ itan** to eat one's fill (of: *G*).
fraitan, fret *sv 5 irreg* to devour (*A*).

Nouns:

gabruka *sf* fragment, crumb.
mats *sm(i)* food.
faheþs *sf* (*G* **-dais**) joy, happiness.
tainjo *wf* basket.
fralet *sn* release, delivery, forgiveness.
wein *sn* wine.

[1] The first two principal parts of strong verbs will be given in the vocabularies as an aid to memory.

waihts *sf* thing, matter; **ni waihts** nothing (fully inflected); the *D* **ni waihtai** is used adverbially: not at all, in no way.

Other:

aiwein- *adj* eternal. The weak form appears irregularly in several phrases, including the frequent **libains aiweino** eternal life. These are to be taken as formulaic (so Streitberg, p. 181); cf. Eng *life eternal.*
naqad- *adj* naked.
bai *num adj* both. The only attested forms are masc. *N* **bai**, *D* **baim**, *A* **bans**; neuter *NA* **ba**. The word was presumably inflected like **twai** (two).
janni = **jah ni**; the conjunction **jah** is also used adverbially before another sentence element in the sense of *even, too.*
ak *conj* but, but rather (follows a negative statement).
hwe *interrog adv* how? with what?
fairra *adv* far, distant, at a distance (from: *D*); **fairra wisan** to be distant, far away.
hwaþ *interrog adv* where to? whither?

Exercises

A. Translate the following phrases:

1. twos tainjons gafullidos matis
2. fralet frawaurhte þata atgibano unsis fram Iesua
3. faheþs þizozei fulljand uns waurda is
4. þai dauþans þaimei nasjands unsar gaf libain
5. gabrukos þozei fretun fuglos
6. siponeis saei þahaida janni qaþ waiht
7. tainjo þoei gafullidedun gabruko
8. leik þis unledins þata bigitano ana wiga
9. dauþus sunaus seinis þis liubins
10. harjis saei usqam fijands unsarans
11. ansteis þozei nemum fram fraujin unsaramma þamma godin
12. þai frawaurhtans þaiei fraqiþand witoþ Gudis
13. kas þatei ik gafullida weinis
14. sa gahailida saei gaf wulþu Guda
15. witoþ bi þatei frehum ina
16. sa siuka bi þanei bedum
17. laun þatei gebuþ þaim waurstwjam
18. so widuwo so sitandei nehwa þamma razna
19. sa unhulþa saei fraqiþiþ waurda Fraujins
20. þai ganasidans þaiei gawasjand sik wulþau
21. þai sitandans af taihswon is
22. managei so frawaurhto soei fraqiþana warþ

B. Translate and convert into the past tense.

1. Ik nima þos wastjos.
2. Ni qimand in baurg unsara.
3. Hwar bigitis wein?
4. Hwas atgibiþ þus þos bokos?
5. Ni magum bigitan leik is.
6. Gaggam in land fairra wisando.
7. Is usfulleiþ mel laiseinais seinaizos.
8. Ganasjiþ uns jah gibiþ uns libain aiweinon.
9. Þo sweina fraitand allos þos gabrukos.
10. Hwaþ insandeiþ þana unhulþan jah aggiluns is?
11. Duhwe brikis þo kasa?
12. Gibam izwis twos tainjons matis.
13. Jus ni insandeiþ skalk untriggwana.
14. Merjam bi aflet frawaurhte.
15. Hwe fraqimand fijandam seinaim?
16. Jus saþ itiþ hlaibis jah akranis.
17. Hwas atgaggiþ du stola Gudis?
18. Bidjam ina fraihnan bi ba barna unsara.
19. Is gasaihwiþ þata leik fairra wisando.
20. Ni fraqiþam waurda praufete is.

C. Translate.

1. Jah is qaþ: "Duhwe mik sokeiþ usqiman?" Andhafjandei so managei qeþun: "Unhulþon habais. Ni þuk sokjam usqiman."
2. Nimands þans fimf hlaibans jah twans fiskans, gaþiuþida ins jah gabrak jah gaf siponjam du lagjan faura þizai managein, jah matidedun jah sadai waurþun allai.
3. Þai Fareisaieis jah þai anþarai sokidedun imma usqiman janni mahtedun.
4. Qiþan ist fram sumaim þatei ik qam gatairan witoþ aiþþau praufetuns. Ni qam ik gatairan, ak usfulljan þata gamelido.
5. Jah fon mikil atiddja us himina jah fraqam þaim twaim baurgim.
6. Is nam hlaif jah bidjands gabrak jah qaþ: "Nimiþ, matjiþ, þata is leik mein þata in izwara gibano."
7. Jah qemun þai anþarai fiskjans jah gafullidedun jah eis ba skipa seina fiske.
8. Gahausidedum ina qiþandan: "Ik gataira þo alh jah bi þrins dagans gatimrja þo."
9. Is qiþiþ þaim af hleidumin: "Gaggiþ fairra mis, jus fraqiþanans, in fon þata aiweino þata manwido unhulþin jah aggilum is, unte gredags was janni gebuþ mis matjan, naqaþs was janni wasideduþ mik." Jah eis andhafjand jah qiþand: "Frauja, hwan þuk sehwum gredagana aiþþau naqadana janni gebum þus mat jah wastja?"
10. Saei fijaiþ uns jah sokeiþ usqiman uns atnehwida sik.
11. Hwana bigetun ija sitandan in alh?
12. Rodidedum du im bi þatei sehwum ana fairgunja jainamma.
13. Hwar usbauhteduþ þoei gebuþ gredagaim?
14. Saei gaf uns libain aiweinon ist nasjands unsar.
15. Magus sa halta ist broþar jainaizos maujos.
16. Duhwe atgebuþ uns in handuns fijande unsaraize?
17. Sa hairdeis bigat þata lamb ana haiþjai.

Lesson 13

13.1 The conjunctions *jah, iþ, þan, -uh þan, þanuh, þaruh, nu.*

A. The elaborate system of particles that outline the structure of Classical Greek narrative and discourse survives in a somewhat reduced form in the koine Greek narratives of the New Testament, where the most important non-subordinating conjunctions are καί, δέ, οὖν and γάρ. A brief survey from the point of view of the Greek gospel narratives will, I believe, help clarify the sometimes bewildering uses of Gothic **jah, iþ, -uh,**[1] **þan, -uh þan, þanuh, þaruh,** and **nu.**

1. καί (and) as a simple conjunction is used to join clauses or elements within a clause. It is most often translated by Gothic **jah** and is too frequent to require examples. The conjunction **jah**, like καί, often requires a more nuanced translation in English, sometimes indicating result (*and then, and consequently*), as in

Lk 7:7 **ak qiþ waurda, jah gahailnid sa þiumagus meins** but just say the words, and then my servant will be healed

or to indicate something unexpected or noteworthy, like the second **jah** in

Mk 12:12 **jah sokidedun ina undgreipan jah ohtedun þo managein** and they sought an excuse to seize him, but they were afraid of the masses,

where a translation like *and yet* or *but* is required. We have already mentioned the use of καί = **jah** as an adverb to emphasize a single element of a clause, to be translated *even, also, too,* as in

Lk 10:17 **Frauja, jah** (καί) **unhulþons ufhausjand unsis in namin þeinamma!** Lord, even unclean spirits obey us in your name!

2. Greek δέ is postpositive but not enclitic, following whatever member heads the clause. δέ marks what is termed *fronting* and serves to emphasize the word or words it follows, sometimes indicating a relatively strong contrast with some member of the preceding clause, sometimes indicating no more than a change in focus, e.g. a different subject, object, or venue. English *and* or *but* will usually suffice in translation. The Gothic translator shows some appreciation for the different functions of δέ:

a. Most frequently, when δέ serves merely to move the narrative along with little or no contrast involved, it is translated by **þan** (*then, and then, and*). The Gothic conjunction **þan** is always postpositive,[2] standing after the leading element of its clause. E.g.

Lk 1:34 **Qaþ þan Mariam du þamma aggilau** Then Mary said to the angel

Lk 2:17 **Gasaihwandans þan gakannidedun bi þata waurd** Then, having seen, they made known concerning the matter which ...

For **þan** following **jah** or **iþ**, see below.

[1] The conjunctive particle **-uh** is enclitic to the first word of its clause. The phonetic changes involved in its attachment are discussed fully in §15.2. For the present lesson it will suffice to note **-a + -uh > -uh, -o + -uh > -oh; -s + -uh** sometimes **> -zuh.**

[2] In defining the term *postpositive* in regard to clause structure it should be noted that the coordinating conjunctions **jah** and **iþ**, as well as **jah warþ** (see §14.2.A6) and **ak** (see §14.2.A7) are extra-clausal.

b. When δέ is used to indicate added information, not sequential in the narrative, it is rendered by **-uh þan,** best translated as *now, incidentally, by the way, furthermore,* or the like. **-uh þan** is frequently assimilated to **-uþþan.** E.g.

Lk I:6 (Elizabeth and Zakarias have already been introduced in the narrative) **Wesun-uh þan garaihta ba in andwairþja Gudis.** They were both, furthermore, righteous in the sight of God.

Lk 2:2 **soh þan gilstrameleins frumista warþ...** and this tax registration was, by the way, the first... (**soh** is for **so** + **-uh**)

c. When a change of subject or topic is indicated, δέ is translated by **iþ** (*but, on the other hand*). E.g.

Lk I:80 **Iþ þata barn wohs jah swinþnoda ...** But the child (as opposed to Zakaris et al.) grew and became strong

Lk 4:I **Iþ Iesus, ahmins weihis fulls, gawandida sik fram Iaurdanau...** But Jesus (as opposed to John the Baptist), filled with the holy spirit, returned from the Jordan...

Iþ is sometimes reinforced by suffixing **-uh** to the verb of the clause, as in

Lk 6:8 **Iþ is wiss-uh mitonins ize.** He, however, knew their thoughts. (relatively emphatic change of subject)

Lk 7:6 **Iþ Iesus iddjuh miþ im** So Jesus went with them (simple change of subject)

This is not, however, a frequent construction and about half of the attestations involve description of dialogue exchanges: X said ..., but Y said ..., then X said... etc., as in

Lk I8:2I **Iþ is qaþuh** ... And he (in response to Jesus) said ... (simple change of subject)

Well over a dozen times in Luke and just a few times in Matthew the dialogue formulas ὁ δὲ εἶπεν, ὁ δὲ λέγει are introduced with the conjunction **þaruh.** E.g.

Lk 3:I3 **þaruh qaþ du im** ὁ δὲ εἶπεν πρὸς αὐτούς Then he said to them ...

d. When δέ is used in discourse (as opposed to simple narrative) with a distinct adversative meaning *but, however, on the other hand,* it is usually rendered with Gothic **aþþan,** which is clause initial:

Lk 3:9 **aþþan ju** (ἤδη δέ) **so aqizi at waurtim bagme ligiþ** But already the axe lies against the roots of the trees...

Mk 2:I0 **aþþan ei witeiþ** (ἵνα δέ)... but so that you might know ...

This usage is frequent and fairly consistent. **Aþþan** may be viewed as a discourse equivalent of narrative **iþ,** although the latter occurs fairly frequently in discourse as well as narrative.

3. The combinations δὲ καί and καὶ ... δέ are treated variously, but in general the καί is adverbial, *too, even, also*, and the δέ is in one of the three uses outlined above. E.g.

δέ = **þan**	Lk 16:22	ἀπέθανεν δὲ καὶ ὁ πλούσιος **gaswalt þan jah sa gabeiga** and then the rich man died too
δέ = **-uh þan**	Jn 18:2	ᾔδει δὲ καὶ Ἰούδας **wiss-uh þan jah Iudas** and Judas too, incidentally, knew ...

In καὶ ... δέ constructions δέ marks the whole unit καὶ ... as fronted, as in

Jn 15:27 καὶ ὑμεῖς δὲ μαρτυρεῖτε **jah þan jus weitwodeiþ** but you, too, will bear witness

Note in this example that while the Greek requires the fronting conjunction to follow this particular expression, Gothic allows the insertion of **þan** between the two elements of the member: **jah þan jus** = ***(jah jus) þan.**

4. οὖν in Classical Greek is primarily a postpositive inferential transitional particle, usually to be translated as *therefore, consequently, then.* Its use in NT Greek is partly in accord with this meaning but exhibits some unusual features.

a. As a frequent inferential particle it is usually translated with Gothic postpositive **nu**:

Mt 6:9 **Swa nu bidjaiþ jus** Thus, then, (οὕτως οὖν) shall you pray
Mk 10:9 **þatei nu Guþ gawaþ** what, then, (ὃ οὖν) God has joined together

Note that in this meaning οὖν is more a discourse than a narrative particle.

b. The writer of the Gospel According to John, however, also employs οὖν frequently as an equivalent of δέ, i.e. as a postpositive particle indicating fronting, with all of the nuances of δέ discussed above. The Gothic translator of John renders οὖν in this sense with **þanuh** or **þaruh**, as in

Jn 6:5 **þaruh ushof augona Iesus** Thereupon Jesus raised (ἐπάρας οὖν) his eyes...
Jn 6:13 **þanuh galesun jah gafullidedun**... then they gathered up(συνήγαγον οὖν) and filled...

This use of **þaruh** is like the Lukan use of **þaruh** = δέ noted above. For other uses of **þanuh, þaruh,** and **nu** see B below.

B. Summary and amplification from the Gothic point of view.

1. **þan** alone has three different functions:

a. Postpositive **þan**, corresponding to Gk δέ: *and, and then, subsequently* (see above).

b. Free-standing but often clause-initial **þan** as a temporal adverb *at that time, then,* translating Gk τότε.

c. Clause initial **þan** as a subordinating conjunction *when,* translating Gk ὅταν or ὅτε.

Þan in uses (b) and (c) occupies clause initial position but (cf. footnote I above) follows the coordinating conjunctions **jah** and **iþ** as well as a few other conjunctive phrases to be treated in a later lesson. E.g.

Lk 6:42 **Liuta, uswairp faurþis þamma anza us augin þeinamma, jah þan** (καὶ τότε) **gaumjis uswairpan gramsta þamma in augin broþrs þeinis.** Hypocrite! First remove the log from your own eye, and then you will see clearly to remove the splinter from your brother's eye.

Lk 15:30 **Iþ þan** (ὅτε δέ) **sa sunus þeins, saei ..., qam...** But when that son of yours, who ..., came back ...

These two uses of **þan** may also occur coordinated in two consecutive clauses. E.g.

Lk 5:35 **Aþþan qimand dagos, jah þan** (καὶ ὅταν) **afnimada af im sa bruþfads, jah þan** (τότε) **fastand in jainaim dagam.** But days are coming when the bridegroom will be taken from them, and then they will fast in those days.

Instead of a temporal clause with ὅταν, τότε = **þan** may be coordinated in the same clause with a temporal expression which it resumes or emphasizes. E.g.

Jn 13:27 **jah afar þamma hlaiba þan** (τότε) **galaiþ in jainana Satana...** and after the morsel of bread, at that moment, Satan entered that (disciple)...

Note that the second **þan** in Lk 5:35 above is doubly coordinated.

2. **-uh þan** generally indicates added information not sequential in the narrative: *now, incidentally, furthermore, by the way* (see above). There are a number of instances, however, where it is used in simple sequence in the introductory formula **qaþuh þan** (and he said), as in

Lk 7:48 εἶπεν δὲ αὐτῇ **qaþuh þan izai** and he said to her ...

but more often the speech so introduced is supplementary and not sequential to the preceding clause, e.g. Lk 6:39; 10:2 etc.

3. **iþ** (initial, extra-clausal) corresponds to Gk δέ when a change of subject or topic is given some degree of emphasis: *but, however, on the other hand.* **iþ** ... (verb)-**uh** is a stylistic variant of this associated primarily with description of dialogue exchanges (see above).

4. **þanuh** (initial, extra-clausal):

a. Used regularly in John to translate Johanine οὖν = δέ, overwhelmingly, but not exclusively, in the dialogue formulas εἶπεν οὖν, εἶπον οὖν, ἔλεγεν οὖν, ἔλεγον οὖν *and then he (they) said.*

b. In Matthew **þanuh** is frequent and corresponds regularly to Gk τότε *at that time, then.*

c. **þanuh** is quite infrequent in Luke and Mark and is used indifferently to translate καί, δέ, or τότε.

d. **þanuh** is virtually absent from the epistles.

5. **þaruh** (initial, extra-clausal):

a. Used regularly to translate Johanine οὖν = δέ, especially, like **þanuh**, in the dialogue exchange formulas given just above in 4a.

b. Used quite frequently in Luke and about four times in Mark to render the dialogue formula ὁ δὲ εἶπεν **þaruh qaþ** then he said. Note the curious fact that the pronominal element slightly emphasized in Greek is not overtly present in the Gothic.

c. **þaruh** is occasionally used with or without **sai** (behold) to translate Gk καὶ ἰδού, as in

Mt 9:3 **þaruh sumai þize bokarje qeþun in sis silbam** καὶ ἰδού τινες τῶν γραμματέων εἶπον ἐν ἑαυτοῖς and behold, some of the scribes said among themselves...

Lk 7:12 **þaruh sai, utbaurans was naus**... καὶ ἰδοὺ ἐξεκομίζετο τεθνηκώς and behold,[3] a corpse was being carried out...

d. **þaruh** also means *there, in that place, even there*, translating Gk ἐκεῖ, as in

Mk 16:7 **þaruh ina gasaihwiþ** ἐκεῖ αὐτὸν ὄψεσθε you will see him there

It may also be coordinated with a preceding **þarei** (where, wherever), as in

Mt 6:21 **þarei** (ὅπου) **auk ist huzd izwar, þaruh** (ἐκεῖ) **ist jah hairto izwar** for where your treasure is, there is also your heart

Jn 14:3 **ei þarei** (ὅπου) **im ik, þaruh** (ἐκεῖ) **sijuþ jah jus** so that wherever I am, you too will be there

6. **aþþan** *but, however, on the other hand* (discourse equivalent of narrative **iþ**).

7. **nu** has two distinct uses:

a. Postpositive, as a translation of the Greek postpositive οὖν *therefore, then, so.* (See above.)

b. As a translation of Greek νῦν *now, at this time* or ἄρτι *now, just now.* These are simple temporal adverbs that may occur at any appropriate position in the clause. Note also the expression **fram himma nu** (from now on).

[The discussion of the coordinating conjunctions is continued in Lesson 14, §14.2]

13.2 More on the verbal prefix *ga*-.

In addition to the perfectivizing function of **ga**- discussed in Lesson 5 there are quite a few instances where the original meaning of the prefix is preserved. As a cognate of Gk

[3] The translation *behold* is used to show the literal content of the Greek and Gothic but should be avoided in modern versions of a text. The Greek words καὶ ἰδού are used to introduce a sudden or unexpected event or situation, and the translation should be adjusted to reflect this. *And just at that moment* is a handy English equivalent.

κοινός (shared, held in common, < **komyos*) and Latin *cum* (together with) and the verbal prefix *com- (con-, co-)*, **ga-** has the meaning of *joined together, sharing* in such words as

garazna *wm* neighbor < **razn**; one of the same household
gabaurgja *wm* fellow-citizen < **baurgs**; one of the same city
gawaurstwa *wm* fellow-worker < **waurstw**; one engaged in the same work
gajuk *sn* yoke, **gajuka** *wm* companion; **gajuko** *wf* parable , all from the base **juk** *sn* (yoke).
gajuka and **gajuko** denote a *joining together*, producing *companion* in the one case and a *comparison* or *similitude* in the other.

The following verbs are examples of those with the prefix **ga-** in this meaning:

gahaitan *sv 7* to call together, convoke; **haitan** *sv 7* to call, summon, name
gaqiman *sv 4* to come together, assemble
garinnan *sv 3* to run together, assemble quickly; **rinnan** *sv 3* to run.

Vocabulary 13

Verbs:

wisan, was *sv 5* to be, exist; to remain, dwell, reside.[4]
wrikan, wrak *sv 5* to persecute (*A*).
lisan, las *sv 5 (imperf.)*; **galisan, galas** *sv 5 (perf.)* to gather, collect (*A*); + **sik** intrans. to gather, assemble.
bairan, bar *sv 4 (imperf.)* to bear, carry (*A*); to wear (*A*). **gabairan, gabar** *sv 4 (perf.)* to bring (*A*; to: **du** *D*); to bear (a child: *A*).
atbairan, atbar *sv 4 (perf.)* to bring or take (*A*; to smn: **du** *D*).
usgiban, usgaf *sv 5 (perf.)* to hand (*A*) over (to: *D*); give (*A*) back (to: *D*), pay back.
usniman, usnam *sv 4 (perf.)* to take out, remove (*A*; from: **us** *D*), carry away.
usqistjan *wv 1* to kill, destroy (smn: *A* or *D*). Cf. **fraqistjan.**
ussaihwan, ussahw *sv 5 (perf.)* to look up (at, toward: *A*, **du** *D*), see (*A*); to regain one's sight.
fragiban, fragaf *sv 5* to give (*A*); to grant, allow; to forgive (smn: *D*; sthg: *A*).
frawaurkjan, frawaurhta (± **sis**) *wv 1 irreg* to commit a sin (against: **du** *D*, **in** *A*).
galaubjan *wv 1* to believe (smn or sthg: *D*); to believe in (smn: *D*, less commonly **in** *D* or **du** *D*). **galaubeins** *sf* faith.
drig(g)kan *sv 3* to drink (sthg: *A*; some of sthg: *G*).
gaqiman, gaqam *sv 4* to come together, assemble. **gaqumþs** *sf* assembly.

Nouns:

aikklesjo *wf* church; the Church (< Gk ἐκκλησία).
aiws *sm* (*irreg Apl* **aiwins**) age, era; **sa aiws** this world; **aiws jains** the world to come; **fram aiwa** from the beginning of the world; **du aiwa** forever; **ni aiw** never.
bloþ *sn* (*G* **-þis**) blood.
smakka *wm* fig; **smakkabagms** *sm* fig tree.

---

[4] Streitberg makes a distinction between **wisan**[1] (to be, exist) and **wisan**[2] (to live, reside). **wisan**[2], unlike **wisan**[1], is used in the present tense (**wisa, wisis, wisiþ...**) and regularly translates Gk μένειν (remain, dwell). Strictly speaking, however, it would be more correct to say that the copula (**im, is, ist...**) occurs only in the present indicative and subjunctive and that all other forms are made up from **wisan**[2] (meanings as given in the vocabulary above). In other words, there is no separate **wisan**[1]! There is also a **wisan**[3] used to translate Gk εὐφραίνομαι (to have a good time). See the historical comments on these words.

Lesson 13

aurtja *wm* farmer, vintner; **aurtigards** *sm(i)* garden, farm, orchard (based on Lat *hortus*).
hlaiw *sn* (sing. only) grave, tomb; **hlaiwasnos** *sf* (plural only) graves, tombs.
siuns *sf* sight, ability to see; likeness, appearance; a vision.
missadeþs *sf* (*G* **-dais**) transgression, sin, misdeed.

Personal Names:

Xristus (*G* **-aus**, *D* **-au**, *A* **-u**) (the) Christ. This word is abbreviated *N* **Xs**, *G* **Xaus**, *D* **Xau**, *A* **Xu** in the mss.
Pawlus (*G* **-aus**) Paul.
Marja (*G* **-jins**, *D* **-jin**, *A* **-jin**); **Marja so Magdalene** Mary Magdelene.

Other:

jabai *conj* if.
misso *reflex pron* one another, each other; usually added to the pl. pronouns **izwis**, **unsis**, and **sis**.
swaswe *conj* as, in the same way that, according as. **swe** *prep.* (being) like (takes same case as antecedent).

Exercises

A. Translate the following initial segments of sentences, giving careful attention to the conjunctive elements.

1. Eis þan gaqemun ...
2. Þaruh qaþ du im ...
3. Iþ Iohannes gasaihwands Iesu qaþ ...
4. Þanuh galesun þos gabrukos ...
5. Iþ þan þai dagos qimand, jah þan gasaihwiþ ...
6. Skuld nu ist unsis ...
7. Þan ni gasaihwiþ ...
8. Gafullidedunuh þan þrins tainjos ...
9. Saei nu ni galaubeiþ ...
10. Atnehwjandans þan sik þai bokarjos ...
11. Iþ Iesus gahausjands þo stibna ...
12. Þan atiddja dalaþ du im ...
13. Gaqimandei þan so managei ...
14. Þata nu qiþa izwis ...
15. Wesunuþþan managai gredagai ...
16. Iþ is qaþuh ...
17. Qiþa þan izwis nu þatei ...
18. Jah þan ganam kas weinis ...
19. Aþþan ganasidai wairþiþ ...
20. Þan atnehwida sik so qino ...

B. Translate and convert the verbs and their subjects to the corresponding plural forms.

1. Atbair mis kas watins.
2. Þu ni magt driggkan fram þamma samin kasa.
3. Is was in þizai haimai þrija jera.
4. Ik galagida þos bokos in þamma funin.
5. Ik atbar im twa lamba þoei wilda frabugjan im.
6. Jabai þu habais ubil, goþ ist sokjan leki.
7. Frijonds meins qimiþ her sabbato daga.
8. Duhwe wrakt du mik?
9. Atnehwei þuk und uns.
10. Is galagiþs was in hlaiwa niujamma.
11. Is usbauhta meinana akr jah meinana aurtigard.
12. Wair jains usqam unsarana smakkabagm.
13. Ik ni fragiba izwis.
14. Ik wita waurstwjam þis aurtigardis.
15. Sa praufetus gasahw siun ana þamma fairgunja.
16. Ik ni wiljau þahan.

17. Is ni gafastaida waurda witodis.
18. Ik usnam þana mat ut us þizai tainjon.
19. Is ni wilda dalaþ atgaggan af þamma hrota.
20. Duhwe þu ni wileis lisan smakkans?

C. Translate

1. Saei matjiþ mein leik jah driggkiþ mein bloþ in mis wisiþ, jah ik in imma.
2. Leik þis usqistidins galagiþ was in wiga faur razn unsar.
3. Skuld ist þiuþjan þans wrikandans izwis.
4. Iesus gahailida þans siukans jah blindaim managaim fragaf siun.
5. Jains þiudans wrak aikklesjon Gudis mela lagga.
6. Warþ þan imma in siunai aggilus Fraujins, jah was imma agis mikil.
7. Sa sama Pawlus saei wrak uns in jainaim dagam nu mereiþ galaubein jah nasein.
8. Is fragaf im allos missadedins ize unte idreiga habaidedun.
9. Jah galesun sik du imma manageins filu.
10. Jabai is fijaiþ uns, usqisteiþ uns.
11. Wesunuh þan þai waurstwjans lisandans akran in aurtigarda.
12. Goþ ist izwis fragiban izwis misso swaswe Guþ in Xristau fragaf izwis.
13. Qam þan frauja þis aurtigardis jah usqam jainans aurtjans unwindans.
14. Jabai afletiþ mannam missadedins ize, afletiþ jah izwis atta izwar sa ufar himinam.
15. Ni mahtedum lisan smakkans unte sa winds was kalds filu.
16. Ik gagga du attin meinamma jah qiþa du imma: "Atta, frawaurhta mis in himin jah in andwairþja þeinamma. Gatawei mik swe ainana asnje þeinaize."
17. Du hwamma atbairam akran þatei galesum af þamma smakkabagma?
18. Jabai galaubeiþ imma jah taujiþ waurda þoei rodida izwis, jah jus bigitiþ nasein jah libain aiweinon.
19. Atberun gibos managos du þamma þiudana.
20. Siponjos Iohannis þis daupjandins usnemun leik is jah galagidedun ita in hlaiwa.
21. Niþþan rodida im bi siun þoei gasahw in alh.
22. Usnimam jainos tainjos gafullidos matis jah gibam ijos þaim unledam þis weihsis.
23. Is gibiþ uns libain aiweinon in aiwa jainamma.
24. Usnemun þata dius us þamma aurtigarda jah usqemun ita.
25. Jah eis hausjandans þatei Iesus libaiþ jah gasaihwans warþ fram izai (þat' ist: Marjin þizai Magdalene), ni galaubidedun.
26. So managei sokidedun usqistjan ina, iþ ni mahtedun bigitan ina.
27. Þai ubilans haband sein laun her in þamma aiwa.
28. Is was miþ unsis und þanei dag gawandidedum uns in baurg unsara.
29. Ni qeþum du im ni waiht þizei gasehwum in þamma hlaiwa.
30. Ufdaupjands þan þana hlaif gaf ina du ainamma siponje seinaize þizei namo was Iudas.

Lesson 14

14.1 Strong verbs: class 1.

The principal parts of **beidan** (to await, expect) and **(ga)teihan** (to tell), typical verbs of this class, are as follows:

Infinitive	Preterite Singular	Preterite Plural	Past Participle
beidan	**baiþ**	**bidum**	**bidan-**
(ga)teihan	**(ga)taih**	**(ga)taihum**	**(ga)taihan-**

For an explanation of the ablaut pattern **ei** - **ai** - **i(ai)** see the historical notes to Lesson 12. The regular lowering of -**i**- to -**ai**- (= ε) before -**h**- has already been noted (§12.1).

The other verbs of this class are

beitan	bite	**(ur)reisan**	arise	**sweiban**	cease
dreiban	drive	**skeinan**	shine	**þeihan**	thrive
greipan	seize	**(dis)skreitan**	tear	**þreihan**	press, crowd
hneiwan	bow	**(ga)smeitan**	smear	**weihan**	fight
(bi)leiban	remain	**sneiþan**	cut, harvest	**weipan**	crown
(ga)leiþan	go	**speiwan**	spit	**(in)weitan**	greet, worship
leihwan	lend	**steigan**	ascend		

Also probably to be classified here are **digan** (to knead), with -**i**- for -**ei**-, and **neiwan** (to bear a grudge against), attested only in the 3rd pers. sing. of the preterite, **naiw** (Mk 6:19). The verb **keinan** (to sprout, grow) does not properly belong here: the attested participle -**kijan**- shows that the -**n**- of **keinan** belongs only to the present system (cf. **fraihnan** in Lesson 12.1); the expected preterite **kay* (Gothic ***kai**) has been replaced with **(us)keinoda** (Lk 8:8), showing that the verb was also interpreted as belonging to class 4 of the weak verbs with stem forms in -**na**-.

14.2 Coordinating conjunctions (continued from §13.1).

A. From the point of view of the Greek original.

5. γάρ is a postpositive conjunction introducing a statement which presents the cause or reason for what has just been stated, or an inferential conclusion therefrom. The Gothic translator used a variety of conjunctions to render γάρ:

a. **auk** (postpositive) *for, since, because* is used only to translate γάρ. E.g.

Lk 1:15 ἔσται γὰρ μέγας ἐνώπιον τοῦ κυρίου
wairþiþ auk mikils in andwairþja Fraujins
for he will become great in the presence of the Lord

Lk 1:30 μὴ φοβοῦ, Μαριάμ, εὗρες γὰρ χάριν παρὰ τῷ θεῷ
ni ogs þus, Mariam, bigast auk anst fram Guda,
Do not be afraid, Mary, for you have found favor from God.

b. **unte** (clause initial) *because.* E.g.

Mt 7:25 καὶ οὐκ ἔπεσεν, τεθεμελίωτο γαρ ἐπὶ τὴν πέτραν
jah (scil. **þata razn**) **ni gadraus, unte gasuliþ was ana staina**
and it did not collapse because it had been built on a foundation of stone

c. **allis** (postpositive) *for, since.* E.g.

Lk 6:26 οὐαὶ ὅταν ὑμᾶς καλῶς εἴπωσιν πάντες οἱ ἄνθρωποι,
κατὰ τὰ αὐτὰ γὰρ ἐποίουν τοῖς ψευδοπροφήταις οἱ πατέρες αὐτῶν
wai þan waila izwis qiþand allai mans;
samaleiko allis tawidedun galiugapraufetum attans ize
Woe! when all men speak well of you,
for thus did their fathers treat the false prophets.

d. **raihtis** (postpositive) *for, since.* E.g.

Lk 1:18 κατὰ τί γνώσομαι τοῦτο; ἐγὼ γάρ εἰμι πρεσβύτης ...
Bihwe kunnum þata? Ik raihtis im sineigs ...
How will we know that? For I am old ...

The translator seems to prefer **unte** when dealing with a reason for a simple action in the past, but his reason for choosing among **raihtis, allis,** and **auk** is elusive. The Vulgate nearly uniformly translates γάρ with *enim.*

6. (καὶ) ἐγένετο, ἐγένετο δὲ. These two expressions, traditionally translated *(and) it came to pass,* deserve special mention since they occur frequently in Luke and sporadically elsewhere. The normal past tense narrative sequence in Biblical Hebrew consisted of a series of clauses joined by the conjunction *and* followed immediately by the main verb of the clause:

... *and* Verb^1 + Subject + ... *and* Verb^2 + Subject + ... *and* Verb^3 + Subject + ...

When the speaker (or writer) wanted to insert a temporal clause or phrase into the narrative, he did so by prefacing the clause or phrase with the conjunction *and* + the 3rd person past tense equivalent of the verb *to be;* the main sequence was then continued with another, to us redundant, *and:*

... *and* Verb^1 + ... *and it-was* + temporal element + *and* Verb^2 + ... *and* Verb^3 + ...

This formula became a part of the translation Greek of the Hebrew (and Jewish Aramaic) speaking world and is commonplace, for example, in the Septuagint. In the Greek formula the *and* (καί) introducing the main clause after the temporal element is frequently omitted. Study the following examples and note the Gothic translation. The English translation given is overly literal in order to show the relevant content of the Greek for those readers with no Greek. Normal English would require omission of the formula entirely.

a. With καί:

Lk 8:22 ἐγένετο δὲ ἐν μιᾷ τῶν ἡμερῶν **καὶ** αὐτὸς ἐνέβη εἰς πλοῖον
and it came to pass on one of the days *and* he boarded a boat
warþ þan in ainamma þize dage *jah* is galaiþ in skip

Lk 9:51 ἐγένετο δὲ ἐν τῷ συμπληροῦσθαι τὰς ἡμέρας τῆς ἀναλήψεως αὐτοῦ
καὶ αὐτὸς τὸ πρόσωπον ἐστήριξεν τοῦ πορεύεσθαι εἰς Ἰ.
and it came to pass in the completion of the days of his being-received-up
and he set his face to go to Jerusalem.
warþ þan in þammei usfulnodedun dagos andanumtais is,
***jah* is andwairþi seinata gatulgida du gaggan in I.**

b. Without καί:

Lk 1:23 καὶ ἐγένετο ὡς ἐπλήσθησαν αἱ ἡμέραι τῆς λειτουργίας αὐτοῦ,
ἀπῆλθεν εἰς τὸν οἶκον αὐτοῦ
and it came to pass when the days of his service were completed, he went home
jah warþ, biþe usfullnodedun dagos andbahteis is, galaiþ du garda seinamma

7. ἀλλά. The clause-initial conjunction ἀλλά indicates a fairly strong contrast with the preceding statement and is translated in English as *but, however, and yet, nevertheless.* When preceded by a negative statement or phrase, it is translated in Gothic with **ak**, as in

Jn 14:10 **Þo waurda þoei ik rodja izwis af mis silbin ni rodja, ak atta saei in mis ist,**
sa taujiþ þo waurda
The words I speak to you I do not speak from myself, but rather the father who is in
me (is) the one who produces those words.

Otherwise, it is translated by Gothic **akei**, as in

Lk 6:27 **Akei izwis qiþa þaim hausjandam:** ... Nevertheless, to you who are listening I say: ...
Lk 7:25 **Akei hwa usiddjeduþ saihwan**? But then again, what did you really go out to see?

B. Summary from the Gothic point of view

1. **auk** (postpositive) *for, since, because;* used only to translate γάρ.

2. **unte** (clause initial) *because;* translating the Greek subordinate conjunctions ὅτι, διότι, καθότι, ἐπεί in this sense, as well as γάρ. **unte** is also frequent as a temporal conjunction *until, as long as,* translating Gk ἕως (ἄν, ὅτου, οὗ), ἐν ᾧ.

3. **allis** (postpositive) *for, since;* nearly always translating γάρ. There are three instances of adverbial use in the phrase **ni ... allis** *not at all.*

4. **raihtis** (postpositive) *for, since;* mainly translating γάρ, but also other Greek particles with similar meaning. **raihtis** is also used to translate μέν in the balanced construction μέν .. δέ (on the one hand ... on the other) as in

Mt 9:37 ὁ μὲν θερισμὸς πολύς, οἱ δὲ ἐργάται ὀλίγοι
asans raihtis managa, iþ waurstwjans fawai
the harvest is plentiful, but workers are few

5. **jah warþ** ... (**jah**)...; **warþ þan** ... (**jah**); see above.

6. **ak, akei** *but, however, nevertheless, and yet.* **Ak**, as indicated above, translates Gk ἀλλά when preceded by a negative statement or phrase. There are a few instances, however, where the preceding negative is implied rather than overt, as in Lk 17:8, where **ak** is preceded by a rhetorical question presupposing a negative response.

14.3 The preterite-present verb ***skal*** is inflected as follows:

Present:	**ik skal**	**weis skulum**	Active participle: **skuland-**
	þu skalt	**jus skuluþ**	
	is skal	**eis skulum**	

Preterite:	**ik skulda** ... (inflected as weak preterite)
Past participle:	**skuld-**

Skal may be used as a transitive verb with an accusative direct object in the meaning *to owe (money):*

Lk 7:41 **ains skulda skatte fimf hunda**
one (debtor) owed five hundred denarii

Its most frequent use, however, is as an auxiliary verb translating Gk δεῖ, μέλλειν, ἔχειν, thus English *shall, be obliged to, to have to, must, to be about to, to be destined to* as illustrated by the following examples:

Lk 17:10 **þatei skuldedum taujan tawidedum**
we did that which we were obliged to do (i.e. as our duty)

Lk 2:49 **in þaim attins meinis skulda wisan**
I had to be involved in the affairs of my father

Jn 12:33 **hwileikamma dauþau skulda gadauþnan**
by what sort of death he was destined to die

Jn 9:4 **ik skal waurkjan waurstwa þis sandjandins mik**
I must do the works of the one who sent me

The past participle has already been introduced in the frequent expression **skuld ist** *it is right, proper, lawful (for smn: D; to do: inf.).* It may also be used predicatively with a personal subject, as in

Jn 12:34 **skulds ist ushauhjan sa sunus mans**
the Son of Man is destined to be lifted up

In this infrequent construction the complementary infinitive always has a passive sense.

14.4 The verbal prefix ***af-*** denotes physical or figurative separation and corresponds to various English adverbs such as *away, off, aside.* It sometimes materially alters the meaning of the base verb, as in

afsatjan	set aside, divorce	**afgaggan**	go away
afgiban sik	depart	**afhaban sik**	hold self away from, refrain
afleiþan	go away	**afmaitan**	cut off
afletan	let, leave off, abandon, divorce	**afqiþan**	renounce
afwairpan	cast away	**afwandjan**	turn away, reject

and sometimes simply reinforces the notion of separation already present in the base verb, as in

afskaidan	divide, separate (**skaidan** *idem*)	**afairzjan**	lead astray (**airzjan** *idem*)
afdauþjan	kill (**dauþjan** *idem*)	**affilhan**	hide sthg away (**filhan** *idem*)
afhrainjan	clean sthg off (**hrainjan** *idem*)	**afþliuhan**	flee (**þliuhan** *idem*)

Occasionally **af-** indicates that the action of the base verb is carried to a particular conclusion, as in **afslahan** to kill from **slahan** to strike. Note, too, the use of **af-** with **afblindnan** (become blind), **afdaubnan** (become deaf), and **afdumbnan** (become dumb).

Unfortunately, most of the compound verbs with **af-** are attested only once or twice, and it is therefore impossible to determine the full range of difference in meaning between the simple verb and the compound verb. In some instances the compound verb is probably no more than a perfective form of the imperfective simple verb.

Vocabulary 14

Verbs:

beidan, baiþ *sv 1* to wait for (*G*), look forward to (*G*).
gateihan, gataih *sv 1* to tell (smn: *D*; that: **þatei**; about: **bi** *A*; how: **hwaiwa**...).
urreisan, urrais *sv 1* to rise, arise, get up.
inweitan, inwait *sv 1* to greet respectfully (*A*), pay one's respects; to do obeisance to, to worship (*A*).
usleiþan, uslaiþ *sv 1* to go out of, leave (a place: *A*, **us** *D*); to pass out (through: **þairh** *A*); to set out (across: **hindar** *A*).
afleiþan, aflaiþ *sv 1* to depart, go away, withdraw (from: **af** *D*).
afgaggan, afiddja *sv 7 irreg* to go away (from: **af** *D*).
afniman, afnam *sv 4* to remove, take away (*A*; from: **af** *D*).

Nouns:

karkara *sf* jail, prison (< Lat *carcer*).
hunda *sn pl* hundred(s); the counted noun is in the *Gpl.*
reiks *m* prominent citizen, community leader.
þrutsfill *sn* leprosy; **habands þrutsfill** a leper.

Adjectives:

þrutsfill- *adj* leprous
baud- *adj* deaf, deaf and dumb.

Other:

þatei *conj* is also used to introduce direct quotation (translating Gk ὅτι).
jainþro *adv* from there, thence.
hwaiwa *interrog adv* how? in what manner?

Lesson 14

hwan *interrog adv* when? **hwan filu** how much?
biþe *conj* when.
miþþanei *conj* while.
ni manna (fully inflected) no one.
sundro *adv* aside, in private.
þairh *prep A* (motion) through; through (agency of), by means of; according to (writer or written source).
inn *adv* in, into

And the conjunctions **auk, raihtis, allis, jah warþ, ak,** and **akei** from §14.2.

Exercises

A. Translate. Pluralize the subject and whatever else is required.

1. Ik frabauhta im fimf hunda sweine in twa hunda skatte.
2. Sa magus skal gasitan miþ aiþein seinai jah gaþahan.
3. Is baiþ unsara þar, akei ni mahtedum atgaggan du imma.
4. Duhwe þu ni inwaist þana þiudan?
5. Is usbauht mat jah wein þrim hundam skatte.
6. Sa þrutsfill habands gahailiþs warþ af þamma unhailja.
7. Duhwe þu ni gataiht mis þo alla?
8. Ik skulda im niun hunda skatte.
9. Þu skalt waurkjan goda waurstwa miþþanei wisis in þamma fairhwau.
10. Duhwe ni aflaist biþe gasahwt þata?
11. Hwan qimis jainþro?
12. Is skal wisan miþ izwis twans dagans.
13. Ik wiljau þus kunþi giban bi waurda is.
14. Þu skalt insandjan þana saman asni.
15. Ik gaumida twaim hundam lambe ana jainai haiþjai.

B. Translate, giving particular attention to the conjunctions.

1. Du aiwa auk wisiþ aikklesjo Iesuis Xristaus.
2. Ni mahtedun rodjan unte waurþun gafullidai agisis mikilis.
3. Jah warþ, miþþanei is was rodjands, jah magus ains atiddja du imma.
4. Pawlus gamelida im qiþands þatei, "Ik qima at izwis, þan Makidonja usleiþa."
5. Gagg du garda þeinamma du þeinaim jah gateih im hwan filu þus Frauja gatawida jah gaarmaida þuk.
6. Þanuh qaþ du þamma haltin: "Urreis nim þana ligr þeinana jah gang in gard þeinana." Jah urreisands galaiþ in gard seinana.
7. Jah warþ, biþe ik gahausida bi þo alla þoei gatawidedun, jah urrais jah aflaiþ fairra im.
8. Jah eis þahaidedun jah mann ni gataihun in jainaim dagam ni waiht þizei gasehwun.
9. Jah warþ, biþe Iesus rodida du imma þata waurd, jah suns þata þrutsfill aflaiþ af imma jah gahailiþs warþ.
10. Ni mahta manna usleiþan þairh þana wig jainana faura þaim unhulþons habandam.
11. Jah Iesus aflaiþ miþ siponjam seinaim du marein jah filu manageins laistidedun afar imma.
12. Biþe þan warþ dags, usgaggands Iesus galaiþ ana staþ auþidos du bidjan, iþ manageins sokidedun ina jah qemun und ina du gahailjan imma.
13. Wildedum qiman at izwis, akei ni mahtedum.
14. Jus auk ni sijuþ wairþai libainais aiweinons.

15. Wiljau raihtis gateihan izwis bi taiknins þozei gawaurhta jah hwaiwa gatawida armaion managa siukaim jah unledaim.
16. Duhwe gaþiuþides ainana sunu þeinana, akei ni gaþiuþides þana anþarana?
17. Akei ni goþ ist drigkan watins þizos ahwos.
18. Eis auk haband laun sein in himina.
19. Jah warþ, biþe gahausidedun þatei harjis mikils atnehwida sik, jah urrisun jah afliþun in fairgunja.
20. Swikunþa auk Guda ist gahugds hairtane izwaraize.
21. Ik gawandida mik þairh þana saman wig, akei ni gamotida mann ana wiga.
22. Akei sa sunus mans skal manag winnan in jainamma daga.
23. So widuwo þan gatrauaida du þamma lekja jah gaf imma þans sibun skattans.
24. Wasuþþan Iohannes galagiþs in karkarai.
25. Þaruh galesun sik so managei jah sokidedun usqistjan imma.
26. Nist auk skuld usniman þos bokos us alh.
27. Ni auk galaubidedun broþrjus is imma.
28. Jah andhafjands Iesus wiþra þana unhulþan qaþ: "Gamelid ist þatei ni bi hlaib ainana libaid manna, ak bi all waurde Gudis.
29. Saei allis wili saiwala seina nasjan fraqisteiþ izai; aþþan saei fraqisteiþ saiwalai seinai in meina ganasjiþ þo.

C. Translate.

1. Jah warþ, biþe usfillida Iesus laisjands þans twalif siponjans seinans, aflaiþ jainþro du laisjan jah merjan and baurgs jah haimos anþaraize gauje. Iþ Iohannes gahausjands in karkarai waurstwa Xristaus, insandjands þairh siponjans seinans qaþ du imma: "Þu ist sa qimanda? Aiþþau skulum weis beidan jah anþaris?" Jah andhafjands Iesus qaþ du im: "Gaggandans gateihiþ Iohanne þatei gahauseiþ jah gasaihwiþ: blindai ussaihwand, jah haltai gaggand, þrutsfillai gahailidai wairþand, jah baudai gahausjand, jah dauþai urreisand, jah unledaim faheþs gibana ist.

2. Miþþanei is rodida þata du im, þaruh reiks ains qimands inwait ina, qiþands þatei, "Dauhtar meina nu gaswalt (has died), akei qimands atlagei handu þeina ana ija, jah libaiþ." Jah urreisands Iesus iddja afar imma jah siponjos is. Jah qimands Iesus in garda þis reikis jah gasaihwands managein auhjondein (mourning loudly) qaþ du im: "Afleiþiþ, unte ni gaswalt so mawi, ak slepiþ (is sleeping)." Þanuh þan aflaiþ so managei, atgaggands inn habaida handu izos, jah urrais so mawi. Jah usiddja meriþa so (the report of this) and alla jaina airþa.

3. Atiddjedun þan du imma aiþei jah broþrjus is jah ni mahtedun atnehwjan sik faura managein. Jah gataihan warþ imma þatei, "Aiþei þeina jah broþrjus þeinai sitand uta gasaihwan þuk gairnjandona." Iþ is andhafjands qaþ du im: "Aiþei meina jah broþrjus meinai þai sind, þai waurd Gudis gahausjandans jah taujandans."

4. Jah warþ, miþþanei was is bidjands sundro, gamotidedun imma siponjos is jah frah ins qiþands: "Hwana mik qiþand wisan þos manageins?" Iþ eis andhafjandans qeþun: "Iohannen þana daupjand, anþarai Heleian (Elijah), sumai þan þatei praufetus sums þize airizane (former) is." Qaþ þan du im: "Aþþan jus hwana mik qiþiþ wisan?" Andhafjands Paitrus qaþ: "Þu is Xristus, sunus Gudis."

Lesson 15

15.1 Strong verbs: Class 2. Verbs of this class, typified by **driusan** (to fall) and **tiuhan** (to lead), have the following principal parts:

Present:	Pret. sing.	Pret. pl.:	Past part.
driusan	**draus**	**drusum**	**drusan-**
tiuhan	**tauh**	**tauhum**	**tauhan-**

For a discussion of the ablaut series **iu** - **au** - **u** with the lowering of **u** to **au** [ɔ] before **h**, see the historical comments to Lesson 12. The following verbs belong to this class:

(ana)biudan	bid, offer	**(fra)liusan**	lose
biugan	bend	**liugan**	tell a lie
driugan	be a soldier	**niutan** (2)	enjoy; catch
driusan	fall	**siukan**	be sick
giutan	pour	**(af)skiuban**	push aside
hiufan	mourn	**sliupan**	slip
(dis)hniupan	break, tear apart	**tiuhan**	lead
(ga)kiusan	choose, test; reject	**þliuhan**	flee
kriusan	gnash	**(us)þriutan**	trouble
liudan	grow, spring up		

The verb **galukan, galauk, galukum, galukan-** (to close) also belongs here; the irregular present stem **galuk-**, showing a reduced grade instead of a full grade of the original root, is taken to be based on the old aorist stem (see historical comments).

15.2 The subjunctive (also called the optative). Apart from the weak verbs of class 2, the conjugation of the present and preterite subjunctive is uniform for all of the remaining verb types. The strong verb **niman** is conjugated as follows:

Present Subjunctive:			Preterite Subjunctive:		
	nimau	**nimaima**		**nemjau**	**nemeima**
	nimais	**nimaiþ**		**nemeis**	**nemeiþ**
	nimai	**nimaina**		**nemi**	**nemeina**

As illustrated by **nemjau, nemeis** etc., the preterite subjunctive of all strong verbs is based on the stem of the indicative preterite plural. The same is true of weak verbs, as illustrated by **sokjan** and **haban:**

Present Subjunctive:			Preterite Subjunctive:		
	sokjau	**sokjaima**		**sokidedjau**	**sokidedeima**
	sokjais	**sokjaiþ**		**sokidedeis**	**sokidedeiþ**
	sokjai	**sokjaina**		**sokidedi**	**sokidedeina**
	habau	**habaima**		**habaidedjau**	**habaidedeima**
	habais	**habaiþ**		**habaidedeis**	**habaidedeiþ**
	habai	**habaina**		**habaidedi**	**habaidedeina**

The present and preterite subjunctive stems of the copula, **skal, wiljan,** and **mag** are as follows. Inflection is perfectly regular, but remember that **mag** and **skal** were originally preterite (IE perfect) forms and the subjunctive is inflected accordingly, e.g. **skuljau, skuleis, skuli....**

Present:	**sijau, sijais...**	Preterite:	**wesjau,weseis...**
	magjau, mageis...		**mahtedjau, mahtedeis...**
	---		**wildedjau, wildedeis...**
	skuljau, skuleis ...		**skuldedjau, skuldedeis...**

The **-j-** of **sijau** etc. is sometimes omitted in the spelling, thus **siau** etc.

Our discussion of the use of the subjunctive, which is quite extensive, will be distributed over the next several lessons.

A. The subjunctive in principal clauses

I. Non-interrogative principal clauses

In non-interrogative principal clauses the present subjunctive is employed to express commands and wishes. In the first person plural its use in commands corresponds to English *let us ...*, also termed the cohortative. In the Pauline epistles and the first ten chapters of Luke the subjunctive is employed for the cohortative, but elsewhere one regularly finds a form identical to the first person plural of the indicative. In this use the latter form is always classified in the Gothic grammars under the heading of imperative. The negative of the cohortative always employs the subjunctive. Study the following examples:

Lk 2:15 **þairhgaggaima ju und Beþlahaim jah saihwaima** Let us go then to Bethlehem and see
Lk 9:33 **gawaurkjaima hleiþros þrins** Let us make three booths
Ro 13:13 **garedaba gaggaima** let us conduct ourselves becomingly
Ro 14:13 **ni ... uns misso stojaima** let us not judge one another

but Lk 20:14 **afslah*am* ina** ... let us kill him ...

In the 2nd person the subjunctive command amounts to a polite imperative or injunction, often involving an implication of duty or obligation, as in

Lk 1:13 **jah haitais namo is Iohannen** and you shall call his name John
Lk 1:20 **jah sai, sijais þahands jah ni magands rodjan** and behold, you shall be silent and unable to speak
Lk 4:8 **Fraujan Guþ þeinana inweitais** you shall worship the Lord God

The negative imperative, as well as the negative injunctive, nearly always employs the subjunctive. E.g.

Lk 4:12 **Ni fraisais Fraujan Guþ þeinana.** Do not tempt the Lord your God.

The few exceptions involve commands ordering a cessation of an activity already begun, as in

Lk 8:52 **Ni gretiþ!** Do not weep! (i.e. Stop weeping!)

In the 3rd person there is a separate form for the indirect imperative (*let him ...*), the singular of which (ending in **-adau**) occurs three times and the plural of which (in **-andau**) occurs only once. E.g.

Mt 27:42 **afsteigadau nu af þamma galgin** let him now come down from the cross

It is a bit misleading to include these forms in every verbal paradigm, as is commonly done, although there is no reason to doubt their authenticity (see the historical comments). Otherwise, the subjunctive is employed to express the 3rd person indirect imperatives, both singular and plural, positive and negative. E.g.

Jn 14:27 **ni indrobnaina izwara hairtona nih faurhtjaina** let not your hearts be troubled nor fearful

Jn 9:21 **silba bi sik rodjai** let him speak for himself

2. Direct questions

The use of the subjunctive in direct questions introduces a modality that is variously characterized as potential or dubitative. More often than not it simply translates the Greek future, as in

Lk 1:34 πῶς ἔσται τοῦτο, ἐπεὶ ἄνδρα οὐ γιγνώσκω;
Hwaiwa sijai þata, þandei aban ni kann?
How can that be, since I have no husband?

Lk 1:66 τί ἄρα τὸ παιδίον τοῦτο ἔσται;
Hwa skuli þata barn wairþan?
What can this child be destined to be?

Lk 9:41 ἕως πότε ἔσομαι πρὸς ὑμᾶς καί ἀνέξομαι ὑμῶν;
Und hwa siau at izwis jah þulau izwis?
How long am I to be with you and put up with you?

Lk 20:15 τί οὖν ποιήσει αὐτοῖς ὁ κύριος τοῦ ἀμπελῶνος ;
Hwa nu taujai im frauja þis weinagardis?
What, then, will the owner of the vineyard do to them?

or the Greek subjunctive, as in

Lk 3:10 τί οὖν ποιήσωμεν; **An hwa taujaima**? But what can we do?

Note that in all these and similar instances there is a context of surprise, dismay, or exasperation that is not present in a simple question.

The Gothic translator shows a tendency to introduce the subjunctive in the second element of a double question, apparently feeling a subordinate relationship (conditional, causal, purpose) between the two clauses not apparent in the Greek. E.g.

ICor 9:7 τίς φυτεύει ἀμπελῶνα καὶ τὸν καρπὸν αὐτοῦ οὐκ ἐσθίει;
Hwas satjiþ weinatriwa jah akran þize ni matjai?
Who plants vines and then doesn't eat their fruit?

Lk 7:31 τίνι οὖν ὁμοιώσω τοὺς ἀνθρόπους τῆς γενεᾶς ταύτης, καὶ τίνι εἰσὶν ὅμοιοι;
Hwe nu galeiko þans mans þis kunjis, jah hwe sijaina galeikai?
To what shall I liken the men of this generation (scil. so that you might know) what they are like?

3. In unfulfillable wishes

Occasionally the preterite subjunctive is used in a principle clause to express an unfulfilled or unfulfillable wish, usually introduced by **wainei**... would that ...! E.g.

I Cor 4:8 **Jah wainei þiudanodedeiþ, ei jah weis izwis miþþiudanoma.**
And would that you would become king, so that we too might rule along with you!

B. The subjunctive in subordinate clauses after verbs of *willing, wishing, commanding, prohibiting*, and *allowing*

Verbs expressing a wish, an order, a prohibition, or a caution are followed either by an infinitive construction, as has been indicated in the Lesson vocabularies with particular verbs, or by the conjunction **ei** followed by the subjunctive. The present tense of the main verb is usually followed by present tense in the subjunctive clause, and the preterite by the preterite, although there are exceptions. The principal verbs of this type are **wiljan, bidjan, anabiudan, faurbiudan, qiþan, saihwan,** and **letan**. Study the following examples carefully:

Mk 10:51 **Hwa wileis ei taujau þus**? What do you want me to do for you?

Jn 17:24 **Wiljau ei þarei im ik jah þai sijaina miþ mis**...
I want also these to be with me where I am...

Mk 9:30 **ni wilda ei hwas wissedi** he wanted no one to know (pret. subj. of **witan**)

Lk 8:31 **jah bad ina ei ni anabudi im in afgrundiþa galeiþan**
and he beseeched him not to command them to go into the abyss
[note **bidjan** with **ei**, but **anabiudan** with the infinitive]

Mk 7:36 **jah anabauþ im ei mann ni qeþeina** and he commanded them to tell no one

Mk 6:8 **jah faurbauþ im ei waiht ni nemeina in wig**
and he forbade them to take anything on the road

Lk 4:3 **Qiþ þamma staina ei wairþai hlaibs.** Tell this stone to turn into bread.

Mk 3:9 **jah qaþ þaim siponjam seinaim ei skip habaiþ wesi at imma**
and he told his disciples that a ship should be ready for him

Mk 11:16 **jah ni lailot** (pret. of **letan**) **ei hwas þairhberi kas þairh þo alh**
and he did not allow anyone to carry anything through the temple

Note that in most of these instances an infinitive construction is more idiomatic in the English translation than a clause with *that*... and the English subjunctive (e.g. he ordered him *that he tell* no one).

[The uses of the subjunctive are continued in §16.2]

15.3 The enclitic coordinating conjunction *-uh*.

The conjunction **-uh** (and), usually equivalent to **jah**, is enclitic and to be translated before the word to which it is attached, exactly like Latin *-que*, Greek τε, and Sanskrit *ca*, with which it is directly cognate. Already noted is the frequent appearance of **-uh** with **þan** in the phrase **-uh þan** (§13.1B2) and with **iþ** in **iþ ...uh**

(§13.1.A2c); it is also the second element of **þanuh** and **þaruh**, but these are best taken as unitary lexical items, as is **nih** *nor*, **nih ... nih ...** *neither ... nor ....* Its use otherwise is less frequent and more or less unpredictable except for two situations where **-uh** appears slightly more often than elsewhere:

a. Two verbs in close sequence may be connected with **-uh**, as in

Mk 2:11 **urreis nimuh þata badi þein jah gagg**... arise and pick up your bed and go...
Mk 16:7 **akei gaggiþ qiþiduh du siponjam is** but go and say to his disciples ...

but note

Mk:5:41 **jah fairgraip bi handau þata barn qaþuh du izai** and he took that child by the hand and said to her

where the verbs are not in any special close relationship.

b. When a sentence or clause begins with a prepositional phrase, there seems to be a slight tendency to use **-uh** rather than **jah** as the coordinating conjunction, as in

Lk 10:21 **inuh þizai hweilai swegnida ahmin Iesus**
ἐν αὐτῇ τῇ ὥρᾳ... and in that (same) hour Jesus rejoiced in the Spirit

Lk 6:45 **uzuh allis ufarfullein hairtins rodeid munþs is**
ἐκ γὰρ περισσεύματος...for out of the overflow of his heart does his mouth speak

Lk 10:7 **inuh þan þamma garda wisaiþ...**
ἐν αὐτῇ δὲ τῇ οἰκίᾳ... in that (same) house, then, you shall stay...

The analysis of these and other instances of **-uh** is complicated by the co-occurrence with other conjunctions like **þan** and **allis** and by the simple fact that there are not enough examples to establish any kind of predictive rule. The reader will have to deal with each instance when encountered, especially in reference to the underlying Greek.

The attachment of the enclitic **-uh** causes some phonological changes:

(1) Final **-a** is dropped; thus **þata** + **-uh** becomes **þatuh**.
(2) The **-u-** of **-uh** is dropped after other vowels, thus **so** + **-uh** > **soh**, **ni** + **-uh** > **nih**, etc.
(3) Final **-s** may be replaced with **-z-**, as in **þans** + **-uh** > **þanzuh**, **us** + **-uh** > **uzuh**; but **-s** may be retained, as in **was** + **-uh** > **wasuh**.
(4) Final **-þ** may be replaced with **-d-**, as in **qiþiþ** + **-uh** > **qiþiduh**.
(5) Final **-f** may be replaced with **-b-**, as in **uf** + **-uh** > **ubuh**.

These last three changes may be viewed as an undoing of the Devoicing Rule. Do not confuse **-uh** with the interrogative particle **-u**, attached to the first word of a question and producing these same phonological changes (see §20.5).

15.4 Tmesis (the separation of a verbal prefix from its verb)

When a verb with a prefix begins a clause, the conjunction **-uh**, as well as the combinations **-uh þan** and **-uþþan**, may be attached to the prefix. E.g.

Lk 1:63	**nam gahmelida** (for **ga-uh-melida**) and he took (the tablet) and wrote
Jn 7:32	**inuhsandidedun** and they sent
Jn 16:28	**uzuhiddja** (for **us-uh-iddja**) and I came forth
Gal 2:2	**uzuþþaniddja bi andhuleinai** I went up, furthermore, because of the revelation ...

There are only a dozen or so instances of this phenomenon with **-uh**, **-uh þan, and -uþþan**, and a few others involving the interrogative particle **-u** (§20.6). More unusual occurrences include

Lk 20:25 **Usnugibiþ** (for **us-nu-gibiþ**) **þo kaisaris kaisara jah þo Gudis Guda**
Render, then, what is Caesar's to Caesar, and what is God's, to God.

Jn 6:22 **þatei miþniqam** (for **miþ-ni-qam**) **siponjam seinaim Iesus**
that Jesus had not come with his disciples

Jn 11:25 **saei galaubeiþ du mis, þauh gabadauþniþ** (for **ga-ba-dauþniþ**), **libaid**
the one who believes in me, even though he dies, will live

15.5 The verbal prefix *uf-*.

As a verbal prefix, **uf** sometimes has the meaning *under* associated with its prepositional counterpart, often merely emphasizing a similar component in the semantics of the base verb. E. g.

ufdaupjan	to submerge
ufmeljan	to sign
ufhausjan	to submit, obey
ufhnaiwjan	to subject (**hnaiwjan** to abase)
ufsneiþan	to slaughter (**sneiþan** to cut, harvest)

More often, however, the meaning is *up from under, out from within,* as in

ufblesan	to inflate (***blesan** to blow)
ufgairdan	to gird up (***gairdan** to gird)
ufhaban	to hold up
ufhropjan	to cry out (**hropjan** to call, cry)
ufrakjan	to reach out, stretch forth (***rakjan** reach)
ufgraban	to dig up (**graban** to dig)

Here again, however, it is obvious that **uf-** is merely the appropriate perfectivizer for a meaning already included in the base verb. There are several verbs in which the meaning of the prefix is not readily defined. E.g.

ufkunnan	to become aware of, recognize (**kunnan** to know)
ufbrikan	to despise, reject (**brikan** to break)

Vocabulary 15

Verbs:

anabiudan, anabauþ *sv 2* to order, command (smn: *D*; to do sthg: inf., **du** + inf., **ei** + subj.).

faurbiudan, faurbauþ *sv 2* to forbid (smn: *D*; to do sthg: **ei ni** + subj.); to prevent (same constructions).
driusan, draus (*imperf.* and *perf.*), **gadriusan, gadraus** (*perf.*) *sv 2* to fall (upon: **ana** *D, A*; into: **in** *A*; at the feet of: **du** *D*, **du fotum** *G*).
tiuhan, tauh *sv 2* to lead, conduct (*A*; to smn: *D*, **du** *D*).
attiuhan, attauh *sv 2* to lead, conduct, bring.
ustiuhan, ustauh *sv 2* to lead out, lead away; to go through to the end of, to complete, fulfill, accomplish.
gahrainjan *wv 1* to cleanse, purify (smn: *A*; of: *G*).
ufhausjan *wv 1* to obey (smn: *D*).
hropjan *wv 1*, **ufhropjan** *wv 1* to cry out, to shout.
bileiþan, bilaiþ *sv 1* to abandon, forsake (smn: *D* or *A*); to leave behind at one's death.
þliuhan, þlauh (*imperf.*), **gaþliuhan, gaþlauh** (*perf.*) to flee (from: **af, faura** *D*); to shun, turn aside from (*A*).

Nouns:

gajuko *wf* parable, similitude.
malma *wm* sand.
fotus *sm* foot; **du fotum** *G* at the feet of.
gadrauhts *wm(i)* soldier (cf. **driugan** in §15.I.)
aiwaggeljo *wf* the gospel (Gk εὐαγγέλιον).
rign *sn* rain.
hweila *sf* hour, time, while.
gudja *wm* priest.
haubiþ (*G* **-dis**) *sn* head.
ustauhts *sf* fulfillment, accomplishment.

Adjectives:

galeik- *adj* like, resembling (*D*).
handug- *adj* wise.
swes- *adj* of one's own, belonging to one's self; as noun *sn* one's own property.
dwal- *adj* foolish.
niund- *ordinal adj* ninth. Ordinals are always inflected as weak adjectives.

Other:

suns, sunsaiw *adv* immediately thereupon, straightway, suddenly.
utana *adv* outside; *prep G* outside of.
ei *subordinating conj* that, in order that. Specific uses will be taken up in the lessons.
aftra *adv* back, again.
Peilatus (*D* **-au**) Pilate.
Heleias (*G* **-leiins**, *D* **-lijin**, *A* **-lian**) Elijah.
Iudaius (*G* **-aiaus**) *m* a Jew; **Iudaieis** *pl* (*G* **-aie**, *D* **-aium**, *A* **- uns**) the Jews.

Exercises

A. Translate. Pluralize the subjects and adjust the rest of the sentence accordingly. E.g. (1) **Duhwe jus ni ufhausideduþ laisarja izwaramma?**

1. Duhwe þu ni ufhausides laisarja þeinamma?
2. Gadraus rign mikil jah fraqistida baurg ize.
3. Is attauh þata barn du gudjam þaiei wesun in alh.
4. Jah warþ, biþe sa þrutsfill habands gasahw þatei gahrainiþs warþ, jah ufhropida fahedai mikilai.
5. Is baiþ ustauhtais waurde þizos aiwaggeljons.
6. Sa dwala wair ni ufhauseiþ witoda Gudis.
7. Gateih imma þatei skip is ist full malmins jah watins.
8. Is urrais jah uslaiþ hindar marein.

9. Sa gadrauhts ustauh ina sundro utana weihsis.
10. Qiþan ist fram sumaim þatei jains stains gadraus us himina.
11. Sa gudja afnam þos bokos af imma jah gaf anþaramma.
12. Sa siponeis mahta in namin Iesuis gahrainjan ina þis þrutsfillis.
13. Is gahausida waurda aiwaggeljons akei ni ufhausida im.
14. Hwis beidis? Urreis suns jah fliuh in fairguni!
15. Ik ustauh alla waurstwa þoei þu atgaft mis du waurkjan.
16. Jah suns so unhulþo ufhropida stibnai mikilai uzuhiddja us þamma magau.
17. Ik haba gadrauhtins managans uf mis silbin.
18. Hwaiwa gadraust þu in þo ahwa?

B. Translate.

1. Þliuhaima nu af þaim wilþjam diuzam.
2. Ni bileiþais aiw qen þeina jah barna þeina.
3. Þai skalkos ufhausjaina fraujam seinaim.
4. Beidais meina jainar.
5. Þliuhais af waurdam ubilaize manne.
6. Urreisaima jah galeiþaima du þamma reik.
7. Þeinai andbahtos afnimaina þos tainjos.
8. Ni gateihaiþ mann bi þatei gasehwuþ.
9. Galisaima uns jainar in niundon hweilai.
10. Wainai mahtedeima þliuhan faura þamma mikilin harja!
11. Driusaiþ du fotum is jah bidjaiþ ina giban izwis fralet.
12. Inweitaima uns misso.
13. Wisai þata barn her þrija jera jah þan gawandjai sik in weihs sein.
14. Ni bairais þana malman in razn.
15. Wainai ni fraqemjau allamma swesa meinamma in wein jah qinons!
16. Alla so managei usleiþaina suns þo baurg.
17. Wainai gasehweima jainos taiknins jah galaubidedeima!

C. Translate.

1. Hwa wileiþ ei taujaima izwis?
2. Jah anabauþ seinaim gadrauhtim ei ustauheina ina jah galagidedeina in karkarai.
3. Saihw ei mann ni qiþais bi þana baudan.
4. Jah faurbauþ im ei waiht ni nemeina in wig.
5. Anabiuþ im ei afnimaina jainans stainans mikilans.
6. Ik qaþ siponjam þeinaim ei uswaurpeina þo unhulþon, akei ni mahtedun.
7. Ni wilda ei jah eis biliþeina imma.
8. Ik faurbiuda þus ei ni gaggais miþ jainamma waira dwalamma.
9. Saihwiþ ei atsaihwaiþ faura laiseinai ize ubilai.
10. Ik bidja þuk ei faurbiudais siponjam þeinaim ei þo ubilon laisein ni hausjaina.
11. Duhwe wileiþ ei þo barna wisaina her?
12. Is faurbauþ uns ei ni galiþeima in þata skip.
13. Anabudum imma ei usliþi gawi unsar jah galiþi hindar marein.

D. Translate.

1. Jah qaþ Iesus: "Sai, qimiþ hweila (Jah nu qam!) jah jus mik ainana bileiþiþ. Jah ni im ains, unte Atta miþ mis ist."
2. Iþ Peilatus aftra andhafjands qaþ du im: "Hwa wileiþ ei taujau þammei qiþiþ þiudan Iudaie?"

3. Jah qaþ so mawi du þamma þiudana: "Wiljau ei mis gibais ana mesa (tray) haubiþ Iohannis þis daupjandins."
4. Jah warþ, miþþanei was is in ainai baurge, jah sai, manna fulls þrutsfillis jah gasaihwands Iesu driusands ana andwairþi bad ina qiþands: "Frauja, jabai wileis, magt mik gahrainjan."
5. Gahausjandei raihtis qino bi ina, þizozei habaida dauhtar unhulþon, qimandei draus du fotum is.

6. Jah anabauþ im ei tauheina þana blindan du sis. Biþe nehwa was imma, frah ina qiþands: "Hwa þus wileis ei taujau?" Iþ is qaþ: "Frauja, wiljau ei fragibais mis siun." Jah Iesus qaþ du imma: "Ussaihw! Galaubeins þeina ganasida þuk." Jah suns ussahw.

7. Jah warþ, biþe so managei þizo haimo ni wildedun hausjan laisarja ize, qeþunuh: "Frauja, wileizu[1] ei qiþaima: 'Fon atgaggai dalaþ us himina jah fraqimai im,' swe jah Heleias gatawida?" Gawandjands þan du im Iesus qaþ: "Sunus mans ni qam saiwalom qistjan, ak nasjan." Jah iddjedun in anþara haim.

8. Þanuh Iesus laisida ins gajukom qiþands: "Saei nu hauseiþ waurda meina jah taujiþ þo galeiks ist waira frodamma saei gatimrida razn sein ana staina. Jah atiddja dalaþ rign jah qemun ahwos jah windos jah bistugqun (pounded) bi þamma razna jainamma, jah ni gadraus, unte gatimriþ was ana staina. Akei saei hauseiþ waurda meina jah ni taujiþ þo, galeiks ist mann dwalamma saei gatimrida razn sein ana malmin. Jah atiddja dalaþ rign jah qemun ahwos jah windos jah bistugqun bi jainamma razna, jah gadraus, jah was drus (fall) is mikils!" Jah warþ, þan ustauh Iesus þo waurda, sildaleikidedun manageins ana laiseinai is. Was auk laisjands ins swe waldufni habands, jah ni swaswe bokarjos.

---

[1] for **wileis-u**, where **-u** indicates a question (see §20.5).

Lesson 16

16.1 The subjunctive in purpose clauses.

Purpose, when not expressed by a simple infinitive construction with or without **du**, may be indicated with a full clause beginning with **ei** followed by the subjunctive. The sequence of tenses is the same as that noted with verbs of *commanding* etc.: present follows present, and preterite, preterite. E.g.

Mk 1:38 **Gaggam du þaim bisunjane haimom jah baurgim ei jah jainar merjau, unte duþe qam.**
Let us go to the neighboring villages and towns so that I may preach there too, for I came for that purpose.

Mk 10:17 **Hwa taujau ei libainais aiweinons arbja wairþau?** What should I do so that I may become heir to life eternal?

Mk 9:22 **Jah ufta ina jah in fon atwarp jah in wato ei usqistidedi imma.** And often it (the unclean spirit) would cast him even into fire and water so that it might destroy him.

16.2 Nominal clauses with *þatei, ei,* and *þei.*

Nominal clauses introduced with the conjunctions **þatei, ei** and **þei** function most frequently as the direct object of verbs of *thinking, believing, supposing, saying, knowing,* and the like. Unfortunately, because infinitival rather than clausal constructions predominate for many of the verbs involved, the paucity of relevant examples for any one subgroup of verbs precludes any sort of definitive statement on the occurrence of the subjunctive versus the indicative in those clauses, but the situation is approximately as follows:

a. Verbs of *thinking, supposing, imagining, hoping,* and *expecting* [including **wenjan, hugjan, þugkjan,** and **munan** (for all of which see the Vocabulary)] usually have object clauses introduced with the conjunction **ei** (rarely **þei**) followed by the subjunctive. E. g.

John 13:29 **sumai mundedun ei, unte arka habaida Iudas, þatei qeþi imma Iesus**
some thought that because Judas was in charge of the money-box Jesus was speaking of him [note the resumption of the **ei**-clause with **þatei** after the interruption]

2Cor 13:6 **wenja ei kunneiþ þatei weis ni sijum ungakusanai**
I hope that you will learn that we are not unsuccessful

Jn 11:13 **iþ jainai hugidedun þatei is bi slep qeþi** but they thought that he was speaking of sleep

Lk 19:11 **jah þuhta im ei suns skulda wesi þiudangardi Gudis gaswikunþjan** and they thought that the kingdom of God was due to appear immediately [note the passive sense of the infinitive **gaswikunþjan** (to reveal) after **skuld**]

but note the indicative in , e.g.,

1Cor 4:9 **man auk þei Guþ ... ustaiknida** for I think that God has singled out ...

b. Verbs of *believing* and *trusting* [**trauan, gatrauan, galaubjan**] have either **þatei** or **ei** followed by the indicative unless what is believed or trusted to be true is known by the speaker or writer to be false or contingent upon hypothetical conditions. E.g.

Lk 18:9 **þaiei silbans trauaidedun sis ei weseina garaihtai** who trusted in themselves that they were righteous [subjunctive **weseina** because they were, in fact, not righteous]

2Thess 3:4 **Aþþan gatrauam in Fraujin in izwis ei þatei anabudum izwis jah taujiþ jah taujan habaiþ**
But we trust in you in the Lord that you are doing and will do what we commanded you.

Gal 5:10 **Ik gatraua in izwis in Fraujin þatei ni waiht aljis hugjiþ**
I trust in you in the Lord that you will not think differently

c. Verbs expressing certain knowledge gained by perception or experience [**witan** (to know), **kunnan** (to know), **gamunan** (to remember), **hausjan, saihwan** etc.] are followed by **þatei** or **ei** with the indicative. E.g.

Mt 27:18 **Wissa auk þatei in neiþis atgebun ina.** For he knew that they had handed him over out of envy.

Jn 12:16 **gamundedun þatei þata was du þamma gameliþ** they remembered that that had been written concerning him

John 17:23 **ei ... kunnei so manaseþs þatei þu mik insandides**
so that the world may know that you sent me

But when **hausjan** has the meaning *know by hearsay only,* the subjunctive is used, as in

John 12:34 **weis hausidedum ana witoda þatei Xristus sijai du aiwa**
we have heard, according to the Law, that the Christ is eternal

d. In reported speech after verbs of *stating, saying, replying* [e.g. **qiþan, andhafjan**] the indicative is normal unless there is doubt about the truth of the assertion or the statement on the part of the narrator, as in

Lk 20:7 **jah anhofun ei ni wissedeina hwaþro**
and they replied that they did not know where (it was) from

where the reply is ostensibly deceitful from the context. The reader will do well to go back and reread the *caveat* in the first paragraph of this section (§16.2).

That the conjunction **þatei** was still felt, at least to some extent, to be composed of the neuter demonstrative **þata** plus the relative particle **ei** (cf. **saei**, etc.) is evidenced by the fact that it is replaced by the genitive **þizei** or the dative **þammei** in a number of instances. E.g.

Phil 2:24 **Aþþan gatraua in Fraujin þammei jah silba sprauto qima.** But I trust in the Lord that I too will come shortly. [**gatrauan** requires a direct object in the dative when not used with **in** or **du**]

Lk 17:15	**iþ ains þan ize gaumjands þammei hrains warþ** but then one of them, noticing that he had become cleansed (of his leprousy)... [**gaumjan** regularly requires a direct object in the dative]

Further instances of the inflected forms of **þatei** are found in the conjunction **in þizei** (because, why, for the reason that), as in

Lk 8:6	**in þizei ni habaida qrammiþa** because it had no moisture
Lk 8:47	**in þizei attaitok imma gataih imma** she told him why she had touched him

and in the temporal conjunctions **in þammei** (when), **fram þammei** (from the time that), and **faurþizei** (before).

The conjunction **þei** as an equivalent of **ei** is infrequent. The conjunction **unte** is sometimes used as the equivalent of **þatei** to introduce both direct and indirect quotations and statements.

16.3 The preterite-present verbs *witan* (to know a fact), *kunnan* (to know, recognize, be acquainted with), *munan* (to think, suppose, believe) and *gamunan* (to remember).

witan:	pres. indicative	**wait**	**witum**	pres. subj.	**witjau**	***witeima**
		waist	**wituþ**		**witeis**	**witeiþ**
		wait	**witun**		**witi**	***witeina**
	pret. indicative	**wissa**	***wissedum**	pret. subj.	**wissedjau**	***wissedeima**
		wisseis[1]	**wisseduþ**		**wissedeis**	***wissedeiþ**
		wissa	**wissedun**		**wissedi**	**wissedeina**
	active participle:	**witand-**				
kunnan:	pres. indicative	**kann**	**kunnum**	pres. subj.	**kunnjau**	***kunneima**
		kant	**kunnuþ**		**kunneis**	**kunneiþ**
		kann	**kunnun**		**kunnei**	**kunneina**
	pret. indicative	**kunþa**	**kunþedum**	pret. subj.	**kunþedjau**	***kunþcdcima**
		kunþes	***kunþeduþ**		***kunþedeis**	**kunþedeiþ**
		kunþa	**kunþedun**		**-kunþedi**	***kunþedeina**
	active participle:	**kunnand-**		past (stative) participle: **kunþ-**		

There are not enough attestations for **munan** and **gamunan** to warrant giving a full paradigm, but a comparison of the attested forms with those of **kann, kunnum** above shows an identical patterning:

pres. indicative	**man**	***munum**	pres. subj.	***munjau**	**-muneima**
pret. indicative	**munda**	**-mundedum**	pret. subj.	***mundedjau**	***mundedeima**
active participle:	**munand-**		past (stative) participle: **mund-**		

The present tense forms of **witan** and **kunnan** follow the preterite inflection of the strong verbs of classes I and 3 respectively. Since these are formally preterites, the subjunctive (in sense present) is based on the plural stems **wit-** and **kunn-** respectively, with the normal preterite subjunctive endings **-jau, -eis**, etc. The actual preterite

[1] For the spelling **wisseis** instead of ***wisses** see Intro. IV6, I.

forms **wissa** (for ***witta**) and **kunþa** are newly formed weak preterites, based on the passive adjectives ***witt-** and ***kunþ-** respectively. Fuller lexical information on all of these verbs is given in the Vocabulary below.

The prefixed verbs **anakunnan, atkunnan, gakunnan,** and **ufkunnan** are inflected as class 3 weak verbs, although the preterite of **ufkunnan** is regularly **ufkunþa** and not **ufkunnaida,** which does occur once. **Frakunnan,** on the other hand, follows the inflection of **kunnan.** These irregularities will be noted when the verbs are introduced in the lesson vocabularies and in the final glossary.

16.4 The verbal prefixes *and-* and *und-*.

The verbal prefix **and-**, like its partial successor *ent-* in German, is semantically ambiguous, sometimes indicating that an action involves an exchange, fig. or lit., as in

andwaurdjan	to reply to, dispute (from ***waurdjan**, a denominative verb from **waurd**; cf. **filuwaurdjan** to be wordy)
andstandan	to resist, oppose (**standan** to stand)
andniman	to accept
andhausjan	to obey, listen to

and sometimes denoting the reversal or undoing of an action, as in

andbindan	to untie
andhuljan	to uncover (**huljan** to hide, conceal)

The formal variation between **and-** and **anda-** is primarily that of verbal versus nominal or adjectival usage and presumably rests on a difference in stress: verbs were stressed on the root syllable (e.g. **andháfjan** to answer) and nouns and adjectives on the prefix itself (e.g. **ándahafts** an answer). There are exceptions, however.

The verbal prefix **und-** occurs only on three verbs:

undgreipan	to seize, lay hold of (**greipan** to seize)
undredan	to furnish, provide (***redan** to take counsel over, attend to)
undrinnan	to fall to the lot of

The corresponding prepositions **and** and **und** have already been introduced.

Vocabulary 16

Verbs:

witan *PP* (§16.3) to know (sthg: *A*; that ...: **þatei,** less commonly **ei,** + the indicative).
kunnan *PP* (§16.3) to know (smn: *A*; sthg: *A*; that ...: **þatei** + the indicative); the Gothic present tense often requires a present perfect in the English translation.
ufkunnan (pres.: *wv 3;* pret.: **-kunþa, -kunþes** etc.) to know, recognize, realize (sthg: *A*; that ...: **þatei** + the indic.).
frakunnan *PP* to despise, hate (smn or sthg: *D*).
wenjan *wv 1* to hope, expect (that...: inf. construction or **ei** + the subjunctive).
hugjan *wv 1* to think, suppose, believe (that...: inf. construction or **ei** + the subjunctive).
þugkjan *wv 1* (pret. irreg.: **þuhta, þuhtes,** etc.) to think, believe, suppose (that...: inf. construction or **ei** + the subjunctive); also used impersonally with logical subject in dative, e.g. **þugkeiþ mis** I think (cf. *methinks,*

Ger *es dünkt mir*).
munan *PP* (§16.3) to think, believe, suppose (that...: inf. construction or **ei** + the subjunctive).
gamunan *PP* (§16.3) to remember (sthg: *G*; that...: **þatei** + the indicative).
atsteigan, atstaig *sv 1* (±**dalaþ**) to descend, come or go down (from: **af** *D*; out of: **us** *D*; into: **in** *A*).
ussteigan, usstaig *sv 1* to ascend, go up (into: **in** *A*; onto: **ana** *A*).

Nouns:

kindins *sm* governor.
hundafaþs *sm(i)* (*G* -**fadis**) centurion.
augo *wn* eye.
anabusns *sf* commandment, order.
auso *wn* ear.
fri(j)aþwa *sf* love; **friaþwa haban miþ** to love.

Other:

ju *adv* already; still, yet; with negative: not yet, no longer.
niu = **ni** + -**u**, an enclitic particle used to indicate a question when no question word appears in the sentence (for details see §§20.5; 21.2).
aufto *adv* perhaps, probably.
duþe *adv* therefore, for that reason, thus; the **du-** is separable with tmesis: ***duþe** + -**uh** > ***duhþe** > **duþþe**.
bisunjane *adv* roundabout; used quasi-adjectivally: **þata bisunjane land** the surrounding land.

Exercises

A. Translate. Pluralize the singular pronominal subjects of the main clauses and adjust accordingly. E.g. (1) **Weis witum ... ana hrot raznis unsaris.**

1. Ik wait þatei þo barna wileina ussteigan ana hrot raznis meinis.
2. Is kann þatei þu ni wileis witan sabbate daga.
3. Ik wenja ei magjau wisan miþ izwis hweila langa in þizai baurg.
4. Niu þu hugjis ei þata sijai bloþ is?
5. Þu waist þatei is ni rodida du siponjam seinaim gajukom.
6. Þu kunþes þatei laisareis unsar was in alh miþ þaim gudjam.
7. Imma þugkeiþ ei habai frijonds managans, akei bi sunjai ni habaiþ.
8. Niu gamant þatei is fraqistida smakkabagma unsaramma?
9. Ik hugja ei is atbairai du im þans skattans.
10. Duhwe þu wenides ei ik gamotidedjau þus jainar?
11. Is wissa þatei imma atgiban was kunþi bi þiudangardja himinis.
12. Niu gamundes þatei is fijands unsar ist janni frijonds?
13. Sumai galaubidedun þatei is bi sunjai was sunus Gudis jah nasjands fairhwaus.
14. Ik kann þatei so aikklesjo wisiþ du aiwa.
15. Mis þuhta ei þai anþarai galeseina þos tainjos.
16. Hwa izwis þugkeiþ? Wileiþ atsteigan miþ uns in þata skip?
17. Þu wisses þatei is mahta fragiban þus missadedins þeinos.
18. Ni galaubida þatei is mahtedi gahailjan þans unhailans.
19. Sa blinda weneiþ ei magi aftra ussaihwan.
20. Ik hugida ei sa kindins atgebi mis laun mikil.
21. Ik gamunda armaions fraujins unsaris.
22. Sa kindins þuhta ei þai gadrauhteis usnemeina þana wair jah usqistidedeina imma.
23. Duhwe ni ufkunþa broþar þeins þatei qens is ju gawandida sik in gard attins seinis.
24. Sumai þize Fareisaie jah bokarje munun sik wisan garaihtans.

25. Þai siponjos gamundedun þatei is qaþ du im: "Ik im hlaifs sa atsteigands us himina."
26. So managei þuhtedun ei so stibna usiddjedi ut us himina.
27. Mis þuhta ei wesjau in auþidai mikilai malmins jah watins gafullidai.
28. Sa hundafaþs wenida ei Iesus gahailidedi sunu is.

B. Translate. Convert the preterite verbs of the principal clauses into present-futures and vice versa; adjust the remainder of the sentence accordingly. E.g. (6) **Gafastand ina bandjom handuns jah fotuns ei ni þliuhai.**

1. Ik insandida þus þos bokos ei wissedeis anabusnins kindinis unsaris.
2. Sa magus usstaig in hauhana bagm ei gasehwi skipa ana marein.
3. Galiþun in baurg ei usbauhtedeina hlaif jah wein.
4. Sa hundafaþs sandida seinana skalk du Iesua ei bedi ina ei qemi jah ganasidedi barn is.
5. Jah gaqemun sunsaiw ei waurpeina ina stainam, akei ni bigetun ina jainar.
6. Gafastaidedun ina bandjom handuns jah fotuns ei ni þlauhi.
7. Ik wiljau ei wisais her ei witais laisarja jainamma jah siponjam is.
8. Is waurhta þo managein anakumbjan ei matidedeina þana mat.
9. Is bar þos gabrukos ut us razna ei gebi fuglam matjan.
10. Ik laisja þuk laisein is ei ni sijais galeiks þaim dwalam þaiei ni galaubidedun imma.
11. Qimiþ sa þiudans miþ harja seinamma ei fraqimai haimom unsaraim.
12. Ni qam Iesus ei gateri witoþ ak ei usfullidedi ita.
13. Biliþun gardins seinans jah gaþlauhun ei ganasidedeina sik.
14. Ik atiddja du imma ei frehjau ina bi waurda þis gamelidins.

C. Translate.

1. Rodidedun þan þai Fareisaieis miþ sis misso bi Iesu unte qaþ, "Ik im hlaifs sa atsteigands us himina," jah qeþun, "Niu sa ist Iesus sa sunus Iosefis þizei weis kunþedum attan jah aiþein? Hwaiwa nu qiþiþ þatei us himina atstaig?"
2. Gatraua auk þatei ni dauþus ni libains nih aggiljus himinis ni mahteis þis fairhwaus magi uns afskaidan (separate) af friaþwai Gudis þizai in Xristau Iesu, Fraujin unsaramma.
3. Saihwiþ ei manna ni witi þo waurda þoei qaþ izwis her.
4. Iesus wilda ei so managei witeina þatei waldufni habaiþ sa sunus mans ana airþai afletan frawaurhtins.
5. Kunnuþ þatei nehwa ist asans!
6. Ik wiljau ei frijaþwa habaiþ miþ sis misso.
7. Jah usstigun þai siponjos in skip iddjedunuh ufar marein in gawi anþar.
8. Qaþ þan Iesus du sumaim þaiei silbans trauaidedun sis ei weseina garaihtai jah frakunnandans þaim anþaraim þo gajuko bi þans twans mannans þaiei usiddjedun in alh bidjan, ains Fareisaius jah anþar motareis.
9. Bi akranam ize ufkunnaiþ ins.
10. Augona habandans ni gasaihwiþ, jah ausona habandans ni gahauseiþ jah ni gamunuþ!
11. Þan jus gasaihwiþ sunu mans ussteigan in wulþau in himin.
12. Unte ik anabusnins attins meinis fasta, wisa ik in friaþwai is.
13. Sildaleikidedun þan qiþandans du sis misso: "Hwas sijai sa ei jah windam faurbiudiþ jah watnam, jah ufhausjand imma?"
14. Gawandei þuk du garda þeinamma jah gateih hwan filu gatawida þus Guþ.

Lesson 17

17.1 Strong verbs: Class 3. The verbs of this class have a present stem with the pattern **CiNC-**, where **N** represents **r, l,** or dental or palatal **n**, and exhibit the ablaut series **i - a - u**:

Present	Preterite Sing.	Preterite Plural	Past Participle	
bindan	**band**	**bundum**	**bundan-**	to bind
siggwan	**saggw**	**suggwum**	**suggwan-**	to sing
filhan	**falh**	**fulhum**	**fulhan-**	to conceal
wairþan	**warþ**	**waurþum**	**waurþan-**	to become

Note the usual lowering of **i** to [ɛ] and **u** to [ɔ] before **r.** As may be seen from the following full list of the verbs belonging to this class, there are two verbs whose present stems end in **-isk-** and **-isq-** that are also assigned to this class on the basis of forms attested elsewhere in Germanic; the preterite forms necessary for identifying their class do not occur in Gothic. **bliggwan,** where **-ggw-** does not represent -[ŋgw]-, did not originally belong to this class; see p. 231, §III(4).

bairgan	hide; preserve	**sigqan**	sink
bindan	bind	**(fra)slindan**	devour
bliggwan	beat	**spinnan**	spin
brinnan	burn	**stigqan**	thrust
drig(g)kan	drink	**(af)swairban**	wipe off
filhan	conceal, bury	**swiltan**	be dying
finþan	learn of	**(ana)trimpan**	tread
(uf)gairdan	gird up	**(ga)þairsan**	wither
(us)gildan	pay back	**(at)þinsan**	attract
(du)ginnan	begin	**þriskan**	thresh
hilpan	help	**wairpan**	throw
(fra)hinþan	capture, arrest	**wairþan**	become
hwairban	walk	**wilwan**	rob
(af)linnan	depart	**windan**	wind
rinnan	run	**winnan**	suffer pain
siggwan	sing, read aloud	**(ga)wrisqan**	bear fruit

17.2 i-stem adjectives. There is a small group of adjectives whose stems originally ended in *-i-*, e.g. **hraini-** (pure, clean). Their inflection differs from that of **-ja-** stem adjectives like **niuj-** and **wilþj-** (Lesson 3) only in the masculine and neuter *Ns* and *Gs,* the neuter *As,* and the feminine *Ns.* Contrast the following singular paradigms:

	masculine		neuter		feminine	
N	**wilþeis**	***hrains***	**wilþi**	***hrain***	**wilþja**	***hrains***
G	**wilþeis**	***hrainis***	**wilþeis**	***hrainis***	**wilþjaizos**	***hrainjaizos**
D	**wilþjamma**	**hrainjamma**	**wilþjamma**	**hrainjamma**	**wilþjai**	**hrainjai**
A	**wilþana**	**hrainjana**	**wilþi**	***hrain***	**wilþja**	**hrainja**

The strong plural forms and all weak forms are the same for the two types. The following adjectives, denoted in the lesson vocabularies and final glossary with final -**i**- (e.g. **hraini**-) and not -**j**- (like **wilþj**-), are usually assigned to this type, although crucial forms are not attested for **auþi**- or **skauni**-:

analaugni-	hidden	**bruki-**	useful	**seli-**	kind
anasiuni-	visible	**gafauri-**	well-behaved	**skauni-**	beautiful
andanemi-	pleasant	**gamaini-**	common	**skeiri-**	clear
auþi-	desolate(d)	**hraini-**	clean, pure	**suti-**	mild, sweet

17.3. Indefinite pronouns and adjectives (I). The simple interrogative pronouns **hwas, hwa, hwo** (Lesson 6.3) also function as indefinite pronouns (*anyone, someone, anything, something*) and interrogative adjectives. As indefinite pronouns their use is uncomplicated, as illustrated by the following examples:

Mt 5:23 **jah jainar gamuneis þatei broþar þeins habaiþ hwa bi þuk**
and you remember there that your brother has something (i.e. a complaint) against you

Lk 9:23: **jabai hwas wili afar mis gaggan** ... if anyone wishes to follow me ...

Lk 20:28 **jabai hwis broþar gadauþnai** ... if someone's brother dies ...

Lk 19:8 **jah jabai hwis hwa afholoda** and if I (inadvertently) defrauded someone out of something [**afholon** requires the *G* of the person defrauded]

As the equivalents of the English interrogative adjective *what* (as in *what book? what man?)*, two constructions are possible in Gothic. The pronoun may be used adjectivally, as in English, e.g.

Lk 14:31 **aiþþau hwas þiudans, gaggands** ... or what king, going forth ...

Lk 15:3 **hwas manna izwara aigands tehuntehund lambe** ...
what man of you, possessing a hundred sheep ...

More frequently, however, the pronoun is used substantively with the genitive plural of the following noun, as in

Lk 20:2 **in hwamma waldufnje þata taujis** through what power you do this

Lk 9:55 **Niu wituþ hwis ahmane sijuþ**? Do you not know of what sort of spirit you are?

When the noun is further modified by an adjective, a rather unusual pattern emerges, requiring the double use of the definite article (i.e. **sa, þata, so**). E.g.

Mk 1:27 **hwo so laiseino so niujo** what new doctrine?
Mk 6:6 **hwo so handugeino so gibano imma** what wisdom granted to him?

[The reader should not be confused by all the -**o**'s: only **laiseino** and **handugeino** are genitive plural; everything else is nominative singular.]

Unrelated to the above, but worth mentioning at this point, is the very frequent use of **hwa** as the interrogative adverb *why?*, as in

Lk 2:48 **Magau, hwa gatawides uns swa**? Boy, why have you done this to us?

Lk 6:46 **Aþþan hwa mik haitid "Frauja, frauja?"** But why do you call me "Master, master?"

17.4 The verbal prefix ***bi-***. The prefix **bi-** denotes primarily *adjacency, encirclement, enclosure.* E.g.

bibindan	to wrap up in	**bigairdan**	gird on (cf. **ufgairdan** gird up)
bigraban	to surround with earthwork (**graban** to dig)	**bihwairban**	crowd around (**hwairban** to walk)
		bimaitan	to circumcise (**maitan** to cut)
biqiman	befall	**birinnan**	to run about (**rinnan** to run)
bisaihwan	to look about, look around	**bisatjan**	to beset with, set around
bisitan	sit with or near		

It also serves to focus the activity of the more general simple verb on a specific object or person, usually in a denigratory sense:

bidomjan	to judge, condemn (**domjan** idem)
bifaihon	to deceive, defraud (**gafaihon** idem)
bihlahjan	to deride, mock (**hlahjan** to laugh)
birodjan	to murmur against
bispeiwan	to spit upon (**speiwan** to spit).

Vocabulary 17

Verbs:

bindan, band *sv 3;* **gabindan, gaband** *sv 3 (perf.)* to bind, tie up, tether (smn: *A*; with: *D*).
andbindan, andband *sv 3* to untie, unbind, release (from: **af** *D*); to explain.
finþan, fanþ *sv 3* to find out, learn, discover (from: **at** *D*).
duginnan, dugann *sv 3* to begin (to do: inf.).
rinnan, rann *sv 3* to run.
urrinnan, urrann *sv 3* (for ***us-rinnan**) to go or come forth (from: **fram** *D*, **us** *D*); (of seed) to sprout; (of sun) to rise.
andniman, andnam *sv 4* to accept, receive.
filhan, falh *sv 3;* **gafilhan, gafalh** *sv 3 (perf.)* to hide, conceal (sthg: *A*; from: **faura** *D*); to bury (smn: *A*).
anafilhan, anafalh *sv 3* to hand (sthg or smn: *A*) over (to: *D*); to hand (sthg: *A*) down (to: *D*) as tradition.
gahaban *wv 3* to lay hold of, hold fast to; to seize, take prisoner; + **sik** to refrain (from: **af** *D*).
swiltan, swalt *sv 3 (imperf.)* to be dying; **gaswiltan, gaswalt** *sv 3 (perf.)* to die.
uslaubjan *wv 1* to allow, permit (smn: *D*; to do: inf.).
ganisan, ganas *sv 5* to be saved (in spiritual sense); to recover, be healed.
ataugjan *wv 1* to show (sthg: *A*; to smn: *D*); + **sik** to appear, become manifest.
hazjan *wv 1* to praise (smn: *A*; for: **in** *G*).

Nouns:

ufkunþi *sn* knowledge, perception, realization.
fraiw *sn* seed; offspring.
þiuda *sf* people, nation.
daur *sn* door.

Lesson 17

Adjectives:

hraini- *adj* pure, clean; **unhraini-** *adj* unclean, impure.
andanemi- *adj* pleasant, acceptable.
auþi- *adj* desolated, deserted; (of persons) childless.
eisarnein- *adj* of iron.
midj- *adj* middle, mid. Expressions translating English *in their midst, in the middle of the city,* etc. are always construed adjectivally in Gothic: *in mid them* **in midjaim im**, *in mid city* **in midjai baurg**.
maht- *part adj* (of **magan**) able, capable; used predicatively with an infinitive often in passive sense, e.g. **ni maht ist gasaihwan** *it cannot be seen, it is invisible.*

Other:

frumist *adv* first(ly).
Lazarus (*D* **-au**, *A* **-u**, *V* **-u**) Lazarus.
Israel (*G* **-is**, *D* **-a**, *A* -) Israel.
samaþ *adv* together, to the same place.
Moses (*G* **Mosezis**, *D* **Moseza**, **Mose**) Moses.

Exercises

A. Translate. Convert to the singular.

1. hairtona hrainja
2. bandjos eisarneinos
3. lekje handugaize
4. stadeis auþjai
5. aurtjans baudai
6. skadjus diupai
7. ausona hrainja
8. weihsa auþja
9. karkaros unhrainjos
10. leika naqada
11. weina andanemja
12. waurstwjans untriggwai
13. bagmos hauhai
14. stadeis unhrainjai
15. kindinos sineigai
16. þiudos wilþjos
17. aiweina rigna funins
18. eisarneina daura
19. hlaiwa niuja
20. reiks frodai
21. fairhwjus auþjai
22. tainjos fairnjos
23. hundafadeis swinþai
24. missadedeis fulginos
25. siuneis weihos
26. laisarjos handugai
27. smakkabagmos wilþjai
28. aurtigardeis mikilai
29. fraiwa leitila
30. widuwons gauros
31. fairgunja auþja
32. blindans unledai
33. anabusneis fairnjos

B. Translate. Pluralize the subjects of the first clauses and adjust accordingly.

1. Hwa fanst þu biþe inn iddjes þairh þata daur?
2. Is dugann hazjan unsis in waurstwe unsaraize.
3. Þata fraiw ni urrann, ak þata fretun fuglos himinis.
4. Ik gaband þana hund ei ni usiddjedi ut us garda.
5. Is anafalh manag faihu þaim gadrauhtim.
6. Ik andnam waurda aiwaggeljons ei habaidedjau libain aiweinon.
7. Is gahabaida unsarana laisarei jah anafalh ina þamma kindina.
8. Duhwe ni rannt fram akra biþe gasahwt þana wulf?
9. Is munda ei dauhtar seina gaswulti.
10. Ik gafalh þans skattans ei þai gadrauhteis ni bigeteina ins.
11. Is andband þana hund jah ustauh ina ut us weihsa.
12. Si ni uslaubida barnam seinaim usleiþan ut us razna.
13. Ik fanþ at aiþein þeinai þatei þu afiddjes.
14. Is warþ siuks jah ni ganas.
15. Sa wair urrann us þamma hlaiwa.
16. Ik ataugida þaim gudjam handuns meinos gahrainidos þis þrutsfillis.

17. Ik man ei gahabaina þans þliuhandans.
18. Is rann ut us weihsa jah gaþlauh ufar marein.
19. Ik anafalh þos bokos meinaim siponjam.
20. Hwar gadraus þata fraiw?
21. Niu gamant þatei ik anabaud þus ei gabundeis ina handuns jah fotuns?
22. Duhwe þu ni hropides biþe dugannt driusan?
23. Ik ni uslaubida im saihwan bokos þos weihons.
24. Is wissa þatei si gaswalt.
25. Duhwe þu ni hazides waurda þis frodins?
26. Ik dugann laisjan im bi ufkunþi sunjos.

C. Translate.

1. Þatuþþan ist god jah andanem in andwairþja nasjandis unsaris Gudis, saei allans mans wili ganisan jah in ufkunþja sunjos qiman.
2. Jah qaþ Iesus du þamma þrutsfill habandin: "Wiljau. Wairþ hrains!" Jah suns hrain warþ þata þrutsfill is. Jah qaþ imma Iesus: "Saihw ei mann ni qiþais, ak gagg, þuk silban ataugei gudjin jah atbair giba þoei anabauþ Moses."
3. Biþe gahausida þata, usiddja sundro ana staþ auþjana baurgs.
4. Gaswalt þan jah sa reiks jah gafulhans warþ.
5. Biþe þan warþ dags, usgaggands galaiþ ana auþjana stad, jah manageins sokidedun ina jah qemun und ina jah gahabaidedun ina ei ni afliþi fairra im.
6. Samaleiko þan jah waurstwa goda swikunþa sind jah filhan ni mahta sind.
7. Jah warþ biþe sa þrutsfill habands gaumida þammei hrains warþ, jah ufhropida jah rann jah gadraus du fotum Iesuis.
8. Ni bandjom eisarneinaim manna mahta ina gabindan.
9. Jah Peilatus finþands at þamma hundafada þatei Iesus ju gaswalt, fragaf þata leik Iosefa ei gafulhi ita in seinamma niujamma hlaiwa.
10. Þata rodida Iesus jah galaiþ jah gafalh sik faura im.
11. Jah qaþ Peilatus du imma: "So þiuda þeina jah gudjans anafulhun þuk mis. Hwa gatawides?"
12. Jah ahmans þai unhrainjans, þai þan ina gasehwun, drusun du imma jah hropidedun qiþandans þatei, "Þu is sunus Gudis."
13. Qaþ du im Iesus: "Andbind ina ei gaggai."
14. Iþ inuh gajukon ni rodida þizai managein, iþ sundro siponjam seinaim andband allata.
15. Anþaruh þan siponje is qaþ du imma: "Frauja, uslaubei mis frumist galeiþan jah gafilhan attan meinana." Iþ Iesus qaþ du imma: "Laistei afar mis jah let (let) þans dauþans filhan seinans dauþans."
16. Þata ist witoþ þatei attans unsarai anafulhun unsis.
17. In þamma mela dugann Iesus insandjan siponjans seinans und anþara gauja jah anþaros haimos, jah gaf im waldufni ahmane unhrainjaize.
18. Ik hazja izwis, broþrjus, þei allata mein waurd gamunandans sijuþ, jasswaswe anafalh izwis, anabusnins gafastaiþ.
19. Fanþ þan manageins filu Iudaie þatei Iesus jainar ist, jah qemun, ni in Iesuis ainis, ak ei jah Lazaru sehweina, saei urrais us dauþaim.
20. Þanuh nemun stainans ei waurpeina ana ina, iþ Iesus þan gafalh sik jah usiddja us alh usleiþands þairh midjans ins.
21. Iþ nu, sai, andbundanai sijum af witoda.
22. Jah gabindandans ina gatauhun ina jah anafulhun ina Peilatau kindina.
23. Jah urrann sa dauþa ut us þamma hlaiwa gabundans handuns jah fotuns faskjam (linen wrappings).
24. Duhwe ni fastais anabusn þoei anafalh þus?
25. Gasaihwands þan Iesus þatei samaþ rann managei, wilda taujan taikn in andwairþja ize ei galaubidedeina imma jah andnemeina aiwaggeljon.

26. Qaþ Iesus: "Ik fram Guda urrann jah qam; nih þan auk fram mis silbin ni qam, ak is mik insandida."
27. Jah sum þize fraiwe gadraus in airþa goda jah urran jah gaf akran manag.
28. Jah gawandidedun sik þai hairdjos hazjandans Guþ in allaize þizeei gahausidedun jah gasehwun swaswe rodiþ was du im fram þaim aggilum.
29. Andhafjands Iesus qaþ du im: "Managa goda waurstwa ataugida izwis us Attin."
30. Jah nemun astans peikabagme (palm-) jah urrunnun wiþra ina hropjandans, "Osanna, þiuþida (cf. §8.2.e) sa qimanda in namin Fraujins, þiudans Israelis.
31. Dugunnun managei siponje hazjan Guþ stibnai mikilai in allaizo þozei sehwun mahte.
32. Qaþ Iesus: "Ik im daur. Þairh mik jabai hwas inn gaggiþ, ganisiþ.
33. Im þuhta ei Helias sa praufetus ataugidedi sik im.
34. Qeþun þan þai gahausjandans: "Jah hwas mag ganisan?"
35. Hazjiþ, allos þiudos, Fraujan, jah hazjaina ina allos manageins!
36. Jah sa hundafaþs baþ Iesus ei qimands lagidedi handuns ana dauhtr is ei ganesi jah libaidedi.
37. Bedun þos unhulþons Iesu ei uslaubidedi im galeiþan in þo sweina, jah uslaubida im.

Lesson 18

18.1 Strong verbs: Class 6.

The verbs of this class are characterized by the ablaut pattern **a-o-o-a**:

Present	Preterite Singular	Preterite Plural	Past Participle	
faran	**for**	**forum**	**faran-**	to travel, go
fraþjan	**froþ**	**froþum**	**fraþan-**	to understand
standan	**stoþ**	**stoþum**	***staþan-**	to stand.

There are seven verbs like **fraþjan,** with present stems in **-j-**. The verb **standan** is alone in having an infixed **-n-** in the present stem. See the historical notes to this lesson for parallels to these forms in other IE languages. The following verbs are assigned to this class, although several are poorly attested in Gothic:

alan	to grow	**(ga)raþjan**	to count
(us)asan	to die, expire	**sakan**	to dispute, contend
(ga)daban	to be fitting	**skaban**	to shave
(ga)draban	to hollow out	**(ga)skapjan**	to create
(ga)dragan	to heap up	**skaþjan**	to injure
faran	to travel, go	**slahan**	to strike
fraþjan	to understand	**standan**	to stand
graban	to dig	**swaran**	to swear
hafjan	to raise	**þwahan**	to wash
hlahjan	to laugh	**wahsjan**	to grow
(af)hlaþan	to load	**wakan**	to wake
malan	to grind		

18.2 The dative absolute.

Frequent use is made in NT Greek of the construction known as the genitive absolute, wherein a nominal subject (noun, pronoun, nominalized adjective or participle) joined to a participial predicate, both in the genitive case, functions as the equivalent of a subordinate clause, usually temporal in meaning. These constructions are imitated slavishly by the Gothic translator, who renders them with the Gothic equivalent, the dative absolute. Study the following examples carefully. Note that the distinction between imperfective and perfective verbs is significant here, constructions with the former usually corresponding to English *while*-clauses, and the latter to *when*- or *after*-clauses with punctual verbs. This distinction is clear in Greek, but, as discussed in Lesson 5, is only partially preserved in Gothic because of the ambiguity concerning aspect with unprefixed verbs. The construction may optionally be introduced with the preposition **at**.

Lk 3:1 — ἡγεμονεύοντος Ποντίου Πιλάτου τῆς Ἰουδαίας
raginondin Puntiau Peilatau Iudaia
while Pontius Pilate was governing Judaea (imperfective)

Lk 3:15 — προσδοκῶντος δὲ τοῦ λαοῦ καὶ διαλογιζομένων πάντων ἐν ταῖς καρδίαις αὐτῶν
at wenjandein þan allai managein jah þagkjandam allaim in hairtam seinam
while all the people were expectant and all were thinking in their hearts (two imperfectives)

Lk 3:21 καὶ Ἰησοῦ βαπτισθέντος καὶ προσευχομένου
jah at Iesu ufdaupidamma jah bidjandin
and when Jesus had been baptized and was praying (perfective passive + imperfective active)

Lk 7:24 ἀπελθόντων δὲ τῶν ἀγγέλων Ἰωάννου
at galeiþandam þan þaim airum Iohannes
when John's messengers had left (perfective)

Lk 7:6 ἤδη δὲ αὐτοῦ οὐ μακρὰν ἀπέχοντος ἀπὸ τῆς οἰκίας, ἔπεμψεν πρὸς αὐτὸν ...
jah juþan ni fairra wisandin imma þamma garda, insandida du imma
and he sent him (a message) when he was already near the house (imperfective)

Note that the context may require a more nuanced interpretation of the exact relationship between the subordination and the main clause, temporal relationships often verging on concessive, adversative, or causal.

It is possible in many instances to see the dative absolute as a fronted modifier of some dative element later on in the main clause, but a comparison with the Greek shows that this is probably coincidental. The omission of the pronominal "subject" in Gothic, however, does introduce a genuine ambiguity. E.g.

Lk 7:42 **ni habandam þan hwaþro usgebeina, *baim* fragaf**
since they did not have the wherewithal to pay him back, he forgave both of them
μὴ ἐχόντων αὐτῶν ἀποδοῦναι ἀμφοτέροις ἐχαρίσατο

But in Luke 8:27, where the Greek does have a fronted dative object of the verb ὑπαντάω, the repetition of the pronoun **imma** suggests that the Gothic translator is employing a dative absolute:[1]

Lk 8:27 ἐξελθόντι δὲ αὐτῷ ἐπὶ τὴν γὴν ὑπήντησεν ἀνήρ τις ...
a man met him having just disembarked ...
usgaggandin þan imma ana airþa, gamotida imma wair sums...
when he had disembarked, a man met him ...

Occasionally the Gothic translator renders a Greek genitive absolute with a full temporal clause, as in

Mt 9:18 ταῦτα αὐτοῦ λαλοῦντος αὐτοῖς **miþþanei is rodida þata du im**
while he was saying that to them

Lk4:40 δύνοντος δὲ τοῦ ἡλίου **miþþanei þan sagq sunno**
while the sun was setting.

18.3 Temporal clauses.

Temporal clauses introduced by conjunctions offer no particular problem in Gothic syntax. Listed below are the more important conjunctions used in a temporal sense. **Faurþizei** (before) is always followed by the subjunctive, and **unte** (until, etc.) occasionally; when **þan** is used with the subjunctive, the sense is quasi-conditional: *whenever, if, should.* The indicative is normal with the remaining conjunctions.

---

[1] Streitberg (§260) offers a different assessment of these constructions, viewing preposed dative modifiers as the origin of the dative absolute. He can hardly mean that this is a development within Gothic itself, however, since there is clear evidence of dative absolutes in OHG and ON as well.

biþe	when, while; as soon as; after. Also used as a simple temporal adverb: later on, afterward, then, next.
þan	when (indicative); whenever, if (subjunctive); see also §13.1.B.1.
þande	until, as long as. Frequently conditional (if, when) or causal (because, since).
miþþanei	while, as. Regularly with imperfective verbs.
sunsei	as soon as.
faurþizei	before. Always followed by a verb in the subjunctive.
unte	until, as long as. Regularly with an indicative verb, occasionally with subjunctive.
und þatei	while.
swe	as, when. Also used in the non-temporal sense: as, like.
in þammei	when. Also non-temporally: because.

18.4 The demonstrative pronoun *sah, þatuh, soh.*

There is an extended form of the demonstrative **sa, þata, so** used only as a pronoun and not as a noun determinant. It consists of the inflected forms of **sa** plus a suffix **-uh**, with the same combinatory rules as the conjunction **-uh** of Lessons 13 and 15. The attested forms are

masc. sing. *N* **sah**, *G* **þizuh**, *D* **þammuh**, *A* **þanuh**
neuter sing. *N* **þatuh**, *G* **þizuh**, *D* **þammuh**, *A* **þatuh**
fem. sing. *N* **soh**

The use of this pronoun as an emphatic demonstrative (he, as opposed to anyone else) is clearly attested in such instances as

Lk 3:16 **sah izwis daupeiþ in ahmin weihamma jah funin**
he (as opposed to me) will baptize you with the holy spirit and fire

John 8:40 **þatuh Abraham ni tawida** That, however, Abraham did not do!

and where it is used as a resumptive pronoun after some preposed element, as in

Mt 5:19 **iþ saei taujiþ jah laisjai swa, sah mikils haitada in þiudangardjai himine**
but (as for him) who acts and teaches thus, he will be called great in the kingdom of heaven

In a large number of occurrences, however, **sah** functions more like a combination of **sa** and **-uh**, especially when followed by **þan**, namely as a simple demonstrative plus the conjunction **-uh** (**þan**) indicating additional descriptive information not sequential to the narrative and bordering, in some instances, on parenthesis or editorial comment. Compare our remarks on the use of **-uh þan** in Lesson 13. E.g.

John 6:6 **þatuh þan qaþ fraisands ina; iþ silba wissa þatei habaida taujan**
He said that, by the way, merely to test him; he himself knew exactly what he was going to do.

John 8:35 **Sah þan skalks ni wisiþ in garda du aiwa, sunus wisiþ du aiwa.**
A slave, as you know, has no permanent standing in a household, but a son does.

In this last example, if **sah**, rather than the **sa** of **sa** + **-uh**, were taken as a modifier of **skalks**, it would be contrary to the otherwise consistent use of these forms as pronouns and not adjectives.

18.5 Causative verbs in *-jan*.

As was noted in the Historical Grammar Lesson 5, one subclass of the weak verbs, class I, consists of causative verbs based on the IE pattern R(o) + *-éye-*, i.e. the o-grade of the verbal root + the causative suffix. Because the o-grade of the verbal root also underlies the form of the preterite singular of strong verbs, classes I-6, there is an obvious formal relationship between these preterites and the causative verbs. The following list is a sampling of these lexical pairs:

Class	Strong Verb				Causative Verb	
I	**urreisan**	to rise	pret.:	**urrais**	**urraisjan**	to raise
	hneiwan	to bow		**hnaiw**	**hnaiwjan**	to cause to bow
	bileiban*	to remain		**bilaif**	**bilaibjan**	to leave behind
2	**driusan**	to fall		**draus**	**drausjan**	to throw down
3	**brinnan**	to burn (intr.)		**brann**	**brannjan**	to burn (tr.)
	drigkan	to drink		**dragk**	**dragkjan**	to give to drink
	urrinnan	to rise (of sun)		**urrann**	**urrannjan**	to cause to rise
5	**sitan**	to sit		**sat**	**satjan**	to set, cause to sit
	ganisan	to be saved, get well		**ganas**	**ganasjan**	to save, cure
	ligan	to lie		**lag**	**lagjan**	to lay

Sometimes the formal relationship survives, but changes in connotation have altered the original simple semantic relationship, as in

kiusan	to test, try, taste	**kaus**	**kausjan**	to taste, experience
dreiban	to drive	**draif**	**draibjan**	to bother

Vocabulary 18

Verbs:

fraþjan, froþ *sv 6* to understand (sthg: *D*); to realize (that...: **þatei...**); to think, suppose (sthg: *A*).
andhafjan, andhof *sv 6* see Vocabulary 7.
ushafjan, ushof *sv 6* to raise, lift, pick up (*A*); **ushafjan augona du** look up toward.
sakan, sok *sv 6 (imperf.)*, **gasakan, gasok** *sv 6 (perf.)* to rebuke, scold (smn: *D*); to argue, contend (with: **miþ** *D*).
standan, stoþ *sv 6* to stand; **gastandan, gastoþ** *sv 6 (perf.)* to stop (intrans.), come to a stop, cease; + **aftra** to recover.
andstandan, andstoþ *sv 6* to oppose, resist (*D*).
usstandan, usstoþ *sv 6* to stand up, get up, rise; to get up and leave (a place: **us** *D*); to rise from the dead.
ligan, lag *sv 5* to lie, be situated.
satjan *wv 1 (imperf.)*, **gasatjan** *wv 1 (perf.)* to put, place, set (*A*; on: **ana** *D* or *A*); to plant; **satid- uf** charged with.
ussatjan *wv 1* to put, set, provide; to plant, lay out; to beget (children).
urraisjan *wv 1* to raise up, lift up; to arouse, awaken.
sigqan, sagq *sv 3 (imperf.)*, **gasigqan, gasagq** *sv 3 (perf.)* to sink.
sweran, sweraida *wv 3* to honor, respect, esteem (smn: *A*).

Lesson 18

Nouns:

sunno *irreg* (*N* fem., *D* **-in** neuter, *A* **sunnon** fem.) the sun.
sauil *sn* the sun.
liuhaþ (*G* **-dis**) *sn* light.
asans *sf* harvest.
synagoge *f* (*G* **-ais, -eis;** *D* **-e, -en, -ein;** *A* **-en, -ein**) synagogue. (< Gk συναγωγή) .

sinista *wm* an elder.
þiumagus *sm* servant.
usliþa *wm* paralytic, one hopelessly ill.
weinagards *sm(i)* vineyard.
Abraham *m* (*G* **-is,** *D* **-a,** *A* -) Abraham.

Other:

spedist- *adj* latest, last.
juþan *adv* still, yet, already.
usdaudo *adv* earnestly.
fairraþro *adv* from afar, far off.

The new temporal conjunctions in §18.3: **þande, sunsei, faurþizei, und þatei, swe.**

Exercises

A. Translate. Convert the clauses into dative absolutes. E.g. (I) **finþandein izai þatei is was jainar**

I. biþe si fanþ þatei is was jainar
2. miþþanei so managei rann þairh þata weihs
3. sunsei ik gasahw þata liuhaþ
4. biþe is gafalh þans skattans
5. miþþanei ik hazida ina bi waurstwa suniwe is
6. biþe weis gamotidedum im ana wiga
7. miþþanei þu wast miþ im
8. biþe ija bigetun ina
9. biþe eis gabundun ina handuns jah fotuns
I0. miþþanei þan sagq sunno
I I. miþþanei so mawi swalt
I2. biþe gahabaidedun þana skalk
I3. und þatei sa kindins uslaubida uns galeiþan
I4. sunsei eis gahausidedun stibna is
I5. biþe þu qimis du baurg unsarai

B. Translate. Convert the dative absolutes into temporal clauses. E.g. (I) **biþe þos bandjos andbundanos waurþun**

I. andbundanaim þaim bandjom
2. at sunnin þan urrinnandin
3. fraþjandein þizai qinon þatei gahailida warþ
4. duginnandam im hazjan ina
5. standandam þaim gadrauhtim jainar
6. ni wiljandin imma anastandan waldufnja þis kindinis
7. anafulhanamma allamma swesa is
8. usstandandam im us jainamma stada
9. unsis ligandam ana haiþjai
I0. ussatidamma þamma aurtigarda
I I. ushafjandin imma þata barn
I2. þus jainar wisandin
I3. sitandam im nehwa imma
I4. galagjandin Iosefa leik Iesuis in seinamma niujamma hlaiwa
I5. ni magandein izai andhafjan im

C. Translate.

l. Þanuh atberun du imma usliþan ana ligra ligandan.

2. Qiþa auk izwis þatei mag Guþ us stainam þaim urraisjan barna Abrahama.
3. In jainamma jera ni was asans mikila, jah warþ so þiuda filu gredaga.
4. Is qaþ siponjam seinaim: "Izwis atgiban ist fraþjan sunjai bi þiudangardja Gudis, iþ þaim anþaraim qiþa in gajukom ei saihwandans ni gasaihwaina jah gahausjandans ni fraþjaina."
5. Þata rodida Iesus uzuhhof augona seina du himina jah qaþ: "Atta, qam hweila!"
6. Jah Iesus nimands þata barn gasatida ina in midjaim im.
7. Jah sai, in þamma daga managa leika weihaize þize ligandane in hlaiwasnom seinaim urrisun.
8. Jah sumai Fareisaie us þizai managein qeþun du imma: "Laisari, sak þaim siponjam þeinaim!"
9. Iþ marei winda mikilamma urraisida was. Siponjos is þan atgaggandans urraisidedun ina qiþandans: "Frauja, nasei unsis!" Þanuh urreisands gasok windam jah marein, jah warþ wis (a calm) mikil.
10. Urreis jah stand in midjaim unsis!
11. Qaþuh þan du siponjam seinaim: "Asans managa, iþ waurstwjans fawai. Bidjiþ nu fraujan asanais ei ussatjai waurstwjans in þo asan seina."
12. Jah sokun miþ sis misso qiþandans: "Niu fraþjiþ jus þaim waurdam?"
13. Ushof seina augona jah gasahw twa skipa standandona jainar.
14. Weinagard ussatida manna jah anafalh ina waurstwjam jah silba aflaiþ in anþar land fairra wisando.
15. Hauseiþ mis allai, jah fraþjaiþ!
16. Gawandjands þan gasok im jah qaþ du im: "Ni wituþ hwis ahmane sijuþ?"
17. Þiumagus meins ligiþ in garda usliþa. Ik bidja þuk usdaudo qiman ei gahailjais ina.
18. Qaþ Iesus: "Saei matjiþ mein leik jah driggkiþ mein bloþ habaiþ libain aiweinon, jah ik urraisja ina in þamma spedistin daga."
19. Jah sa motareis fairraþro standands, ni munands sik silban fraletis wairþana, ni wilda augona seina ushafjan du himina miþþanei baþ.
20. Usiddjedun þan saihwan þata waurþano, jah qemun at Iesua jah bigetun sitandan þana mannan af þammei unhulþons usiddjedun, gawasidana jah fraþjandan, faura fotum Iesuis.
21. Ni skuld ist unsis andstandan waldufnja þis kindinis.
22. Qaþ Iesus du swistr þis dauþins: "Amen qiþa þus, usstandiþ broþar þeins."
23. Sa manna nist fram Guda þande sabbate daga ni witaiþ.
24. Þaruh was manna jainar þizei namo Symaion, jah sa manna was garaihts, jah ahma weihs was ana imma, jah was imma gataihan fram ahmin þamma weihamma ni saihwan dauþu faurþize sehwi Xristu Fraujins.
25. Jainai ni froþun hwa was þatei rodida du im.
26. Hwa qiþa du managein þizai ungalaubjandein jah andstandein?
27. Ushof augona meina jah gaumida þiumagau þis hundafadis gaggandin ana wiga.
28. Jah usstoþ jainþro jah qam in landa seinamma, jah laistidedun afar imma siponjos is.
29. Duhwe andstost laiseinai nasjandis unsaris?

30. Biþe þan usfullida alla þo waurda seina hausjandein þizai managein, galaiþ in Kafarnaum. Hundafade þan sumis skalks swalt, þanei sa hundafaþs filu sweraida. Gahausjands þan bi Iesu insandida du imma sinistans Iudaie, bidjandans ina ei qemi jah ganasidedi þana skalk is. Iþ eis qimandans at Iesua bedun ina usdaudo, qiþandans þatei, "Wairþs ist þammei fragibis þata, unte frijonds þiudos unsaraizos ist jah synagogein is gatimrida unsis." Iþ Iesus iddjuh miþ im. Jah juþan ni fairra wisandin imma þamma garda, insandida du imma sa hundafaþs frijonds seinans qiþands du imma: "Frauja, ni draibei þuk (do not trouble yourself), unte ni im wairþs ei uf hrot mein inn gaggais. Duþei ni mik silban wairþana munda at þus qiman. Ak qiþ waurda, jah ganisiþ sa skalks meins. Jah þan auk ik manna im uf waldufnja gasatids, habands uf mis silbin gadrauhtins. Jah qiþa du þamma, 'Gagg,' jah gaggiþ; jah anþaramma, 'Qim,' jah qimiþ; jah du skalka meinamma, 'Tawei þata,' jah taujiþ." Gahausjands þan þata Iesus sildaleikida ina jah wandjands sik du þizai laistjandein sis managein qaþ: "Amen qiþa izwis, ni in Israela swalauda (such great) galaubein bigat." Jah gawandjandans sik þai insandidans du garda bigetun þana siukan skalk hailana.

Lesson 19

19.1 Weak verbs: class 2.

Verbs of this class are characterized by a suffix **-o-** which appears in all forms (paradigm verb: **salbon** to anoint):

	Present Indicative				Present Subjunctive		
sing.	**salbo**	pl.	**salbom**	sing.	**salbo**	pl.	**salboma**
	salbos		**salboþ**		**salbos**		**salboþ**
	salboþ		**salbond**		**salbo**		**salbona**

Imperative: sing. **salbo**, pl. **salboþ**

Preterite indicative: **salboda** (like **nasida**) Preterite subjunctive: **salbodedjau** (like **nasidedjau**)

Present (active) participle: **salbond-**; past (passive) participle: **salbod-**.

All verbs of this class are denominative, formed on nominal or adjectival bases which in some cases have not survived in Gothic. For the relationship of this class to the Latin first conjugation *(amo, amare)* and Greek verbs in -άω, see the historical notes to this lesson. The following verbs belong to this class:

(ga)aiginon	take possession	**holon**	violate	**(ga)paidon**	clothe
aihtron	beg	**horinon**	commit adultery	**qainon**	mourn
airinon	be messenger	**hwarbon**	stroll about	**raginon**	rule
aljanon	be jealous	**idreigon**	repent	**rahton**	offer
auhjon	cry out	**iudaiwiskon**	follow Jewish custom	**(bi)raubon**	rob
awiliudon	give thanks			**reikinon**	rule
drauhtinon	wage war	**kapillon**	cut off hair	**salbon**	anoint
dwalmon	rage	**karon**	care for	**sidon**	practice
faginon	rejoice	**kaupon**	trade with	**skalkinon**	serve
(bi)faihon	outwit	**(ga)kroton**	smash	**spillon**	narrate
fairinon	accuse, charge	**(bi)laigon**	lick	**sunjon**	justify
fiskon	fish	**laþon**	invite	**supon**	season
fraujinon	be lord over	**(ga)leikinon**	cure	**swiglon**	pipe
frijon	love	**(ga)leikon**	liken to	**þiudanon**	be king
(ga)friþon	reconcile	**liuþon**	sing praise	**(and)tilon**	be devoted to
gaunon	lament, grieve	**luston**	desire	**(ga)wadjon**	betroth
gredon	be hungry	**luton**	deceive	**(ga)weison**	attend to
gudjinon	serve as priest	**militon**	be a soldier	**(ga)wundon**	wound
(af)hamon	doff	**miton**	think, suppose	**(ga)sibjon**	make up with
hatizon	be angry	**mundon**	note, mark		
hausjon	hear	**(ufar)munnon**	forget		

Verbal nouns, though only a few are attested, are formed with the suffix **-ons**, e.g. **laþons** (invitation), **mitons** (thinking), **frijons** (a kiss), **salbons** (ointment), inflected like the verbal nouns in **-ains** associated with weak verbs of class 3. Verbs in **-inon** and **-anon** have related abstract nouns in **-inassus**, e.g. **leikinassus** (healing); see §21.4.5 for further examples.

19.2 Conditional sentences.

The protasis of a conditional sentence is introduced, for the most part, with the conjunction **jabai** (if); the apodosis is either unmarked or is introduced with **aiþþau** or **þau**, the latter being postpositive. Three types of sentences are distinguished, depending on the moods of the verbs involved:

a. Real conditions, with an indicative verb in the protasis and with an apodosis consisting of a simple declarative, interrogative or exclamatory clause with an indicative verb or of an imperative. The tense of the verb in the protasis may be present or preterite. E.g.

Mk 5:28 **jabai wastjom is atteka, ganisa** if I touch his garments I will be healed.

Mk 10:12 **jabai qino afletiþ aban seinana jah liugada anþaramma, horinoþ**
if a woman leaves her husband and marries another, she is committing adultery

Lk 14:34 **jabai salt baud wairþiþ, hwe gasupoda**? if salt loses its flavor, with what can it be seasoned?

Mt 6:23 **jabai nu liuhaþ þata in þus riqiz ist, þata riqiz hwan filu**!
for if the light which is in you is darkness, how great is that darkness!

Lk 19:8 **jabai hwis hwa afholoda, fidurfalþ fragilda**
if I have cheated anyone of anything, I pay him back fourfold.

b. Potential or hypothetical conditions, with a present subjunctive verb in the protasis and with an imperative or injunctively used subjunctive in the apodosis. E.g.

Mt 5:29 **jabai augo þein þata taihswo marzjai þuk, usstagg ita jah wairp af þus**
if your right eye offends you, pluck it out and cast it away from you

Mt 5:41 **jabai hwas þuk ananauþjai rasta aina, gaggais miþ imma twos**
if anyone forces you (to go) one mile, you should go two with him

c. Contrary-to-fact conditions, with preterite subjunctive verbs in both protasis and apodosis; the apodosis is frequently introduced with **aiþþau** or postpositive **þau**. E.g.

Lk 17:6 **jabai habaidedeiþ glaubein swa kaurno sinapis, aiþþau jus qiþeiþ du bairabagma þamma ...., jah andhausidedi þau izwis**
if you had faith (even) the size of a mustard seed, you could say to this mulberry tree ...., and it would obey you [**qiþeiþ** is for **qeþeiþ** ; CA has a second and erroneous **jabai** before **qiþeiþ**]

Jn 5:46 **jabai allis Mose galaubidedeiþ, gaþaulaubidedeiþ mis**
for if you had believed Moses, you would have believed me [note the tmesis with **ga-þau-laubidedeiþ**]

The distinction between real and potential conditions is defined above purely on a formal basis, since the semantic difference between the two is difficult to characterize, and even the formal distinction is sometimes blurred. Compare, for example, the three successive protases in Luke 6:32-34 all with the same apodosis "**hwa izwis laune ist**? (what credit is there for you?):

aþþan jabai frijod þans frijondans izwis ... for if you love those who love you ...

jabai þiuþ taujaid þaim þiuþ taujandam izwis ... if you do good unto those who do good to you
jah jabai leihwid fram þaimei weneid andniman ... and if you lend (to those) from whom you expect to receive back

where **taujaid** is subjunctive, **leihwid** is indicative, and **frijod** is ambiguous. Even protases with **hwas** (anyone), usually followed by the subjunctive, appear occasionally with the indicative, e.g.

Lk 14:26 **jabai hwas gaggiþ du mis jah ni fijaiþ ..., ni mag meins siponeis wisan**
if anyone come to me and does not repudiate ..., he cannot be my disciple

Contrary-to-fact protases are occasionally introduced with the conjunction **iþ** or, if negated, with **nih** (**ni** + **-uh**). It is not clear whether this **iþ** is a specialized use of the coordinating conjunction **iþ** or a completely different word. The latter is more likely. E.g.

Jn 18:30 **nih wesi sa ubiltojis, ni þau atgebeima þus ina**
if he were not a criminal, we would not have turned him over to you

Jn 18:36 **iþ us þamma fairhwau wesi meina þiudangardi, aiþþau andbahtos meinai usdaudidedeina ei ...**
if my kingdom were of this world, my servants would have seen to it that ...

Closely related to conditional sentences are those containing subordinations introduced with **niba(i)** (unless), usually followed by the indicative, as in

Mt 5:20 **nibai managizo wairþiþ izwaraizos garaihteins**[1] **þau þize bokarje jah Fareisaie, ni þau qimiþ in þiudangardjai himine**
unless your righteousness surpasses that of the scribes and Farisees, you will not enter the kingdom of heaven

Occasionally, however, **niba(i)** is clearly the equivalent of **jabai ni** in a contrary-to-fact protasis, as in

Jn 14:2 **In garda attins meinis saliþwos managos sind, aþþan niba weseina, aiþþau qeþjau du izwis, 'Gagga manwjan stad izwis'?**
In my father's house there are many rooms, for if there were not, would I have said to you, 'I go to prepare a place for you'?

19.3 The dual.

There are distinct dual forms of the first and second person pronouns and of the corresponding verbal forms:

N	**wit**	we two	---	you two
G	---		**igqara**	
D	**ugkis, uggkis**		**igqis**	
A	**ugkis, uggkis**		**igqis**	

[1] ***managizo wairþiþ***, translating Gk περισσεύῃ, is impersonal: *there surpasses, there is an excess.* The genitive ***izwaraizos garaihteins*** is used partitively with this idiom, which is not attested elsewhere in our corpus. Cf., however, 2Cor 1:5, where the same Greek verb is translated with the phrase ***ufarassus ist*** *there is an excess* followed by the partitive genitive ***þulaine*** *of patience.* For ***þau*** with comparative constructions, see §20.4.

The possessive adjective **iggqar-** (belonging to you two) also occurs.

The dual forms of the first and second persons of all active verbs may be obtained conveniently from the first person plural forms of the respective paradigms as follows:

(a) For the lst person dual: replace the lst person plural endings

-am and **-om**	with	**-os**	thus: pres. indic. **sokjos, salbos, habos, nimos**
-um		**-u**	pret. indic. **sokidedu, salbodedu, habaidedu, nemu**
-ma		**-wa**	pres. subj. **nimaiwa, salbowa;**
			pret. subj. **sokidedeiwa, salbodedeiwa, habaidedeiwa, nemeiwa**

(b) For the 2nd person dual: replace the 1st person plural endings **-m** and **-ma** with **-ts**. Thus: pres. indic. **sokjats, salbots, habats, nimats**; pret. indic. **sokideduts, salbodeduts, habaideduts, nemuts**; pres. subj. **sokjaits, salbots, habaits, nimaits**; pret. subj. **sokidedeits, salbodedeits, habaidedeits, nemeits.**

(c) The imperative dual is the same as the present indicative dual of the 2nd person: **sokjats, salbots, habats, nimats.**

19.4 The verbal prefix *miþ-*.

As a verbal prefix, **miþ-** denotes that an activity is performed together with someone else; the direct object of verbs with this prefix is always in the dative case. E.g.

miþinngaggan to enter in along with (*D*)
miþstandan to stand along with (*D*)
miþswiltan to die together with (*D*).

There is frequently an apparently free interchange of **miþ** as a preposition and **miþ-** as a verbal prefix. Compare the following lexical pairs:

Lk 1:58	**jah miþfaginodedun izai** and they rejoiced along with her
Lk 15:6	**faginoþ miþ mis!** rejoice with me!
Lk 7:11	**jah mididdjedun imma siponjos is** and his disciples went with him
Lk 2:51	**jah iddja miþ im** and he went with them
Mk 1:27	**sokidedun miþ sis misso** they argued among themselves
Mk 8:11	**dugunnun miþsokjan imma** they began to argue with him

The extent to which this interchange was restricted or unrestricted cannot, of course, be determined from our limited corpus.

19.5 Final remarks on relative constructions: *ei, þei, izei* and *sei.*

a. **ei** is occasionally used alone as an uninflected relative pronoun immediately following a temporal expression. E.g.

Lk I:20 **... und þana dag ei wairþai þata** ... until the day when that takes place (note the subjunctive)

There is also a single occurrence of relative **ei** after **haidus** (way, manner):

2Tim 3:8 **þamma haidau ei ...** in the manner in which ...

b. With a single exception, **þei** is used as a relative pronoun only in conjunction with the indefinite pronoun **þatahwah** (whatever) and the indefinite adverbs **þishwaruh, þishwaduh** (wherever), for which see §22.2.

c. The poorly attested relative forms of the 1st and 2nd person pronouns were presented in §12.3c. Similar forms exist for the 3rd person singular, namely masc. **izei, ize** and fem. **sei**, which have become generalized as relative pronouns. The following points should be noted concerning their use:

(1) Both **izei** and **sei** function only as the subject of their clauses; no oblique cases are attested.

(2) **izei** may be added to plural forms of the demonstrative **þai** etc., forming what is essentially a compound relative form with a simple relative meaning. E.g.

Mk 9:1 **sind sumai þize her standandane þai ize ni kausjand dauþaus** there are some of those standing here who will not taste death [the parallel passage in Lk 9:27 has simply **þaiei**]

Mt 7:15 **atsaihwiþ sweþauh faura liugnapraufetum þaim izei qimand at izwis in wastjom lambe** Beware then of false prophets who come to you in sheep's clothing

These same forms, as well as the singular **sa izei**, may, like the ordinary relatives **saei** etc., be used pronominally. E.g.

John 11:37 **sa izei uslauk augona þamma blindin** he who opened the eyes of the blind man

Eph 2:17 **gawairþi þaim izei nehwa** peace (be) unto those who are nearby

Note in particular that when **þai izei** etc. are used as simple relatives, the first element reflects the syntax of the main clause. This is in contrast with the usage of the ordinary relatives **saei** etc. Contrast, for example, the phrases **liugnapraufetum þaim ize** of Mt 7:15 cited above with the **liugnapraufetum þaiei** of the parallel passage in Lk 9:27.

Vocabulary 19

Verbs:

aihtron *wv 2* to beg (as a beggar); to pray (on behalf of: **faur** *D*).
awiliudon *wv 2* to thank (smn: *D*; for: **faur** *A*, **fram** *D*, **in** *G*).
faginon *wv 2* to rejoice (at: *D*, **in** *G*).
hwarbon *wv 2* to walk about.
idreigon *wv 2* ± **sik** to repent (of: **ana** *D*).
wopjan *wv 1*, **ufwopjan** *wv 1* (*perf.*) to cry out, call (to, upon: *D*, **du** *D*).
insaihwan *sv 5* to look at, regard (*D*); to give heed to, pay attention to (*D*).
faurgaggan *sv 7* (pret. **-iddja**) to pass by; **fauragaggan** *sv 7* (pret. **-iddja**) to precede (smn: **faura** *D*), go in front; to take charge of, manage (sthg: *D*).

duatgaggan *sv 7*(pret. **-iddja**) to approach (smn: *D*).
þairhgaggan *sv 7*(pret. **-iddja**) to pierce (*A*); to pass (along: **and** *A*; through: **þairh** *A*).
innatgaggan *sv 7*(pret. **-iddja**) to enter (into: **in** *A*).
hweilan *wv 3* to cease (doing: participle).
frijon *wv 2* to love (smn: *A*).

Nouns:

staiga *sf* road, way, path.
barnilo *wn* small child; the vocative, like Gk τέκνε, may be used as an affectionate address to a male of any age.
aipiskaupei *wf* the office of bishop (< Gk ἐπισκοπή).
nahts *f* (*irreg.* *G* **nahts,** *D* **naht,** *A* **naht;** *Dpl* **nahtam**) night.
gabaurþs *sf* (*G* **-þais**) birth; generation; birth-place.
sinþs* *sm* used to form the numerical adverbs: **ainamma sinþa** once; **twaim sinþam** twice; **anþaramma sinþa** once more; **þrim, fimf, sibun sinþam** three, five, seven times.

Adjectives:

ainah- *adj* only-begotten; **ainaha** *wm* only son.
auhumist- *adj* highest; **auhumisto** *wn* highest point, summit.

Proper Names:

Esaias, Esaeias, *G* **Esaeiins,** *D* **Esaiin,** *A* **Esaiau** *m* Isaiah.
Iairiko* (*G* **-ons,** *D* **-on,** *A* **-on**) Jericho.
Seimon (*G* **-is, -aus,** *D* **-a, -au,** *A* **-, -u**) *m* Simon.
Nazorenus* (*D* **-au** *m*); **Nazoraius** (*D* **-au,** *A* **-u**) *m* Nazorene
Daweid (*G* **-dis**) *m* David.
Iudaia (*G* **-as,** *D* **-a,** *A* **-an**) *f* Judaea.
Andraias (*G* **-aiins,** *D* **-aiin,** *A* **-aian**) *m* Andreas.
Diabaulus, Diabulus (*G* **-laus,** *D* **-lau**) *m* the Devil.

Other:

hiri *quasi-imperative interj* come here! *pl.* **hirjiþ,** *dual* **hirjats.**
und filu mais *adv* all the more.
hwaþro *interrog adv* from where? whence?

Exercises

A. Translate.

1. Jah qaþ Diabulus du Iesua: "Jabai sunus sijais Gudis, qiþ þamma staina ei wairþai hlaibs."
2. Jabai hwarbots and staigos þis weihsis, gasaihwats managans aihtrondans.
3. Jabai ufwopidedeis du imma anþaramma sinþa, gahausidedi þus.
4. Jabai sa manns ist frauja þeins, skuld ist þus ina sweran jah inweitan.
5. Jabai wileis, magt ugkis gahrainjan.
6. Jabai fraihnats ina usdaudo, andhafjiþ igqis.
7. Jabai sa hundafaþs ni habaidedi galaubein, þiumagus seins ni ganesi.
8. Jabai awiliudodedeits im, ni biliþeina igqis.
9. Aþþan jabai frijoþ þans frijondans izwis ainans, hwo mizdono habaiþ?
10. Jabai gahausidedeiþ meinaize waurde, þai sinistans þau ni gasokeina izwis.
11. Jabai wit ni þlauheiwa faura gadrauhtim, usqemeina ugkis.

12. Jabai ushafjiþ augona izwara du himinam, gasaihwiþ liuhaþ sauilis jah faginoþ.
13. Jabai wissedi þata, aiþþau usstodi us þamma stada.
14. Jabai ni magt andstandan imma, usstand jah þliuh.
15. Jabai afletiþ mannam missadedins ize, afletiþ jah izwis atta izwar sa ufar himinam.
16. Jabai faurgaggands gaumeis usliþin ligandin ana ligra, gastand jah rodei miþ imma mel leitil.
17. Jabai þo barna gasehweina mik, aiþþau atstigeina dalaþ af þamma hrota.
18. Jabai hwarbonds þairhgaggis þairh þata fairguni, gamoteis diuzam managaim.
19. Jabai swerandei duatiddjedeis imma, ni gasoki þus jah ganasidedi þuk.
20. Jabai hwas gibai igqis mat, awiliudots imma.
21. Nibai ufhausjiþ imma jah taujiþ anabusnins is, ni qimiþ in libain aiweinon.
22. Jabai fauragaggands gamoteis imma, gawandi þuk her jah gateih unsis.
23. Jabai frawaurkjai broþar þeins, gasak imma, jah þan jabai idreigo sik, afletais imma frawaurhtins is.
24. Jabai sa blinda galaubidedi, ganesi þau jah mahtedi ussaihwan.
25. Jabai idreigots, is afletiþ igqis.

C. Translate.

1. Swaswe gamelid ist in bokom waurde Esaeiins praufetaus qiþandins: "Stibna wopjandins in auþidai: 'Manweid wig Fraujins; raihtos (straight) waurkeiþ staigos is.'"
2. Jah hwarboda Iesus afar þata in Galilaia; ni auk wilda in Iudaia gaggan unte sokidedun ina þai Iudaieis usqiman.
3. Jah draus faur fotum is awiliudonds imma.
4. Qaþ Zakarias du Iohannen sunau seinamma: "Þu, barnilo, fauragaggis faura andwairþja Fraujins manwjan wigans imma, du giban kunþi naseinais managein is in fraleta frawaurhte ize."
5. Jah jabai sibun sinþam ana dag frawaurkjai broþar þeins du þus, jah sibun sinþam ana dag gawandjai sik qiþands, "Idreigo mik," afletais imma.
6. Qaþ þan sa aggilus du Zakariin bi Iohannen, sunu is: "Wairþiþ þus faheds jah swegniþa (rejoicing), jah managai in gabaurþai is faginond."
7. Þata þan qiþands ufwopida: "Saei habai ausona du hausjan, gahausjai!"
8. Fram þamma daga ei hausidedum bi þizai wrakai ni hweilaidedum faur izwis bidjandans jah aihtrondans.
9. Sa Fareisaius standands sis þo bad: "Guþ, awiliudo þus unte ni im swaswe þai anþarai mans."
10. Jah qaþ Iesus du siponjam seinaim: "Hausideduþ ei ik qaþ izwis, 'Galeiþa, jah qima aftra at izwis.' Jabai frijodedeiþ mik, aiþþau jus faginodedeiþ ei ik gagga du Attin."
11. Jah hwarbonds faur marein Galeilaias gasahw Seimonu jah Andraian broþar is, þis Seimonis, wairpandans nati in marein; wesun auk fiskjans. Jah qaþ im Iesus: "Hirjats afar mis, jah gatauja igqis wairþan nutans (catchers) manne."
12. Iþ sumai þize jainar standandane gahausjandans qeþun þatei, "Helian wopeiþ sa."
13. Idreigoþ jah galaubeiþ in aiwaggeljon!
14. Jabai hwas aipiskaupeins gairneiþ, sah skal seinamma garda waila fauragaggan, barna habands ufhausjandona. Iþ jabai hwas seinamma garda fauragaggan ni mag, hwaiwa aikklesjon Gudis fauragaggiþ?
15. Afaruh þan þata innatgaggandin imma in Kafarnaum, duatiddja imma hundafaþs.
16. Jah nimands þans sibun hlaibans jah awiliudonds gabrak jah atgaf siponjam seinaim ei atlagidedeina faur þo managein.
17. Jah sai, manna us þizai managein ufwopida qiþands: "Laisari, bidja þuk insaihwan du sunu meinamma, unte ainaha mis ist."
18. Skuld is wopjan du Guda bidom dagam jah nahtam.
19. Jah insaihwandei aina þiwi du Petrau, duatgaggandei imma qaþ: "Jah þu miþ Iesua þamma Nazoreinau wast!"
20. Jah warþ, unte Zakkaius was wair leitils, jah usstaig ana smakkabagm ei gasehwi Iesu biþe sah þairhiddja and þana wig.
21. Atta, awiliudo þus unte gahausides bido meinaizo.

22. Warþ þan, miþþanei nehwa was is Iaireikon, blinda sums sat faur wig du aihtron. Gahausjands þan managein faurgaggandein frah qiþands: "Hwa ist þata?" Gataihun þan imma þatei, "Iesus Nazoraius þairhgaggiþ." Iþ is ubuhwopida qiþands: "Iesu, sunu Daweidis, armai mik!" Jah þai fauragaggandans anabudun imma ei þahaidedi, iþ is und filu mais hropida, "Sunu Daweidis, armai mik!" Gastandands þan Iesus anabauþ ei tauheina ina du sis. Biþe nehwa was imma, frah ina qiþands: "Hwa þus wileis ei taujau?" Iþ is qaþ: "Frauja, wiljau ei taujais ei ussaihwau." Jah Iesus qaþ du imma: "Ussaihw! Galaubeins þeina ganasida þuk." Jah suns ussahw jah laistida Iesu awiliudonds Guda. Jah alla managei gasaihwandei gaf hazein Guda.

23. Jah hwarbondin Iesua jainþro, laistidedun afar imma twai blindans, hropjandans jah qiþandans: "Armai uggkis, sunu Daweidis!" Qimandin þan in garda duatiddjedun imma þai blindans jah qaþ im Iesus: "Gaulaubjats þatei magjau þata taujan?" Qeþun du imma: "Jai, frauja!" Þanuh attaitok (he touched) augam ize qiþands: "Bi galaubeinai iggqarai wairþai iggqis."

24. Jah in allh hwarbondin Iesua atiddjedun du imma þai auhumistans gudjans jah bokarjos jah sinistans, jah qeþun du imma: "In hwamma waldufnje þata taujis? Jah hwas þus þata waldufni atgaf ei þata taujis?" Iþ Iesus andhafjands qaþ du im: "Fraihna jah ik izwis ainis waurdis, jah andhafjiþ mis, jah qiþa izwis in hwamma waldufnje þata tauja. Daupeins Iohannis uzuh himina was þau uzuh mannam? Andhafjiþ mis." Jah þahtedun (they thought) du sis misso qiþandans: "Jabai qiþam, 'Us himina,' qiþiþ, 'Aþþan duhwe ni galaubideduþ imma?' Iþ jabai qiþam, 'Us mannam,' alla so managei stainam afwairpiþ unsis, unte allai galaubjand Iohannen praufetu wisan." Jah andhofun ei ni wissedeina hwaþro. Jah Iesus qaþ im: "Ni ik izwis qiþa in hwamma waldufnje þata tauja."

Lesson 20

20.1 Preterite-present verbs.

The preterite-present verbs **magan, witan, kunnan, *skulan, munan**, and **gamunan** have already been introduced. The remaining verbs in this category are much less well attested, but their paradigms may be reconstructed easily from the following attested forms:

(a) ***þaurban** to need, be in need

Present Indicative		Present Subjunctive		Preterite Indicative	
þarf	**þaurbum**	---	**þaurbeima**	---	---
þarft	**þaurbuþ**	---	**þaurbeiþ**	---	---
---	**þaurbun**	---	---	**þaurfta**	---

Present (active) participle: **þaurband-**
Past (passive, stative) participle: **þaurft-** (needed, necessary).

(b) **gadaursan** to dare, venture

gadars	**gadaursum**	**gadaursjau**	---	**gadaursta**	---
---	---	---	---	---	---
gadars	---	---	---	---	**gadaurstedun**

(c) ***ogan** to fear, be afraid

og	---	---	---	**ohta**	---
---	---	**ogeis**	**ogeiþ**	---	---
---	---	---	---	**ohta**	**ohtedun**

Present (active) participles: **ogand-**
Imperative singular: **ogs** (!)

(d) ***aigan, -aihan** (in cpd **fairaihan**) to own

aih	**aigum, aihum**	---	---	**aihta**	---
---	**aihuþ**	---	**aigeiþ**	---	---
aih	**aigun**	**aigi**	**aigeina**	---	**aihtedun**

Present (active) participles: **aigand-, aihand-**. Pret. subjunctive 2nd pers. sing. **aihtedeis.**
[See the historical notes for a comment on the variation between **-g-** and **-h-**.]

The following PP verbs are attested in even fewer forms: **lais** (I know); **daug** (it is useful), **gamot** (is accommodated), lst pers. pl. pres. subj. **gamoteima,** 3rd pers. pl. pret. indic. **gamostedun**; **ganah** (it is enough); **binah** (it is necessary, sufficient, lawful), past participle **binauht-** (sufficient).

20.2 u-stem adjectives

There is a small group of adjectives whose stems originally ended in *-u* and which were inflected like the nouns **sunus, handus,** and **faihu.** The only trace of the original inflection is in the strong nominative singular of all three genders and in the neuter accusative singular. Otherwise these adjectives follow exactly the inflection of **ja**-stem adjectives (i.e. **wilþj**-):

N	masc.	**hardus**	fem.	**hardus**	neuter	**hardu, hardjata**
A		**hardjana**		**hardja**		**hardu, hardjata**

Belonging to this group, but for the most part very poorly attested, are

aggwu-	narrow	**kauru-**	heavy	**tulgu-**	stable, steadfast
aglu-	difficult	**manwu-**	ready	**twalibwintru-**	12 years old
hardu-	hard	**qairru-**	gentle	**þaursu-**	withered
hnasqu-	soft	**seiþu-**	late	**þlaqu-**	soft

20.3 The comparative and superlative of adjectives

The comparative degree of adjectives is formed with the suffix **-iz**- or **-oz**-. No rule can be given for the choice between the two suffixes, but on the basis of the rather sparse evidence available a given adjective is limited to one form only; attestations are about evenly distributed. The comparative adjective is always inflected weak, but like the active participle, the feminine follows the paradigm of **managei**, not **qino**. The masculine singular nominative always ends in **-a**. Following is a list of all attested stems:

alþiz-	older	**framaldroz**-	older
azetiz-	easier	**frodoz**-	wiser
fawiz-	fewer	**garaihtoz**-	more just
hardiz-	harder	**handugoz**-	wiser
juhiz-	younger	**hlasoz**-	more cheerful
managiz-	more	**swinþoz**-	stronger
raþiz-	easier	**þaurftoz**-	needier
spediz-	later	**unswikunþoz**-	less known
sutiz-	sweeter		
wulþriz-	worthier		

The superlative degree of adjectives is formed with the suffix **-ist**- or **-ost**-, probably parallelling the choice of **-iz**- and **-oz**- in the comparative, but the evidence is insufficient for certainty on this point. Unlike the comparative, the superlative has both strong and weak inflections. Attested regular stems are

hauhist-	highest	**spedist-**	latest	**lasiwost-**	weakest, laziest
reikist-	mightiest	**undarist-**	innermost	**armost-**	poorest
smalist-	smallest				

A few adjectives have comparative and superlative forms based on a lexical stem different from that of the positive:

god-	good	**batiz-**	better	**batist-**	best
leitil-	little	**minniz-**	smaller, less	**minnist-**	smallest, least
mikil-	big	**maiz-**	bigger	**maist-**	biggest

ubil-	bad	**wairsiz-**	worse	***wairst-**	worst

The noun **sinista** (elder) is regarded as the superlative of **sineig-** (old).

A second, non-productive set of superlative endings contains **-um-**, **-tum-**, **-dum-**, which are used as comparatives, always with weak inflection. These are limited to nine adjectives denoting spacial relationships. A secondary superlative in **-ist-** was created on the older superlative stem:

auhum-	higher	**auhumist-**	highest
frum-	former, prior	**frumist-**	first
aftum-	next, following	**aftumist-**	last
iftum-	next, following	---	
innum-	inner	---	
hleidum-	left (not right)	---	
---		**spedumist-**	last
---		**hindumist-**	hindmost

20.4 The syntax of the comparative adjective.

Like ordinary adjectives, comparative adjectives may be used attributively, as in

Lk 15:25 **sunus is sa alþiza** his elder son
Lk 15:13 **sa juhiza sunus** the younger son

or predicatively (but always weak), as in

John 14:28 **Atta meins maiza mis ist** My Father is greater than I
Mt 10:31 **managaim sparwam batizans sijuþ jus** you are better (i.e. worthier) than many sparrows

As seen in these examples, the expressed basis of the comparison, if a noun or pronoun, is placed in the dative. A comparative adjective may be nominalized, as in

Rom 9:12 **sa maiza skalkinoþ þamma minnizin** the greater will serve the lesser
Lk 3:16 **iþ gaggiþ swinþoza mis** but there shall come one who is stronger than I

When the basis of the comparison is phrasal or clausal, it is introduced with **þau**. This is the case especially with the comparisons involving impersonal neuter predications like **raþizo ist** (it is easier), as in

Lk 18:25 **raþizo allis ist ulbandau þairh þairko neþlos þairhleiþan þau gabigamma in þiudangardja Gudis galeiþan**
it is easier for a camel to go through the eye of a needle than for a rich man to go into the Kingdom of God

Other such impersonal expressions are **azetizo ist** (it is easier), **sutizo ist** (it is sweeter), and **batizo ist** (it is better). Note that the dative, without a preposition, is used here to express the logical subject of the infinitival phrase; the accusative, which is the norm in the underlying Greek, is also found in Gothic, as in

Lk 16:17 **iþ azetizo ist himin jah airþa hindarleiþan þau witodis ainana writ gadriusan**
for it is easier for heaven and earth to pass away than for one stroke of the law to fall.

20.5 The verbal prefixes *ana-* and *in(n)-*.

The prefix **ana-** retains its prepositional meaning of *on, onto, down onto, to, against* with most of the verbs to which it is added. E.g.

analagjan	to lay (sthg: *A*) on (sthg: *D*)
anaqiman	to come or go to (smn: *A*), approach
anahaban	to take hold of, seize
anaaukan	to add (sthg: *A*) to (sthg: **ana** *D*) [**aukan** to increase (intrans.)]
anameljan	to register (intrans.)
anahnaiwjan	to lay down (one's head) [**hnaiwjan** to cause to bow, humble]
anaqiþan	to talk down, slander, blaspheme
anahaitan	to call down, rebuke, scold (smn: *D*); to call to (smn: *A*) [**haitan** to call, name]

ana- may also emphasize the notion of imposition or oppression already present in the simple verb, as in

anakaurjan	to importune, bother [**kaurjan** to burden, make heavy]
ananauþjan	to force, compel [**nauþjan** idem]

A more extensive corpus would probably reveal that in these verbs as well as others, such as **slepan** (to sleep) vs. **anaslepan** (to fall asleep), **ana-** was often simply the semantically appropriate prefix for forming an ingressive perfective counterpart to an imperfective simple verb, or for forming a perfective denominative verb, as in **ananiujan** (to renew), **anaqiujan** (to bring to life; cf. **qiw-** alive), and **anaþiwan** (to enslave; cf. **þius** slave).

The verbal prefix **in-** also appears occasionally as **inn-**, formally indistinguishable from the adverb **inn**, as can be see from its usage in pairs like the following:

Jn 18:16	**jah attauh inn Paitru** and he brought Peter in
Lk 2:27	**jah miþþanei innattauhun berusjos þata barn Iesu** and when the parents were bringing in the child Jesus
Lk 1:28	**jah galeiþands inn sa aggilus du izai qaþ** and having entered, the angel said to her
Mt 7:13	**jah managai sind þai inngaleiþandans þairh þata (daur)** and many are those who enter through that (door)

With verbs of motion and conveyance the literal sense of **in-** as *in, into* prevails:

inngaggan	to enter	**insandjan**	to send in
inngaleiþan	to enter	**insaian**	to sow in, on
innattiuhan	to bring in , lead in		

As with other prefixes, **in** may only intensify a semantic component already present in the simple verb, as in

insaihwan	to direct one's gaze at (usually with **du**)
inweitan	idem, to greet, honor

or be used to form perfective or ingressive counterparts to the simple verb, as in

inreiran	to begin to tremble	[**reiran** to tremble]
intandjan	to burn up, consume with fire	[**tandjan** to burn]

or to form denominative /causative verbs, as in

inliuhtjan	to enlighten	[**liuhaþ** light]
inbrannjan	to burn (trans.)	[**brinnan** to burn intrans.]
insailjan	to tie with rope	[***sail** rope].

20.6 Direct questions.

Direct questions, when not merely implicit, are marked as such in one of two ways: (1) by the presence of interrogative pronouns, adjectives, or adverbs, or (2) by the presence of an interrogative particle, either enclitic **-u** or sentence initial **ibai.** The enclitic particle **-u**, accompanied by the same phonological changes that characterize **-uh** (see §15.3), is attached to the first word of its clause. E.g.

Lk 7:20 **þu is sa qimanda þau anþaranu wenjaima**? Are you the one who is to come or should we await another? [**þu** is probably for **þu-u; anþaranu** is regular for **anþarana** + **-u**]

Lk 9:54 **Wileizu ei qiþaima** ... Do you want us to say ...? [**wileizu** is regular for **wileis** + **-u**]

The combined form **niu** is quite frequent, introducing a negative question expecting a positive answer. E.g.

Lk 2:49 **Niu wisseduþ þatei in þaim attins meinis skulda wisan?**
Didn't you know that I was obliged to be involved in my Father's affairs?

Elipsis is sometimes involved in the use of **niu.** E.g.

Lk 20:22 **Skuldu ist unsis Kaisara gild giban þau niu**? Is it right for us to pay taxes to Caesar or not?

The particle **ibai** placed before a positive question indicates an expected negative answer, and vice versa. E.g.

John 6:67 **Ibai jah jus wileiþ galeiþan**? You don't want to go too, do you?

John 7:51 **Ibai witoþ unsar stojiþ mannan nibai faurþis hauseiþ fram imma jah ufkunnaiþ hwa taujai?**
Our law does not judge a man unless it first hears his testimony and discovers what he has done, does it?

I Cor 9:4 **Ibai ni habam waldufni matjan jah driggkan?**
We have the right to eat and drink, don't we?

The reversal of the negation in the English translation is idiomatic. One may also translate simply "Do you want to go too?" and leave the tenor of the question to the context.

Vocabulary 20

Verbs:

***þaurban** PP (§20.1) to need, be in need of (sthg: *G*), to require (that ...: **ei** + subj.).
gadaursan PP (§20.1) to dare, venture (to do: inf.).

***ogan** PP (§20.1) (± **sis**) to fear, be afraid of (smn: *A*); + **agis mikil** or **agisa mikilamma** to be greatly afraid.
***aigan** PP (§20.1) to own, possess, have (*A*).
atwopjan *wv 1* to summon (smn: *A*).
ushramjan *wv 1* to hang, crucify (smn: *A*).
haitan *sv 7* to name, call (smn: *A*); to order, command.
birodjan *wv 1* to mutter, murmur (sthg: *A*) in disapproval (concerning: **bi** *A*).
fraliusan *sv 2* to lose (sthg: *D*); **fralusan-** *pp* lost.
uslagjan *wv 1* to lay, place (*A*); mostly in the phrase **uslagjan handuns ana** to place one's hands on (smn: *A*).
laþon, galaþon *wv 2* to invite (smn: *A*).
fraletan *sv 7* to release, set free (smn: *A*); to forgive (smn: *D*; one's sins: *A*); to allow, permit (smn: *A*; to do: inf.); to leave, withdraw from (*A*).

Nouns:

garazna *wm* neighbor; **garazno** *wf* idem (female).
nehwundja *wm* neighbor, a close associate.
drakma *wm* drachma (a coin) < Gk δραχμή.
lukarn *sn* lamp (< Lat *lucerna*).
manaseþs *sf* (*G* **-dais**) the world, mankind; usually with **so.**

Adjectives:

aftumist- *superl adj* last, in last place.
frum- *comp adj* previous, prior, coming before; **fram fruma** *adv* from the very first; **frumist-** *superl adj* first; **fram frumistin** from the first, from the start.
wairsiz- *comp adj* worse.
spediz- *comp adj* later, latter; **spedist-** *superl adj* last, latest.
juhiz- *comp adj* (of **jugg-**) younger.
alþiz- *comp adj* older, elder.
maiz- *comp adj* more, greater; **mais** *adv* more; **hwan filu ... mais þamma** the more ... the more ...; **maist-** *superl adj* greatest, most.
hardu- *adj* strict, severe; difficult to understand.
batiz- *comp adj* better; **batist-** *superl adj* best.
[and the comparative adjectives **fawiz-**, **managiz-**, **frodoz-**, and **swinþoz-**]

Other:

taihuntehund *card num indecl* hundred.
iupaþro *adv* from above, from on high.
þarei *rel adv* where, (to, at, in) the place where
ibai *interrog particle* §20.6.
niuntehund *card num indecl* or *G* **-is** ninety.
swa *adv* so, to such an extent; **swa ... swe ...** as ... as ....
þau than (in comparative constructions involving phrases or clauses) §20.4.

Exercises

Translate.

1. Ik ohta mis auk þuk, unte manna hardus is.
2. Weis gebum imma þans skattans jah anabudum imma qiþandans, "Bugei þizei þaurbeima."
3. Ibai mag blinds blindana tiuhan?
4. Jah warþ biþe þata gahausidedun ni gadaurstedun fraihnan ina ni waihtis.
5. Niþþan qam laþon garaihtans ak frawaurhtans in idreiga.
6. Nist skalks maiza fraujin seinamma, nih apaustaulus maiza þamma sandjandin sik.

7. Waituþþan atta izwar sa ufar himinam þatei þaurbeiþ faurþizei jus bidjaiþ ina.
8. Birodidedun þan Iudaieis bi ina unte qaþ, "Ik im hlaifs sa atsteigands us himina, " jah qeþun, "Niu ist Iesus sa sunus Iosefis þizei weis kunþedum attan jah aiþein? Hwaiwa nu qiþiþ sa þatei us himina atstaig?"
9. Ainana attan aigum: Guþ.
10. Atwopidedun þan anþaramma sinþa þana mannan saei was blinds jah frehun ina hwaiwa mahtedi ussaihwan.
11. Ni manwus im galaistjan afar þus.
12. Nim libain aiweinon du þizaiei laþoþs is.
13. Manne sums aihta twans sununs: namo þis alþizins Iosef jah namo þis juhizins Iohannes.
14. Þai bokarjos jah auhumistans gudjans þahaidedun unte ohtedun þo managein.
15. Amen, amen qiþa izwis: saei galaubeiþ du mis aih libain aiweinon.
16. Þanuh managai þize siponje is gahausjandans qeþun: "Hardu ist þata waurd. Hwas mag þamma fraþjan?"
17. Ni þaurbun hailai lekeis, ak þai unhaili habandans.
18. Saei galaubeid mis þo waurstwa þoei ik tauja jah is taujiþ, jah maizona þaim taujiþ.
19. Jah anabauþ im ei mann ni qeþeina waiht bi jainos mahtins. Hwan filu is im anabauþ, mais þamma eis meridedun.
20. Jah galaiþ aftra ufar Iaurdanu in þana stad þarei was Iohannes frumist daupjands.
21. Jah ohtedun sis agis mikil jah qeþun du sis misso: "Hwas sa sijai, unte jah winds jah marei ufhausjand imma?"
22. Maizein þizai friaþwai manna ni habaiþ, ei hwas saiwala seina lagjiþ faur frijonds seinans.
23. Ibai þai blindans saihwand jah þai baudans hausjand?
24. Ni ogeiþ izwis þans fraqistjandans leika þatainei (only), iþ saiwalai ni magandans fraqistjan; iþ ogeiþ mais þana magandan jah saiwalai jah leika fraqistjan.
25. Jah sitands atwopida þans twalif jah qaþ du im: "Jabai hwas wili frumists wisan, sijai allaize aftumists jah allaim andbahts."
26. Þata rodida izwis þei in mis gawairþi (peace) aigeiþ.
27. Ni ogs þus!

28. Jah qaþ Iesus: "Ik im hairdeis sa goda jah kann meina lamba jah kunnun mik þo meina swaswe kann mik Atta jah ik kann Attan, jah saiwala meina lagja faur þo lamba. Jah anþara lamba aih þoei ni sind þis awistris (sheepfold). Jah þo skal ik briggan (bring), jah stibnos meinaizos hausjand, jah wairþand ain aweþi (flock of sheep) jah ains hairdeis."

29. Jah qaþ Iesus du siponjam seinaim: "Jabai so manaseþs izwis fijai, kunneiþ ei mik fruman izwis fijaida. Jabai þis fairhwaus weseiþ, aiþþau so manaseþs izwis swaswe swesans frijodedi. Aþþan unte us þamma fairhwau ni sijuþ, ak ik gawalida (selected) izwis us þamma fairhwau, duþþe fijaid izwis so manaseþs.

30. Jah andhofun Peilatau Iudaieis: "Weis witoþ aihum, jah bi þamma witoda unsaramma skal sa manna gaswiltan, unte sik silban Gudis sunu gatawida." Biþe gahausida Peilatus þata waurd, mais ohta sis, jah galaiþ in praitauriaun (praetorium) aftra jah qaþ du Iesua: "Hwaþro is þu?" Iþ Iesus ni andhof imma. Þaruh qaþ imma Peilatus: "Du mis ni rodeis? Niu waist þatei waldufni aih ushramjan þuk jah waldufni aih fraletan þuk?" Andhof Iesus: "Ni aihtedeis waldufnje ainhun (any) ana mik nih wesi þus atgiban iupaþro."

31. Wesunuþþan imma nehwjandans sik allai motarjos jah frawaurhtai hausjan imma. Jah birodidedun Fareisaieis jah bokarjos qiþandans þatei, "Sa frawaurhtans andnimiþ jah miþmatjiþ im."

Qaþ þan du im þo gajukon qiþands: "Hwas manna izwara aigands taihuntehund lambe jah fraliusands ainamma þize niu bileiþiþ þo niuntehund jah niun ana auþidai jah gaggiþ afar þamma fralusanin unte bigitiþ þata? Jah bigitands uslagjiþ ana amsans (shoulders) seinans faginonds, jah qimands in garda galaþoþ frijonds jah garaznans qiþands du im: 'Faginoþ miþ mis þammei bigat lamb mein þata fralusano.' Qiþa izwis þatei swa faheds wairþiþ in himina in ainis frawaurhtis idreigondins þau in niuntehundis jah niune garaihtaize þaiei ni þaurbun idreigos.

"Aiþþau suma qino drakmans habandei taihun, jabai fraliusiþ drakmin ainamma, niu tandeiþ (lights) lukarn jah usbaugeiþ (sweeps) razn jah sokeiþ glaggwaba (diligently) unte bigitiþ? Jah bigitandei gahaitiþ frijondjos (fem. friends) jah garaznons qiþandei: 'Faginoþ miþ mis, unte bigat drakman þammei fralaus.' Swa, qiþa izwis, faheds wairþiþ in andwairþja aggile Gudis in ainis idreigondins frawaurhtis."

32. Iþ Iesus andhof imma þatei, "Frumista allaizo anabusns ist so: Hausei, Israel! Frauja Guþ unsar Frauja ains ist, jah frijos Fraujan Guþ þeinana us allamma hairtin þeinamma jah us allai saiwalai þeinai jah us allai gahugdai þeinai jah us allai mahtai þeinai. So frumista anabusns. Jah anþara galeika þizai: Frijos nehwundjan þeinana swe þuk silban. Maizei þaim anþara anabusns nist."

Lesson 21

21.1 Strong verbs: class 7.

Verbs of this class are characterized by reduplication in the preterite stem and are conveniently divided into two groups: (1) those showing no change (ablaut) in the vowel of the stem syllable, and (2) those with the stem vowel **-e-** in the present stem and **-o-** in the preterite stem. The vowel of the reduplicating syllable is **-ai-** (< PG **i*) in both groups. The following list contains all verbs assigned to this class, quite a few of which are poorly attested:

	Present (Infinitive)	Preterite	Past Participle	
(1)	**falþan**	**faifalþ**	**falþan-**	to fold
	haldan	**haihald**	**haldan-**	to tend (cattle); to hold
	(ga)staldan	**(ga)staistald**	**(ga)staldan-**	to possess, acquire
	fahan	**faifah**	**fahan-**	to seize
	hahan	**haihah**	**hahan-**	to hang
	(af)aikan	**(af)aiaik**	**(af)aikan-**	to deny
	fraisan	**faifrais**	**fraisan-**	to tempt
	haitan	**haihait**	**haitan-**	to call, name
	laikan	**lailaik**	**laikan-**	to play, leap
	maitan	**maimait**	**maitan-**	to cut
	skaidan	**skaiskaiþ**	**skaidan-**	to divide
	slepan	**saislep**	**slepan-**	to sleep
	***flokan**	**faiflok**	***flokan-**	to bewail
	***lauan**	**lailo**	***lauan-**	to revile
	aukan	**aiauk**	**aukan-**	to increase
	hwopan	**hwaihwop**	**hwopan-**	to boast

The following verbs are assigned to Group I on the basis of cognates elsewhere in Germanic; the crucial forms of the preterite are not attested in Gothic itself.

(us)alþan	to grow old	**waldan**	to rule, prevail	**blotan**	to worship
blandan	to mix	**gaggan**	to go	**hlaupan**	to leap
(ana)praggan	to press	**(ga)þlaihan**	to console	**stautan**	to strike
saltan	to salt	**(uf)blesan**	to blow, puff up		

(2)	**gretan**	**gaigrot**	**gretan-**	to weep
	letan	**lailot**	**letan-**	to let, allow, leave
	(ga)redan	**(ga)rairod**	**(ga)redan**	to reflect on
	tekan	**taitok**	**tekan-**	to touch
	saian	**saiso**	**saian-**	to sow
	waian	**waiwo**	**waian-**	to blow

21.2 Indirect questions

Like direct questions, indirect questions are distinguishable by the presence of interrogative pronouns and adjectives or interrogative adverbs, including the interrogative suffix **-u.** The choice between indicative and subjunctive for the verb of indirect questions is determined by two criteria. The first criterion is how the question would be cast if it were a direct question, where the subjunctive is used when there is an element of surprise, dismay, doubt, or exasperation present (see the examples in §15.2A2). The second criterion is the meaning of the verb governing the indirect question. Verbs of simple assertion, knowing, and understanding are usually followed by the indicative, while verbs of inquiring, doubting, and wondering tend to require the subjunctive. The reader should study the following examples carefully, noting that even with these two criteria there remains a large element of unpredictability. Note too that generally present follows present and preterite follows preterite, although exceptions do occur. Both tense and mood are best understood by casting the question in direct form.

Lk 3:15 **jah þagkjandam allaim in hairtam seinaim bi Iohannein niu aufto sa wesi Xristus**
and when all were wondering inwardly about John (as to) whether he was perhaps the Christ [the governing verb, although participial in a dative absolute, is past tense in effect]

Lk 6:9 **fraihna izwis hwa skuld ist sabbato dagam**
I ask you what is proper for sabbaths

Lk 14:28 **Izwara hwas raihtis wiljands kelikn timbrjan niu frumist gasitands rahneiþ manwiþo habai-u du ustiuhan?**
Who among you, desiring to build a watchtower, does not first sit down and calculate whether he has the means to complete it? [**manwiþo** is *Gpl* used as partitive object ; see §23.3]

Mk 3:2 **jah witaidedun imma hailidedi-u sabato daga**
and they kept an eye on him (to see) whether he would do healing on the Sabbath

Mk 8:23 **frah ina gauhwasehwi** he asked him whether he could see anything
[note the unusual tmesis with **ga-u-hwa-sehwi**]

Mk 9:6 **Ni auk wissa hwa rodidedi.** For he did not know what he was saying.

Mk 10:2 **frehun ina skuld-u sijai mann qen afsatjan**
they asked him whether it is lawful for a man to divorce a wife [note present following preterite because of the general non-temporal nature of the question]

Mk 11:18 **sokidedun hwaiwa imma usqistidedeina**
they sought a way in which they might kill him [lit., they sought how...]

Mt 6:3 **Ni witi hleidumei þeina hwa taujiþ taihswo þeina**
Don't let your left hand know what your right hand is doing.

John 13:24 **du fraihnan hwas wesi** to ask who it was [context is past tense]

John 18:21 **fraihn þans hausjandans hwa rodidedjau du im**
ask those who were listening (to me) what I said to them [the question, if direct, would have to be asked in the preterite: **hwa rodida du im?**]

21.3 Interrogative and indefinite pronouns and adjectives (II)

The interrogative pronoun **hwarjis** (which one?), inflected like a strong adjective (cf. **niujis**), occurs almost entirely in indirect questions, though this is undoubtedly accidental. It may be used alone, as in

John 13:18 **Ik wait hwarjans gawalida.** I know which ones I have chosen.

John 13:22 **þagkjandans bi hwarjana qeþi** wondering which one he was talking about

or, like **hwas** (§17.3), may be followed by the genitive plural of a noun, as in

John 10:32 **In hwarjis þize waurstwe staineiþ mik?** Which of these deeds are you stoning me for?

There are also several attestations of an interrogative pronoun **hwaþar** (which one?), used only when there is a choice of two possibilities. **hwaþar**, both masc. *Ns* and neuter *Ns*, is the only form attested, as in

Mt 9:5 **hwaþar ist raihtis azetizo...?** Which (of the two) is easier ....?

The interrogative adjectives **hwileik-** (what sort of?) and **hwelaud-** (how great a, how much?) are inflected as strong adjectives.

There are three indefinite pronouns formed by the addition of the particle **-uh** to the interrogative pronouns **hwas** (who?), **hwarjis** (which one?), and **hwaþar** (which one of the two?). The indefinite form **hwaþaruh** occurs only once in a questionable reading (Sk 5). The inflections of **hwazuh** and **hwarjizuh**, both meaning *each one, every one*, are as follows:

	masculine	neuter	feminine	masculine	neuter	feminine
N	**hwazuh**	**hwah**	**hwoh**	**hwarjizuh**	**hwarjatoh**	---
G	**hwizuh**	**hwizuh**	---	**hwarjizuh**	---	---
D	**hwammeh**	**hwammeh**	---	**hwarjammeh**	---	---
A	**hwanoh**	**hwah**	---	**hwarjanoh**	---	**hwarjoh**

A masculine plural form **hwanzuh** survives in the distributive phrase (**insandida ins**) **twans hwanzuh** (he sent them out) two by two (Mk 6:7; Lk 10:1).

Hwazuh may be used adjectivally, as in the temporal expressions **jera hwammeh** (every year) and **dag hwanoh** (every day), or substantivally with the *Gpl,* as in

Lk 6:30 **Hwammeh þan bidjandane þuk gif** ... Give to everyone who begs from you ...

Its most frequent use is in the phrase **hwazuh saei** (whoever, everyone who, anyone who) with a finite verb or, less commonly, with an active participle, as in

John 11:26 **Jah hwazuh saei libaiþ jah galaubeiþ du mis ni gadauþniþ aiw.**
And everyone who lives and believes in me will never die.

Lk 16:18 **Hwazuh saei afletands qen seina jah liugands anþara horinoþ.**
Everyone who leaves his wife and marries another is committing adultery.

Hwazuh sa with a participle also occurs:

John 6:45 **Hwazuh nu sa gahausjands at attin jah ganam gaggiþ du mis.**
Whoever, then, has heeded the Father and accepted Him will come to me.

Hwarjizuh is much less frequent, but its attested usage seems to parallel that of **hwazuh,** as in

Mk 15:24	**disdailjand wastjos is, wairpandans hlauta ana þos, hwarjizuh hwa nemi** they divided up his garments, casting lots for them (to see) what each one would take
Lk 2:3	**Jah iddjedun allai ei melidai weseina, hwarjizuh in seinai baurg.** And they all went to be registered, each one to his own city.

The only adjectival occurrences require textual emendation, suggesting that the form was becoming obsolete and puzzled the scribe:

Mt 27:15	**and dulþ þan hwarjoh** (corrected from **hwarjanoh**) on the occasion of each holiday
Mk 15:6	**and dulþ hwarjoh** (corrected from **hwarjo**).

21.4 Noun formation.

Most of the unprefixed nouns belonging to the various inflectional categories (a-stems, ya-stems, i-stems etc.) were inherited as such from IE and no longer represent productive types within PG or Gothic. The principal exception is the group of derived nouns in **-jan-** < PG *-*yan-* discussed in Historical Lesson 6. Many of these are derived from nouns with meanings which developed specifically within Germanic and undoubtedly represent a productive type in PG and Gothic. For examples see that discussion. There are several other suffixes that appear to be productive in Gothic, although some of them may have been limited to the words actually attested in our corpus.

1. By far the most frequent is the suffix **-ei(n)**- (type **managei**, Lesson 6) used to form abstract feminine nouns from adjectival bases. There are about a hundred of these nouns, and since their formation is quite regular, a few samples will suffice:

Adjectives:	**frod-**	wise	Nouns:	**frodei**	wisdom
	gaur-	sad		**gaurei**	sadness
	lagg-	long		**laggei**	length
	hauh-	high		**hauhei**	height(s)
	hraini-	pure, clean		**hrainei**	purity
	airzj-	erring		**airzei**	heresy

In a number of instances the underlying adjective is not actually attested in Gothic, e.g.

***bairgah-**	hilly	**bairgahei**	hill-country
***balþ-**	bold	**balþei**	boldness
***digr-**	thick, abundant	**digrei**	abundance

2. In addition to the weak masculine nouns inherited from IE (e.g. **guma** man, **ahma** spirit), there are quite a few that seem to be Gothic or PG formations because of their specifically Germanic meanings. Among these are the nouns with prefixed **ga-** designating one who shares something, introduced in §13.2. Further examples include

gadaila	partner, sharer (lit., portion [**dail-**]-sharer)
gahlaiba	comrade (lit., bread-sharer)
galaista	follower (lit., path [***laisti-**]-sharer; cf. **laistjan** Historical Lesson 8)

3. Nouns ending in **-ands** and **-onds** represent original active participles that became nominalized at an early period and retain a consonantal inflection in Gothic, i.e. the inflection of **frijonds** given in Lesson 10. Attested are

bisitands	neighbor	**fraweitands**	avenger
frijonds	friend	**gardawaldands**	master of the house
fijands	enemy	**gibands**	giver
allwaldands	the Almighty	**merjands**	preacher
daupjands	baptist, baptizer	**saiands**	sower
nasjands	saviour	**talzjands**	teacher

4. Another agent suffix is **-areis** *sm*, both deverbal and denominative, designating a person associated with the base word:

bokareis	scribe
laisareis	teacher
motareis	tax-collector (**mota**, customs house)
sokareis	disputant
daimonareis	demoniac (< Gk δαίμων)
wullareis	wool-cleaner, fuller (**wulla** wool)

5. **-assus** *sm* is used to form abstract nouns primarily from nominal bases; most of the attested words have the fuller form **-inassus**, where the **-in-** has been clipped from the stem of weak masculine nouns like **gudjin-** (priest), **gudjinassus** (office of priesthood):

drauhtinassus	warfare	**gudjinassus**	priestly office
fraujinassus	lordship	**leikinassus**	healing
þiudinassus	kingship	**horinassus**	whoredom, adultery (**hors** adulterer)
skalkinassus	service	**kalkinassus**	harlotry (***kalkjo** harlot)

but note also	**ibnassus**	evenness (cf. adjective **ibn-** even, level)
	ufarassus	excess (cf. preposition **ufar**)
	blotinassus	worship (cf. verb **blotan** to worship).

Vocabulary

Verbs:

letan, lailot *sv 7* to allow, let, permit (smn: *A*; to do: inf. or rarely **ei** + subj.); to let remain, to leave behind (at one's death); to let go, utter (*A*).

gretan, gaigrot *sv 7* to weep (over, about: **bi** *A*).

tekan, taitok *sv 7;* **attekan, attaitok** *sv* 7 (*perf.*) to touch (sthg, smn: *D*).

maitan, maimait *sv 7* to cut (A); **afmaitan, afmaimait** *sv 7* (*perf.*) to cut off; + **haubiþ** to behead (smn: *D*); **usmaitan, usmaimait** *sv 7* (*perf.*) to cut out, off.

slepan, saislep (also spelled **saizlep**) *sv 7* to sleep; **gaslepan, gasaislep** *sv 7* (*perf.*) and **anaslepan, anasaislep** *sv 7* (*perf.*) to go to sleep.

gakunnan *wv 3* to find out, learn, experience (*A*).

horinon *wv 2* to commit adultery, be sexually promiscuous.

andbahtjan *wv 1* to serve (as a servant, cf. **andbahts**) (smn: *D*).

marzjan *wv 1;* **gamarzjan** *wv 1* (*perf.*) to offend, hinder, cause trouble for, lead astray (smn: *A*).

ufrakjan *wv 1* + **handu** to reach out, hold one's hand out.

þagkjan *wv 1* (*P* **þahta**) (± **sis**) to think, suppose; to ponder; to wonder, speculate.

Lesson 21

Nouns:

sleps *sm* sleep.
bandja *wm* prisoner, captive.
brinno *wf* fever.
skaut *sn* hem.
swaihro *wf* mother-in-law.
wens *sf* hope.
heito *wf* fever, heat

Adjectives:

unweis- *adj* ignorant (of: **bi** *A*).
hwileik- *interrog adj* of what sort? Also used pronominally: what sort of thing or person?
swaleik- *adj* such, of this sort. Also pronominal: such a thing or person.
þaursu- *adj* withered, dried up.

Other:

aftaro *adv* behind; **du aftaro** up from behind.
baitraba *adv* bitterly.
Iairusalem uninflected or with *G* **-ms** Jerusalem.
Iairusaulyma *sf* (*G* **-os**, *D* **-ai**) Jerusalem.
þau *adv* but just, only just.
jai *interj* yea, yes.
niu *conj* (in indirect questions) whether.

Exercises

A. Translate.

1. Þahtedun so managei bi Iesu niu aufto is wesi Heleias.
2. Ni witum hwis þaurbeina þai bandjans.
3. Gateih mis af hwamma usbauhtes þo lukarna.
4. Ni magum finþan bi hwa gaigrot swa baitraba.
5. Hwan gakunnaideduþ þatei sa kindins imma haubiþ afmaimait?
6. Ni skuld ist tekan kasam þaim unhrainjam.
7. Sa triggwa skalks andbahtida seinamma fraujin jera managa.
8. Ufrakida handu seina jah attaitok haubida is.
9. Ni wissedum hwileika waurda skuldedeima qiþan.
10. Usmaitaima þana þaursjan smakkabagm jah wairpaima in funin.
11. Hwaþar þize broþre ist sa alþiza?
12. Swaihro hwarjis siponje was ligandei in brinnon?
13. Ik ni wissa hwaiwa gamarzidedeina þuk swaleika waurda.
14. Jabai þo barna þaurbun slepis, letiþ þo anaslepan.
15. Fraihnam ina hwas aih jainana gard mikilana.
16. Þaiei sind unweisai bi sunja ni aigun libain aiweinon.
17. Ni wissedun hwas qimands du aftaro attaitoki skauta wastjos þis laisareis.
18. Ik ni wissa hwo jains wair liugaidedi.
19. Hwarjata þize razne ist þata maisto?
20. Gateih unsis hwa rodidedun bi garaznans þeinans horinondans.
21. In hwarjamma þize weihse wesuþ?

B. Translate.

1. Atwopida sa frauja seinans skalkans ei gakunnaidedi hwa hwarjizuh gawaurhtedi.

2. Gasaihwands Iesus þo baurg Iairusalem gaigrot bi þo qiþands: "Ni letand þeinai fijands stain ana staina."
3. Jah qaþ sa Fareisaius: "Sa iþ wesi praufetus, ufkunþedi þau hwo jah hwileika so qino sei tekiþ imma, þatei frawaurhta ist."
4. Hwazuh sa gaggands du mis jah hausjands waurda meina jah taujands þo habaiþ libain aiweinon.
5. Baþ þan ina sa wair af þammei þos unhulþons usiddjedun ei wesi miþ imma. Fralailot þan ina Iesus qiþands: "Gawandei þuk du gard þeinamma jah gateih hwan filu gatawida þus Guþ."
6. Qaþ Iesus þaim twaim blindam: "Galaubjats þatei magjau þata taujan?" Qeþun du imma: "Jai, frauja." Þanuh attaitok augam ize qiþands: "Bi galaubeinai iggqarai wairþai iggqis."
7. Hwazuh sa afletands qen seina jah liugands anþara horinoþ, jah hwazuh saei afletana liugaiþ horinoþ.
8. Sumai astans maimaitun us bagmam jah waurpun ana wiga.
9. Ana wiga lagidedun siukans jah bedun ina ei þau skauta wastjos is attaitokeina, jah swa managai swe attaitokun imma ganesun.
10. Jah gamunda Paitrus waurdis Iesuis qiþanis du sis, jah usgaggands ut gaigrot baitraba.
11. Qaþ þan Paitrus: "Sai, weis aflailotum allata jah laistidedum þuk."
12. Þaruh is qaþ: "Taitok mis sums; ik auk ufkunþa maht usgaggandein af mis."
13. Andhof im Iesus: "Amen, amen qiþa izwis þatei hwazuh saei taujiþ frawaurht skalks ist frawaurhtai."
14. Atgaggandei so qino du aftaro attaitok skauta wastjos is jah suns warþ haila.
15. Jabai taihswo þeina handus marzjai þuk, afmait þo jah wairp af þus.
16. Jah qimands Iesus in garda Paitraus jah gasahw swaihron is ligandein in heitom. Jah attaitok handau izos jah aflailot ija so heito, jah urrais jah andbahtida imma.
17. Qaþ Iesus: "Ik liuhaþ in þamma fairhwau qam, ei hwazuh saei galaubjai du mis in riqiza ni wisai."
18. Jah fralailot Iesus þo managein jah galaiþ sunsaiw in skip miþ siponjam seinaim.
19. Gaigrotun allai bi dauþu þizos maujos, iþ qaþ Iesus im: "Ni gretiþ, unte ni gaswalt, ak slepiþ."
20. Jah qaþ Iesus: "Letiþ þo barna gaggan du mis, unte þize swaleikaize ist þiudangardi Gudis."
21. Managans auk gahailida, swaswe drusun ana ina ei imma attaitokeina.
22. Duhwe aflailost gard þeinana jah qen þeina ei laistidedeis afar þamma laisarja?
23. Gahausida þan Herodis þo waurþanona fram Iesua alla jah þahta, unte qeþun sumai þatei Iohannes urrais us dauþaim. Jah qaþ Herodis: "Iohannau ik haubiþ afmaimait, iþ hwas sa bi þanei ik hausja swaleik?" Jah sokida Iesu gasaihwan.
24. Iþ Peilatus, wiljands þizai managein fullafahjan (to placate), fralailot im þana anþarana bandjan, iþ Iesu atgaf ei ushramiþs wesi.
25. Gasaihwandans þai anþarai þatei Marja, swistar Lazaraus, sprauto usstoþ jah usiddja, iddjedunuh afar izai qiþandans þatei, "Gaggiþ du hlaiwa broþrs seinis ei gretai jainar."
26. Jah qaþ Iesus þamma waira þizei handus so taihswo was þaursus: "Ufrakei þo handu þeina." Þaruh is ufrakida, jah gastoþ so handus is swaswe so anþara.
27. Let ija gawandjan sik du garda attins seinis.
28. Aþþan ni wileima izwis unweisans, broþrjus, bi þans anaslepandans, ei ni saurgaiþ (grieve) swe þai anþarai þaiei ni haband wen, unte jabai galaubjam þatei Iesus gaswalt jah usstoþ, swa jah Guþ þans þaiei anasaislepun þairh Iesu tiuhiþ miþ imma.
29. Jah afar þata qaþ Iesus du siponjam seinaim: "Lazarus, frijonds unsar, gasaizlep. Akei, gaggam, ei uswakjau (awaken) ina." Þanuh qeþun þai siponjos is: "Frauja, jabai slepiþ, hails wairþiþ." Qaþuh þan Iesus bi dauþu is, iþ jainai hugidedun þatei is bi slep qeþi.

Lesson 22

22.1 The Passive

The passive is found only in the present indicative and present subjunctive. Past tense meanings, when required, are expressed periphrastically with the past (passive) participle plus the appropriate forms of **wisan** or **wairþan**, already discussed in §9.4 q.v.

		Present Indicative	Present Subjunctive
Strong Verbs:	1s	**nimada**	**nimaidau**
	2s	**nimaza**	**nimaizau**
	3s	**nimada**	**nimaidau**
	1-3pl	**nimanda**	**nimaindau**

Weak Verbs:	Present Indicative	Present Subjunctive
Class 1	**nasjada, nasjaza, nasjada** **nasjanda**	**nasjaidau, nasjaizau, nasjaidau** **nasjaindau**
Class 2	**salboda, salboza, salboda** **salbonda**	**salbodau, salbozau, salbodau** **salbondau**
Class 3	**habada, habaza, habada** **habanda**	**habaidau, habaizau, habaidau** **habaindau**

The use of the passive is uncomplicated, as may be seen from the following examples:

Lk 1:15 **jah ahmins weihis gafulljada nauhþan in wambai aiþeins seinaizos**
and he will be filled with the Holy Spirit while still in his mother's womb

Lk 1:26 **þanuh þan in menoþ saihstin insandiþs was aggilus Gabriel fram Guda in baurg Galeilaias sei haitada Nazaraiþ**
Subsequently, then, in the sixth month the angel Gabriel was sent by God to the city of Galilee which is called Nazareth

Lk 6:21 **Audagai jus gretandans nu, unte ufhlohjanda.**
Blessed are you who now weep, for you shall be made to laugh.

Lk 7:22 **þrutsfillai gahrainjanda** lepers are cleansed

Lk 8:17 **nih (ist) fulgin þatei ni gakunnaidau**
nor is there anything hidden that will not be known

Lk 15:19 **ju þanaseiþs ni im wairþs ei haitaidau sunus þeins**
from now on I am not worthy to be called (lit., that I be called) your son

In the rare instances where an agent is expressed, it is introduced with the preposition **fram**, as in Lk 1:26 above. The relative infrequency of the passive is due in part to the existence of a large number of inchoative stative verbs belonging to Class 4 of the weak verbs (see Lesson 23).

22.2 Indefinite pronouns and adjectives (III).

In addition to the phrase **hwazuh saei** (whosoever, everyone who) introduced in §21.3, there are two equivalent phrases, **sahwazuh saei** and **sahwazuh izei**, which, like **hwazuh saei**, occur only in the nominative singular. A neuter counterpart **þatahwah** (whatsoever, everything that) occurs only in the accusative singular. The possible full range of their usage in other cases is unknown.

A further combination with the same meaning is **þishwazuh saei**:

masculine:	N	**þishwazuh saei**	neuter:	**þishwah þei/þatei**
	G	**þishwizuh saei**		**þishwizuh þei**
	D	**þishwammeh saei**		**þishwammeh þei**
	A	**þishwanoh saei**		**þishwah þatei**

The following examples illustrate the typical uses of these phrases:

Lk 18:14 **unte sahwazuh saei hauheiþ sik silba gahnaiwjada**
for everyone who exalts himself shall himself be humbled

Lk 4:6 **jah þishwammeh þei wiljau giba þata**
and I give it to whomever I wish

Mk 6:22 **Bidei mik þishwizuh þei wileis**
Ask me for whatever you wish

A final group of indefinite pronouns is formed by suffixing the particle **-hun** to **hwas, manna,** or **ains.** These always co-occur with the negative adverb **ni** in the sense of *no one, nothing.*

(1) **ni hwashun** is attested only in the nominative singular.

(2) masc. sing. only:	N	**ni mannahun**	no one
	G	**ni manshun**	of no one
	D	**ni mannhun**	to no one
	A	**ni mannanhun**	no one

(3)

	masculine	neuter	feminine
N	**ainshun**	**ainhun**	**ainohun**
G	**ainishun**	**ainishun**	***ainaizoshun**
D	**ainummehun**	**ainummehun**	**ainaihun**
A	**ain(n)ohun**	**ainhun**	**ainohun**

Examples of their use:

Mk 10:18 **Hwa mik qiþis þiuþeigana? Ni hwashun þiuþeigs alja ains Guþ.**
Why do you call me blessed? No one is blessed except God alone.

Mk 9:39 **Ni mannahun auk ist saei taujiþ maht in namin meinamma jah magi sprauto ubilwaurdjan mis**
For there is no one who will perform a miracle in my name and would then immediately be able to speak ill of me.

Lk 1:61	**Ni ainshun ist in kunja þeinamma saei haitaidau þamma namin** There is no one in your family who is called by that name.

The forms of **ainshun** may also be used quasi-adjectivally with a following genitive plural:

Lk 9:50	**Ni ainshun auk ist manne saei ni gawaurkjai maht in namin meinamma** For there is no man who may not work a miracle in my name
Mk 13:20	**ni þauh ganesi ainhun leike** nor yet would any person (lit., body) be saved

Note also the related adverbial phrases **þishwaduh þadei** (whithersoever) and **þishwaruh þei** (wheresoever):

Lk 9:57	**Laistja þuk þishwaduh þadei gaggis.** I shall follow you whithersoever you go.
Mk 9:18	**jah þishwaruh þei ina gafahiþ** and wherever it seizes him

22.3 Noun formation (II)

1. The suffix **-iþa** *sf* is used to form abstract nouns from adjectival bases. After a stem-final **-þ-** it is dissimilated to **-ida.** Attested are

afgrundiþa	abyss	**kauriþa**	burden (**kauru-** heavy)
aggwiþa	anguish (**aggwu-** narrow)	**manwiþa**	preparation
agliþa	difficulty (**aglu-** difficult)	**meriþa**	fame (**-merj-** in **wailamerj-**)
ainamundiþa	unanimity	**mildiþa**	mildness (PG **mild-*)
airziþa	heresy (**airzj-** erring)	**niujiþa**	newness
ananiujiþa	renewal	**swegniþa**	joy
armahairtiþa	mercy	**sweriþa**	honor (**swer-** honored)
auþida	wilderness (**auþi-** wild, deserted)	**swikniþa**	purity (**swikn-** pure)
daubiþa	deafness (**daub-** deaf, mute)	**tulgiþa**	firmness
diupiþa	depth	**þwastiþa**	certainty
dwaliþa	foolishness	**unhrainiþa**	impurity
fairniþa	oldness	**unsweriþa**	dishonor
garaihtiþa	justice	**wairþida**	worthiness
gauriþa	sadness	**wargiþa**	condemnation
hauniþa	meekness, humbleness	**weihiþa**	holiness
hlutriþa	purity	**airkniþa**	purity

It is possible that some of these are derived from nouns rather than adjectives, but the limited nature of our corpus precludes certainty.

2. The suffixes **-eins, -ons,** and **-ains,** used regularly to form the verbal nouns of weak verbs, classes 1-3, have already been introduced. See §§10.3; 19.1.

3. Much less frequent are the suffixes **-oþus,** dissimilated to **-odus** after a voiceless stem-final consonant:

gabaurjoþus	pleasure (cf. the adverb **gabaurjaba** willingly)
auhjodus	tumult (cf. **auhjon** to riot, make a tumult)
wratodus	journey (cf. **wraton** to travel)

manniskodus	humanity (cf. the adjective **mannisk-** human)

-ufni *sn* or *sf*, dissimilated to **-ubni** after a voiceless stem-final consonant:

fastubni *sn*	fasting (cf. **fastan**)
fraistubni *sf*	temptation (cf. **fraisan** to tempt)
witubni *sn*	knowledge (cf. **witan**)
waldufni *sn*	power (cf. **waldan** to govern)
wundufni *sf*	wound (cf. **gawundon** to wound)

and **-duþs** *sf*:

ajukduþs	eternity (cf. **aiws** time, eternity, the world)
managduþs	abundance
mikilduþs	greatness
gamainduþs	community (cf. **gamaini-** in common).

22.4 Adjective Formation. There are five fairly frequent suffixes in Gothic used to form adjectives from nominal bases. Because all of these are inherited from IE, it is impossible to determine where along the line these adjectives came into being. See the accompanying Historical Grammar lesson for a discussion of the cognate forms elsewhere in IE.

(I) **-aga-**:	**audag-**	blessed (PG **aud-* wealth, good fortune)
	gredag-	hungry (**gredus** hunger)
	hailag-	holy
	modag-	angry (**moþs**, G **modis** *sm* anger)
	unhunslag-	implacable (lit., unoffering-able; **hunsl** *sn* offering)
	wulþag-	splendid, glorious
(2) **-aha-**:	**ainah-**	single, sole
	niuklah-	childlike, underage
	stainah-	stony
	unbarnah	childless
	waurdah-	verbal
	***bairgah-**	hilly, mountainous (in the noun **bairgahei** hill-country)
	***broþrah-**	brotherly (in the nominalized **broþrahans** brethren)
(3) **-eig-**	**ananemeig-**	holding fast
	ansteig-	gracious
	gawairþeig-	peaceful (**gawairþi** peace)
	gawizneig-	sharing joy (***wizns** enjoyment)
	hroþeig-	victorious (PG **hrōþ-* fame, victory)
	laiseig-	good at teaching
	listeig-	cunning (**lists** *sf* cunning)
	mahteig-	mighty
	sineig-	old
	þiuþeig-	blessed, good
	usbeisneig-	long-suffering (**usbeisns** *sf* patience, *vn* of **usbeidan**)
	waurstweig-	real, actual, effective

(4) **-ein-**:	**ahmein-**	spiritual
	airþein-	earthen, made of earth
	barizein-	made of barley (PG **bariz-* barley)
	eisarnein-	made of iron
	fillein-	made of leather (PG **fell-* leather, hide; cf. **þrutsfill-**, Lesson 14)
	gulþein-	made of gold (**gulþ** *sn* gold)
	gumein-	male (**guma** *wm* man)
	leikein-	of the body (not spiritual)
	muldein-	made of dust (**mulda** *sf* dust, earth)
	pistikein-	pure, genuine (loanword modified from Gk πιστικός)
	qinein-	female
	riqizein-	dark
	seitein-	daily (cf. ?PG **sīđ-* late, late part of day)
	silubrein-	made of silver (**silubr** *sn* silver)
	stainein-	made of stone
	sunjein-	true
	triwein-	made of wood (**triu** *sn* tree, wood)
	þaurnein-	made of thorns (**þaurnus** *sm* thorn)
(5) **-isk-**	**barnisk-**	childish
	funisk-	fiery
	gudisk-	divine
	mannisk-	human
	iudaiwisk-	Jewish
	haiþiwisk-	wild, of the fields (**haiþi**)

Many adjectives, including participles, have negative counterparts formed by the prefixing of **un-**. E.g.

frod-	wise	**unfrod-**	lacking understanding
hail-	sound, whole	**unhail-**	sick
hraini-	pure, clear	**unhraini-**	impure, unclean
mahteig-	mighty, able; possible	**unmahteig-**	weak, incapable; impossible

Such adjectives, when formed from active or passive participles, often have the added nuance of inability or impossibility. E.g.

unhwapnand-	unquenchable (***hwapnan** to be quenched)
unbilaistid-	inscrutable (***bilaistjan** to track down, or sim.)
ungasaihwan-	unseeable, invisible
ungawagid-	immovable (**gawagjan** to move, shake)
unrodjand-	dumb, mute
unusspillod-	unexpoundable, beyond understanding (**usspillon** to expound, state)
unbairand-	sterile, barren, incapable of bearing

Lesson 22

Vocabulary 22

Verbs:

bisaihwan *sv 5* to look about (at: *A*); to notice, perceive (*A*); to look after (*G*).
mitan, *mat; gamitan, gamat *sv 5 (perf.)* to measure (sthg: *A*). **mitaþs** *f* measure, grain measure.
andhaitan, andhaihait *sv 7* to confess, acknowledge (sthg: *D*, smn to be smn: *A* + *A*); to call upon (smn: *D*) in thanksgiving or prayer; to declare.
galukan, galauk *sv 2 irreg* to close, shut (*A*); to confine (smn: *A*), snare, net; to consign (smn: *A*; to: **in** *D*).
uslukan, uslauk *sv 2 irreg* to open (*A*); to draw (e.g. a sword).
fraisan, faifrais *sv 7* to tempt, test, try (smn: *A*); **fraistubni** *sf* temptation.
slahan, sloh *sv 6* to strike (*A*).
saian, saiso *sv 7* to sow (seed: *D*); **saiands** *m* sower. Note the irreg. 2nd pers. sing. pret. **saisost**.
sneiþan, snaiþ *sv 1* to cut down, reap.
lewjan *wv 1*, **galewjan** *wv 1 (perf.)* to betray, hand over (smn: *A*); to turn (e.g. the other cheek).
briggan, bringan *sv 3 irreg* (P **brahta**, like **bauhta** p. 21) to bring, lead (sthg, smn: *A*; to a person: **at, du** *D;* to a place: **und, ana** *A*; into a place: **in** *D*). For idiomatic uses see the Glossary under **aljan, frei-, þwairhei, wairþ-**, and **wundan**.

Nouns:

andanahti *sn* evening.
maurgins *sm* morning, morrow; **in maurgin** on the next morning; **du maurgina** tomorrow.
waurts *sf* root(s); sing. when figurative, pl. when literal.
gamunds *sf* remembrance, memory; **du gamundai** *G* in remembrance of.
sarwa *sn pl* weapons, armor.
hairus *sm* sword.

Other:

Beþania (*G* **-ias**, *D* **-iin**, *A* **-ian**) Bethany.
rabbei < Gk ῥαββει < Hebrew *rabbî* (my) teacher (voc.).
unmahteig- *adj* powerless, weak; impossible.
unbairand- *part adj* not bearing, sterile, barren.
framis *adv* further on; of the night: advanced, nearly over.
nehwis *adv* nearer.
raiht- *adj* straight.
Satana (*G* **-nins**, *D* **-nin**, *A* **-nan**) Satan.
ni þatain(ei)... ak jah *conj phrase* not only ... but even ....
ni hwanhun *adv phrase* never, at no time.

Exercises

A. Translate. Convert the verbs to the past tense of the passive. E.g. (1) Aurtigards ussatiþs ist (*or* was *or* warþ)....

1. Aurtigards ussatjada in jainamma stada.
2. Þai garaihtans wrikanda fram þamma kindina jah gadrauhtim is.
3. So asans galisada fram þaim waurstwjam.
4. Þos gibos atbairanda du þiudana.

5. Þata wein gadrigkada in gamundai is.
6. Þata daur uslukada du izwis.
7. Alla waurstwa þeina hazjanda.
8. Þai þliuhandans gahabanda.
9. Þata witoþ anafilhaidau barnam þeinaim.
10. Missadedeis þeinos ni fragibanda.
11. Sa bauda gahailjada.
12. So anabusns atgibada unsis.
13. Jus fraisanda fram þamma ubilin.
14. Sa usliþa galagjada faur þata razn.
15. Þai handugans ni sweranda fram þizai ubilon þiudai.
16. In þamma daga urraisjanda þai dauþans.
17. Namo is haitada Iohannes.
18. Sunus is sa ainaha ushramjada.
19. Managai galaþonda, akei fawai galeiþand.
20. Þai dwalans jah þai ungalaubjandans ni galaþonda in þiudangardja himinis.
21. Astos þis bagmis afmaitaindau jah galagjaindau in þamma funin.
22. Swaihro is ganasjada sunsaiw.
23. Wens mikila gibada izwis.
24. Þrutsfillai gahrainjanda.
25. Þata leik gafilhada sundro fairra þizai baurg.

B. Translate.

1. Nimiþ þan sarwa Gudis ei mageiþ in þamma daga ubilin andstandan allaim waldufnjam Satanins jah aggile is.
2. Manna auk þatei saiiþ þatuh jah sneiþiþ.
3. Frauja Iesus in þizaiei naht galewiþs was nam hlaif jah awiliudonds gabrak jah qaþ: "Nimiþ, matjiþ. Þata ist mein leik þata faur izwis gibano. Þata waurkjaiþ du gamundai meina."
4. Mel ist uns ju us slepa urreisan, unte nu nehwis ist naseins unsara þau þan galaubidedum. Nahts framis galaiþ, iþ dags atnehwida; uswairpam nu waurstwam riqizis, iþ gawasjam sarwam liuhadis.
5. Bisaihwaiþ godis ni þatainei in andwairþja Gudis, ak jah in andwairþja manne allaize.
6. Sahwazuh nu saei andhaitiþ mis in andwairþja manne andhaita jah ik imma in andwairþja attins meinis saei in himinam ist.
7. Urran saiands du saian fraiwa seinamma, jah miþþanei saiso, sum gadraus faur wig, jah fuglos himinis fretun þata.
8. Galauk auk Guþ allans mannans in unglaubeinai ei allans gaarmai.
9. Iþ Seimon Paitrus habands hairu uslauk ina jah sloh þis auhumistins gudjins skalk jah afmaimait imma auso taihswo (sah þan haitans was namin Malkus).
10. Ni fraisais Fraujan Guþ þeinana!
11. Nist skuld izwis briggan sarwa in þizai alh.
12. Jah us þaim reikam managai galaubidedun du imma, akei faur Fareisaium ni andhaihaitun, ei us synagogei ni uswaurpanai waurþeina.
13. Wissuh þan Iesus fram frumistin hwas ist saei galeweiþ ina.
14. Qaþ þan Iesus: "Amen izwis qiþa þatei ni ainshun praufete andanems ist in gabaurþai seinai."
15. Amen qiþa izwis: þishwaruh þei merjada so aiwaggeljo and alla manaseþ jah þatei gatawida so qino rodjada du gamundai izos.
16. Qaþ Iesus Peilatau: "Sa galewjands mik þus maizein frawaurht habaid."
17. At andanahtja þan waurþanamma gawandidedun sik so managei und haimos seinos.
18. Jabai brahtedeina þans siukans at imma, gahailidedi ins.
19. Insaihwiþ du fuglam himinis þei ni saiand nih sneiþand.
20. Nist unmahteig Guda ainhun waurde.

21. Jah was in auþidai dage fidwor tiguns fraisans fram Satanin.
22. Jah þan andhaita im þatei, "Ni hwanhun kunþa izwis. Afleiþiþ fairra mis, jus waurkjandans ubilona."[1]
23. Aþþan ju so aqizi (axe) at waurtim bagme ligiþ; all nu bagme unbairandane akran god usmaitada jah in fon galagjada.
24. Ni sneiþis þatei ni saisost.
25. Qaþ Iesus du siponjam seinaim: "Sai, galewjada sunus mans in handuns frawaurhtaize. Urreisiþ, gangam! Sai, sa lewjands mik atnehwida."
26. Þizai samon mitad þizaiei mitid mitada izwis.
27. Jah duatgaggandans Fareisaieis frehun ina skuldu sijai mann qen afsatjan, fraisandans ina.
28. Jah brahtedun þana fulan (foal) at Jesua jah galagidedun ana[2] wastjos seinos jah (Jesus) gasat ana ina.

See Mark 11:11-14; 20-26 for the following:

Jah galaiþ in Iairusaulyma Iesus in alh, jah bisaihwands alla, at andanahtja juþan wisandin hweilai[3] usiddja in Beþanian miþ þaim twalibim. Jah iftumin daga usstandandam im us Beþaniin gredags was. Jah gasaihwands smakkabagm fairraþro habandan lauf atiddja ei aufto bigeti hwa ana imma, jah qimands at imma ni waiht bigat ana imma niba laub. Ni auk was mel smakkane... Jah usbairands (exclaiming)[4] qaþ du imma: "Ni þanaseiþs (henceforth) us þus aiw manna akran matjai!" Jah gahausidedun þai siponjos is.

Jah in maurgin faurgaggandans gasehwun þana smakkabagm þaursjana us waurtim. Jah gamunands Paitrus qaþ du imma: "Rabbei, sai smakkabagms þanei fraqast þaursus warþ." Jah andhafjands Iesus qaþ du im: "Habaiþ galaubein Gudis! Amen auk qiþa izwis: þishwazuh ei qiþai du þamma fairgunja, 'Ushafei þuk jah wairp þus in marein,' jah ni tuzwerjai (harbor doubts) in hairtin seinamma, ak galaubjai þata, ei þatei qiþiþ gagaggiþ, wairþiþ imma þishwah þei qiþiþ. Duþþe qiþa izwis: allata þishwah þei bidjandans sokeiþ, galaubeiþ þatei nimiþ, jah wairþiþ izwis. Jah þan standaiþ bidjandans, afletaiþ jabai hwa habaiþ wiþra hwana, ei jah Atta izwar sa in himinam afletai izwis missadedins izwaros. Iþ jabai jus ni afletiþ, ni þau Atta izwar sa in himinam afletiþ izwis missadedins izwaros."

---

[1] Note **ubilo** (evil) as a *wn* noun.

[2] Note the adverbial use of **ana** here: *thereon, thereupon.* Some would amend to **ana ina** *on it.*

[3] Apparently a slight mistranslation of the Greek ὀψίας ἤδη οὔσης τῆς ὥρας *since the hour was already late.* ὀψίας is the adjective ὄψιος, modifying ὥρας, and not the noun ἡ ὀψία *evening,* as taken by the Gothic translator. If the passage is correct as it stands, **at** must be taken here as a prep. governing **andanahtja** and not as the optional marker of the dative absolute: "the time being already *toward* evening." **wisandin** would have to be for **wisandein**, modifying **hweilai**. There is undoubtedly some contamination here with the frequent phrase **at andanahtja waurþanamma** *when it was evening.*

[4] **usbairan** has this meaning only here.

Lesson 23

23.1 Weak verbs: class 4. Verbs of this class are characterized by a suffixed **-n-** (infinitive **-nan**) and are inflected regularly in the present, but like verbs of class 2 (**salboda...**) in the preterite. The inflection of **fullnan** (to become full, be filled) is as follows:

Present	indicative:	**fullna, fullnis, fullniþ, ...**
	subjunctive:	**fullnau, fullnais, fullnai, ...**
	imperative:	**fulln; fullniþ**
	participles:	**fullnand-**
Preterite	indicative:	**fullnoda, fullnodes, fullnoda, fullnodedum, ...**
	subjunctive:	**fullnodedjau, fullnodedeis, fullnodedi, ...**

These verbs are derived variously from nominal, adjectival, and verbal bases and always denote entering into the particular state indicated by the lexical base, hence the designations *inchoative* and *inceptive.* They are all intransitive and therefore there is no passive inflection, nor is there a past (passive) participle.[1] The following verbs belong to this class; note that other prefixed verbs exist for several of the base verbs involved.

auknan	to increase
gabatnan	to profit, be bettered
afblindnan	to become blind
usbruknan	to be broken
andbundnan	to be unbound
afdaubnan	to become deaf
gadauþnan	to die
afdobnan	to become silent
drobnan	to become troubled, anxious
afdumbnan	to hold one's peace, be still
infeinan	to be moved to pity
gafrisahtnan	to copy, imitate
fullnan	to be filled, become full
gabignan	to become rich
ganipnan	to become sad, dejected
ganohnan	to be satisfied, sated
gagawairþnan	to become reconciled
usgeisnan	to be aghast, dismayed
usgutnan	to gush out, pour out
ufarhafnan	to be exalted
gahaftnan	to become attached
gahailnan	to become healed
ushauhnan	to be exalted
dishnupnan	to be torn, broken
afhwapnan	to be quenched, choked
andletnan	to depart, die
aflifnan	to be left over
galuknan	to be shut up
fralusnan	to be lost, perish
managnan	to become numerous
usmernan	to be proclaimed
mikilnan	to be magnified
minznan	to become less, diminish
fraqistnan	to be destroyed, perish
gaqiunan	to come alive, be brought to life
urrumnan	to spread, expand
bisaulnan	to be defiled
gaskaidnan	to become divided
disskritnan	to be torn, ripped
afslauþnan	to be filled with fear or anxiety
gastaurknan	to become stiff
swinþnan	to become strong
aftaurnan	to be torn away
tundnan	to catch fire
gaþaursnan	to wither, dry up
gawaknan	to awaken, wake up
weihnan	to become holy

---

[1] Technically speaking, the absence of a past (passive) participle is due not only to the intransitive nature of these verbs, but also to the fact that they are by definition perfective, and hence the active participles denote *having become* as well as *becoming.*

23.2 Adverb formation. There are several productive suffixes used for the formation of adverbs from nominal or adjectival bases. For the IE antecedents of these endings see the Historical Grammar.

1. **-ba**, the most frequent suffix, attested on the following words:

abraba	strongly	**glaggwuba, -aba**	accurately, carefully
agluba	with difficulty	**harduba, -aba**	grievously
analaugniba	secretly	**hauhaba**	highly
andaugiba	openly	**hwassaba**	sharply
arniba	safely, surely	**manwuba**	in readiness
azetaba	easily	**mikilaba**	greatly
bairhtaba	brightly	**raihtaba**	rightly
baitraba	bitterly	**sunjaba**	truly
balþaba	boldly	**swikunþaba**	manifestly
frodaba	wisely	**triggwaba**	truly
gabaurjaba	willingly	**ubilaba**	evilly
gafehaba	properly	**unanasiunaba**	invisibly
gagudaba	in a godly fashion	**unfairinodaba**	blamelessly
garaihtaba	justly	**unsahþaba**	uncontestedly
garedaba	properly	**unwairþaba**	in an unworthy fashion
gatilaba	conveniently	**usstiuriba**	licentiously
gatemiba	fitly		

2. **-o**, next in frequency, also added to prepositional bases:

aftaro	behind	**sniumundo**	quickly
alakjo	collectively	**sprauto**	quickly
allandjo	fully	**sundro**	apart, privately
analeiko	in like manner	**þiubjo**	secretly
andaugjo	openly	**þiudisko**	in a non-Jewish way
anþarleiko	in another way	**þridjo**	for the third time
arwjo	in vain	**ufaro**	above
aufto, ufto	perhaps	**uhteigo**	opportunely
gahahjo	coherently	**undaro**	below
galeiko	in like manner	**unuhteigo**	inopportunely
glaggwo	diligently	**unweniggo**	unexpectedly
iudaiwisko	according to Jewish law	**usdaudo**	zealously
laþaleiko	willingly	**ussindo**	especially
misso	one another, mutually	**wairaleiko**	in a manly fashion
samaleiko	in like manner	**witodeigo**	lawfully
sinteino	continually		

3. **-þro**, denoting motion from a place:

aljaþro	from elsewhere	**iupaþro**	from above
allaþro	from all directions	**jainþro**	from there, thence
dalaþro	from below	**hwaþro**	from where, whence
fairraþro	from afar	**þaþro**	from there, thence
innaþro	from within	**utaþro**	from outside

4. **-þ**, denoting motion toward a place:

aljaþ	in another direction	**dalaþ**	down
hwaþ	in what direction, whither	**samaþ**	to the same place, together

5. **-dre**, denoting motion toward a place:

hwadre	in what direction, whither	**jaindre**	to that place, thither
hidre	to here, hither		

6. **-e**, denoting an adverb of manner:

sware	in vain	**simle**	once before
swe	so, thus	**bisunjane**	roundabout
hwe	how, with what	**duhwe**	why

7. **-na**, denoting motion from a place:

aftana	from behind	**hindana**	from behind
utana	from outside	**iupana**	from above
innana	from within		

8. **-r**, denoting rest in a place, as in **jainar** (there), **her** (here), **hwar** (where?), **þar** (there)

9. **-is**, **-os**, used regularly to form a comparative degree of adverbs; most of these are originally the neuter of the corresponding comparative adjective used adverbially:

airis	earlier	**mais**	more
faurþis	previously, beforehand	**nehwis**	nearer
framis	further on	**mins** (***minnis**)	less
haldis	rather	**wairs** (***wairsis**)	worse
aljaleikos	otherwise	**sniumundos**	with greater haste

The remaining adverbs are either (1) simple lexical items, such as **air** (early), **hwan** (when, at what time), **ju** (already), **nu** (therefore), **þan** (then, at that time), **nauh** (still, yet), or various combinations of the same; (2) a few genitive case forms used adverbially, such as **allis** (indeed, therefore), **raihtis** (idem), **andwairþis** (facing, over against), **nahts** (at night); (3) miscellaneous adverbial phrases or compounds, such as **himma daga** (today), **gistradagis** (tomorrow).

23.3 The partitive genitive.

The regular use of the partitive genitive with **all** (§8.4), cardinal numbers (§9.2), **sums** (§9.3), and the indefinite pronouns (§§17.3; 21.3) has already been noted. In addition, note the following:

(1) The genitive instead of the accusative is occasionally used with verbs of *taking, giving, consuming,* and the like to indicate that only a portion of the object is involved. E.g.

John 6:51 **jabai hwas matjiþ þis hlaibis** if anyone eats any (*or* some) of this bread

(2) In negative predications the partitive genitive corresponds to English *not... any.* E.g.

Lk 1:7 **Ni was im barne**. They didn't have any children.
Lk 20:31 **ni biliþun barne** they didn't leave behind any children
Mt 9:36 **swe lamba ni habandona hairdeis** like lambs that don't have any shepherd

Neither of these constructions is frequent.

23.4 Final remarks on the subjunctive. There are several remaining uses of the subjunctive that deserve special mention, although they are more difficult to classify and predict than those previously introduced.

I. In relative clauses.

a. Nominalized **saei** + subjunctive as the subject of an injunctively used subjunctive is the virtual equivalent of a conditional protasis. Compare

Lk 8:8 **saei habai ausona du hausjan gahausjai** let him who has ears to hear hear
Mk 4:23 **jabai hwas habai ausona hausjandona gahausjai** if anyone has hearing ears, let him hear

It is interesting to note that **sa** + active participle may have the same nuance. Compare, e.g., the parallel statements in

Lk 3:11 **saei habai matins samaleiko taujai** let him who has food do likewise
sa habands twos paidos gibai þamma unhabandin let him who has two tunics give (one) to him who does not have any

In general, the subjunctive verb may be seen as imparting a specifically indefinite meaning to the preceding **saei** or **þatei**, as in

Mk 7:10 **saei ubil qiþai attin seinamma aiþþau aiþein seinai dauþau afdauþjaidau**
anyone who speaks evil to his father or his mother shall surely be put to death
Lk 3:13 **ni waiht ufar þatei garaid sijai izwis lausjaiþ**
you should not collect anything more than whatever is allotted to you

b. The indefinite negative predications **ni ainshun ist ... saei** (there is no one ... who), **ni ist ... þatei** (there is nothing ... that), and similar expressions are followed by the subjunctive. E.g.

L1:61 **jah qeþun du izai þatei ni ainshun ist in kunja þeinamma saei haitaidau þamma namin**
and they said to her, "There is no one in your family who is called by that name."

Lk 18:29-30 **ni ainshun ist þize... saei ni andnimai managfalþ...**
there is no one of these ... who will not receive manyfold

Lk 8:17 **ni auk ist analaugn þatei swikunþ ni wairþai, nih fulgin þatei ni gakunnaidau jah in swekunþamma qimai**
there is nothing hidden that will not become manifest, nor secret that will not be known and come into the open

c. Unlike this last example, where the verb phrases **gakunnaidau** and **in swekunþamma qimai** are synonymous and hence parallel, other examples where two verbs are temporally sequential show an unusual feature, in that only the second verb is placed in the subjunctive. This is true for the constructions discussed in both a and b above; note the similar usage in direct questions (p. 74 bottom). E.g.

Mk 9:39 **ni mannahun auk ist saei taujiþ maht in namin meinamma jah magi sprauto ubilwaurdjan mis**
there is no one who will perform a miracle in my name and then immediately slander me

Mt 5:19 **saei nu gatairiþ ... jah laisjai** anyone who relaxes ... and (then) teaches...
Mt 10:38 **saei ni nimiþ ... laistjai** anyone who does not take up ... and follow

2. Nominal clauses introduced with **ei** followed by the subjunctive often function as the virtual subject of various impersonal expressions, alternating with the more frequent infinitival constructions already noted. E.g.

Mk 9:42 **goþ ist imma mais ei galagjaidau asiluqairnus ana balsaggan is jah frawaurpans wesi in marein**
it is better for him if a millstone were placed on his neck (usually corrected to ***halsaggan**) and that he were cast into the sea

Mt 5:29 **batizo ist auk þus ei fraqistnai ains liþiwe þeinaize jah ni allata leik þein gadriusai in Gaiainnan**
for it is better for you that one of your limbs perish and your whole body not fall into Gehenna

Mt 10:25 **ganah siponi ei wairþai swe laisareis is**
it is enough for a disciple that he become like his teacher

Closely related is the complementary (or appositional) use of such **ei**-clauses:

Lk 1:43 **Jah hwaþro mis þata, ei qemi aiþei Fraujins meinis at mis?**
And why is this granted to me (lit., whence this to me) that the mother of my Lord should come to me?

Lk 7:6 **ni im wairþs ei uf hrot mein inngaggais**
I am not worthy that you should enter under my roof

23.5 Final remarks on the infinitive.

1. We have noted in passing that the infinitive of transitive verbs is used in a passive sense in various constructions, e.g. with **skuld- ist, goþ ist, maht- ist**. This usage is encountered elsewhere, usually translating a passive infinitive in the underlying Greek, but no firm rules can be given for its occurrence; the reader must simply always be aware of this possibility when an active translation makes no sense, as, for example, in

Lk 5:15 **garunnun hiuhmans managai hausjon jah leikinon**
vast throngs congregated to listen and be healed

where **leikinon** *wv 2* is normally transitive: to heal, cure. The Greek has the passive infinitive θεραπεύεσθαι (to be healed).

2. There are a number of instances of the construction **warþ** + inf. + dative translating Greek ἐγένετο + inf. + accusative. E.g.

Lk 6:6 **jah warþ þan in anþaramma daga sabbato galeiþan imma in synagogein jah laisjan**
ἐγένετο δὲ καὶ ἐν ἑτέρῳ σαββάτῳ εἰσελθεῖν αὐτὸν εἰς τὴν συναγωγὴν καὶ διδάσκειν
and on another Sabbath he entered the synagogue and taught

The interpretation of this unusual construction is disputed, but it looks as though, in Gothic at least, the infinitive is taken nominally as the subject of **warþ**, literally: an entering ... and a teaching happened to him. For other examples see Lk 6:1 (**warþ ... gaggan imma**), Lk 16:22 (**warþ gaswiltan þamma unledin**), and Mk 2:23.

3. **swaswe** + an infinitive is sometimes used to indicate consequence or result, in imitation of the underlying Greek construction with ὥστε. Note the accusative subject of the infinitive, just as in the Greek. E.g.

Mt 8:24 **Jah sai, wegs mikils warþ in marein, swaswe þata skip gahuliþ wairþan fram wegim.**
καὶ ἰδοὺ σεισμὸς μέγας ἐγένετο ἐν τῇ θαλάσσῃ, ὥστε τὸ πλοῖον καταλύπτεσθαι ὑπὸ τῶν κυμάτων.
And suddenly there was a great disturbance in the sea, so that the ship was swamped by the waves.

Mk 4:1 **jah galesun sik du imma manageins filu, swaswe ina galeiþan in skip gasitan in marein**
καὶ συνήχθη πρὸς αὐτὸν ὄχλος πολύς, ὥστε αὐτὸν ἐμβάντα εἰς τὸ πλοῖον καθῆσθαι ἐν τῇ θαλάσσῃ
and great crowds gathered around him, so that he boarded a ship to sit in the sea

Streitberg emends **galeiþan** to **galeiþandan** (= ἐμβάντα), but the Gothic translator does not always slavishly follow the Greek and may have been more comfortable with the rendering given, with **gasitan** dependent, quite idiomatically, on **galeiþan** and expressing purpose.

23.6 Final remarks on absolutes.

Occasionally there are participial phrases that seem to require interpretation as nominative or accusative absolutes. E.g.

Mk 6: 21 **jah waurþans dags gatils ...**
καὶ γενομένης ἡμέρας εὐκαίρου ...
and when an appropriate day arrived ...

Mk 9:28 **jah galeiþandan ina in gard, siponjos is frehun ina sundro**
καὶ εἰσελθόντα αὐτὸν εἰς οἶκον, οἱ μαθηταὶ αὐτοῦ ἐπηρώτων αὐτὸν κατ' ἰδίαν
and when he had gone indoors, his disciples questioned him privately

Mt 6:3 **iþ þuk taujandan armaion ni witi hleidumei þeina ...**
σοῦ δὲ ποιοῦντος ἐλεημοσύνην μὴ γνώτω ἡ ἀριστερά σου ...
but when you perform a charity, do not let your left hand know ...

The second example could just as well be interpreted as a preposed modifier of the second **ina** (= αὐτὸν), but the repetition of the pronoun suggests the interpretation as an absolute. Wright (p. 292) takes **þuk taujandan** in the third example as the object of **witi**, but this is difficult to reconcile with the rest of the verse, q.v.

23.7 Final remarks on the numbers.

1. The extant cardinals above ten are

***ainlif** (*D* **ainlibim**)	11	**twa hunda**	200
twalif (*G* **-be,** *D* **-bim**)	12	**þrija hunda**	300
fidwortaihun *indecl*	14	**fimf hunda**	500
fimftaihun *indecl*	15	**niun hunda**	900
twai tigjus	20	**þusundi**	1000
***þreis tigjus** (*A* **þrins tiguns**)	30	**twos þusundjos**	2000
fidwor tigjus	40	**.g. þusundjos**	3000
fimf tigjus	50	**fimf þusundjos**	5000
saihs tigjus	60	**miþ taihun þusundjom**	with 10,000
		miþ twaim tigun þusundjom	with 20,000
sibuntehund	70		
ahtautehund	80		
niuntehund (*G* **-dis**)	90		
taihuntehund, taihuntaihund	100		

The singular of **tigjus** (tens) from which the tens through sixty are formed is not attested; this element was felt as a separate word and was fully inflected, as attested by *G* **þrije tigiwe,** *D* **twaim tigum, saihs tigum,** in addition to the *A* **þrins tiguns** cited above. The **-tehund** of seventy through a hundred, however, seems to be compounded with the initial element and the whole inflected like a strong neuter singular; on the problematic origin of **-tehund** see the historical grammar. **þusundi** is a strong feminine noun of the type **bandi** and is fully inflected.

2. Attested ordinals are

frum-	first	**ahtud-**	eighth
anþar-	second	**niund-**	ninth
þridj-	third	**taihund-**	tenth
fimft-	fifth	**fimftataihund-**	fifteenth
saihst-	sixth		

The ordinals **þridj-** and above follow the regular weak adjectival inflection; **frum-**, however, follows **managei** in the weak feminine like the active participles. **Anþar-**, of course, is always inflected strong (§4.2c).

3. For **bai, ba** (both) see Voc. 12. Note also the appositional pronominal *N* **bajoþs,** *D* **bajoþum** (both of us, you, them).

4. Numerical adverbs indicating the number of times an action occurs are formed from the noun ***sinþs** (see Voc. 19).

5. Multiplicatives are formed by suffixing the adjective **-falþ-** (-fold) to a form of the cardinal. Attested are **ainfalþs** (simple > unimpaired), **fidurfalþ-** (fourfold), **taihuntaihundfalþ-** (hundredfold).

6. Of the sparsely attested distributive expressions, only the twice attested base **tweihn-** merits note because of its ambiguity:

Lk 9:3 **nih þan tweihnos paidos haban** μήτε ἀνὰ δύο χιτῶνας ἔχειν nor even have two tunics apiece

Lesson 23

Mk 7:31 **miþ tweihnaim markom** ἀνὰ μέσον τῶν ὁρίων between the two regions (of ...)

Vocabulary 23

Verbs:

anastodjan *wv 1* to begin, commence (intrans.). **dustodjan** *wv 1* idem. **anastodeins** *sf vn* beginning; a new beginning, first-fruits of a new age or undertaking.
usluknan *wv 4* to open (intrans.), be opened.
usfullnan, usfulnan *wv 4* to be fulfilled, completed, brought to completion.
bandwjan *wv 1*; **gabandwjan** *wv 1 (perf.)* to communicate (with smn: *D*) through a gesture (e.g. nod, hand-signal); to indicate, show, single out (*A*).
laugnjan *wv 1* to deny; **galaugnjan** *wv 1 (perf.)* (± **sik**) to hide oneself, withdraw into seclusion.
hauhjan *wv 1*; **ushauhjan** *wv 1 (perf.)* to raise up, exalt; used frequently with deliberate word play on the secondary meanings: to raise up on the cross, to raise up to heaven (i.e. the Ascension).
andhausjan *wv 1* to obey (smn: *D*); to heed, pay attention to (smn: *D*).
goljan *wv 1* to greet (smn: *A*). **goleins** *sf vn* greeting, salutation.
infeinan *wv 4* to take pity on (smn: **du** *D*).
fraqistnan *wv 4* to be destroyed, perish, die.
talzjan *wv 1* to teach (smn: *A*). **talzjands*** *m* teacher (occurs only in the vocative: **talzjand**).
gadauþjan *wv 1;* **afdauþjan** *wv 1* to kill, put to death, execute (*A*).
gadauþnan *wv 4* to die.
usgeisnan *wv 4* to be frightened, dismayed, astonished, amazed.

Nouns:

garaihtei *wf* (1) commandment; (2) righteousness.
hiuhma *wm* throng, crowd.
gawairþi *sn* peace; **gawairþi taujan** to make peace.
andbahti *sn* (*G* **-teis** or **-tjis**) service; liturgy.
armahairtei *wf* mercy, pity.

Other:

audag- *adj* blessed, fortunate.
þadei *rel adv* to where, whither; **þishwaduh þadei** whithersoever
nauh, nauhþan(uh), nauhuþþan *adv* still, yet.
duþ(þ)e ei *conj* because; with subjunctive: so that; *adv* therefore, for that reason.

Exercises

Translate.

1. Sa manna dustodida timrjan razn jah ni mahta ustiuhan.
2. Sa kindins anabaud þamma hundafada ei galuki þans bandjans in karkarai.
3. Bandwida þan Seimon Paitrus siponja þamma saei nehwa was Iesu du fraihnan hwas wesi bi þanei qaþ Iesus biþe rodida bi þana lewjandan ina.
4. Jah þata warþ, ei usfullnodedi waurd þata gamelido in witoda ize.
5. Her anastodeiþ aiwaggeljo so þairh Lukan.
6. Jah atgibanos wesun Iesua bokos praufetaus jah uslukands þos bokos bigat stad þarei wesun gamelida þo waurda.
7. Iþ Paitrus uta sat ana rohsnai (courtyard), jah duatiddja imma aina þiwi qiþandei, "Jah þu wast miþ Iesua þamma Galeilaiau." Iþ is laugnida faura þaim allaim qiþands, "Ni wait hwa qiþis."

8. Iþ nu Xristus urrais us dauþaim, anastodeins gaslepandane waurþans.
9. Hwazuh saei hauheiþ sik silba gahnaiwjada, jah saei hnaiweiþ sik silba ushauhjada.
10. Herodis ohta sis Iohannen, kunnands ina wair garaihtana jah weihana, jah witaida imma, jah hausjands imma manag gatawida, jah gabaurjaba (willingly) imma andhausida.
11. Jah bandwidedun þaim fiskjam þaiei wesun in anþaramma skipa ei atiddjedeina hilpan ize.
12. Qaþuh þan im Iesus, "Þan jus ushauheiþ þana sunu mans, þanuh ufkunnaiþ þatei ik im, jah af mis silbin tauja ni waiht, ak swaswe laisida mik atta meins, þata rodja.
13. Gibai Frauja izwis bigitan armahairtein at Fraujin in jainamma daga!
14. Jah Xristus ist faura allaim jah alla in imma ussatida sind; jah is ist haubiþ leikis (þat' ist aikklesjons), saei ist anastodeins.
15. Jah in þamma daga hlaiwasnos usluknodedun, jah managa leika þize ligandane weihaize[2] urrisun.
16. Jah galeiþands in gard ni wilda witan mannan, jah ni mahta galaugnjan.
17. Usfullnoda þata mel jah atnehwida sik þiudangardi Gudis.
18. Witumuh þan þatei Guþ frawaurhtaim ni andhauseiþ.
19. Swa rodida Guþ þairh munþ weihaize þize fram anastodeinai aiwis praufete seinaize.
20. Afaruh þan þans dagans inkilþo (pregnant) warþ Aileisabaiþ qens is, jah galaugnida sik menoþs (months) fimf.
21. Jah eis gaggandans galukun þata hlaiw.
22. Swa liuhtjai (let shine) liuhaþ izwar in andwairþja manne, ei gasaihwaina izwara goda waurstwa jah hauhjaina attan izwarana þana in himinam.
23. Jah þai Faireisaieis frehun þana blindan qiþandans: "Hwaiwa usluknodedun þus þo augona?"
24. Biþe usfullnodedun dagos andbahteis is, gawandida sik du garda seinamma.
25. Þugkeiþ im auk ei in filuwaurdein (verbosity) seinai andhausjaindau.
26. Gadrausida (he cast down) mahteigans af stolam, jah ushauhida gahnaiwidans.
27. Jah þahta sis Marja hwileika wesi so goleins <jah> þatei swa þiuþida izai.
28. Jah at Iesu ufdaupidamma jah bidjandin usluknoda himins jah atiddja ahma sa weiha leikis siunai swe ahaks (dove), jah stibna us himina warþ qiþandei, "Þu is sunus meins sa liuba in þuzei waila galeikaida."
29. Iþ Aileisabaiþ usfullnoda mel du bairan, jah gabar sunu. Jah hausidedun ganiþjos (kinsmen) izos unte gamikilida Frauja armahairtein seina bi izai jah miþfaginodedun izai.
30. Gabandwidedun þan attin is, saei ni mahta rodjan in þamma mela, þata hwaiwa wildedi haitan þata barn.
31. Þan nu taujais armaion, ni haurnjais (trumpet) faura þus, ei hauhjaizau fram mannam.
32. Iþ Iesus uzuhhof augona iup jah qaþ, "Atta, awiliudo þus unte mis andhausides."
33. Jah ussaihwands Iesus du himina gaswogida (sighed), jah qaþ du þamma baudin, "Aiffaþa," [þatei ist: "Uslukn!"] jah sunsaiw usluknodedun ausona is jah andbundnoda bandi tuggons is jah rodida raihtaba.
34. Jah þahtedun allai in hairtam seinaim bi Iohannein niu aufto sa wesi Xristus.
35. Jah galaiþ Marja in gard Zakariins jah golida Aileisabaiþ.
36. Jah ik jabai ushauhjada af airþai, alla atþinsa (I draw) du mis." --þatuþþan qaþ Iesus bandwjands hwileikamma dauþau skulda gadauþnan.
37. Andhof Iesus, "Jabai ik hauhja mik silban, so hauheins meina ni waihts ist; ist atta meins saei hauheiþ mik, þanei jus qiþiþ þatei Guþ unsar ist."
38. Ni ogs þus, Zakaria, duþe ei andhausida ist bida þeina."
39. Jah dugunnun so managei goljan ina: "Hails, þiudan Iudaie!"
40. Jah gasaihwands qinon þo gretandein Frauja Iesus infeinoda du izai jah qaþ du izai, "Ni gret!"
41. Dugunnun ana badjam þans ubil habandans bairan þadei hausidedun ei is wesi.
42. Jah wesun þai apaustauleis talzjandans all manne jah laisjandans all manne in allai handugein jah sunjai.
43. So goleins gamelida ist meinai handau, þat' ist Pawlaus.
44. At maurgin þan waurþanana, runa (counsel) nemun allai gudjans jah þai sinistans manageins bi Iesu, ei afdauþidedeina ina.
45. Laisari, ik brahta sunu meinana þana juhizan du þus ei gahailjaidau fram þus.
46. Iþ Iesus infeinands ufrakjands handu seina attaitok imma jah qaþ imma, "Wiljau. Wairþ hrains!"

---

2 **weihaize** is used nominally here: "the bodies of the deceased (lit. lying) holy ones."

47. Moses auk raihtis qaþ, "Swerai attan þeinana jah aiþein þeina, jah saei ubil qiþai attin seinamma aiþþau aiþein seinai dauþau afdauþjaidau."
48. Ik im sa hlaifs libainais. Attans izwarai matidedun manna in auþidai jah gaswultun. Sa ist hlaifs saei us himina atstaig, ei saei þis matjai ni gadauþnai.
49. Lamba meina stibnai meinai hausjand, jah ik kann þo, jah laistjand mik, jah ik libain aiweinon giba im, jah ni fraqistnand aiw.
50. Iþ jabai hwas ni ufhausjai waurda unsaramma, talzjaiþ ina swe broþar ei ufkunnai sunja aiwaggeljons unsaraizos.
51. Warþ þan gaswiltan þamma unledin jah briggan fram aggilum in barma (bosom) Abrahamis.
52. Usgeisnodedun þan allai þai hausjandans is[3] ana frodein jah andawaurdjam (responses) is.
53. Iþ þai auhimistans gudjans sokidedun ana Iesu weitwodiþa (testimony) du afdauþjan ina, jah ni bigetun.
54. Jah was Iesus ana notin (prow) þis skipis slepands, jah þai siponjos urraisida ina jah qeþun du imma, "Talzjand, fraqistnam!"
55. Gaqumanaim þan hiuhmam managaim jah þaim þaiei us baurgim gaiddjedun du imma, qaþ Iesus du im þairh gajukon þo bi þana mannan saei urrann du saian fraiwa seinamma.
56. Iþ þan qimiþ jains, ahma sunjos, briggiþ izwis in allai sunjai.
57. Usgeisnodedun allai jah hauhidedun mikiljandans Guþ, qiþandans þatei aiw swa ni gasehwun.
58. Gawairþi taujandans sijaiþ!
59. Wulþus in hauhistjam Guda, jah ana airþai gawairþi in mannam godis wiljins.
60. Duþþe jah weis, fram þamma daga ei hausidedum, ni hweilaidedum faur izwis bidjandans jah aihtrondans, ei fullnaiþ kunþjis wiljins Gudis in allai handugein jah frodein ahmeinai.
61. Gagg in gawairþi.
62. Ni hwanhun brahteduts du ugkis mat.
63. Jah andhafjands sa aggilus qaþ du Marjin: "Ahma weihs atgaggiþ ana þuk. Duþe ei saei gabairada weihs haitada, sunus Gudis.
64. Jah audags ist sahwazuh saei ni gamarzjada in mis.
65. Þadei ik gagga jus ni maguþ qiman. Jus us þaim dalaþro sijuþ, iþ ik us þaim iupaþro im. Jus us þamma fairhwau sijuþ, iþ ik ni im us þamma fairhwau.
66. Qiþa auk izwis þatei nibai managizo wairþiþ (there be more) izwaraizos garaihteins þau þize bokarje jah Fareisaie, ni þau qimiþ in þiudangardjai himine.
67. Jah qaþ du im: "Ibai lukarn qimiþ duþe ei undar ligr satjaidau? Niu ei ana lukarnastaþan (lampstand) satjaidau?"
68. Audags saei matjiþ hlaif in þiudangardjai Gudis.
69. Wesunuh þan Zakarias jah qens is garaihta ba in andwairþja Gudis, gaggandona in allaim anabusnim jah garaihteim Fraujins.
70. Insandiþs was in þamma fairhwau ei brahtedi wen du manasedai.

[3] The sole use of a *G* of person with **hausjan**.

Texts

The texts that follow include all extant portions of the four gospels from the Codex Argenteus together with a brief portion of Matthew XXV and XXVI from the Codex Ambrosianus C. The texts of the ***Epistle to the Romans*** and the ***First Epistle to Timothy*** are based on the extant portions of these two epistles in Codex Ambrosianus A with occasional help from Codex Carolinus and Codex Ambrosianus B respectively. The texts follow those given in Streitberg but without his emendations; obvious manuscript errors, however, have been corrected as indicated in the notes, and a few conjectures have been included.

The *Gospel According to Luke* has been fully glossed: all words that have not appeared previously in the Lesson Vocabularies are given at the foot of the page together with brief notes on difficult passages. Both of the epistles have been supplied with a literal English translation as an aid to the reader. The language of the epistles and the logic of their discourse are sufficiently obtuse in both Greek and Gothic to justify such assistance.

Aiwaggeljo þairh Lukan anastodeiþ

Chapter I

[1]Unte raihtis managai dugunnun meljan insaht bi þos gafullaweisidons in uns waihtins, [2]swaswe anafulhun
unsis þaiei fram frumistin silbasiunjos jah andbahtos wesun þis waurdis, [3]galeikaida jah mis jah ahmin weihamma
fram anastodeinai allaim glaggwuba afarlaistjandin gahahjo þus meljan, batista Þaiaufeilu, [4]ei gakunnais þize bi þoei
galaisiþs is waurde astaþ.

[5]Was in dagam Herodes þiudanis Iudaias gudja namin Zakarias, us afar Abijins, jah qeins is us dauhtrum
Aharons, jah namo izos Aileisabaiþ. [6]Wesunuh þan garaihta ba in andwairþja Gudis, gaggandona in allaim
anabusnim jah garaihteim Fraujins unwaha. [7]Jah ni was im barne, unte was Aileisabaiþ stairo, jah ba framaldra dage
seinaize wesun.

[8]Warþ þan, miþþanei gudjinoda is in wikon kunjis seinis in andwairþja Gudis, [9]bi biuhtja gudjinassaus
hlauts imma urrann du saljan, atgaggands in alh Fraujins, [10]jah alls hiuhma was manageins beidandans uta hweilai
þymiamins. [11]Warþ þan imma in siunai aggilus Fraujins standands af taihswon hunslastadis þymiamins. [12]Jah
gadrobnoda Zakarias gasaihwands, jah agis disdraus ina. [13]Qaþ þan du imma sa aggilus: "Ni ogs þus, Zakaria, duþe
ei andhausida ist bida þeina, jah qens þeina Aileisabaiþ gabairid sunu þus, jah haitais namo is Iohannen.

[14]Jah wairþiþ þus faheds jah swegniþa,
jah managai in gabaurþai is faginond.
[15]Wairþiþ auk mikils in andwairþja Fraujins,
jah wein jah leiþu ni drigkid,
jah ahmins weihis gafulljada
nauhþan in wambai aiþeins seinaizos.
[16]Jah managans suniwe Israelis gawandeiþ du Fraujin Guda ize.
[17]Jah silba fauraqimid in andwairþja is in ahmin jah mahtai Haileiins
gawandjan hairtona attane du barnam
jah untalans in frodein garaihtaize,
manwjan Fraujin managein gafahrida."

[18]Jah qaþ Zakarias du þamma aggilau: "Bihwe kunnum þata? Ik raihtis im sineigs, jah qens meina
framaldrozei in dagam seinaim." [19]Jah andhafjands sa aggilus qaþ du imma: "Ik im Gabriel sa standands in
andwairþja Gudis, jah insandiþs im rodjan du þus jah wailamerjan þus þata. [20]Jah <sai>, sijais þahands jah ni

I *insahts sf* narrative. *(ga)fullaweisjan wv 1* persuade, bring into common agreement. 2 *silbasiuneis sm* eye-witness. 3 *glaggwuba adv* carefully, accurately [note *glaggwo, glaggwaba* idem]. *gahahjo adv* coherently, in an orderly fashion. *Þaiaufilus* (*V -u*) Theophilus. 4 *astaþ* = Gk ἀσφάλεια (certainty, truth), but is otherwise quite obscure. It is probably the result of a simple copying error (haplography) wherein the original sequence of letters **þwastiþawas* was simplified to **astiþwas*, with subsequent garbling. The noun *þwastiþa sf* (certainty) translates Gk ἀσφαλές in Ph 3:I. 5 *Herodes* (*G -des, D -da*) Herod. *gudja* corr. from CA *gudji*. *afar* is unclear; one expects a noun equivalent to Gk ἐφημερία (a priestly order or division). *Abia** (*G Abijins*) Abijah. *Aharon** (*G -ns*) Aaron. *Ailesabaiþ indecl* Elizabeth. 6 *unwah- adj* flawless, blameless. 7 *stairo wf* barren woman. *framaldr- adj* advanced in age; *comp framaldroz-*. 8 *gudjinon wv 2* to exercise priestly office. *wiko wf* time cycle, week. *kuni sn* kind, species, race, family. *in wikon kunjis seinis* in the cycle of his (priestly) phyle (Gk ἐν τῇ τάξει τῆς ἐφημερίας αὐτοῦ). 9 *biuhti sn* custom, habit. *gudjinassus sm* priesthood. *hlauts sm* lot; *hlauts imma urrann* it fell to his lot. 10 *alls hiuhma ... manageins* the whole crowd of people (Gk πᾶν τὸ πλῆθος ... τοῦ λαοῦ). *þymiama wm* incense offering < Gk θυμίαμα. 11 *hunslastaþs sm(i)* altar. 12 *gadrobnan wv 4* be troubled, agitated. *disdriusan sv 2* fall upon, seize. 14 *swegniþa sf* rejoicing. 15 *leiþu As* strong drink. *wamba sf* womb; belly, stomach; also fig. glutton. 17 *fauraqiman sv 4* go forward. *untal- adj* disobedient. *gafahrid- adj* ready (< **gafahrjan wv 1*). 18 *bihwe interrog adv* how?

magands rodjan und þana dag ei wairþai þata, duþe ei ni galaubides waurdam meinaim, þoei usfulljanda in mela
seinamma." [21]Jah was managei beidandans Zakariins, jah sildaleikidedun hwa latidedi ina in þizai alh. [22]Usgaggands
þan ni mahta du im rodjan, jah froþun þammei siun gasahw in alh; jah silba was bandwjands im jah was dumbs.
[23]Jah warþ, biþe usfullnodedun dagos andbahteis is, galaiþ du garda seinamma.

[24]Afaruh þan þans dagans inkilþo warþ Aileisabaiþ qens is jah galaugnida sik menoþs fimf, qiþandei
[25]þatei, "Swa mis gatawida Frauja in dagam þaimei insahw afniman idweit mein in mannam." [26]Þanuh þan in
menoþ saihstin insandiþs was aggilus Gabriel fram Guda in baurg Galeilaias sei haitada Nazaraiþ, [27]du magaþai in
fragibtim abin, þizei namo Iosef, us garda Daweidis, jah namo þizos magaþais Mariam. [28]Jah galeiþands inn sa
aggilus du izai qaþ: "Fagino, anstai audahafta, Frauja miþ þus; þiuþido þu in qinom." [29]Iþ si gasaihwandei
gaþlahsnoda bi innatgahtai is jah þahta sis hweleika wesi so goleins þatei swa þiuþida izai. [30]Jah qaþ aggilus du izai:
"Ni ogs þus, Mariam, bigast auk anst fram Guda. [31]Jah sai, ganimis in kilþein jah gabairis sunu, jah haitais namo is
Iesu.

[32]Sa wairþiþ mikils jah sunus hauhistins haitada,
jah gibid imma Frauja Guþ stol Daweidis attins is.
[33]Jah þiudanoþ ufar garda Iakobis in ajukduþ,
jah þiudinassaus is ni wairþiþ andeis.

[34]Qaþ þan Mariam du þamma aggilau: "Hwaiwa sijai þata, þandei aban ni kann?" [35]Jah andhafjands sa aggilus qaþ
du izai:

"Ahma weihs atgaggiþ ana þuk,
jah mahts hauhistins ufarskadweid þus,
duþe ei saei gabairada weihs haitada,
sunus Gudis.

[36]Jah sai, Aileisabaiþ niþjo þeina, jah so inkilþo sunau in aldomin seinamma, jah sa menoþs saihsta ist izai sei haitada
stairo, [37]unte nist unmahteig Guda ainhun waurde. [38]Qaþ þan Mariam: "Sai, þiwi Fraujins, wairþai mis bi waurda
þeinamma." Jah galaiþ fairra izai sa aggilus.

[39]Usstandandei þan Mariam in þaim dagam iddja in baurgahein sniumundo in baurg Iudins, [40]jah galaiþ in
gard Zakariins jah golida Aileisabaiþ. [41]Jah warþ, swe hausida Aileisabaiþ golein Mariins, lailaik barn in qiþau izos,
jah gafullnoda ahmins weihis Aileisabaiþ, [42]jah ufwopida stibnai mikilai jah qaþ: "Þiuþido þu in qinom, jah þiuþido
akran qiþaus þeinis. [43]Jah hwaþro mis þata, ei qemi aiþei Fraujins meinis at mis? [44]Sai allis, sunsei warþ stibna
goleinais þeinaizos in ausam meinaim, lailaik þata barn in swigniþai in wambai meinai. [45]Jah audaga so galaubjandei
þatei wairþiþ ustauhts þize rodidane izai fram Fraujin." [46]Jah qaþ Mariam:

"Mikileid saiwala meina Fraujan,
[47]jah swegneid ahma meins du Guda nasjand meinamma,
[48]unte insahw du hnaiweinai þiujos seinaizos.
Sai allis, fram himma nu audagjand mik alla kunja,
[49]unte gatawida mis mikilein sa mahteiga,
jah weih namo is.

---

21 *latjan wv 1* delay, detain. 22 *dumb- adj* mute, dumb. 23 *dagos* corr. from CA *dagis.* 24 *inkilþ- adj* pregnant. *menoþs m* month. 25 *insaihwan* in sense: to show concern for someone and act thereon. *idweit sn* disapproval, reproach. 26 *Galeilaia* (*G -aias, D -aia, A -aian*) Galilee. *Nazaraiþ indecl* Nazareth. 27 *magaþs sf* virgin. *in fragibtim D* betrothed to. 28 *audahaft- adj* blessed (with: *D*). 29 *gaþlahsnan wv 4* be frightened. *innatgahts* sf* entry, approach. *innatgahtai* corr. from CA *innagahtai.* 31 *kilþei wf* womb. 33 *Iakob* (*G -bis, D -ba, A -b*) Jacob. *ajukduþs sf* eternity. 35 *ufarskadwjan wv 1* shade, protect. 36 *niþjo wf* female relative. *aldomin Ds* old age. *swigniþa = swegniþa.* 39 *baurgahei wf* hill-country. *sniumundo adv* quickly, in haste. 41 *laikan sv 7* (pret. *lailaik*) jump, leap. *qiþus sm* belly, womb. 45 *ustauhts sf* fulfillment. 46 *mikiljan wv 1, gamikiljan wv 1* (*perf*) magnify; *mikileins vn* greatness, a great thing. 47 *swegnjan wv 1* rejoice. *hnaiweins sf* lowly state. 48 *audagjan wv 1* to deem or call blessed. 50 *alds sf* age, generation; *in aldins alde* from generation to generation.

[50]Jah armahairtei is in aldins alde þaim ogandam ina.
[51]Gatawida swinþein in arma seinamma,
distahida mikilþuhtans gahugdai hairtins seinis.
[52]Gadrausida mahteigans af stolam
jah ushauhida gahnaiwidans;
[53]gredagans gasoþida þiuþe
jah gabignandans insandida lausans.
[54]Hleibida Israela þiumagu seinamma,
gamunands armahairteins,
[55]swaswe rodida du attam unsaraim Abrahama
jah fraiwa is und aiw.

[56]Gastoþ þan Mariam miþ izai swe menoþs þrins jah gawandida sik du garda seinamma.

[57]Iþ Aileisabaiþ usfullnoda mel du bairan jah gabar sunu. [58]Jah hausidedun bisitands jah ganiþjos izos
unte gamikilida Frauja armahairtein seina bi izai, jah miþfaginodedun izai. [59]Jah warþ in daga ahtudin, qemun
bimaitan þata barn, jah haihaitun ina afar namin attins is Zakarian. [60]Jah andhafjandei so aiþei is qaþ: "Ne, ak
haitaidau Iohannes." [61]Jah qeþun du izai þatei, "Ni ainshun ist in kunja þeinamma saei haitaidau þamma namin."
[62]Gabandwidedun þan attin is, þata hwaiwa wildedi haitan ina. [63]Iþ is sokjands spilda nam gahmelida qiþands:
"Iohannes ist namo is." Jah sildaleikidedun allai. [64]Usluknoda þan munþs is suns jah tuggo is, jah rodida þiuþjands
Guþ. [65]Jah warþ ana allaim agis þaim bisitandam ina, jah in allai bairgahein Iudaias merida wesun alla þo waurda.
[66]Jah galagidedun allai þai hausjandans in hairtin seinamma qiþandans: "Hwa skuli þata barn wairþan?" Jah þan
handus Fraujins was miþ imma.

[67]Jah Zakarias, atta is, gafullnoda ahmins weihis jah praufetida jah qaþ:

[68]"Þiuþeigs Frauja Guþ Israelis,
unte gaweisoda jah gawaurhta uslausein managein seinai,
[69]jah urraisida haurn naseinais unsis
in garda Daweidis þiumagaus seinis,
[70]swaswe rodida þairh munþ weihaize þize
fram anastodeinai aiwis praufete seinaize,
[71]giban nasein us fijandam unsaraim
jah us handau allaize þize hatandane unsis,
[72]taujan armahairtiþa bi attam unsaraim
jah gamunan triggwos weihaizos seinaizos,
[73]aiþis þanei swor wiþra Abraham attan unsarana,
ei gebi unsis [74]unagein us handau fijande unsaraize
galausidaim skalkinon imma [75]in sunjai jah garaihtein
in andwairþja is allans dagans unsarans.
[76]Jah þu, barnilo, praufetus hauhistins haitaza;
fauragaggis auk faura andwairþja Fraujins, manwjan wigans imma,

---

51 *swinþei wf* a show of strength. *arms sm(i)* arm. *distahjan wv 1* to scatter. *mikilþuht- adj* proud, arrogant. 52 *gadrausjan wv 1* throw down, depose. *gahnaiwjan wv 1* to humble. 53 *gasoþjan wv 1* to sate, satisfy (with: *G*). *gabignan wv 4* become rich. *laus- adj* empty, empty-handed. 54 *hleibjan wv 1* take care of *D*. 55 *fraiwa* corr. from CA *fraiw*. 58 *bisitands m* neighbor. *ganiþjis sm* kinsman. Note *unte* in the unusual sense "that..." 59 *ahtud- ord adj* eighth. *bimaitan sv 7* circumcise. 60 *ne interj* no. 63 *spilda sf* writing tablet. 64 *tuggo wf* tongue. 65 *bisitandam* corr. from CA *bisitandandam*. 67 *praufetjan wv 1* prophesy. 68 *gaweison wv 2* visit, attend to. *uslauseins sf vn* redemption, release. 69 *haurn sn* horn (here in OT sense of power, plenitude). 71 *hatan wv 3* to hate; note also *hatjan wv 1* idem. 72 *armahairtiþa sf* mercy, charity. *triggwa sf* covenant. 73 *aiþs sm* (*G -þis*) oath. *swaran sv 6* swear. *Abraham* corr. from CA *Abrahama*. 74 *unagein adv* fearlessly; modifies *skalkinon wv 2* serve. *galausjan wv 1* set free, release (from: *us D*).

77 du giban kunþi naseinais managein is
in afleta frawaurhte ize,
78 þairh infeinandein armahairtein Gudis unsaris,
in þammei gaweisoþ unsara urruns us hauhiþai,
79 gabairhtjan þaim in riqiza jah skadau dauþaus sitandam,
du garaihtjan fotuns unsarans in wig gawairþjis."

80 Iþ þata barn wohs jah swinþnoda ahmin jah was ana auþidom und dag ustaikneinais seinaizos du Israela.

Chapter II

1 Warþ þan in dagans jainans, urrann gagrefts fram kaisara Agustau gameljan allana midjungard. 2 Soh þan
gilstrameleins frumista warþ at [wisandin kindina Syriais] raginondin Saurim Kyreinaiau. 3 Jah iddjedun allai ei
melidai weseina, hwarjizuh in seinai baurg. 4 Urrann þan jah Iosef us Galeilaia, us baurg Nazaraiþ in Iudaian, in
baurg Daweidis sei haitada Beþlaihaim, duþe ei was us garda fadreinais Daweidis, 5 anameljan miþ Mariin sei in
fragiftim was imma qeins, wisandein inkilþon. 6 Warþ þan, miþþanei þo wesun jainar, usfullnodedun dagos du
bairan izai. 7 Jah gabar sunu seinana þana frumabaur, jah biwand ina jah galagida ina in uzetin, unte ni was im rumis
in stada þamma.

8 Jah hairdjos wesun in þamma samin landa þairhwakandans jah witandans wahtwom nahts ufaro hairdai
seinai. 9 Iþ aggilus Fraujins anaqam ins jah wulþus Fraujins biskain ins, jah ohtedun agisa mikilamma. 10 Jah qaþ du
im sa aggilus: "Ni ogeiþ, unte sai, spillo izwis faheid mikila, sei wairþiþ allai managein, 11 þatei gabaurans ist izwis
himma daga nasjands, saei ist Xristus Frauja, in baurg Daweidis. 12 Jah þata izwis taikns: bigitid barn biwundan jah
galagid in uzetin. 13 Jah anaks warþ miþ þamma aggilau managei harjis himinakundis hazjandane Guþ jah qiþandane:

14 "Wulþus in hauhistjam Guda
jah ana airþai gawairþi in mannam godis wiljins.

15 Jah warþ, biþe galiþun fairra im in himin þai aggiljus, jah þai mans þai hairdjos qeþun du sis misso:
"Þairhgaggaima ju und Beþlahaim jah saihwaima waurd þata waurþano, þatei Frauja gakannida unsis." 16 Jah qemun
sniumjandans, jah bigetun Marian jah Iosef jah þata barn ligando in uzetin. 17 Gasaihwandans þan gakannidedun bi
þata waurd þatei rodiþ was du im bi þata barn. 18 Jah allai þai gahausjandans sildaleikidedun bi þo rodidona fram
þaim hairdjam du im. 19 Iþ Maria alla gafastaida þo waurda, þagkjandei in hairtin seinamma. 20 Jah gawandidedun
sik þai hairdjos mikiljandans jah hazjandans Guþ in allaize þizeei gahausidedun jah gasehwun swaswe rodiþ was du
im. 21 Jah biþe usfulnodedun dagos ahtau du bimaitan ina, jah haitan was namo is Iesus, þata qiþano fram aggilau
faurþizei ganumans wesi in wamba.

---

78 *urruns sm* dawn (used figuratively here, but sense of verse is obscure). *hauhiþa sf* heights. *skadus sm* shade, shadow. *dauþaus* corr. from CA *dauþus.* 79 *gabairhtjan wv 1* bring light. *garaihtjan wv 1* set straight, guide. 80 *wahsjan sv 6 irreg* (pret. *wohs*) grow. *swinþnan wv 4* become strong. *ustaikneins sf vn* designation, being singled out. I *gagrefts sf* decree. *kaisar* sm* (the) Caesar. *midjungards sm(i)* the world. 2 *gilstr sn* tax. *gilstrameleins sf* tax registration. *wisandin kindina Syriais* is a gloss on the phrase *raginondin Saurim* that has found its way into the text. *raginon wv 2* to rule, govern *D. Saur sm(i)* a Syrian. *Kyreinaius (D -aiau)* Quirinius. 4 *Beþla(i)haim indecl* Bethlehem. *fadreins sf* family; cf. *fadrein sn* family, tribe, race; parent. 5 *anameljan wv 1* register. 7 *biwindan sv 3* to wrap. *frumabaur sm* first-born son. *uzeta* wm(?)* crib, manger. *rum sn* room, space. 8 *þairhwakan sv 6* remain awake, keep watch. *wahtwo* wf* watch. *hairda sf* herd, flock. 9 *anaqiman sv 4* approach (smn: *A*). *biskeinan sv 1* shine round about, illumine. 10 *spillon wv 2* tell, declare. 13 *anaks adv* suddenly. *himinakund- adj* of heaven, heavenly. 14 *hauhisti sn* highest place, height. *wilja wm* will, desire. 16 *sniumjan wv 1* hasten, hurry. 21 *ganiman sv 4* learn (of); receive, keep; here = to conceive.

[22]Jah biþe usfulnodedun dagos hraineinais ize bi witoda Mosezis, brahtedun ina in Iairusalem atsatjan faura Fraujin, [23]swaswe gamelid ist in witoda Fraujins, þatei "Hwazuh gumakundaize uslukands qiþu weihs Fraujins haitada," [24]jah ei gebeina fram imma hunsl swaswe qiþan ist in witoda Fraujins, "gajuk hraiwadubono aiþþau twos juggons ahake." [25]Þaruh was manna in Iairusalem þizei namo Symaion, jah sa manna was garaihts jah gudafaurhts, beidands laþonais Israelis, jah ahma weihs was ana imma. [26]Jah was imma gataihan fram ahmin þamma weihin ni saihwan dauþu, faurþizei sehwi Xristu Fraujins. [27]Jah qam in ahmin in þizai alh; jah miþþanei innattauhun berusjos þata barn Iesu ei tawidedeina bi biuhtja witodis bi ina, [28]jah is andnam ina ana armins seinans, jah þiuþida Guda jah qaþ:

[29]"Nu fraleitais skalk þeinana, fraujinond Frauja,
bi waurda þeinamma in gawairþja;
[30]þande sehwun augona meina nasein þeina,
[31]þoei manwides in andwairþja allaizo manageino,
[32]liuhaþ du andhuleinai þiudom,
jah wulþu managein þeinai Israela."

[33]Jah was Iosef jah aiþei is sildaleikjandona ana þaim þoei rodida wesun bi ina, [34]jah þiuþida ina Symaion jah qaþ du Mariin, aiþein is:

"Sai, sa ligiþ du drusa jah usstassai managaize in Israela
jah du taiknai andsakanai.
[35]Jah þan þeina silbons saiwala þairhgaggiþ hairus
ei andhuljaindau us managaim hairtam mitoneis."

[36]Jah was Anna praufeteis, dauhtar Fanuelis, us kunja Aseris; soh framaldra dage managaize libandei miþ abin jera sibun fram magaþein seinai, [37]soh þan widuwo jere ahtautehund jah fidwor, soh ni afiddja fairra alh fastubnjam jah bidom blotandei Fraujan nahtam jah dagam. [38]Soh þizai hweilai atstandandei andhaihait Fraujin, jah rodida bi ina in allaim þaim usbeidandam laþon Iairusaulymos. [39]Jah biþe ustauhun allata bi witoda Fraujins, gawandidedun sik in Galeilaian, in baurg seina Nazaraiþ. [40]Iþ þata barn wohs jah swinþnoda ahmins fullnands jah handugeins, jah ansts Gudis was ana imma.

[41]Jah wratodedun þai birusjos is jera hwammeh in Iairusalem at dulþ Paska. [42]Jah biþe warþ twalibwintrus, usgaggandam þan im in Iairusaulyma bi biuhtja dulþais, [43]jah ustiuhandam þans dagans, miþþane gawandidedun sik aftra, gastoþ Iesus sa magus in Iairusalem jah ni wissedun Iosef jah aiþei is. [44]Hugjandona in gasinþjam ina wisan qemun dagis wig jah sokidedun ina in ganiþjam jah in kunþam. [45]Jah ni bigitandona ina gawandidedun sik in Iairusalem sokjandona ina. [46]Jah warþ afar dagans þrins, bigetun ina in alh sitandan in midjaim laisarjam jah hausjandan im jah fraihnandan ins. [47]Usgeisnodedun þan allai þai hausjandans is ana frodein jah andawaurdjam is. [48]Jah gasaihwandans ina sildaleikidedun, jah qaþ du imma so aiþei is: "Magau, hwa gatawides uns swa? Sai, sa atta þeins jah ik winnandona sokidedun þuk. [49]Jah qaþ du im: "Hwa þatei sokideduþ mik? Niu wisseduþ þatei in þaim attins meinis skulda wisan? [50]Jah ija ni froþun þamma waurda þatei rodida du im. [51]Jah iddja miþ im jah qam in Nazaraiþ, jah was ufhausjands im; jah aiþei is gafastaida þo waurda alla in hairtin seinamma. [52]Jah Iesus þaih frodein jah wahstau jah anstai at Guda jah mannam.

---

23 *gumakund- adj* male. 24 *hunsl sn* sacrifice, offering. *gajuk sn* pair. *hraiwadubo wf* turtledove. *ahaks sf(?)* dove. 25 *gudafaurht- adj* god-fearing, devout. 27 *berusjos, birusjos sm pl* parents. 29 Delete *fraujinond* (so Streitberg). 31 *andwairþja* corr. from CA *anandwairþja.* 32 *andhuleins vn* of *andhuljan wv 1* uncover, reveal. 34. *sa ligiþ du drusa...* renders Gk κεῖται εἰς πτῶσιν. he is appointed for the fall. *usstass sf* resurrection, rising up. *andsakan- part adj* opposed, spoken against. 35 *hairus sm* sword. *mitons vn* of *miton wv 2* think, ponder, consider. 36 *praufeteis f* prophetess. *magaþei wf* virginity, maidenhood. 37 *fastubni sn* fasting; observance (of the Law). *blotan sv 7* to worship; *blotandei* corr. from CA *blotande.* 38 *atstandan sv 7* stand by or near. 40 *handugei wf* wisdom, cleverness. 41 *wraton wv 2* to journey, travel. *dulþs sf* feast, festival. *Paska, Pasxa indecl* Passover. 42. *twalibwintru- adj* twelve years old. 43 *wissedun* corr. from CA *wisedun.* 44 *gasinþ(j)a wm* companion. *kunþ-* used as noun: friends and acquaintances. 46 *alh* corr. from CA *allh.* 47 *usgeisnan wv 4* be astonished, amazed. *andawaurdi sn* response, answer. 48 *winnan wv 3* suffer, grieve, worry. 52 *þeihan sv 1* grow, prosper, progress. *wahstus sm* stature.

Chapter III

[1]In jera þan fimftataihundin þiudinassaus Teibairiaus kaisaris, raginondin Puntiau Peilatau Iudaia, jah
fidurraginja þis Galeilaias Herodeis, Filippauzuh þan broþrs is fidurraginja þis Ituraias jah Trakauneitidaus landis,
jah Lysaniaus Abeilenes fidurraginja, [2]at auhmistam gudjam Annin jah Kajafin, warþ waurd Gudis at Iohannen,
Zaxariins sunau, in auþidai. [3]Jah qam and allans gaujans Iaurdanaus merjands daupein idreigos du fraleta frawaurhte,
[4]swaswe gamelid ist in bokom waurde Esaeiins praufetaus qiþandins:

"Stibna wopjandins in auþidai,
manweid wig Fraujins,
raihtos waurkeiþ staigos is.
[5]All dalei usfulljada
jah all fairgunje jah hlaine gahnaiwjada,
jah wairþiþ þata wraiqo du raihtamma,
jah usdrusteis du wigam slaihtaim.
[6]Jah gasaihwiþ all leike nasein Gudis.

[7]Qaþ þan du þaim atgaggandeim manageim daupjan fram sis: "Kuni nadre, hwas gataiknida izwis þliuhan
faura þamma anawairþin hatiza? [8]Waurkjaiþ nu akran wairþata idreigos jah ni duginnaiþ qiþan in izwis, 'Attan
aigum Abraham.' Qiþa auk izwis þatei mag Guþ us stainam þaim urraisjan barna Abrahama. [9]Aþþan ju so aqizi at
waurtim bagme ligiþ: all nu bagme unbairandane akran god usmaitada jah in fon galagjada.

[10]Jah frehun ina manageins qiþandans: "An hwa taujaima?" [11]Andhafjands þan qaþ: "Sa habands twos
paidos gibai þamma unhabandin, jah saei habai matins, samaleiko taujai." [12]Qemun þan <jah> motarjos daupjan
jah qeþun du imma: "Laisari, hwa taujaima?" [13]Þaruh qaþ du im: "Ni waiht ufar þatei garaid sijai izwis lausjaiþ."
[14]Frehun þan ina jah þai militondans qiþandans: "Jah weis hwa taujaima?" Jah qaþ du im: "Ni mannanhun holoþ, ni
mannanhun anamahtjaid jah waldaiþ annom izwaraim."

[15]At wenjandein þan allai managein jah þagkjandam allaim in hairtam seinaim bi Iohannein niu aufto sa
wesi Xristus, [16]andhof þan Iohannes allaim qiþands: "Ik allis izwis watin daupja, iþ gaggiþ swinþoza mis, þizei ik ni
im wairþs andbindan skaudaraip skohis is. Sah izwis daupeiþ in ahmin weihamma jah funin. [17]Habands
winþiskauron in handau seinai jah gahraineiþ gaþrask sein jah briggiþ kaurn in bansta seinamma, iþ ahana intandeiþ
funin unhwapnandin." [18]Managuþþan jah anþar þrafstjands þiuþspilloda managein. [19]Iþ Herodes sa taitrarkes
gasakans fram imma bi Herodiadein, qen broþrs is, jah bi alla þoei gawaurhta ubila Herodes, [20]anaaiauk jah þata ana
alla jah galauk Iohannen in karkarai.

III.1 *þiudinassus sm* kingdom; rule, reign. *Teibairius** (*G -aus*) Tiberius. *Pauntius** (*D -tiau, -teau*) Pontius. *fidurragini sn* tetrarchate. *Filippus* (*G -aus, D -au, A -u*) Philip. 2 *auhmist-, auhumist- superl adj* highest. *Annas* (*D -in*) Annas. *Kajaf* (*D -in*) Caiaphas. Note *Zaxariins* for *Zakariins.* 3 *gauja wm* country-man; pl. surrounding region. *Iaurdanus* (*G -aus, D -au, A -u*) the Jordan. 5 *dals* sm* valley, trench; note *dalei* for *dale. hlaine Gpl* (only here) hills. *wraiq- adj* crooked. *usdrusts* sf* rough road. *slaiht- adj* smooth, even. 7 *nadr* sm* adder, viper. *gataiknjan wv 1* indicate by a sign, warn. *hatis sn* wrath, hatred. *anawairþ- adj* future, coming. 9 *aqizi sf* axe. 11 *paida sf* tunic. 10 *an interrog particle* and then? 13 *garaid- adj* apportioned, assigned. *lausjan wv 1* set free, deliver; reclaim, collect (taxes). 14 *militon* wv 2* to soldier (<Lat *militare*). *holon wv 2* harrass, oppress. *waldan sv 7* occurs once elsewhere (ITim 5:14) in the expected sense "administer, control;" its peculiar use here to translate ἀρκεῖσθε (be satisfied with) occasioned a marginal gloss on the part of the scribe: *ganohidai sijaiþ* (be satisfied). *anamahtjan wv 1* do harm or damage to (*A*). *anno wf(?)* yearly wages (Lat *annona*). 16 *skaudaraip As* strap, (shoe)lace. *skohs sm* shoe. 17 *winþiskauro wf* winnowing fork. *gaþrask sn* threshing-floor. *kaurn sn* grain, wheat. *bansts sm(i)* barn, granary. *ahana sf* chaff. *intandjan wv 1* set fire to, burn. *unhwapnand- part adj* unquenchable. 18 *þrafstjan wv 1* console, comfort. *þiuþspillon wv 2* tell as good news. 19 *taitrarkes* tetrarch Gk τετράρχης. *Herodia* (*G -dins, A -dein*) Herodia. 20 *anaaukan sv 7* (pret. *anaaiauk*) add (to: *ana*).

[21]Warþ þan, biþe daupida alla managein, jah at Iesu ufdaupidamma jah bidjandin usluknoda himins, [22]jah
atiddja ahma sa weiha leikis siunai swe ahaks ana ina, jah stibna us himina warþ qiþandei: "Þu is sunus meins sa
liuba, in þuzei waila galeikaida." [23]Jah silba was Iesus swe jere þrije tigiwe uf gakunþai, swaei sunus munds was
Iosefis ... [the long genealogy going back to Adam and God, vss. 23-38, is here omitted]

Chapter IV

[1]Iþ Iesus, ahmins weihis fulls, gawandida sik fram Iaurdanau jah tauhans was in ahmin in auþidai [2]dage
fidwor tiguns fraisans fram diabulau. Jah ni matida waiht in dagam jainaim, jah at ustauhanaim þaim dagam, biþe
gredags warþ, [3]jah qaþ du imma diabulus: "Jabai sunus sijais Gudis, qiþ þamma staina ei wairþai hlaibs." [4]Jah
andhof Iesus wiþra ina qiþands: "Gamelid ist þatei ni bi hlaib ainana libaid manna, ak bi all waurde Gudis." [5]Jah
ustiuhands ina diabulus ana fairguni hauhata ataugida imma allans þiudinassuns þis midjungardis in stika melis. [6]Jah
qaþ du imma sa diabulus: "Þus giba þata waldufni þize allata jah wulþu ize, unte mis atgiban ist, jah þishwammeh
þei wiljau, giba þata. [7]Þu nu jabai inweitis mik in andwairþja meinamma, wairþiþ þein all." [8]Jah andhafjands imma
Iesus qaþ: "Gamelid ist:

> Fraujan Guþ þeinana inweitais
> jah imma ainamma fullafahjais."

[9]Þaþroh gatauh ina in Iairusalem, jah gasatida ina ana giblin alhs, jah qaþ du imma: "Jabai sunus sijais Gudis, wairp
þuk þaþro dalaþ. [10]Gamelid ist auk þatei,

> 'Aggilum seinaim anabiudiþ bi þuk du gafastan þuk,'

[11]jah þatei,

> 'Ana handum þuk ufhaband,
> ei hwan ni gastagqjais bi staina fotu þeinana.'"

[12]Jah andhafjands qaþ imma Iesus þatei, "Qiþan ist: 'Ni fraisais Fraujan Guþ þeinana.' [13]Jah ustiuhands all fraist-
ubnjo diabulus afstoþ fairra imma und mel.

[14]Jah gawandida sik Iesus in mahtai ahmins in Galeilaian jah meriþa urrann and all gawi bisitande bi ina.
[15]Jah is laisida in gaqumþim ize, mikilids fram allaim. [16]Jah qam in Nazaraiþ þarei was fodiþs, jah galaiþ inn bi
biuhtja seinamma in daga sabbato in synagogein, jah usstoþ siggwan bokos. [17]Jah atgibanos wesun imma bokos
Eisaeiins praufetaus, jah uslukands þos bokos bigat stad þarei was gamelid:

> [18]"Ahma Fraujins ana mis
> in þizei gasalboda mik du wailamerjan unledaim,
> insandida mik du ganasjan þans gamalwidans hairtin
> [19]merjan frahunþanaim fralet jah blindaim siun,
> fraletan gamaidans in gaþrafstein,
> merjan jer Fraujins andanem."

---

23 *us gakunþai* seems to translate Gk ἀρχόμενος, which, unfortunately, is itself somewhat unclear: καὶ αὐτὸς ἦν Ἰησοῦς ἀρχόμενος ὡσεὶ ἐτῶν τριάκοντα ὢν υἱός, ὡς ἐνομίζετο, Ἰωσὴφ... and Jesus himself was thirty years old beginning (his ministry ?), being the son, as was supposed, of Joseph... The noun *gakunþ-* is not attested elsewhere. *swaei conj* so that; inasmuch as. IV 3 *sunus* corr. from CA *sunaus.* 5 *diabulus* corr. from CA *diabulaus. stiks sm(i)* point; *in stika melis* in an instant. 8 *fullafahjan wv 1* serve, satisfy. 9 *gibla wm* pinnacle, pediment. 11 *ufhaban wv 3* bear up, hold up. *hwan ni* = never. *gastagqjan wv 1* stumble and strike (*A*) against (*bi*). 13 *fraistubnjo* corr. from CA *fraistobnjo. und mel* until (another) time, for the present. 15 *gaqumþs sf* assembly. 16 *fodjan wv 1* raise, rear, nourish. *siggwan, saggw sv 3*; *ussiggwan sv 3 (perf)* sing, read, recite. 17 *praufetaus* corr. from CA *praufetus.* 18 *gamalwid- part adj* crushed, bruised. 19 *frahinþan sv 3* take captive. *gamaid- adj* crippled, wounded, oppressed. *gaþrafsteins vn* consolation.

[20]Jah faifalþ þos bokos jah usgibands andbahta gasat. Jah allaim in þizai synagogein wesun augona fairweitjandona du imma. [21]Dugann þan rodjan du im þatei, "Himma daga usfullnodedun mela þo in ausam izwaraim." [22]Jah allai alakjo weitwodidedun imma jah sildaleikidedun bi þo waurda anstais þo usgaggandona us munþa is jah qeþun: "Niu sa ist sunus Iosefis?" [23]Jah qaþ du im: "Aufto qiþiþ mis þo gajukon: 'Þu leiki, hailei þuk silban. Hwan filu hausidedum waurþan in Kafarnaum, tawei jah her in gabaurþai þeinai.'" [24]Qaþ þan: "Amen izwis qiþa þatei ni ainshun praufete andanems ist in gabaurþai seinai: [25]aþþan bi sunjai qiþa izwis þatei managos widuwons wesun in dagam Heleiins in Israela, þan galuknoda himins du jeram þrim jah menoþs saihs, swe warþ huhrus mikils and alla airþa; [26]jah ni du ainaihun þizo insandiþs was Helias, alja in Saraipta Seidonais du qinon widuwon. [27]Jah managai þrutsfillai wesun uf Haileisaiu praufetau in Israela, jah ni ainshun ize gahrainids was alja Naiman sa Saur." [28]Jah fullai waurþun allai modis in þizai synagogein hausjandans þata. [29]Jah usstandandans uskusun imma ut us baurg jah brahtedun ina und auhmisto þis fairgunjis ana þammei so baurgs ize gatimrida was du afdrausjan ina þaþro. [30]Iþ is þairhleiþands þairh midjans ins iddja.

[31]Jah galaiþ in Kafarnaum, baurg Galeilaias, jah was laisjands ins in sabbatim. [32]Jah sildaleikidedun bi þo laisein is, unte in waldufnja was waurd is. [33]Jah in þizai synagogein was manna habands ahman unhulþons unhrainjana, jah ufhropida [34]qiþands: "Let! Hwa uns jah þus, Iesu Nazorenu? Qamt fraqistjan unsis? Kann þuk, hwas is, sa weiha Gudis." [35]Jah gahwotida imma Iesus qiþands: "Afdobn jah usgagg us þamma." Jah gawairpands ina sa unhulþa in midjaim urrann af imma, ni waihtai gaskaþjands imma. [36]Jah warþ afslauþnan <ana> allans, jah rodidedun du sis misso qiþandans: "Hwa waurde þata, þatei miþ waldufnja jah mahtai anabiudiþ þaim unhrainjam ahmam jah usgaggand?" [37]Jah usiddja meriþa fram imma and allans stadins þis bisunjane landis.

[38]Usstandands þan us þizai synagogai galaiþ in gard Seimonis. Swaihro þan þis Seimonis was anahabaida brinnon mikilai, jah bedun ina bi þo. [39]Jah atstandands ufar ija gasok þizai brinnon, jah aflailot ija. Sunsaiw þan usstandandei andbahtida im.

[40]Miþþanei þan sagq sunno, allai swa managai swe habaidedun siukans sauhtim missaleikaim brahtedun ins at imma; iþ is ainhwarjammeh ize handuns analagjands gahailida ins. [41]Jah usiddjedun þan jah unhulþons af managaim hropjandeins jah qiþandeins þatei "Þu is Xristus, sunus Gudis." Jah gasakands im ni lailot þos rodjan, unte wissedun silban Xristu ina wisan.

[42]Biþeh þan warþ dags, usgaggands galaiþ ana auþjana stad, jah manageins sokidedun ina jah qemun und ina jah gahabaidedun ina, ei ni afliþi fairra im. [43]Þaruh is qaþ du im þatei "Jah þaim anþaraim baurgim wailamerjan ik skal bi þiudangardja Gudis, unte duþe mik insandida." [44]Jah was merjands in synagogim Galeilaias.

Chapter V

[1]Jah warþ, miþþanei managei anatramp ina du hausjan waurd Gudis, jah is silba was standands nehwa saiwa Gainnesaraiþ, [2]jah gasahw twa skipa standandona at þamma saiwa, iþ fiskjans afgaggandans af im usþwohun

20 *falþan sv 7* (*P faifalþ*) to fold, close. *fairweitjan wv 1* look at, look around at. 22 *alakjo adv* collectively, altogether. *weitwodjan wv 1* bear witness. 23 *leiki* = *leki. Kafarnaum indecl* Capernaum. 25 *huhrus sm* hunger, famine. 26 *Sairapta* Zarephath. *Sidona* (*G -ais, D -ai, A -a*) Sidon. 27 *Haileisaius* (*D -aiu*) Elisha. 28 *moþs* sm* anger. *auhmisto wn* peak, highest point. 29 *uskiusan sv 2* single out, test; cast out, reject (*D*). *afdrausjan wv 1* cast down. 35 *hwotjan, gahwotjan wv 1* rebuke, warn not to do sthg. *afdobnan wv 4* be silent. *skaþjan, gaskaþjan wv 1* to harm, injure. 36 *afslauþnan wv 4* be frightened; the inf. is used here as a noun: fright, fear. 38 *anahaban wv 3* take hold of; pass.: be gripped (by). 40 *siggan sv 3* to sink. *sauhts sf* illness, disease. *missaleik- adj* various. V.1 *anatrimpan sv 3* press, crowd. *saiws sm* sea. *Gainnesaraiþ indecl* Gennesaret. 2. *þwahan, þwoh sv 6; usþwahan sv 6* wash. 3 *aftiuhan sv 2* pull, draw, lead away. *staþ sn* or *staþs sm* (*D -þa*) shore. 4 *gananþjan wv 1* to end, finish. This sole attestation is sometimes emended

natja. [3]Galaiþ þan in ain þize skipe, þatei was Seimonis; haihait ina aftiuhan fairra staþa leitil jah gasitands laisida us þamma skipa manageins. [4]Biþeh þan gananþida rodjands, qaþ du Seimonau: "Brigg ana diupiþa, jah athahid þo natja izwara du fiskon. [5]Jah andhafjands Seimon qaþ du imma: "Talzjand, alla naht þairharbaidjandans waiht ni nemum; iþ afar waurda þeinamma wairpam natja." [6]Jah þata taujandans galukun managein fiske filu, swe natja dishnupnodedun ize. [7]Jah bandwidedun gamanam þoei wesun in anþaramma skipa, ei atiddjedeina hilpan ize. Jah qemun jah gafullidedun ba þo skipa, swe sugqun. [8]Gaumjands þan Seimon Paitrus draus du kniwan Iesuis qiþands: "Bidja þuk, usgagg fairra mis, unte manna frawaurhts im, frauja." [9]Sildaleik auk dishabaida ina jah allans þans miþ imma in gafahis þize fiske þanzei ganutun; [10]samaleikoh þan jah Iakobau jah Iohannen, sununs Zaibaidaiaus, þaiei wesun gadailans Seimona. Jah qaþ du Seimona Iesus: "Ni ogs þus, fram himma nu manne siud nutans." [11]Jah gatiuhandans þo skipa ana airþa afleiþandans allata laistidedun afar imma.

[12]Jah warþ, miþþanei was is in ainai baurge, jah sai, manna fulls þrutsfillis jah gasaihwands Iesu driusands ana andwairþi bad ina qiþands: "Frauja, jabai wileis, magt mik gahrainjan." [13]Jah ufrakjands handu attaitok imma qiþands: "Wiljau, wairþ hrains." Jah suns þata þrutsfill aflaiþ af imma. [14]Jah is faurbaud imma ei mann ni qeþi; "Ak gagg jah ataugei þuk silban gudjin jah atbair imma fram þizai gahraineinai þeinai þatei anabaud Moses du weitwodiþai im." [15]Usmernoda þan þata waurd mais bi ina, jah garunnun hiuhmans managai hausjon jah leikinon fram imma sauhte seinaizo. [16]Jah is was afleiþands ana auþidos jah bidjands.

[17]Jah warþ in ainamma dage, jah is was laisjands. Jah wesun sitandans Fareisaieis jah witodalaisarjos þaiei wesun gaqumanai us allamma haimo Galeilaias jah Iudaias jah Iairusaulymon, jah mahts Fraujins was du hailjan ins. [18]Jah sai mans bairandans ana ligra mannan saei was usliþa, jah sokidedun hwaiwa ina innatbereina jah galagidedeina in andwairþja is. [19]Jah ni bigitandans hwaiwa innatbereina ina in manageins, ussteigandans ana hrot and skaljos, gasatidedun ina miþ þamma badja in midjaim faura Iesua. [20]Jah gasaihwands galaubein ize qaþ du þamma usliþin: "Manna, afleitanda þus frawaurhteis þeinos." [21]Jah dugunnun þagkjan þai bokarjos jah Fareisaieis qiþandans: "Hwas ist sa, saei rodeiþ naiteinins? Hwas mag afletan frawaurhtins alja ains Guþ?" [22]Ufkunnands þan Iesus mitonins ize andhafjands qaþ du im: "Hwa biþagkeiþ in hairtam izwaraim? [23]Hwaþar ist azetizo qiþan, 'Afletanda þus frawaurhteis,' þau qiþan, 'Urreis jah gagg'? [24]Aþþan ei witeid þatei waldufni habaid sa sunus mans ana airþai afletan frawaurhtins," -- qaþ du þamma usliþin: "Du þus qiþa, urreis jah ushafjands þata badi þeinata gagg in gard þeinana." [25]Jah sunsaiw usstandands in andwairþja ize, ushafjands ana þammei lag, galaiþ in gard seinana mikiljands Guþ. [26]Jah usfilmei dissat allans, jah mikilidedun Guþ jah fullai waurþun agisis qiþandans þatei "Gasaihwam wulþaga himma daga."

[27]Jah afar þata usiddja jah gasahw motari, namin Laiwwi, sitandan ana motastada, jah qaþ du imma: "Laistei afar mis." [28]Jah bileiþands allaim, usstandands iddja afar imma. [29]Jah gawaurhta dauht mikila Laiwweis imma in garda seinamma, jah was managei motarje mikila jah anþaraize, þaei wesun miþ im anakumbjandans. [30]Jah birodideun bokarjos ize jah Fareisaieis du siponjam is qiþandans: "Duhwe miþ þaim motarjam jah frawaurhtaim matjid jah drigkid?" [31]Jah andhafjands Iesus qaþ du im: "Ni þaurbun hailai leikeis, ak þai unhailans. [32]Ni qam laþon garaihtans, ak frawaurhtans in idreiga."

---

to **gaandida, P* of **gaandjan,* which is nowhere attested in Gothic. Since the verbal root *-nanþ-* is known from *ananan þjan* (to take courage), there is no convincing reason for rejecting the manuscript reading. *diupiþa sf* depth, deep part. *athahan sv* 7 (*P -haihah*) to lower (nets). *fiskon wv 2* to fish. 5 *arbaidjan wv 1* to work, labor; *þairharbaidjan wv 1* work through. 6 *dishupnan wv 4* to tear (intr.). 7 *gaman sn* partner, fellow-worker. *hilpan sv 3* to help (smn: *G*). 9 *sildaleik sn* amazement. *dishaban wv 3* seize. *gafah sn* catch (of fish). *ganiutan sv 2* catch, seize. 10 *gadaila wm* partner, companion. *nuta wm* fisherman. 11 Because *afleiþan* is not otherwise attested with an accusative direct object in the transitive sense "leave, abandon," *afleiþands* is usually emended (so Streitberg) to *afleitands= afletands.* But since this usage is found with *bileiþan* from the same root verb, this emendation seems unnecessary. 14 *weitwodiþa sf* testimony, witness. 15 *usmernan wv 4* be spread abroad. *garinnan sv 3* assemble quickly. *hausjon wv 2 = hausjan. le(i)kinon wv 2* to heal, cure (of: *G*); used here in passive sense. 17 *witodalaisareis sm* teacher of the law. *Iairusaulymon* read *-mos?* 18 *usliþa wm* a paralytic. *galagidedeina* corr. from CA *-dideina.* 19 *skalja sf* tile. *badi sn* bed. 21 *naiteins vn* blasphemy. *alja conj* except (quasi-prepositional like Eng *but (except)*, but requires case of antecedent). 22 *biþagkjan wv 1* ponder, consider. 23 *hwaþar ... þau ... conj* whether ... or .... 26 *usfilmei wf* awe, dread. *dissitan sv 5* seize. *wulþag- adj* wondrous; neut. pl. wondrous things. 27 *motastaþs sm(i)* customs house. *Laiwweis* (*G -eis, A -i*) Levi. 29 *dauhts sf* feast, banquet.

[33]Iþ eis qeþun du imma: "Duhwe siponjos Iohannes fastand ufta jah bidos taujand, samaleiko jah Fareisaie,
iþ þai þeinai siponjos matjand jah drigkand?" [34]Þaruh is qaþ du im: "Ni magud sununs bruþfadis, unte sa bruþfads
miþ im ist, gataujan fastan. [35]Aþþan qimand dagos, jah þan afnimada af im sa bruþfads, jah þan fastand in jainaim
dagam." [36]Qaþuh þan jah gajukon du im, þatei "Ainshun plat snagins niujis ni lagjid ana snagan fairnjana, aiþþau
jah sa niuja aftaurnid, jah þamma fairnjin ni gatimid þata af þamma niujin. [37]Jah ainshun ni giutid wein niujata in
balgins fairnjans, aiþþau distairid þata niujo wein þans balgins jah silbo usgutniþ, jah þai balgeis fraqistnand. [38]Ak
wein juggata in balgins niujans giutand, jah bajoþs gafastanda. [39]Jah ainshun drigkandane fairni, ni suns wili jugg,
qiþiþ auk: 'Þata fairnjo batizo ist.'"

Chapter VI

[1]Jah warþ in sabbato anþaramma frumin gaggan imma þairh atisk, jah raupidedun ahsa siponjos is jah
matidedun bnauandans handum. [2]Iþ sumai Fareisaie qeþun du im: "Hwa taujid þata ni skuld ist taujan in sabbato
dagam?" [3]Jah andhafjands wiþra ins Iesus qaþ: "Ni þata ussuggwud þatei gatawida Daweid, þan gredags was, silba
jah þaiei miþ imma wesun? [4]Hwaiwa inngalaiþ in gard Gudis jah hlaibans faurlageinais usnam jah matida jah gaf
þaim miþ sis wisandam, þanzei ni skuld is matjan, nibai ainaim gudjam?" [5]Jah qaþ du im þatei "Frauja ist sa sunus
mans jah þamma sabbato daga."

[6]Jah warþ þan in anþaramma daga sabbato galeiþan imma in synagogein jah laisjan. Jah was jainar manna,
jah handus is so taihswo was þaursus. [7]Witaidedunuh þan þai bokarjos jah Fareisaieis, jau in sabbato daga
leikinodedi, ei bigeteina til du wrohjan ina. [8]Iþ is wissuh mitonins ize jah qaþ du þamma mann, þamma þaursja
habandin handu: "Urreis jah stand in midjaim." Þaruh is urreisands gastoþ. [9]Qaþ þan Iesus du im: "Fraihna izwis
hwa skuld ist sabbato dagam, þiuþ taujan þau unþiuþ taujan, saiwala ganasjan þau usqistjan?" [10]Jah ussaihwands
allans ins qaþ du imma: "Ufrakei þo handu þeina." Þaruh is ufrakida, jah gastoþ so handus is, swaswe so anþara.
[11]Iþ eis fullai waurþun unfrodeins jah rodideun du sis misso hwa tawidedeina þamma Iesua.

[12]Jah warþ in dagam þaim, ei usiddja Iesus in fairguni bidjan, jah was naht þairhwakands in bidai Gudis.
[13]Jah biþe warþ dags, atwopida siponjans seinans jah gawaljands us im twalib, þanzei jah apaustuluns namnida:
[14]Seimon þanei jah namnida Paitru, jah Andraian broþar is; Iakobu jah Iohannen, Filippu jah Barþulomaiu;
[15]Maþþaiu jah Þoman, Iakobu þana Alfaius jah Seimon þana haitanan Zeloten; [16]Judan Iakobaus jah Iudan
Iskarioten, saei jah warþ galewjands ina.

---

33 *Fareisaie* corr. from CA *-saiei.* 34 *bruþfaþs sm(i)* bridegroom. *sununs bruþfadis* = the wedding guests. 36 *plat sn(?)* patch. *snaga wm* cloak, coat. *aftaurnan wv 4* be torn. *gatiman sv 5* suit, fit, match (*D*). 37 *giutan sv 2* pour. *balgs sm(i)* leather bottle. *distairan sv 4* to tear. *usgutnan wv 4* gush out. 38 *bajoþs pron* (*D -þum*) both of them. 39 *drigkandane* corr. from CA *driggandane.* VI.1 *in sabbato anþaramma frumin* = Gk ἐν σαββάτῳ δευτεροπρώτῳ, the meaning of which is much disputed. One school of thought holds to the view that the Jewish Sabbath, i.e. Saturday, was referred to as the First Sabbath, and the Christian Sabbath, i.e. Sunday, as the Second Sabbath. Our expression, then, could be interpreted as either the first Sunday or the second Saturday of some understood period of time, but its use here would be completely anachronistic as well as being an utterly pointless reference. The context makes it clear that the Jewish Sabbath is meant. One suspects a weary scribe garbling and then rewriting, without erasing his error, the next word in the Greek text, διαπορεύεσθαι. *gaggan*: on inf. see §23.5. *atisk As* field of grain. *raupjan wv 1* pluck. *ahs sn* ear of grain. *bnauan sv 7* rub, grind. 4 *faurlageins sf* exhibiting, showing; *hlaibans faurlageinais* the Temple Show-Bread (cf. I Samuel 21:1-7). 6 *galeiþan*; on inf. see §23.5. 7 *jau conj* whether. *til As* reason, cause, occasion. *wrohjan wv 1* bring charges against. 9 *usqistjan wv 1* kill, destroy. 11 *unfrodei wf* folly; frustration, rage. *tawidedeina* corr. from CA *-dideina.* 12 *þairhwakands* corr. from CA *þairwakands.* 13 *gawaljan wv 1* choose, select. *apaust(a)ulus* (*G -aus, A -u; Npl -eis, G -e, D -um, A -uns*) apostle. 14 *Barþulomaius, Barþaulaumaius* (*A -aiu*) Bartholomew. *Maþþaiaus* (*A -aiu*) Matthew. 15 *Þomas* (*A -an*) Thomas. *Alfaius* (*G -aus, -us*) Alphaeus. *Zelotes* = Gk Ζηλωτής zealot. 16 *Iudas* (*G -dins, A -in, A -an*) Judas. *Iskariotes* (*D -au, A -en, -u*) Iscariot.

17 Jah atgaggands dalaþ miþ im gastoþ ana stada ibnamma jah hiuhma siponje is jah hansa mikila manageins
af allamma Iudaias jah Iairusalem jah þize faur marein Tyre jah Seidone jah anþaraizo baurge, 18 þaiei qemun hausjan
imma jah hailjan sik sauhte seinaizo; jah þai anahabaidans fram ahmam unhrainjaim, jah gahailidai waurþun. 19 Jah
alla managei sokidedun attekan imma, unte mahts af imma usiddja jah ganasida allans. 20 Jah is ushafjands augona
seina du siponjam seinaim qaþ:

"Audagai jus unledans ahmin, unte izwara ist þiudangardi himine.
21 Audagai jus gredagans nu, unte sadai wairþiþ.
Audagai jus gretandans nu, unte ufhlohjanda.
22 Audagai sijuþ, þan fijand izwis mans jah afskaidand izwis jah idweitjand jah uswairpand namin
izwaramma swe ubilamma in sunaus mans; 23 faginod in jainamma daga jah laikid, unte sai, mizdo izwara managa in
himinam; bi þamma auk tawidedun praufetum attans ize.

24 Aþþan wai izwis þaim gabeigam, unte ju habaid gaþlaiht izwara.
25 Wai izwis, jus sadans nu, unte gredagai wairþiþ; wai izwis, jus hlahjandans nu, unte gaunon jah gretan
duginnid.
26 Wai, þan waila izwis qiþand allai mans; samaleiko allis tawidedun galiugapraufetum attans ize.

27 Akei izwis qiþa þaim hausjandam: Frijod þans hatandans izwis; waila taujaid þaim fijandam izwis.
28 Þiuþjaiþ þans fraqiþandans izwis; bidjaid fram þaim anamahtjandam izwis. 29 Þamma stautandin þuk bi kinnu,
galewei imma jah anþara; jah þamma nimandin af þus wastja, jah paida ni warjais. 30 Hwammeh þan bidjandane þuk
gif jah af þamma nimandin þein ni lausei. 31 Jah swaswe wileid ei taujaina izwis mans, jah jus taujaid im samaleiko.

32 Aþþan jabai frijod þans frijondans izwis, hwa izwis laune ist? Jah auk þai frawaurhtans þans frijondans
sik frijond. 33 Jah jabai þiuþ taujaid þaim þiuþ taujandam izwis, hwa izwis laune ist? Jah auk þai frawaurhtans þata
samo taujand. 34 Jah jabai leihwid fram þaimei weneid andniman, hwa izwis laune ist? Jah auk frawaurhtai
frawaurhtaim leihwand, ei andnimaina samalaud. 35 Sweþauh frijod þans fijands izwarans, þiuþ taujaid jah leihwaid
ni waihtais uswenans, jah wairþiþ mizdo izwara managa, jah wairþiþ sunjus hauhistins, unte is gods ist þaim
unfagram jah unseljam. 36 Wairþaid bleiþjandans, swaswe jah atta izwar bleiþs ist.

37 Jah ni stojid, ei ni stojaindau; ni afdomjaid, jah ni afdomjanda; fraletaid, jah fraletanda. 38 Gibaid, jah
gibada izwis, mitads goda jah ufarfulla jah gawigana jah ufargutana gibada in barm izwarana; þizai auk samon
mitadjon þizaiei mitid mitada izwis."

39 Qaþuh þan gajukon im: "Ibai mag blinds blindana tiuhan? Niu bai in dal gadriusand? 40 Nist siponeis
ufar laisairi seinana; iþ gamanwids hwarjizuh wairþai swe laisareis is. 41 Aþþan hwa gaumeis gramsta in augin broþrs
þeinis, iþ anza in þeinamma augin ni gaumeis? 42 Aiþþau hwaiwa magt qiþan du broþr þeinamma: 'Broþar let, ik
uswairpa gramsta þamma in augin þeinamma,' silba in augin þeinamma anza ni gaumjands? Liuta, uswairp faurþis
þamma anza us augin þeinamma , jah þan gaumjais uswairpan gramsta þamma in augin broþrs þeinis.

---

17 *ibn- adj* even, level. *hansa sf* crowd; military company. 17 *atgaggands* corr. from CA *atgaggaggands. hiuhma* corr. from CA *hiuma.* 21 *ufhlohjan wv 1* make laugh. 22 *afskaidan sv 7* separate, divide. *idweitjan wv 1* revile, reproach. 23 *bi þamma* thus, in the same way. 24 *gabeig-, gabig- adj* rich. *gaþlaihts sf* consolation. 25 *wai interj* woe! *hlahjan sv 6* irreg to laugh. *gaunon wv 2* weep, lament. 26 *waila qiþan* speak well of (*D*). 27 *waila taujan* to treat well (*D*). 29 *stautan sv 7* to strike. *kinnus sf* cheek. 29 *warjan wv 1* forbid, refuse. 30 *lausjan* in the special sense: ask back, reclaim. 34 *leihwjan wv 1* lend; + *sis af* borrow from. *samalaud- adj* equally great; here used nominally: a like amount. 35 *sweþauh adv* however, rather. *uswen- adj* without hope (of: *G*); note double negative. *unfagr- adj* ungrateful. *unseli- adj* wicked, impious. 36 *bleiþjan wv 1* be merciful. *swaswe* corr. from CA *swawe. bleiþ- adj* merciful. 37 *stojan wv 1* (pret. *stawida*) to judge. *afdomjan wv 1* to judge, condemn. 38 *gawigan- part adj* shaken down. *barms sm(i)* bosom, lap. *mitaþs* (*Gpl -de*) *f* measure. *ufarfull- adj* full to overflowing. *mitadjo wf* measure. *mitid* corr. from CA *mitad.* 40 *gamanwids* (once fully) prepared (i.e. instructed). *laisareis* corr. from CA *-ris.* 41 *gramsta Ds* splinter. *anza Ds* beam, log. 42 *liuta wm* hypocrite.

[43]Ni auk ist bagms gods taujands akran ubil, nih þan bagms ubils taujands akran god. [44]Hwarjizuh raihtis
bagme us swesamma akrana uskunþs ist; ni auk us þaurnum lisanda smakkans, nih þan us aihwatundjai trudanda
weinabasja. [45]Þiuþeigs manna us þiuþeigamma huzda hairtins seinis usbairid þiuþ, jah ubils manna us ubilamma
hairtins seinis usbairid ubil: uzuh allis ufarfullein hairtins rodeid munþs is.

[46]Aþþan hwa mik haitid 'Frauja, frauja!' jah ni taujid þatei qiþa? [47]Hwazuh sa gaggands du mis jah
hausjands waurda meina jah taujands þo, ataugja izwis hwamma galeiks ist. [48]Galeiks ist mann timrjandin razn, saei
grob jah gadiupida jah gasatida grunduwaddju ana staina. At garunjon þan waurþanai bistagq ahwa bi jainamma
razna jah ni mahta gawagjan ita; gasulid auk was ana þamma staina. [49]Iþ sa hausjands jah ni taujands galeiks ist
mann timrjandin razn ana airþai inuh grunduwaddju, þatei bistagq flodus, jah suns gadraus, jah warþ so uswalteins
þis raznis mikila."

Chapter VII

[1]Biþe þan usfullida alla þo waurda seina in hliumans manageins, galaiþ in Kafarnaum. [2]Hundafade þan
sumis skalks siukands swultawairþja <was>, saei was imma swers. Gahausjands þan bi Iesu insandida du imma
sinistans Iudaie, bidjands ina ei qimi jah ganasidedi þana skalk is. [4]Iþ eis qimandans at Iesua bedun ina usdaudo,
qiþandans þatei wairþs ist þammei fragibis þata, [5]unte frijoþ þiuda unsara, jah synagogein is gatimrida unsis. [6]Iþ
Iesus iddjuh miþ im. Jah juþan ni fairra wisandin imma þamma garda, insandida du imma sa hundafads frijonds,
qiþands du imma: "Frauja, ni draibei þuk, unte ni im wairþs ei uf hrot mein inngaggais. [7]Duþei ni mik silban
wairþana rahnida at þus qiman; ak qiþ waurda, jah gahailnid sa þiumagus meins. [8]Jah þan auk ik manna im uf
waldufnja gasatids, habands uf mis silbin gadrauhtins. Jah qiþa du þamma, 'Gagg,' jah gaggid; jah anþaramma, 'Qim
her,' jah qimid, jah du skalka meinamma, 'Tawei þata,' jah taujid. [9]Gahausjands þan þata Iesus sildaleikida ina jah
wandjands sik du þizai afarlaistjandein sis managein qaþ: "Amen, qiþa izwis, ni in Israela swalauda galaubein bigat."
[10]Jah gawandjandans sik þai insandidans du garda bigetun þana siukan skalk hailana.

[11]Jah warþ in þamma afardaga, iddja in baurg namnida Naem, jah mididdjedun imma siponjos is ganohai
jah manageins filu. [12]Biþe þan nehwa was daura þizos baurgs, þaruh sai, utbaurans was naus, sunus ainaha aiþein
seinai, jah si silbo widowo, jah managei þizos baurgs ganoha miþ izai. [13]Jah gasaihwands þo Frauja Iesus infeinoda
du izai jah qaþ du izai: "Ni gret!" [14]Jah duatgaggands attaitok hwilftrjom; iþ þai bairandans gastoþun; jah qaþ:
"Juggalaud, du þus qiþa, 'Urreis!'" [15]Jah ussat sa naus jah dugann rodjan. Jah atgaf ina aiþein is. [16]Dissat þan allans
agis, jah mikilidedun Guþ, qiþandans þatei praufetus mikils urrais in unsis, jah þatei gaweisoda Guþ manageins
seinaizos. [17]Jah usiddja þata waurd and alla Iudaia bi ina jah and allans bisitands

[18]Jah gataihun Iohannen siponjos is bi alla þo. [19]Jah athaitands twans siponje seinaize Iohannes insandida
ins du Iesua qiþands: "Þu is sa qimanda þau anþaranu wenjaima?" [20]Qimandans þan at imma þai wairos qeþun:
"Iohannes sa daupjands insandida ugkis du þus qiþands: 'Þu is sa qimanda þau anþaranu wenjaima?'" ([21]Inuh þan
þizai hweilai gahailida managans af sauhtim jah slahim jah ahmane ubilaize jah blindaim managaim fragaf siun.)
[22]Jah andhafjands Iesus qaþ du im: "Gaggandans gateihats Iohannen þatei gasehwuts jah gahausideduts, þatei blindai
ussaihwand, haltai gaggand, þrutsfillai gahrainjanda, baudai gahausjand, naweis urreisand, unledai wailamerjanda.
[23]Jah audags ist sahwazuh saei ni gamarzjada in mis."

---

44 *uskunþ- adj* known, manifest. *þaurnus sm* thornbush. *aihwatundi sf* thornbush. *trudan sv 4 irreg* tread. *weinabasi sn* grape. 45 *þiuþeig- adj* good, blessed. *ufarfullei wf* overflow. 48 *graban sv 6* dig, till. *gadiupjan wv 1* deepen. *grunduwaddjus sm* foundation wall. *-waddju* corr. from CA *-waddjau*. *garunjo wf* flood. *bistigqan sv 3* stumble, strike (against: *A, du, bi D*). *gawagjan wv 1* shake, stir. *gasulid- part adj* (firmly) grounded, founded (< **gasuljan* to found). 49 *flodus sm(?)* flood, river. *uswalteins sf vn* collapse. VII.1 *hliuma wm* hearing. 2 *swultawairþja wm* one on the point of death. *swer- adj* honored, highly esteemed. 4 *usdaudo adv* earnestly, seriously. 6 *draibjan wv 1* drive, press; + *sik* bother oneself. 7 *rahnjan wv 1* count, reckon, consider. 9 *swalaud- adj* so great, such. 11 *afardags sm* the following day. *Naem* corr. from CA *Maen*. *mididdjedun* for *miþiddjedun*. *ganoh- adj* enough, many. 12 *naus sm(i)* corpse. *widowo* for *widuwo*. 14 *hwilftrjom Dpl* coffin. *juggalauþs sm(i)* (*G -dis*) young man. 21 *slahs sm(i)* blow, wound.

[24]At galeiþandam þan þaim airum Iohannes dugann rodjan du manageim bi Iohannen: "Hwa usiddjeduþ in auþida saihwan? Raus fram winda wagid? [25]Akei hwa usiddjeduþ saihwan? Mannan in hnasqjaim wastjom gawasidana? Sai, þai in wastjom wulþagaim jah fodeinai wisandans in þiudangardjom sind. [26]Akei hwa usiddjeduþ saihwan? Praufetu? Jai, qiþa izwis, jah mais praufetu. [27]Sa ist, bi þanei gamelid ist:

Sai, ik insandja aggilu meinana faura andwairþja þeinamma,
saei gamanweid wig þeinana faura þus.

[28]Qiþa allis izwis, maiza in baurim qinono praufetus Iohanne þamma daupjandin ainshun nist; iþ sa minniza in þiudangardjai Gudis maiza imma ist." [29]Jah alla managei gahausjandei jah motarjos garaihtana domidedun Guþ, ufdaupidai daupeinai Iohannis. [30]Iþ Fareisaieis jah witodafastjos runa Gudis fraqeþun ana sik, ni daupidai fram imma.

[31]"Hwe nu galeiko þans mans þis kunjis, jah hwe sijaina galeikai? [32]Galeikai sind barnam þaim in garunsai sitandam jah wopjandam seina misso jah qiþandam:

'Swiglodedum izwis jah ni plinsideduþ,
gaunodedum izwis janni gaigrotuþ.'

[33]Urrann raihtis Iohannes sa daupjands, nih hlaif matjands nih wein drigkands, jah qiþiþ: 'Unhulþon habaiþ.' [34]Urrann sunus mans matjands jah drigkands, jah qiþiþ: 'Sai, manna afetja jah weindrugkja, frijonds motarje jah frawaurhtaize.' [35]Jah gasunjoda warþ handugei fram barnam seinaim allaim."

[36]Baþ þan ina sums Fareisaie ei matidedi miþ imma; jah atgaggands in gard þis Fareisaiaus anakumbida. [37]Þaruh sai, qino in þizai baurg, sei was frawaurhta, jah ufkunnandei þatei anakumbida in razna þis Fareisaiaus, briggandei alabalstraun balsanis [38]jah standandei faura fotum is aftaro greitandei, dugann natjan fotuns is tagram jah skufta haubidis seinis biswarb jah kukida fotum is jah gasalboda þamma balsana. [39]Gasaihwands þan sa Fareisaius, saei haihait ina, rodida sis ains qiþands: "Sa iþ wesi praufetus, ufkunþedi þau hwo jah hwileika so qino sei tekiþ imma, þatei frawaurhta ist." [40]Jah andhafjands Iesus qaþ du Paitrau: "Seimon, skal þus hwa qiþan." Iþ is qaþ: "Laisari, qiþ!" [41]"Twai dulgis skulans wesun dulgahaitjin sumamma: ains skulda skatte fimf hunda, iþ anþar fimf tiguns. [42]Ni habandam þan <im> hwaþro usgebeina, baim fragaf. Hwaþar nu þize, qiþ, mais ina frijod?" [43]Andhafjands þan Seimon qaþ: "Þana gawenja þammei managizo fragaf." Þaruh is qaþ du imma: "Raihtaba stauides." [44]Jah gawandjands sik du þizai qinon qaþ du Seimona: "Gasaihwis þo qinon? Atgaggandin in gard þeinana wato mis ana fotuns meinans ni gaft. Iþ si tagram seinaim ganatida meinans fotuns jah skufta seinamma biswarb. [45]Ni kukides mis; iþ si, fram þammei innatiddja, ni swaif bikukjan fotuns meinans. [46]Alewa haubid meinata ni salbodes; iþ si balsana gasalboda fotuns meinans. [47]In þizei qiþa þus: afletanda frawaurhteis izos þos managons, unte frijoda filu; iþ þammei leitil fraletada, leitil frijod." [48]Qaþuh þan du izai: "Afletanda þus frawaurhteis þeinos." [49]Jah dugunnun þai miþanakumbjandans qiþan in sis silbam: "Hwa sa ist saei frawaurhtins afletai?" [50]Iþ is qaþ þan du þizai qinon: "Galaubeins þeina ganasida þuk. Gagg in gawairþi."

---

24 *airus sm* messenger. *raus sn* reed. *wagjan wv 1* shake. 25 *hnasqj- adj* soft. *fodeins sf* nourishment; apparently an error of the translator, who confused Gk τρυφῇ (splendor) and τροφῇ (nourishment). Note *þiudangardja* in sense of *palace*. 28 *baur sm(i)* one born, child. A meaningless *imma* following *minniza* has been deleted (so Streitberg). 29 *domjan wv 1* deem, judge. 30 *witodafasteis sm* lawyers, experts in the law. *runa sf* secret, mystery. 31 *galeikon wv 2* liken, compare. *garuns sf* (*G -nsais*) street, market-place. 32 *wopjan* occurs with *G* direct object (*seina misso*) only here. *swiglon wv 2* play the flute. *plinsjan wv 1* to dance. 34 *afetja wm* glutton. *weindrugkja wm* drunkard. *gasunjon wv 2* justify, excuse. The meaning of this proverb is somewhat obscure. 37 *alabalstraun* = Gk ἀλάβαστρον an alabaster container. *balsan sn* ointment < Lat *balsamum*. 38 *natjan wv 1* to moisten; *ganatjan* idem. *skufta Ds* hair. *biswairban sv 3* wipe dry. *tagr sn* tear. *kukjan wv 1* to kiss. *salbon wv 2* anoint. 41 *dulgis Gs* debt. *dulgahaitja wm* creditor. 42 *usgiban sv 5* give out, pay; restore. *hwaþar interrog pron* which one? 43. *gawenjan wv 1* to think, suppose. *raihtaba adv* rightly, correctly. 45 *sweiban (P swaif) sv 1* cease. *bikukjan wv 1* to cover *A* with kisses. 46 *alew sn* olive oil.

Chapter VIII

[1]Jah warþ biþe afar þata, ei jah is wratoda and baurgs jah haimos merjands jah wailaspillonds þiudangardja Gudis, jah þai twalib miþ imma. [2]Jah qinons þozei wesun galeikinodos ahmane ubilaize jah sauhte, jah Marja sei haitana was Magdalene, us þizaiei usiddjedun unhulþons sibun, [3]jah Iohanna, qens Kusins, fauragaggjins Herodes, jah Susanna jah anþaros managos, þozei andbahtidedun im us aiginam seinaim.

[4]Gaqumanaim þan hiuhmam managaim jah þaim þaiei us baurgim gaiddjedun du imma, qaþ þairh gajukon: [5]"Urrann saiands du saian fraiwa seinamma; jah miþþanei saiso, sum gadraus faur wig jah gatrudan warþ, jah fuglos himinis fretun þata. [6]Jah anþar gadraus ana staina jah uskijanata gaþaursnoda, in þizei ni habaida qrammiþa. [7]Jah sum gadraus in midumai þaurniwe, jah miþuskeinandans þai þaurnjus afhwapidedun þata. [8]Jah anþar gadraus ana airþai godai jah uskeinoda jah tawida akran taihuntaihundfalþ." Þata þan qiþands ufwopida: "Saei habai ausona du hausjan gahausjai." [9]Frehun þan ina siponjos is qiþandans hwa sijai so gajuko. [10]Iþ is qaþ: "Izwis atgiban ist kunnan runos þiudinassaus Gudis, iþ þaim anþaraim in gajukom, ei saihwandans ni gasaihwaina, jah gahausjandans ni fraþjaina. [11]Aþþan þata ist so gajuko: þata fraiw ist waurd Gudis. [12]Iþ þai wiþra wig sind þai hausjandans; þaþroh qimiþ diabulus jah usnimiþ þata waurd af hairtin ize, ei galaubjandans ni ganisaina. [13]Iþ þai ana þamma staina, ize þan hausjand, miþ faheidai andnimand þata waurd, jah þai waurtins ni haband, þaiei du mela galaubjand jah in mela fraistubnjos afstandand. [14]Iþ þata in þaurnuns gadriusando þai sind þaiei gahausjandans jah af saurgom jah gabein jah gabaurjoþum þizos libainais gaggandans afhwapnand jah ni gawrisqand. [15]Iþ þata ana þizai godon airþai þai sind þai ize in hairtin godamma jah seljamma gahausjandans þata waurd gahaband jah akran bairand in þulainai.

[16]Aþþan ni manna lukarn tandjands dishuljiþ ita kasa aiþþau uf ligr gasatjiþ, ak ana lukarnastaþin satjiþ, ei þai inngaggandans saihwaina liuhad. [17]Ni auk ist analaugn þatei swikunþ ni wairþai, nih fulgin þatei ni gakunnaidau jah in swekunþamma qimai. [18]Saihwiþ nu hwaiwa hauseiþ; unte saei habaiþ, gibada imma, jah saei ni habaiþ, jah þatei þugkeiþ haban afnimada af imma."

[19]Atiddjedun þan du imma aiþei jah broþrjus is jah ni mahtedun andqiþan imma faura managein. [20]Jah gataihan warþ imma þatei "Aiþei þeina jah broþrjus þeinai standand uta gasaihwan þuk gairnjandona." [21]Iþ is andhafjands qaþ du im: "Aiþei meina jah broþrjus meinai þai sind þai waurd Gudis gahausjandans jah taujandans."

[22]Warþ þan in ainamma þize dage, jah is galaiþ in skip jah siponjos is, jah qaþ du im: "Galeiþam hindar þana marisaiw!" Jah galiþun. [23]Þaruh þan swe faridedun, anasaislep; jah atiddja skura windis in þana marisaiw, jah gafullnodedun jah birekjai waurþun. [24]Duatgaggandans þan urraisidedun ina qiþandans: "Talzjand, fraqistnam!" Iþ is urreisands gasok winda jah þamma wega watins; jah anaslawaidedun jah warþ wis. [25]Qaþ þan du im: "Hwar ist galaubeins izwara?" Ogandans þan sildaleikidedun qiþandans du sis misso: "Hwas siai sa, ei jah windam faurbiudiþ jah watnam, jah ufhausjand imma?"

[26]Jah atfaridedun in gawi Gaddarene, þatei ist wiþrawairþ Galeilaia. [27]Usgaggandin þan imma ana airþa,

---

1 *biþe* is adverbial here: afterward. The following *afar þata* is probably a marginal gloss that has found its way into the text. 2 *andbahtidedun* corr. from CA *andbahtededun*. *Kusa* (*G -sins*) Chuza. *fauragaggja wm* administrator. *fauragaggjins* corr. from CA *-gagjins*. *aigin sn* property, inheritance. 4 *hiuhmam* corr. from CA *hiumam*. *gagaggan sv 7 irreg* (pret. *gaiddja*) gather, assemble. 5 *faur wig* along the path (i.e. not in the field). 6 *uskijan- part adj* having sprouted; *keinan sv 1 irreg* to sprout. *gaþaursnan wv 4* dry up, wither. 6 *qrammiþa sf* moisture. 7 *miþuskeinan sv 1 irreg* grow up along with. *miduma sf* middle, midst. *afhwapjan wv 1* choke, quench. 12 *þaþro adv* from there; then. 13 *fraistubni sf* temptation. *afstandan sv 7* fall away. 14 *saurga sf* grief, sorrow. *gabei wf* riches, wealth. *gabaurjoþus sm* pleasure. *afhwapnan wv 4* be extinguished, choked off, drowned. *gawriskan sv 3(?)* bear fruit. 15 *seli- adj* good, kind. *þulains vn* patience. 16 *tandjan wv 1* to light, ignite. *dishuljan wv 1* hide, conceal. *lukarnastaþa wm* lampstand. 17 *in swekunþamma qiman* become manifest. 17 *analaugn- adj* hidden, concealed. 19 *andqiþan sv 5* speak with; (Lk 9:61) take leave of. 22 *marisaiws* m* sea, lake. 23 *farjan wv 1* travel, sail; *atfarjan wv 1 (perf)* sail to (a place: *in A*). *skura sf* shower; *skura windis* storm. *birekj- adj* in danger. 24 *wegs sm(a/i)* wave; movement of waves. *anaslawan wv 3* fall silent, quiet down. *wis sn* calm sea. 26 *wiþrawairþ- adj* situated opposite.

gamotida imma wair sums us baurg saei habaida unhulþons mela lagga jah wastjom ni gawasiþs was jah in garda ni gawas, ak in hlaiwasnom. [28]Gasaihwands þan Iesu jah ufhropjands draus du imma jah stibnai mikilai qaþ: "Hwa mis jah þus, Iesu, sunau Gudis hauhistins? Bidja þuk, ni balwjais mis." ([29]Unte anabaud ahmin þamma unhrainjin usgaggan af þamma mann; manag auk mel frawalw ina, jah bundans was eisarnabandjom jah fotubandjom fastaiþs was, jah dishniupands þos bandjos draibiþs was fram þamma unhulþin ana auþidos.) [30]Frah þan ina Iesus qiþands: "Hwa ist namo þein?" Þaruh qaþ: "Harjis," unte unhulþons managos galiþun in ina. [31]Jah bad ina ei ni anabudi im in afgrundiþa galeiþan. [32]Wasuþþan jainar hairda sweine managaize haldanaize in þamma fairgunja; jah bedun ina ei uslaubidedi im in þo galeiþan. Jah uslaubida im. [33]Usgaggandans þan suns þai unhulþans af þamma mann galiþun in þo sweina, jah rann sa wriþus and driuson in þana marisaiw jah afhwapnodedun.

[34]Gasaihwandans þan þai haldandans þata waurþano gaþlauhun jah gataihun in baurg jah in weihsa. [35]Usiddjedun þan saihwan þata waurþano jah qemun at Iesua jah bigetun sitandan þana mannan af þammei unhulþons usiddjedun, gawasidana jah fraþjandan faura fotum Iesuis, jah ohtedun. [36]Gataihun þan im jah þai gasaihwandans hwaiwa ganas sa daimonareis. [37]Jah bedun ina allai gaujans þize Gaddarene galeiþan fairra sis, unte agisa mikilamma dishabaidai wesun. Iþ is galeiþands in skip gawandida sik. [38] Baþ þan ina sa wair af þammei þos unhulþons usiddjedun, ei wesi miþ imma; fralailot þan ina Iesus qiþands: [39]Gawandei þuk du garda þeinamma jah usspillo hwan filu gatawida þus Guþ. Jah galaiþ and baurg alla merjands hwan filu gatawida imma Iesus.

[40]Warþ þan, miþþanei gawandida sik Iesus, andnam ina managei; wesun auk allai beidandans is. [41]Jah sai, qam wair þizei namo Iaeirus, sah fauramaþleis synagogais was, jah driusands faura fotum Iesuis bad ina gaggan in gard seinana; [42]unte dauhtar ainoho was imma swe wintriwe twalibe, jah so swalt. Miþþanei þan iddja is, manageins þraihun ina. [43]Jah qino wisandei in runa bloþis jera twalif, soei in lekjans fraqam allamma aigina seinamma, jah ni mahta was fram ainomehun galeikinon, [44]atgaggandei du aftaro attaitok skauta wastjos is, jah suns gastoþ sa runs bloþis izos. [45]Jah qaþ Iesus: "Hwas sa tekands mis?" Laugnjandam þan allaim qaþ Paitrus jah þai miþ imma: "Talzjand, manageins bihwairband þuk jah þreihand, jah qiþis: 'Hwas sa tekands mis?'" [46]Þaruh is qaþ: "Taitok mis sums; ik auk ufkunþa maht usgaggandein af mis." [47]Gasaihwandei þan so qino þatei ni galaugnida, reirandei jah atdriusandei du imma, in þizei attaitok imma gataih imma in andwairþja allaizos manageins jah hwaiwa gahailnoda suns. [48]Iþ Iesus qaþ du izai: "Þrafstei þuk, dauhtar. Galaubeins þeina ganasida þuk. Gagg in gawairþja."

[49]Nauhþan imma rodjandin gaggiþ sums manne fram þis fauramaþleis synagogais, qiþands du imma þatei "Gadauþnoda dauhtar þeina. Ni draibei þana laisari." [50]Iþ is gahausjands andhof imma qiþands: "Ni faurhtei. Þatainei galaubei, jah ganasjada." [51]Qimands þan in garda ni fralailot ainohun inngaggan alja Paitru jah Iakobu jah Iohannen jah þana attan þizos maujos jah aiþein. [52]Gaigrotun þan allai jah faiflokun þo. Þaruh qaþ: "Ni gretiþ, unte ni gaswalt, ak slepiþ." [53]Jah bihlohun ina gasaihwandans þatei gaswalt. [54]Þanuh is usdreibands allans ut jah fairgreipands handu izos wopida qiþands: "Mawi, urreis!" [55]Jah gawandida ahman izos, jah usstoþ suns. Jah anabaud izai giban mat. [56]Jah usgeisnodedun fadrein izos; iþ is faurbaud im ei mann ni qiþeina þata waurþano.

---

27 *hlaiwasnos Npl* tombs, graves. 28 *Hwa mis jah þus* = What have you to do with me? (literal rendering of the Greek Τί ἐμοὶ καὶ σοί). *balwjan wv 1* to torment. 29 *eisarn sn* iron; *eisarnabandi sf* iron fetters. *dishniupan sv 2* to tear off. *frawilwan sv 3* rob, plunder, seize. 31 *afgrundiþa sf* abyss. 32 *haldan sv 7* tend (cattle). 33 *wriþus sm* herd. *driuso wf* cliff 36 *daimonareis sm* demoniac < Gk δαιμον- + Goth *-areis.* 37 *gauja wm* countryman, resident of a *gawi.* 38 *fraletan* here has the meaning "dismiss, send away," translating Gk ἀπολύω. *usspillon wv 2* declare, expound. 41 *fauramaþleis sm* leader, ruler. 42 *ainoho* for *ainaho* (*ainah- adj*). *wintrus sm* winter; *swe wintriwe twalibe* about 12 yrs. old. *þreihan sv 1* press, crowd. 43 *runs sm* flow, run; *in runa bloþis* hemorrhaging. *skaut sn* hem. *ainomehun* for *ainummehun.* 45 *laugnjan wv 1* deny. *bihwairban sv 3* press around, crowd around. 47 *galaugnjan wv 1* remain hidden. *reiran wv 3* tremble. *faurhtjan wv 1* (± *sis*) be afraid, frightened. 50 *þataini adv* only. 52 *flokan sv 7* (*P faiflok*) mourn for. 53 *bihlahjan sv 6 irreg* (*P bihloh*) laugh at, mock. 55 *ahman A* cannot be the subject of *gawandida*; since an impersonal construction is unlikely, the subject must be Jesus. The Gk is ambiguous: ἐπέστρεψεν τὸ πνεῦμα αὐτῆς "he brought back her spirit" or "her spirit returned." *usstoþ* corr. from CA *ustoþ*.

Chapter IX

[1]Gahaitands þan þans twalif apaustauluns atgaf im maht jah waldufni ufar allaim unhulþom jah sauhtins gahailjan. [2]Jah insandida ins merjan þiudangardja Gudis jah gahailjan allans þans unhailans. [3]Jah qaþ du im: "Ni waiht nimaiþ in wig, nih waluns nih matibalg nih hlaib nih skattans, nih þan tweihnos paidos haban. [4]Jah in þanei gard gaggaiþ, þar saljiþ jah þaþroh usgaggaiþ. [5]Jah swa managai swe ni andnimaina izwis, usgaggandans us þizai baurg jainai jah mulda af fotum izwaraim afhrisjaiþ du weitwodiþai ana ins." [6]Usgaggandans þan þairhiddjedun and haimos wailamerjandans jah leikinondans and all.

[7]Gahausida þan Herodis sa taitrarkes þo waurþanona fram imma alla jah þahta, unte qeþun sumai þatei Iohannes urrais us dauþaim. [8]Sumai þan qeþun <þatei> Helias ataugida sik; sumaiuþþan þatei praufetus sums þize airizane usstoþ. [9]Jah qaþ Herodes: "Iohannau ik haubiþ afmaimait, iþ hwas is sa bi þanei ik hausja swaleik?" Jah sokida ina gasaihwan.

[10]Jah gawandjandans sik apaustauleis usspillodedun imma swa filu swe gatawidedun. Jah andnimands ins afiddja sundro ana staþ auþjana baurgs namnidaizos Baidsaiidan. [11]Iþ þos manageins finþandeins laistidedun afar imma, jah andnimands ins rodida du im þo bi þiudangardja Gudis jah þans þarbans leikinassaus gahailida. [12]Þanuh dags juþan dugann hneiwan. Atgaggandans þan du imma þai twalif qeþun du imma: "Fralet þo managein, ei galeiþandans in þos bisunjane haimos jah weihsa saljaina jah bugjaina sis matins, unte her in auþjamma stada sium." [13]Þanuh qaþ du im: "Gibiþ im jus matjan." Iþ eis qeþun du imma: "Nist hindar uns maizo fimf hlaibam jah fiskos twai, niba þau þatei weis gaggandans bugjaima allai þizai manaseidai matins." [14]Wesun auk swe fimf þusundjos waire. Qaþ þan du siponjam seinaim: "Gawaurkeiþ im anakumbjan kubituns, ana hwarjanoh fimf tiguns." [15]Jah gatawidedun swa jah gatawidedun anakumbjan allans. [16]Nimands þan þans fimf hlaibans jah twans fiskans, insaihwands du himina gaþiuþida ins jah gabrak jah gaf siponjam du faurlagjan þizai managein. [17]Jah matidedun jah sadai waurþun allai; jah ushafan warþ þatei aflifnoda im gabruko tainjons twalif.

[18]Jah warþ, miþþanei was is bidjands sundro, gamotidedun imma siponjos is, jah frah ins qiþands: "Hwana mik qiþand wisan þos manageins?" [19]Iþ eis andhafjandans qeþun: "Johannen þana daupjand, anþarai þan Heleian, sumai þan þatei praufetus sums þize airizane usstoþ." [20]Qaþ þan du im: "Aþþan jus hwana mik qiþiþ wisan? Andhafjands þan Paitrus qaþ: "Þu is Xristus, sunus Gudis." [21]Iþ is þan gahwotjands im faurbauþ ei mann ni qiþeina þata, [22]qiþands þatei skal sunus mans manag winnan jah uskusans fram sinistam wairþan jah gudjam jah bokarjam jah usqiman jah þridjin daga urreisan."

[23]Qaþ þan du allaim: "Jabai hwas wili afar mis gaggan, afaikai sik silban jah nimai galgan seinana dag hwanoh jah laistjai mik. [24]Saei allis wili saiwala seina nasjan, fraqisteiþ izai; aþþan saei fraqisteiþ saiwalai seinai in meina, ganasjiþ þo. [25]Hwo allis þaurfte gataujiþ sis manna, gageigands þo manased alla, iþ sis silbin fraqistjands aiþþau gasleiþjands? [26]Saei allis skamaiþ sik meina aiþþau meinaize waurde, þizuh sunus mans skamaid sik, biþe qimiþ in wulþu seinamma jah attins jah þize weihane aggile. [27]Qiþuh þan izwis sunja: sind sumai þize her standandane þaiei ni kausjand dauþau, unte gasaihwand þiudinassau Gudis."

[28]Waurþun þan afar þo waurda swe dagos ahtau, ganimands Paitru jah Iakobu jah Iohannen usiddja in fairguni bidjan. [29]Jah warþ, miþþanei baþ is, siuns andwairþjis is anþara jah gawaseins is hweita skeinandei. [30]Jah

---

IX. 3 *walus sm* staff. *matibalgs sm(i)* food bag. *tweihn- num adj* two apiece. *mulda sf* dust, dirt. *afhrisjan wv 1* shake off. 4 *saljan wv 1* (1) dwell, reside, remain; (2) bring an offering, sacrifice. 6 *and all* everywhere. 7 *taitrarkes* corr. from CA *taitarkes.* 8 *airiz- comp adj* former. 11 *þarb- adj* in need of (*G*). 12 *hneiwan sv 1* bend, incline; (of day) wear on, decline. 13 *Gibiþ im jus matjan,* a verbatim rendering of the Gk Δότε αὐτοῖς ὑμεῖς φαγεῖν. The use of *hindar* to indicate possession is not attested elsewhere. *manaseþs* (*G -dais*) *sf* mankind, the world; multitude. 14 *kubitus sm* group at a meal < Lat *cubitus. ana hwarjanoh fimf tiguns* fifty apiece. 17 *aflifnan wv 4* be left over. 23 *afaikan sv 7* deny. *galga wm* gallows, cross. 25 *þaurfts sf* need, necessity. *gageigan wv 3* win, gain as profit. *gasleiþjan wv 1* to harm, damage; + *sik* suffer harm or loss. 26 *skaman sik wv 3* be ashamed of (*G*). 27 *kausjan wv 1* to taste, experience. 29 *skeinan sv 1* shine.

sai, wairos twai miþrodidedun imma, þaiei wesun Moses jah Helias; [31]þai gasaihwanans in wulþau qeþun urruns is,
þoei skulda usfulljan in Iairusalem. [32]Iþ Paitrus jah þai miþ imma wesun kauridai slepa: gawaknandans þan
gasehwun wulþu is jah þans twans wairans þans miþstandandans imma. [33]Jah warþ, miþþanei afskaiskaidun sik af
imma, qaþ Paitrus du Iesua: "Talzjand, god ist unsis her wisan, jah gawaurkjaima hleiþros þrins, aina þus jah aina
Mose jah aina Helijin," ni witands hwa qiþiþ. [34]Þata þan imma qiþandin warþ milhma jah ufarskadwida ins;
faurhtidedun þan in þammei jainai qemun in þamma milhmin. [35]Jah stibna warþ us þamma milhmin qiþandei: "Sa
ist sunus meins sa liuba, þamma hausjaiþ." [36]Jah miþþanei warþ so stibna, bigitans warþ Iesus ains. Jah eis
þahaidedun jah mann ni gataihun in jainaim dagam ni waiht þizei gasehwun.

[37]Warþ þan in þamma <afar>daga, dalaþ atgaggandam im af fairgunja, gamotida imma manageins filu.
[38]Jah sai, manna us þizai managein ufwopida qiþands: "Laisari, bidja þuk insaihwan du sunu meinamma, unte ainaha
mis ist. [39]Jah sai, ahma nimiþ ina unhrains jah anaks hropeiþ jah tahjiþ ina miþ hwaþon jah halisaiw aflinniþ af
imma gabrikands ina. [40]Jah baþ siponjans þeinans ei usdribeina imma, jah ni mahtedun." [41]Andhafjands þan Iesus
qaþ: "O kuni ungalaubjando jah inwindo, und hwa siau at izwis jah þulau izwis? Attiuh þana sunu þeinana hidrei."
[42]Þaruh nauhþan duatgaggandin imma, gabrak ina sa unhulþa jah tahida. Gahwotida þan Iesus ahmin þamma
unhrainjin jah gahailida þana magu jah atgaf ina attin is. [43]Usfilmans þan waurþun allai ana þizai mikilein Gudis.
At allaim þan sildaleikjandam bi alla þoei gatawida Iesus qaþ Paitrus: "Frauja, duhwe weis ni mahtedum usdreiban
þamma? Iþ Iesus qaþ: "Þata kuni ni usgaggiþ, nibai in bidom jah in fastubnja."

Qaþ þan du siponjam seinaim: [44]"Lagjiþ jus in ausona izwara þo waurda, unte sunus mans skulds ist
atgiban in handuns manne." [45]Iþ eis ni froþun þamma waurda, jah was gahuliþ faura im, ei ni froþeina imma; jah
ohtedun fraihnan ina bi þata waurd. [46]Galaiþ þan mitons in ins, þata hwarjis þau ize maists wesi. [47]Iþ Iesus
gasaihwands þo miton hairtins ize, fairgreipands barn gasatida faura sis [48]jah qaþ du im: "Sahwazuh saei andnimiþ
þata barn ana namin meinamma, mik andnimiþ; jah sahwazuh saei mik andnimiþ, andnimiþ þana sandjandan mik;
unte sa minnista wisands in allaim izwis, sa wairþiþ mikils." [49]Andhafjands þan Iohannes qaþ: "Talzjand, gasehwum
sumana ana þeinamma namin usdreibandan unhulþons jah waridedum imma, unte ni laisteiþ miþ unsis." [50]Jah qaþ
du im Iesus: "Ni warjiþ, unte saei nist wiþra izwis, faur izwis ist; ni ainshun auk ist manne saei ni gawaurkjai maht
in namin meinamma."

[51]Warþ þan in þammei usfulnodedun dagos andanumtais is, jah is andwairþi seinata gatulgida du gaggan in
Iairusalem. [52]Jah insandida airuns faura sis, jah gaggandans galiþun in haim Samareite, swe manwjan imma. [53]Jah ni
andnemun ina, unte andwairþi is was gaggando du Iairusalem. [54]Gasaihwandans þan siponjos is Iakobus jah
Iohannes qeþun: "Frauja, wileizu ei qiþaima, fon atgaggai us himina jah fraqimai im, swe jah Heleias gatawida?
[55]Gawandjands þan gasok im jah qaþ du im: "Niu wituþ hwis ahmane sijuþ? [56]unte sunus mans ni qam saiwalom
qistjan, ak nasjan." Jah iddjedun in anþara haim.

[57]Warþ þan gaggandam im in wiga qaþ sums du imma: "Laistja þuk þishwaduh þadei gaggis, Frauja." [58]Jah
qaþ du imma Iesus: "Fauhons grobos aigun jah fuglos himinis sitlans; iþ sunus mans ni habaiþ hwar haubiþ
galagjai." [59]Qaþ þan du anþaramma: "Laistei mik." Iþ is qaþ: "Frauja, uslaubei mis galeiþan faurþis jah usfilhan
attan meinana." [60]Qaþ þan du imma Iesus: "Let þans dauþans usfilhan seinans nawins, iþ þu gagg jah gaspillo
þiudangardja Gudis." [61]Qaþ þan jah anþar: "Laistja þuk, Frauja, iþ faurþis uslaubei mis andqiþan þaim þaiei sind in
garda meinamma." [62]Qaþ þan du imma Iesus: "Ni manna uslagjands handu seina ana hohan jah saihwands aftra
gatils ist in þiudangardja Gudis."

---

31 *urruns* here = departure, ascension. 32 *kaurjan wv 1* to burden, weigh down. *gawaknan wv 4* wake up. 33 *hleiþra sf* tent, booth. 34 *milhma wm* cloud. *ufarskadwjan wv 1* overshadow. 36 *miþþanei warþ* reversed in CA. 39 *tahjan wv 1* to tear, rend. *hwaþo wf* foam. *halisaiw adv* reluctantly, hardly. *aflinnan sv 3* go away. 40 *usdreiban sv 1* drive out, send away. 41 *hidrei* = *hidre adv* hither. 43 *usfilm- adj* amazed. 45 *huljan wv 1, gahuljan wv 1 (perf)* hide, conceal. 47 *fairgreipan sv 1* seize, catch hold of. 51 *andanumts sf* acceptance; assumption (into heaven). *gatulgjan wv 1* strengthen; fix, set. 52 *Samareites (Gpl -e)* the Samaritans. 54 *Iakobus* corr. from CA *-bos*. 58 *fauho wf* fox. *groba sf* den, lair. 59 *usfilhan sv 3* bury. 62 *hoha wm* plow. *gatil- adj* suitable, fit; opportune.

Chapter X

1Afaruþþan þata ustaiknida Frauja jah anþarans sibuntehund jah insandida ins twans hwanzuh faura
andwairþja seinamma in all baurge jah stade, þadei munaida is gaggan. 2Qaþuh þan du im: "Asans managa, iþ
waurstwjans fawai. Bidjiþ nu Fraujan asanais ei ussatjai waurstwjans in þo asan seina. 3Gaggiþ, sai ik insandja izwis
swe lamba in midumai wulfe. 4Ni bairaiþ pugg nih matibalg nih gaskohi, ni mannanhun bi wig goljaiþ. 5In þane
gardei inngaggaiþ, frumist qiþaiþ, 'Gawairþi þamma garda.' 6Jah jabai sijai jainar sunus gawairþjis, gahweilaiþ sik
ana imma gawairþi izwar; iþ jabai ni, du izwis gawandjai. 7Inuh þan þamma garda wisaiþ matjandans jah
driggkandans þo at im; wairþs auk is waurstwja mizdons seinaizos. Ni faraiþ us garda in gard. 8Jah in þoei baurge
gaggaiþ jah andnimaina izwis, matjaiþ þata faurlagido izwis. 9Jah lekinoþ þans in izai siukans jah qiþiþ du im:
'Atnehwida ana izwis þiudangardi Gudis.' 10Iþ in þoei baurge inngaggaiþ jah ni andnimaina izwis, usgaggandans ana
fauradaurja izos qiþaiþ: 11'Jah stubju þana gahaftnandan unsis us þizai baurg izwarai ana fotuns unsarans afhrisjam
izwis; sweþauh þata witeiþ þatei atnehwida sik ana izwis þiudangardi Gudis.' 12Qiþa izwis þatei Saudaumjam in
jainamma daga sutizo wairþiþ þau þizai baurg jainai.

13"Wai þus Kaurazein, wai þus Baiþsaidan! Unte iþ in Tyrai jah Seidonai waurþeina mahteis þozei
waurþun in izwis, airis þau in sakkum jah azgon sitandeins gaidreigodedeina. 14Sweþauh Tyrai jah Seidonai sutizo
wairþiþ in daga stauos þau izwis. 15Jah þu Karafnaum, þu und himin ushauhido, und halja gadrausjaza. 16Saei
hauseiþ izwis, mis hauseiþ, jah saei ufbrikiþ izwis, mis ufbrikiþ, iþ saei ufbrikiþ mis, ufbrikiþ þamma sandjandin
mik.

17Gawandidedun þan sik þai sibuntehund miþ fahedai qiþandans: "Frauja, jah unhulþons ufhausjand unsis
in namin þeinamma." 18Qaþ þan du im: "Gasahw Satanan swe lauhmunja driusandan us himina. 19Sai, atgaf izwis
waldufni trudan ufaro waurme jah skaurpjono jah ana allai mahtai fijandis, jah waihte ainohun izwis ni gaskaþjiþ.
20Sweþauh þamma ni faginoþ, ei þai ahmans izwis ufhausjand, iþ faginod in þammei namna izwara gamelida sind in
himinam." 21Inuh þizai hweilai swegnida ahmin Iesus jah qaþ: "Andhaita þus, atta, Frauja himinis jah airþos, unte
affalht þo faura snutraim jah frodaim jah andhulides þo niuklahaim. Jai, atta, unte swa warþ galeikaiþ in andwairþja
þeinamma." Jah gawandiþs du siponjam seinaim qaþ: 22"All mis atgiban ist fram attin meinamma, jah ni hwashun
kann hwas ist sunus, alja atta, jah hwas ist atta, alja sunus, jah þammei wili sunus andhuljan." 23Jah gawandiþs du
siponjam seinaim sundro qaþ: "Audaga augona, þoei saihwand þoei jus saihwiþ. 24Qiþa auk izwis þatei managai
praufeteis jah þiudanos wildedun saihwan þatei jus saihwiþ jah ni gasehwun, jah hausjan þatei jus gahauseiþ jah ni
hausidedun."

25Jah sai, witodafasteis sums ustoþ fraisands ina jah qiþands: "Laisari, hwa taujands libainais aiweinons
arbja wairþa?" 26Þaruh qaþ du imma: "In witoda hwa gameliþ ist? Hwaiwa ussiggwis?" 27Iþ is andhafjands qaþ:
"Frijos Fraujan Guþ þeinana us allamma hairtin þeinamma jah us allai saiwalai þeinai jah us allai mahtai þeinai jah
us allai gahugdai þeinai; jah nehwundjan þeinana swe þuk silban." 28Þanuh qaþ du imma: "Raihtaba andhoft. Þata
tawei jah libais." 29Iþ is wiljands uswaurhtana sik domjan qaþ du Iesua: "An hwas ist mis nehwundja?"
30Andhafjands þan Iesus qaþ: "Manna <sums> galaiþ af Iairusalem in Iaireikon jah in waidedjans frarann, þaiei jah
biraubodedun ina jah banjos analag[...the text is missing from X: 30 b to XIV:9a].

X.1 *ustaiknjan wv 1* appoint, designate. *twans hwanzuh* two by two. 2 *ussatjan wv 1* set, place; lay out; beget. *waurstwjans* corr. from CA *-wjands.* 4 *puggs* sm* purse. *gaskohi sn* shoe, sandal. 5 *in þane gardei* for *in þanei garde*; see §23.3. 6 *gahweilan sik wv 3* stop, rest (upon: *ana*). 7 *þo at im* what they have (lit. what [is] to them). *faran sv 6* wander, go. 10 *fauradauri sn* street. 11 *stubjus sm* dust. *gahaftnan wv 4* cling to. 12 *sutj- adj* pleasant, agreeable; *comp sutiz-.* 13 *airis comp adv* sooner. *sakkus sm* sackcloth < Lat *saccus.* *azgo wf* ashes. 14 *staua sf* judgement. 15 *halja sf* Hell, Hades. 16 *ufbrikan sv 4* reject, despise (D). 18 *lauhmuni sf* lightning. *waurms m* snake. *skaurpjo wf* scorpion < Lat *scorpio.* *gaskaþjan wv 1* to harm, injure. 21 *affilhan sv 3* hide, conceal. *snutr- adj* wise. *niuklah- adj* childlike, young. *galeikaid- part adj* pleasing; pleased. 25 *arbja wm* heir. 29 *uswaurht- adj* righteous. *uswaurhtana sik domjan* to show oneself as righteous, justify oneself. 30 *waidedja wm* criminal, thief. *frarinnan sv 3* encounter by chance. *biraubon wv 2* rob. *banja sf* blow, stroke; wound, sore.

Chapter XIV

9"...na aftumistan haban staþ. 10Ak þan haitaizau, atgaggands anakumbei ana þamma aftumistin stada, ei biþe qimai saei haihait þuk, qiþai du þus: 'Frijond, usgagg hauhis.' Þanuh ist þus hauhiþa faura þaim miþanakumbjandam þus. 11Unte hwazuh saei hauheiþ sik silba gahnaiwjada, jah saei hnaiweiþ sik silban ushauhjada."

12Qaþuþþan jah þamma haitandin sik: "Þan waurkjais undaurnimat aiþþau nahtamat, ni haitais frijonds þeinans nih broþruns þeinans nih niþjans þeinans nih garaznans gabeigans, ibai aufto jah eis aftra haitaina þuk jah wairþiþ þus usguldan; 13ak þan waurkjais dauht, hait unledans, gamaidans, haltans, blindans. 14Jah audags wairþis, unte eis ni haband usgildan þus; usgildada auk þus in usstassai þize uswaurhtane.

15Gahausjands þan sums þizei anakumbjandane þata qaþ du imma: "Audags saei matjiþ hlaif in þiudangardjai Gudis." 16Þaruh qaþ imma Frauja: "Manna sums gawaurhta nahtamat mikilana jah haihait managans. 17Jah insandida skalk seinana hweilai nahtamatis qiþan þaim haitanam: 'Gaggiþ, unte ju manwu ist allata.' 18Jah dugunnun suns faurqiþan allai. Sa frumista qaþ: 'Land bauhta, jah þarf galeiþan jah saihwan þata; bidja þuk, habai mik faurqiþanana.' 19Jah anþar qaþ: "Juka auhsne usbauhta fimf, jah gagga kausjan þans; bidja þuk, habai mik faurqiþanana." 20Jah sums qaþ: 'Qen liugaida, jah duþe ni mag qiman.' 21Jah qimands sa skalks gataih fraujin seinamma þata. Þanuh þwairhs sa gardawaldands qaþ du skalka seinamma: 'Usgagg sprauto in gatwons jah staigos baurgs, jah unledans jah gamaidans jah blindans jah haltans attiuh hidre.' 22Jah qaþ sa skalks: 'Frauja, warþ swe anabaust, jah nauh stads ist.' 23Jah qaþ sa frauja du þamma skalka: 'Usgagg and wigans jah faþos jah nauþei innatgaggan, ei usfulnai gards meins. 24Qiþa allis izwis þatei ni ainshun manne jainaize þize faura haitanane kauseiþ þis nahtamatis meinis.'"

25Miþiddjedun þan imma hiuhmans managai, jah gawandjands sik qaþ du im: 26"Jabai hwas gaggiþ du mis, jah ni fijaiþ attan seinana jah aiþein jah qen jah barna jah broþruns jah swistruns, nauhuþþan seina silbins saiwala, ni mag meins siponeis wisan. 27Jah saei ni bairiþ galgan seinana jah gaggai afar mis, ni mag wisan meins siponeis. 28Izwara hwas raihtis wiljands kelikn timbrjan niu frumist gasitands rahneiþ manwiþo habaiu du ustiuhan? 29Ibai aufto, biþe gasatidedi grunduwaddju jah ni mahtedi ustiuhan, allai þai gasaihwandans duginnaina bilaikan ina, 30qiþandans þatei 'Sa manna dustodida timbrjan jah ni mahta ustiuhan.' 31Aiþþau hwas þiudans gaggands stigqan wiþra anþarana þiudan du wiganna niu gasitands faurþis þankeiþ, siaiu mahteigs miþ taihun þusundjom gamotjan þamma miþ twaim tigum þusundjo gaggandin ana sik? 32Eiþþau jabai nist mahteigs, nauhþanuh fairra imma wisandin insandjands airu bidjiþ gawairþjis. 33Swah nu hwarjizuh izwara saei ni afqiþiþ allamma aigina seinamma ni mag wisan meins siponeis.

34"God salt. Iþ jabai salt baud wairþiþ, hwe gasupoda? 35Nih du airþai, ni du maihstau fagr ist; utuswairpand imma. Saei habai ausona gahausjandona, gahausjai."

XIV.10 *hauhis comp adv* higher. 12 *undaurnimats sm(i)* breakfast, noonday meal. *nahtamats sm(i)* evening meal, supper. *niþjis sm* kinsman. *usgildan sv 3* repay (smn: *D*). 14 *usstassai* corr. from CA *ustassai*. 18 *faurqiþan sv 5* excuse, make excuses. 19 *juk sn* yoke. *auhsa sm* ox (Gpl *auhsne*). 21 *þwairh- adj* angry. *gardawaldands part m* master of the house. *sprauto adv* quickly. *gatwo wf* street. 23 *faþa sf* fence, hedge. *nauþjan wv 1* compel. 28 *kelikn sn* tower; upper room. *manwiþa sf* means, wherewithal; *manwiþo* is presumably a partitive *G* object of *habai*. 29 *mahtedi* corr. from CA *mahtide*. *bilaikan sv 7* mock, deride. 30 *dustodjan wv 1* begin. 31 *stigqan sv 3* push, thrust; march against (*wiþra*). *wiganna* (read *wigana* or *wigan* <*i*>*na*): the reading and meaning of this phrase are uncertain; the Gk has εἰς πόλεμον (to encounter) for war. 32 *eiþþau* occurs only here and should perhaps be emended to *aiþþau* (so Streitberg, following others), which is used elsewhere to translate the underlying Gk εἰ δὲ μήγε (if not, otherwise). Streitberg deletes the following *jabai nist mahteigs* as an interpolated gloss. 33 *afqiþan sv 5* renounce (*D*). 34 *gasupon wv 2* to season. 35 *maihstus sm* dunghill. *fagr- adj* suitable.

The Gospel According to Luke

Chapter XV

1Wesunuþþan imma nehwjandans sik allai motarjos jah frawaurhtai hausjan imma. 2Jah birodidedun
Fareisaieis jah bokarjos, qiþandans þatei "Sa frawaurhtans andnimiþ jah miþmatjiþ im." 3Qaþ þan du im þo
gajukon qiþands: "Hwas manna izwara aigands taihuntehund lambe jah fraliusands ainamma þize niu bileiþiþ þo
niuntehund jah niun ana auþidai jah gaggiþ afar þamma fralusanin unte bigitiþ þata? 5Jah bigitands uslagjiþ ana
amsans seinans faginonds, 6jah qimands in garda galaþoþ frijonds jah garaznans qiþands du im: 'Faginoþ miþ mis
þammei bigat lamb mein þata fralusano.' 7Qiþa izwis þatei swa faheds wairþiþ in himina in ainis frawaurhtis
idreigondins þau in niuntehundis jah niune garaihtaize þaiei ni þaurbun idreigos.

8"Aiþþau suma qino drakmans habandei taihun, jabai fraliusiþ drakmin ainamma, niu tandeiþ lukarn jah
usbaugeiþ razn jah sokeiþ glaggwaba unte bigitiþ? 9Jah bigitandei gahaitiþ frijondjos jah garaznons qiþandei:
'Faginoþ miþ mis, unte bigat drakman þammei fralaus.' 10Swa, qiþa izwis, faheds wairþiþ in andwairþja aggile Gudis
in ainis idreigondins frawaurhtis."

11Qaþuþþan: "Manne sums aihta twans sununs. 12Jah qaþ sa juhiza ize du attin: 'Atta, gif mis sei undrinnai
mik dail aiginis;' jah disdailida im swes sein. 13Jah afar ni managans dagans brahta samana allata sa juhiza sunus, jah
aflaiþ in land fairra wisando, jah jainar distahida þata swes seinata libands usstiuriba. 14Biþe þan frawas allamma,
warþ huhrus abrs and gawi jainata, jah is dugunn alaþarba wairþan. 15Jah gaggands gahaftida sik sumamma baurgjane
jainis gaujis, jah insandida ina haiþjos seinaizos haldan sweina. 16Jah gairnida sad itan haurne þoei matidedun
sweina, jah manna imma ni gaf. 17Qimands þan in sis qaþ: 'Hwan filu asnje attins meinis ufarassau haband hlaibe, iþ
ik huhrau fraqistna?' 18Usstandands gagga du attin meinamma jah qiþa du imma: 'Atta, frawaurhta mis in himin jah
in andwairþja þeinamma. 19Ju þanaseiþs ni im wairþs ei haitaidau sunus þeins. Gatawei mik swe ainana asnje
þeinaize.' 20Jah usstandands qam at attin seinamma. Nauhþanuh þan fairra wisandan gasahw ina atta is jah infeinoda,
jah þragjands draus ana hals is jah kukida imma. 21Jah qaþ imma sa sunus: 'Atta, frawaurhta in himin jah in
andwairþja þeinamma; ju þanaseiþs ni im wairþs ei haitaidau sunus þeins.' 22Qaþ þan sa atta du skalkam seinaim:
'Sprauto bringiþ wastja þo frumiston jah gawasjiþ ina jah gibiþ figgragulþ in handu is jah gaskohi ana fotuns is; 23jah
bringandans stiur þana alidan ufsneiþiþ jah matjandans wisam waila, 24unte sa sunus meins dauþs was jah gaqiunoda,
jah fralusans was jah bigitans warþ.' Jah dugunnun wisan.

25"Wasuþþan sunus is sa alþiza ana akra, jah qimands atiddja nehw razn, jah gahausida saggwins jah laikins.
26Jah athaitands sumana magiwe frahuh hwa wesi þata. 27Þaruh is qaþ du imma þatei 'Broþar þeins qam jah afsnaiþ
atta þeins stiur þana alidan unte hailana ina andnam. 28Þanuh modags warþ jah ni wilda inngaggan, iþ atta is
usgaggands ut bad ina. 29Þaruh is andhafjands qaþ du attin: 'Sai, swa filu jere skalkinoda þus, jah ni hwanhun
anabusn þeina ufariddja, jah mis ni aiw atgaft gaitein, ei miþ frijondam meinaim biwesjau; 30iþ þan sa sunus þeins,
saei fret þein swes miþ kalkjom qam, ufsnaist imma stiur þana alidan.' 31Þaruh qaþ du imma: 'Barnilo, þu sinteino
miþ mis wast jah is, jah all þata mein þein ist; 32waila wisan jah faginon skuld was, unte broþar þeins dauþs was jah
gaqiunoda, jah fralusans jah bigitans warþ.'

XV.5 *amsans Apl* shoulders. 8 *drakma* wm* drachma < Gk δραχμή. *usbaugjan wv 1* sweep out. *glaggwaba adv* assiduously. 9 *frijondi sf* female friend. *garazno wf* female neighbor. *drakman* corr. from CA *drakmein.* 12 *undrinnan sv 3* to fall to one's (*A*) lot. *dails sf* portion, share. *disdailjan wv 1* divide up. 13 *samana adv* together. *distahjan wv 1* tear apart; waste, squander. *usstiuriba adv* aimlessly, dissolutely. 14 *frawisan sv 5* spend, use up. *abr- adj* strong, severe. *alaþarba wm* one lacking everything, a destitute person. 15 *gahaftjan sik wv 1* attach oneself (to: *D*). *baurgja wm* citizen. Because *haiþjos seinaizos* translate εἰς τοὺς ἀγροὺς αὐτοῦ, it is usually taken as an example of the genitive used to express "place to which," an otherwise very rare (and questionable) usage. 16 *sad itan* to eat his fill. *haurn*[2] *sn* carob pod. 17 *qiman in sis* to come to his senses. *ufarassau adv* in abundance. 19 *þanaseiþs adv* henceforth, further. 20 *þragjan wv 1* to run. *hals m* neck 22 *figgragulþ sn* finger-ring. 23 *stiur sm* calf. *alid- adj* fatted (**aljan wv 1* fatten) *ufsneiþan sv 1* to slaughter. *wisan* (± *waila*) *sv 5, biwisan sv 5* to make merry, have a party. 24 *gaqiunan wv 4* be brought back to life. 25 *alþiz- comp adj* elder; *alþj-* old (in age). The accusative *razn* after *atiddja nehw* is difficult to explain. *saggws sm(i)* song, music. *laiks sm(i)* leaping, dancing. 27 *afsnaiþ* is usually corrected to *ufsnaiþ*; cf. *ufsneiþiþ* in v. 23 above and *ufsnaist* in v. 30 below. 28 *modag- adj* angry. 29 *ufargaggan sv 7 irreg* transgress. *gatein sn* kid; *gaits sf* goat. 30 *kalkjom Dpl* harlots. 31 *sinteino adv* always, continually.

Chapter XVI

[1]Qaþuþþan du siponjam seinaim: "Manne sums was gabeigs, saei aihta fauragag<g>jan jah sa frawrohiþs warþ du imma ei distahidedi aigin is. [2]Jah atwopjands ina qaþ du imma: 'Duhwe þata hausja fram þus? Usgif raþjon fauragaggjis þeinis; ni magt auk ju þanamais fauragaggja wisan.' [3]Qaþ þan in sis sa fauragaggja: 'Hwa taujau, þandei frauja meins afnimiþ fauragaggi af mis? Graban ni mag; bidjan skama mik. [4]Andþahta mik hwa taujau ei þan, biþe afsatjaidau us fauragaggja, andnimaina mik in gardins seinans.' [5]Jah athaitands ainhwarjanoh faihuskulane fraujins seinis qaþ þamma frumistin: 'Hwan filu skalt fraujin meinamma?' [6]Þaruh qaþ: 'Taihuntaihund kase alewis.' Jah qaþ du imma: 'Nim þus bokos jah gasitands sprauto gamelei fim tiguns.' [7]Þaþro þan du anþaramma qaþ: 'Aþþan þu, hwan filu skalt?' Iþ is qaþ: 'Taihuntaihund mitade kaurnis.' Jah qaþ du imma: 'Nim þus bokos jah melei ahtautehund.' [8]Jah hazida sa frauja þana fauragaggjan inwindiþos, unte frodaba gatawida; unte þai sunjus þis aiwis frodozans sunum liuhadis in kunja seinamma sind. [9]Jah ik izwis qiþa: Taujaiþ izwis frijonds us faihuþraihna inwindiþos, ei þan ufligaiþ, andnimaina izwis in aiweinos hleiþros.

[10]"Saei triggws ist in leitilamma jah in managamma triggws ist; jah sa in leitilamma untriggwa jah in managamma untriggws ist. [11]Jabai nu in inwindamma faihuþraihna triggwai ni waurþuþ, þata sunjeino hwas izwis galaubeiþ? [12]Jah jabai in þamma framaþjin triggwai ni waurþuþ, þata izwar hwas izwis gibiþ? [13]Ni ainshun þiwe mag twaim fraujam skalkinon; andizuh ainana fijaiþ jah anþarana frijoþ, aiþþau ainamma andtiloþ, iþ anþaramma frakann. Ni maguþ Guda skalkinon jah faihuþraihna."

[14]Gahausidedun þan þo alla jah þai Fareisaieis, faihufrikai wisandans, jah bimampidedun ina. [15]Jah qaþ du im: "Jus sijuþ juzei garaihtans domeiþ izwis silbans in andwairþja manne; iþ Guþ kann hairtona izwara, unte þata hauho in mannam andaset in andwairþja Gudis. [16]Witoþ jah praufeteis und Iohannen; þaþroh þiudangardi Gudis wailamerjada jah hwazuh in izai nauþjada. [17]Iþ azetizo ist himin jah airþa hindarleiþan þau witodis ainana writ gadriusan. [18]Hwazuh saei afletands qen seina jah liugands anþara horinoþ, jah hwazuh saei afleitana liugaiþ, horinoþ.

[19]Aþþan manne sums was gabigs jah gawasids was paurpaurai jah byssaun jah waila wisands daga hwammeh bairhtaba. [20]Iþ unleds sums was namin haitans Lazarus; sah atwaurpans was du daura is, banjo fulls. [21]Jah gairnida saþ itan drauhsno þizo driusandeino af biuda þis gabeigins, akei jah hundos atrinnandans bilaigodedun banjos is. [22]Warþ þan gaswiltan þamma unledin jah briggan fram aggilum in barma Abrahamis; gaswalt þan jah sa gabeiga jah gafulhans warþ. [23]Jah in Haljai ushafjands augona seina wisands in balweinim gasahw þan Abraham fairraþro jah Lazaru in barmim is. [24]Jah is ufhropjands [remainder of chapter missing].

XVI. 1 *fauragaggja wm* administrator, chief steward; *fauragaggi sn* administration, stewardship. *frawrohjan wv 1* accuse, charge. 2 *raþjo wf* account, records. *þanamais adv* henceforth. 4 *andþagkjan sik wv 1* become aware of, realize. *afsatjan wv 1* remove, divorce. 5 *ainhwarjanoh* each one singly. *faihuskula wm* debtor. 8 *inwindiþa sf* injustice, crime. The genitive *inwindiþos* here and in vs. 9 is a literal rendering of the Greek (τῆς ἀδικίας); the adj. *inwind-* would seem to be more appropriate in Gothic. Note the same construction below in Lk. 18:6. *frodaba adv* wisely. *sunjus* corr. from CA *sunjos.* Verses 8 and 9 make little or no sense as they stand. 9 *faihuþraihna Ds* worldly wealth, mammon. *faihuþraihna* is glossed in the margin as *mammonim. ufligan sv 5* to fail, faint. 11 *sunjein- adj* true, belonging to the Truth. *galaubjan* in sense: to entrust *A* to *D*, trust *D* with *A*. *framaþj- adj* foreign, belonging to someone else. Again, the sense of the verse is obscure. 13 *andizuh ... aiþþan* either ... or. *andtilon wv 2* be devoted to *D*. 14 *faihufrik- adj* greedy, covetous. *bimampjan wv 1* deride. 15 *andaset- adj* abominable. 17 *hindarleiþan sv 1* (1) perish; (2) go or come up to. *writs sm(i)?* stroke, point (in written text). On the use of the infinitives *hindarleiþan* and *gadriusan* see §20.4. 19 *paurpura sf* purple < Gk πορφύρα. *byssaun Asg* fine linen < Gk βύσσος. *bairhtaba adv* clearly; here = ostentatiously. 20 *atwairpan sv 3* cast down. 21 *biuþ(s) sm* or *sn* table. *drauhsna sf* crumb. *atrinnan sv 3* run up to. *bilaigon wv 2* to lick. 23 *balweins vn* torment, pain.

Chapter XVII

[vss I-3a missing] 3...jabai frawaurkjai broþar þeins, gasak imma; jah þan jabai idreigo sik, fraletais imma. 4Jah jabai sibun sinþam ana dag frawaurkjai du þus, jah sibun sinþam ana dag gawandjai sik qiþands, idreigo mik, fraletais imma." 5Jah qeþun apaustauleis du Fraujin: "Biauk uns galaubein." 6Qaþ þan Frauja: "Jabai habaidedeiþ galaubein swe kaurno sinapis, aiþþau jus jabai qiþeiþ du bairabagma þamma: 'Uslausei þuk us waurtim jah ussatei þuk in marein,' jah andhausidedi þau izwis.

7"Hwas þan izwara skalk aigands arjandan aiþþau haldandan, saei atgaggandin af haiþjai qiþai: 'Suns hindarleiþ anahkumbei'? 8Ak niu qiþiþ du imma: 'Manwei hwa du naht matjau jah bigaurdans andbahtei mis, unte matja jah drigka, jah biþe gamatjis jah gadrigkais þu'? 9Iba þank þu fairhaitis skalka jainamma, unte gatawida þatei anabudan was? Ni man. 10Swa jah jus, þan taujaiþ alla þo anabudanona izwis, qiþaiþ þatei skalkos unbrukjai sijum, unte þatei skuldedum taujan gatawidedum."

11Jah warþ, miþþanei iddja is in Iairusalem, jah is þairhiddja þairh midja Samarian jah Galeilaian. 12Jah inngaggandin imma in suma haimo, gamotidedun imma taihun þrutsfillai mans, þaih gastoþun fairraþro. 13Jah silbans ushofun stibna qiþandans: "Iesu, talzjand, armai unsis!" 14Jah gaumjands qaþ du im: "Gaggandans ataugeiþ izwis gudjam." Jah warþ, miþþanei galiþun, gahrainidai waurþun. 15Iþ ains þan ize gaumjands þammei hrains warþ, gawandida sik miþ stibnai mikilai, hauhjands Guþ, 16jah draus ana andawleizn faura fotum is awiliudonds imma (sah was Samareites). 17Andhafjands þan Iesus qaþ: 'Niu taihun þai gahrainidai waurþun? Iþ þai niun hwar? 18Ni bigitanai waurþun gawandjandans giban wulþu Guda, niba sa aljakunja?" 19Jah qaþ du imma: "Usstandands gagg, galaubeins þeina ganasida þuk."

20Fraihans þan fram Fareisaium: "Hwan qimiþ þiudangardi Gudis?" andhof im jah qaþ: "Ni qimiþ þiudangardi Gudis miþ atwitainai. 21Nih qiþand: 'Sai her,' aiþþau 'Sai jainar,' sai auk þiudangardi Gudis in izwis ist." 22Qaþ þan du siponjam: "Aþþan qimand dagos, þan gairneiþ ainana þize dage sunaus mans gasaihwan jah ni gasaihwiþ. 23Jah qiþand izwis: 'Sai her,' aiþþau 'Sai jainar.' Ni galeiþaiþ nih laistjaiþ. 24Swaswe raihtis lauhmuni lauhatjandei us þamma uf himina in þata uf himina skeiniþ, swa wairþiþ sunus mans in daga seinamma. 25Aþþan faurþis skal manag gaþulan jah uskiusada fram þamma kunja. 26Jah swaswe warþ in dagam Nauelis, swah wairþiþ jah in dagam sunaus mans. 27Etun jah drugkun, liugaidedun jah liugaidos wesun, und þanei dag galaiþ Nauel in arka; jah qam midjasweipains jah fraqistida allans. 28Samaleiko jah swe warþ in dagam Lodis; etun jah drugkun, bauhtedun jah frabauhtedun, satidedun, timridedun; 29iþ þammei daga usiddja Lod us Saudaumim, rignida swibla jah funin us himina jah fraqistida allaim. 30Bi þamma wairþiþ þamma daga, ei sunus mans andhuljada. 31In jainamma daga, saei sijai ana hrota jah kasa is in razna, ni atsteigai dalaþ niman þo; jah saei ana haiþjai, samaleiko ni gawandjai sik ibukana. 32Gamuneiþ qenais Lodis. 33Saei sokeiþ saiwala seina ganasjan, fraqisteiþ izai, jah saei fraqisteiþ izai in meina ganasjiþ þo. 34Qiþa izwis þatei þizai naht twai wairþand ana ligra samin, ains usnimada jah anþar bileiþada; 35twos wairþand malandeins samana, aina usnimada jah anþara bileiþada." 37Jah andhafjandans qeþun du imma: "Hwar, Frauja?" Iþ is qaþ im: "Þarei leik, jaindre galisand sik arans."

XVII.5 *biaukan sv 7* increase, add to. 6 *sinaps sm(?)* mustard. *bairabagms sm* mulberry tree. *uslausjan wv 1* set free, redeem; here: uproot yourself. 7 *arjan wv 1* to plow. 8 *bigairdan sik sv 3* gird oneself, get dressed. *þank As* thanks; *þank fairhaitan* to thank *D. unbrukj- adj* unworthy. 13 *ufhofun* corr. from CA *ufhofon. andawleizn sn(?)* face. 18 *aljakunja wm* stranger, outsider. 20 *atwitains sf vn* observation, scrutiny. 22 *ainana ... sunaus* corr. from CA *ainamma ... sununs.* 24 *lauhmuni* corr. from CA *-moni. lauhatjan wv 1* to flash. *us þamma ... in þata* from one side ... to the other. 26 *Nauel (G -is)* Noah. 27 *arka sf* the Ark; box. *midjasweipains sf* The Deluge. 29 *rignjan wv 1* to rain. *swibla Ds* sulfur, brimstone. 30 *bi þamma* accordingly, so, thus. 31 *ibuk- adj* facing backward; *gawandjan sik ibukana* turn back, look back. 35 *malan sv 6* grind grain. 37 *jaindre adv* thither, there. *ara wm* vulture, eagle.

Chapter XVIII

1Qaþuþþan jah gajukon im du þammei sinteino skulun bidjan jah ni wairþan usgrudjans, 2qiþands: "Staua
was sums in sumai baurg, Guþ ni ogands jah mannan ni aistands. 3Wassuþþan jah widuwo in þizai baurg jainai jah
atiddja du imma qiþandei: "Fraweit mik ana andastaþja meinamma." 4Jah ni wilda laggai hweilai. Afaruþþan þata
qaþ in sis silbin: "Jabai jah Guþ ni og jah mannan ni aista, 5iþ in þizei usþriutiþ mis so widuwo, fraweita þo, ibai
und andi qimandei usagljai mis." 6Qaþ þan Frauja: "Hauseiþ hwa staua inwindiþos qiþiþ. 7Iþ Guþ niu gawrikai
þans gawalidans seinans, þans wopjandans du sis dagam jah nahtam, jah usbeidands ist ana im? 8Aþþan qiþa izwis
þatei gawrikiþ ins sprauto. Iþ sweþauh sunus mans qimands bi-u-gitai galaubein ana airþai?"

9Qaþ þan du sumaim, þaiei silbans trauaidedun sis ei weseina garaihtai jah frakunnandans þaim anþaraim,
þo gajukon: 10"Mans twai usiddjedun in alh bidjan, ains Fareisaius jah anþar motareis. 11Sa Fareisaius standands sis
þo bad: 'Guþ, awiliudo þus, unte ni im swaswe þai anþarai mans, wilwans, inwindai, horos, aiþþau <jah> swaswe sa
motareis. 12Fasta twaim sinþam sabbataus jah afdailja taihundon dail allis þize gastalda." 13Jah sa motareis fairraþro
standands ni wilda nih augona seina ushafjan du himina, ak sloh in brusts seinos qiþands: 'Guþ, hulþs sijais mis
frawaurhtamma.' 14Qiþa izwis: atiddja sa garaihtoza gataihans du garda seinamma þau raihtis jains; unte sahwazuh
saei hauheiþ sik silba gahnaiwjada, iþ saei hnaiweiþ sik silba ushauhjada."

15Berun þan du imma barna, ei im attaitoki. Gasaihwandans þan siponjos andbitun ins. 16Iþ Iesus
athaitands ins qaþ: "Letiþ þo barna gaggan du mis jah ni warjiþ þo, unte þize swaleikaize ist þiudangardi Gudis.
17Amen qiþa izwis, saei ni andnimiþ þiudangardja Gudis swe barn, ni qimiþ in izai."

18Jah frah ina sums reike qiþands: 'Laisari þiuþeiga, hwa taujands libainais aiweinons arbja wairþau?" 19Qaþ
þan du imma Iesus: "Hwa mik qiþis þiuþeigana? Ni ainshun þiuþeigs niba ains Guþ. 20Þos anabusnins kant: Ni
horinos; ni maurþrjais; ni hlifais; ni galiugaweitwods sijais; swerai attan þeinana jah aiþein." 21Iþ is qaþuh: "Þata
allata gafastaida us jundai meinai." 22Gahausjands þan þata Iesus qaþ du imma: "Nauh ainis þus wan ist: all þatei
habais frabugei jah gadailei unledaim, jah habais huzd in himina, jah hiri laistjan mik." 23Iþ is gahausjands þata
gaurs warþ; was auk gabeigs filu. 24Gasaihwands þan ina Iesus gaurana waurþanana qaþ: "Hwaiwa agluba þai faihu
habandans inngaleiþand in þiudangardja Gudis! 25Raþizo allis ist ulbandau þairh þairko neþlos þairhleiþan þau
gabigamma in þiudangardja Gudis galeiþan." 26Qeþun þan þai gahausjandans: "An hwas mag ganisan?" 27Iþ is qaþ:
"Þata unmahteigo at mannam mahteig ist at Guda." 28Qaþ þan Paitrus: "Sai, weis aflailotum allata jah laistidedum
þuk." 29Iþ is qaþuh du im: "Amen, qiþa izwis þatei ni ainshun ist þize afletandane gard aiþþau fadrein aiþþau
broþruns aiþþau qen aiþþau barna in þiudangardjos Gudis, 30saei ni andnimai managfalþ in þamma mela jah in aiwa
þamma qimandin libain aiweinon."

31Ganimands þan þans .ib. qaþ du im: "Sai, usgaggam in Iairusalem, jah ustiuhada all þata gamelido þairh
praufetuns bi sunu mans. 32Atgibada auk þiudom jah bilaikada jah anamahtjada jah bispeiwada, 33jah
usbliggwandans usqimand imma, jah þridjin daga usstandiþ." 34Jah eis ni waihtai þis froþun, jah was þata waurd
gafulgin af im, jah ni wissedun þo qiþanona.

XVIII.1 *du þammei conj* to the end that, so that. *usgrudja wm* a despondent person. 2 *staua wm* judge. *aistan wv 3* to show proper respect for. 3 *fraweitan sv 1* avenge, vindicate. *andastaþjis sm* adversary. 5 *usþriutan sv 2* bother, annoy. *usagljan wv 1* wear out, drive to distraction. 6 *staua inwindiþos* for *unjust judge* is a literal rendering of the Greek ὁ κριτὴς τῆς ἀδικίας. 7 *gawrikan sv 5* vindicate, avenge, take revenge on behalf of. *usbeidan sv 1* be patient, delay long (over: *ana*). *wilwa wm* robber, *inwindai* corr. from CA *inwinda*. *hors sm* adulterer. 12 *afdailjan wv 1* divide up, apportion. *taihundo dails* one-tenth. *gastaldan sv 7* acquire, earn. 13 *slahan, sloh sv 6* strike, beat. *brusts fpl* breast, chest. *hulþ- adj* merciful. 14 *sa* is pronominal: "the latter;" *jains* = "the former." *garaihtoza gataihans* "designated" as more righteous. 15 *andbeitan sv 1* reproach, charge (not to do). 20 *maurþrjan wv 1* to murder. *hlifan sv 5* steal. *galiug sn* falsehood; as prefix: false, pseudo-. *galiugaweitwoþs* (*G -dis*) false witness. 21 *junda sf* youth. 22 *wan sn* lack. *dailjan, wv 1*, *gadailjan wv 1* (*perf*) divide up, distribute. *hiri inter* come here! come and (+ inf.)! 24 *agluba adv* with difficulty. 25 *raþizo comp adj neuter* easier. *ulbandus* camel. *þairko wn* hole; eye (of a needle). *neþla sf* needle. *þairhleiþan* corr. from CA *þairþleiþan*. 30 *managfalþ adv* many-fold. 32 *bispeiwan sv 1* to spit upon. 33 *bliggwan, usbliggwan sv 3* beat severely, scourge.

[35]Warþ þan miþþanei nehwa was is Iaireikon, blinda sums sat faur wig du aihtron. [36]Gahausjands þan managein faurgaggandein frah hwa wesi þata. [37] Gataihun þan imma þatei "Iesus Nazoraius þairhgaggiþ." [38]Iþ is ubuhwopida qiþands: "Iesus, sunu Daweidis, armai mik!" [39]Jah þai faur<a>gaggandans andbitun ina ei þahaidedi, iþ is und filu mais hropida: "Sunau Daweidis, armai mik!" [40]Gastandands þan Iesus haihait ina tiuhan du sis. Biþe nehwa was þan imma, frah ina [41]qiþands: "Hwa þus wileis ei taujau?" Iþ is qaþ: "Frauja, ei ussaihwau." [42]Jah Iesus qaþ du imma: "Ussaihw, galaubeins þeina ganasida þuk." [43]Jah suns ussahw jah laistida ina awiliudonds Guda. Jah alla managei gasaihwandei gaf hazein Guda.

Chapter XIX

[1]Jah inngaleiþands þairhlaiþ Iaireikon. [2]Jah sai, guma namin haitans Zakkaius, sah was fauramaþleis motarje jah was gabigs, [3]jah sokida gasaihwan Iesus, hwas wesi, jah ni mahta faura managein, unte wahstau leitils was. [4]Jah biþragjands faur usstaig ana smakkabagm ei gasehwi ina, unte is and þata munaida þairhgaggan. [5]Jah biþe qam ana þamma stada, insaihwands iup Iesus gasahw ina jah qaþ du imma: "Zakkaiu, sniumjands dalaþ atsteig: himma daga auk in garda þeinamma skal ik wisan." [6]Jah sniumjands atstaig jah andnam ina faginonds. [7]Jah gasaihwandans allai birodidedun, qiþandans þatei "Du frawaurhtis mans galaiþ in gard ussaljan." [8]Standands þan Zakkaius qaþ du Fraujin: "Sai, halbata aiginis meinis, Frauja, gadailja unledaim, jah jabai hwis hwa afholoda, fidurfalþ fragilda." [9]Qaþ þan du imma Iesus þatei "Himma daga naseins þamma garda warþ, unte jah sa sunus Abrahamis ist; qam auk sunus mans sokjan jah nasjan þans fralusanans."

[11]At gahausjandam þan im þata, biaukands qaþ gajukon, bi þatei nehwa Iairusalem was, jah þuhta im ei suns skulda wesi þiudangardi Gudis gaswikunþjan. [12]Qaþ þan: "Manna sums godakunds gaggida landis franiman sis þiudangardja jah gawandida sik. [13]Athaitands þan taihun skalkans seinans atgaf im taihun dailos jah qaþ du im: 'Kaupoþ, unte ik qimau.' [14]Iþ baurgjans is fijaidedun ina jah insandidedun airu afar imma qiþandans: 'Ni wileima þana þiudanon ufar unsis.' [15]Jah warþ, biþe atwandida sik aftra andnimands þiudangardja, jah haihait wopjan du sis þans skalkans þaimei atgaf þata silubr, ei gakunnaidedi hwa hwarjizuh gawaurhtedi. [16]Qam þan sa frumista qiþands: 'Frauja, skatts þeins gawaurhta taihun skattans.' Jah qaþ du imma: 'Waila, goda skalk, unte in leitilamma wast triggws, sijais waldufni habands ufar taihun baurgim.' [18]Jah qam anþar qiþands: 'Frauja, skatts þeins gawaurhta fimf skattans.' [19]Qaþ þan jah du þamma: 'Jah þu sijais ufaro fimf baurgim.' [20]Jah sums qam qiþands: 'Frauja, sai, sa skatts þeins þanei habaida galagidana in fanin. [21]Ohta mis auk þuk, unte manna hardus is. Nimis þatei ni lagides jah sneiþis þatei ni saisost.' [22]Jah qaþ du imma: 'Us munþa þeinamma stoja þuk, unselja skalk jah lata. Wisses þatei ik manna hardus im, nimands þatei ni lagida jah sneiþands þatei ni saiso. [23]Jah duhwe ni atlagides þata silubr mein du skattjam? Jah qimands miþ wokra galausidedjau þata.' [24]Jah du þaim faurastandandam qaþ: 'Nimiþ af imma þana skatt jah gibiþ þamma þos taihun dailos habandin. ([25]Jah qeþun du imma: 'Frauja, habaiþ taihun dailos.') [26]Qiþa allis izwis þatei hwarjammeh habandane gibada, iþ af þamma unhabandin jah þatei habaiþ afnimada af imma. [27]Aþþan sweþauh fijands meinans jainans, þaiei ni wildedun mik þiudanon ufar sis, briggiþ her jah usqimiþ faura mis.'" [28]Jah qiþands þata iddja fram, usggaggands in Iairusaulyma.

---

38 *ubuh-* = *ufuh-*. XIX.2 *guma wm* man. 4 *biþragjan* (*wv 1*) *faur* run on ahead. 5 *iup adv* up(ward). 7 *ussaljan wv 1* (*perf*) stop over with. The syntax of *du* ... *ussaljan* is difficult to account for; the Greek has simply παρὰ ἁμαρτωλῷ ἀνδρὶ εἰσῆλθεν καταλῦσαι. Streitberg sees *in gard* as an incorporated marginal gloss originally made to clarify an ellipsis, but this does not explain the apparent (and unique) use of *du* with the genitive to translate Greek παρά (here = *chez*). 8 *halb- adj* half. *afholon wv 2* to defraud *G* of *A*. *fidurfalþ adv* fourfold. *fragildan sv 3* pay back, compensate. 11 *gaswikunþjan wv 1* make known. 12 *godakund- adj* of noble birth. *gaggida*: the sole occurrence of a weak preterite form of *gaggan*. *franiman sv 4* receive, take. 13 *kaupon wv 2* invest, engage in trade with; based on Lat *caupo* shopkeeper. 14 *þiudanon wv 2* reign, rule. 15 *silubr sn* silver. 16 *goda*: a rare occurrence of the vocative adjective; note also *unselja* and *lata* in verse 22 below. These forms appear to be weak, although the grammars are sketchy on vocative forms. 20 *galagidana*: conjectured for CA *galagida ina* on the basis of the Greek: ἰδοὺ ἡ μνᾶ σου ἣν εἶχον **ἀποκειμένην** ἐν σουδαρίῳ (Here is your money, which I have had stored away in a towel). *fana wm* piece of cloth. 22 *lat- adj* lazy. *wisses* corr. from CA *wisseis*. 23 *atlagjan du skattam* to invest. *wokra Ds* interest (on money). 25 Verse 25 seems to be parenthetical since the nobleman of the parable is still speaking in verse 26.

29 Jah warþ, biþe nehwa was Beþsfagein jah Beþanijin, at fairgunja þatei haitada alewjo, insandida twans
siponje seinaize 30 qiþands: "Gaggats in þo wiþrawairþon haim, in þizaiei inngaggandans bigitats fulan asilaus
gabundanana, ana þammei ni ainshun aiw manne sat; andbindandans ina attiuhiþ. 31 Jah jabai hwas inqis fraihnai,
'Duhwe andbindiþ?' swa qiþaits du imma þatei Frauja þis gairneiþ." 32 Galeiþandans þan þai insandidans bigetun
swaswe qaþ du im. 33 Andbindandam þan im <þana fulan> qeþun þai fraujans þis du im: "Duhwe andbindats þana
fulan?" 34 Iþ eis qeþun: "Fraujin þaurfts þis ist." 35 Jah attauhun þana fulan Iesua jah uswairpandans wastjos seinos
ana þana fulan ussatidedun Iesu. 36 Gaggandin þan imma ufstrawidedun wastjom seinaim ana wiga. 37 Biþe þan is
nehwa was, juþan at ibdaljin þis faurgunjis alewabagme, dugunnun alakjo managei siponje faginondans hazjan Guþ
stibnai mikilai in allaizo þoze sehwun mahte, 38 qiþandans: "Þiuþida sa qimanda þiudans in namin Fraujins; gawairþi
in himina jah wulþus in hauhistjam." 39 Jah sumai Fareisaie us þizai managein qeþun du imma: "Laisari, sak þaim
siponjam þeinaim." 40 Jah andhafjands qaþ du im: "Qiþa izwis þatei jabai þai slawand, stainos hropjand." 41 Jah
sunsei nehwa was, gasaihwands þo baurg gaigrot bi þo, qiþands: 42 þatei "Iþ wissedeis jah þu in þamma daga
þeinamma þo du gawairþja þeinamma! Iþ nu gafulgin ist faura augam þeinaim, 43 þatei qimand dagos ana þus, jah
bigraband fijands þeinai grabai þuk jah bistandand þuk jah biwaibjand þuk allaþro. 44 Jah airþai þuk gaibnjand jah
barna þeina in þus jah ni letand in þus stain ana staina, in þizei ni ufkunþes þata mel niuhseinais þeinaizos."

45 Jah galeiþands in alh dugann uswairpan þans frabugjandans in izai jah bugjandans, 46 qiþands du im:
"Gameliþ ist þatei 'Gards meins gards bido ist;' iþ jus ina gatawideduþ du filegrja þiube." 47 Jah was laisjands daga
hwammeh in þizai alh, iþ þai auhmistans gudjans jah bokarjos sokidedun ina usqistjan jah þai frumistans manageins.
48 Jah ni bigetun hwa gatawidedeina; managei auk alakjo hahaida du hausjan imma.

Chapter XX

1 Jah warþ in sumamma dage jainaize at laisjandin imma þo managein in alh jah wailamerjandin, atstoþun
þai gudjans jah bokarjos miþ þaim sinistam, 2 jah qeþun du imma qiþandans: "Qiþ unsis, in hwamma waldufnje þata
taujis, aiþþau hwas ist saei gaf þus þata waldufni?" 3 Andhafjands þan qaþ du im: "Fraihna izwis jah ik ainis waurdis
jah qiþiþ mis: 4 Daupeins Iohannis uzuh himina was þau uzuh mannam?" 5 Iþ eis þahtedun miþ sis misso qiþandans
þatei "Jabai qiþam, 'Us himina,' qiþiþ, 'Aþþan duhwe ni galaubideduþ imma?' 6 Iþ jabai qiþam, 'Us mannam,' alla so
managei stainam afwairpiþ unsis. Triggwaba galaubjand auk allai Iohannen praufetu wisan." 7 Jah andhofun ei ni
wissedeina hwaþro. 8 Jah Iesus qaþ im: "Ni ik izwis qiþa, in hwamma waldufnje þata tauja."

9 Dugann þan du managein qiþan þo gajukon: "Manna ussatida weinagard, jah anafalh ina waurstwjam jah
aflaiþ jera ganoha. . 10 Jah in mela insandida du þaim aurtjam skalk, ei akranis þis weinagardis gebeina imma. Iþ þai
aurtjans usbliggwandans ina insandidedun lausana. 11 Jah anaaiauk sandjan anþarana skalk; iþ eis jah jainana
bliggwandans jah unswerandans insandidedun lausana. 12 Jah anaaiauk sandjan þridjan: iþ eis jah þana
gawundondans uswaurpun. 13 Qaþ þan sa frauja þis weinagardis: 'Hwa taujau? Sandja sunu meinana þana liuban;
aufto þana gasaihwandans aistand.' 14 Gasaihwandans þan ina þai aurtjans þahtedun miþ sis misso qiþandans: 'Sa is
sa arbinumja. Afslaham ina, ei uns wairþai þata arbi.' 15 Jah uswairpandans ina ut us þamma weinagarda usqemun.

---

28 *fram adv* forward. 29 *alewj- adj* olive-tree-, of olive trees; *alewjo* is *Ns* neuter modifying *fairguni*. 30 *fula wm* foal. *asilus sm* ass. Note the grammatical lapses (plural for dual) in *attiuhiþ* and (vs. 31) *andbindiþ*. 36 *ufstraujan wv 1* spread, strew *D* on (*ana D*). 37 *ibdaljin Ds* downward slope. *slawan wv 3* be silent. 42 *þo du gawairþja þeinamma* the things that would lead to peace for you. 43 *bigraban sv 6* surround with an embankment or palisade. *graba sf* ditch, embankment. *bistandan sv 7* surround, stand around. *allaþro adv* from all sides. *biwaibjan wv 1* to wind sthg (*D*) around *A*, surround *A*. 44 *ga-ibnjan wv 1* make level with *D*. *niuhseins sf* visitation. 46 *filigri,* filegri* sn* den, lair. *þiufs sm* (*G -bis*) thief. 47 *auhmist-* occurs several times as a variant of *auhumist-*. 48 *hahan wv 3* to hang. The Gothic here renders Gk ὁ λαὸς ἐξεκρέματο αὐτοῦ ἀκούων the people hung upon his words (lit. were suspended hearing him). XX.6 *triggwaba adv* truly. 10 *gebeina* corr. from CA *gebena*. 11 *unsweran wv 3* to dishonor, treat shamefully. 12 *gawundon wv 2* to wound, injure.

Hwa nu taujai im frauja þis weinagardis? [16]Qimiþ jah usqisteiþ aurtjam þaim jah gibiþ þana weinagard anþaraim."
Gahausjandans qeþun þan: "Nissijai." [17]Iþ is insaihwands du im qaþ: "Aþþan hwa ist þata gamelido:

'Stains þammei uskusun timrjans,
sah warþ du haubida waihstins?'

[18]Hwazuh saei driusiþ ana þana stain gakrotoda; iþ ana þanei driusiþ, diswinþeiþ ina."

[19]Jah sokidedun þai bokarjos jah auhumistans gudjans uslagjan ana ina handuns in þizai hweilai jah ohtedun
þo managein; froþun auk þatei du im þo gajukon qaþ. [20]Jah afleiþandans insandidedun ferjans, þans us liutein
taiknjandans sik garaihtans wisan, ei gafaifaheina is waurdei jah atgebeina ina reikja jah waldufnja kindinis. [21]Jah
frehun ina qiþandans: "Laisari, witum þatei raihtaba rodeis jah laiseis jah ni andsaihwis andwairþi, ak bi sunjai wig
Gudis laiseis: [22]Skuldu is unsis kaisara gild giban þau niu?" [23]Bisaihwands þan ize unselein Iesus qaþ du im: "Hwa
mik fraisiþ? [24]Ataugeiþ mis skatt. Hwis habaiþ manleikan jah ufarmeli?" Andhafjandans þan qeþun: "Kaisaris."
[25]Iþ is qaþuh du im: "Usnugibiþ þo Kaisaris Kaisara jah þo Gudis Guda." [26]Jah ni mahtedun gafahan is waurde in
andwairþja manageins jah sildaleikjandans andawaurde is gaþahaidedun.

[27]Duatgaggandans þan sumai Saddukaie, þaiei qiþand usstass ni wisan, frehun ina [28]qiþandans: "Laisari,
Moses gamelida uns, jabai hwis broþar gadauþnai aigands qen, jah sa unbarnahs gadauþnai, ei nimai broþar is þo
qen jah urraisjai fraiw broþr seinamma. [29]Sibun nu broþrjus wesun, jah sa frumista nimands qen gadauþnoda
unbarnahs. [30] Jah nam anþar þo qen, jah sa gaswalt unbarnahs. [31]Jah þridja nam þo samaleiko; samaleiko þan jah
þai sibun, jah ni biliþun barne jah gaswultun. [32]Spedista allaize gadauþnoda jah so qens. [33]In þizai usstassai nu,
hwarjis þize wairþiþ qens? Þai auk sibun aihtedun þo du qenai."

[34]Jah andhafjands qaþ du im Iesus: "Þai sunjus þis aiwis liugand jah liuganda; [35]iþ þaiei wairþai sind jainis
aiwis niutan jah usstassais us dauþaim ni liugand ni liuganda; [36]nih allis gaswiltan þanaseiþs magun, ibnans aggilum
auk sind jah sunjus sind Gudis, usstassais sunjus wisandans. [37]Aþþan þatei urreisand dauþans, jah Moses bandwida
ana aihwatundjai, swe qiþiþ: 'Sahw Fraujan Guþ Abrahamis jah Guþ Isakis jah Guþ Iakobis.' [38]Aþþan Guþ nist
dauþaize, ak qiwaize; allai auk imma liband." [39]Andhafjandans þan sumai þize bokarje qeþun: "Laisari, waila qast."
[40]Niþþan þanaseiþs gadaurstedun fraihnan ina ni waihtais.

[41]Qaþ þan du im: "Hwaiwa qiþand Xristu sunu Daweidis wisan? [42]Jah silba Daweid qiþiþ in bokom
Psalmo: 'Qaþ Frauja du Fraujin meinamma: sit af taihswon meinai, [43]unte ik galagja fijands þeinans fotubaurd fotiwe
þeinaize.' [44]Daweid ina 'Fraujan' haitiþ, jah hwaiwa sunus imma ist?" [45]At gahausjandein þan allai managein qaþ du
siponjam seinaim: [46]"Atsaihwiþ faura bokarjam þaim wiljandam gaggan in hweitaim ... [The remainder of the
Gospel of Luke is missing.]

---

14 ***arbinumja*** *wm* heir. ***afslahan*** *sv 6* kill, slay. ***arbi*** *sn* inheritance. 16 ***nissijai*** = ***nih sijai.*** 17 ***waihsta*** *wm* corner. ***haubiþ waihstins*** corner-stone. 18 ***gakrotoda*** corr. from CA ***gakrotuda. gakroton*** *wv 2* smash, crush. ***diswinþjan*** *wv 1* crush. 19 ***du im*** against them, i.e. the scribes and chief priests. 20 ***ferja**** *wm* spy. ***liutei*** *wf* hypocrisy, guile. ***taiknjan*** *wv 1* point out, indicate; + ***sik*** act as. ***waurdei*** for ***waurde. fahan*** *sv 2* (pret. ***faifah***), ***gafahan*** *sv 7* (*perf*) catch, seize ***gafahan is waurde*** occurs only here and in verse 26 below. It is a verbatim rendering of Gk ἐπιλαμβάνομαι + *G* of person + *G* of thing = to catch someone up with something. The Greek construction is rare, attested only in these two places. ***reiki*** *sn* power, rule, authority. 21 ***andsaihwan andwairþi*** to show partiality (lit. take note of face). 22 ***gild*** *sn* tax, tribute. 23 ***unselei*** *wf* wickedness, craftiness. 24 ***manleika*** *wm* likeness, image. ***ufarmeli*** *sn* inscription. 26 ***andawaurde*** is probably for *A* ***andawaurdi.*** 28 ***unbarnah-*** *adj* childless. 35 ***niutan*** *sv 2* reach, attain *G*. 37 ***bandwida*** corr. from CA ***banwida. aihwatundi*** *sf* thornbush. 38 ***qiu-*** *adj* alive, living. 42 ***Psalmo*** *Gpl* psalms < Gk ψαλμός. The other attested forms of this irregular noun are *As psalmon, Dpl psalmom.* 43 ***fotubaurd*** *sn* footboard, footstool.

Aiwaggeljo þairh Marku anastodeiþ:

Chapter I

1 Anastodeins aiwaggeljons Iesuis Xristaus sunaus Gudis. 2 Swe gameliþ ist in Esaiin praufetau:

"Sai, ik insandja aggilu meinana faura þus,
saei gamanweiþ wig þeinana faura þus.
3 Stibna wopjandins in auþidai:
manweiþ wig Fraujins;
raihtos waurkeiþ staigos Gudis unsaris."

4 Was Iohannes daupjands in auþidai jah merjands daupein idreigos du aflageinai frawaurhte. 5 Jah usiddjedun du imma all Iudaialand jah Iairusaulymeis, jah daupidai wesun allai in Iaurdane ahwai fram imma, andhaitandans frawaurhtim seinaim. 6 Wasuþ-þan Iohannes gawasiþs taglam ulbandaus jah gairda filleina bi hup seinana, jah matida þramsteins jah miliþ haiþiwisk.[1] 7 Jah merida qiþands: "Qimiþ swinþoza mis sa afar mis, þizei ik ni im wairþs anahneiwands andbindan skaudaraip skohe is. 8 Aþþan ik daupja izwis in watin, iþ is daupeiþ izwis in ahmin weihamma.

9 Jah warþ in jainaim dagam, qam Iesus fram Nazaraiþ Galeilaias, jah daupiþs was fram Iohanne in Iaurdane. 10 Jah suns usgaggands us þamma watin gasahw usluknans[2] himinans jah ahman swe ahak atgaggandan ana ina. 11 Jah stibna qam us himinam: "Þu is sunus meins sa liuba, in þuzei waila galeikaida."[3]

12 Jah suns sai, ahma ina ustauh in auþida. 13 Jah was in þizai auþidai dage fidwor tiguns fraisans fram Satanin, jah was miþ diuzam, jah aggileis andbahtidedun imma. 14 Iþ afar þatei atgibans warþ Iohannes, qam Iesus in Galeilaia merjands aiwaggeljon þiudangardjos Gudis, 15 qiþands þatei "Usfullnoda þata mel jah atnehwida sik þiudangardi Gudis. Idreigoþ jah galaubeiþ in aiwaggeljon."

16 Jah hwarbonds faur marein Galeilaias gasahw Seimonu jah Andraian broþar is, þis Seimonis, wairpandans nati in marein: wesun auk fiskjans. 17 Jah qaþ im Iesus: "Hirjats afar mis, jah gatauja igqis wairþan nutans manne." 18 Jah suns afletandans þo natja seina laistidedun afar imma. 19 Jah jainþro inngaggands framis leitil[4] gasahw Iakobu þana Zaibaidaiaus jah Iohanne broþar is, jah þans in skipa manwjandans natja. 20 Jah suns haihait ins. Jah afletandans attan seinana Zaibaidaiu in þamma skipa miþ asnjam, galiþun afar imma.

21 Jah galiþun in Kafarnaum, jah suns sabbato daga galeiþands in synagogen laisida ins. 22 Jah usfilmans waurþun ana þizai laiseinai is, unte was laisjands ins swe waldufni habands jah ni swaswe þai bokarjos. 23 Jah was in þizai synagogen ize manna in unhrainjamma ahmin, jah ufhropida 24 qiþands: "Fralet, hwa uns jah þus, Iesu Nazorenai? Qamt fraqistjan uns? Kann þuk, hwas þu is, sa weiha Gudis." 25 Jah andbait ina Iesus qiþands: "Þahai, jah usgagg ut us þamma, ahma unhrainja." 26 Jah tahida ina ahma sa unhrainja, jah hropjands stibnai mikilai usiddja us imma. 27 Jah afslauþnodedun allai sildaleikjandans, swaei sokidedun miþ sis misso qiþandans: "Hwa sijai þata? Hwo so laiseino so niujo, ei miþ waldufnja jah ahmam þaim unhrainjam anabiudiþ jah ufhausjand imma?" 28 Usiddja þan meriþa is suns and allans bisitands Galeilaias.

29 Jah suns us þizai synagogen usgaggandans qemun in garda Seimonis ja Andraiins miþ Iakobau jah Iohannen. 30 Iþ swaihro Seimonis lag in brinnon, jah suns qeþun imma bi ija. 31 Jah duatgaggands urraisida þo undgreipands handu izos, jah aflailot þo so brinno suns, jah andbahtida im.

32 Andanahtja þan waurþanamma, þan gasaggq sauil, berun du imma allans þans ubil habandans jah unhulþons habandans. 33 Jah so baurgs alla garunnana was at daura. 34 Jah gahailida managans ubil habandans missaleikaim sauhtim, jah unhulþons managos uswarp, jah ni fralailot rodjan þos unhulþons, unte kunþedun ina.

35 Jah air uhtwon usstandands usiddja, jah galaiþ ana auþjana staþ, jah jainar baþ. 36 Jah galaistans waurþun imma Seimon jah þai miþ imma. 37 Jah

[1] There is a marginal gloss to *haiþiwisk: wilþi.*

[2] If from *uslukan* (transitive), read *uslukanans*; if from *usluknan* (intransitive), read *usluknandans.*

[3] There is a marginal gloss to the last clause: *þukei wilda.*

[4] Streitberg has *leit<ilat>a*; it is not clear whether the ms has *leita* or *leit....a.* One expects simply *leitil*, as elsewhere; an adverbial fem. acc. *leitila* would presuppose a suppressed noun of extent.

bigitandans ina qeþun du imma þatei "Allai þuk sokjand." 38Jah qaþ du im: "Gaggam du þaim bisunjane haimom[5] jah baurgim, ei jah jainar merjau, unte duþe qam. 39Jah was merjands in synagogim ize and alla Galeilaian jah unhulþons uswairpands.

40Jah qam at imma þrutsfill habands, bidjands ina jah kniwam knussjands jah qiþands du imma þatei "Jabai wileis, magt mik gahrainjan." 41Iþ Iesus infeinands, ufrakjands handu seina attaitok imma jah qaþ imma: "Wiljau. Wairþ hrains." 42Jah biþe qaþ þata Iesus, suns þata þrutsfill aflaiþ af imma, jah hrains warþ. 43Jah gahwotjands imma suns ussandida ina, 44jah qaþ du imma: "Saihw, ei mannhun ni qiþais waiht; ak gagg þuk silban ataugjan gudjin, jah atbair fram gahraineinai þeinai þatei anabauþ Moses du weitwotiþai im." 45Iþ is usgaggands dugann merjan filu jah usqiþan þata waurd, swaswe is juþan ni mahta andaugjo in baurg galeiþan, ak uta ana auþjaim stadim was; jah iddjedun du imma allaþro.

Chapter II

1Jah galaiþ aftra in Kafarnaum afar dagans, jah gafrehun þatei in garda ist. 2Jah suns gaqemun managai swaswe juþan ni gamostedun nih at daura, jah rodida im waurd. 3Jah qemun at imma usliþan bairandans, hafanana fram fidworim.[6] 4Jah ni magandans nehwa qiman imma faura manageim, andhulidedun hrot þarei was Iesus, jah usgrabandans insailidedun þata badi jah fralailotun ana þammei lag sa usliþa. 5Gasaihwands þan Iesus galaubein ize qaþ du þamma usliþin: "Barnilo, afletanda þus frawaurhteis þeinos." 6Wesunuh þan sumai þize bokarje jainar sitandans jah þagkjandans sis in hairtam seinaim: 7"Hwa sa swa rodeiþ naiteinins? Hwas mag afletan frawaurhtins niba ains Guþs?" 8Jah suns ufkunnands Iesus ahmin seinamma þatei swa þai mitodedun sis, qaþ du im: "Duhwe mitoþ þata in hairtam izwaraim? 9Hwaþar ist azetizo du qiþan þamma usliþin, 'Afletanda[7] þus frawaurhteis þeinos,' þau qiþan, 'Urreis jah nim þata badi þeinata jah gagg'? 10Aþþan ei witeiþ þatei waldufni habaiþ sunus mans ana airþai afletan frawaurhtins..." Qaþ du þamma usliþin: 11"Þus qiþa: urreis nimuh þata badi þein jah gagg du garda þeinamma." 12Jah urrais suns jah ushafjands badi usiddja faura andwairþja allaize, swaswe usgeisnodedun allai jah hauhidedun mikiljandans Guþ, qiþandans þatei aiw swa ni gasehwun.

13Jah galaiþ aftra faur marein, jah all manageins iddjedun du imma, jah laisida ins. 14Jah hwarbonds gasahw Laiwwi þana Alfaiaus sitandan at motai, jah qaþ du imma: "Gagg afar mis." Jah usstandands iddja afar imma.

15Jah warþ, biþe is anakumbida in garda is, jah managai motarjos jah frawaurhtai miþanakumbidedun Iesua jah siponjam is; wesun auk managai, jah iddjedun afar imma. 16Jah þai bokarjos jah Fareisaieis gasaihwandans ina matjandan miþ þaim motarjam jah frawaurhtaim, qeþun du þaim siponjam is: "Hwa ist þatei miþ motarjam jah frawaurhtaim matjiþ jah driggkiþ?" 17Jah gahausjands Iesus qaþ du im: "Ni þaurbun swinþai lekeis, ak þai ubilaba habandans; ni qam laþon uswaurhtans, ak frawaurhtans."

18Jah wesun siponjos Iohannis jah Fareisaieis fastandans; jah atiddjedun jah qeþun du imma: "Duhwe siponjos Iohannes jah Fareisaieis fastand, iþ þai þeinai siponjos ni fastand?" 19Jah qaþ im Iesus: "Ibai magun sunjus bruþfadis, und þatei miþ im ist bruþfaþs, fastan? Swa lagga hweila swe miþ sis haband bruþfad, ni magun fastan. 20Aþþan atgaggand dagos þan afnimada af im sa bruþfaþs, jah þan fastand in jainamma daga. 21Ni manna plat fanins niujis siujiþ ana snagan fairnjana; ibai afnimai fullon af þamma sa niuja þamma fairnjin, jah wairsiza gataura wairþiþ. 22Ni manna giutiþ wein juggata in balgins fairnjans; ibai aufto distairai wein þata niujo þans balgins, jah wein usgutniþ, jah þai balgeis fraqistnand; ak wein juggata in balgins niujans giutand."

23Jah warþ þairhgaggan imma sabbato daga þairh atisk, jah dugunnun siponjos is skewjandans raupjan ahsa. 24Jah Fareisaieis qeþun du imma: "Sai, hwa taujand siponjos þeinai sabbatim þatei ni skuld ist." 25Jah is qaþ du im: "Niu ussuggwuþ aiw hwa gatawida Daweid, þan þaurfta ja gredags was, is jah þai miþ imma, 26hwaiwa galaiþ in gard Gudis uf Abiaþara gudjin jah hlaibans faurlageinais matida, þanzei ni skuld ist matjan niba ainaim gudjam, jah gaf jah þaim miþ sis wisandam?"

---

[5] Corrected from CA *haimon.*

[6] Corrected from CA *fidworin.*

[7] Corrected from CA *afleþanda.*

[27]Jah qaþ im: "Sabbato in mans warþ gaskapans, ni manna in sabbato dagis; [28]swaei frauja ist sa sunus mans jah þamma sabbato."

Chapter III

[1]Jah galaiþ aftra in synagogen, jah was jainar manna gaþaursana habands handu. [2]Jah witaidedun imma hailidediu sabbato daga, ei wrohidedeina ina. [3]Jah qaþ du þamma mann þamma gaþaursana habandin handu: "Urreis in midumai." [4]Jah qaþ du im: "Skuldu ist in sabbatim þiuþ taujan aiþþau unþiuþ taujan, saiwala nasjan aiþþau usqistjan?" Iþ eis þahaidedun. [5]Jah ussaihwands ins miþ moda, gaurs in daubiþos hairtins ize, qaþ du þamma mann: "Ufrakei þo handu þeina!" Jah ufrakida, jah gastoþ aftra so handus is. [6]Jah gaggandans þan Fareisaieis sunsaiw miþ þaim Herodianum garuni gatawidedun bi ina, ei imma usqemeina.

[7]Jah Iesus aflaiþ miþ siponjam seinaim du marein, jah filu manageins us Galeilaia laistidedun afar imma, [8]jah us Iudaia jah us Iairusaulymim jah us Idumaia jah hindana Iaurdanaus; jah þai bi Tyra jah Seidona, manageins filu, gahausjandans hwan filu is tawida, qemun at imma. [9]Jah qaþ þaim siponjam seinaim ei skip habaiþ wesi at imma in þizos manageins, ei ni þraiheina ina. [10]Managans auk gahailida, swaswe drusun ana ina ei imma attaitokeina, jah swa managai swe habaidedun wundufnjos [11]jah ahmans unhrainjans, þaih þan ina gasehwun, drusun du imma jah hropidedun qiþandans þatei, "Þu is sunus Gudis." [12]Jah filu andbait ins ei ina ni gaswikunþidedeina.

[13]Jah usstaig[8] in fairguni jah athaihait þanzei wilda is, jah galiþun du imma. [14]Jah gawaurhta twalif du wisan miþ sis, jah ei insandidedi ins merjan, [15]jah haban waldufni du hailjan sauhtins jah uswairpan unhulþons. [16]Jah gasatida Seimona namo Paitrus; [17]jah Iakobau þamma Zaibaidaiaus, jah Iohanne broþr Iakobaus, jah gasatida im namna Bauanairgais, þatei ist: sunjus þeihwons. [18]Jah Andraian jah Filippu ja Barþaulaumaiu jah Matþaiu jah Þoman jah Iakobu þana Alfaiaus, jah Þaddaiu jah Seimona þana Kananeiten, [19]jah Iudan Iskarioten, saei jah galewida ina.

[20]Jah atiddjedun in gard, jah gaiddja sik managei swaswe ni mahtedun nih hlaif matjan. [21]Jah hausjandans fram imma bokarjos jah anþarai usiddjedun gahaban ina; qeþun auk þatei usgaisiþs ist. [22]Jah bokarjos þai af Iairusaulymai qimandans qeþun þatei Baiailzaibul habaiþ jah þatei in þamma reikistin unhulþono uswairpiþ þaim unhulþom. [23]Jah athaitands ins in gajukom qaþ du im: "Hwaiwa mag Satanas Satanan uswairpan? [24]Jah jabai þiudangardi wiþra sik gadailjada, ni mag standan so þiudangardi jaina. [25]Jah jabai gards wiþra sik gadailjada, ni mag standan sa gards jains. [26]Jah jabai Satana usstoþ ana sik silban jah gadailiþs warþ, ni mag gastandan, ak andi habaiþ. [27]Ni manna mag kasa swinþis galeiþands in gard is wilwan, niba fauris þana swinþan gabindiþ; jah <þan> þana gard is diswilwai.

[28]"Amen qiþa izwis þatei allata afletada þata frawaurhte sunum manne, jah naiteinos swa managos swaswe wajamerjand; [29]aþþan saei wajamereiþ ahman weihana ni habaiþ fralet aiw, ak skula ist aiweinaizos frawaurhtais." --[30]Unte qeþun: "Ahman unhrainjana habaiþ." [31]Jah qemun þan aiþei is jah broþrjus is jah uta standandona insandidedun du imma, haitandona ina. [32]Jah setun bi ina managei; qeþun þan du imma: "Sai, aiþei þeina jah broþrjus þeinai jah swistrjus þeinos uta sokjand þuk." [33]Jah andhof im qiþands: "Hwo ist so aiþei meina aiþþau þai broþrjus meinai?" [34]Jah bisaihwands bisunjane þans bi sik sitandans qaþ: "Sai, aiþei meina jah þai broþrjus meinai. [35]Saei allis waurkeiþ wiljan Gudis, sa jah broþar meins jah swistar jah aiþei ist."

Chapter IV

[1]Jah aftra Iesus dugann laisjan at marein, jah galesun sik du imma manageins filu, swaswe ina galeiþan in skip gasitan in marein; jah alla so managei wiþra marein ana staþa was. [2]Jah laisida ins in gajukom manag, jah qaþ im in laiseinai seinai: [3]"Hauseiþ! Sai, urrann sa saiands du saian fraiwa seinamma. [4]Jah warþ, miþþanei saiso, sum raihtis gadraus faur wig, jah qemun

[8] Corrected from CA *ustaig*.

fuglos jah fretun þata. 5Anþaruþþan gadraus ana stainahamma, þarei ni habaida airþa managa, jah suns urrann, in þizei ni habaida diupaizos airþos, 6at sunnin þan urrinnandin ufbrann, jah unte ni habaida waurtins, gaþaursnoda. 7Jah sum gadraus in þaurnuns; jah ufarstigun þai þaurnjus jah afhwapidedun þata, jah akran ni gaf. 8Jah sum gadraus in airþa goda, jah gaf akran urrinnando jah wahsjando, jah bar ain .l. jah ain .j. jah ain .r.." 9Jah qaþ: "Saei habai ausona hausjandona, gahausjai."

10Iþ biþe warþ sundro, frehun ina þai bi ina miþ þaim twalibim þizos gajukons. 11Jah qaþ im: "Izwis atgiban ist kunnan runa þiudangardjos Gudis, iþ jainaim þaim uta in gajukon allata wairþiþ, 12ei saihwandans saihwaina jah ni gaumjaina, jah hausjandans hausjaina jah ni fraþjaina, nibai hwan gawandjaina sik jah afletaindau im frawaurhteis." 13Jah qaþ du im: "Ni wituþ þo gajukon, jah hwaiwa allos þos gajukons kunneiþ? 14Sa saijands waurd saijiþ. 15Aþþan þai wiþra wig sind, þarei saiada þata waurd, jah þan gahausjand unkarjans, suns qimiþ Satanas jah usnimiþ waurd þata insaiano in hairtam ize. 16Jah sind samaleiko þai ana stainahamma saianans, þaiei þan hausjand þata waurd, suns miþ fahedai nimand ita, 17jah ni haband waurtins in sis, ak hweilahwairbai sind; þaþroh, biþe qimiþ aglo aiþþau wrakja in þis waurdis, suns gamarzjanda. 18Jah þai sind þai in þaurnuns saianans, þai waurd hausjandans, 19jah saurgos þizos libainais jah afmarzeins gabeins jah þai bi þata anþar lustjus innatgaggandans afhwapjand þata waurd jah akranalaus wairþiþ. 20Jah þai sind þai ana airþai þizai godon saianans, þaiei hausjand þata waurd jah andnimand, jah akran bairand, ain .l. jah ain .j. jah ain .r.."

21Jah qaþ du im: "Ibai lukarn qimiþ duþe ei uf melan satjaidau aiþþau undar ligr? Niu ei ana lukarnastaþan satjaidau? 22Nih allis ist hwa fulginis þatei ni gabairhtjaidau: nih warþ analaugn, ak ei swikunþ wairþai. 23Jabai hwas habai ausona hausjandona, gahausjai." 24Jah qaþ du im: "Saihwiþ hwa hauseiþ! In þizaiei mitaþ mitiþ, mitada izwis jah biaukada izwis þaim galaubjandam. 25Unte þishwammeh saei habaiþ gibada imma; jah saei ni habaiþ jah þatei habaiþ afnimada imma."

26Jah qaþ: "Swa is þiudangardi Gudis, swaswe jabai manna wairpiþ fraiwa ana airþa, 27jah slepiþ jah urreisiþ naht jah daga, jah þata fraiw keiniþ jah liudiþ, swe ni wait is. 28Silbo auk airþa akran bairiþ: frumist gras, þaþroh ahs, þaþroh fulleiþ kaurnis in þamma ahsa. 29Þanuh biþe atgibada akran, suns insandeiþ gilþa, unte atist asans." 30Jah qaþ: "Hwe galeikom þiudangardja Gudis, aiþþau in hwileikai gajukon gabairam þo? 31Swe kaurno sinapis, þatei þan saiada ana airþa, minnist allaize fraiwe ist þize ana airþai; 32jah þan saiada, urrinniþ, jah wairþiþ allaize grase maist, jah gataujiþ astans mikilans, swaswe magun uf skadau is fuglos himinis gabauan.

33Jah swaleikaim managaim gajukom rodida du im þata waurd, swaswe mahtedun hausjon. 34Iþ inuh gajukon ni rodida im, iþ sundro siponjam seinaim andband allata.

35Jah qaþ du im in jainamma daga at andanahtja þan waurþanamma: "Usleiþam jainis stadis." 36Jah afletandans þo managein andnemun ina, swe was, in skipa; jah þan anþara skipa wesun miþ imma. 37Jah warþ skura windis mikila jah wegos waltidedun in skip, swaswe ita juþan gafullnoda. 38Jah was is ana notin ana waggarja slepands, jah urraisidedun ina jah qeþun du imma: "Laisari, niu kara þuk þizei fraqistnam?" 39Jah urreisands gasok winda jah qaþ du marein: "Gaslawai, afdumbn!" Jah anasilaida sa winds, jah warþ wis mikil. 40Jah qaþ du im: "Duhwe faurhtai sijuþ swa? Hwaiwa ni nauh habaiþ galaubein?" 41Jah ohtedun sis agis mikil, jah qeþun du sis misso: "Hwas þannu sa sijai, unte jah winds jah marei ufhausjand imma?"

Chapter V

1Jah qemun hindar marein in landa Gaddarene. 2Jah usgaggandin imma us skipa suns gamotida imma manna us aurahjom in ahmin unhrainjamma, 3saei bauain habaida in aurahjom: jah ni naudibandjom eisarneinaim manna mahta ina gabindan. 4Unte is ufta eisarnam bi fotuns gabuganaim jah naudibandjom eisarneinaim gabundans was, jah galausida af sis þos naudibandjos, jah þo ana fotum eisarna gabrak, jah manna ni mahta ina gatamjan. 5Jah sinteino nahtam jah dagam in aurahjom jah in fairgunjam was hropjands jah bliggwands sik stainam. 6Gasaihwands[9] þan Iesu fairraþro rann jah inwait ina, 7jah hropjands stibnai mikilai qaþ "Hwa mis jah þus, Iesu, sunau Gudis þis hauhistins? Biswara þuk bi Guda, ni balwjais mis!"

9 Corrected from CA *gasaisaihwands.*

8Unte qaþ imma: "Usgagg, ahma unhrainja, us þamma mann!" 9Jah frah ina: "Hwa namo þein? Jah qaþ du imma: "Namo mein Laigaion, unte managai sijum." 10Jah baþ ina filu ei ni usdrebi im us landa. 11Wasuh þan jainar hairda sweine haldana at þamma fairgunja. 12Jah bedun ina allos þos unhulþons qiþandeins: "Insandei unsis in þo sweina ei in þo galeiþaima." 13Jah uslaubida im Iesus suns. Jah usgaggandans ahmans þai unhrainjans galiþun in þo sweina, jah rann so hairda and driuson in marein; wesunuþþan swe twos þusundjos, jah afhwapnodedun in marein.

14Jah þai haldandans þo sweina gaþlauhun, jah gataihun in baurg jah in haimom, jah qemun saihwan hwa wesi þata waurþano. 15Jah atiddjedun du Iesua, jah gasaihwand þana wodan sitandan jah gawasidana jah fraþjandan, þana saei habaida laigaion, jah ohtedun. 16Jah spillodedun im þaiei gasehwun, hwaiwa warþ bi þana wodan jah bi þo sweina. 17Jah dugunnun bidjan ina galeiþan hindar markos seinos. 18Jah inngaggandan ina in skip baþ ina, saei was wods, ei miþ imma wesi. 19Jah ni lailot ina, ak qaþ du imma: "Gagg du garda þeinamma du þeinaim, jah gateih im hwan filu þus Frauja gatawida jah gaarmaida þuk." 20Jah galaiþ jah dugann merjan in Daikapaulein, hwan filu gatawida imma Iesus; jah allai sildaleikidedun. 21Jah usleiþandin Iesua in skipa aftra hindar marein, gaqemun sik manageins filu du imma, jah was faura marein. 22Jah sai, qimiþ ains þize synagogafade namin Jaeirus; jah saihwands ina gadraus du fotum Iesuis, 23jah baþ ina filu, qiþands þatei "Dauhtar meina aftumist habaiþ, ei qimands lagjais ana þo handuns, ei ganisai jah libai." 24Jah galaiþ miþ imma, jah iddjedun afar imma manageins filu jah þraihun ina.

25Jah qinono suma wisandei in runa bloþis jera twalif, 26jah manag gaþulandei fram managaim lekjam jah fraqimandei allamma seinamma jah ni waihtai botida, ak mais wairs habaida, 27gahausjandei bi Iesu, atgaggandei in managein aftana attaitok wastjai is. 28Unte qaþ þatei "Jabai wastjom is atteka, ganisa." 29Jah sunsaiw gaþaursnoda sa brunna bloþis izos, jah ufkunþa ana leika þatei gahailnoda af þamma slaha. 30Jah sunsaiw Iesus ufkunþa in sis silbin þo us sis maht usgaggandein; gawandjands sik in managein qaþ: "Hwas mis taitok wastjom?" 31Jah qeþun du imma siponjos is: "Saihwis þo managein þreihandein þuk jah qiþis: 'Hwas mis taitok?'" 32Jah wlaitoda saihwan þo þata taujandein. 33Iþ so qino ogandei jah reirandei, witandei þatei warþ bi ija, qam jah draus du imma, jah qaþ imma alla þo sunja. 34Iþ is qaþ du izai: "Dauhtar, galaubeins þeina ganasida þuk; gagg in gawairþi, jah sijais haila af þamma slaha þeinamma."

35Nauhþanuh imma rodjandin qemun fram þamma synagogafada, qiþandans þatei "Dauhtar þeina gaswalt. Hwa þanamais draibeis þana laisari?" 36Iþ Iesus sunsaiw gahausjands þata waurd rodiþ, qaþ du þamma synagogafada: "Ni faurhtei; þatainei galaubei." 37Jah ni fralailot ainohun ize miþ sis afargaggan, nibai Paitru jah Iakobu jah Iohannen broþar Iakobis. 38Jah galaiþ in gard þis synagogafadis, jah gasahw auhjodu jah gretandans jah waifairhwjandans filu. 39Jah inn-atgaggands qaþ du im: "Hwa auhjoþ jah gretiþ? Þata barn ni gadauþnoda, ak slepiþ. 40Jah bihlohun ina. Iþ is uswairpands allaim ganimiþ attan þis barnis jah aiþein jah þans miþ sis, jah galaiþ inn þarei was þata barn ligando. 41Jah fairgraip bi handau þata barn, qaþuh du izai: "Taleiþa kumei." (þatei ist gaskeiriþ: "Mawilo, du þus qiþa: urreis.") 42Jah suns urrais so mawi jah iddja; was auk jere twalibe; jah usgeisnodedun faurhtein mikilai. 43Jah anabauþ im filu ei manna ni funþi þata; jah haihait izai giban matjan.

Chapter VI

1Jah usstoþ jainþro jah qam in landa seinamma, jah laistidedun afar imma siponjos is. 2Jah biþe warþ sabbato, dugann in synagoge laisjan, jah managai hausjandans sildaleikidedun qiþandans: "Hwaþro þamma þata, jah hwo so handugeino so gibano imma, ei mahteis swaleikos þairh handuns is wairþand? 3Niu þata ist sa timrja, sa sunus Marjins, iþ broþar Iakoba[10] jah Iuse jah Iudins jah Seimonis? Jah niu sind swistrjus is her at unsis?" Jah gamarzidai waurþun in þamma. 4Qaþ þan im Iesus þatei "Nist praufetus unswers, niba in gabaurþai seinai jah in ganiþjam jah in garda seinamma." 5Jah ni mahta jainar ainohum mahte gataujan, niba fawaim siukaim handuns galagjands gahailida. 6Jah sildaleikida in ungalaubeinais ize, jah bitauh weihsa bisunjane laisjands.

7Jah athaihait þans twalif jah dugann ins insandjan twans hwanzuh, jah gaf im waldufni ahmane unhrainjaize. 8Jah faurbauþ im ei waiht ni nemeina in wig, niba hrugga aina, nih matibalg nih hlaif nih in

[10]One expects the genitives *Iakobaus* (or *Iakobis*) and *Iosezis* here as elsewhere.

gairdos aiz, [9]ak gaskohai suljom; "Jah ni wasjaiþ twaim paidom." [10]Jah qaþ du im: "Þishwaduh þei gaggaiþ in gard, þar saljaiþ, unte usgaggaiþ[11] jainþro. [11]Jah swa managai swe ni andnimaina izwis nih hausjaina izwis, usgaggandans jainþro ushrisjaiþ mulda þo undaro fotum izwaraim du weitwodiþai im. Amen qiþa izwis: sutizo ist Saudaumjam aiþþau Gaumaurjam in daga stauos þau þizai baurg jainai.[12]" [12]Jah usgaggandans meridedun ei idreigodedeina. [13]Jah unhulþons managos usdribun, jah gasalbodedun alewa managans siukans, jah gahailidedun.

[14]Jah gahausida þiudans Herodes -- swikunþ allis warþ namo is -- jah qaþ þatei "Iohannis sa daupjands us dauþaim urrais; duþþe waurkjand þos mahteis in imma." [15]Anþarai þan qeþun þatei "Helias ist;" anþarai þan qeþun þatei "Praufetes ist swe ains þize praufete." [16]Gahausjands þan Herodes qaþ þatei "Þammei ik haubiþ afmaimait Iohanne sa ist: sah urrais us dauþaim". [17]Sa auk raihtis Herodes insandjands gahabaida Iohannen jah gaband ina in karkarai in Hairodiadins qenais Filippaus broþrs seinis, unte þo galiugaida. [18]Qaþ auk Iohannes du Heroda þatei, "Ni skuld is þus haban qen broþrs þeinis." [19]Iþ so Herodia naiw imma jah wilda imma usqiman, jah ni mahta, [20]unte Herodis ohta sis Iohannen, kunnands ina wair garaihtana jah weihana, jah witaida imma, jah hausjands imma manag gatawida, jah gabaurjaba imma andhausida. [21]Jah waurþans dags gatils, þan Herodis mela gabaurþais seinaizos nahtamat waurhta þaim maistam seinaize jah þusundifadim jah þaim frumistam Galeilaias, [22]jah atgaggandein inn dauhtar[13] Herodiadins jah plinsjandein jah galeikandein Heroda jah þaim miþanakumbjandam qaþ þiudans du þizai maujai: "Bidei mik þishwizuh þei wileis, jah giba þus." [23]Jah swor izai þatei, "Þishwah þei bidjais mik, giba þus und halba þiudangardja meina." [24]Iþ si usgaggandei qaþ du aiþein seinai: "Hwis bidjau." Iþ si qaþ: "Haubidis Iohannis þis daupjandins." [25]Jah atgaggandei sunsaiw sniumundo du þamma þiudana baþ qiþandei: "Wiljau ei mis gibais ana mesa haubiþ Iohannis þis daupjandins." [26]Jah gaurs waurþans sa þiudans in þize aiþe jah in þize miþanakumbjandane ni wilda izai ufbrikan. [27]Jah suns insandjands sa þiudans spaikulatur, anabauþ briggan haubiþ is. Iþ is galeiþands afmaimait imma haubiþ in karkarai, [28]jah atbar þata haubiþ is ana mesa, jah atgaf ita þizai maujai, jah so mawi atgaf ita aiþein seinai. [29]Jah gahausjandans siponjos is qemun jah usnemun leik is jah galagidedun ita in hlaiwa. [30]Jah gaiddjedun apaustauleis du Iesua jah gataihun imma allata jah swa filu swe gatawidedun... (vss. 30b-53a are missing) [53]... jah duatsniwun.

[54]Jah usgaggandam im us skipa, sunsaiw ufkunnandans ina [55]birinnandans all þata gawi dugunnun ana badjam þans ubil habandans bairan, þadei hausidedun ei is wesi. [56]Jah þishwaduh þadei iddja in haimos aiþþau baurgs aiþþau in weihsa, ana gagga lagidedun siukans jah bedun ina ei þau skauta wastjos is attaitokeina; jah swa managai swe attaitokun imma ganesun.

Chapter VII

[1]Jah gaqemun sik du imma Fareisaieis jah sumai þize bokarje, qimandans us Iairusaulymim. [2]Jah gasaihwandans sumans þize siponje is gamainjaim handum (þat' ist unþwahanaim) matjandans hlaibans ([3]Iþ Fareisaieis jah allai Iudaieis, niba ufta þwahand handuns, ni matjand, habandans anafilh þize sinistane, [4]jah af maþla niba daupjand ni matjand, jah anþar ist manag þatei andnemun du haban: daupeinins stikle jah aurkje jah katile jah ligre), [5]þaþroh þan frehun ina þai Fareisaieis jah þai bokarjos: "Duhwe þai siponjos þeinai ni gaggand bi þammei anafulhun þai sinistans, ak unþwahanaim handum matjand hlaif?" [6]Iþ is andhafjands qaþ du im þatei "Waila praufetida Esaias bi izwis þans liutans, swe gameliþ ist: 'So managei wairilom mik sweraiþ, iþ hairto ize fairra habaiþ sik mis; [7]iþ sware mik blotand, laisjandans laiseinins anabusnins manne.' [8]Afletandans raihtis anabusn Gudis habaiþ þatei anafulhun mannans, daupeinins aurkje jah stikle, jah anþar galeik swaleikata manag taujiþ."

[9]Jah qaþ du im: "Waila inwidiþ anabusn Gudis, ei þata anafulhano izwar fastaiþ. [10]Moses auk raihtis qaþ: 'Swerai attan þeinana jah aiþein þeina; jah saei ubil qiþai attin seinamma aiþþau aiþein seinai, dauþau afdauþjaidau.' [11]Iþ jus qiþiþ: 'Jabai qiþai manna attin seinamma aiþþau aiþein: 'Kaurban (þatei ist maiþms) þishwah þatei us mis gabatnis --' [12]jah ni fraletiþ ina ni waiht taujan attin seinamma aiþþau aiþein seinai, [13]blauþjandans waurd Gudis þizai anabusnai

[11]Corrected from CA *usgaggaggaiþ*.

[12]Corrected from CA *janai*.

[13]So CA; apparently to be taken as an accusative absolute. A dative absolute would require *dauhtr*.

izwarai, þoei anafulhuþ. Jah galeik swaleikata manag taujiþ."

[14]Jah athaitands alla þo managein qaþ im: "Hauseiþ mis allai jah fraþjaiþ: [15]Ni waihts ist utaþro mans inngaggando in ina þatei magi ina gamainjan, ak þata utgaggando us mann þata ist þata gamainjando mannan. [16]Jabai hwas habai ausona hausjandona, gahausjai." [17]Jah þan galaiþ in gard us þizai managein, frehun ina siponjos is bi þo gajukon. [18]Jah qaþ du im: "Swa jah jus unwitans sijuþ? Ni fraþjiþ þammei all þata utaþro inngaggando in mannan ni mag ina gamainjan, [19]unte ni galeiþiþ imma in hairto, ak in wamba jah in urrunsa usgaggiþ (gahraineiþ allans matins)." [20]Qaþuþþan þatei "Þata us mann usgaggando þata gamaineiþ mannan. [21]Innaþro auk us hairtin manne mitoneis ubilos usgaggand: kalkinassjus, horinassjus, maurþra, [22]þiubja, faihufrikeins, unseleins, liutei, aglaitei, augo unsel, wajamereins, hauhhairtei, unwiti. [23]Þo alla ubilona innaþro usgaggand jah gagamainjand mannan."

[24]Jah jainþro usstandands galaiþ in markos Tyre jah Seidone, jah galeiþands in gard ni wilda witan mannan jah ni mahta galaugnjan. [25]Gahausjandei raihtis qino bi ina, þizozei habaida dauhtar ahman unhrainjana, qimandei draus du fotum is. [26]Wassuþ-þan so qino haiþno, Saurini Fynikiska gabaurþai, jah baþ ina ei þo unhulþon uswaurpi us dauhtr izos. [27]Iþ Iesus qaþ du izai: "Let faurþis sada wairþan barna, unte ni goþ ist niman hlaib barne jah wairpan hundam." [28]Iþ si andhof imma jah qaþ du imma: "Jai frauja; jah auk hundos undaro biuda matjand af drauhsnom barne." [29]Jah qaþ du izai: "In þis waurdis gagg, usiddja unhulþo us dauhtr þeinai." [30]Jah galeiþandei du garda seinamma bigat unhulþon usgaggana jah þo dauhtar ligandein ana ligra.

[31]Jah aftra galeiþands af markom Tyre jah Seidone qam at marein Galeilaie miþ tweihnaim markom Daikapaulaios. [32]Jah berun du imma baudana stammana, jah bedun ina ei lagidedi imma handau. [33]Jah afnimands ina af managein sundro, lagida figgrans seinans in ausona imma ja spewands attaitok tuggon is. [34]Jah ussaihwands du himina gaswogida, jah qaþ du imma: "Aiffaþa." (Þatei ist "uslukn.") [35]Jah sunsaiw usluknodedun imma hliumans jah andbundnoda bandi tuggons is jah rodida raihtaba. [36]Jah anabauþ im ei mann ni qeþeina. Hwan filu is im anabauþ, mais þamma eis meridedun. [37]Jah ufarassau sildaleikidedun qiþandans: "Waila allata gatawida, jah baudans gataujiþ gahausjan jah unrodjandans rodjan."

Chapter VIII

[1]In jainaim þan dagam aftra at filu managai managein wisandein jah ni habandam hwa matidedeina, athaitands siponjans qaþuh du im: [2]"Infeinoda du þizai managein, unte ju dagans þrins miþ mis wesun, jah ni haband hwa matjaina, [3]jah jabai fraleta ins lausqiþrans du garda ize, ufligand ana wiga; sumai raihtis ize fairraþro qemun." [4]Jah andhofun imma siponjos is: "Hwaþro þans mag hwas gasoþjan hlaibam ana auþidai?" [5]Jah frah ins: "Hwan managans habaiþ hlaibans?" Iþ eis qeþun: "Sibun." [6]Jah anabauþ þizai managein anakumbjan ana airþai, jah nimands þans sibun hlaibans jah awiliudonds gabrak jah atgaf siponjam seinaim, ei atlagidedeina faur. Jah atlagidedun faur þo managein. [7]Jah habaidedun fiskans fawans, jah þans gaþiuþjands qaþ ei atlagidedeina jah þans. [8]Gamatidedun þan jah sadai waurþun; jah usnemun laibos gabruko sibun spyreidans. [9]Wesunuþþan þai matjandans swe fidwor þusundjos, jah fralailot ins. [10]Jah galaiþ sunsaiw in skip miþ siponjam seinaim, jah qam ana fera Magdalan.

[11]Jah urrunnun Fareisaieis jah dugunnun miþsokjan imma sokjandans du imma taikn us himina, fraisandans ina. [12]Jah ufswogjands ahmin seinamma qaþ: "Hwa þata kuni taikn sokeiþ? Amen, qiþa izwis: jabai gibaidau kunja þamma taikne." [13]Jah afletands ins, galeiþands aftra in skip uslaiþ hindar marein.

[14]Jah ufarmunnodedun niman hlaibans jah niba ainana hlaif ni habaidedun miþ sis in skipa. [15]Jah anabauþ im qiþands: "Saihwiþ ei atsaihwiþ izwis þis beistis Fareisaie jah beistis Herodis." [16]Jah þahtedun miþ sis misso qiþandans unte "Hlaibans ni habam." [17]Jah fraþjands Iesus qaþ du im: "Hwa þaggkeiþ unte hlaibans ni habaiþ? Ni nauh fraþjiþ nih wituþ, unte daubata habaiþ hairto izwar. [18]Augona habandans ni gasaihwiþ, jah ausona habandans ni gahauseiþ, jah ni gamunuþ. [19]Þan þans fimf hlaibans gabrak fimf þusundjom, hwan managos tainjons fullos gabruko usnemuþ" Qeþun du imma: "Twalif." [20]"Aþþan þan þans sibun hlaibans fidwor þusundjom, hwan managans spyreidans fullans gabruko usnemuþ?" Iþ eis qeþun: "Sibun." [21]Jah qaþ du im: "Hwaia ni nauh fraþjiþ?"

[22]Jah qemun in Beþaniin, jah berun du imma blindan jah bedun ina ei imma attaitoki. [23]Jah fairgreipands handu þis blindins ustauh ina utana weihsis jah speiwands in augona is, atlagjands ana

handuns seinos frah ina gauhwasehwi. [24]Jah ussaihwands qaþ: "Gasaihwa mans, þatei swe bagmans gasaihwa gaggandans." [25] Þaþro aftra galagida handuns ana þo augona is jah gatawida ina ussaihwan; jah aftra gasatiþs warþ jah gasahw bairhtaba allans. [26]Jah insandida ina du garda is qiþands: "Ni in þata weihs gaggais, ni mannhun qiþais in þamma wehsa."

[27]Jah usiddja Iesus jah siponjos is in weihsa[14] Kaisarias þizos Filippaus. Jah ana wiga frah siponjans seinans qiþands du im: "Hwana mik qiþand mans wisan?" [28]Iþ eis andhofun: "Iohannen þana daupjand, jah anþarai Helian; sumaih þan ainana praufete." [29]Jah is qaþ du im: "Aþþan jus, hwana mik qiþiþ wisan?" Andhafjands þan Paitrus qaþ du imma: "Þu is Xristus." [30]Jah faurbauþ im ei mannhun ni qeþeina bi ina.

[31]Jah dugann laisjan ins þatei skal sunus mans filu winnan jah uskiusan skulds ist fram þaim sinistam jah þaim auhumistam gudjam jah bokarjam, jah usqiman jah afar þrins dagans usstandan. [32]Jah swikunþaba þata waurd rodida; jah aftiuhands ina Paitrus dugann andbeitan ina. [33]Iþ is gawandjands sik jah gasaihwands þans siponjans seinans andbait Paitru qiþands: "Gagg hindar mik, Satana, unte ni fraþjis þaim Gudis, ak þaim manne."

[34]Jah athaitands þo managein miþ siponjam seinaim qaþ du im: "Saei wili afar mis laistjan, inwidai sik silban, jah nimai galgan seinana jah laistjai mik. [35]Saei allis wili saiwala seina ganasjan, fraqisteiþ izai; iþ saei fraqisteiþ saiwalai seinai in meina jah in þizos aiwaggeljons, ganasjiþ þo. [36]Hwa auk boteiþ mannan, jabai gageigaiþ þana fairhwu allana jah gasleiþeiþ sik saiwalai seinai? [37]Aiþþau hwa gibiþ manna inmaidein saiwalos seinaizos? [38]Unte saei skamaiþ sik meina jah waurde meinaize in gabaurþai þizai horinondein jah frawaurhton, jah sunus mans skamaiþ sik is, þan qimiþ in wulþau attins seinis miþ aggilum þaim weiham."

Chapter IX

[1]Jah qaþ du im: "Amen qiþa izwis þatei sind sumai þize her standandane þai ize ni kausjand dauþaus, unte gasaihwand þiudinassu Gudis qumanana in mahtai." [2]Jah afar dagans saihs ganam Iesus Paitru jah Iakobu jah Iohannen, jah ustauh ins ana fairguni hauh sundro ainans, jah inmaidida sik in andwairþja ize. [3]Jah wastjos is waurþun glitmunjandeins, hweitos swe snaiws, swaleikos swe wullareis ana airþai ni mag gahweitjan. [4]Jah ataugiþs warþ im Helias miþ Mose; jah wesun rodjandans miþ Iesua. [5]Jah andhafjands Paitrus qaþ du Iesua: "Rabbei, goþ ist unsis her wisan, jah gawaurkjam hlijans þrins, þus ainana jah Mose ainana jah ainana Helijin." [6]Ni auk wissa hwa rodidedi; wesun auk usagidai. [7]Jah warþ milhma ufarskadwjands im, jah qam stibna us þamma milhmin: "Sa ist sunus meins sa liuba, þamma hausjaiþ." [8]Jah anaks insaihwandans ni þanaseiþs ainohun gasehwun, alja Iesu ainana miþ sis.

[9]Dalaþ þan atgaggandam im af þamma fairgunja, anabauþ im ei mannhun ni spillodedeina þatei gasehwun, niba biþe sunus mans us dauþaim usstoþi. [10]Jah þata waurd habaidedun du sis misso sokjandans: "Hwa ist þata us dauþaim usstandan?" [11]Jah frehun ina qiþandans unte "Qiþand þai bokarjos þatei Helias skuli qiman faurþis?" [12]Iþ is andhafjands qaþ du im: "Helias sweþauh qimands faurþis aftra gaboteiþ alla; jah hwaiwa gameliþ ist bi sunu mans, ei manag winnai jah frakunþs wairþai. [13]Akei qiþa izwis þatei ju Helias qam jah gatawidedun imma swa filu swe wildedun, swaswei gameliþ ist bi ina.

[14]Jah qimands at siponjam gasahw filu manageins bi ins, jah bokarjans sokjandans miþ im. [15]Jah sunsaiw alla managei gasaihwandans ina usgeisnodedun, jah durinnandans inwitun ina. [16]Jah frah þans bokarjans: "Hwa sokeiþ miþ þaim?" [17]Jah andhafjands ains us þizai managein qaþ: "Laisari, brahta sunu meinana du þus habandan ahman unrodjandan. [18]Jah þishwaruh þei ina gafahiþ, gawairpiþ ina, jah hwaþjiþ jah kriustiþ tunþuns seinans, jah gastaurkniþ; jah qaþ siponjam þeinaim ei usdreibeina ina, jah ni mahtedun." [19]Iþ is andhafjands im qaþ: "O kuni ungalaubjando! Und hwa at izwis sijau? Und hwa þulau izwis? Bairiþ ina du mis." [20]Jah brahtedun ina at imma. Jah gasaihwands ina sunsaiw sa ahma tahida ina; jah driusands ana airþa walwisoda hwaþjands. [21]Jah frah þana attan is: "Hwan lagg mel ist ei þata warþ imma?" Iþ is qaþ: "Us barniskja. [22]Jah ufta ina jah in fon atwarp jah in wato, ei usqistidedi imma; akei jabai mageis, hilp unsara, gableiþjands unsis." [23]Iþ Iesus qaþ du imma: "Þata jabai mageis galaubjan,[15] allata mahteig þamma

[14]Corr. from CA *wehsa*. [15] The text *þata jabai mageis galaubjan* (Gk τὸ εἰ δύνασαι πιστεῦσαι) is difficult to interpret. Some delete πιστεῦσαι (*galaubjan*) and take the remainder as an exclamation of exasperation: "That 'If you can'!"

galaubjandin." 24Jah sunsaiw ufhropjands sa atta þis barnis miþ tagram qaþ: "Galaubja. Hilp meinaizos ungalaubeinais!" 25Gasaihwands þan Iesus þatei samaþ rann managei, gahwotida ahmin þamma unhrainjin, qiþands du imma: "Þu ahma, þu unrodjands jah bauþs, ik þus anabiuda: Usgagg us þamma jah þanaseiþs ni galeiþais in ina." 26Jah hropjands jah filu tahjands ina usiddja. Jah warþ swe dauþs, swaswe managai qeþun þatei gaswalt. 27Iþ Iesus undgreipands ina bi handau urraisida ina; jah usstoþ. 28Jah galeiþandan ina in gard siponjos is frehun ina sundro: "Duhwe weis ni mahtedum[15] usdreiban þana?" 29Jah qaþ du im: "Þata kuni in waihtai ni mag usgaggan, niba in bidai jah fastubnja."

30Jah jainþro usgaggandans iddjedun þairh Galeilaian, jah ni wilda ei hwas wissedi, 31unte laisida siponjans seinans, jah qaþ du im þatei sunus mans atgibada in handuns manne, jah usqimand imma, jah usqistiþs þridjin daga usstandiþ. 32Iþ eis ni froþun þamma waurda, jah ohtedun ina fraihnan.

33Jah qam in Kafarnaum, jah in garda qumans frah ins: "Hwa in wiga miþ izwis misso mitodeduþ?" 34Iþ eis slawaidedun; du sis misso andrunnun, hwarjis maists wesi. 35Jah sitands atwopida þans twalif jah qaþ du im: "Jabai hwas wili frumists wisan, sijai allaize aftumists jah allaim andbahts." 36 Jah nimands barn gasatida ita in midjaim im, jah ana armins nimands ita qaþ du im: 37"Saei ain þize swaleikaize barne andnimiþ ana namin meinamma, mik andnimiþ; jah sahwazuh saei mik andnimiþ, ni mik andnimiþ, ak þana sandjandan mik."

38Andhof þan imma Iohannes qiþands: "Laisari, sehwum sumana in þeinamma namin usdreibandan unhulþons, saei ni laisteiþ unsis, jah waridedum imma, unte ni laisteiþ unsis. 39Iþ is qaþ: "Ni warjiþ imma. Ni mannahun auk ist saei taujiþ maht in namin meinamma jah magi sprauto ubilwaurdjan mis, 40unte saei nist wiþra izwis, faur izwis ist. 41Saei auk allis gadragkjai izwis stikla watins in namin meinamma, unte Xristaus sijuþ, amen qiþa izwis ei ni fraqisteiþ mizdon seinai.

42"Jah sahwazuh saei gamarzjai ainana þize leitilane þize galaubjandane du mis, goþ ist imma mais ei galagjaidau asiluqairnus ana balsaggan is jah frawaurpans wesi in marein. 43Jah jabai marzjai þuk handus þeina, afmait þo; goþ þus ist hamfamma in libain galeiþan, þau twos handuns habandin galeiþan in Gaiainnan, in fon þata unhwapnando, 44þarei maþa ize ni gaswiltiþ jah fon ni afhwapniþ. 45Jah jabai fotus þeins marzjai þuk, afmait ina; goþ þus ist galeiþan in libain haltamma, þau twans fotuns habandin gawairpan in Gaiainnan, in fon þata unhwapnando, 46þarei maþa ize ni gaswiltiþ jah fon ni afhwapniþ. 47Jah jabai augo þein marzjai þuk, uswairp imma; goþ þus ist haihamma galeiþan in þiudangardja Gudis, þau twa augona habandin atwairpan in Gaiainnan funins, 48þarei maþa ize ni gadauþniþ jah fon ni afhwapniþ. 49Hwazuh auk funin saltada jah hwarjatoh hunsle salta saltada. 50Goþ salt; iþ jabai salt unsaltan wairþiþ, hwe supuda?[16] Habaiþ in izwis salt, jah gawairþeigai sijaiþ miþ izwis misso."

Chapter X

1Jah jainþro usstandands qam in markom Iudaias hindar Iaurdanau; jah gaqemun sik aftra manageins du imma, jah, swe biuhts, aftra laisida ins. 2Jah duatgaggandans Fareisaieis frehun ina skuldu sijai mann qen afsatjan, fraisandans ina. 3Iþ is andhafjands qaþ: "Hwa izwis anabauþ Moses?" 4Iþ eis qeþun: "Moses uslaubida unsis bokos afsateinais meljan jah afletan." 5Jah andhafjands Iesus qaþ du im: "Wiþra harduhairtein izwara gamelida izwis þo anabusn. 6Iþ af anastodeinai gaskaftais gumein jah qinein gatawida Guþ. 7Inuh þis bileiþai manna attin seinamma jah aiþein seinai, 8jah sijaina þo twa du leika samin, swaswe þanaseiþs ni sind twa, ak leik ain. 9Þatei nu Guþ gawaþ, manna þamma ni skaidai." 10Jah in garda aftra siponjos is bi þata samo frehun ina. 11Jah qaþ du im: "Sahwazuh saei afletiþ qen seina jah liugaiþ anþara, horinoþ du þizai. 12Jah jabai qino afletiþ aban seinana jah liugada anþaramma, horinoþ."

13Þanuh atberun du imma barna ei attaitoki im, iþ þai siponjos is sokun þaim bairandam du. 14Gasaihwands þan Iesus unwerida jah qaþ du im: "Letiþ þo barna gaggan du mis jah ni warjiþ þo, unte þize ist þiudangardi Gudis. 15Amen qiþa izwis: Saei ni andnimiþ þiudangardja Gudis swe barn, ni þauh qimiþ in izai." 16Jah gaþlaihands im, lagjands handuns ana þo þiuþida im. 17Jah usgaggandin imma in wig,

[15]Corr. from CA *mahtedun*.

[16]Corr. from CA *supuda*.

duatrinnands ains jah knussjands baþ ina qiþands:
"Laisari þiuþeiga, hwa taujau ei libainais aiweinons arbja
wairþau?" [18]Iþ is qaþ du imma: "Hwa mik qiþis
þiuþeigana? Ni hwashun þiuþeigs, alja ains Guþ. [19]Þos
anabusnins kant: ni horinos; ni maurþrjais; ni hlifais; ni
sijais galiugaweitwods; ni anamahtjais; swerai attan
þeinana jah aiþein þeina." [20]Þaruh andhafjands qaþ du
imma: "Laisari, þo alla gafastaida us jundai meinai."
[21]Iþ Iesus insaihwands du imma frijoda ina jah qaþ du
imma: "Ainis þus wan ist: gagg, swa filu swe habais
frabugei jah gif þarbam, jah habais huzd in himinam; jah
hiri laistjan mik nimands galgan." [22]Iþ is gahnipnands
in þis waurdis galaiþ gaurs; was auk habands faihu
manag.

[23]Jah bisaihwands Iesus qaþ siponjam seinaim:
"Sai, hwaiwa agluba þai faihu[17] gahabandans in
þiudangardja Gudis galeiþand!" [24]Iþ þai siponjos
afslauþnodedun in waurde is. Þaruh Iesus aftra
andhafjands qaþ im: "Barnilona, hwaiwa aglu ist þaim
hugjandam afar faihau in þiudangardja Gudis galeiþan.
[25]Azitizo ist ulbandau þairh þairko neþlos galeiþan, þau
gabigamma in þiudangardja Gudis galeiþan." [26]Iþ eis
mais usgeisnodedun qiþandans du sis misso: "Jah hwas
mag ganisan?" [27]Insaihwands du im Iesus qaþ: "Akei
fram mannam unmahteig ist, ni fram Guþa; allata auk
mahteig ist fram Guþa." [28]Dugann þan Paitrus qiþan du
imma: "Sai, weis aflailotum alla jah laistidedum þuk."
[29]Andhafjands im Iesus qaþ: "Amen qiþa izwis: ni
hwashun ist saei aflailoti[18] gard aiþþau broþruns aiþþau
aiþein aiþþau attan aiþþau qen aiþþau barna aiþþau
haimoþlja in meina jah in þizos aiwaggeljons, [30]saei ni
andnimai .r. falþ nu in þamma mela gardins jah
broþruns jah swistruns jah attan jah aiþein jah barna jah
haimoþlja miþ wrakom, jah in aiwa þamma anawairþin
libain aiweinon. [31]Aþþan managai wairþand frumans
aftumans, jah aftumans frumans."

[32]Wesunuþþan ana wiga gaggandans du
Iairusaulymai jah faurbigaggands ins Iesus, jah
sildaleikidedun jah afarlaistjandans faurhtai waurþun.
Jah andnimands aftra þans twalif dugann im qiþan þoei
habaidedun ina gadaban, [33]þatei: "Sai, usgaggam in
Iairusaulyma jah sunus mans atgibada þaim ufargudjam
jah bokarjam, jah gawargjand ina dauþau, [34]jah
bilaikand ina jah bliggwand ina, jah speiwand ana ina jah
usqimand imma, jah þridjin daga us<s>tandiþ." [35]Jah
athabaidedun sik du imma Iakobus jah Iohannes, sunjus
Zaibaidaiaus, qiþandans: "Laisari, wileima ei þatei þuk
bidjos, taujais uggkis." [36]Iþ Iesus qaþ im: "Hwa wileits
taujan mik igqis?" [37]Iþ eis qeþun du imma: "Fragif
ugkis ei ains af taihswon þeinai jah ains af hleidumein
þeinai sitaiwa in wulþau þeinamma." [38]Iþ Iesus qaþuh
du im: "Ni wituts[19] hwis bidjats. Magutsu driggkan
stikl þanei ik driggka, jah daupeinai þizaiei ik daupjada
ei daupjaindau?" [39]Iþ eis qeþun du imma: "Magu." Iþ
Iesus qaþuh du im: "Sweþauh þana stikl þanei ik
driggka driggkats, jah þizai daupeinai þizaiei ik daupjada
<daupjanda>, [40]iþ þata du sitan af taihswon meinai
aiþþau af hleidumein nist mein du giban, alja þaimei
manwiþ was. [41]Jah gahausjandans þai taihun dugunnun
unwerjan bi Iakobu jah Iohannen. [42]Iþ is athaitands ins
qaþ du im: "Wituþ þatei <þaiei> þuggkjand reikinon
þiudom, gafraujinond im, iþ þai mikilans ize gawaldand
im. [43]Iþ ni swa sijai in izwis; ak sahwazuh saei wili
wairþan mikils in izwis, sijai izwar andbahts; [44]jah saei
wili izwara wairþan frumist<s>, sijai allaim skalks.
[45]Jah auk sunus mans ni qam at andbahtjam, ak
andbahtjan jah giban saiwala seina faur managans lun."

[46]Jah qemun in Iairikon. Jah usgaggandin imma
jainþro miþ siponjam seinaim jah managein ganohai,
sunus Teimaiaus, Barteimaiaus blinda, sat faur wig du
aihtron. [47]Jah gahausjands þatei Iesus sa Nazoraius ist,
dugann hropjan jah qiþan: "Sunau Daweidis, Iesu, armai
mik!" [48]Jah hwotidedun imma managai ei gaþahaidedi;
iþ is filu mais hropida: "Sunau Daweidis, armai mik!"
[49]Jah gastandands Iesus haihait atwopjan ina. Jah
wopidedun þana blindan, qiþandans du imma: "Þrafstei
þuk. Urreis, wopeiþ þuk." [50]Iþ is afwairpands wastjai
seinai ushlaupands qam at Iesu. [51]Jah andhafjands qaþ
du imma Iesus: "Hwa wileis ei taujau þus?" Iþ sa blinda
qaþ du imma: "Rabbaunei, ei ussaihwau." [52]Iþ Iesus qaþ
du imma: "Gagg, galaubeins þeina ganasida þuk." Jah
sunsaiw ussahw jah laistida in wiga Iesu."

Chapter XI

[1]Jah biþe nehwa wesun Iairusalem, in
Beþsfagein jah Biþaniin at Fairgunja Alewjin, insandida
twans siponje seinaize, [2]jah qaþ du im: "Gaggats in

[17]Corrected from CA *faiho*.

[18]Corrected from CA *aflailailoti*. *attan* is corrected from CA *attin*.

[19]Corrected from CA *wituþs*.

haim þo wiþrawairþon iggqis, jah sunsaiw inngaggandans in þo baurg bigitats fulan gabundanana, ana þammei nauh ainshun manne ni sat; andbindandans ina attiuhats. [3]Jah jabai hwas iggqis qiþai: 'Duhwe þata taujats?' qiþaits þatei 'Frauja þis gairneiþ, jah sunsaiw ina insandeiþ hidre.'" [4]Galiþun þan jah bigetun fulan gabundanana at daura uta ana gagga, jah andbundun ina. [5]Jah sumai þize jainar standandane qeþun du im: "Hwa taujats andbindandans þana fulan?" [6]Iþ eis qeþun du im swaswe anabauþ im Iesus, jah lailotun ins. [7]Jah brahtedun þana fulan at Iesua, jah galagidedun ana wastjos seinos, jah gasat ana ina. [8]Managai þan wastjom seinaim strawidedun ana wiga. Sumai astans maimaitun us bagmam jah strawidedun ana wiga. [9]Jah þai fauragaggandans hropidedun qiþandans: "Osanna, þiuþida sa qimanda in namin fraujins! [10]Þiuþido so qimandei þiudangardi in namin <Fraujins> attins unsaris Daweidis. Osanna in hauhistjam!"

[11]Jah galaiþ in Iairusaulyma Iesus jah in alh, jah bisaihwands alla, at andanahtja juþan wisandin hweilai usiddja in Beþanian miþ þaim twalibim. [12]Jah iftumin daga usstandandam im us Beþaniin gredags was. [13]Jah gasaihwands smakkabagm fairraþro habandan lauf atiddja, ei aufto bigeti hwa ana imma; jah qimands at imma ni waiht bigat ana imma niba lauf; ni auk was mel smakkane. [14]Jah usbairands qaþ du imma: "Ni þanaseiþs us þus aiw manna akran matjai." Jah gahausidedun þai siponjos is.

[15]Jah iddjedun du Iairusaulymai. Jah atgaggands Iesus in alh dugann uswairpan þans frabugjandans jah bugjandans in alh, jah mesa skattjane jah sitlans þize frabugjandane ahakim uswaltida. [16]Jah ni lailot ei hwas þairhberi kas þairh þo alh. [17] Jah laisida qiþands du im: "Niu gameliþ ist þatei 'Razn mein razn bido haitada allaim þiudom'? Iþ jus gatawideduþ ita du filigrja waidedjane." [18]Jah gahausidedun þai bokarjos jah gudjane auhumistans jah sokidedun hwaiwa imma usqistidedeina. Ohtedun auk ina, unte alla managei sildaleikidedun in laiseinais is. [19]Jah biþe andanahti warþ, usiddja ut us þizai baurg.

[20]Jah in maurgin faurgaggandans gasehwun þana smakkabagm þaursjana us waurtim. [21]Jah gamunands Paitrus qaþ du imma: "Rabbei, sai smakkabagms þanei fraqast gaþaursnoda." [22]Jah andhafjands Iesus qaþ du im: "Habaiþ galaubein Gudis! [23]Amen auk qiþa izwis, þishwazuh ei qiþai du þamma fairgunja: 'Ushafei þuk jah wairp þus in marein,' jah ni tuzwerjai in hairtin seinamma, ak galaubjai þata, ei þatei qiþiþ gagaggiþ, wairþiþ imma þishwah þei qiþiþ. [24]Duþþe qiþa izwis: Allata þishwah þei bidjandans sokeiþ, galaubeiþ þatei nimiþ, jah wairþiþ izwis. [25]Jah þan standaiþ bidjandans, afletaiþ, jabai hwa habaiþ wiþra hwana, ei jah atta izwar sa in himinam afletai izwis missadedins izwaros. [26]Iþ jabai jus ni afletiþ, ni þau atta izwar sa in himinam afletiþ izwis missadedins izwaros."

[27]Jah iddjedun aftra du Iairusaulymai. Jah in alh hwarbondin imma atiddjedun du imma þai auhumistans gudjans jah bokarjos jah sinistans. [28]Jah qeþun du imma: "In hwamma waldufnje þata taujis? Jah hwas þus þata waldufni atgaf, ei þata taujis?" [29]Iþ Iesus andhafjands qaþ du im: "Fraihna jah ik izwis ainis waurdis jah andhafjiþ mis, jah qiþa izwis in hwamma waldufnje þata tauja. [30]Daupeins Iohannis uzuh himina was þau uzuh mannam? Andhafjiþ mis." [31]Jah þahtedun du sis misso qiþandans: "Jabai qiþam: 'Us himina,' qiþiþ: 'Aþþan duhwe ni galaubideduþ imma?' [32]Ak qiþam: 'Us mannam'...." --Ohtedun[20] þo managein; allai auk alakjo habaidedun Iohannen þatei bi sunjai praufetes was. [33]Jah andhafjandans qeþun du Iesua: "Ni witum." Jah andhafjands Iesus qaþ du im: "Nih ik izwis qiþa in hwamma waldufnje þata tauja."

Chapter XII

[1]Jah dugann im in gajukom qiþan: "Weinagard ussatida manna, jah bisatida ina faþom, jah usgrof dal uf mesa, jah gatimrida kelikn, jah anafalh ina waurstwjam, jah aflaiþ aljaþ. [2]Jah insandida du þaim waurstwjam at mel skalk, ei at þaim waurstwjam nemi akranis þis weinagardis. [3]Iþ eis nimandans ina usbluggwun jah insandidedun laushandjan. [4]Jah aftra insandida du im anþarana skalk. Jah þana stainam wairpandans gaaiwiskodedun jah haubiþ wundan brahtedun, jah insandidedun ganaitidana. [5]Jah aftra insandida anþarana. Jah jainana afslohun, jah managans anþarans, sumans usbliggwandans, sumanzuh þan usqimandans. [6]Þanuh nauhþanuh ainana sunu aigands liubana sis, insandida jah þana du im spedistana, qiþands þatei gaaistand sunu meinana. [7]Iþ jainai þai waurstwjans

[20]Corrected from CA *uhtedun.*

qeþun du sis misso þatei "Sa is sa arbinumja. Hirjiþ, usqimam imma, jah unsar wairþiþ þata arbi." [8]Jah undgreipandans ina usqemun, jah uswaurpun imma ut us þamma weinagarda. [9]Hwa nuh taujai frauja þis weinagardis? Qimiþ jah usqisteiþ þans waurstwjans, jah gibiþ þana weinagard anþaraim. [10]Nih þata gamelido ussuggwuþ:

"Stains þammei uswaurpun þai timrjans,
sah warþ du haubida waihstins.
[11]Fram fraujin warþ sa,
jah ist sildaleiks in augam unsaraim."

[12]Jah sokidedun ina undgreipan, jah ohtedun þo managein; froþun auk þatei du im þo gajukon qaþ. Jah afletandans ina galiþun.

[13]Jah insandidedun du imma sumai þize Fareisaie jah Herodiane, ei ina ganuteina waurda. [14]Iþ eis qimandans qeþun du imma: "Laisari, witum þatei sunjeins is jah ni kara þuk manshun. Ni auk saihwis in andwairþja manne, ak bi sunjai wig Gudis laiseis. Skuldu ist kaisaragild giban kaisara, þau niu gibaima?" [15]Iþ Iesus gasaihwands ize liutein qaþ du im: "Hwa mik fraisiþ? Atbairiþ mis skatt, ei gasaihwau." [16]Iþ eis atberun jah qaþ du im: "Hwis ist sa manleika jah so ufarmeleins?" Iþ eis qeþun du imma: "Kaisaris." [17]Jah andhafjands Iesus qaþ du im: "Usgibiþ þo Kaisaris Kaisara jah þo Gudis Guda." Jah sildaleikidedun ana þamma.

[18]Jah atiddjedun Saddukaieis du imma, þaiei qiþand usstass ni wisan, jah frehun ina qiþandans: [19]"Laisari, Moses gamelida unsis þatei jabai hwis broþar gadauþnai, jah bileiþai qenai, jah barne ni bileiþai, ei nimai broþar is þo qen is, jah ussatjai barna broþr seinamma. [20]Sibun broþrahans wesun. Jah sa frumista nam qen jah gaswiltands ni bilaiþ fraiwa. [21]Jah anþar nam þo, jah gadauþnoda, jah ni sa bilaiþ fraiwa. Jah þridja samaleiko. [22]Jah nemun þo samaleiko þai sibun, jah ni biliþun fraiwa. Spedumista allaize gaswalt jah so qens. [23]In þizai usstassai, þan usstandand, hwarjamma ize wairþiþ qens, þai auk sibun aihtedun þo du qenai? [24]Jah andhafjands Iesus qaþ du im: "Niu duþe airzjai sijuþ, ni kunnandans mela[21] nih maht Gudis? [25]Allis þan usstandand us dauþaim, ni liugand ni liuganda, ak sind swe aggiljus þai in himinam. [26]Aþþan bi dauþans þatei urreisand, niu gakunnaideduþ ana bokom Mosezis ana aihwatundjai, hwaiwa imma qaþ Guþ qiþands: 'Ik im Guþ Abrahamis jah Guþ Isakis jah Iakobis'? [27]Nist Guþ dauþaize, ak qiwaize. Aþþan jus filu airzjai sijuþ."

[28]Jah duatgaggands ains þize bokarje, gahausjands ins samana sokjandans, gasaihwands þatei waila im andhof, frah ina: "Hwarja ist allaizo anabusne frumista?" [29]Iþ Iesus andhof imma þatei frumista allaizo anabusns: "Hausei Israel, Frauja Guþ unsar Frauja ains ist. [30]Jah frijos Fraujan Guþ þeinana us allamma hairtin þeinamma jah us allai saiwalai þeinai jah us allai gahugdai þeinai jah us allai mahtai þeinai. So frumista anabusns. [31] Jah anþara galeika þizai: frijos nehwundjan þeinana swe þuk silban. Maizei þaim anþara anabusns nist." [32]Jah qaþ du imma sa bokareis: "Waila, laisari, bi sunjai qast þatei ains ist, jah nist anþar alja imma; [33]jah þata du frijon ina us allamma hairtin jah us allamma fraþja jah us allai saiwalai jah us allai mahtai, jah þata du frijon nehwundjan swe sik silban managizo ist allaim þaim alabrunstim jah saudim." [34]Jah Iesus gasaihwands ina þatei frodaba andhof, qaþ du imma: "Ni fairra is þiudangardjai Gudis." Jah ainshun þanaseiþs ni gadaursta ina fraihnan.

[35]Jah andhafjands Iesus qaþ laisjands in alh: "Hwaiwa qiþand þai bokarjos þatei Xristus sunus ist Daweidis? [36]Silba auk Daweid qaþ in ahmin weihamma: 'Qiþiþ Frauja du Fraujin meinamma, sit af taihswon meinai, unte ik galagja fijands þeinans fotaubaurd fotiwe þeinaize." [37]Silba raihtis Daweid qiþiþ ina Fraujan, jah hwaþro imma sunus ist?" Jah alla so managei hausidedun imma gabaurjaba. [38]Jah qaþ du im in laiseinai seinai: "Saihwiþ faura bo[karjam --- (text missing)]

Chapter XIII

(vss 1-16a missing) . . . wastja seina. [17]Aþþan wai þaim qiþuhaftom jah daddjandeim in jainaim dagam. [18]Aþþan bidjaiþ ei ni wairþai sa þlauhs izwar wintrau. [19]Wairþand auk þai dagos jainai aglo swaleika, swe ni was swaleika fram anastodeinai gaskaftais þoei gaskop Guþ und hita, jah ni wairþiþ. [20]Jah ni Frauja gamaurgidedi þans dagans, ni þauh ganesi ainhun leike; akei in þize gawalidane þanzei gawalida, gamaurgida þans dagans. [21]Jah þan jabai hwas izwis qiþai, 'Sai, her Xristus, aiþþau sai, jainar,' ni galaubjaiþ; [22]unte urreisand galiugaxristjus jah galiugapraufeteis, jah giband taiknins

[21]Glossed marginally as *bokos*.

jah fauratanja du afairzjan, jabai mahteig sijai, jah þans gawalidans. [23]Iþ jus saihwiþ, sai, fauragataih izwis allata.

[24]Akei in jainans dagans afar þo aglon jaina sauil riqizeiþ jah mena ni gibiþ liuhaþ sein. [25]Jah stairnons himinis wairþand driusandeins jah mahteis þos in himinam gawagjanda. [26]Jah þan gasaihwand sunu mans qimandan in milhmam miþ mahtai managai jah wulþau. [27]Jah þan insandeiþ aggiluns seinans jah galisiþ þans gawalidans seinans af fidwor windam fram andjam airþjos und andi himinis. [28]Aþþan af smakkabagma ganimiþ þo gajukon. Þan þis juþan asts þlaqus wairþiþ jah uskeinand laubos, kunnuþ þatei nehwa ist asans. [29]Swah jah jus, þan gasaihwiþ þata wairþan, kunneiþ þatei nehwa sijuþ at . . . (vss 29b-37 missing)

Chapter XIV

(vss 1-4a missing) 4... "<fraqis>teins þis balsanis warþ? [5]Maht wesi auk þata balsan frabugjan in managizo þau þrija hunda skatte jah giban unledaim." Jah andstaurraidedun þo. [6]Iþ Iesus qaþ: "Letiþ þo. Duhwe izai usþriutiþ? Þannu goþ waurstw waurhta bi mis. [7]Sinteino auk þans unledans habaiþ miþ izwis, jah þan wileiþ, maguþ im waila taujan, iþ mik ni sinteino habaiþ. [8]Þatei habaida so gatawida: faursnau salbon mein leik du usfilha. [9]Amen qiþa izwis: þishwaruh þei merjada so aiwaggeljo and alla manaseþ, jah þatei gatawida so rodjada du gamundai izos."

[10]Jah Iudas Iskarioteis, ains þize twalibe, galaiþ du þaim gudjam ei galewidedi ina im. [11]Iþ eis gahausjandans faginodedun jah gahaihaitun imma faihu giban. Jah sokida hwaiwa gatilaba ina galewidedi.

[12]Jah þamma frumistin daga Azyme, þan Paska salidedun, qeþun du imma þai siponjos is: "Hwar wileis ei galeiþandans manwjaima ei matjais Paska?" [13]Jah insandida twans siponje seinaize qaþuh du im: "Gaggats[22] in þo baurg jah gamoteiþ igqis manna kas watins bairands. Gaggats afar þamma, [14]jah þadei inngaleiþai, qiþaits þamma heiwafraujin þatei laisareis qiþiþ: 'Hwar sind saliþwos þarei Paska miþ siponjam meinaim matjau?' [15]Jah sa izwis taikneiþ kelikn mikilata gastrawiþ manwjata, jah jainar manwjaiþ unsis." [16]Jah usiddjedun þai sipon<jos>... [vss 16b- 41a missing]

[41]..."sai, galewjada sunus mans in handuns frawaurhtaize. [42]Urreisiþ, gaggam! Sai, sa lewjands mik atnehwida." [43]Jah sunsaiw nauhþanuh at imma rodjandin qam Iudas, sums þize twalibe, jah miþ imma managei miþ hairum jah triwam fram þaim auhumistam gudjam jah bokarjam jah sinistam. [44]Atuhþangaf sa lewjands im bandwon qiþands: "Þammei kukjau, sa ist. Greipiþ þana jah tiuhiþ arniba." [45]Jah qimands sunsaiw, atgaggands du imma qaþ: "Rabbei, rabbei!" jah kukida imma. [46]Iþ eis uslagidedun handuns ana ina jah undgripun ina. [47]Iþ ains sums þize atstandandane imma uslukands hairu sloh skalk auhumistins gudjins jah afsloh imma auso þata taihswo. [48]Jah andhafjands Iesus qaþ du im: "Swe du waidedjin urrunnuþ miþ hairum jah triwam greipan mik? [49]Daga hwammeh was at izwis in alh laisjands jah ni gripuþ mik. Ak ei usfullnodedeina bokos..." [50]Jah afletandans ina gaþlauhun allai.

[51]Jah ains sums juggalauþs laistida afar imma biwaibiþs leina ana naqadana. Jah gripun is þai[23] juggalaudeis, [52]iþ is bileiþands þamma leina naqaþs gaþlauh faura im.

[53]Jah gatauhun Iesu du auhumistin gudjin, jah garunnun miþ imma auhumistans gudjans allai jah þai sinistans jah bokarjos. [54]Jah Paitrus fairraþro laistida afar imma, unte qam in garda þis auhumistins gudjins, jah was sitands miþ andbahtam jah warmjands sik at liuhada. [55]Iþ þai auhumistans gudjans jah alla so gafaurds sokidedun ana Iesu weitwodiþa du afdauþjan ina, jah ni bigetun. [56]Managai auk galiug weitwodidedun ana ina, jah samaleikos þos weitwodiþos ni wesun. [57]Jah sumai usstandandans galiug weitwodidedun ana ina qiþandans [58]þati "Weis gahausidedum qiþandan ina þatei 'Ik gataira alh þo handuwaurhton, jah bi þrins dagans anþara unhanduwaurhta gatimrja.'" [59]Jah ni swa samaleika was weitwodiþa ize. [60]Jah usstandands sa auhumista gudja in midjaim frah Iesu qiþands: "Niu andhafjis waiht, hwa þai ana þuk weitwodjand?" [61]Iþ is þahaida jah waiht ni andhof. Aftra sa auhumista gudja frah ina jah qaþ du imma: "Þu is Xristus sa sunus þis þiuþeigins?" [62]Iþ is qaþuh: "Ik im, jah gasaihwiþ þana sunu mans af taihswon sitandan mahtais, jah qimandan miþ milhmam

[22]Corrected from CA *gaggast.*

[23]*þai juggalaudeis* is not in the Greek and should probably be deleted, especially since it makes no sense.

himinis." 63Iþ sa auhumista gudja disskreitands wastjos seinos qaþ: "Hwa þanamais þaurbum weis weitwode? 64Hausideduþ þo wajamerein is. Hwa izwis þugkeiþ?" Þaruh eis allai gadomidedun ina skulan wisan dauþau. 65Jah dugunnun sumai speiwan ana wlit is jah huljan andwairþi is jah kaupatjan ina, jah qeþun du imma: "Praufetei!" Jah andbahtos gabaurjaba lofam slohun ina.

66Jah wisandin Paitrau in rohsnai dalaþa jah atiddja aina þiujo þis auhumistins gudjins, 67jah gasaihwandei Paitru warmjandan sik insaihwandei du imma qaþ: "Jah þu miþ Iesua þamma Nazoreinau wast." 68Iþ is afaiaik qiþands: "Ni wait, ni kann hwa þu qiþis." Jah galaiþ faur gard, jah hana wopida. 69Jah þiwi gasaihwandei ina aftra dugann qiþan þaim faurastandandam þatei, "Sa þizei ist." 70Iþ is aftra laugnida. Jah afar leitil aftra þai atstandandans qeþun du Paitrau: "Bi sunjai, þizei is, jah auk razda þeina galeika ist." 71Iþ is dugann afaikan jah swaran þatei "Ni kann þana mannan þanei qiþiþ." 72Jah anþaramma sinþa hana wopida. Jah gamunda Paitrus þata waurd, swe qaþ imma Iesus, þatei faurþize hana hrukjai twaim sinþam, inwidis mik þrim sinþam. Jah dugann greitan.

Chapter XV

1Jah sunsaiw in maurgin garuni taujandans þai auhumistans gudjans miþ þaim sinistam jah bokarjam, jah alla so gafaurds gabindandans Iesu brahtedun ina at Peilatau. 2Jah frah ina Peilatus: "Þu is þiudans Iudaie?" Iþ is andhafjands qaþ du imma: "Þu qiþis." 3Jah wrohidedun ina þai auhumistans gudjans filu. 4Iþ Peilatus aftra frah ina qiþands: "Niu andhafjis ni waiht? Sai, hwan filu ana þuk weitwodjand." 5Iþ Iesus þanamais ni andhof, swaswe sildaleikida Peilatus.

6Iþ and dulþ hwarjo<h> fralailot im ainana bandjan þanei bedun. 7Wasuh þan sa haitana Barabbas miþ þaim miþ imma drobjandam gabundans, þaiei in auhjodau maurþr gatawidedun. 8Jah usgaggandei alla managei dugunnun bidjan, swaswe sinteino tawida im. 9Iþ Peilatus andhof im qiþands: "Wileid-u fraleitan izwis þana þiudan Iudaie?" 10Wissa auk þatei in neiþis atgebun ina þai auhumistans gudjans. 11Iþ þai auhumistans gudjans inwagidedun þo managein ei mais Barabban fralailoti im. 12Iþ Peilatus aftra andhafjands qaþ du im: "Hwa nu wileiþ ei taujau þammei qiþiþ þiudan Iudaie?" 13Iþ eis aftra hropidedun: "Ushramei ina!" 14Iþ Peilatus qaþ du im: "Hwa allis ubilis gatawida?" Iþ eis mais hropidedun: "Ushramei ina!" 15Iþ Peilatus wiljands þizai managein fullafahjan, fralailot im þana Barabban, iþ Iesu atgaf usbliggwands, ei ushramiþs wesi.

16Iþ gadrauhteis gatauhun ina innana gardis, þatei ist praitoriaun, jah gahaihaitun alla hansa, 17jah gawasidedun ina paurpurai, jah atlagidedun ana ina þaurneina wipja uswindandans, 18jah dugunnun goljan ina: "Hails, þiudan Iudaie!" 19Jah slohun is haubiþ rausa, jah bispiwun ina, jah lagjandans kniwa inwitun ina. 20Jah biþe bilailaikun ina andwasidedun ina þizai paurpurai, jah gawasidedun ina wastjom swesaim, jah ustauhun ina ei ushramidedeina ina.

21Jah undgripun sumana manne, Seimona Kyreinaiu, qimandan af akra, attan Alaiksandraus jah Rufaus, ei nemi galgan is. 22Jah attauhun ina ana Gaulgauþa staþ (þatei ist gaskeiriþ "hwairneins staþs"). 23Jah gebun imma drigkan wein miþ smyrna, iþ is ni nam. 24Jah ushramjandans ina disdailjand[24] wastjos is wairpandans hlauta ana þos, hwarizuh hwa nemi. 25Wasuh þan hweila þridjo, jah ushramidedun ina. 26Jah was ufarmeli fairinos is ufarmeliþ: "Sa þiudans Iudaie." 27Jah miþ imma ushramidedun twans waidedjans, ainana af taihswon jah ainana af hleidumein is. 28Jah usfullnoda þata gamelido þata qiþan<d>o: "Jah miþ unsibjaim rahniþs was." 29Jah þai faurgggandans wajameridedun ina, wiþondans haubida seina jah qiþandans: "O sa gatairands þo alh jah bi þrins dagans gatimrjands þo, 30nasei þuk silban jah atsteig af þamma galgin!" 31Samaleiko jah þai auhumistans gudjans bilaikandans ina miþ sis misso miþ þaim bokarjam qeþun: "Anþarans ganasida, iþ sik silban ni mag ganasjan. 32Sa Xristus, sa þiudans Israelis, atsteigadau nu af þamma galgin, ei gasaihwaima jah galaubjaima." Jah þai miþushramidans imma idweitidedun imma.

33Jah biþe warþ hweila saihsto, riqis warþ ana allai airþai und hweila niundon. 34Jah niundon hweilai wopida Iesus stibnai mikilai qiþands: "Ailoe, ailoe, lima sibakþanei?" (Þatei is gaskeiriþ: "Guþ meins, Guþ meins, duhwe mis bilaist?") 35Jah sumai þize atstandandane gahausjandans qeþun: "Sai, Helian wopeiþ." 36Þragjands þan ains jah gafulljands swam[m] akeitis, galagjands ana raus, dragkida ina qiþands: "Let,

[24]Corrected from CA *disdailjandans.*

ei saihwam qimaiu Helias athafjan ina." 37Iþ Iesus aftra letands stibna mikila uzon. 38Jah faurahah al<h>s disskritnoda in twa iupaþro und dalaþ. 39Gasaihwands þan sa hundafaþs sa atstandands in andwairþja is þatei swa hropjands uzon, qaþ: "Bi sunjai, sa manna sa sunus was Gudis."

40Wesunuþþan qinons fairraþro saihwandeins, in þaimei was Marja so Magdalene jah Marja Iakobis þis minnizins jah Iosezis aiþei jah Salome, (41Jah þan was in Galeilaia, jah laistidedun ina jah andbahtidedun imma) jah anþaros managos þozei miþiddjedun imma in Iairusalem. 42Jah juþan at andanahtja waurþanamma, unte was Paraskaiwe, saei ist fruma sabbato, 43qimands Iosef af Areimaþaias, gaguds ragineis, saei was silba beidands þiudangardjos Gudis, ananan þjands galaiþ inn du Peilatau jah baþ þis leikis Iesuis. 44Iþ Peilatus sildaleikida ei is juþan gaswalt; jah athaitands þan<a> hundafaþ frah ina juþan[25] gadauþnodedi. 45Jah finþands at þamma hundafada fragaf þata leik Iosefa. 46Jah usbugjands lein jah usnimands ita biwand þamma leina jah galagida ita in hlaiwa þatei was gadraban us staina, jah atwalwida stain du daura þis hlaiwis. 47Iþ Marja so Magdalene jah Marja Iosezis sehwun hwar galagiþs wesi.

Chapter XVI

1Jah inwisandin sabbate daga[26] Marja so Magdalene jah Marja so Iakobis jah Salome usbauhtedun aromata ei atgaggandeins gasalbodedeina ina. 2Jah filu air þis dagis afarsabbate atidd<j>edun du þamma hlaiwa at urrinnandin sunnin. 3Jah qeþun du sis misso: "Hwas afwalwjai unsis þana stain af daurom þis hlaiwis?" 4Jah insaihwandeins gaumidedun þammei afwalwiþs ist sa stains, was auk mikils abraba. 5Jah atgaggandeins in þata hlaiw gasehwun juggalauþ sitandan in taihswai biwaibidana wastjai hweitai, jah usgeisnodedun. 6Þaruh qaþ du im: "Ni faurhteiþ izwis, Iesu sokeiþ Nazoraiu þana ushramidan. Nist her, urrais, sai þana staþ þarei galagidedun ina. 7Akei gaggiþ qiþiduh du siponjam is jah du Paitrau þatei faurbigaggiþ izwis in Galeilaian. Þaruh ina gasaihwiþ, swaswe qaþ izwis." 8Jah usgaggandeins af þamma hlaiwa gaþlauhun. Dizuhþansat ijos reiro jah usfilmei, jah ni qeþun mannhun waiht; ohtedun sis auk.

9Usstandands þan in maurgin frumin sabbato ataugida <sik> frumist Marjin þizai Magdalene, af þizaiei uswarp sibun unhulþons. 10Soh gaggandei gataih þaim miþ imma wisandam, qainondam jah gretandam. 11Jah eis hausjandans þatei libaiþ jah gasaihwans warþ fram izai ni galaubidedun. 12Afaruh þan þata [remainder missing]

[25] Perhaps to be understood as **ju-u-þan*, with *-u* marking the indirect question.

[26] CA has *inwisandinsabbatedagis*. The choice is between a dative absolute, as given in the text, or a genitive absolute *inwisandins sabbate dagis*, a construction not attested elsewhere in Gothic.

The Gospel According to Matthew

Chapter V

(I:I to V:15a are missing) [15]".... ak ana lukarnastaþin, jah liuteiþ[1] allaim þaim in þamma garda. [16]Swa liuhtjai liuhaþ izwar in andwairþja manne, ei gasaihwaina izwara goda waurstwa jah hauhjaina attan izwarana þana in himinam."

[17]"Ni hugjaiþ ei qemjau gatairan wiþoþ aiþþau praufetuns; ni qam gatairan, ak usfulljan. [18]Amen auk qiþa izwis: und þatei usleiþiþ himins jah airþa, jota ains aiþþau ains striks ni usleiþiþ af witoda, unte allata wairþiþ. [19]Iþ saei nu gatairiþ aina anabusne þizo minnistono jah laisjai swa mans, minnista haitada in þiudangardjai himine; iþ saei taujiþ jah laisjai swa, sah mikils haitada in þiudangardjai himine. [20]Qiþa auk izwis þatei nibai managizo wairþiþ izwaraizos garaihteins þau þize bokarje jah Fareisaie, ni þau qimiþ in þiudangardjai himine.

[21] "Hausideduþ þatei qiþan ist þaim airizam: 'Ni maurþrjais, iþ saei maurþreiþ skula wairþiþ stauai.' [22]Aþþan ik qiþa izwis þatei hwazuh modags broþr seinamma sware skula wairþiþ stauai. Iþ saei qiþiþ broþr seinamma 'raka' skula wairþiþ gaqumþai; aþþan saei qiþiþ 'dwala' skula wairþiþ in Gaiainnan funins. [23]Jabai nu bairais aibr[2] þein du hunslastada jah jainar gamuneis þatei broþar þeins habaiþ hwa bi þuk, [24]aflet jainar þo giba þeina in andwairþja hunslastadis jah gagg faurþis gasibjon broþr þeinamma, jah biþe atgaggands atbair þo giba þeina. [25]Sijais waila hugjands andastauin þeinamma sprauto, und þatei is in wiga miþ imma, ibai hwan atgibai þuk sa andastaua stauin, jah sa staua þuk atgibai andbahta, jah in karkara galagjaza. [26]Amen qiþa þus: ni usgaggis jainþro unte usgibis þana minnistan kintu.

[27] "Hausideduþ þatei qiþan ist: 'Ni horinos.' [28]Aþþan ik qiþa izwis þatei hwazuh saei saihwiþ qinon du luston izos ju gahorinoda izai in hairtin seinamma. [29]Iþ jabai augo þein þata taihswo marzjai þuk, usstagg ita jah wairp af þus. Batizo ist auk þus ei fraqistnai ains liþiwe þeinaize jah ni allata leik þein gadriusai in Gaiainnan. [30]Jah jabai taihswo þeina handus marzjai þuk, afmait þo jah wairp af þus. Batizo ist auk þus ei fraqistnai ains liþiwe þeinaize jah ni allata leik þein gadriusai in Gaiainnan.

[31]"Qiþanuh þan ist þatei, 'Hwazuh[3] saei afletai qen gibai izai afstassais bokos.' [32]Iþ ik qiþa izwis þatei hwazuh saei afletiþ qen seina - inuh fairina kalkinassaus - taujiþ þo horinon; jah sa ize afsatida liugaiþ horinoþ.

[33]"Aftra hausideduþ þatei qiþan ist þaim airizam: 'Ni ufarswarais, iþ usgibais Fraujin aiþans þeinans.' [34]Aþþan ik qiþa izwis ni swaran allis, ni bi himina, unte stols ist Gudis; [35]nih bi airþai, unte fotubaurd ist fotiwe is; nih bi Iairusaulymai, unte baurgs ist þis mikilins þiudanis. [36]nih bi haubida þeinamma swarais, unte ni magt ain tagl hweit aiþþau swart gataujan. [37]Sijaiþþan waurd izwar: 'Ja, ja; ne, ne.' Iþ þata managizo þaim us þamma ubilin ist.

[38]"Hausideduþ þatei qiþan ist: 'Augo und augin, jah tunþu und tunþau.' [39]Iþ ik qiþa izwis: ni andstandan allis þamma unseljin; ak jabai hwas þuk stautai bi taihswon þeina kinnu, wandei imma jah þo anþara. [40]Jah þamma wiljandin miþ þus staua jah paida þeina niman, aflet imma jah wastja. [41]Jah jabai hwas þuk ananauþjai rasta aina, gaggaiþ miþ imma twos. [42]Þamma bidjandin þuk gibais, jah þamma wiljandin af þus leihwan sis ni uswandjais.

[43]"Hausideduþ þatei qiþan ist: 'Frijos nehwundjan þeinana, jah fiais fiand þeinana.' [44]Aþþan ik qiþa izwis: frijoþ fijands izwarans, þiuþjaiþ þans wrikandans izwis, waila taujaiþ þaim hatjandam izwis, jah bidjaiþ bi þans usþriutandans izwis, [45]ei wairþaiþ sunjus attins izwaris þis in himinam, unte sunnon seina urranneiþ ana ubilans jah godans, jah rigneiþ ana garaihtans jah ana inwindans. [46]Jabai auk frijoþ þans frijondans izwis ainans, hwo mizdono habaiþ? Niu jah þai þiudo þata samo taujand? [47]Jah jabai goleiþ þans frijonds izwarans þatainei, hwe managizo taujiþ? Niu jah motarjos þata samo taujand? [48]Sijaiþ nu jus fullatojai swaswe atta izwar sa in himinam fullatojis ist."

---

[1] Probably to be corrected to *liuhteiþ*.

[2] Usually corrected to **tibr* on the basis of OE *tifer*, OHG *zebar* (offering).

[3] Corrected from CA *hwahwazuh*.

Chapter VI

[1]"Atsaihwiþ armaion izwara ni taujan in andwairþja manne du saihwan im; aiþþau laun ni habaiþ fram attin izwaramma þamma in himinam. [2]Þan nu taujais armaion, ni haurnjais faura þus, swaswe þai liutans taujand in gaqumþim jah in garunsim, ei hauhjaindau fram mannam. Amen qiþa izwis: andnemun mizdon seina. [3]Iþ þuk taujandan armaion ni witi hleidumei þeina hwa taujiþ taihwso þeina, [4]ei sijai so armahairtiþa þeina in fulhsnja, jah atta þeins saei saihwiþ in fulhsnja[4] usgibiþ þus in bairhtein.

[5]"Jah þan bidjaiþ, ni sijaiþ swaswe þai liutans, unte frijond in gaqumþim jah waihstam plapjo standandans bidjan, ei gaumjaindau mannam. Amen qiþa izwis þatei haband mizdon seina. [6]Iþ þu þan bidjais, gagg in heþjon þeina, jah galukands haurdai þeinai bidei du attin þeinamma in fulhsnja, jah atta þeins saei saihwiþ in fulhsnja usgibiþ þus in bairhtein.

[7]"Bidjandansuþþan ni filuwaurdjaiþ, swaswe þai þiudo; þugkeiþ im auk ei in filuwaurdein seinai andhausjaindau. [8]Ni galeikoþ nu þaim, wait auk atta izwar þizei jus þaurbuþ, faurþizei jus bidjaiþ ina. [9]Swa nu bidjaiþ jus:

Atta unsar þu in himinam, weihnai namo þein.
[10]Qimai þiudinassus þeins.
Wairþai wilja þeins, swe in himina, jah ana airþai.
[11]Hlaif unsarana þana sinteinan gif us himma daga.
[12]Jah aflet uns þatei skulans sijaima
swaswe jah weis afletam þaim skulam unsaraim.
[13]Jah ni briggais uns in fraistubnjai,
ak lausei uns af þamma ubilin;
unte þeina ist þiudangardi jah mahts jah wulþus in aiwins. Amen.

[14]Unte jabai afletiþ mannam missadedins ize, afletiþ jah izwis atta izwar sa ufar himinam. [15]Iþ jabai ni afletiþ mannam missadedins ize, ni þau atta izwar afletiþ missadedins izwaros. [16]Aþþan biþe fastaiþ, ni wairþaiþ swaswe þai liutans gaurai; frawardjand auk andwairþja seina ei gasaihwaindau mannam fastandans. Amen qiþa izwis, þatei andnemun mizdon seina. [17]Iþ þu fastands salbo haubiþ þein, jah ludja þeina þwah, [18]ei ni gasaihwaizau mannam fastands, ak attin þeinamma þamma in fulhsnja, jah atta þeins saei saihwiþ in fulhsnja, usgibiþ þus.

[19]"Ni huzdjaiþ izwis huzda ana airþai, þarei malo jah nidwa frawardeiþ, jah þarei þiubos ufgraband jah hlifand. [20]Iþ huzdjaiþ izwis huzda in himina, þarei nih malo nih nidwa frawardeiþ, jah þarei þiubos ni ufgraband nih stiland. [21]Þarei auk ist huzd izwar, þaruh ist jah hairto izwar.

[22]"Lukarn leikis ist augo: jabai nu augo þein ainfalþ ist, allata leik þein liuhadein wairþiþ; [23]iþ jabai augo þein unsel ist, allata leik þein riqizein wairþiþ. Jabai nu liuhaþ þata in þus riqiz ist, þata riqiz hwan filu!

[24]"Ni manna mag twaim fraujam skalkinon: unte jabai fijaiþ ainana, jah anþarana frijoþ; aiþþau ainamma ufhauseiþ, iþ anþaramma frakann. Ni maguþ Guda skalkinon jah mammonin.

[25]"Duþþe qiþa izwis: Ni maurnaiþ saiwalai izwarai hwa matjaiþ jah hwa drigkaiþ, nih leika izwaramma hwe wasjaiþ; niu saiwala mais ist fodeinai jah leik wastjom? [26]Insaihwiþ du fuglam himinis, þei ni saiand nih sneiþand, nih lisand in banstins, jah atta izwar sa ufar himinam fodeiþ ins. Niu jus mais wulþrizans sijuþ þaim? [27]Iþ hwas izwara maurnands mag anaaukan ana wahstu seinana aleina aina? [28]Jah bi wastjos hwa saurgaiþ? Gakunnaiþ blomans haiþjos, hwaiwa wahsjand; nih arbaidjand nih spinnand. [29]Qiþuh þan izwis þatei nih Saulaumon in allamma wulþau seinamma gawasida sik swe ains þize. [30]Jah þande þata hawi haiþjos himma daga wisando jah gistradagis in auhn galagiþ Guþ swa wasjiþ, hwaiwa mais izwis leitil galaubjandans? [31]Ni maurnaiþ nu qiþandans: 'Hwa matjam aiþþau hwa drigkam, aiþþau hwe wasjaima?' [32]All auk þata þiudos sokjand; waituh þan atta izwar sa ufar himinam þatei þaurbuþ... (text missing)

Chapter VII

[12] "... <tau>jaina izwis mans, swa jah jus taujaiþ im. Þata auk ist witoþ jah praufeteis.

[4] Corrected here and in vs. 6 from CA *fulhsja.*

[13]"Inngaggaiþ þairh aggwu daur, unte braid daur jah rums wigs[5] sa brigganda in fralustai, jah managai sind þai inngaleiþandans þairh þata. [14]Hwan aggwu þata daur jah þraihans wigs sa brigganda in libainai, jah fawai sind þai bigitandans þana.

[15]"Atsaihwiþ sweþauh faura liugnapraufetum þaim izei qimand at izwis in wastjom lambe, iþ innaþro sind wulfos wilwandans. [16]Bi akranam ize ufkunnaiþ ins. Ibai lisanda af þaurnum weinabasja aiþþau af wigadeinom smakkans? [17]Swa all bagme godaize akrana goda gataujiþ, iþ sa ubila bagms akrana ubila gataujiþ. [18]Ni mag bagms þiuþeigs akrana ubila gataujan, nih bagms ubils akrana þiuþeiga gataujan. [19]All bagme ni taujandane akran god usmaitada jah in fon atlagjada. [20]Þannu bi akranam ize ufkunnaiþ ins.

[21]"Ni hwazuh saei qiþiþ mis, 'Frauja, frauja,' inngaleiþiþ in þiudangardja himine, ak sa taujands wiljan attins meinis þis in himinam. [22]Managai qiþand mis in jainamma daga, 'Frauja, frauja, niu þeinamma namin praufetidedum, jah þeinamma namin unhulþons uswaurpum, jah þeinamma namin mahtins mikilos gatawidedum?' [23]Jah þan andhaita im þatei, 'Ni hwanhun kunþa izwis. Afleiþiþ fairra mis, jus waurkjandans unsibjona.'

[24]"Hwazuh nu saei hauseiþ waurda meina jah taujiþ þo, galeiko ina waira frodamma, saei gatimrida razn sein ana staina. [25]Jah atiddja dalaþ rign jah qemun ahwos jah waiwoun windos jah bistugqun bi þamma razna jainamma, jah ni gadraus, unte gasuliþ was ana staina. [26]Jah hwazuh saei hauseiþ waurda meina jah ni taujiþ þo, galeikoda mann dwalamma, saei gatimrida razn sein ana malmin. [27]Jah atiddja dalaþ rign jah qemun ahwos jah waiwoun windos jah bistugqun bi jainamma razna, jah gadraus, jah was drus is mikils."

[28]Jah warþ, þan ustauh Iesus þo waurda, biabridedun manageins ana laiseinai is. [29]Was auk laisjands ins swe waldufni habands, jah ni swaswe bokarjos.

Chapter VIII

[1]Dalaþ þan atgaggandin imma af fairgunja, laistidedun afar imma iumjons managos. [2]Jah sai, manna þrutsfill habands durinnands inwait ina qiþands: "Frauja, jabai wileis, magt mik gahrainjan." [3]Jah ufrakjands handu attaitok imma qiþands: "Wiljau, wairþ hrains!" Jah suns hrain warþ þata þrutsfill is. [4]Jah qaþ imma Iesus: "Saihw ei mann ni qiþais, ak gagg, þuk silban ataugei gudjin, jah atbair giba þoei anabauþ Moses du weitwodiþai im.

[5]Afaruh þan þata innatgaggandin imma in Kafarnaum, duatiddja imma hundafaþs bidjands ina [6]jah qiþands: "Frauja, þiumagus meins ligiþ in garda usliþa, harduba balwiþs." [7]Jah qaþ du imma Iesus: "Ik qimands gahailja ina." [8]Jah andhafjands sa hundafaþs qaþ: "Frauja, ni im wairþs ei uf hrot mein inngaggais, ak þatainei qiþ waurda jah gahailniþ sa þiumagus meins. [9]Jah auk ik manna im habands uf waldufnja meinamma gadrauhtins, jah qiþa du þamma: 'Gagg,' jah gaggiþ, jah anþaramma: 'Qim!' jah qimiþ, jah du skalka meinamma: 'Tawei þata!' jah taujiþ." [10]Gahausjands þan Iesus sildaleikida jah qaþ du þaim afarlaistjandam: "Amen qiþa izwis, ni in Israela swalauda galaubein bigat. [11]Aþþan qiþa izwis þatei managai fram urrunsa jah saggqa qimand, jah anakumbjand miþ Abrahama jah Isaka jah Iakoba in þiudangardjai himine; [12]iþ þai sunjus þiudangardjos uswairpanda in riqis þata hindumisto; jainar wairþiþ grets ja krusts tunþiwe." [13]Jah qaþ Iesus þamma hundafada: "Gagg, jah swaswe galaubides wairþai þus." Jah gahailnoda sa þiumagus is in jainai hweilai.

[14]Jah qimands Iesus in garda Paitraus, jah gasahw swaihron is ligandein in heitom. [15]Jah attaitok handau izos jah aflailot ija so heito; jah urrais jah andbahtida imma. [16]At andanahtja þan waurþanamma, atberun du imma daimonarjans managans, jah uswarp þans ahmans waurda, jah allans þans ubil habandans gahailida, [17]ei usfullnodedi þata gamelido þairh Esaian praufetu qiþandan: 'Sa unmahtins unsaros usnam jah sauhtins usbar.'"

[18]Gasaihwands þan Iesus managans hiuhmans bi sik, haihait galeiþan siponjans hindar marein. [19]Jah duatgaggands ains bokareis qaþ du imma: "Laisari, laistja þuk, þishwaduh þadei gaggis." [20]Jah qaþ du imma Iesus: "Fauhons grobos aigun, jah fuglos himinis sitlans, iþ sunus mans ni habaiþ hwar haubiþ sein anahnaiwjai." [21]Anþaruh þan siponje is qaþ du imma: "Frauja, uslaubei mis frumist galeiþan jah gafilhan attan meinana." [22]Iþ

[5] Corrected from CA *wigss.*

Iesus qaþ du imma: "Laistei afar mis, jah let þans dauþans filhan seinans dauþans."

23Jah innatgaggandin imma in skip, afariddjedun imma siponjos is. 24Jah sai, wegs mikils warþ in marein, swaswe þata skip gahuliþ wairþan fram wegim; iþ is saislep. 25Jah duatgaggandans siponjos is urraisidedun ina qiþandans: "Frauja, nasei unsis, fraqistnam." 26Jah qaþ du im Iesus: "Hwa faurhteiþ, leitil galaubjands?" Þanuh urreisands gasok windam jah marein, jah warþ wis mikil. 27Iþ þai mans sildaleikidedun qiþandans: "Hwileiks ist sa, ei jah windos jah marei ufhausjand imma?"

28Jah qimandin imma hindar marein in gauja Gairgaisaine, gamotidedun imma twai daimonarjos us hlaiwasnom rinnandans, sleidjai filu, swaswe ni mahta manna usleiþan þairh þana wig jainana. 29Jah sai, hropidedun qiþandans: "Hwa uns jah þus, Iesu, sunau Gudis? Qamt her faur mel balwjan unsis?" 30Wasuh þan fairra im hairda sweine managaize haldana. 31Iþ þo skohsla bedun ina qiþandans: "Jabai uswairpis uns, uslaubei uns galeiþan in þo hairda sweine." 32Jah qaþ du im: "Gaggiþ!" Iþ eis usgaggandans galiþun in hairda sweine; jah sai, run gawaurhtedun sis alla so hairda and driuson in marein, jah gadauþnodedun in watnam. 33Iþ þai haldandans gaþlauhun jah galeiþandans gataihun in baurg all bi þans daimonarjans. 34Jah sai, alla so baurgs usiddja wiþra Iesu, jah gasaihwandans ina bedun ei usliþi hindar markos ize.

Chapter IX

1Jah atsteigands in skip ufarlaiþ jah qam in seinai baurg. 2Þanuh atberun du imma usliþan ana ligra ligandan. Jah gasaihwands Iesus galaubein ize qaþ du þamma usliþin: "Þrafstei þuk, barnilo! Afletanda þus frawaurhteis þeinos." 3Þaruh sumai þize bokarje qeþun in sis silbam: "Sa wajamereiþ." 4Jah witands Iesus þos mitonins ize qaþ: "Duhwe jus mitoþ ubila in hairtam izwaraim? 5Hwaþar ist raihtis azetizo qiþan 'Afletanda þus frawaurhteis,' þau qiþan 'Urreis jah gagg?' 6Aþþan ei witeiþ þatei waldufni habaiþ sa sunus mans ana airþai afleitan frawaurhtins..." Þanuh qaþ du þamma usliþin: "Urreisands nim þana ligr þeinana jag gagg in gard þeinana." 7Jah urreisands galaiþ in gard seinana. 8Gasaihwandeins þan manageins ohtedun sildaleikjandans jah mikilidedun Guþ þana gibandan waldufni swaleikata mannam.

9Jah þairhleiþands Iesus jainþro gasahw mannan sitandan at motai, Maþþaiu haitanana, jah qaþ du imma: "Laistei afar mis." Jah usstandands iddja afar imma. 10Jah warþ, biþe is anakumbida in garda, jah sai, managai motarjos jah frawaurhtai qimandans miþanakumbidedun Iesua jah siponjam is. 11Jah gaumjandans Fareisaieis qeþun du þaim siponjam is: "Duhwe miþ motarjam jah frawaurhtaim matjiþ sa laisareis izwar?" 12Iþ Iesus gahausjands qaþ du im: "Ni þaurbun hailai lekeis, ak þai unhaili habandans. 13Aþþan gaggaiþ, ganimiþ hwa sijai: 'Armahairtiþa wiljau jah ni hunsl.' Niþþan qam laþon uswaurhtans, ak frawaurhtans."

14Þanuh atiddjedun siponjos Iohannes qiþandans: "Duhwe weis jah Fareisaieis fastam filu, iþ þai siponjos þeinai ni fastand?" 15Jah qaþ du im Iesus: ibai magun sunjus bruþfadis qainon und þata hweilos þei miþ im ist bruþfaþs? Iþ atgaggand dagos, þan afnimada af im sa bruþfaþs, jah þan fastand. 16Aþþan ni hwashun lagjiþ du plata fanan þarihis ana snagan fairnjana, unte afnimiþ fullon af þamma snagin, jah wairsiza gataura wairþiþ. 17Niþþan giutand wein niujata in balgins fairnjans, aiþþau distaurnand balgeis; biþeh þan jah wein usgutniþ jah balgeis fraqistnand; ak giutand wein juggata in balgins niujans, jah bajoþum gabairgada."

18Miþþanei is rodida þata du im, þaruh reiks ains qimands inwait ina, qiþands þatei, "Dauhtar meina nu gaswalt; akei qimands atlagei handu þeina ana ija, jah libaiþ." 19Jah urreisands Iesus iddja afar imma jah siponjos is. 20Jah sai, qino bloþarinnandei .ib. wintruns duatgaggandei aftaro attaitok skauta wastjos is; 21qaþuh auk in sis: "Jabai þatainei atteka wastjai is ganisa." 22Iþ Iesus gawandjands sik jah gasaihwands þo qaþ: "Þrafstei þuk dauhtar! Galaubeins þeina ganasida þuk." Jah ganas so qino fram þizai hweilai jainai. 23Jah qimands Iesus in garda þis reikis jah gasaihwands swigljans jah haurnjans haurnjandans jah managein auhjondein, qaþ du im: 24"Afleiþiþ, unte ni gaswalt so mawi, ak slepiþ." Jah bihlohun ina. 25Þanuh þan usdribana warþ so managei, atgaggands inn habaida handu izos, jah urrais so mawi. 26Jah usiddja meriþa so and alla jaina airþa.

27Jah hwarbondin Iesua jainþro, laistidedun afar imma twai blindans, hropjandans jah qiþandans: "Armai uggkis, sunau Daweidis!" 28Qimandin þan in garda duatiddjedun imma þai blindans jah qaþ im Iesus: "Gaulaubjats þatei magjau þata taujan?" Qeþun du imma: "Jai, frauja!" 29Þanuh attaitok augam ize qiþands: "Bi galaubeinai iggqarai wairþai iggqis." 30Jah usluknodedun im augona, jah inagida ins Iesus qiþands: "Saihwats ei manna ni witi. 31Iþ eis usgaggandans usmeridedun ina in allai airþai jainai.

32Þanuh biþe utusiddjedun eis, sai, atberun imma mannan baudana daimonari. 33Jah biþe usdribans warþ unhulþo, rodida sa dumba, jah sildaleikidedun manageins qiþandans: "Ni aiw swa uskunþ was in Israela." 34Iþ Fareisaieis qeþun: "In fauramaþlja unhulþono usdreibiþ unhulþons."

35Jah bitauh Iesus baurgs allos jah haimos laisjands in gaqumþim ize, jah merjands aiwaggeljon þiudangardjos jah hailjands allos sauhtins jah alla unhailja. 36Gasaihwands þan þos manageins infeinoda in ize, unte wesun afdauidai jah frawaurpanai swe lamba ni habandona hairdeis. 37Þanuh qaþ du siponjam seinaim: "Asans raihtis managa, iþ waurstwjans fawai. 38Bidjiþ nu fraujan asanais ei ussandjai waurstwjans in asan seina."

Chapter X

1Jah athaitands þans twalif si[ponjans ...[vss. 1-23a missing].

23 "... þizai baurg, þliuhaiþ in anþara: amen auk qiþa izwis, ei ni ustiuhiþ baurgs Israelis, unte qimiþ sa sunus mans.

24"Nist siponeis ufar laisarja, nih skalks ufar fraujin seinamma. 25Ganah siponi ei wairþai swe laisareis is jah skalks swe frauja is; jabai gardawaldand Baiailzaibul haihaitun, und hwan filu mais þans innakundans is.

26"Ni nunu ogeiþ izwis ins; ni waiht auk is gahuliþ, þatei ni andhuljaidau, jah fulgin, þatei ni ufkunnaidau. 27Þatei qiþa izwis in riqiza, qiþaiþ in liuhada, jah þatei in auso gahauseiþ, merjaiþ ana hrotam. 28Jah ni ogeiþ izwis þans usqimandans leika þatainei, iþ saiwalai ni magandans usqiman, iþ ogeiþ mais þana magandan jah saiwalai jah leika fraqistjan in Gaiainnan. 29Niu twai sparwans assarjau bugjanda? Jah ains ize ni gadriusiþ ana airþa inuh attins izwaris wiljan. 30Aþþan izwara jah tagla haubidis alla garaþana sind. 31Ni nunu ogeiþ; managaim sparwam batizans sijuþ jus. 32Sahwazuh nu saei andhaitiþ mis in andwairþja manne, andhaita jah ik imma in andwairþja attins meinis saei in himinam ist. 33Iþ þishwanoh saei afaikiþ mik in andwairþja manne, afaika jah ik ina in andwairþja attins meinis þis saei in himinam ist.

34"Nih ahjaiþ þatei qemjau lagjan gawairþi ana airþa; ni qam lagjan gawairþi, ak hairu. 35Qam auk skaidan mannan wiþra attan is jah dauhtar wiþra aiþein izos jah bruþ wiþra swaihron izos; 36jah fijands mans innakundai is. 37Saei frijoþ attan aiþþau aiþein ufar mik, nist meina wairþs; jah saei frijoþ sunu aiþþau dauhtar ufar mik, nist meina wairþs. 38Jah saei ni nimiþ galgan seinana jah laistjai afar mis, nist meina wairþs. 39Saei bigitiþ saiwala seinana, fraqisteiþ izai; jah saei fraqisteiþ saiwalai seinai in meina, bigitiþ þo.

40"Sa andnimands izwis mik andnimiþ, jah sa mik andnimands andnimiþ þana sandjandan mik. 41Sa andnimands praufetu in namin praufetaus[6] mizdon praufetaus nimiþ, jah sa andnimands garaihtana in namin garaihtis mizdon garaihtis nimiþ. 42Jah saei gadragkeiþ ainana þize minnistane stikla kaldis watins þatainei in namin siponeis, amen qiþa izwis, ei ni fraqisteiþ mizdon seinai."

Chapter XI

1Jah warþ, biþe usfullida Iesus anabiudands þaim twalif siponjam seinaim, ushof sik jainþro du laisjan jah merjan and baurgs ize. 2Iþ Iohannes gahausjands in karkarai waurstwa Xristaus, insandjands bi siponjam seinaim qaþ du imma: 3"Þu is sa qimanda þau anþarizuh beidaima?" 4Jah andhafjands Iesus qaþ du im: "Gaggandans gateihiþ Iohanne þatei gahauseiþ jah gasaihwiþ. 5Blindai ussaihwand, jah haltai gaggand, þrusfillai hrainjai wairþand, jah baudai gahausjand, jah dauþai urreisand, jah unledai wailamerjanda. 6Jah audags ist hwazuh saei ni gamarzjada in mis."

7At þaim þan afgaggandam, dugann Iesus qiþan þaim manageim bi Iohannen: "Hwa usiddjeduþ ana auþida saihwan? Raus fram winda wagidata? 8Akei

---

6 Corrected from CA *praufetis*.

hwa usiddjeduþ saihwan? Mannan hnasqjaim wastjom gawasidana? Sai, þaiei hnasqjaim wasidai sind in gardim þiudane sind. 9Akei hwa usiddjeduþ saihwan? Praufetu? Jai, qiþa izwis, jah managizo praufetau. 10Sa ist auk bi þanei gameliþ ist:

> 'Sai, ik insandja aggilu meinana[7] faura þus,
> saei gamanweiþ wig þeinana faura þus.'

11Amen qiþa izwis: Ni urrais in baurim qinono maiza Iohanne þamma daupjandin, iþ sa minniza in þiudangardjai himine maiza imma ist. 12Framuh þan þaim dagam Iohannis þis daupjandins und hita þiudangardi himine anamahtjada, jah anamahtjandans frawilwand þo. 13Allai auk praufeteis jah witoþ und Iohanne fauraqeþun, 14jah jabai wildedeiþ miþniman, sa ist Helias, saei skulda qiman. 15Saei habai au[sona haujsandona, ga]hausja[i.]

[Remainder of the chapter is too fragmentary to include here.]

[Chapters XI:25 toXXVI:70 are missing in Codex Argenteus; a portion of the intervening text is found in Ambrosianus C: XXV:38 to XXVI:2; XXVI65-70; CA resumes at XXVI:71]

Chapter XXV

38"'Hwanuh þan þuk sehwum gast jah galaþodedum? Aiþþau naqadana jah wasidedum? 39Hwanuh þan þuk sehwum siukana aiþþau in karkarai jah atiddjedum du þus?' 40Jah andhafjands sa þiudans qiþiþ du im: 'Amen, qiþa izwis: jah þanei tawideduþ ainamma þize minnistane broþre meinaize, mis tawideduþ.' 41Þanuh qiþiþ jah þaim af hleidumein ferai: 'Gaggiþ fairra mis, jus fraqiþanans, in fon þata aiweino, þata manwido unhulþin jah aggilum is. 42Unte gredags was janni gebuþ mis matjan; afþaursiþs was janni dragkideduþ mik; 43gasts, janni galaþ*ode*duþ mik; naqaþs, janni waside*duþ* mik; siuks jah in karkarai, janni gaweisodeduþ meina.' 44Þanuh andhafjand jah þai qiþandans: 'Frauja, hwan þuk sehwum gredagana aiþþau afþaursidana aiþþau gast aiþþau naqadana aiþþau siukana aiþþau in karkarai janni andbahtidedeima þus?' 45Þanuh andhafjiþ im qiþands: 'Amen qiþa izwis, jah þanei ni tawideduþ ainamma þize leitilane, mis ni tawideduþ.' 46Jah galeiþand þai in balwein aiweinon, iþ þai garaihtans in libain aiweinon."

Chapter XXVI

1Jah warþ, biþe ustauh Iesus alla þo waurda, qaþ siponjam sein*aim*: 2"Wituþ þatei afar twans dagans p*aska* wairþiþ, jassa sunus mans atgibada du ushramjan. 3Þanuh... [text missing from XXVI.3 - 65a]

...66"Hwa izwis þugkeiþ?" Iþ eis andhafjandans qeþun: "Skula dauþaus ist." 67Þanuh spiwun ana andawleizn is jah kaupastedun ina; sumaiþþan lofam slohun, 68qiþandans: "Praufetei unsis, Xristu, hwas ist sa slahands þuk?"

69Iþ Paitrus uta sat ana rohsnai, jah duatiddja imma aina þiwi qiþandei: "Jah þu wast miþ Iesua þamma Galeilaiau." 70Iþ is laugnida faura þaim allaim qiþands: "Ni wait (CA resumes here) hwa qiþis." 71Usgaggandan þan ina in daur, gasahw ina anþara jah qaþ du þaim jainar: "Jah sa was miþ Iesua þamma Nazoraiau." 72Jah aftra afaiaik miþ aiþa swarands þatei "Ni kann þana mannan." 73Afar leitil þan atgaggandans þai standandans qeþun Paitrau: "Bi sunjai, jah þu þize is, jah auk razda þeina bandweiþ þuk." 74Þanuh dugann afdomjan jah swaran þatei "Ni kann þana mannan." Jah suns hana hrukida. 75Jah gamunda Paitrus waurdis Iesuis qiþanis du sis, þatei "Faur hanins hruk þrim sinþam afaikis mik." Jah usgaggands ut gaigrot baitraba.

Chapter XXVII

1At maurgin þan waurþanana, runa nemun allai gudjans jah þai sinistans manageins bi Iesu, ei afdauþidedeina ina. 2Jah gabindandans ina gatauhun jah anafulhun ina Pauntiau Peilatau kindina.

3Þanuh gasaihwands Iudas sa galewjands ina þatei du stauai gatauhans warþ, idreigonds gawandida þans þrins tiguns silubrinaize gudjam jah sinistam 4qiþands: "Frawaurhta mis galewjands bloþ swikn." Iþ eis qeþun: "Hwa kara unsis? Þu witeis." 5Jah atwairpands þaim silubr<ein>am in alh aflaiþ, jah galeiþands ushaihah sik. 6Iþ þai gudjans nimandans

[7] Corrected from CA *meinna*.

þans skattans qeþun: "Ni skuld ist lagjan þans in kaurbanau,[8] unte andawairþi[9] bloþis ist." 7Garuni þan nimandans usbauhtedun us þaim þana akr kasjins du usfilhan ana gastim. 8Duþþe haitans warþ akrs jains 'akrs bloþis' und hina dag. 9Þanuh usfullnoda þata qiþano þairh Iairaimian praufetu qiþandan: "Jah usnemun þrins tiguns silubreinaize andawairþi þis wairþodins, þatei garahnidedun fram sunum Israelis, 10jah atgebun ins und akra kasjins, swaswe anabauþ mis Frauja."

11Iþ Iesus stoþ faura kindina, jah frah ina sa kindins qiþands: "Þu is þiudans Iudaie?" Iþ Iesus qaþ du imma: "Þu qiþis." 12Jah miþþanei wrohiþs was fram þaim gudjam jah sinistam, ni waiht andhof. 13Þanuh qaþ du imma Peilatus: "Niu hauseis hwan filu ana þuk weitwodjand?" 14Jah ni andhof imma wiþra ni ainhun waurde, swaswe sildaleikida sa kindins filu.

15And dulþ þan hwarjoh[10] biuhts was sa kindins fraletan ainana þizai managein bandjan, þanei wildedun. 16Habaidedunuh þan bandjan gatarhidana <haitanana> Barabban. 17Gaqumanaim þan im, qaþ im Peilatus: "Hwana wileiþ ei fraletau izwis? Barabban þau Iesus, saei haitada Xristus?" 18Wissa auk þatei in neiþis atgebun ina. 19Sitandin þan imma ana stauastola, insandida du imma qens is qiþandei: "Ni waiht þus jah þamma garaihtin [.... text missing]

42"...Israelis ist, atsteigadau nu af þamma galgin ei gasaihwaima jah galaubjam imma. 43Trauida du Guda. Lausjadau nu ina, jabai wili ina. Qaþ auk þatei 'Gudis im sunus.'" 44Þatuh samo jah þai waidedjans þai miþ-ushramidans imma idweitidedun imma.

45Fram saihston þan hweilai warþ riqis ufar allai airþai und hweila niundon. 46Iþ þan bi hweila niundon ufhropida Iesus stibnai mikilai qiþands: "Helei, Helei, lima sibakþani." (Þatei ist: "Guþ meins, Guþ meins, duhwe mis bilaist?") 47Iþ sumai þize jainar standandane gahausjandans qeþun þatei "Helian wopeiþ sa." 48Jah suns þragida ains us im jah nam swamm fulljands aketis, jah lagjands ana raus draggkida ina. 49Iþ þai anþarai qeþun: "Let, ei saihwam, qimaiu Helias nasjan ina." 50Iþ Iesus aftra hropjands stibnai mikilai aflailot ahman.

51Jah þan faurhah alhs diskritnoda in twa, iupaþro und dalaþ, jah airþa inreiraida, jah stainos disskritnodedun, 52jah hlaiwasnos usluknodedun, jah managa leika þize ligandane weihaize urrisun. 53Jah usgaggandans us hlaiwasnom afar urrist is innatgaggandans in þo weihon baurg jah ataugidedun sik managaim. 54Iþ hundafaþs jah þai miþ imma witandans Iesua, gasaihwandans þo reiron jah þo waurþanona, ohtedun abraba, qiþandans: "Bi sunjai Gudis sunus ist sa."

55Wesunuh þan jainar qinons managos fairraþro saihwandeins, þozei laistidedun afar Iesua fram Galeilaia, andbahtjandeins imma, 56in þaimei was Marja so Magdalene, jah Marja so Iakobis jah Iosez<is> aiþei, jah aiþei suniwe Zaibaidaiaus. 57Iþ þan seiþu warþ, qam manna gabigs af Areimaþaias þizuh namo Iosef, saei jah silba siponida Iesua. 58Sah atgaggands du Peilatau baþ þis leikis Iesuis. Þanuh Peilatus uslaubida giban þata leik. 59Jah nimands þata leik Iosef biwand ita sabana hrainjamma 60jah galagida ita in niujamma seinamma hlaiwa þatei ushuloda ana staina, jah faurwalwjands staina mikilamma daurons þis hlaiwis galaiþ. 61Wasuh þan jainar Marja Magdalene jah so anþara Marja sitandeins andwairþis þamma hlaiwa.

62Iftumin þan daga, saei ist afar Paraskaiwein, gaqemun auhumistans gudjans jah Fareisaieis du Peilatau 63qiþandans: "Frauja, gamundedum þatei jains airzjands qaþ nauh libands: 'Afar þrins dagans urreisa.' 64Hait nu witan þamma hlaiwa und þana þridjan[11] dag, ibai ufto qimandans þai siponjos is binimaina imma jah qiþaina du managein: 'Urrais us dauþaim,' jah ist so speidizei airziþa wairsizei þizai frumein." 65Qaþ im Peilatus: "Habaiþ wardjans. Gaggiþ witaiduh swaswe kunnuþ." 66Iþ eis gaggandans galukun þata hlaiw, faursigljandans þana... [The remainder of the Gospel According to Matthew is missing.]

8 Corrected from CA ***kaurbanaun.***

9 Corrected from CA ***andwairþi*** (cf. vs 9 below).

10 Corrected from CA ***hwarjanoh.***

11 Corrected from CA ***þridjin.***

The Gospel According to John

Chapter V

45 ...þatei ik wrohidedjau izwis du attin; ist saei wrohida izwis Moses, du þammei jus weneiþ. 46Jabai allis Mose galaubidedeiþ, gaþaulaubidedeiþ mis; bi mik auk jains gamelida. 47Þande nu jainis melam ni galaubeiþ, hwaiwa meinaim waurdam galaubjaiþ?"

Chapter VI

1Afar þata galaiþ Iesus ufar marein þo Galeilaie jah Tibairiade. 2Jah laistida ina manageins filu, unte gasehwun taiknins þozei gatawida bi siukaim. 3Usiddja þan ana fairguni Iesus jah jainar gasat miþ siponjam seinaim. 4Wasuh þan nehwa Pasxa, so dulþs Iudaie. 5Þaruh ushof augona Iesus jah gaumida þammei manageins filu iddja du imma, qaþuh du Filippau: "Hwaþro bugjam hlaibans ei matjaina þai?" 6(Þatuh þan qaþ fraisands ina; iþ silba wissa þatei habaida taujan.) 7Andhof imma Filippus: "Twaim hundam skatte hlaibos ni ganohai sind þaim, þei nimai hwarjizuh leitil." 8Qaþ ains þize siponje is, Andraias, broþar Paitraus Seimonaus: 9"Ist magula ains her, saei habaiþ .e. hlaibans barizeinans jah .b. fiskans. Akei þata hwa ist du swa managaim?" 10Iþ Iesus qaþ: "Waurkeiþ þans mans anakumbjan." Wasuh þan hawi manag ana þamma stada. Þaruh anakumbidedun wairos raþjon swaswe fimf þusundjos. 11Namuh þan þans hlaibans Iesus awiliudonds gadailida þaim anakumbjandam; samaleiko jah þize fiske swa filu swa wildedun. 12Þanuh, biþe sadai waurþun, qaþ du siponjam seinaim. "Galisiþ þos aflifnandeins drauhsnos, þei waihtai ni fraqistnai." 13Þanuh galesun jah gafullidedun .ib. tainjons gabruko us fimf hlaibam þaim barizeinam þatei aflifnoda þaim matjandam. 14Þaruh þai mans gasaihwandans þoei gatawida taikn Iesus, qeþun þatei: "Sa ist bi sunjai praufetus sa qimanda in þo manaseþ." 15Iþ Iesus kunnands þatei munaidedun usgaggan jah wilwan ei tawidedeina ina du þiudana, afiddja aftra in fairguni is ains.

16Iþ swe seiþu warþ, atiddjedun siponjos is ana marein, jah usstigun in skip, iddjedunuh afar marein in Kafarnaum. Jah riqis juþan warþ jah ni atiddja nauhþan du im Iesus. 18Iþ marei winda mikilamma waiandin urraisida was. 19Þaruh farjandans swe spaurde .k. jah .e. aiþþau .l. gasaihwand Iesu gaggandan ana marein jah nehwa skipa qimandan jah ohtedun sis. 20Þaruh is qaþ: "Ik im. Ni ogeiþ izwis." 21Þaruh wildedun ina niman in skip, jah sunsaiw þata skip warþ ana airþai ana þoei eis iddjedun.

22Iftumin daga managei sei stoþ hindar marein sehwun þatei skip anþar ni was jainar alja ain, jah þatei miþ-ni-qam siponjam seinaim Iesus in þata skip, ak ainai siponjos is galiþun. 23Anþara þan skipa qemun us Tibairiadau nehwa þamma stada, þarei matidedun hlaif, ana þammei awiliudoda Frauja. 24Þaruh þan gasahw managei þatei Iesus nist jainar nih siponjos is, gastigun in skipa jah qemun in Karafnaum sokjandans Iesu.

25Jah bigetun ina hindar marein qeþunuh du imma: "Rabbei, hwan her qamt?" 26Andhof im Iesus jah qaþ: "Amen, amen qiþa izwis, sokeiþ mik, ni þatei sehwuþ taiknins jah fauratanja, ak þatei matideduþ þize hlaibe jah sadai waurþuþ. 27Waurkjaiþ ni þana mat þana fralusanan, ak mat þana wisandan du libainai aiweinon, þanei sunus mans gibiþ izwis; þanuh auk atta gasiglida Guþ." 28Þaruh qeþun du imma: "Hwa taujaima ei waurkjaima waurstwa[1] Gudis?" 29Andhof Iesus jah qaþ du im: "Þatist waurstw Gudis, ei galaubjaiþ þammei insandida jains." 30Qeþun du imma: "Aþþan hwa taujis þu taikne, ei saihwaima jah galaubjaima þus? Hwa waurkeis? 31Attans unsarai manna matidedun ana auþidai swaswe ist gameliþ: 'Hlaif us himina gaf im du matjan.'" 32Þaruh qaþ im Iesus: "Amen, amen qiþa izwis, ni Moses gaf izwis hlaif us himina, ak atta meins gaf izwis hlaif us himina þana sunjeinan. 33Sa auk hlaifs Gudis ist saei atstaig us himina jah gaf libain þizai manasedai." 34Þanuh qeþun du imma: "Frauja, framwigis gif unsis þana hlaif."

35Jah qaþ du im Iesus: "Ik im sa hlaifs libainais; þana gaggandan du mis ni huggreiþ jah þana galaubjandan du mis ni þaurseiþ hwanhun. 36Akei qaþ izwis þatei gasehwuþ mik jah ni galaubeiþ. All þatei gaf mis atta, du mis qimiþ, jah þana gaggandan du mis ni uswairpa ut, 38 unte atstaig us himina, nih þeei taujau wiljan meinana, ak wiljan þis sandjandins mik. 39... (text

[1] Corrected from CA *waurswa.*

missing) 40Þatuh þan ist wilja[2] þis sandjandins mik, ei hwazuh saei saihwiþ þana sunu jah galaubeiþ du imma, aigi libain aiweinon, jah urraisja ina ik in spedistin daga."

41Birodidedun þan Iudaieis bi ina, unte qaþ: "Ik im hlaifs sa atsteigands us himina." 42 Jah qeþun: "Niu sa ist Iesus sa sunus Iosefis, þizei weis kunþedum attan jah aiþein? Hwaiwa nu qiþiþ sa þatei us himina atstaig?" 43Andhof þan Iesus jah qaþ du im: "Ni birodeiþ miþ izwis misso. 44Ni manna mag qiman at mis, nibai atta saei sandida mik atþinsiþ ina, jah ik urraisja ina in þamma spedistin daga. 45Ist gameliþ ana praufetum: 'Jah wairþand allai laisidai Gudis.' Hwazuh nu sa gahausjands at attin jah ganam gaggiþ du mis. 46Ni þatei attan sehwi hwas, nibai saei was fram attin, sa sahw attan. 47Amen, amen qiþa izwis: Saei galaubeiþ du mis aih libain aiweinon. 48Ik im sa hlaifs libainais. 49Attans izwarai matidedun manna in auþidai jah gaswultun. 50Sa ist hlaifs saei us himina atstaig, ei saei þis matjai, ni gadauþnai. 51Ik im hlaifs sa libanda, sa us himina qumana. Jabai hwas matjiþ þis hlaibis, libaiþ in ajukduþ. Jah þan sa hlaifs þanei ik giba, leik mein ist þatei ik giba in þizos manasedais libainais."

52Þanuh sokun miþ sis misso Iudaieis qiþandans: "Hwaiwa mag sa unsis leik giban du matjan?" 53Þaruh qaþ du im Iesus: "Amen, amen qiþa izwis, nibai matjiþ leik þis sunaus mans jah driggkaiþ is bloþ, ni habaiþ libain in izwis silbam. 54Saei matjiþ mein leik jah driggkiþ mein bloþ, aih libain aiweinon, jah ik urraisja ina in þamma spedistin daga. 55Þata auk leik meinata bi sunjai ist mats jah þata bloþ mein bi sunjai is draggk. 56Saei matjiþ mein leik jah driggkiþ mein bloþ in mis wisiþ jah ik in imma. 57Swaswe insandida mik libands atta, jah ik liba in attins, jah saei matjiþ mik jah sa libaiþ in meina. 58Sa ist hlaifs saei us himina atstaig, ni swaswe matidedun attans izwarai manna jah gadauþnodedun, iþ saei matjiþ þana hlaif libaiþ in ajukduþ." 59Þata qaþ in synagoge laisjands in Kafarnaum.

60Þanuh managai gahausjandans þize siponje is qeþun: "Hardu ist þata waurd. Hwas mag þis hausjon? 61Iþ witands Iesus in sis silbin þatei birodidedun þata þai siponjos is, qaþ du im: "Þata izwis gamarzeiþ? 62Jabai nu gasaihwiþ sunu mans ussteigan, þadei was faurþis? 63Ahma ist saei liban taujiþ, þata leik ni boteiþ waiht. Þo waurda þoei ik rodida izwis ahma ist jah libains ist, 64akei sind izwara sumai þaiei ni galaubjand." Wissuh þan us frumistja Iesus hwarjai sind þai ni galaubjandans, jah hwas ist saei galeiweiþ ina. 65Jah qaþ: "Duþe qaþ izwis þatei ni ainshun mag qiman at mis, nibai ist atgiban imma fram attin meinamma." 66Uzuh þamma mela managai galiþun siponje is ibukai jah þanaseiþs miþ imma ni iddjedun. 67Þaruh qaþ Iesus du þaim twalibim: "Ibai jah jus wileiþ galeiþan?" 68Þanuh andhof imma Seimon Paitrus: "Frauja, du hwamma galeiþaima? Waurda libainais aiweinons habais. 69Jah weis galaubidedum jah ufkunþedum þatei þu is Xristus, sunus Gudis libandins." 70Andhof im Iesus: "Niu ik izwis .ib. gawalida jah izwara ains diabaulus ist?" 71Qaþuh þan þana Iudan Seimonis, Iskariotu, sa auk habaida ina galewjan, ains wisands þize twalibe.

Chapter VII

1Jah hwarboda Iesus afar þata in Galeilaia. Ni auk wilda in Iudaia gaggan, unte sokidedun ina þai Iudaieis usqiman. 2Wasuh þan nehwa dulþs Iudaie, so Hleþrastakeins. 3Þanuh qeþun du imma broþrjus is: "Usleiþ þaþro jah gagg in Iudaian, ei jah þai siponjos <þeinai> saihwaina waurstwa þeina þoei þu taujis. 4Ni manna auk in analaugnein hwa taujiþ jah sokeiþ sik uskunþana wisan. Jabai þata taujis, bairhtei þuk silban þizai manasedai." 5Ni auk þai broþrjus is galaubidedun imma. 6Þaruh qaþ im Iesus: "Mel mein ni nauh ist, iþ mel izwar sinteino is manwu. 7Ni mag so manaseþs fijan izwis, iþ mik fijaiþ unte ik weitwodja bi ins þatei waurstwa ize ubila sind. 8Jus galeiþiþ in dulþ þo, iþ ik ni nauh galeiþa in þo dulþ unte meinata mel ni nauh usfulliþ ist." 9Þatuh þan qaþ du im wisands in Galeilaia.

10Iþ biþe galiþun þai broþrjus is, þanuh jah is galaiþ in þo dulþ ni andaugjo, ak swe analaugniba. 11Þanuh Iudaieis sokidedun ina in þizai dulþai jah qeþun: "Hwar ist jains?" 12Jah birodeins mikila <bi ina> was in managein: sumaih qeþun þatei sunjeins ist; anþarai qeþun, "Ne, ak airzeiþ þo managein." 13Nih þan ainshun sweþauh balþaba rodida bi ina in agisis Iudaie. 14Iþ juþan ana midjai dulþ usstaig Iesus in alh jah laisida. 15Jah sildaleikidedun manageins qiþandans: "Hwaiwa sa bokos kann unuslaisiþs?" 16Andhof þan Iesus jah qaþ: "So meina laiseins nist meina, ak þis sandjandins mik. 17Jabai hwas wili wiljan is taujan,

2 Corrected from CA *wiljan.*

ufkunnaiþ bi þo laisein framuh Guda sijai, þau iku fram mis silbin rodja. [18]Saei fram sis silbin rodeiþ, hauhiþa seina sokeiþ, iþ saei sokeiþ hauhiþa þis sandjandins sik, sah sunjeins ist jah inwindiþa in imma nist. [19]Niu Moses gaf izwis witoþ? Jah ni ainshun izwara taujiþ þata witoþ. Hwa mik sokeiþ usqiman?" [20]Andhof so managei jah qeþun: "Unhulþon habais. Hwas þuk sokeiþ usqiman?" [21]Andhof Iesus jah qaþ du im: "Ain waurstw gatawida jah allai sildaleikeiþ. [22]Duþþe Moses atgaf izwis bimait (ni þatei fram Mose sijai, ak us attam) jah in sabbato bimaitiþ mannan. [23]Jabai bimait nimiþ manna in sabbato, ei ni gatairaidau witoþ þata Mosezis, iþ mis hatizoþ unte allana mannan hailana gatawida in sabbato? [24]Ni stojaiþ bi siunai, ak þo garaihton staua stojaiþ."

[25]Qeþunuh þan sumai þize Iairusaulymeite: "Niu sa ist þammei sokjand usqiman? [26]Jah sai, andaugiba rodeiþ jah waiht du imma ni qiþand. Ibai aufto bi sunjai ufkunþedun þai reiks þatei sa ist bi sunjai Xristus? [27]Akei þana kunnum, hwaþro ist, iþ Xristus, biþe qimiþ, ni manna wait hwaþro ist." [28]Hropida þan in alh laisjands Iesus jah qiþands: "Jah mik kunnuþ jah wituþ hwaþro im. Jah af mis silbin ni qam, ak ist sunjeins saei sandida mik, þanei jus ni kunnuþ. [29]Iþ ik kann ina, unte fram imma im, jah is mik insandida." [30]Sokidedun þan ina gafahan, jah ni ainshun uslagida ana ina handu, unte nauhþanuh ni atiddja hweila is. [31]Iþ managai þizos manageins galaubidedun imma jah qeþun: "Xristus, þan qimiþ, ibai ei managizeins taiknins taujai þaimei sa tawida?"

[32]Hausidedun þan Fareisaieis þo managein birodjandein bi ina þata. Inuhsandidedun andbahtans þai Fareisaieis jah þai auhumistans gudjans, ei gafaifaheina ina. [33]Þanuh qaþ Iesus: "Nauh leitila hweila miþ izwis im, jah þan gagga du þamma sandjandin mik. [34]Sokeiþ mik jah ni bigitiþ, jah þarei im ik, jus ni maguþ qiman." [35]Þaruh qeþun þai Iudaieis du sis misso: "Hwadre sa skuli gaggan, þei weis ni bigitaima ina? Nibai in distahein þiudo skuli gaggan jah laisjan þiudos? [36]Hwa sijai þata waurd þatei qaþ: "Sokeiþ mik jah ni bigitiþ, jah þarei im ik, jus ni maguþ qiman?"

[37]Iþ in spedistin daga þamma mikilin dulþais stoþ Iesus jah hropida qiþands: "Jabai hwana þaursjai, gaggai du mis jah driggkai. [38]Saei galaubeiþ du mis, swaswe qaþ gameleins, ahwos us wambai is rinnand watins libandins." [39]Þatuh þan qaþ bi ahman þanei skuldedun niman þai galaubjandans du imma, unte ni nauhþanuh was ahma sa weiha ana im, unte Iesus nauhþanuh ni hauhiþs was. [40]Managai þan þizos manageins hausjandans þize waurde qeþun: "Sa ist bi sunjai sa praufetes." [41]Sumaih qeþun: "Sa ist Xristus." Sumaih qeþun: "Ibai þau[3] us Galeilaia Xristus qimiþ? [42]Niu gameleins qaþ þatei us fraiwa Daweidis jah us Beþlaihaim weihsa, þarei was Daweid, Xristus qimiþ?" [43]Þanuh missaqiss in þizai managein warþ bi ina. [44]Sumaih þan ize wildedun fahan ina, akei ni ainshun uslagida ana in handuns.

[45]Galiþun þan þai andbahtos du þaim auhumistam gudjam jah Fareisaium. Þaruh qeþun du im jainai: "Duhwe ni attauhuþ ina?" [46]Andhofun þai andbahtos: "Ni hwanhun aiw rodida manna swase sa manna." [47]Andhofun þan im þai Fareisaieis: "Ibai jah jus afairzidai sijuþ? [48]Sai, jah ainshun þize reike galaubidedi imma aiþþau Fareisaie? [49]Alja so managei, þaiei ni kunnun witoþ, fraqiþanai sind." [50]Qaþ Nikaudemus du im (saei atiddja du imma in naht, sums wisands izei): [51]"Ibai witoþ unsar stojiþ mannan[4] nibai faurþis hauseiþ fram imma jah ufkunnaiþ hwa taujai?" [52]Andhofun jah qeþun du imma: "Ibai jah þu us Galeilaia is? Ussokei jah saihw þatei praufetus us Galeilaia ni urreisiþ." (Verses 7:53-8:11are not in the Gothic text nor in many of the ancient Greek versions.)

Chapter VIII

[12]Aftra du im Iesus rodida qaþuh: "Ik im liuhaþ manasedais. Saei laisteiþ mik ni gaggiþ in riqiza, ak habaiþ liuhaþ libainais." [13]Þanuh qeþun du imma þai Fareisaieis: "Þu bi þuk silban weitwodeis. So weitwodiþa þeina nist sunjeina." [14]Andhof Iesus jah qaþ du im: "Jah jabai ik weitwodja bi mik silban, sunja ist so weitwodiþa meina, unte wait hwaþro qam jah hwaþ galeiþa, iþ jus ni wituþ hwaþro qima, aiþþau hwaþ galeiþa. [15]Jus bi leika stojiþ, iþ ik ni stoja ainnohun. [16]Jaþþan jabai stoja ik, staua meina sunjeina ist unte ains ni im, ak ik jah saei sandida mik atta. [17]Jah þan in witwoda izwaramma gameliþ ist þatei twaddje manne weitwodiþa sunja ist. [18]Ik im saei weitwodja bi mik silban, jah weitwodeiþ bi mik saei sandida mik atta."

[3] Corrected from CA *þu*.

[4] Corrected from CA *manna*.

[19]Qeþun þan du imma: "Hwar ist sa atta þeins?" Andhof Iesus: "Ni mik kunnuþ nih attan meinana. Iþ mik kunþedeiþ, jah þau attan meinana kunþedeiþ." [20]Þo waurda rodida in gazaufylakio, laisjands in alh, jah ainshun ni faifah ina unte nauhþanuh ni qam hweila is.

[21]Þanuh qaþ aftra du im Iesus: "Ik galeiþa, jah sokeiþ mik, jah in frawaurhtai izwarai gadauþniþ. Þadei ik gagga, jus ni maguþ qiman." [22]Qeþun þan Iudaieis: "Nibai usqimai sis silbin, ei qiþiþ: 'Þadei ik gagga jus ni maguþ qiman'?" [23]Jah qaþ du im Iesus: "Jus us þaim dalaþro sijuþ, iþ ik us þaim iupaþro im. Jus us þamma fairhwau sijuþ, iþ ik ni im us þamma fairhwau. [24]Qaþ nu izwis þatei gadauþniþ in frawaurhtim izwaraim. Jabai auk ni galaubeiþ þatei ik im, gadauþniþ in frawaurhtim izwaraim." [25]Þaruh qeþun du imma: "Þu hwas is?" Jah qaþ du im Iesus: "Anastodeins þatei jah rodja du izwis. [26]Manag skal bi izwis rodjan jah stojan, akei saei sandida mik sunjeins ist, jah ik þatei hausida at imma þata rodja in þamma fairhwau." [27]Ni froþun þatei attan im qaþ. [28]Qaþuh þan du im Iesus: "Þan ushauheiþ þana sunu mans, þanuh ufkunnaiþ þatei ik im, jah af mis silbin tauja ni waiht, ak swaswe laisida mik atta meins, þata rodja. [29]Jah saei sandida mik miþ mis ist. Ni bilaiþ mis ainamma atta unte ik þatei leikaiþ imma tauja sinteino." [30]Þata imma rodjandin managai galaubidedun imma.

[31]Þanuh qaþ Iesus du þaim galaubjandam sis Iudaium: "Jabai jus gastandiþ in waurda meinamma, bi sunjai siponjos meinai sijuþ, [32]jah ufkunnaiþ sunja, jah so sunja frijans izwis briggiþ." [33]Andhofun imma: "Fraiw Abrahamis sijum jah ni mannhun skalkinodedum aiw hwanhun. Hwaiwa þu qiþis þatei 'Frijai wairþiþ'?" [34]Andhof im Iesus: "Amen, amen, qiþa izwis þatei hwazuh saei taujiþ frawaurht skalks ist frawaurhtai. [35]Sah þan skalks ni wisiþ in garda du aiwa, sunus wisiþ du aiwa. [36]Jabai nu sunus izwis frijans briggiþ, bi sunjai frijai sijuþ. [37]Wait þatei fraiw Abrahamis sijuþ, akei sokeiþ mis usqiman, unte waurd mein ni gamot in izwis. [38]Ik þatei gasahw at attin meinamma rodja, jah jus þatei hausideduþ fram attin izwaramma taujiþ."

[39]Andhofun jah qeþun du imma: "Atta unsar Abraham ist." Qaþ im Iesus: "Iþ barna Abrahamis weseiþ, waurstwa Abrahamis tawidedeiþ. [40]Iþ nu sokeiþ mik usqiman, mannan izei sunja izwis rodida, þoei hausida fram Guda. Þatuh Abraham ni tawida. [41]Jus taujiþ toja attins izwaris." Þanuh qeþun imma: "Weis us horinassau ni sijum gabauranai; ainana attan aigum, Guþ." [42]Qaþ du im Iesus: "Jabai Guþ atta izwar wesi, friodedeiþ þau mik, unte ik fram Guda urrann jah qam. Nih þan auk fram mis silbin ni qam, ak is mik insandida. [43]Duhwe maþlein meina ni kunnuþ? Unte ni maguþ hausjan waurd mein. [44]Jus us attin diabaulau sijuþ jah lustuns þis attins izwaris wileiþ taujan. Jains manamaurþrja was fram frumistja, jah in sunjai ni gastoþ, unte nist sunja in imma. Þan rodeiþ liugn, us seinaim rodeiþ, unte liugnja ist jah atta is. [45]Iþ ik, þatei sunja rodida, ni galaubeiþ mis. [46]Hwas izwara gasakiþ mik bi frawaurht? Þande sunja qiþa, duhwe ni galaubeiþ mis? [47]Sa wisands us Guda waurda Gudis hauseiþ; duþe jus ni hauseiþ, unte us Guda ni sijuþ."

[48]Andhofun þan þai Iudaieis jah qeþun du imma: "Niu waila qiþam weis þatei Samareites is þu jah unhulþon habais?" [49]Andhof Iesus: "Ik unhulþon ni haba, ak swera attan meinana, jah jus unsweraiþ mik. [50]Ik ni sokja hauhein meina. Ist saei sokeiþ jah stojiþ. [51]Amen, amen qiþa izwis: jabai hwas waurd mein fastaiþ, dauþu ni gasaihwiþ aiwa dage." [52]Þanuh qeþun du imma þai Iudaieis: "Nu ufkunþedum þatei unhulþon habais. Abraham gadauþnoda jah praufeteis, jah þu qiþis: 'Jabai hwas mein waurd fastai, ni kausjai dauþau aiwa dage. [53]Ibai þu maiza is attin unsaramma Abrahama, saei gadauþnoda? Jah praufeteis gadauþnodedun. Hwana þuk silban taujis þu?" [54]Andhof Iesus: "Jabai ik hauhja mik silban, so hauheins meina ni waihts ist; ist atta meins saei hauheiþ mik, þanei jus qiþiþ þatei 'Guþ unsar ist.' [55]Jah ni kunnuþ ina, iþ ik kann ina. Jah jabai qeþjau þatei ni kunnjau ina, sijau galeiks izwis liugnja, ak kann ina jah waurd is fasta. [56]Abraham atta izwar sifaida ei gasehwi dag meinana, jah gasahw jah faginoda." [57]Þanuh qeþun þai Iudaieis du imma: "Fimf tiguns jere nauh ni habais jah Abraham sahwt?" [58]Qaþ im Iesus: "Amen, amen qiþa izwis: faurþizei Abraham waurþi im ik." [59]Þanuh nemun stainans ei waurpeina ana ina, iþ Iesus þan gafalh sik jah usiddja us alh usleiþands þairh midjans ins jah hwarboda swa.

Chapter IX

[1]Jah þairhgaggands gaumida mann blindamma us gabaurþai. [2]Þaruh frehun ina siponjos is qiþandans: "Rabbei, hwas frawaurhta, sau þau fadrein is, ei blinds gabaurans warþ?" [3]Andhof Iesus: "Nih sa frawaurhta nih fadrein is, ak ei bairhta waurþeina waurstwa Gudis ana imma. [4]Ik skal waurkjan waurstwa þis sandjandins mik, unte dags ist. Qimiþ nahts, þanei ni manna mag

waurkjan. 5Þan in þamma fairhwau im, liuhaþ im þis fairhwaus." 6Þata qiþands gaspaiw dalaþ jah gawaurhta fani us þamma spaiskuldra, jah gasmait imma ana augona þata fani þamma blindin, 7jah qaþ du imma: "Gagg þwahan in swumsl Siloamis." (Þatei gaskeirjada "insandiþs.") Galaiþ jah afþwoh jah qam saihwands. 8Þanuh garaznans jah þai saihwandans ina faurþis, þatei is bidagwa was, qeþun: "Niu sa ist saei sat aihtronds?" 9Sumaih qeþun þatei, "Sa ist," sumaih þatei, "Galeiks þamma ist." Iþ is qaþ þatei, "Ik im." 10Þanuh qeþun du imma: "Hwaiwa usluknodedun þus þo augona?" 11Andhof jains jah qaþ: "Manna haitans Iesus fani gawaurhta jah bismait mis augona jah qaþ mis: 'Gagg afþwahan in þata swumfsl Siloamis.' Iþ ik galaiþ jah biþwahands ussahw." 12Qeþun þan du imma: "Hwar ist sa?" Iþ is qaþ: "Ni wait."

13Gatiuhand ina du Fareisaium, þana saei was blinds. 14Wasuh þan sabbato þan þata fani gawaurhta Iesus jah uslauk imma augona. 15Aftra þan frehun ina jah þai Fareisaieis hwaiwa ussahw, iþ is qaþ jah þaim: "Fani galagida mis ana augona jah afþwoh jah saihwa." 16Qeþun þan sumai þize Fareisaie: "Sa manna nist fram Guda, þande sabbate daga ni witaiþ." Sumaih qeþun: "Hwaiwa mag manna frawaurhts swaleikos taiknins taujan?" Jah missaqiss warþ miþ im. 17Qeþunuh du þamma faurþis blindin aftra: "Þu hwa qiþis bi þana ei uslauk þus augona?" Iþ is qaþuh þatei, "Praufetus ist."

18Ni galaubidedun þan Iudaieis bi ina þatei is blinds wesi jah ussehwi, unte atwopidedun þans fadrein is, þis ussaihwandins, 19jah frehun ins qiþandans: "Sau ist sa sunus izwar þanei jus qiþiþ þatei blinds gabaurans waurþi? Hwaiwa nu saihwiþ?" 20Andhofun þan im þai fadrein is jah qeþun: "Witum þatei sa ist sunus unsar, jah þatei blinds gabaurans warþ. 21Iþ hwaiwa nu saihwiþ ni witum, aiþþau hwas uslauk imma þo augona weis ni witum. Silba uswahsans ist. Ina fraihniþ; silba bi sik rodjai." 22Þata qeþun þai fadrein is, unte ohtedun sis Iudaiuns, juþan auk gaqeþun sis Iudaieis ei jabai hwas ina andhaihaiti Xristu, utana synagogais wairþai. 23Duhþe þai berusjos is qeþun þatei, "Uswahsans ist; silban fraihniþ."

24Atwopidedun þan anþaramma sinþa þana mannan saei was blinds, jah qeþun du imma: "Gif hauhein Guda! Weis witum þatei sa manna frawaurhts ist." 25Þanuh andhof jains: "Jabai frawaurhts ist, ik ni wait. Þatain wait ei blinds was, iþ nu saihwa." 26Þanuh qeþun aftra: "Hwa gatawida þus? Hwaiwa uslauk þus augona?" 27Andhof im: "Qaþ izwis ju jah ni hausideduþ. Hwa aftra wileiþ hausjan? Ibai jah jus wileiþ þamma siponjos wairþan?" 28Þanuh lailoun imma jah qeþun: "Þu is siponeis þamma, iþ weis Moses siponjos sijum. 29Weis witum þatei du Mose rodida Guþ, iþ þana ni kunnum hwaþro ist." 30Andhof sa manna jah qaþ du im: "Auk in þamma sildaleik ist, þatei jus ni wituþ hwaþro ist, jah uslauk mis augona. 31Witumuh þan þatei Guþ frawaurhtaim ni andhauseiþ, ak jabai hwas gudblostreis[5] ist jah wiljan is taujiþ, þamma hauseiþ. 32Fram aiwa ni gahausiþ was þatei uslukiþ hwas augona blindamma gabauranamma. 33Nih wesi sa fram Guda, ni mahtedi taujan ni waiht." 34Andhofun jah qeþun du imma: "In frawaurhtim þu gabaurans warst alls jah þu laiseis unsis?" Jah uswaurpun imma ut.

35Hausida Iesus þatei uswaurpun imma ut, jah bigat ina qaþuh du imma: "Þu gaulaubeis du sunau Gudis?" 36Andhof jains jah qaþ: "An hwas ist, frauja, ei galaubjau du imma?" 37Qaþ þan imma Iesus: "Jah gasahwt ina jah saei rodeiþ miþ þus sa ist." 38Iþ is qaþuh: "Galaubja, frauja." Jah inwait ina. 39Jah qaþ Iesus: "Du stauai ik in þamma fairhwau qam, ei þai unsaihwandans saihwaina jah þai saihwandans blindai wairþaina." 40Jah hausidedun þize Fareisaie sumai þata, þai wisandans miþ imma, jah qeþun du imma: "Ibai jah weis blindai sijum?" 41Qaþ im Iesus: "Iþ blindai weseiþ, ni þau habaidedeiþ frawaurhtais. Iþ nu qiþiþ[6] þatei, "Gasaihwam," eiþan frawaurhts izwara þairhwisiþ.

Chapter X

1"Amen, amen qiþa izwis: saei inn ni atgaggiþ þairh daur in gardan lambe, ak steigiþ aljaþro, sah hliftus ist jah waidedja. 2Iþ sa inngaggands þairh daur hairdeis ist lambe. 3Þammuh daurawards uslukiþ, jah þo lamba stibnai is hausjand, jah þo swesona lamba haitiþ bi namin jah ustiuhiþ þo. 4Jah þan þo swesona ustiuhiþ, faura im gaggiþ, jah þo lamba ina laistjand, unte kunnun stibna is. 5Iþ framaþjana ni laistjand, ak þliuhand faura imma, unte ni kunnun þize framaþjane

5 Written *gþblostreis* in CA.

6 Corrected from CA *qiþiþiþ*.

stibna." 6Þo gajukon qaþ im Iesus, iþ jainai ni froþun hwa was þatei rodida du im.

7Þanuh qaþ aftra du im Iesus: "Amen, amen qiþa izwis þatei ik im daur þize lambe. 8Allai swa managai swe qemun þiubos sind jah waidedjans; akei ni hausidedun im þo lamba. 9Ik im þata daur; þairh mik jabai hwas inngaggiþ, ganisiþ, jah inngaggiþ jah utgaggiþ jah winja bigitiþ. 10Þiubs ni qimiþ, nibai ei stilai jah ufsneiþai jah fraqistjai; iþ ik qam ei libain aigeina jah managizo aigeina. 11Ik im hairdeis gods. Hairdeis sa goda saiwala seina lagjiþ faur lamba. 12Iþ asneis jah saei nist hairdeis, þizei ni sind lamba swesa, gasaihwiþ wulf qimandan jah bileiþiþ þaim lambam jah þliuhiþ, jah sa wulfs frawilwiþ þo jah distahjiþ þo lamba. 13Iþ sa asneis afþliuhiþ, unte asneis ist jah ni kar' ist ina þize lambe. 14Ik im hairdeis sa goda jah kann meina jah kunnun mik þo meina, 15swaswe kann mik atta jah ik kann attan, jah saiwala meina lagja faur þo lamba. 16Jah anþara lamba aih þoei ni sind þis awistris, jah þo skal briggan, jah stibnos meinaizos hausjand, jah wairþand ain aweþi, ains hairdeis. 17Duhþe atta mik frijoþ, unte ik lagja saiwala meina, ei aftra nimau þo. 18Ni hwashun nimiþ þo af mis silbin. Waldufni haba aflagjan þo, jah waldufni haba aftra niman þo. Þo anabusn nam at attin meinamma."

19Þanuh missaqiss aftra warþ miþ Iudaium in þize waurde. 20Qeþunuh managai ize: "Unhulþon habaiþ jah dwalmoþ. Hwa þamma hauseiþ?" 21Sumaih qeþun: "Þo waurda ni sind unhulþon habandins. Ibai mag unhulþo blindaim augona uslukan?"

22Warþ þan Inniujiþa in Iairusaulymai, jah wintrus was. 23Jah hwarboda Iesus in alh in ubizwai Saulaumonis. 24Þanuh birunnun ina Iudaieis jah qeþun du imma: "Und hwa saiwala unsara hahis? Jabai þu sijais Xristus, qiþ unsis andaugiba." 25Andhof Iesus: "Qaþ izwis, jah ni galaubeiþ. Waurstwa þoei ik tauja in namin attins meinis, þo weitwodjand bi mik. 26Akei jus ni galaubeiþ unte ni sijuþ lambe meinaize, swaswe qaþ izwis. 27Lamba meina stibnai meinai hausjand, jah ik kann þo, jah laistjand mik. 28Jah ik libain aiweinon giba im, jah ni fraqistnand aiw, jah ni frawilwiþ hwashun þo us handau meinai. 29Atta meins þatei fragaf mis maizo allaim ist, jah ni aiw ainshun mag frawilwan þo us handau attins meinis. 30Ik jah atta meins ain siju."

31Nemun aftra stainans þai Iudaieis ei waurpeina ana ina. 32Andhof im Iesus: "Managa goda waurstwa ataugida izwis us attin meinamma. In hwarjis þize waurstwe staineiþ mik?" 33Andhofun imma þai Iudaieis: "In godis waurstwis ni stainjam þuk, ak in wajamereins, jah þatei þu manna wisands taujis þuk silban du Guda." 34Andhof im Iesus: "Niu ist gameliþ in witoda izwaramma: "Ik qaþ, guda sijuþ"? 35Jabai jainans qaþ guda, du þaimei waurd Gudis warþ, jah ni maht ist gatairan þata gamelido. 36Þanei atta gaweihaida jah insandida in þana fairhwu jus qiþiþ þatei wajamerjau unte qaþ, 'Sunus Gudis im'? 37Niba taujau waurstwa attins meinis, ni galaubeiþ mis. 38Iþ jabai taujau, niba mis galaubjaiþ, þaim waurstwam galaubjaiþ, ei ufkunnaiþ jah galaubjaiþ þatei in mis atta jah ik in imma." 39Sokidedun ina aftra gafahan, jah usiddja us handum ize. 40Jah galaiþ aftra ufar Iaurdanu in þana stad þarei was Iohannes frumist daupjands, jah salida jainar. 41Jah managai qemun at imma jah qeþun þatei Iohannes gatawida taikne ni ainohun, iþ allata þatei qaþ Iohannes bi þana sunja was." 42Jah galaubidedun managai du imma jainar.

Chapter XI

1Wasuh þan sums siuks, Lazarus af Beþanias, us haimai Marjins jah Marþins, swistrs izos. 2Wasuh þan Marja, soei salboda Fraujan balsana jah biswarb fotuns is skufta seinamma, þizozei broþar Lazarus siuks was. 3Insandidedun þan þos swistrjus is du imma qiþandeins: "Frauja, sai, þanei frijos siuks ist." 4Iþ is gahausjands qaþ: "So siukei nist du dauþau, ak in hauheinais Gudis, ei hauhjaidau sunus Gudis þairh þata."

5Frijoduh þan Iesus Marþan jah swistar izos jah Lazaru. 6Swe hausida þatei siuks was, þanuh þan salida in þammei was stada twans dagans. 7Þaþro þan afar þata qaþ du siponjam: "Gaggam in Iudaian aftra." 8Qeþun du imma þai siponjos: "Rabbei, nu sokidedun þuk afwairpan stainam Iudaieis, jah aftra gaggis jaind?" 9Andhof Iesus: "Niu twalif sind hweilos dagis? Jabai hwas gaggiþ in dag, ni gastiggqiþ, unte liuhaþ þis fairhwaus gasaihwiþ; 10aþþan jabai hwas gaggiþ in naht, gastiggqiþ, unte liuhad nist in imma." 11Þo qaþ jah afar þata qiþiþ du im: "Lazarus, frijonds unsar, gasaizlep; akei gaggam ei uswakjau ina." 12Þanuh qeþun þai siponjos is: "Frauja, jabai slepiþ, hails wairþiþ." 13Qaþuh þan Iesus bi dauþu is, iþ jainai hugidedun þatei is bi slep qeþi. 14Þanuh þan qaþ du im Iesus swikunþaba: "Lazarus gaswalt, 15jah fagino in izwara ei galaubjaiþ unte ni was jainar. Akei gaggam du imma." 16Þanuh qaþ Þomas, saei haitada Didimus, þaim gahlaibam seinaim: "Gaggam jah weis, ei gaswiltaima miþ imma."

17Qimands þan Iesus bigat ina juþan fidwor dagans habandan in hlaiwa. 18Wasuh þan Beþania nehwa Iairusaulymim,[7] swaswe ana spaurdim fimftaihunim. 19Jah managai Iudaie gaqemun bi Marþan jah Marjan ei gaþrafstidedeina ijos bi þana broþar izo. 20Iþ Marþa, sunsei hausida þatei Iesus qimiþ, wiþraiddja ina; iþ Marja in garda sat. 21Þanuh qaþ Marþa du Iesua: "Frauja, iþ weseis her, ni þau gadauþnodedi broþar meins. 22Akei jah nu wait ei þishwah þei bidjis Guþ gibiþ þus Guþ." 23Qaþ izai Iesus: "Usstandiþ broþar þeins." 24Qaþ du imma Marþa: "Wait þatei usstandiþ in usstassai in þamma spedistin[8] daga." 25Qaþ þan Iesus: "Ik im so usstass jah libains. Saei galaubeiþ du mis, þauh ga-ba-dauþniþ, libaid, 26Jah hwazuh saei libaiþ jah galaubeiþ du mis ni gadauþniþ aiw. Galaubeis þata?" 27Qaþ imma: "Jai, frauja, ik galaubida þatei þu is Xristus, sunus Gudis, sa in þana fairhwu qimanda."

28Jah þata qiþandei galaiþ jah wopida Marjan, swistar seina, þiubjo qiþandei: "Laisareis qam jah haitiþ þuk." 29Iþ jaina, sunsei hausida, urrais sprauto jah iddja du imma. 30Niþþan nauhþanuh qam Iesus in weihsa, ak was nauhþanuh in þamma stada þarei gamotida imma Marþa. 31Iudaieis þan þai wisandans miþ izai in garda þrafstjandans ija, gasaihwandans Marjan þatei sprauto usstoþ jah usiddja, iddjedunuh afar izai qiþandans þatei gaggiþ du hlaiwa ei greitai jainar. 32Iþ Marja, sunsei qam þarei was Iesus, gasaihwandei ina draus imma du fotum qiþandei du imma: "Frauja, iþ weiseis her, ni þauh gaswulti meins broþar." 33Þanuh Iesus, sunsei gasahw ija greitandein jah Iudaiuns þaiei qemun miþ izai gretandans, inrauhtida ahmin jah inwagida sik silban. 34Jah qaþ: "Hwar lagideduþ ina?" Qeþun du imma: "Frauja, hiri jah saihw." 35Jah tagrida Iesus. 36Þaruh qeþun þai Iudaieis: "Sai hwaiwa frioda ina." 37Sumai þan ize qeþun: "Niu mahta sa izei uslauk augona þamma blindin gataujan ei jah sa ni gadauþnodedi?"

38Þanuh Iesus aftra inrauhtiþs in sis silbin gaggiþ du þamma hlaiwa. Wasuh þan hulundi jah staina ufarlagida was ufaro. 39Qaþ Iesus: "Afnimiþ þana stain." Qaþ du imma swistar þis dauþins Marþa: "Frauja, ju fuls ist; fidurdogs auk ist." 40Qaþ izai Iesus: "Niu qaþ þus þatei jabai galaubeis, gasaihwis wulþu Gudis?" 41Ushofun þan þana stain þarei was. Iþ Iesus uzuhhof augona iup jah qaþ: "Atta, awiliudo þus, unte andhausides mis, 42jah þan ik wissa þatei sinteino mis andhauseis. Akei in manageins þizos bistandandeins qaþ, ei galaubjaina þatei þu mik insandides." 43Jah þata qiþands stibnai mikilai hropida: "Lazaru, hiri ut!" 44Jah urrann sa dauþa gabundans handuns jah fotuns faskjam, jah wlits is auralja bibundans. Qaþ du im Iesus: "Andbindiþ ina jah letiþ gaggan."

45Þanuh managai þize Iudaiei þai qimandans at Marjin jah saihwandans þatei gatawida, galaubidedun imma. 46Sumaiþþan ize galiþun du Fareisaium jah qeþun du im þatei gatawida Iesus. 47Galesun þan þai auhumistans gudjans jah þai Farei<saieis...> (remainder of chapter missing)

Chapter XII

1...]in Beþanijin, þarei was Lazarus sa dauþa, þanei urraisida us dauþaim Iesus. 2Þaruh gawaurhtedun imma nahtamat jainar, jah Marþa andbahtida; iþ Lazarus was sums þize anakumbjandane miþ imma. 3Iþ Marja nam pund balsanis nardaus pistikeinis filugalaubis jah gasalboda fotuns Iesua, jah biswarb fotuns is skufta seinamma; iþ sa gards fulls warþ daunais þizos salbonais. 4Qaþ þan ains þize siponje is, Judas Seimonis sa Iskariotes, izei skaftida sik du galewjan ina: 5"Duhwe þata balsan ni frabauht was in .t. skatte jah fradailiþ wesi þarbam?" 6Þatuh-þan qaþ, ni þeei ina þize þarbane kara wesi, ak unte þiubs was jah arka habaida jah þata innwaurpano bar. 7Qaþ þan Iesus: "Let ija. In dag gafilhis meinis fastaida þata. 8Iþ þans unledans sinteino habaiþ miþ izwis, iþ mik ni sinteino habaiþ."

9Fanþ þan manageins filu Iudaie þatei Iesus jainar ist, jah qemun ni in Iesuis ainis ak ei jah Lazaru sehweina þanei urraisida us dauþaim. 10Munaidedunuþ-þan auk þai auhumistans gudjans ei jah Lazarau usqemeina, 11unte managai in þis garunnun Iudaiei jah galaubidedun Iesua.

---

[7] Corrected from CA *Lairusaulymiam.*

[8] Corrected from CA *spedistan.*

12Iftumin daga manageins filu sei qam at dulþai, gahausjandans þatei qimiþ Iesus in Iairausaulymai, 13nemun astans peikabagme, jah urrunnun wiþragamotjan imma, jah hropidedun: "Osanna, þiuþida sa qimanda in namin Fraujins, þiudans Israelis." 14Bigat þan Iesus asilu, <jah> gasat ana ina, swaswe ist gameliþ:

15"Ni ogs þus, dauhtar Sion.
Sai, þiudans þeins qimiþ
sitands ana fulin asilaus."

16Þatuþþan ni kunþedun siponjos is frumist; ak biþe gasweraiþs was Iesus, þanuh gamundedun þatei þata was du þamma gameliþ, jah þata gatawidedun imma. 17Weitwodida þan so managei sei was miþ imma þan Lazaru wopida us hlaiwa jah urraisida ina us dauþaim. 18Duþþe iddjedun gamotjan imma managei, unte hausidedun ei gatawidedi þo taikn. 19Þanuh þai Fareisaieis qeþun du sis misso: "Saihwiþ þatei ni boteiþ waiht; sai, so manaseds afar imma galaiþ."

20Wesunuþþan sumai þiudo þize urrinnandane ei inwiteina in þizai dulþai. 21Þai atiddjedun du Filippau, þamma fram Beþsaeida Galeilaie, jah bedun ina qiþandans: "Frauja, wileima Iesu gasaihwan." 22Gaggiþ Filippus jah qiþiþ du Andraiin, jah aftra Andraias jah Filippus qeþun du Iesua. 23Iþ Iesus andhof im qiþands: "Qam hweila ei sweraidau sunus mans. 24Amen, amen, qiþa izwis: Nibai kaurno hwaiteis gadriusando in airþa gaswiltiþ, silbo ainata aflifniþ, iþ jabai gaswiltiþ, manag akran bairiþ. 25Saei frijoþ saiwala seina fraqisteiþ izai, jah saei fiaiþ saiwala seina in þamma fairhwau, in libainai aiweinon bairgiþ izai. 26Jabai mis hwas andbahtjai, mik laistjai; jah þarei im ik, þaruh sa andbahts meins wisan habaiþ. Jah jabai hwas mis andbahteiþ, sweraiþ ina atta.

27"Nu saiwala meina gadrobnoda, jah hwa qiþau? 'Atta, nasei mik us þizai hweilai?' Akei duþþe qam in þizai hweilai. 28Atta, hauhei namo þeinata!" Qam þan stibna us himina: "Jah hauhida, jah aftra hauhja." 29Managei þan sei stoþ gahausjandei qeþun þeihwon wairþan; sumaih qeþun: "Aggilus du imma rodida." 30Andhof Iesus jah qaþ: "Ni in meina so stibna warþ, ak in izwara. 31Nu staua ist þizai manasedai; nu sa reiks þis fairhwaus uswairpada ut. 32Jah ik jabai ushauhjada af airþai alla atþinsa du mis." 33Þatuþþan qaþ bandwjands hwileikamma dauþau skulda gadauþnan. 34Andhof imma so managei: "Weis hausidedum ana witoda þatei Xristus sijai du aiwa. Jah hwaiwa þu qiþis þatei skulds ist ushauhjan sa sunus mans? Hwas ist sa sunus mans?" 35Qaþ þan du im Iesus: "Nauh leitil mel liuhaþ in izwis ist. Gaggiþ þande liuhaþ habaiþ, ei riqiz izwis ni gafahai. Jah saei gaggiþ in riqiza ni wait hwaþ gaggiþ. 36Þande liuhaþ habaiþ, galaubeiþ du liuhada ei sunjus liuhadis wairþaiþ."

Þata rodida Iesus, jah galaiþ jah gafalh sik faura im. 37Swa filu imma taikne gataujandin in andwairþja ize, ni galaubidedun imma, 38ei þata waurd Esaeiins praufetaus usfullnodedi þatei qaþ:

"Frauja, hwas galaubida hauseinai unsarai?
Jah arms Fraujins hwamma andhuliþs warþ?"

39Duþþe ni mahtedun galaubjan, unte aftra qaþ Esaeias:

40"Gablindida ize augona
jah gadaubida ize hairtona,
ei ni gaumidedeina augam
jah froþeina hairtin,
jah gawandidedeina jah ganasidedjau ins."

41Þata qaþ Esaeias, þan sahw wulþu is jah rodida bi ina. 42Þanuh þan sweþauh jah us þaim reikam managai galaubidedun du imma, akei faura Fareisaium ni andhaihaitun, ei us synagogei<n> ni uswaurpanai waurþeina. 43Frijodedun auk mais hauhein manniska þau hauhein Gudis.

44Iþ Iesus hropida jah qaþ: "Saei galaubeiþ du mis ni galaubeiþ du mis, ak du þamma sandjandin mik. 45Jah saei saihwiþ mik, saihwiþ þana sandjandan mik. 46Ik liuhad in þamma fairhwau qam, ei hwazuh saei galaubjai du mis in riqiza ni wisai. 47Jah jabai hwas meinaim hausjai waurdam jah galaubjai, ik ni stoja ina; nih þan qam ei stojau manased, ak ei ganasjau manased. 48Saei frakann mis jah ni andnimiþ waurda meina habaid þana stojandan sik. Waurd þatei rodida, þata stojiþ ina in spedistin daga. 49Unte ik us mis silbin ni rodida, ak saei sandida mik atta, sah mis anabusn at[gaf ..." (Text missing to XIII:11).

Chapter XIII

11...qaþ: "Ni allai hrainjai sijuþ."

12Biþeh þan usþwoh fotuns ize jah nam wastjos seinos, anakumbjands aftra qaþ du im: "Witudu[9] hwa gatawida izwis? 13Jus wopeid mik 'Laisareis'[10] jah 'Frauja.' Waila qiþiþ; im auk. 14Jabai nu usþwoh izwis fotuns, frauja jah laisareis, jah jus skuluþ izwis misso þwahan fotuns. 15Du frisahtai auk atgaf izwis, ei swaswe ik gatawida izwis, swa jus taujaiþ. 16Amen, amen qiþa izwis: nist skalks maiza fraujin seinamma, nih apaustaulus maiza þamma sandjandin sik. 17Þande þata wituþ, audagai sijuþ, jabai taujiþ þata. 18Ni bi allans izwis qiþa. Ik wait hwarjans gawalida. Ak ei usfulliþ waurþi þata gamelido: 'Saei matida miþ mis hlaib ushof ana mik fairzna seina.' Fram himma qiþa izwis faurþizei waurþi, ei biþe wairþai galaubjaiþ þatei ik im. 20Amen, amen qiþa izwis: Saei andnimiþ þana þanei ik insandja mik andnimiþ, iþ saei mik andnimiþ, andnimiþ þana sandjandan mik."

21Þata qiþands Iesus indrobnoda ahmin jah weitwodida jah qaþ: "Amen, amen qiþa izwis þatei ains izwara galeweiþ mik." 22Þanuh sehwun du sis misso þai siponjos, þagkjandans bi hwarjana qeþi. 23Wasuh þan anakumbjands ains þize siponje is in barma Iesuis, þanei frijoda Iesus. 24Bandwiduh þan þamma Seimon Paitrus du fraihnan hwas wesi bi þanei qaþ. 25Anakumbida þan jains swa ana barma Iesuis qaþuh imma: "Frauja, hwas ist?" 26Andhof Iesus: "Sa ist þammei ik ufdaupjands þana hlaif giba." Jah ufdaupjands þana hlaif gaf Iudin Seimons, Skariotau. 27Jah afar þamma hlaiba þan galaiþ in jainana Satana. Qaþ þan du imma Iesus: "Þatei taujis, tawi sprauto." 28Þatuh þan ainshun ni wissa þize anakumbjandane duhwe qaþ imma. 29Sumai mundedun ei unte arka habaida Iudas þatei qeþi imma Iesus: "Bugei þizei þaurbeima du dulþai," aiþþau "þaim unledam ei hwa gibau." 30Biþe andnam þana hlaib jains, suns galaiþ ut. Wasuh þan nahts þan galaiþ ut. 31Qaþ þan Iesus: "Nu gasweraids warþ sunus mans, jah Guþ hauhiþs ist in imma. 32Jabai nu Guþ hauhiþs ist in imma, jah Guþ hauheiþ ina in sis jah suns hauhida ina. 33Barnilona, nauh leitil mel miþ izwis im. Sokeiþ mik, jah swaswe qaþ du Iudaium, ei þadei ik gagga, jus ni maguþ qiman, jah izwis qiþa nu. 34Anabusn niuja giba izwis, ei frijoþ izwis misso swe ik frijoda izwis, þei jah jus frijoþ misso izwis. 35Bi þamma ufkunnand[11] allai þei meinai siponjos sijuþ, jabai friaþwa habaid miþ izwis misso."

36Þanuh qaþ du imma Seimon Paitrus: "Frauja, hwad gaggis?" Andhafjands Iesus qaþ: "Þadei ik gagga ni magt mik nu laistjan, iþ biþe laisteis." 37Þaruh Paitrus qaþ du imma: "Frauja, duhwe ni mag þuk laistjan nu? Saiwala meina faur þuk lagja. 38Andhof Iesus: "Saiwala þeina faur mik lagjis? Amen, amen qiþa þus þei hana ni hrukeiþ unte þu mik afaikis kunnan þrim sinþam."

Chapter XIV

1"Ni indrobnai izwar hairto. Galaubeiþ du Guda jah du mis galaubeiþ. 2In garda attins meinis saliþwos managos sind. Aþþan niba weseina, aiþþau qeþjau du izwis: 'Gagga manwjan stad izwis'? 3Jah þan jabai gagga <jah> manwja izwis stad, aftra qima jah franima izwis du mis silbin, ei þarei im ik þaruh sijuþ jah jus. 4Jah þadei ik gagga kunnuþ, jah þana wig kunnuþ. 5Þaruh qaþ imma Þomas: "Frauja, ni witum hwaþ gaggis, jah hwaiwa magum þana wig kunnan?" 6Qaþ imma Iesus: "Ik im sa wigs jah sunja jah libains. Ainshun ni qimiþ at attin niba þairh mik. 7Iþ kunþedeiþ mik, aiþþau kunþedeiþ jah attan meinana; jah þan fram himma kunnuþ ina jah gasaihwiþ ina."

8Iþ Filippus qaþuh du imma: "Frauja, augei unsis þana attan. Þatuh ganah unsis." 9Þaruh qaþ imma Iesus: "Swalaud melis miþ izwis was, jah ni ufkunþes mik, Filippu? Saei gasahw mik, gasahw attan, jah hwaiwa þu qiþis: 'Augei unsis þana attan'? 10Niu galaubeis þatei ik in attin jah atta in mis ist? Þo waurda þoei ik rodja izwis, af mis silbin ni rodja, ak atta saei in mis ist, sa taujiþ þo waurstwa. 11Galaubeiþ mis þatei ik in attin jah atta in mis. Iþ jabai ni,[12] in þize waurstwe galaubeiþ mis.

12"Amen, amen qiþa izwis: Saei galaubeid mis, þo waurstwa þoei ik tauja jah is taujiþ, jah maizona þaim taujiþ unte ik du attin gagga. 13Jah þatei hwa bidjiþ in namin meinamma, þata tauja ei hauhjaidau atta in sunau. 14Jabai hwis bidjiþ mik in namin meinamma, ik tauja.

---

[9] Corrected from CA *witadu;* for *wituþ-u.*

[10] Corrected from CA *laisareisareis.*

[11] Corrected from CA *ufkunnanda.*

[12] *ni* is incorrectly placed after *waurstwe* in CA.

15"Jabai mik frijoþ, anabusnins meinos fastaid. 16Jah ik bidja attan jah anþarana parakletu gibiþ izwis ei sijai miþ izwis du aiwa, 17ahma sunjos, þanei so manaseiþs ni mag niman, unte ni saihwiþ ina, nih kann ina; iþ jus kunnuþ ina, unte is miþ izwis wisiþ jah in izwis ist.

18"Ni leta izwis widuwairnans; qima at izwis. 19Nauh leitil, jah so manaseiþs mik ni þanaseiþs saihwiþ; iþ jus saihwiþ mik þatei ik liba, jah jus libaiþ. 20In jainamma daga ufkunnaiþ jus þatei ik in attin meinamma jah jus in mis jah ik in izwis. 21Saei habaid anabusnins meinos jah fastaiþ þos, sa ist saei frijoþ mik; jah þan saei frijoþ mik, frijoda fram attin meinamma, jah ik frijo ina, jah gabairhtja imma mik silban." 22Þaruh qaþ imma Iudas, ni sa Iskarjotes: "Frauja, hwa warþ ei unsis munais gabairhtjan þuk silban, iþ þizai manasedai ni?" 23Andhof Iesus jah qaþ du imma: "Jabai hwas mik frijoþ jah waurd mein fastaiþ, jah atta meins frijoþ ina, jah du imma galeiþos jah saliþwos at imma gataujos. 24Iþ saei ni frioþ mik, þo waurda meina ni fastaiþ. Jah þata waurd þatei hauseiþ nist mein, ak þis sandjandins mik attins.

25"Þata rodida izwis at izwis wisands. 26Aþþan sa parakletus, ahma sa weiha, þanei sandeiþ atta in namin meinamma, sa izwis laiseiþ allata jah gamaudeiþ izwis allis þatei qaþ du izwis. 27Gawairþi bileiþa izwis, gawairþi mein giba izwis; ni swaswe so manaseþs gibiþ, ik giba izwis. Ni indrobnaina izwara hairtona nih faurhtjaina. 28Hausideduþ ei ik qaþ izwis: 'Galeiþa jah qima at izwis.' Jabai frijodedeiþ mik, aiþþau jus faginodedeiþ ei ik gagga du attin, unte atta meins maiza mis ist. 29Jah nu qaþ izwis faurþizei waurþi, ei biþe wairþai galaubjaiþ. 30Þanaseiþs filu ni maþlja miþ izwis. Qimiþ saei þizai manasedai reikinoþ, jah in mis ni bigitiþ waiht. 31Ak ei ufkunnai so manaseþs þatei ik frijoda attan meinana, jah swaswe anabaud mis atta, swa tauja. Urreisiþ, gaggam þaþro."

Chapter XV

1"Ik im weinatriu þata sunjeino, jah atta meins waurstwja ist. 2All taine in mis unbairandane akran goþ usnimiþ ita, jah all akran bairandane gahraineiþ ita, ei managizo akran bairaina. 3Ju jus hrainjai sijuþ in þis waurdis þatei rodida du izwis. 4Wisaiþ in mis, jah ik in izwis. Swe sa weinatains ni mag akran bairan af sis silbin, niba ist ana weinatriwa, swah nih jus niba in mis sijuþ. 5Ik im þata weinatriu, iþ jus weinatainos; saei wisiþ in mis jah ik in imma, swa bairiþ akran manag þatei inuh mik ni maguþ taujan ni waiht. 6Niba saei wisiþ in mis, uswairpada ut swe weinatains, jah gaþaursniþ jah galisada, jah in fon galagjand jah inbrannjada.[13] 7Aþþan jabai sijuþ in mis, jah waurda meina in izwis sind, þatahwah þei wileiþ, bidjiþ, jah wairþiþ izwis. 8In þamma hauhiþs ist atta meins, ei akran manag bairaiþ jah wairþaiþ meinai siponjos. 9Swaswe frijoda mik atta, swah ik frijoda izwis; wisaiþ in friaþwai meinai. 10Jabai anabusnins meinos fastaid, sijuþ in friaþwai meinai, swaswe ik anabusnins attins meinis fastaida jah wisa in friaþwai is. 11Þata rodida izwis ei faheþs meina in izwis sijai, jah faheds izwara usfulljaidau.

12"Þata ist anabusns meina: ei frijoþ izwis misso swaswe ik frijoda izwis. 13Maizein þizai friaþwai manna ni habaiþ, ei hwas saiwala seina lagjiþ faur frijonds seinans. 14Jus frijonds meinai sijuþ, jabai taujiþ þatei ik anabiuda izwis. 15Þanaseiþs izwis ni qiþa skalkans, unte skalks ni wait hwa taujiþ is frauja, iþ ik izwis qaþ frijonds unte all þatei hausida at attin meinamma gakannida izwis. 16Ni jus mik gawalideduþ, ak ik gawalida izwis ei jus sniwaiþ jah akran bairaiþ, jah akran izwar du aiwa sijai ei þatahwah þei bidjaiþ attan in namin meinamma gibiþ izwis. 17Þata anabiuda izwis: ei frijoþ izwis misso.

18"Jabai so manaseds izwis fijai, kunneiþ ei mik fruman izwis fijaida. 19Jabai þis fairhwaus weseiþ, aiþþau so manaseds swesans frijodedi; aþþan unte us þamma fairhwau ni sijuþ, ak ik gawalida izwis us þamma fairhwau, duþþe fijaid izwis so manaseþs. 20Gamuneiþ þis waurdis þatei ik qaþ du izwis: 'Nist skalks maiza fraujin seinamma.' Jabai mik wrekun, jah izwis wrikand; jabai mein waurd fastaidedeina, jah izwar fastaina. 21Ak þata allata taujand izwis in namins meinis unte ni kunnun þana sandjandan mik. 22Nih qemjau jah rodidedjau du im, frawaurht ni habaidedeina; iþ nu inilons ni haband bi frawaurht seina. 23Saei mik fijaiþ, jah attan meinana fijaiþ. 24Iþ þo waurstwa ni gatawidedjau in im þoei anþar ainshun ni gatawida, frawaurht ni habaidedeina; iþ nu jah gasehwun mik jah fijaidedun jah mik jah attan meinana. 25Ak ei usfullnodedi waurd þata gamelido in witoda ize: ei 'Fijaidedun mik arwjo.' 26Aþþan þan qimiþ parakletus þanei ik insandja izwis

13Corrected from CA *inbranjada.*

fram attin, ahman sunjos izei fram attin urrinniþ, sa weitwodeiþ bi mik. [27]Jah þan jus weitwodeiþ, unte fram fruma miþ mis sijuþ."

Chapter XVI

[1]"Þata rodida izwis, ei ni afmarzjaindau. [2]Us gaqumþim dreiband izwis; akei qimiþ hweila, ei sahwazuh izei usqimiþ izwis þuggkeiþ hunsla saljan Guda. [3]Jah þata taujand unte ni ufkunþedun attan nih mik. [4]Akei þata rodida izwis, ei biþe qimai so hweila ize, gamuneiþ þize þatei ik qaþ izwis. Iþ þata izwis fram fruma ni qaþ unte miþ izwis was. [5]Iþ nu gagga du þamma sandjandin mik, jah ainshun us izwis ni fraihniþ mik: 'Hwaþ gaggis?' [6]Akei unte þata rodida izwis, gauriþa gadaubida izwar hairto. [7]Akei ik sunja izwis qiþa: batizo ist izwis ei ik galeiþau, unte jabai ik ni galeiþa, parakletus ni qimiþ at izwis; aþþan jabai gagga, sandja ina du izwis. [8]Jah qimands is gasakiþ þo manaseþ bi frawaurht jah bi garaihtiþa jah bi staua: [9]bi frawaurht raihtis þata þatei ni galaubjand du mis; [10]iþ bi garaihtiþa, þatei du attin meinamma gagga, jah ni þanaseiþs saihwiþ mik; [11]iþ bi staua, þatei sa reiks þis fairhwaus afdomiþs warþ.

[12]"Nauh ganoh skal qiþan izwis, akei ni maguþ frabairan nu; [13]iþ þan qimiþ jains, ahma sunjos, briggiþ izwis in allai sunjai; nih þan rodeiþ af sis silbin, ak swa filu swe hauseiþ, rodeiþ; jah þata anawairþo gateihiþ izwis. [14]Jains mik hauheiþ, unte us meinamma nimiþ jah gateihiþ izwis. [15]All þatei aih atta mein ist; duhþe qaþ þatei us meinamma nimiþ jah gateihiþ izwis.

[16]"Leitil nauh jah ni saihwiþ mik; jah aftra leitil jah gasaihwiþ mik, unte ik gagga du attin." [17]Þaruh qeþun us þaim siponjam du sis misso: "Hwa ist þata þatei qiþiþ unsis: 'Leitil ei ni saihwiþ mik, jah aftra leitil jah gasaihwiþ mik,' jah þatei: 'Ik gagga du attin'?" [18]Qeþunuh: "Þata hwa sijai þatei qiþiþ 'Leitil'? Ni witum hwa qiþiþ." [19]Iþ Iesus wissuh þatei wildedun ina fraihnan jah qaþ im: "Bi þata sokeiþ miþ izwis misso þatei qaþ: 'Leitil, jah ni saihwiþ mik, jah aftra leitil jah gasaihwiþ mik.' [20]Amen, amen qiþa izwis þei greitiþ jah gaunoþ jus, iþ manaseþs faginoþ. Jus saurgandans wairþiþ, akei so saurga izwara du fahedai wairþiþ. [21]Qino þan bairiþ, saurga habaid, unte qam hweila izos. Iþ biþe gabauran ist barn, ni þanaseiþs ni gaman þizos aglons faura fahedai, unte gabaurans warþ manna in fairhwau. [22]Jah þan jus auk nu saurga habaiþ; iþ aftra saihwa izwis, jah faginoþ izwar hairto, jah þo fahed izwara ni ainshun nimiþ af izwis. [23]Jah in jainamma daga mik ni fraihniþ waihtais. Amen, amen qiþa izwis þatei þishwah þei bidjiþ attan in namin meinamma gibiþ izwis. [24]Und hita ni beduþ ni waihtais in namin meinamma. Bidjaiþ jah nimiþ, ei faheþs izwara sijai usfullida.

[25]"Þata in gajukom rodida izwis, akei qimiþ hweila þanuh izwis ni þanaseiþs in gajukom rodja, ak andaugiba bi attan gateiha izwis. [26]In jainamma daga in namin meinamma bidjiþ, jah ni qiþa izwis þei ik bidjau attan bi izwis, [27]ak silba atta frijoþ izwis, unte jus mik frijodeduþ jah galaubideduþ þatei ik fram Guda urrann. [28]Uzuhiddja fram attin jah atiddja in þana fairhwu; aftra bileiþa þamma fairhwau jah gagga du attin."

[29]Þaruh qeþun þai siponjos is: "Sai, nu andaugiba rodeis jah gajukono ni ainohun qiþis. [30]Nu witum ei þu kant alla, jah ni þarft ei þuk hwas fraihnai. Bi þamma galaubjam þatei þu fram Guda urrant. [31]Andhof im Iesus: "Nu galaubeiþ? [32]Sai, qimiþ hweila, jah nu qam, ei distahjada hwarjizuh du seinaim,[14] jah mik ainana bileiþiþ. Jah ni im ains, unte atta miþ mis ist. [33]Þata rodida izwis þei in mis gawairþi aigeiþ; in þamma fairhwau aglons habaid, akei þrafsteiþ izwis, ik gajiukaida þana fairhwu."

Chapter XVII

[1]Þata rodida Iesus uzuhhof augona seina du himina jah qaþ: "Atta, qam hweila, hauhei þeinana sunu ei sunus þeins hauhjai þuk, [2]swaswe atgaft imma waldufni allaize leike ei all þatei atfgaft imma gibai im libain aiweinon. [3]Soh þan ist so aiweino libains: ei kunneina þuk ainana sunjana[15] Guþ jah þanei insandides, Iesu Xristu. [4]Ik þuk hauhida ana airþai; waurstw ustauh þatei atgaft mis du waurkjan. [5]Jah nu hauhei mik, þu atta, at þus silbin þamma wulþau, þanei habaida at þus, faurþizei sa fairhwus wesi.

---

[14]Corrected from CA *seina.*

[15]Corrected from CA *sunja.*

6"Gabairhtida þeinata namo mannam þanzei
atgaft mis us þamma fairhwau. Þeinai wesun jah mis
atgaft ins, jah þata waurd þeinata gafastaidedun. 7Nu
ufkunþa ei alla þoei atgaft mis, at þus sind, 8unte þo
waurda þoei atgaft mis atgaft im, jah eis nemun bi sunjai
þatei fram þus urrann, jah galaubidedun þatei þu mik
insandides. 9Ik bi ins bidja; ni bi þo manaseþ bidja, ak bi
þans þanzei atgaft mis unte þeinai sind. 10Jah meina alla
þeina sind jah þeina meina, jah hauhiþs im in þaim.
11Ni þanaseiþs im in þamma fairhwau; iþ þai in þamma
fairhwau sind, jah ik du þus gagga. Atta weiha, fastai
ins in namin þeinamma, þanzei atgaft mis, ei sijaina ain
swase wit. 12Þan was miþ im in þamma fairhwau, ik
fastaida ins in namin þeinamma. Þanzei atgaft mis
gafastaida, jah ainshun us im ni fraqistnoda niba sa
sunus fralustais ei þata gamelido usfulliþ waurþi. 13Iþ
nu du þus gagga, jah þata rodja in manasedai, ei habaina
fahed meina usfullida in sis. 14Ik atgaf im waurd
þeinata; jah so manaseþs fijaida ins, unte ni sind us
þamma fairhwau, swaswe ik us þamma fairhwau ni im.
15Ni bidja ei usnimais ins us þamma fairhwau, ak ei
bairgais im faura þamma unseljin. 16Us þamma fairhwau
ni sind, swaswe ik us þamma fairhwau ni im. 17Weihai
ins in sunjai: waurd þeinata sunja ist. 18Swaswe mik
insandides in manaseþ, swah ik insandida ins in þo
manased. 19Jah fram im ik weiha mik silban, ei sijaina
jah eis weihai in sunjai. 20Aþþan ni bi þans bidja ainans,
ak bi þans galaubjandans þairh waurda ize du mis, 21ei
allai ain sijaina, swaswe þu, atta, in mis jah ik in þus, ei
jah þai in uggkis ain sijaina, ei so manaseþs galaubjai
þatei þu mik insandides. 22Jah ik wulþu þanei gaft mis
gaf im, ei sijaina ain swaswe wit ain siju. 23Ik in im jah
þu in mis, ei sijaina ustauhanai du ainamma, jah kunnei
so manaseþs þatei þu mik insandides jah frijodes ins,
swaswe mik frijodes. 24Atta, þatei atgaft mis, wiljau ei
þarei im ik, jah þai sijaina miþ mis, ei saihwaina wulþu
meinana þanei gaft mis, unte frijodes mik faur gaskaft
fairhwaus. 25Atta garaihta, jah so manaseþs þuk ni
ufkunþa; iþ ik þuk kunþa. Jah þai ufkunþedun þatei þu
mik insandides. 26Jah gakannida im namo þeinata jah
kannja, ei friaþwa þoei frijodes mik in im sijai jah ik in
im."

Chapter XVIII

1Þata qiþands Iesus usiddja miþ siponjam
seinaim ufar rinnon þo Kaidron, þarei was aurtigards in
þanei galaiþ Iesus jah siponjos is. 2Wissuh þan jah Iudas
sa galewjands ina þana stad þatei ufta gaiddja Iesus
jainar miþ siponjam seinaim. 3Iþ Iudas nam hansa jah
þize gudjane jah Fareisaie andbahtans, iddjuh
jaindwairþs miþ skeimam jah haizam jah wepnam. 4Iþ
Iesus witands alla þoei qemun ana ina, usgaggands ut
qaþ im: "Hwana sokeiþ?" 5Andhafjandans imma
qeþun: "Iesu þana Nazoraiu." Þaruh qaþ im Iesus: "Ik
im." Stoþuh þan jah Iudas sa lewjands ina miþ im.
6Þaruh swe qaþ im þatei "Ik im," galiþun ibukai jah
gadrusun dalaþ. 7Þaþroh þan ins aftra frah: "Hwana
sokeiþ?" Iþ eis qeþun: "Iesu, þana Nazoraiu."
8Andhof Iesus: "Qaþ izwis þatei ik im. Jabai nu mik
sokeiþ, letiþ þans gaggan." (9Ei usfullnodedi þata
waurd þatei qaþ ei "þanzei atgaft[16] mis ni fraqistida ize
ainummehun.") 10Iþ Seimon Paitrus habands hairu
uslauk ina jah sloh þis auhumistins gudjins skalk jah
afmaimait imma auso taihswo, sah þan haitans was
namin Malkus. 11Þaruh qaþ Iesus du Paitrau: "Lagei
þana hairu in fodr. Stikl þanei gaf mis atta, niu drigkau
þana?"

12Þaruh hansa jah sa þusundifaþs jah andbahtos
Iudaie undgripun Iesu jah gabundun ina, jah gatauhun
ina du Annin frumist; sa was auk swaihra Kajafin saei
was auhumists weiha þis ataþnjis. (14Wasuh þan Kajafa
saei garaginoda Iudaium þatei batizo ist ainana mannan
fraqistjan faur managein.)

15Þaruh laistida Iesu Seimon P<ait>rus jah
anþar siponeis. Sah þan siponeis was kunþs þamma
gudjin jah miþinngalaiþ miþ Iesua in rohsn þis gudjins.
16Iþ Paitrus stoþ at daurom uta. Þaruh usiddja ut sa
siponeis anþar, saei was kunþs þamma gudjin, jah qaþ
daurawardai jah attauh inn Paitru. 17Þaruh qaþ jaina
þiwi, so daurawardo, du Paitrau: "Ibai jah þu þize
siponje is þis mans?" Iþ is qaþ: "Ni im." 18Þaruh
stoþun skalkos jah andbahtos haurja waurkjandans, unte
kald was, jah warmidedun sik. Jah þan was miþ im
Paitrus standands jah warmjands sik.

19Iþ sa auhumista gudja frah Iesu bi siponjans is
jah bi laisein is. 20Andhof imma Iesus: "Ik andaugjo
rodida manasedai; ik sinteino laisida in gaqumþai jah in
gudhusa, þarei sinteino Iudaieis gaqimand, jah þiubjo ni
rodida waiht. 21Hwis mik fraihnis? Fraihn þans
hausjandans hwa rodidedjau du im. Sai, þai witun þatei
qaþ ik." 22Iþ þata qiþandin imma sums andbahte
standands gaf slah lofin Iesua, qaþuh: "Swau andhafjis
þamma reikistin gudjin?" 23Andhof Iesus: "Jabai

16Corrected from CA *atgaf*.

ubilaba rodida, weitwodei bi þata ubil. Aiþþau jabai
waila, duhwe mik slahis?" [24]Þanuh insandida ina Annas
gabundanana du Kajafin þamma maistin gudjin. [25]Iþ
Seimon Paitrus was standands jah warmjands sik. Þaruh
qeþun du imma: "Niu jah þu þize siponje þis is?" Iþ is
afaiaik jah qaþ: "Ne, ni im." [26]Qaþ sums þize skalke
þis maistins gudjins, sah niþjis was þammei afmaimait
Paitrus auso; "Niu þuk sahw ik in aurtigarda miþ
imma?" [27]Þaruh aftra afaiaik Paitrus, jah suns hana
hrukida.

[28]Iþ eis tauhun Iesu fram Kajafin in praitoriaun.
Þanuh was maurgins. Iþ eis ni iddjedun in praitoria ei ni
besaulnodedeina, ak matidedeina Pasxa. [29]Þaruh atiddja
ut Peilatus du im jah qaþ: "Hwo wrohe bairiþ ana þana
mannan?" [30]Andhofun jah qeþun du imma: "Nih wesi
sa ubiltojis, ni þau weis atgebeima þus ina." [31]Þaruh
qaþ im Peilatus: "Nimiþ ina jus jah bi witoda
izwaramma stojiþ ina." Iþ eis qeþunuh du imma
Iudaieis: "Unsis ni skuld ist usqiman manne
ainummehun." [32](Ei waurd Fraujins usfullnodedi þatei
qaþ, bandwjands hwileikamma dauþau skulda
gaswiltan.) [33]Galaiþ in praitauria aftra Peilatus jah
wopida Iesu qaþuh imma: "Þu is þiudans Iudaie?"
[34]Andhof Iesus: "Abu þus silbin þu þata qiþis þau
anþarai þus qeþun bi mik?" [35]Andhof Peilatus: "Waitei
ik Iudaius im? So þiuda þeina jah gudjans anafulhun
þuk mis. Hwa gatawides?" [36]Andhof Iesus:
"Þiudangardi meina nist us þamma fairhwau. Iþ us
þamma fairhwau wesi meina þiudangardi, aiþþau
andbahtos meinai usdaudidedeina[17] ei ni galewiþs wesjau
Iudaium. Iþ nu þiudangardi meina nist þaþro." [37]Þaruh
qaþ imma Peilatus: "An nuh þiudans is þu?"
Andhafjands Iesus <qaþ>: "Þu qiþis ei þiudans im ik.
Ik du þamma gabaurans im jah du þamma qam in
þamma fairhwau: ei weitwodjau sunjai. Hwazuh saei ist
sunjos hauseiþ stibnos meinaizos." [38]Þanuh qaþ imma
Peilatus: "Hwa ist so sunja?"

Jah þata qiþands galaiþ ut du Iudaium jah qaþ
im: "Ik ainohun fairino ni bigita in þamma." [39]Iþ ist
biuhti izwis ei ainana izwis fraletau in Pasxa. Wileidu
nu ei fraletau izwis þana þiudan Iudaie?" [40]Iþ eis
hropidedun aftra allai qiþandans: "Ne þana, ak
Barabban." (Sah þan was sa Barabba waidedja.)

Chapter XIX

[1]Þanuh þan nam Peilatus Iesu jah usblaggw.
[2]Jah þai gadrauhteis uswundun wipja[18] us þaurnum jah
galagidedun imma ana haubid jah wastjai paurpurodai
gawasidedun ina, [3]jah qeþun: "Hails þiudans Iudaie!"
Jah gebun imma slahins lofin. [4]Atiddja aftra ut Peilatus
jah qaþ im: "Sai, attiuha izwis ina ut, ei witeiþ þatei in
imma ni ainohun fairino bigat." [5]Þaruh usiddja ut Iesus
bairands þana þaurneinan waip jah þo paupurodon
wastja. Jah qaþ im: "Sa ist sa manna." [6]Þaruh biþe
sehwun ina þai maistans gudjans jah andbahtos,
hropidedun qiþandans: "Ushramei, ushramei ina!" Qaþ
im Peilatus: "Nimiþ ina jus jah hramjiþ. Iþ ik fairina in
imma ni bigita." [7]Andhofun imma Iudaieis: "Weis
witoþ aihum, jah bi þamma witoda unsaramma skal
gaswiltan unte sik silban Gudis sunu gatawida." [8]Biþe
gahausida Peilatus þata waurd, mais ohta sis, [9]jah galaiþ
in praitauria aftra jah qaþ du Iesua: "Hwaþro is þu?" Iþ
Iesus andawaurdi ni gaf imma. [10]Þaruh qaþ imma
Peilatus: "Du mis ni rodeis? Niu waist þatei waldufni
aih ushramjan þuk jah waldufni aih fraletan þuk?"
[11]Andhof Iesus: "Ni aihtedeis waldufnje ainhun ana mik
nih wesi þus atgiban iupaþro. Duhþe sa galewjands mik
þus maizein frawaurht habaid." [12]Framuh þamma
sokida Peilatus fraletan ina, iþ Iudaieis hropidedun
qiþandans: "Jabai þana fraletis, ni is frijonds Kaisara.
Sahwazuh izei þiudan sik silban taujiþ andstandiþ
Kaisara. [13]Þanuh Peilatus hausjands þize... (remainder
missing)

[17]Corrected from CA *usdaudedideina.*

[18]Corrected from CA *wippja.*

The Epistle of Paul to the Romans

[Vss. I:1 to VI:22 are missing.][1]

Chapter VI

23. Þo auk launa frawaurhtais dauþus;
iþ ansts Gudis libains aiweino in Xristau Iesu, Fraujin unsaramma.

23. For the wages of sin are death,
but the favor of God is eternal life in Christ Jesus, our Lord.

Chapter VII

1. Þau niu wituþ, broþrjus, --
kunnandam auk witoþ rodja --
þatei witoþ fraujinoþ mann swa lagga hweila swe libaiþ?

1. Do you not know, brothers --
for I am speaking to those who know the law --
that the law is binding on a man only as long as he is alive?

2. Jah auk ufwaira qens at libandin abin gabundana ist witoda; aþþan jabai gaswiltiþ aba,
galausjada af þamma witoda abins.

2. For a married woman is bound by the law while her husband is alive, but if the husband dies,
she is freed from the law regarding a husband.

3. Þannu þan at libandin abin haitada horinondei,
jabai wairþiþ waira anþaramma;
iþ jabai gaswiltiþ wair, frija ist þis witodis,
ei ni sijai horinondei waurþana abin anþaramma.

3. When then her husband is alive she is called an adulteress if she lives with another man;
but if the man dies, she is free of this law,
lest she be (regarded as) an adulteress having taken up with another husband.

4. Swaei nu jah jus, broþrjus meinai, afdauþidai waurþuþ witoda þairh leik Xristaus,
ei wairþaiþ anþaramma, þamma us dauþaim urreisandin,
ei akrana bairaima guda.

4. Likewise now even you, my brothers, have died as far as the law is concerned through the body of Christ,
so that you may belong to another, (namely) the one risen from the dead,
that we may bear good fruit.

5. Þan auk wesum in leika,
winnons frawaurhte[2] þos þairh witoþ waurhtedun in liþum unsaraim du akran bairan dauþau.

5. For while we were in the flesh,
the passions of sins produced by the law worked in our bodies for the production of fruit for death.

6. Iþ nu, sai, andbundanai waurþum af witoda,
gadauþnandans in þammei gahabaidai wesum,
swaei skalkinoma in niujiþai ahmins jah ni fairniþai bokos.

6. But now, we are freed from the law,
dead in regard to that by which we were held captive,
so that we may serve in newness of spirit and not in the staleness of written works.

7. Hwa nu qiþam?
Witoþ frawaurhts ist? Nissijai!
Ak frawaurht ni ufkunþedjau nih þairh witoþ,
unte lustu nih wissedjau,
nih witoþ qeþi: Ni gairnjais.

7. What shall we now say?
The law is sin? By no means!
But I would not have known sin except through the law,
because I would not have known covetousness
if the law had not said: Thou shalt not covet.

8. Iþ lew nimandei[2] frawaurhts þairh anabusn gawaurhta in mis allana lustu;

8. But sin, finding opportunity through the commandments, produced in me all covetousness;

---

[1] The text is that of Ambrosianus A (siglum A) unless otherwise indicated.

[2] Corr. from A *frawaurhti. nimandei* in verse 8 below is corr. from A *nimands.*

unte inu witoþ frawaurhts was nawis.[3]

since without the law sin was dead.

9. Iþ ik qius <was> inu witoþ simle,
iþ qimandein anabusnai frawaurhts gaqiunoda,

9. But I was once alive apart from the law,
but with the arrival of the law sin came alive,

10. iþ ik gadauþnoda, jah bigitana warþ mis anabusns,
sei was du libainai, wisan du dauþau.

10. and I died, and the commandment which was for
life proved to be for death for me.

11. Unte frawaurhts lew nimandei þairh anabusn
uslutoda mik,
jah þairh þo usqam.

11. Because sin, seizing the opportunity through the
commandment, deceived me,
and through it I perished.

12. Aþþan nu sweþauh witoþ weihata
jah anabusns weiha jah garaihta jah þiuþeiga.

12. But then the law is indeed holy
and the commandment is holy and just and good.

13. Þata nu þiuþeigo warþ mis dauþus?
Nissijai! ak frawaurhts, ei uskunþa waurþi frawaurhts,
þairh þata þiuþeigo mis gawaurkjandei dauþu,
ei waurþi ufarassau frawaurhta frawaurhts þairh
anabusn.

13. Did that then which is good become death to me?
By no means! but rather it was sin, so that it might be
recognized as sin, producing death for me through that
which is good, so as to become exceedingly sinful sin
through the commandment.

14. Witum auk þatei witoþ ahmein ist,
iþ ik leikeins im, frabauhts uf frawaurht.

14. For we know that the law is spiritual,
but I am carnal, sold into the subjection of sin.

15. Þatei waurkja ni fraþja,
unte ni þatei wiljau tauja,
ak þatei fija þata tauja.

15. That which I do I do not understand,
for I do not do what I will,
but rather do I do what I hate.

16. Iþ jabai þatei ni wiljau þata tauja,
gaqiss im witoda þatei goþ,

16. But if I do that which I do not will,
and (yet) I am in accord with the law that is good,

17. iþ nu ju ni ik waurkja þata,
ak so bauandei in mis frawaurhts.

17. then no longer is it I who do it,
but rather sin which dwells in me.

18. Wait auk þatei ni bauiþ in mis,
þatist in leika meinamma, þiuþ,
unte wiljan atligiþ mis, iþ gawaurkjan goþ ni,

18. For I know that good does not dwell in me,
that is, in my physical being,
because I am capable of willing, but not of doing, good,

19. unte ni þatei wiljau waurkja goþ,
ak þatei ni wiljau ubil <þata> tauja.

19. because I do not do the good that I want to do,
but rather do I do the evil that I do not want to do.

20. Jabai nu þatei ni wiljau ik þata tauja,
ju ni ik waurkja ita, ak sei bauiþ in mis frawaurhts.

20. If when I do that which I do not will,
no longer is it I who do it, but rather is it sin which
resides in me.

21. Bigita nu witoþ:
wiljandin mis goþ taujan, unte mis atist ubil.

21. I find then a law:
whenever I want to do good, evil lies close at hand.

22. Gawizneigs im auk witoda Gudis bi þamma innumin
mann,

22. For I am delighted with the law of God in my inner-
most being,

---

3 *nawi- adj(i)* dead; the fem sing. form is *-is* is not normal (see §17.2); one expects *naus* or *nauja*.

23. aþþan gasaihwa anþar witoþ in liþum meinaim,
andweihando witoda ahmins meinis
jah frahinþando mik in witoda frawaurhtais
þamma wisandin in liþum meinaim.

23. But I see another law in my limbs
warring with the law of my spirit
and making me captive to the law of sin
which is in my limbs.

24. Wainahs ik manna!
Hwas mik lauseiþ us þamma leika dauþaus þis?

24. Wretched man that I am!
Who will set me free from this body of this death?

25. Awiliudo Guda þairh Iesu Xristu, Fraujan unsarana;
jau nu silba ik skalkino gahugdai witoda Gudis,
iþ leika witoda frawaurhtais.

25. I give thanks to God through Jesus Christ our Lord;
so then I myself serve the law of God with (my) thoughts,
but (I serve) the law of sin with (my) body.

Chapter VIII

Chapter VIII

1. Ni waiht þannu nu wargiþos þaim in Xristau Iesu ni gaggandam bi leika.

1. Now then (there is) nothing of condemnation for those in Christ Jesus who do not go according to the flesh.

2. Unte witoþ ahmins libainais in Xristau Iesu frijana brahta mik witodis frawaurhtais jah dauþaus.

2. For the law of the spirit of life in Christ Jesus set me free from the law of sin and death.

3. Unte þata unmahteigo witodis,
in þammei siuks was þairh leik,
Guþ seinana sunu insandjands in galeikja leikis frawaurhtais jah bi frawaurht gawargida frawaurht in leika,

3. For that which (was) impossible for the law,
inasmuch as it was sick because of the body,
God, sending his son in the bodily form of sin, even through sin condemned as sin in the body,

4. ei garaihtei witodis usfulljaidau in uns þaim ni bi leika gaggandam, ak bi ahmin.

4. so that the righteousness of the law might be fulfilled in us who go not by the body, but by the spirit.

5. Unte þai bi leika wisandans þo þoei leikis sind mitond,
iþ þai bi ahmin þo þoei ahmins.

5. For those living by the flesh think about the things which are of the flesh,
but those (who live) by the spirit (think about) the things which are of the spirit.

6. Aþþan fraþi leikis dauþus,
iþ fraþi ahmins libains jah gawairþi;

6. For concentration on the body is death,
but concentration on the spirit is life and peace;

7. unte fraþi leikis fijands du Guda;
witoda Gudis ni ufhauseiþ, iþ ni mag;

7. for concentration on the body is an enemy to God;
it does not obey the law of God, indeed it cannot.

8. Aþþan þai in leika wisandans Guda galeikan ni magun.

8. For those living in the flesh cannot please God.

9. Iþ jus ni sijuþ in leika, ak in ahmin,
sweþauh jabai ahma Gudis bauiþ in izwis;
iþ jabai hwas ahman Xristaus ni habaiþ, sa nist is.

9. But you are not in the flesh, but in the spirit,
if the spirit of God really dwells in you;
but if anyone does not have the spirit of Christ,
he is not of him (*or* of it).

10. Jabai auk Xristus in izwis, leik raihtis [text missing from here to 34b]

10. For if Christ is in you...

34b. ..saei ist in taihswon Gudis, saei jah bidjiþ faur uns.

35. Hwas uns afskaidai af friaþwai Xristaus? Aglo?
þau aggwiþa? þau wrakja? þau huhrus? þau naqadei?
þau sleiþei? þau hairus?

36. Swaswe gameliþ ist þatei
"In þuk gadauþjanda all dagis,
rahnidai wesum swe lamba slauhtais."

37. Akei in þaim allaim jiukam þairh þana frijondan uns.

38. Gatraua auk þatei ni dauþus <ni libains> nih aggiljus ni reikja ni mahteis nih andwairþo nih anawairþo,

39. nih hauhiþa, nih diupiþa nih gaskafts anþara magi uns afskaidan af friaþwai Gudis þizai in Xristau Iesu, Fraujin unsaramma.

34b. ...who is on the right hand of God, who indeed intercedes for us.

35. What will separate us from the love of Christ?
Tribulation? distress? persecution? hunger?
nakedness? danger? the sword?

36. As it is written:
"For your sake we are being killed all day long;
We have been reckoned as sheep to be slaughtered."

37. But in all these things we are victorious through him who loves us.

38. For I trust that neither death nor life nor angels nor governments nor powers nor present things nor future things,

39. nor height nor depth nor any other creation can separate us from the love of God in Christ Jesus, our Lord.

Chapter IX

I. Sunja qiþa, ni waiht liuga,
miþweitwodjandein mis miþwissein meinai in ahmin weihamma,

2. þatei saurga mis ist mikila jah unhweilo aglo hairtin meinamma.

3. Usbida auk anaþaima wisan silba ik af Xristau faur broþruns meinans þans samakunjans bi leika,

4. þaiei sind Israeleitai, þizeei ist frastisibja jah wulþus jah witodis garaideins jah triggwos jah skalkinassus jah gahaita,

5. þizeei attans, jah us þaimei Xristus bi leika.
Saei is ufar allaim, Guþ þiuþiþs in aiwam, Amen!

6. Aþþan sweþauh ni usdraus waurd Gudis.
Ni auk allai þai us Israela, [þai] sind Israel;

7. niþ-þatei sijaina fraiw Abrahamis allai barna,
ak "in Isaka haitada þus fraiw."

8. Þat-ist: ni þo barna leikis barna Gudis,
ak barna gahaitis rahnjanda du fraiwa.

Chapter IX

1. I am speaking the truth, I am not lying,
my conscience bearing witness for me in the Holy Spirit,

2. that I have great sorrow and unceasing anguish in my heart.

3. For I would pray to be myself anathema to Christ for the sake of my brethren, kinsmen in the flesh,

4. who are Israelites, to whom belong the adoption (by God), the glory, the readying of the law, the covenants, the service, and the promises,

5. to whom belong the patriarchs, and out of whom, according to the flesh, was Christ.
(May) God, who is over all, (be) blessed forever. Amen.
6. But the word of God has not, however, failed.
For not all those (descended) from Israel (belong to) Israel;
7. nor, because they may be the seed of Abraham, are they all (his) children,
but "through Isaac shall a lineage be named for you."
8. That is, (it is) not the children of the flesh that are the children of God, but (it is) the children of the promise that are reckoned as (his) seed.

9. Gahaitis auk waurd þat' ist: "Bi þamma mela qima,
jah wairþiþ Sarrin sunus;"

9. For this is the word of the promise: "I shall return at
this season, and Sarah will have a son."

10. aþþan ni þat' ain, ak jah Raibaikka us ainamma
galigrja habandei Isakis, attins unsaris.

10. But not only that, but (there was) also Rebecca,
conceiving from the sole intercourse of Isaac, our father.

11. Aþþan nauhþanuh <ni> gabauranai wesun,
aiþþau tawidedeina hwa þiuþis aiþþau unþiuþis,
-- ei bi gawaleinai muns Gudis wisai,

11. But when they had not yet even been born,
that they might do any good or evil,
-- in order that God's intention might come about by
election,

12. nih us waurstwam, ak us þamma laþondin--
qiþan ist izai þatei "Sa maiza skalkinoþ þamma
minnizin,"

12. not from works, but from (his) call --
she was told: "The elder will serve the younger."

13. swaswe gameliþ ist: "Iakob frijoda, iþ Esaw fijaida."

13. As it is written: "Jacob I loved, but Esau I hated."

14. Hwa nu qiþam? Ibai inwindiþa fram Guda? Nis-
sijai!

14. What, then, shall we say? There is not injustice from
God, is there? Of course not.

15. Du Mose auk qiþiþ: "Gaarma þanei arma,
jah gableiþja þanei bleiþja."

15. For he says to Moses: "I will have mercy on him on
whom I have mercy, and I will show com-
-passion to him to whom I show compassion.

16. Þannu nu ni wiljandins ni rinnandins, ak armandins
Gudis.

16. Therefore, then, (it is) not (a matter) of one wishing
(salvation) or of one running (after salvation),
but rather of God showing mercy.

17. Qiþiþ auk þata gamelido du Faraoni:
"Unte in þize jah raisida þuk,
ei gabairhtjau bi þus maht meina
jah gateihaidau namo mein and alla airþa."

17. For the scripture says to Pharaoh:
"I have raised you up for these (reasons):
that I might make my might manifest through
you and that my name might be proclaimed
throughout all the earth."

18. Þannu nu jai þanei wili armaiþ,
iþ þanei wili gahardeiþ.

18. Therefore, then, he has mercy on whomsoever he
wills, and he makes obdurate whomsoever he wills.

19. Qiþis mis nu: "Aþþan hwa nauh faianda?
Unte wiljin is hwas andstandiþ?"

19. You will say to me then: "But why are they still
found fault with?
For who can resist his will?"

20. Þannu nu jai, manna, þu hwas is,
ei andwaurdjais Guda?
Ibai qiþiþ gadigis du þamma digandin:
"Hwa mik gatawides swa?"

20. But then indeed, man, who are you
that you talk back to God?
Does what is molded say to the molder:
"Why have you made me so?"?

21. Þau niu habaiþ kasja waldufni þahons
us þamma samin daiga
taujan sum du galaubamma kasa,
sumuþþan du ungal<a>ubamma?

21. But has not the potter power over (lit. of) the clay to
make out of the same lump
one piece into a precious vessel, but another piece into
an ordinary vessel?

22. Iþ jabai wiljands Guþ ustaiknjan þwairhein
jah uskannjan þata mahteigo
usbeidands <was> in managai laggamodein bi kasam
þwairheins gamanwidaim du fralustai,

22. But (what) if God, wanting to show (his) wrath and
make known (his) power,
has tolerated with great patience the vessels of wrath
fashioned for destructive purposes,

23. ei gakannidedi gabein wulþaus seinis bi kasam armaions
þoei fauragamanwida du wulþau?

23. so that he might make known the wealth of his glory toward the vessels of mercy
which he has prepared beforehand for glory,

24. þanzei jah laþoda uns ni þatainei us Iudaium,
ak jah us þiudom,

24. even us, whom he has called not only from the Jews
but also from the Gentiles,

25. swaswe jah in Osaiin qiþiþ:
"Haita þo ni managein meina managein meina,
jah þo unliubon liubon;
26. jah wairþiþ in þamma stada þarei qiþada im: 'Ni managei meina jus,'
þai haitanda sunjus Gudis libandins."

25. as he says in Hosea:
"Those not-my-people I shall call my people,
the not-beloved (I shall call) beloved.
26. And it will happen that in the (very) place where it was said to them "You are not my people" they will be called "the sons of the Living God."

27. Iþ Esaias hropeiþ bi Israel:
"Jabai wesi raþjo suniwe Israelis swaswe malma mareins, laibos ganisand.

27. But Isaiah proclaims concerning Israel:
"Even if the number of the sons of Israel were like the sand of the sea, only a remnant will be saved.

28. Waurd auk ustiuhands jah gamaurgjands in garaihtein,
unte waurd gamaurgiþ taujiþ Frauja ana airþai."

28. For (he is) finishing off the matter in short order with righteousness;
for the Lord is settling a shortened affair on earth."

29. Jah swaswe fauraqaþ Esaias:
"Nih Frauja Sabaoþ biliþi unsis fraiwa,
swe Saudauma þau waurþeima
jah swe Gaumaurra þau galeikai waurþeima."

29. And as Isaiah predicted:
"If the Lord of Hosts had not left us seed,
we would either have become like Sodom
or become like Gomorrah."

30. Hwa nu qiþam?
Þatei þiudos þos ni laistjandeins garaihtein gafaifahun garaihtein,
aþþan garaihtein þo us galaubeinai;

30. What then shall we say?
That those peoples who did not pursue righteousness have attained righteousness,
that is, righteousness through faith;

31. iþ Israel laistjands witoþ garaihteins
bi witoþ garaihteins ni gasnau.

31. but Israel, pursuing law-righteousness, did not achieve law-righteousness.

32. Duhwe? Unte ni us galaubeinai ak us waurstwam witodis.
Bistuggqun du staina bistuggqis,

32. Why? Because (they pursued it) not through faith but through works of the law.
They stumbled over the stumbling-block,

33. swaswe gameliþ ist:
"Sai, galagja in Sion stain bistuggqis,
jah hallu gamarzeinais,
jah <sa> galaubjands du imma ni gaaiwiskoda.

33. as it is written:
"Behold I am laying a stumbling-block in Zion,
and a rock of offense,
and the one who believes in him will not be put to shame."

Chapter X

Chapter X

1. Broþrjus, sa raihtis wilja meinis hairtins jah bida du Guda bi ins du naseinai.

1. Brothers, the desire of my heart and (my) prayer to God concerning them (is) for (their) salvation.

2. Weitwodja auk im þatei aljan Gudis haband,
akei ni bi kunþja.

2. For I will bear witness for them that they have a zeal for God,
but not with clear understanding.

3. Unkunnandans auk Gudis garaihtein jah seina garaihtein sokjandans stiurjan,
garaihtein Gudis ni ufhausidedun.

3. For, being ignorant of the justification of God and seeking to establish their own justification,
they have not heeded the justification of God.

4. Ustauhts auk witodis Xristus du garaihtein allaim þaim galaubjandam.

4. For the perfection of the law is Christ, for the justification of all those believing.

5. Moses auk meleiþ þo garaihtein us witoda,
þatei "Sa taujands þo manna libaiþ in izai."

5. For Moses writes of justification from the law,
namely: "The man who performs it will live in it."

6. Iþ so us galaubeinai garaihtei swa qiþiþ:
"Ni qiþais in hairtin þeinamma
'Hwas ussteigiþ in himin?'
(Þat' ist Xristu dalaþ attiuhan)

6. But justification which originates in faith says thus:
"Do not say in your heart
'Who can go up to heaven?'
(i.e. to bring Christ down from there)

7. Aiþþau: 'Hwas gasteigiþ in afgrundiþa?'
(Þat' ist Xristu us dauþaim iup ustiuhan)"

7. Or 'Who can go down into the abyss?'
(i.e. to lead Christ up from the dead)."

8. Akei hwa qiþiþ?
Nehwa þus þata waurd ist, in munþa þeinamma jah in hairtin þeinamma
(þat' ist waurd galaubeinais þatei merjam),

8. But what *does* it say?
That answer is near you, in your heart and in your mouth
(i.e. the word of faith which we preach),

9. þei jabai andhaitis in munþa þeinamma Fraujin Iesu
jah galaubeis in hairtin þeinamma
þatei Guþ ina urraisida us dauþaim, ganisis.

9. namely that if you confess with your mouth the Lord
Jesus and believe in your heart
that God raised him up from the dead, you will be saved.

10. Hairto auk galaubeiþ du garaihtiþai,
iþ munþa andhaitada du ganistai.

10. For the heart believes and the result is justification;
and the mouth confesses, with salvation as the result.

11. Qiþiþ auk þata gameliþ:
"Hwazuh sa galaubjands du imma ni gaaiwiskoda."

11. For the scripture says:
"Whosoever believes in him will not be put to shame."

12. Ni auk is gaskaideins Iudaiaus jah Krekis:
sa sama auk Frauja allaize, gabigs in allans þans bidjandans sik.

12. For there is no distinction between Jew and Greek:
for the same (Lord) is the Lord of all, generous to all those calling upon him.

13. "Hwazuh auk saei anahaitiþ bidai namo Fraujins ganisiþ."

13. For "whosoever calls on the name of the Lord in prayer will be saved."

14. Hwaiwa nu bidjand du þammei ni galaubidedun?
Aiþþau hwaiwa galaubjand þammei ni hausidedun?
Iþ hwaiwa hausjand inu[4] merjandan?

14. How then will they pray to him in whom they have
not believed? Or how will they believe in him of whom they have not heard?
But how will they hear without a preacher?

15. Iþ hwaiwa merjand niba insandjanda?
Swaswe gameliþ ist:

15. But how will they preach unless they are sent?
As it is written:

---

[4] Corr. from A *ina*.

"Hwaiwa skaunjai fotjus þize spillondane gawairþi, þize spillondane þiuþ!"

"How beautiful (are) the feet of those telling of peace, of those telling good (tidings)."

16. Akei ni allai ufhausidedun aiwaggeljon;
Esaias auk qiþiþ: "Frauja, hwas galaubida hauseinai unsarai?"

16. But not all have heeded the gospel,
for Isaiah says: "Lord, who has believed our preaching?"

17. Þannu galaubeins us gahauseinai,
iþ gahauseins þairh waurd Xristaus.

17. For belief (comes) from preaching,
and preaching (comes) by the word of Christ.

18. Akei qiþa: "Ibai ni hausidedun?" Raihtis!
"And alla airþa galaiþ drunjus ize,
jah and andins midjungardis waurda ize."

18. But I say: "Haven't they heard?" Of course!
"Their voice has gone to all the earth,
and their word to the ends of the world."

19. Akei qiþa: "Ibai Israel ni fanþ?"
Frumist Moses qiþiþ: "Ik in aljana izwis brigga in unþiudom,
in þiudai unfraþjandein in þwairhein izwis brigga."

19. But I say: "Didn't Israel find out?"
First, Moses says: "I will make you envious of a non-people;
I shall make you angry with an ignorant people."

20. Iþ Esaias ananannþeiþ jah qiþiþ"
"Bigitans warþ þaim mik ni gasokjandam,
Swikunþs warþ þaim mik ni gafraihnandam."

20. Then, Isaiah dared to say:
"I was found by those who did not seek me;
"I became known to those who did not inquire of me.

21. Iþ du Israela qiþiþ:
"Allana dag usbraidida þos handuns meinos du managein ungalaubjandein jah andstandandein."

21. But he says regarding Israel:
"All day have I extended my hands to an unbelieving and rebellious multitude."

Chapter XI

1. Qiþa nu: "Ibai afskauf Guþ arbja seinamma?"
Nissijai! Jah auk ik Israeleites im [...text missing to 11b]

11. ...ei gadruseina? Nissijai! Ak þizai ize missadedai ganists þiudom du in aljana briggan ins.

12. Iþ jabai missadeds ize gabei fairhwau
jah wanains ize gabei þiudom,
hwan mais fullo ize?

13. Izwis auk qiþa þiudom.
Swa lagga swe ik im þiudo apaustaulus, andbahtei mein mikilja,

14. ei hwaiwa in aljana briggau leik mein jah ganasjau sumans us im.

Chapter XI

1. I say then: "Has God rejected his heritage?"
God forbid! For I am an Israelite [... ...]

11. ...so as to fall? God forbid! But through this misdeed of theirs salvation (has come) to the Gentiles, so as to make them (i.e. Israel) envious.

12. But if their misdeed (means) wealth for the world
and their failure (means) wealth for the Gentiles,
how much more so their fullness (i.e. full inclusion among the faithful)?

13. For I am speaking to you Gentiles.
As long as I am an apostle to the Gentiles, I will increase my ministry,

14. so as somehow to make my flesh (i.e. fellow-Israelites) envious and save some of them.

15. Jabai auk uswaurpa ize gabei fairhwaus,
hwa so andanumts, nibai libains us dauþaim?

15. For if their rejection (means) wealth for the world,
what (does) their acceptance (mean) but life from the dead?

16. Þandei ufarskafts weiha, jah daigs,
jah jabai waurts weiha, jah astos.

16. If the (portion of dough set aside as an offering of) first-fruits is holy, then the (entire lump of) dough is holy; and if the root is holy, then the branches (are too).

17. Iþ jabai sumai þize aste usbruknodedun,
iþ þu wilþeis alewabagms wisands intrusgiþs warst in ins
jah gamains þizai waurtai[5] jah smairþra alewabagmis warst,

17. But if some of these branches were broken off,
and you, being a wild olive-tree, were grafted on in their stead
and became one with the root and richness of the olive-tree,

18. ni hwop ana þans astans.[6]
Iþ jabai hwopis, ni þu þo waurt[6] bairis,
ak so waurts þuk.

18. do not boast over those (other) branches.
But if you boast, (remember that) you do not support that root,
but rather that root (supports) you.

19. Qiþais nu: "Usbruknodedun astos ei ik intrusgjaidau."

19. But you will say: "The branches were broken off so that I might be grafted on."

20. Waila! Ungalaubeinai usbruknodedun,
iþ þu galaubeinai gastost;
ni hugei hauhaba, ak ogs,

20. Very well! They were broken off for their lack of faith, but you have remained firm (only) through faith.
Do not think proudly, but be fearful;

21. þandei Guþ þans us gabaurþai astans ni freidida,
ibai aufto ni þuk freidjai.

21. if God did not spare the natural (lit. from-birth) branches,
he will not spare you either, will he?

22. Sai nu selein jah hwassein garaihta Gudis;
aþþan ana þaim þaiei gadrusun, hwassein,
iþ ana þus selein, jabai þairhwisis in selein.
Aiþþau[7] jah þu usmaitaza,

22. Behold then the goodness and just severity of God:
on the one hand, severity for those who have fallen;
on the other, goodness for you, if you remain in (his) kindness.
Otherwise even you will be cut off,

23. jah jainai, nibai gatulgjand sik in ungalaubeinai, intrusgjanda;
mahteigs auk ist Guþ aftra intrusgjan ins.

23. and those (other branches), unless they persist in (their) unbelief, will be grafted (back) on,
for God is able to graft them back on.

24. Jabai auk þu, us wistai usmaitans þis wilþins[8] alewabagmis jah aljakuns wisands, intrusgans warst in godana alewabagm,
hwan filu mais þai bi wistai intrusgjanda in swesana alewabagm.

24. For if you, cut from this olive-tree, wild by nature, were unnaturally grafted onto the good (i.e. cultivated) olive-tree,
how much more so will those natural (branches) be grafted (back) onto their own olive-trees?

25. Ni auk wiljau izwis unweisans, broþrjus, þizos runos, ei ni sijaiþ in izwis silbam frodai,
unte daubei <bi> sumata Israela warþ,
und þatei fullo þiudo inngaleiþai,

25. I do not want you to be ignorant of this mystery,
lest you be wise in yourself (i.e. conceited, arrogant),
for obduracy has come upon some of Israel
until the full number of Gentiles come in,

26. jah swa allai Israel ganisand, swaswe gameliþ ist:

26. and so all Israel will be saved, as it is written:

---

[5] Corr. from A *waurhtai.*

[6] Corr. from A *anstans.* *waurt* corr. from A *waurts.*

[7] Corr. from A *aþþan.*

[8] Corr. from A *wilþeis.*

"Urrinniþ us Sion sa lausjands du afwandjan
afgudein af Iakoba,

27. jah so im fram mis triggwa,
þan afnima frawaurhtins ize."

"The Deliverer will come out of Zion for the
banishing of ungodliness from Jacob;

27. and this (will be) the covenant from me to
them
when I take away their sins."

28. Aþþan bi aiwaggeljon fijandans in izwara,
iþ bi gawaleinai liubai ana attans.

28. For as regards the gospel, they are your enemies;
but as regards election (they are) beloved because of
(their) forefathers.

29. Inu idreiga sind auk gibos jah laþons Gudis.

29. For the gifts and invitation of God are irrevocable
(lit. without repentance).

30. Swaswe raihtis jus suman ni galaubideduþ Guda,
iþ nu gaarmaidai waurþuþ þizai ize ungalaubeinai,

30. Just as you once did not obey God, but now have
been shown mercy because of their disobedience,

31. swa jah þai nu ni galaubidedun,
izwarai armaion ei jah eis gaarmaindau.

31. even so they now have been disobedient
so that even they may be shown mercy because of your
being shown mercy.

32. Galauk auk Guþ allans in ungalaubeinai,
ei allans gaarmai.

32. For God consigned all to disobedience,
so that he might have mercy on all.

33. O diupiþa gabeins handugeins[9] jah witubnjis
Gudis!
Hwaiwa unusspillodos[10] sind stauos is jah unbilaistidai
wigos is!

33. Oh the depth of God's wealth, wisdom, and
knowledge!
How inscrutable are his judgements and how un-
searchable (are) his ways!

34. "Hwas auk ufkunþa fraþi Frauins,
aiþþau hwas imma ragineis was?"

34. "For who has understood the mind of the
Lord,
or who has been a counsellor to Him?

35. Aiþþau
"Hwas imma fruma gaf,
jah fragildaidau imma?"

35. Or
"Who has first given something to Him
so that it might be paid back to him?"

36. Unte us imma, jah þairh ina, jah in imma, alla!
Immuh wulþus du aiwam! Amen.

36. Because all things are from him, through him, and in
him.
And glory be to him forever! Amen.

Chapter XII

1. Bidja nu izwis, broþrjus, þairh bleiþein Gudis,
usgiban leika izwara saud qiwana, weihana,
waila galeikaidana Guda, andaþahtana
blotinassu izwarana.

Chapter XII

1. I ask you then, brothers, by the mercy of God,
to present your bodies as a living sacrifice,
holy, well pleasing to God, (as) your reasonable
service.

2. Ni galeikoþ izwis þamma aiwa,
<ak inmaidjaiþ> ananiujiþai fraþjis izwaris
du gakiusan hwa sijai wilja Gudis,
þatei goþ jah galeikaiþ jah ustauhan.

2. Do not liken yourselves to this world,
but be transformed by renewal of your understanding
to prove what is the will of God,
namely what is good, pleasing, and perfect.

---

[9] A breaks off here and resumes at XII.8. The intervening text to XII.5 is from Car.

[10] Corr. from A *unusspilloda.*

3. Qiþa auk þairh anst Gudis sei gibana ist mis allaim wisandam in izwis ni mais fraþjan þau skuli fraþjan, ak fraþjan du waila fraþjan, hwarjammeh swaswe Guþ gadailida mitaþ galaubeinais.	3. For by the grace of God given to me I ask all who are among you not to think more than he should think, but to think to think well, each according as God has apportioned to him the measure of faith.
4. Swaswe raihtis in ainamma leika liþuns managans habam, þaiþþan liþjus allai ni þata samo taui haband,	4. For as in a single body we have many limbs, and those limbs do not all have the same function,
5. swa managai ain leik sijum in Xristau, aþþan ainhwarjizuh anþar ...	5. even so we, though many, are one body in Christ, and of one another ... (text missing)
8. ... sa dailjands in allawerein, sa faurastandands in usdaudein, sa armands in hlasein.	8. ... the distributor in honesty, the administrator in seriousness, the alms-giver in cheerfulness.
9. Friaþwa unliuta, fiandans ubila, haftjandans godamma.	9. (Let) love (be) genuine, hating evil, holding fast to what is good.
10. Broþralubon in izwis misso friaþwamildjai, sweriþai izwis misso faurarahnjandans.	10. Be loving with brotherly affection to one another, outdoing one another in honoring.
11. Usdaudein ni latai; ahmin wulandans; Frauin skalkinondans;	11. Do not grow lax in zeal, glowing with the spirit, serving the Lord,
12. wenai faginondans; aglons usþulandans; bidai haftjandans;	12. rejoicing in hope, bearing tribulations patiently, holding fast to prayer,
13. andawiznim weihaize gamainjandans; gastigodein galaistjandans.	13. contributing to the needs of the saints, pursuing hospitality.
14. Þiuþjaiþ þans wrikandans izwis. Þiuþjaiþ, jah ni unþiuþjaiþ.	14. Bless those who persecute you. Bless and do not curse.
15. Faginon miþ faginondam; gretan miþ gretandam,	15. Rejoice with those who rejoice; weep with those who weep,
16. þata samo in izwis misso fraþjandans; ni hauhaba hugjandans, ak þaim hnaiwam miþgawisandans. Ni wairþiþ inahai bi izwis silbam,	16. comprehending that which is the same among you, not thinking haughtily, but associating with the lowly. Do not be conceited (lit. wise) among yourselves,
17. ni ainummehun ubil und ubilamma usgibandans, bisaihwandans godis ni þatainei in andwairþja Gudis, ak jah in andwairþja manne allaize,	17. repaying evil for evil to no one, seeing to the good not only in the presence of God but even in the presence of all men,
18. jabai magi wairþan us izwis, miþ allaim mannam gawairþi habandans.	18. if it is possible of you, having peace with all men,
19. ni izwis silbans gawrikandans, liubans,	19. never avenging yourselves, beloved,

ak gibiþ staþ þwairhein.

Gameliþ ist auk: "Mis fraweit leitaidau,
ik fragilda, qiþiþ Frauja."

20. Jabai gredo fijand þeinana, mat gif imma.
Iþ jabai þaursjai, dragkei ina;
þata auk taujands haurja funins rikis ana haubiþ is.

21. Ni gajiukaizau af unþiuþa,
ak gajiukais af þiuþa unþiuþ.

but give place to the wrath (of God).

For it is written: "Let vengeance be left to me;
I shall repay, says the Lord."

20. If your enemy is hungry, give him food.
And if he is thirsty, give him something to drink;
for by doing that you are heaping coals of fire on his head.

21. Do not be overcome by evil,
but overcome evil with good.

Chapter XIII

1. All saiwalo waldufnjam ufarwisandam ufhausjai;
unte nist waldufni alja fram Guda,
iþ þo wisandona fram Guda gasatida sind.[11]

2. Swaei sa andstandands waldufnja Gudis garaideinai andstoþ;
iþ þai andstandandans silbans sis wargiþa nimand.

3. Þai auk reiks ni sind agis godamma waurstwa, ak ubilamma;
aþþan wileis ei ni ogeis waldufni,
þiuþ taujais jah habais hazein us þamma;

4. unte Gudis andbahts ist þus in godamma.
Iþ jabai ubil taujis, ogs;
unte ni sware þana hairau bairiþ;
Gudis auk andbahts ist,
fraweitands in þwairhein þamma ubil taujandin.

5. Duþþe ufhausjaiþ ni þatainei in þwairheins,
ak jah in miþwisseins.

6. Inuþþis auk jah gilstra ustiuhaiþ;
unte andbahtos Gudis sind in þamma silbin skalkinondans.

7. Usgibiþ nu allaim skuldo: þammei gabaur gabaur, þammei mota mota, þammei agis agis þammei sweriþa sweriþa.

8. Ni ainummehun waihtais skulans sijaiþ,
niba þatei izwis misso frijoþ;
unte saei frijoþ nehwundjan witoþ usfullida.

Chapter XIII

1. Let every soul be subject to the governing authorities,
for there is no authority except from God,
and those that exist have been put there by God.

2. So that he who resists authority opposes what God has ordained;
and those who oppose will themselves incur judgement.

3. For the rulers are not a source of terror to good conduct, but rather to evil;
so if you wish not to fear authority,
do what is good and you will have praise from him;

4. for he is the servant of God for your good.
But if you do evil, be afraid,
for not in vain does he bear that sword;
for he is the servant of God,
punishing in wrath him doing evil.

5. Therefore obey, not only because of the wrath,
but also because of your own conscience.

6. Moreover, fulfill also your tax obligations;
for those serving in this same (capacity) are the servants of God.

7. Pay then all of them what is due; taxes to whom taxes are due; customs to whom customs, respect to whom respect, honor to whom honor.

8. Do not be indebted for anything to anyone,
except that you love each other;
for he who loves his neighbor has fulfilled the law.

---

[11] Corr. from A *ist.*.

9. Þata auk: ni horinos, ni maurþrjais, ni hlifais,
nih faihugeigais,
jah jabai hwo anþaraizo anabusne ist,
in þamma waurda usfulljada, þamma:
frijos nehwundjan þeinana swe þuk silban.

10. Friaþwa nehwundjins ubil ni waurkeiþ;
usfulleins nu witodis ist friaþwa.

11. Jah þata witandans þata þeihs,
þatei mel ist uns ju us slepa urreisan;
unte nu nehwis ist naseins unsara þau þan galaubidedum

12. Nahts framis galaiþ, iþ dags atnehwida;
uswairpam nu waurstwam riqizis,
iþ gawasjam sarwam liuhadis.

13. Swe in daga garedaba gaggaima,
ni gabauram jah drugkaneim,[12]
ni ligram jah aglaitjam ni haifstai jah aljana.

14. Ak gahamoþ Fraujin unsaramma Xristau Iesua
jah leikis mun ni taujaiþ in lustuns.

Chapter XIV

1. Iþ unmahteigana galaubeinai andnimaiþ, ni du
tweifleinai mitone.

2. Sums raihtis galaubeiþ matjan allata;
iþ saei unmahteigs ist, gras matjiþ.

3. Sa matjands þamma ni matjandin ni frakun<n>i,
iþ sa ni matjands þana matjandan[13] ni stojai;
Guþ auk ina andnam.

4. Þu hwas is, þuei stojis framaþjana skalk?
Seinamma fraujin standiþ aiþþau driusiþ.
Aþþan standiþ; mahteigs auk ist frauja gastoþan[14] ina.

5. Sums raihtis stojiþ dag hindar daga...(text missing[15])

9. ... jah qiwaim jah dauþaim fraujinoþ.

9. Moreover: do not commit adultery, do not murder,
do not steal, do not covet,
and whatever other commandment there is,
it is fulfilled in this saying, namely:
you shall love your neighbor as yourself.

10. Loving a neighbor produces no evil;
love, then, is the fulfillment of the law.

11. Knowing moreover the time,
that it is time for us now to rise up from sleep;
for now our redemption is nearer than we then thought.

12. The night has gone past, and day has drawn nigh;
let us cast aside now the works of darkness,
and let us gird on the armor of light.

13. Let us conduct ourselves becomingly as in daylight,
not in revelries and drunkenness,
not in debauchery and licentiousness, not in quarreling
and jealousy.

14. But put on our Lord Jesus Christ
and make no provision for the flesh for gratifications.

Chapter XIV

1. But receive one who is weak in faith, not however
for disputes about opinions.

2. Some indeed believe (it proper) to eat everything;
but he who is weak eats (only) vegetables.

3. Let not the eater despise the non-eater,
nor let the non-eater pass judgement on the eater;
for God has accepted him.

4. Who are you that you judge the servant of another?
He stands or falls for his own master.
And he will stand, for the master is capable of making
him stand.

5. Some indeed judge one day better than another...

9. ... and he rules both the quick and the dead.

---

[12] Corr. from A *dragkaneim.*

[13] Corr. from A *matjandin.*

[14] Conjectured for A *gastoþanana.*

[15] A breaks off here and resumes at XVI.21. The intervening text is from Car.

10. Iþ þu, hwa stojis broþar þeinana?
Aiþþau jah þu, hwa frakant broþr þeinamma?
Allai auk gasatjanda faura stauastola Xristaus.

10. But you, why do you judge your brother?
Or you too, why do you despise your brother?
For all will be placed before the judgement seat of Christ.

11. Gameliþ ist auk:
"Liba ik, qiþiþ Frauja,
þatei mis all kniwe biugiþ
jah andhaitiþ all razdo Guda."

11. For it is written:
"As I live, says the Lord,
every knee shall bow to me
and every tongue shall confess to God."

12. Þannu nu hwarjizuh unsara fram sis raþjon usgibiþ Guda.

12. So then, each of us will give an account for himself to God.

13. Ni þanamais nu uns misso stojaima,
ak þata stojaiþ mais,
ei ni satjaiþ bistugq broþr aiþþau gamarzein.

13. Moreover, then, let us not judge one another,
but rather judge (as proper)
not to set a stumbling-block or hindrance in a brother's way.

14. Wait jaggatraua in Fraujin Iesua,
þatei ni waiht gawamm þairh sik silbo,
niba þamma munandin hwa unhrain wisan[16]
þamma gamain ist.

14. I know and am persuaded in the Lord Jesus
that nothing is of itself impure,
except that something is unclean to the one who thinks it is unclean.

15. Iþ jabai in matis broþar þeins gaurjada,
ju ni bi friaþwai gaggis.
Ni nunu mata þeinamma jainamma fraqistjais, faur þanei Xristus gaswalt.

15. But if your brother is offended by (your) food,
you no longer walk in love.
Do not, then, destroy with your food one for whom Christ died.

16. Ni wajamerjaidau unsar þiuþ.

16. Do not let our welfare be slandered.

17. Nist auk þiudangardi Gudis mats jah dragk,
ak garaihtei jah gawairþi jah faheþs in ahmin weihamma.

17. For the Kingdom of God is not food and drink,
but righteousness and peace and joy in the Holy Spirit.

18. Saei auk in þaim skalkinoþ Xristau waila galeikaiþ Guda jah gakusans ist mannam.

18. For he who serves Christ in these pleases God and is approved of by men.

19. Þannu nu þoei gawairþjis sind laistjaima
jah þoei timreinais sind in uns misso.

19. Therefore, then, let us pursue the things of peace
and of edification in one another.

20. Ni nunu in matis gatair waurstw Gudis...
(text missing)

20. Do not, then, for the sake of food destroy the work of God...

Chapter XV

Chapter XV

3. ...þize idweitjandane þuk gadrusun ana mik.

3...(the reproaches) of those reproaching you fell on me.

4. Swa filu auk swe fauragameliþ warþ du unsarai laiseinai gameliþ warþ,

4. For so much as was written formerly was written for our instruction,

---

[16]*hwa unhrain wisan* restored from traces on basis of Greek τι κοινὸν εἶναι.

ei þairh þulain jah gaþrafstein boko wen habaima.

that by the patience and consolation of the scripture we might have hope.

5. Iþ Guþ þulainais jah þrafsteinais gibai izwis þata samo fraþjan in izwis misso bi Xristu Iesu,

5. But may the God of patience and consolation allow you to live in harmony with one another in accord with Christ Jesus,

6. ei gawiljai ainamma munþa hauhjaiþ Guþ jah attan Fraujins unsaris, Iesuis Xristaus.

6. that willingly with one voice you may extol God and the Father of our Lord, Jesus Christ.

7. In þizei andnimaiþ izwis misso,
swaswe jah Xristus andnam izwis du wulþau Gudis.

7. Therefore, accept one another
as even Christ accepted you for the glory of God.

8. Qiþa auk Xristu Iesu andbaht waurþanana fram sunjai Gudis
du gatulgjan gahaita attane,

8. For I say that Christ Jesus was made a servant by the truth of God
to confirm the promise to the patriarchs,

9. iþ þiudos in armahairteins hauhjan Guþ,
swaswe gameliþ ist:
"Duþþe andhaita þus in þiudom, Frauja,
jah namin þeinamma liuþo."

9. but ...[17]
as it is written:
"For this reason I praise you among the Gentiles, O Lord, and I sing to your name."

10. Jah aftra qiþiþ: "Sifaiþ þiudos miþ managein is."

10. And again it says: "Rejoice O Gentiles with his people."

11. Jah aftra qiþiþ:
"Hazjiþ allos þiudos Fraujan
jah hazjaina ina allos manageins."

11. And again it says:
"Praise the Lord, all ye people,
and let all the peoples praise him."

12. Jah aftra Esaeias qiþiþ:
"Wairþiþ waurts Iaissaizis,
jah sa usstandands reikinoþ þiudom;
du imma þiudos wenjand.

12. And again Isaiah says:
"The root of Jesse shall come,
and he who arises will rule the Gentiles;
in him will the Gentiles hope."

13. Iþ Guþ lubainais fulljai izwis allaizos fahedais... (text missing)

13. But may the God of hope fill you with every joy...

Chapter XVI

Chapter XVI

21. ...jah Lukius jah Iasson jah Soseipatrus, þai niþjos meinai.

21. ... and Lucius and Jason and Sosipater, the kinsmen of mine.

22. Golja izwis ik Tairtius sa meljands þo aipistaulein in Fraujin.

22. I, Tertius, the one writing this letter, greet you in the Lord.

[17] The Greek of vss. 8-9a reads: λέγω γὰρ Χριστὸν Ἰησοῦν διάκονον γεγενῆσθαι περιτομῆς ὑπὲρ ἀληθείας θεοῦ, εἰς τὸ βεβαιῶσαι τὰς ἐπαγγελίας τῶν πατέρων, (9) τὰ δὲ ἔθνη ὑπὲρ ἐλέους δοξάσαι τὸν θεόν, καθὼς γέγραπται... The Vulgate reads: *Dico enim Christum Iesum ministrum fuisse circumcisionis, propter veritatem Dei, ad confirmandas promissiones patrum: (9) gentes autem super misericordiam honorare Deum, sicut scriptum est...* I invite the reader to make his own sense of this. The Gothic translator may have deliberately omitted the reference to circumcision in his attempt to understand these two verses.

23. Goleiþ izwis Gaius, wairdus meins jah allaizos aikklesjons.
Goleiþ izwis Airastus, fauragaggja baurgs, jah Qartus sa broþar.

23. Gaius, my host and (that) of the whole church, greets you.
Erastus, the administrator of the city, greets you, as does Quartus, his brother.

24. Ansts Fraujins unsaris Iesuis Xristaus miþ ahmin izwaramma. Amen.

24. (May) the grace of Our Lord Jesus Christ (be) with your spirit. Amen.

Du Rumonim ustauh.
Du Rumonim meliþ ist us Kaurinþon.

(The Epistle) to the Romans has ended.
(The Epistle) to the Romans was written from Corinth

The First Epistle of Paul to Timothy

Du Teimauþaiau .a. dustodeiþ[1]

I. Pawlus apaustaulus Xristaus Iesuis
bi anabusnim Gudis nasjandis unsaris jah Xristaus Iesuis, wenais unsaraizos,

2. Teimauþaiau, walisin barna in galaubeinai:
ansts, armaio, gawairþi fram Guda Attin jah Xristau Iesu Fraujin unsaramma.

3. Swaswe[2] baþ þuk saljan in Aifaison galeiþands Makedonais
ei faurbiudais sumaim ei anþarleiko ni laisjaina,

4. niþþan atsaihwaina spille jah gabaurþiwaurde andalausaize,
þoei soknim andstaldand mais þau timreinai Gudis þizai wisand<e>in in galaubeinai,

5. aþþan andeis ist anabusnais friaþwa us hrainjamma hairtin jah miþwissein godai jah galaubeinai unhindarweisai,

6. af þaimei sumai afairzidai uswandidedun du lausawaurdein,

7. wiljandans wisan witodalaisarjos,
nih fraþjandans nih hwa rodjand nih bi hwa stiurjand.

8. Aþþan witum þatei goþ ist witoþ,
jabai hwas is witoda[3] brukeiþ,

9. witands þatei garaihtamma nist witoþ satiþ,
ak witodalausaim jah untalaim jah unsibjaim jah frawaurhtaim jah unairknaim jah usweihaim, attans bliggwandam jah aiþeins[4] bliggwandam, mannans maurþrjandam,

IO. horam,[5] mannans gaþiwandam, liugnjam, ufarswaram,
jah jabai hwa aljis þizai hailon laiseinai andstandand,

II. sei ist bi aiwaggeli wulþaus þis audagins Gudis
þatei gatrauaiþ ist mis.

To Timothy I begins:

I. Paul, the apostle of Christ Jesus
by the commands of God our saviour and Christ Jesus, our hope,

2. to Timothy, (my) true child in the faith:
grace, mercy, peace from God the Father and Christ Jesus our Lord.

3. {As} I asked you to remain at Ephesus while I was going to Macedonia,
so that you may prevent some from teaching otherwise (i.e. contrary to our doctrine),

4. and from pursuing legends and endless genealogies,
which provide them with speculation rather than the disciplined divine training that exists in faith,

5. whereas the aim of (our) command is love from a pure heart and good conscience and sincere faith,

6. from which certain erring persons have turned away to vain discussion,

7. desiring to be teachers of the law,
understanding neither what they say nor about what they make assertions.

8. Now we know that the law is good
if anyone uses it (solely) as law,

9. knowing that the law was not laid down for the righteous,
but for the lawless and rebellious and criminal and sinful and unholy and profane, strikers of father and mothers, murderers of men,

IO. adulterers, enslavers of men, liars, perjurers,
and whatever else is contrary to this sound doctrine

II. which is in accordance with the gospel of glory of the blessed God
that has been entrusted to me.

---

1 Main text is Ambrosianus A; Ambrosianus B only where indicated.

2 *Swaswe* (Gk καθώς) makes no sense here, unless it is part of an epistolary formula like, e.g. "to wit:"

3 B has the adverb *witodeigo* (lawfully) here for A's adverbial dative *witoda.*

4 A has gap here; we follow B to *faura* in vs. 18.

5 The Gothic translator omitted "sodomites" (Gk ἀρσενοκοίταις); Streitberg (p. 412) remarks "offenbar mit Absicht."

12. Jah awiliudo þamma inswinþjandin mik Xristau Iesu Fraujin unsaramma,
unte triggwana mik rahnida, gasatjands in andbahtja,

12. I thank him who has strengthened me, Christ Jesus our Lord,
because he judged me faithful by setting me in his service,

13. ikei faura was wajamerjands jah wraks jah ufbrikands;
akei gaarmaiþs was unte unwitands gatawida in ungalaubeinai,

13. though I was formerly a blasphemer and persecutor and despiser;
but I received mercy because I had acted ignorantly in unbelief,

14. iþ ufarassiþ ansts Fraujins
miþ galaubeinai jah friaþwai þizai in Xristau Iesu.

14. and the grace of our Lord became abundant for me
with the faith and love that are in Christ Jesus.

15. Triggw þata waurd jah allaizos andanumtais wairþ,
þatei Xristus Iesus qam in þamma fairhwau
frawaurhtans nasjan, þizeei frumists im ik;

15. The saying is sure and worthy of full acceptance,
that Christ came into the world to save sinners,
of whom I am the foremost;

16. akei duþþe gaarmaiþs warþ,
ei in mis frumistamma ataugidedi Xristaus[6] Iesus alla usbeisnein
du frisahtai þaim ize anawairþai wesun du galaubjan imma du libainai aiweinon.

16. but I received mercy for this reason,
that in me, as the foremost, Jesus Christ might display all his patience
as an example to those who were to believe in him for eternal life.

17. Aþþan þiudana aiwe, unriurjamma,[7] ungasaihwanamma, ainamma, frodamma Guda sweriþa jah wulþus in aldins aiwe. Amen.

17. To the King of ages, immortal, invisible, the sole, wise God be honor and glory for ever and ever. Amen.

18. Þo anabusn anafilha þus, barnilo Teimauþaiu,
bi þaim faura faursniwandam[8] ana þuk praufetjam,
ei driugais in þaim þata godo drauhtiwitoþ,

18. This charge I commit to you, Timothy, my son,
in accordance with the prophetic utterances made long ago concerning you,
so that in them you may wage the good battle,

19. habands galaubein jah goda miþwissein,
þizaiei sumai afskiubandans bi galaubein naqadai waurþun,

19. having faith and a good conscience.
by the rejection of which, certain persons have become naked in regard to their faith,

20. þizeei ist Hymainaius jah Alaiksandrus,
þanzei anafalh Satanin,
ei gatalzjaindau [jah][9] ni wajamerjan.

20. among them Hymenaeus and Alexander,
whom I delivered to Satan
that they may learn not to blaspheme.

Chapter II

1. Bidja nu frumist allis taujan bidos, aihtronins, liteinins, awiliuda fram[10] allaim mannam,

1. First of all, then, I urge
that supplications, prayers, petitions, and thanksgivings be made for all men,

---

6 *Xristaus* for *Xristus*. *ize* for *izei* (rel. pron.).

7 Conjectured by Streitberg for *u....jamma*. The Gk has ἀφθάρτῳ, an adjective translated elsewhere, e.g. ICor 9:25, by *unriurj-*.

8 *faura faursniwandam* = Gk προαγούσας which were made long ago.

9 Delete *jah* (so B).

10 *fram* is idiomatic with *bidjan* and related words: to pray *for*.

2. fram þiudanam jah fram allaim þaim in ufarassau wisandam,
ei slawandein jas-sutja ald bauaima in allai gagudein jag-gariudja.

2. for kings and all who are in high position,
that we may lead a quiet and peaceful life, godly and respectful in every way.

3. Þatuþþan ist god jah andanem in andwairþja nasjandis unsaris Gudis,

3. For this is good and acceptable in the sight of our saviour God,

4. saei allans mans wili ganisan jah in ufkunþja sunjos qiman.

4. who desires all men to be saved and to come into the knowledge of the truth.

5. Ains allis Guþ, ains jah midumonds Gudis jah manne, manna Xristus Iesus,

5. For God is one, and one too is the mediator of God and man, the man Jesus Christ,

6. sa gibands sik silban andabauht faur allans,
þizei weitwodein melam swesaim,

6. who gave himself as the ransom for all,
the testimony of which (is to be) at its own times,

7. du þammei gasatiþs im ik merjands jah apaustaulus,
(sunja qiþa in Xristau, ni liuga)
laisareis þiudo in galaubeinai jas-sunjai.

7. to which I was appointed as preacher and apostle,
(I speak the truth in Christ; I am not lying)
teacher of the non-Jewish peoples in faith and truth.

8. Wiljau nu wairans bidjan in allaim stadim,
ushafjandans swiknos handuns inuh þwairhein jah tweiflein,

8. I desire, then, that men in all places pray,
raising pure hands without anger or dissension,

9. samaleiko jah qinons in gafeteinai hrainjai miþ gariudein jah inahein fetjandeins sik,
ni in flahtom aiþþau gulþa aiþþau marikreitum aiþþau wastjom galaubaim,

9. likewise too women adorning themselves in clean attire with modesty and good sense
not with braids or gold or pearls or expensive clothes.

10. ak þatei gadob ist qinom gahaitandeim Guþ blotan þairh waurstwa goda.

10. but by that which is fitting for women professing to worship God, i.e. through good works.

11. Qino in hauniþai galaisjai sik in allai ufhauseinai.

11. Let a woman learn humbly in all submissivesness.

12. Iþ galaisjan qinon ni uslaubja,
nih fraujinon faura waira,
ak wisan in þahainai.

12. But I will not allow a woman to teach,
nor to have authority over men,
but rather to be in silence.

13. Adam auk fruma gadigans warþ, þaþro Aiwwa;

13. For Adam was created first, then Eve;

14. jah Adam ni warþ uslutoþs,
iþ qino uslutoda in missadedai warþ.

14. and Adam was not deceived,
but woman was deceived into misdeeds.

15. Iþ ganisiþ þairh barne gabaurþ,
jabai gastandand in galaubeinai jah frijaþwai jah weihiþai miþ gafraþjein.

15. But (woman) will be saved through bearing children,
if they stand firm in faith and love and holiness with prudence.

Chapter III

1. Triggw þata waurd:
jabai hwas aipiskaupeins gairneiþ,
godis waurstwis gairneiþ.

2. Skal nu aipiskaupus ungafairinonds wisan,
ainaizos qenais aba, andaþahts, gariuds, froþs,
gafaurs, gastigods, laiseigs,

3. ni weinnas, nis-slahuls, ak sutis, qairrus, ni sakuls,
ni faihufriks,

4. seinamma garda waila fauragaggands,
barna habands ufhausjandona[11] miþ allai anawiljein.

5. Iþ jabai hwas seinamma garda fauragaggan ni mag,
hwaiwa aikklesjon Gudis gakaroþ?

6. Nih niujasatidana, ibai aufto ufarhauhiþs
in stauai atdriusai unhulþins.

7. Skal auk is weitwodiþa goda haban fram þaim uta,
ei ni atdriusai in idweit jah hlamma unhulþins.

8. Jah swa diakaununs gariudans, nih faihufrikans,
ni weina filu haftjandans, nih aglaitgastaldans,

9. habandans runa galaubeinais in hrainjai gahugdai.

10. Jaþþai þan gakiusaindau frumist;
jas-swa andbahtjaina ungafairinodai wisandans.

11. Qinons samaleiko gariudos, ni diabulos,
gafaurjos,[12] triggwos in allamma.

12. Diakaunjus sijaina ainaizos qenais abans,
barnam waila fauragaggandans jah seinaim gardim.

13. Þai auk waila andbahtjandans grid goda sis faur-
waurkjand
jah managa balþein <in> galaubeinai þizai in Xristau
Iesu.

14. Þata þus melja, wenjands qiman at þus sprauto;

15. aþþan jabai sainjau,

Chapter III

1. The saying is sure:
If anyone aspires to the office of bishop,
he aspires to a good task.

2. Now a bishop must be above reproach,
the husband of one wife, temperate, modest, intelligent,
well-behaved, hospitable, good at teaching,

3. not a drunkard, not a bully, but pleasant, gentle, not
quarrelsome, not greedy for property,

4. managing his household well,
having obedient children with every respectfulness.

5. For if someone cannot manage his own household,
how will he care for the church of God?

6. Nor (would I have) a recent convert, for indeed
(being) conceited he may fall into the judge-
ment of the devil.

7. For he shall also have good testimony from outsiders,
lest he fall into reproach and the snare of the devil.

8. And so (would I have) deacons modest, not greedy
for property, not much addicted to wine, nor shamefully
acquisitive,

9. keeping the mystery of the faith in good conscience.

10. And they shall be tested first;
and so let them serve being (found) blameless.

11. (I would have) the women likewise modest, not
slanderous, well-behaved, faithful in everything.

12. Let the deacons be husbands of one wife,
managing their children and households well.

13. For those serving well acquire good standing for
themselves,
and much confidence in the faith that is in Christ
Jesus.

14. I write this to you, hoping to come to you soon,

15. but if I am delayed,

---

[11] Corr. from A *ufhausjanjandona.*

[12] Glossed in margin with *andaþahtos.*

ei witeis hwaiwa skuld ist in garda Gudis usmitan,
saei ist aikklesjo Gudis libandins, sauls jah tulgiþa
sunjos.

that you may know how it is proper to behave in the
house of God, which is the church of the living God,
the pillar and stronghold of the truth.

16 Jah unsahtaba [13] mikils ist gagudeins runa:
saei gabairhtiþs warþ in leika,
garaihts gadomiþs warþ in ahmin,
ataugids warþ þaim aggilum,
merids warþ in þiudom,
galaubiþs warþ in fairhwau,
andnumans warþ in wulþau.

16. And incomprehensively great is the mystery of piety:
He was manifested in flesh,
was deemed just in the Spirit,
was shown to the angels
was preached about among the nations,
was believed in in the world,
was taken up in glory.

Chapter IV

Chapter IV

I. Aþþan ahma swikunþaba qiþiþ
þatei in spedistaim dagam afstandand sumai galaubeinai
atsaihwandans ahmane airziþos jah laiseino unhulþono,

I. Now the Spirit explicitly says
that in later days some will leave the faith,
giving heed to spirits of deception and the doctrines of
demons,

2. in liutein liugnawaurde jah gatandida habandane
swesa miþwissein,

2. through the hypocrisy of liars and those who have
their consciences seared,

3. warjandane liugos, gaþarban mate,
þanzei Guþ gaskop du andniman miþ awiliudam
galaubjandam jah ufkunnandam sunja.

3. who forbid marriage and to abstain from foods
which God created to be received with thanksgiving
for those who believe and know the truth.

4. Unte all gaskaftais Gudis goþ
jah ni waiht du uswaurpai miþ awiliudam andnuman;

4. Because all of God's creation is good
and nothing received with thanksgiving is to be rejected;

5. gaweihada auk þairh waurd Gudis jah bida.

5. for it is consecrated through the word of God and
prayer.

6. Þata insakands broþrum goþs wairþis andbahts
Xristaus Iesuis,
alands waurdam galaubeinais jah godaizos laiseinais
þoei galaistides.

6. Charging the brethren with this, you will become a
good minister of Christ Jesus,
nourished with the words of faith and the good doctrine
which you have followed.

7. Iþ þo usweihona swe usalþanaizo[14] spilla biwandei,
iþ þroþei þuk silban du gagudein,

7. But shun unholy tales as though old women's,
and train yourself in piety,

8. aþþan leikeina usþroþeins du fawamma ist bruks,
iþ gagudei du allamma ist bruks,
gahaita habandei libainais þizos nu jah þizos
anawairþons.

8. for while physical training is useful to some extent,
piety is useful for all occasions,
having the promise of the present life and of the life to
come.

9.[15] Triggw þata waurd jah allaizos andanumtais wairþ.

9. The saying is sure and worthy of all acceptance.

I0. Duþþe allis arbaidjam jah idweitjanda,

I0. Therefore, indeed, we labor and suffer reproach,

---

[13] *mikils* and *saei* are masculine because *runa gagudeins* refers to Christ.

[14] *Gpl* of nominalized *usalþana* old woman. Note the ellipsis: "unholy tales as though (they are tales) of old women.

[15] B from here to V.5.

unte wenidedum du Guda libandin,
saei ist nasjands allaize manne, þishun galaubjandane.

because we have set our hope on the living God,
who is the savior of all men, especially of believers.

11. Anabiud þata jah laisei.

11. Command and teach this.

12. Ni manna þeinai jundai frakunni,
ak frisahts sijais þaim galaubjandam in waurda,
in usmeta, in friaþwai, in galaubeinai, in swikniþai.

12. Let no one despise your youth,
but be an example to believers in word,
in conduct, in love, in faith, in purity.

13. Unte qima, gaumei saggwa boko, gaþlaihtai,
laiseinai.

13. Until I come, attend to the reading of scripture,
to admonishing, and to teaching.

14. Ni sijais unkarja þizos in þus anstais,
sei gibana warþ þus þairh praufetjans afar analageinai
handiwe praizbytairei<n>s.

14. Do not be neglectful of the grace which is in you,
which was given to you through prophecies after the
laying on of the elders' hands.

15. Þo sido þus, inuþþaim sijais, ei þatei þeihais þu
swikunþ sijai allaim.

15. Practice this, be (devoted) to them, so that it be-
come known to all that you are progressing.

16. Atsaihw du þus silbin jah du laiseinai usdaudo,
þairhwis in þaim;
þatuh auk taujands jah þuk silban ganasjis
jah hausjandans þus.

16. Attend to yourself and to teaching seriously,
persist in them;
for by so doing you will save both yourself and
those listening to you.

Chapter V

Chapter V

1. Seneigana[16] ni andbeitais,
ak gaþlaih swe attin, juggans[17] swe broþruns;

1. Do not rebuke an old man, but rather admonish
him as (you would) a father, and young men as
brothers;

2. sineigos swe aiþeins, juggos swe swistruns in allai
swiknein.

2. old women as mothers, young women as sisters
in all purity.

3. Widuwons swerai, þozei bi sunjai sijaina widuwons.

3. Honor widows who are actually widows.

4. Iþ jabai hwo widuwono barna aiþþau barne barna
habai,
galaisjaina <sik> faurþis swesana gard barusnjan
jah andalauni usgiban fadreinam;
þata auk ist god jah andanem in andwairþja Gudis.

4. But if some widow has children or grandchildren,
let them learn first to honor their own house
and restore some compensation to their parents;
for that is good and acceptable in the sight of God.

5. Aþþan soei bi sunjai widuwo <ist> jah ainakla
wenida du Guda jah þairhwisiþ in bidom nahtam jah
dagam.

5. Then she who is truly a widow and alone (is one)
who has set her hope on God and persists in prayer
night and day.

6. Iþ so wizondei in azetjam jah libandei dauþa ist.

6. But the one who indulges herself in easy ways, even
though alive, is dead.

---

[16] *seneigana* for *sineigana.*

[17] The curious mixture of cases here results from a slavish rendering of the Greek. One expects a continuation of the dative objects of an understood *gaþlaihan.*

7. Jah þata anabiud ei ungafairinodos sijaina.

7. And command this so that they be blameless.

8. Aþþan jabai hwas swesaim þishun ingardjam ni gaþlaihiþ,
galaubein inwidiþ jah ist ungalaubjandin wairsiza.

8. If, then, anyone does not take care even of his own family,
he has rejected the faith and is worse than an unbeliever.

9. Widuwo gawaljaidau ni mins saihs tigum jere,
sei wesi ainis abins qens,

9. Let a widow be enrolled (only if) not less than sixty,
who has been the wife of (only) one husband,

10. in waurstwam godaim weitwodiþa habandei,
jah barna fodidedi, jah gastins andnemi,
jah weihaim fotuns þwohi, jah aglons winnandam andbahtidedi,
jah allamma waurstwe godaize afarlaistidedi.

10. having testimony for good works,
and who has raised children, received guests,
has washed the feet of the saints, and has served those suffering afflictions,
and has pursued every good work.

11.[18] Iþ juggos widuwons biwandei;
þan auk gairnidedeina wiþra Xristu, liugan wileina.

11. But shun young widows; for when they conceive
desires against Christ, they wish to marry,

12. habandeins staua,
unte frumein galaubein wana gatawidedun.

12. being subject to condemnation
because they have made their first vow worthless.

13. Aþþan samana jah unwaurstwons laisjand sik þairhgaggan gardins,
aþþan ni þatain unwaurstwons,
ak jah unfaurjos jah fairweitjandeins,
rodjandeins þoei ni skulda sind.

13. And in addition, as idlers, they learn to go from house to house,
and not only as idlers,
but even as gossipers and busybodies,
saying those thing that are not proper.

14-17 fragmentary

18. Qaþ auk gameleins:
"Auhsau þriskandin munþ ni faurwaipjais;"
jah: "Wairþs sa waurstw<j>a[19] mizdons is."

18. For the scripture says:
"You shall not muzzle the mouth of a threshing ox,"
and "The worker is worthy of his wages."

19. Bi praizbytairein wroh ni andnimais,
niba in andwairþja twa<d>dje aiþþau þrije weitwode.

19. Do not accept a charge against an elder
unless in the presence of two or three witnesses.

20. Iþ þans frawaurhtans in andwairþja allaize gasak,
ei jah þai anþarai agis habaina.

20. But rebuke the sinful in the presence of all
so that the others have fear as well.

21. Weitwodja in andwairþja Gudis jah Fraujins unsaris Iesuis Xristaus jah þize gawalidane aggile,
ei þata fastais inu faurdomein,
ni waiht taujands bi wiljahalþein.

21. I bear witness in the presence of God and of our Lord Jesus Christ and of the elect angels,
that you hold to these (rules) without prejudice,
doing nothing out of partiality.

22. Handuns sprauto ni mannhun lagjais,
ni gamainja siais frawauhtim framaþjaim;
þuk silban swiknana fastais.

22. Do not be hasty in laying hands on anyone,
and do not partake of another's sins;
keep yourself pure.

---

[18]vss. 11-12 are from B.

[19]Streitberg prefers to read the hapax *waurstwa* (worker) here and defends the form by citing the noun *gawaurstwa wm* (fellow-worker). But *gawaurstwa* belongs to another derivational pattern (cf. *gahlaiba* etc.) and is derived from *waurstw*.

23. Ju ni drigkais þanamais wato,
ak weinis leitil brukjais in qiþaus þeinis
jah þizo ufta sauhte þeinaizo.

24. Sumaize manne frawaurhteis swikunþos sind,
faurbisniwandeins du stauai;
sumaizeh þan jah afargaggand.

25. Samaleiko þan jah waurstwa goda swikunþa sind,
jah þoei aljaleikos sik habandona filhan ni mahta sind.

23. No longer drink (only) water,
but use a little wine for the sake of your stomach
and your frequent ailments.

24. The sins of some men are manifest,
leading quickly to judgement;
but (the sins) of others appear later on.

25. Likewise, then, good deeds too are manifest,
and those which are not cannot remain hidden.

Chapter VI

1. Swa managai swe sijaina uf jukuzjai skalkos[20]
seinans fraujans allaizos sweriþos wairþans rahnjaina,
ei namo Fraujins jah laiseins ni wajamerjaidau.

2. Aþþan þaiei galaubjandans haband fraujans,
ni frakunneina, unte broþrjus sind,
ak mais skalkinona, unte galaubjandans sind jah liubai,
þaiei wailadedais gadailans sind.
Þata laisei jah gaþlaih.

3. Jabai hwas aljaleikos laisjai
janni atgaggiþ du hailaim waurdam þaim fraujins
unsaris Iesuis Xristaus
jah þizai bi gagudein laiseinai,

4. iþ hauhþuhts, ni waiht witands,
ak siukands bi soknins jah waurdajiukos,
us þaimmei wairþand neiþa,
maurþra, haifsteis, anaqisseis, anamindeis ubilos,

5. usbalþeins frawardidaize manne ahin,
at þaimei gatarniþ ist sunja,
hugjandane faihugawaurki wisan gagudein;
afstand af þaim swaleikaim.

6. Aþþan ist gawaurki mikil gagudei miþ ganauhin.

7. Ni waiht auk brahtedum in þamma fairhwau;
bi sunjai þatei ni usbairan hwa magum.

8. Aþþan habandans usfodein jah gaskadwein
þaimuh ganohidai sijaima.

9. Aþþan þaiei wileina gabigai wairþan atdriusand in
fraistubnja jah hlamma unhulþins jah

Chapter VI

1. As many as are under the yoke of slavery
shall regard their masters worthy of all honor,
so that the name of the Lord and the doctrine may not
be defamed.

2. And those who have believing masters
shall not be disrespectful because they are brothers,
but shall serve all the more (assiduously) because
they are believers and beloved,
those who partake of the benefit.
Teach this and admonish.

3. If anyone teaches otherwise
and does not follow the holy words of our Lord
Jesus Christ
and the doctrine in regard to piety,

4. (he is) conceited, knowing nothing,
but rather is sick for disputations and word games,
out of which arise envy,
murder, contention, slander, wicked suspicions,

5. the insolence of men depraved in mind,
for whom truth is taken away,
thinking that piety is a means to fortune;
avoid the likes of these.

6. But piety with contentment is a great gain.

7. We brought nothing into this world;
it is certain that we can take nothing out.

8. But having nourishment and clothing,
we should be content with them.

9. But those who desire to be rich fall into
temptation and the snare of the devil and

[20] Corrected from *skalkans*. Lit., slaves under the yoke.

lustuns managans unnutjans jah skaþulans,
þaei saggqjand mans in frawardein jah fralust.

many useless and harmful desires
which sink men into ruin and destruction.

10. Waurts allaize ubilaize is faihugeiro,
þizozei sumai gairnjandans afairzidai waurþun af galaubeinai
jassik silbans gaþiwaidedun sairam managaim.

10. The root of all evils is the love of money
which some desiring are led astray from the faith
and subject themselves to many pains.

11. Iþ þu, jai manna Gudis, þata þliuhais,
iþ laistjais garaihtein, gagudein, galaubein, frijaþwa, þulain, qairrein.

11. But you, even a man of God, flee from that,
but rather follow after righteousness, piety, faith, love, patience, gentleness.

12. Haifstei þo godon haifst galaubeinais,
undgreip libain aiweinon du þizaiei laþoþs is
jah andhaihaist þamma godin andahaita in[21] andwairþja managaize weitwode.

12. Fight the good fight of faith,
take hold of the eternal life to which you were invited
and confessed the good confession in the presence of many witnesses.

13. Anabiuda in andwairþja Gudis þis gaqiujandins alla
jah Xristaus Iesuis þis weitwodjandins uf Paunteau Peilatau þata godo andahait,

14. fastan þuk þo anabusn unwamma ungafairinoda
und qum Fraujins unsaris Iesuis Xristaus,

15. þanei in melam swesaim taikneiþ sa audaga jah ains mahteiga jah þiudans þiudanondane jah frauja fraujinondane,

13. I charge you in the presence of God who gives life to all
and of Christ Jesus who before Pontius Pilate bore witness to the good confession,
14. to keep the commandment unstained and irreproachable
until the coming of our Lord Jesus Christ,
15. which in its proper times the blessed and sole mighty King of kings and Lord of lords will make manifest,

16. saei ains aih undiwanein jah liuhaþ bauiþ unatgaht,
þanei sahw manne ni ainshun nih sai<hwan mag>...

16. who alone possesses immortality and dwells in the unapproachable light,
whom no man has seen nor can ever see...

[remainder missing]

[21]B from here to end of I Timothy.

Introduction

I. The phonological system of Proto-Indo-European

A. The Consonants

The phonological system of PIE (hereafter abbreviated simply as IE) is reconstructed as containing the following consonant phonemes:

		Labial	Dental	Palatal	Velar	Labio-velar
Stops: voiceless unaspirated		*p*	*t*	*k̂*	*k*	k^w
voiceless aspirated		*ph*	*th*	*k̂h*	*kh*	k^wh
voiced unaspirated		*b*	*d*	*ĝ*	*g*	g^w
voiced aspirated		*bh*	*dh*	*ĝh*	*gh*	g^wh
Fricatives (spirants)			*s*			
Resonants	Nasals	*m*	*n*			
	Liquids			*r, l*		
	Semivowels	*w*		*y*		
Laryngeals	h_1 h_2 h_3					

Remarks:

1. The following alternate terminology should be noted: plosives, explosives, occlusives = stops; sibilants = dental fricatives; sonant = voiced; surd, unvoiced = voiceless.

2. The phoneme /n/ probably had three phonetic realizations: [ɲ, ń] before palatal consonants, [ŋ, ñ] before velar consonants, and [n] elsewhere. /s/ was realized as [z] before voiced stops, e.g. /sd/ = [zd].

3. *w* and *y* are frequently represented by the symbols *u̯* and *i̯* respectively.

4. The laryngeals h_1, h_2, and h_3 belong only to the earliest phases of IE. They are reconstructed on the basis of the systematic reflexes they left in the vowel system of the language. The reasoning behind the reconstruction of the three laryngeals is sketched in E below. The sounds represented by these three symbols cannot be reconstructed, but they were presumably in the range of the glottal, pharyngeal, and laryngeal stops and fricatives, voiced and voiceless, found in other language families, e.g. Semitic. When it is necessary to indicate a laryngeal whose identity cannot be established precisely, the cover symbol H is employed. h_1, h_2, and h_3 are also denoted by $ə_1$, $ə_2$, and $ə_3$ and by E, A, and O.

5. The voiceless aspirated stops are now regarded as secondary, resulting from a combination of a voiceless unaspirated stop followed by a laryngeal; thus, *ph* < *pH*, *th* < *tH*, etc. Since they still appear in recent major reference works like Pokorny and LIV, however, they merit inclusion in our table above. Their occurrences in IE were, at any rate, very rare.

B. The Vowels

The vowel inventory usually listed for IE is properly that of the late stage of the language, after the disappearance of the three laryngeals. The plain vowels are as follows:

	Front		Central	Back
High	*i, ī*			*u, ū*
Middle	*e, ē*		*ə*	*o, ō*
Low		*a, ā*		

The short vowels followed by *y* or *w* are generally classified as diphthongs, but their structural status as vowel + consonant is always readily apparent. For this reason, we have adopted the now prevalent notation *iw, ew, aw,* etc. for older *iu, au, au,* etc. or *i̯u, e̯u, a̯u,* etc. The long vowels formed diphthongs similarly but are less frequent in occurrence. *iy* and *uw* are not considered proper diphthongs, being equivalent to *ī* and *ū* respectively.

To these must be added the syllabic resonants *m, n, r, l* discussed in section D below.

The existence of Late IE **ə* is seriously contested by some Indo-Europeanists,[1] but because it appears in standard reference works, it has been included here.

C. Word formation

Most PIE words consisted of a verbal root or a base to which were added formative elements (root extensions and derivational suffixes) and inflectional endings (case endings and personal endings). Stress (accent) was determined by morphological criteria or, in some cases, by meaning, and could fall on any syllable. Verbal roots, which constitute the irreducible minimum of etymologies, had a variety of shapes, but most predominant were those with the patterns C_1eC_2 and C_1eRC_2, where C_1 represents a single consonant or one of a small set of consonant clusters consisting of *s* + a stop or a stop + *r* or *l*; C_2 represents any consonant; *R* represents one of the continuants *r, l, m, n, w, y,* h_1, h_2, h_3. Bases, as opposed to verbal roots, have no uniform patterns and are generally the source of nominal, pronominal, and adjectival forms that cannot be assigned to an extant verbal root, though it is possible that they are derived from verbal roots no longer reconstructable as such.

Nearly any consonant can be added to roots of the type C_1eC_2 to produce a new root $C_1eC_2C_3$. Such additions are known as extensions and are one of the least satisfactory features of IE etymologies since no specific meaning can be assigned to a given consonantal extension. The concept of root extensions originated as a logical necessity when scholars compiling etymological dictionaries ended up, for example, with a dozen or so roots with meanings related to the notion of *bending* and *turning,* all beginning with **wer-* and differing only in the final consonant. It is probable that such root extensions were originally nominal or adjectival suffixes; with the gradual semantic drift of a particular base away from the meaning of the primitive root, a new root was abstracted and the now otiose final consonant was incorporated as part of the new root.

D. Ablaut (apophony)

Qualitative ablaut and quantitative ablaut were characteristic features of the IE phonological system from its earliest reconstructable stages. Qualitative ablaut involved the systematic alteration of a vowel corresponding to a

[1] See, for example, T. Burrow, *The Sanskrit Language* (London, Faber and Faber, 1955), pp. 104-6.

change in morphological function of a particular structural entity. For example, the present tense stem of a given verbal root may have been based on the form C_1eC_2-, while the stem of the perfect was based on C_1oC_2-. C_1eC_2 is referred to as the e-grade of the root, and C_1oC_2 as the o-grade. This interchange of the two vowels *e* and *o* was fundamental to the phonological system, occurring not only in verbal roots (see below) but also in a wide variety of suffixes, e.g. **-men-/-mon-*, **-es-/-os-*. Many English strong verbs, like *sing/sang* and *sit/sat* still preserve this extremely ancient feature of the parent language.

It is customary to speak of *ablaut series* in the phonological structure of late PIE, wherein the more frequent alterations characteristic of certain inflected forms are singled out. In the case of Germanic, the strong verb provides excellent examples of such series. Since these and others form the subject of a number of the lessons that follow, there is no need to discuss them here. It is important to note, however, that ablaut variation pervades the structure of late IE, including roots, suffixes, and endings.

Quantitative ablaut affected the length of vowels and was dependent on the original position of the stress. The normal or full grade of a vowel is the simple short vowel, e.g. *e* or *o;* the lengthened grade is the same vowel lengthened, e.g. *ē, ō;* the reduced grade or zero-grade is the disappearance of the vowel completely or the retention of a syllabic element notated with a subscript. For example, the root √*sed* (to sit) has e-grade *sed-*, o-grade *sod-*, reduced grade s_ed- or *sd-*, lengthened e-grade *sēd-*, lengthened o-grade *sōd-*. These gradations are usually introduced without further comment in presenting etymologies.

Special note should be made of the reduced form of syllables containing one of the resonants. When the *e* or *o* of such syllables was reduced to zero, the resonant functioned as a vowel, making a syllable. These vocalic resonants are denoted with a subscript dot: *ṛ, ḷ, ṃ, ṇ, ẉ, ỵ* and are listed with the vowels of the language; *w* and *y* were realized phonetically as *u* and *i* respectively.

E. The laryngeals

It was the tendency toward uniformity in verbal root structure that originally led scholars to posit the existence of laryngeal consonants at an early stage of IE: if C_1eC_2 is a prevailing type, could not the roots reconstructed with final long vowels, e.g. √*stā* (to stand), √*pā* (to protect), √*dō* (to give), √*dhē* (to put, place, do), have originated in earlier forms like **steX, *peX, *deY, *dheZ,* where the unknown sounds *X, Y,* and *Z* affected the quality of the preceding vowel prior to their disappearance, which resulted further in lengthening the vowel when in syllable-closing position. The application of this basic hypothesis coupled with intensive sorting of data led to the currently accepted laryngeal theory, or the recognition that PIE had two phases, a laryngeal phase and a post-laryngeal phase. The roots mentioned above are now represented as √$steh_2$, √peh_2, √deh_3, and √$dheh_1$ respectively. Acceptance of the laryngeal theory was furthered substantially when one of the laryngeals, h_2, turned up as a phonetic reality in Hittite.

Because there is a lack of concensus on many details concerning the effect of earlier laryngeals on the development of the late IE vowel system with its various ablaut series, we shall limit ourselves in this work to the following basic set of assumptions:

1. In word initial position h_1e- > *e-*, h_2e- > h_2a- > *a-*, h_3e- > h_3o- > *o-*.

2. Initially or internally eh_1C- > *ēC*, eh_2C > ah_2C > *āC*, eh_3C > oh_3C > *ōC*, where *C* represents any non-laryngeal consonant. Presumably, *o* from ablaut, *u* from *w*, and *i* from *y* were also lengthened in similar environments: *-oHC* > *-ōC*, *-uHC* > *-ūC*, *-iHC* > *-īC*.

3. In word final position eh_1 > *ē*, eh_2 > ah_2 > *ā*, eh_3 > oh_3 > *ō*.

4. When the vowel preceding the laryngeal was reduced to the zero-grade, the laryngeal was realized as a short vowel, e.g. Ch_1C > *CeC*, Ch_2C > *CaC*, and Ch_3C > *CoC*.

Since the foregoing "rules" account for the genesis of a lengthened grade of *e* and *o*, as well as both grades of *a*, the question arises whether, except for *e* and o, all of the vowels of late IE and all of the so-called ablaut series could not have arisen as a result of the loss of the laryngeals coupled with the process of vowel reduction and a long period of analogical extension. This seems quite probable, but a formal proof of such a hypothesis is impossible with the limited data at our disposal. The possibility of such a process, however, has led to its adoption as an idealization or ordering principle in modern IE studies.

In the historical grammar discussions and etymologies that follow the late IE form of a verbal root is cited with the sign √, e.g. *√stā*, and except for the rewriting of the diphthongs with *y* and *w* is substantially that given in the standard reference work, Julius Pokorny, *Indogermanisches etymologisches Wörterbuch*, 3rd ed., Tübingen 1944 (A. Franke Verlag), hereafter referred to as Pokorny. The earlier, "laryngealized" form of the verbal root is added when appropriate with brackets, e.g. [*steh*$_2$], usually as given in Helmut Rix (gen. ed.), *Lexikon der indogermanischen Verben: Die Wurzeln und ihre Primärstammbildungen*, Wiesbaden 1998 (Dr. Ludwig Reichert Verlag), hereafter referred to as LIV.

II. From Late IE to Proto-Germanic.

The changes that took place in the transition from Late IE to Proto-Germanic are summarized in Tables A-D and the remarks that accompany them. Because several of the major changes are assumed to have occurred sequentially, e.g. the changes designated as Grimm's Law preceded those of Verner's Law, it is useful to speak of changes *within* PG or, as shown in the tables, *between* Early and Late PG. Since all reconstructed proto-languages are logical fictions, there is no harm in expressing their contents in the simplest and most convenient way.

As noted above in §I.C, the stress in IE could occur on any syllable of a word, depending on a number of morphological and/or semantic criteria. It is assumed that this original stress system was still intact in Early PG prior to the working of Verner's Law, but that subsequent to those changes the stress shifted to the root syllable, i.e. the first syllable, of non-prefixed words. In the case of words compounded with prefixes, nouns and adjectives became stressed on the first syllable, but verbs became stressed on the root syllable after the prefix.

The development of the IE labiovelars **k*^{w}, **g*^{w}, **g*^{w}*h* was far less regular than that of the plain velar stops. One may distinguish between a "normal" development, i.e. one which is in conformity with the development of the corresponding plain stops, and an "abnormal" one. The normal development of these sounds is covered by the following rules:

(1) IE **k*^{w} > PG **h*^{w} or, by Verner's Law, *-*γ*^{w}-.
(2) IE **g*^{w} > PG **k*^{w}
(3) IE **g*^{w}*h* > PG initial **g*^{w}-, medial *-*γ*^{w}-.

By Late PG the labial element of PG **h*^{w}, **k*^{w}, and **g*^{w} was lost before PG **u* and **ū* and before a following consonant. PG *-*γ*^{w}- > *-*w*- at the end of a syllable.

The abnormal development of the labiovelars is posited for only a few words, and because the evidence is so sparse, no resolution of the problem can be expected. The change IE **k*^{w} > PG **f* ostensibly occurs in IE **wl̥k*^{w}*ós* (wolf) > Goth *wulfs* (see Lesson 1 below); IE **g*^{w}*h* > PG **w* in PG **warm-* (warm), if taken from IE **g*^{w}*horm-*; IE **g*^{w}*h* > PG **b* in Goth **bidjan** (Lesson 12), if from *√g*^{w}*hedh*. Because alternate etymologies exist for the latter two items, such abnormal correspondences must be viewed with some suspicion.

There are a number of general assimilatory changes in PG that do not appear on the tables and are frequent enough to note here:

(1) PG *-*tt*- and *-*ts*- from any IE source became PG *-*ss*-.
(2) PG *-*nw*- > PG *-*nn*-.
(3) PG *-*md*- > PG *-*nd*-.
(4) PG **s* > PG **z* before a voiced stop. PG **sr*-, -*sr*- > **str*-, -*str*-.

The PG consonants resulting from IE **t* and **d* were lost in final position in unstressed final syllables, i.e. in polysyllabic words; final PG *-*m* > *-*n*, which was then lost in the same situation.

Apart from their involvement in changes already noted above, the IE resonants **r*, **l*, **m*, **n*, **w*, **y* underwent no further changes in PG.

With the exception of **u* all IE short vowels which were or became final and unstressed in PG were dropped in Gothic, as were the short vowels of final unstressed syllables ending in a single consonant. Because some PG short final unstressed vowels show up in early runic (North Germanic) inscriptions, these vowels are generally retained in reconstructed PG; their loss presumably occurred in the transition from PG to the various daughter languages.

III. From Late PG to Gothic

In addition to the changes indicated in Tables A-D, the following should be noted:

(1) As indicated in Table C, IE **ē* > PG **ǣ*. There is another long vowel **ē* reconstructed for PG whose IE origin is obscure. Both of these vowels became **e** in Gothic, but elsewhere in Germanic they remained distinct. Compare, for example, the following sets of cognates:

PG **hēr* (here), Goth **her**, ON *hér*, OHG *hier*, *hēr*, AS *hēr*
PG **sǣtun* (they sat), Goth **setun**, ON *sátu*, OHG *sāzun*, AS *sǣtun*.

(2) As noted at the end of section II above, all unstressed PG short vowels except *u* in final position or in final syllables ending in a single consonant were dropped in Gothic.

(3) The Gothic reflex /w/ of PG **w* alternates between **w** and **u** in Gothic spelling: when /w/ closes a syllable it is written as -**u**, e.g. **triu** (wood), **snau** (> [*snɔ*], he hurried), **taujan** (> [*tɔyan*], to do); when it begins a syllable, it is written as **w**-, e.g. **triwis** (of wood), **sniwan** (to hurry), **tawida** (I did).

(4) PG *-*ww*- and *-*yy*-, as now conventionally reconstructed, are thought to be reflexes of IE *-*wH*- and *-*yH*- respectively. PG *-*ww*- > Goth -**ggw**- [phonetically -*ggw*-, not -*ŋgw*-], as in **treww*- > **triggw**- (true, loyal), ON *trygg*-; in West Germanic, however, PG *-*ww*- > *-*uw*-, as reflected in OHG *gitriuwi*, AS *trīewe*, Eng *true*. PG *-*yy*- > Goth -**ddj**-, ON -*ggj*-, as in Goth *twaddje* (of two), ON *tveggja*. For a summary of the Germanic evidence for these unusual correspondences and their laryngeal antecedents in IE see Winfred P. Lehmann, "Germanic Evidence," in *Evidence for Laryngeals*, ed. by Werner Winter (The Hague, Mouton and Co., 1965), pp. 212-23, and the bibliography cited there.

(5) The development of PG **y* in Gothic is treated in the following lessons in connection with specific morphological problems, e.g. -jo-stem nouns (Lesson 3) and weak verbs, class I (Lesson 5).

(6) The PG *h^w*, *k^w*, and *g^w* that resulted from the changes given for the IE labiovelars in the preceding section developed into Goth **hw**, **q** (= [*kw*]), and **gw** respectively.

(7) Initial PG **pl*- > Goth **þl**-, as in PG **flewhan*- (to flee) > Goth **þliuhan**. Exceptions like **flodus** (flood) and **flokan** (to lament) are thought to be dialectal variants.

Table A

The Gothic development of IE plain voiceless stops and *s

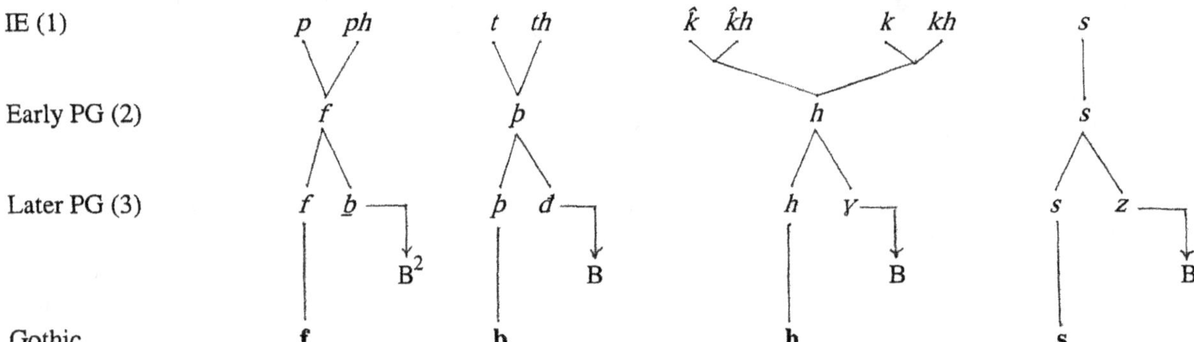

Remarks:

(1) The IE aspirated stops **ph, *th, *k̂h, *kh,* which occurred very infrequently in IE, merged with the unaspirated stops in early PG. The plain velar stops **k, *kh* merged with the plain palatal stops **k̂, *k̂h.*

(2) The spirantization of the voiceless stops in early PG, known as Grimm's Law,[3] did not take place when these sounds occurred immediately after **s* (i.e. in the combinations **sp, *st, *sk̂, *sk*). Only the first stop was affected in the combinations **pt > *ft, *k̂t > *ht, *kt > *ht.* For typographic convenience we use the symbol **h* to denote the PG sound that was probably [χ], i.e. the *ch* of German *Bach, Dach,* etc.

(3) Verner's Law[4] involves the voicing of the PG voiceless spirants **f, *þ, *h, *s* to **ƀ, *đ, *γ, *z* in postvocalic positions when the preceding vowel did not bear the original IE stress. The voiced spirants that resulted from this change merged with those already present as reflexes of the IE voiced aspirates (see Table B). The effects of Verner's Law should show up most clearly in the inflection of the strong verb, where the original stress varied within a single paradigm, e.g. the PG preterite singular **wárþa* (I became) < IE **wórta* and the preterite plural **wurđum* < IE **wr̥tmé* (we became). This distinction is preserved in some Germanic languages, e.g. English *was/were* < PG **was/*wǣzum,* but in Gothic the voiced/voiceless contrast was given up in favor of the voiceless spirant. Even when such a contrast exists, as in Gothic **þarf** (I need)/**þaurbum** (we need), the Devoicing Rule (see Grammar Lesson I) could underlie the distinction, and only a careful study of cognates elsewhere permits a correct assessment of the historical situation. There are abundant examples of Verner's Law elsewhere in Gothic, however, and there is no reason to exempt Gothic from the workings of that law, as has sometimes been suggested. In the etymologies and morphological discussion of the following lessons the reader may assume that Verner's Law is in effect whenever Gothic **b, d, g** correspond to IE **p, *t, *k,* e.g. **winds, fugls, hunds,** and **laufs** in Lesson I. Even when the original stress is not indicated in the etymology the reader should assume that it did not stand on the vowel before the consonant in question.

---

[2]i.e. see Table B.

[3]After the German philologist Jacob Grimm (1785-1863), whose "law," formulated in 1822, dealt with the reflexes of all IE stops throughout Germanic and the other subfamilies of IE then known.

[4]After the Danish philologist Karl Adolf Verner (1846-96).

Table B

The Gothic development of the IE plain voiced stops

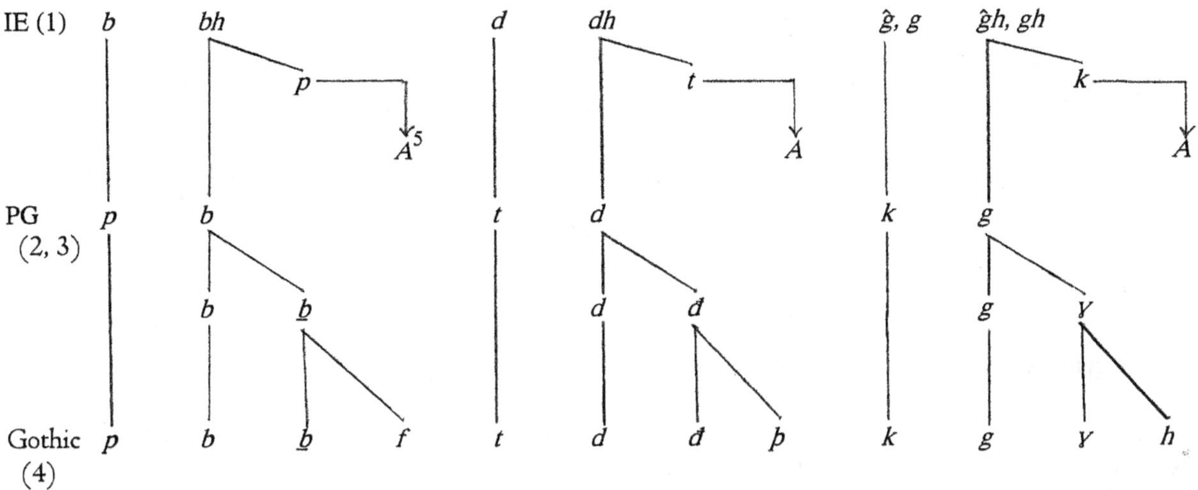

Remarks:

(1) Already in late IE **(bh, dh, ĝh, gh) + *(t, s)* assimilated to **(p, t, k̂, k) + *(t, s).* The resulting **p, *t, *k̂, *k* followed the development of original IE **p, *t, *k̂, *k* (see Table A).

(2) PG **b, *d, *g* remained as stops in word-initial position and medially when preceded by their corresponding nasals (i.e. in the combinations **mb, *nd, *ŋg*). Elsewhere they were spirantized to **ƀ, *đ, *γ.*

(3) The **ƀ, *đ, *γ* that resulted from Verner's Law (see Table A) merged with the **ƀ, *đ, *γ* resulting from step (2) above.

(4) The voiced spirants *ƀ* (written **b**), *đ* (written **d**), and **z** were devoiced in Gothic to **f**, **þ**, and **s** respectively in word-final position and before final **s** (see Grammar Lesson I).

(5) For the development of the IE labialized velar stops see section II of the Introduction.

5 i.e. see Table A.

Table C

The development of the IE long vowels and diphthongs in PG and Gothic

A. In syllables ending up stressed in Gothic, including the vowels of monosyllables:

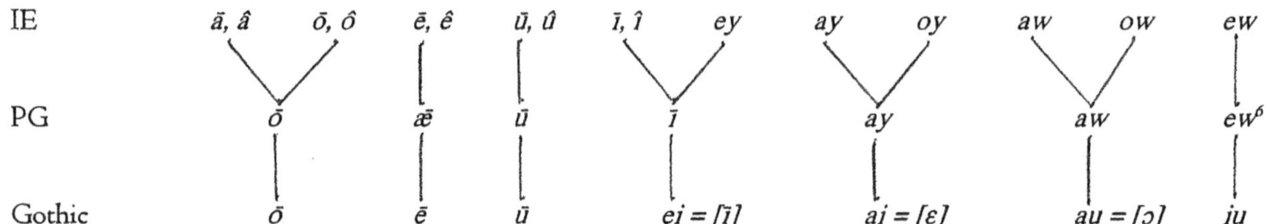

B. In syllables ending up unstressed and final in Gothic:

The rules governing the development of IE long vowels and long diphthongs which end up in final unstressed syllables in PG and Gothic are very difficult to formulate. In the first place, the precise forerunner of a particular Gothic form may be in dispute. For example, does the ending of the dative singular of **dags,** i.e. **-a,** go back to IE dative **-ōi,* or the instrumental **-ō, *-ē,* or the locative **-oi, *-ei?* All have been suggested. In the second place, many of the phonetic combinations occurring in final position are found in only one or two paradigms, and it is only too easy to end up with a separate rule for each form. In view of this indeterminacy, we will adopt the following fairly simple rules as the most general that can be safely formulated:

1. All IE final consonants other than **-s, *-r* and the cluster **-ns* were lost in Gothic.[7]
   a. Before IE final **-s* IE long vowels were preserved in PG and Gothic.
   b. IE final **-ēr* and **-ōr* show up in Gothic as **-ar** and **-or** respectively. See p. 264 for further comments.

2. All IE normal long vowels which became final unstressed in late PG and Gothic were shortened. When a final unstressed long vowel does occur in Gothic, like the **-o** of **tuggo** or **gibo**, or the **-e** of **dage,** it is assumed either that the original IE vowel was trimoric (extra-long) instead of bimoric (normal long) or that it was protected by a final consonant, usually **-d, -*m,* or **-n,* which disappeared at a later date than did the rest of the consonants. Such phenomena will be dealt with individually as they occur.

3. The masculine singular accusative ending **-ana** of **þana** and the strong adjective inflection is taken as evidence that IE final **-m* > PG **-n* prior to its loss. The IE ending in question apparently alternated between **-om* and **-om-ō,* where *-ō* was an optional particle indicating proximity. Late PG **þana* would then result from a fusion of the two developing forms **þan* and **þama.*

C. IE long vowels and ordinary diphthongs ending up in unstressed non-final syllables in Gothic are assumed to have followed the development of their stressed counterparts as given in A above.

D. The rules for final long diphthongs, e. g. **-ēw, *-āy, *-ây,* are indeterminate for the same reasons as given above and will be discussed individually when encountered in the historical comments.

---

[6] But see rule 2a in Table D.

[7] It is convenient to retain some final consonants, especially **-t,* in monosyllabic words in PG and treat their loss individually in describing the transition from PG to the various daughter languages.

Table D

The development of the Indo-European short vowels and short syllabic resonants in syllables ending up stressed in Gothic

1. From Late Proto-Indo-European to Early Proto-Germanic:

Indo-European:	*ə*	*a*	*o*	*e*	*i*	*u*	*ḷ*	*ṃ*	*ṇ*	*ṛ*
Early PG:		*a*		*e*	*i*	*u*	*ul*	*um*	*un*	*ur*

2. Changes which took place within the Proto-Germanic period, in chronological sequence:

a. *e was raised to *i before a nasal (*m, *n, *ñ) + consonant, or (2) when the next syllable contained *i, *ī, or *y.

b. *i and *u, when not followed by a nasal + consonant or by *Cy or *y, were lowered to *e and *o respectively before *a, *o, *ō, *ǣ, or *ē in the following syllable.

c. the sequences *anh, *inh, and *unh became *āh, *īh, and *ūh respectively.

3. From Late Proto-Germanic to Gothic, in chronological sequence:

a. *e and *o were raised to **i** and **u** respectively.

b. *i and *u were lowered to [ε] (spelled **ai**) and [ɔ] (spelled **au**) respectively before **r**, **h**, and **hw**.

Or, in tabular form:

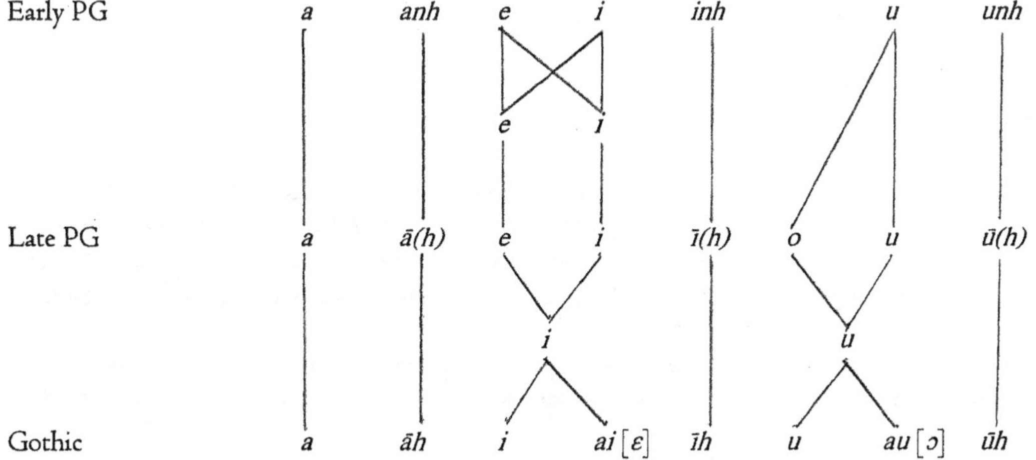

Lesson I

Masculine a-stem (IE o-stem) nouns.

The declension of strong masculine nouns of the type **dags** derives from that of the IE o-stem nouns and corresponds to the Latin second declension (e. g. *servus* servant), the Greek masculine *-os* declension (e. g. ἄνθρωπος man), and the Sanskrit masculine *-as* declension (e. g. *dēvas* god). Taking into consideration all of the related declensions throughout IE, one finds that there is hardly an ending in the entire paradigm that doesn't present problems or, at best, variant forms in reconstruction. Furthermore, the intrusion into the paradigm of analogical forms from other nominal and pronominal inflections is always present. In presenting a full IE paradigm for each type of nominal inflection, we are essentially giving only those forms which were the immediate forerunners of the PG forms and ignoring the variants that a fuller discussion would require.

The IE noun was inflected in three numbers (singular, dual, and plural) and eight cases (nominative, genitive, dative, accusative, vocative, ablative, locative, and instrumental). The dual number in nouns and adjectives did not survive into the PG or Latin nominal systems but is well represented in Greek and Sanskrit. Forms and categories that did not survive into PG will generally not be presented in our schemes. Of the cases, all eight survive in Sanskrit. A merger[1] of ablative, locative, and instrumental reduced the number of cases to six in Latin. A merger of genitive and ablative plus a merger of dative, locative, and instrumental reduced the system to five cases in Classical Greek. In PG the vocative is still a distinct form in some of the paradigms; the functions of the instrumental and locative were subsumed under the PG dative, and the ablative survived only as an adverbial ending (see Lesson 23). Note that in these mergers, the same case forms did not always survive in different paradigms. The IE masculine o-stem noun paradigm with its survivors in Sanskrit, Classical Greek, Latin, *Proto-Germanic, and Gothic is as follows:

Singular	*IE	Skr	Gk	Lat	*PG	Gothic
N	*os*	*as*	*os*	*us*	*az*	**s**
G	*eso, osyo*	*asya*	*ou < oio*	*ī*	*esa*	**is**
D	*ōy*	*āya*	*ōi*	*ō*	*ay*	**a**
A	*om*	*am*	*on*	*um*	*an > a*	Ø[2]
V	*e*	*a*	*e*	*e*	*e*	Ø
Abl	*ôd*	*āt*	--	*ō*	*[ō]*[3]	[**o**]
Instr	*ō*	*ēna*	--	--	*[ē, ō]*	--
Loc	*oy, ey*	*ē*	*[oi, ei]*		*ai*	

Remarks on the singular:

The transition from IE to PG is relatively uncomplicated. With the regular changes of *o* > *a*, final *-Vm* > *-Vn*, and final *-Vs* > *-Vz*, only the dative form requires comment. IE long diphthongs in final unstressed positions were shortened in PG, so that the transition *-ōi* > *-ay* may also be viewed as regular. During the PG period final *-n* was lost after short vowels in polysyllabic words; thus, *-an* > *-a*. Final *-z* reverted to *-s* in Gothic by the Devoicing

[1]When speaking of a merger within a paradigm we are referring to a merger of the functions exercised by the various case forms in the syntactic structure of the language. Obviously only one morpheme among the several involved survived in any given paradigm.

[2]The symbol Ø indicates a zero ending, as in the *As dag*. The symbol -- indicates that the antecedent form did not survive.

[3][ ] enclose endings that survived extra-paradigmatically, usually as isolated adverbial forms.

Rule cited above. That PG **-esa* was not affected by Verner's Law is due probably to the influence of the same ending in the pronominal system, where the vowel before -s- was always stressed; cf. PG **þesa* in the paradigm below.

In the transition from PG to Gothic, short vowels, with the exception of *-u,* were regularly lost in final position and in final syllables before a single consonant. Thus all the forms except the dative are accounted for. As noted on p. 234, the rules governing the development of IE long diphthongs in unstressed final syllables in Gothic are difficult to formulate. IE **-ōy* is reconstructed as the *Ds* ending for masculine o-stem nouns (**daga**), as given above, for the masculine (and neuter) demonstrative (**tosmōy* > **þamma**) and interrogative (**kʷosmōy* > **hwamma**) pronouns, and the 3rd person pronoun (**esmōy* > **imma**). It would appear that final unstressed IE **-ōy* > PG **-ay* > Gothic **-a**. This is in accord with the general rule, Table C, B2, on the shortening of IE final stressed plain long vowels in PG. The transition of PG final **-ay* to Gothic **-a** is also in agreement with the development of the passive forms *bairada, bairanda* from IE **bheretay, *bherontay,* Gk φέρεται, φέρονται (Lesson 22). Possibly contradicting this simple formulation are the *Ds* forms of the indefinite pronouns **hwammeh** (Lesson 21) and **ainummehun** (Lesson 22), where the vowel of the dative ending under discussion is preserved unshortened before the suffixed **-h(un),** i.e. it is no longer in final position. Since Gothic **-e-** regularly presupposes PG **ǣ* < IE **ē,* some scholars are forced to reject the equation of Gothic final **-a** with IE **-ōy* presented above and to look elsewhere for this dative ending, namely in the IE instrumental ending **-ē* found in the **tosmē, *esmē, *kʷosmē.* Corresponding West Germanic forms is *-u* would seem to require a retention in PG of the alternate IE instrumental form in **-ō: *tosmō.* The problem cannot be resolved with the evidence at our disposal.

Plural		*IE	Skr	Gk	Lat	*PG	Gothic	
	N	*ōs*	*ās*	*oi*	*ī*	*ōz*	*ōs*	**os**
	G	*ôm*	*ānām*	*ōn*	*(ōr)um*	*ôn > ō*	*ē*	**e**
	D	*omes, omos*	*ēbhyas*	*ois*	*īs*	*omiz, omoz*	*am*	**am**
	A	*ons*	*ān*	*ous < ons*	*ōs*	*anz*	*ans*	**ans**
	Abl	*omes, omos*	*ēbhyas*	--	*īs*	--	--	
	Instr	*ōys*	*āis*	--	--	--	--	
	Loc	*oysu*	*ēsu*	--	--	--	--	

Remarks on the plural:

The reconstruction of a complete paradigm for the plural in IE poses serious problems: the *N, G, A* and *Instr* are fairly straightforward, but evidence for the *D, Abl,* and *Loc* is conflicting. The dative and ablative forms in *-m-* (*-omes* and *-omos*) underlie the forms in PG and in PBSl; the corresponding forms in Sanskrit, however, derive from IE *-(oy)bhyos* or -(oy)*bhyes.* Equally problematic is the stem final vowel: Gothic **-am** < PG *-omiz* points to IE *-o-,*[4] while Skr *-ē-* would require IE *-oy-,*[5] as in the locative. The origin of the Gothic *Gpl* ending **-e** is completely obscure; the other Germanic languages have forms continuing PG ***-ôn.***

---

[4]As noted in Table C, the general rule for the development in PG of IE plain long vowels which became unstressed in PG is that they were shortened in final position but preserved as long in eventually final syllables when followed by a single consonant which was originally final or became final in Gothic. Thus Gothic ***-am***<PG *-omiz* points to IE *-omis,* not *-ōmis.*

[5]For this *-oy-* as a plural marker, see the discussion of ***sa*** below.

The Demonstrative Adjective **sa**:

Singular:		*IE	Skr	Gk	*PG	Gothic
	N	*so*	*sa(s)*	ὁ	*sa*	**sa**
	G	*tosyo, teso*	*tasya*	τοῦ	*þesa*	**þis**
	D	*tosmōy*	*tasmāi*	τῷ	*þammai*	**þamma**
	A	*tom*	*tam*	τόν	*þan (+ a)*	**þana**
	Abl	*tosmôd*	*tasmād*	--	--	--
	Inst	*tosmē, -ō*	*tēna*	--	--	--
	Loc	*tosmin*	*tasmin*	--	--	--
Plural:	N	*toy*	*tē*	οἱ	*þai*	**þai**
	G	*tōm, toysōm*	*tēṣām*	τῶν	*þō*	**þize**
	D	*toy-mos, -bhyos*	*tēbhyas*	τοῖς	*þaimiz*	**þaim**
	A	*tons*	*tān*	τοῦς < τονς	*þanz*	**þans**
	Abl	*toybhyos*	*tēbhyas*	--	--	--
	Inst	*tōys*	*tāis*	--	--	--
	Loc	*toysu*	*tēṣu*	--	--	--

There are several stems involved here in the IE paradigm:

(1) *so-* appears only in the *Ns*, but is consistently preserved in Skr, Gk, and PG; Gk has extended this stem to the *Npl* as well (remember that IE **sV-* became *hV-* in Greek initially).

(2) The remaining forms are based on a **t-** stem, but further analysis is complicated by our inability to be certain where a stem ends and an ending begins. Detailed analysis of all the possible variants is beyond the scope of these brief comments. Note, however, that the extended stem in *-sm-*, namely **tosm-* is well represented in Skr and underlies PG *Ds* **þammai* > Goth **þamma**. Most scholars prefer to derive **þamma** from the IE instrumental **tosmē*.

The relationship between this pronominal inflection and that of the o-stem nouns above is clear. Precisely which forms are originally nominal and which pronominal is the subject of debate. It is sufficient for our purposes to note that the IE forms given in the *IE column are all legitimate reconstructions accepted by various scholars and that the transition from those forms to PG and thence to Gothic is relatively uncomplicated. The same problems occur here that occur in the o-stem noun paradigm, i. e. the final vowel of the *Ds* (see above) and the maverick *-ē* of the ***Gpl.*** The stem of Gothic **þize** is an extension from the ***Gs* þis**; we will encounter this secondary stem again when we take up the feminine forms in Lesson 3. It is interesting to note that there was a similar secondary stem already in IE, where singular **tos-* and plural **toys-* could, by one analysis, be isolated as alternates to simple **t-*. The *-a* suffixed in PG to the *As* form is presumed to be cognate with Skr *ā* < IE **ō*, a particle co-occurring with various cases, including the accusative, to mark proximity.

Some etymologies:

akrs < PG **akra-* < IE **aĝro-*; probably < √*aĝ* (to drive) [h_2*eĝ*] + *-ro-*, if it referred originally to a "place where cattle are driven." Cf. Lat *ager*, Gk ἀγρός.

þiudans < PG **þewđana-* (Verner) < [**þewđ-* (people) < IE **tewt-*] + [**-an-* < IE *-on-*]; cf. ON *þjóðan-*, AS *ðēoden*; IE **tewt-* is probably the source of Lat *tot-* (all). *Teuton* is this same word, via Latin.

stains < PG **stayna-* < IE **stoy-no-* < √*stāy* (< √*steh*$_2$*-ye-* be stiff) + *-no-*; cf. Gk στία, στῖον pebble, Lat *stiria* icicle; Ger *Stein*, Eng *stone*, ON *stein-*.

sitls < PG **setla-* < IE **sedlo-* < √*sed* (sit) + *-lo-*; cf. Lat *sella* and Gk ἑλλά < **sedla*, Russ *седло*; Ger *Sessel*, Eng *settle*.

himins < PG **himina-* < IE **kemen-* < ?? (metathesis) **akmen-* (sharp stone, tool) < √*ak* be sharp + *-men-*. Semantics: sharp stone > stone, to describe "stony" vault of sky. For meaning *stone* cf. Russ *камень*. Ger *Himmel* and Eng *heaven* both show dissimilations, *-m-n* to *-m-l* and *-m-n* to *-v-n*. Another less artful, but more probably correct, etymology derives PG **himina-* from IE **ḱemno-* < √*ḱem* (to cover) + suffix **-no-*. This root is also attested in PG **hamiþyo-* (shirt) > Ger *Hemd*, borrowed into Latin as *camisia*, and Gothic **gahamon** (to clothe).

winds < PG **winda-* (Verner) < IE **wē-nt-o-* < √*wē* (to blow) [√*h*$_2$*weh*$_1$] + *-nt-* (participial suffix). Cf. Lat *ventus*, Hit *huwant-*.

wair < PG **wera-* < IE **wiro-*. Cf. Lat *vir*, OIr *fer*, Skr *vīras* (hero). IE verbal root not certain; perhaps < √*weyh*$_2$ (be vigorous, strive) + *-ro-*.

bagms < PG **baɣma-*, apparently a variant form of **bawma-* < IE **bhowmo-* < *√*bhew* (be, grow) [√*bhewh*$_2$] + *-mo-*. Cf. Ger *Baum*, MidDutch *boom*, Eng *beam*. The **-g-** of the Gothic form could conceivably be a reflex of a PG sequence *-wX-*, where ***X*** represents an indeterminate reflex of the IE laryngeal *h*$_2$. Reconstruction is further complicated by the presence of ON *baðm-* (tree).

wigs < PG **weɣa-* < IE **weĝho-* < √*weĝh* (to go, transport) + *-o-*. Cf. Ger *Weg*, ON *veg-*, Eng *way*; Lat *vīa* (<IE **weĝ-ya-*).

hlaifs < PG **hlayḇa-* < IE **kloybho-*. Cf. Eng *loaf*, Ger *Laib*, ON *hleif-*. The IE root is not clear. The Germanic word appears as a loan word in Slavic, e. g. Russ *хлеб* (bread, grain). There is a possible association with the PG verb **hlīḇ-* (to protect, look after), Gothic **hleibjan**, ON *hlífa*, OHG *līben*, and the related noun **hlīḇ-* (protection; shield), ON *hlíf*; PG **hlayḇ-* could also have meant *shield*, with a semantic shift to *loaf* on the basis of the shape. As a second and even more remote possibility, I would suggest a derivation from an IE root ***kleybh* as a variant of **gleybh* (to be sticky); **gloybhos* = **kloybhos* would originally have characterized the *sticky dough*. A similar etymology has been suggested in Semitic for Hebrew *léḥem* (bread) = Arabic *laḥm-* (meat).

fugls < PG **fuɣla-* (Verner) < (probably, by dissimilation) PG **flugla-* < IE **pluklo-* < √*plewk* (to fly) + *-lo-*. Cf. Ger *Vogel*, ON *fugl*, Eng *fowl*. The IE root √*plewk* is one of two extensions of the more primitive root √*plew* (to flow, fly); the other is √*plewd* (to flow, float). Both of these were in PG as evidenced, e.g., by ON *fljóta* (to flow) < PG **flewt-* < IE **plewd-* and ON *fljúga* (to fly) < PG **flewg-* < IE **plewk-*.

fisks < PG **fiska-* < IE **pisko-*. Cf. Lat *piscis*, Ir *iasc*. The IE root of the word is obscure.

skalks < PG **skalka-*. Cf. ON *skalk-*, AS *scealc*, Ger *Schalk*. The IE origin of this word is obscure.

asts < PG **asta-* <IE **ozdo-* < **o-* (on) + √*sed* (to sit). Cf. Ger *Ast;* Gk ὄζος.

hunds < PG **hunda-* < IE **kwn̥to-* < **kwon* (dog) + *-to-*. Cf. Gk κύων, Lat *canis* (development obscure); Ger *Hund*, Eng *hound*.

laufs < PG **lawb̠a-* (Verner)< IE **lowpo-* < √*lewp* (to peel off). Cf. Ger *Laube*, Eng *leaf*, ON *lauf*. The verbal root occurs only in BSl, e. g. Russ *лупить* (to peel); the IE root √*lewp* is perhaps a by-form of √*lep* (to peel), e.g. Gk λέπω, Lith *lapas* (leaf).

ligr < PG **leɣra-* < IE **leghro-* < √*legh* (to lie) + *-ro-*. Cf. Eng *lair*, Ger *Lager* (store).

wulfs < PG **wulfa-* < IE **w̥lk*^{w}*o-*. Cf. ON *ulf-*, Ger *Wolf*, Eng *wolf*; Gk λύκος, Lat *lupus*, Skr *vr̥kas*. For the unusual correspondence of IE **k*^{w} > PG **f* see above, p. 230.

hwar < PG **hwar* < IE **k*^{w}*o-* (interrog. stem) + *-r* (adverbial suffix). Cf. Eng *where*, ON *hvar*; related to Lat *cur*.

in < PG **in* < IE **en* (in). Cf. ON *in*, Ger *in*, Eng *in*; Lat *in*, Gk ἐν.

ana < PG **ana* < IE **ana* (on). Cf. Gk ἀνά, Lat *an-* (as prefix); Eng *on*, Ger *an*.

du < PG ? In spite of the similarity in both form and meaning, Gothic **du** seems not to be related to Eng *to* and Ger *zu*. The latter require a PG **tō*, (which would have yielded **tō* in Gothic) from IE * *d-* (a basic demonstrative stem). On the other hand, Gothic **du** requires PG **du* < IE **dhu*, which has no other foundation.

fram < PG **fram* < IE **pro-* + *-mo-*. IE **pro* (or **prō*) is an extended form of √*per*, the base of numerous prepositions and adverbs, as well as being a prolific verbal root (e. g. Gothic **faran**). The primary meaning of √*per* seems to have been *forward, through*.

us < PG **uz* < IE **us* (up, out). Cf. ON *ór*; mainly as a prefix elsewhere in Germanic. Elsewhere in IE as a prefix: OCSl *vŭz-*, Avestan *us-*.

Lesson 2

Neuter a-stem (IE o-stem) nouns:

		IE	Skr	Gr	Lat	PG	Gothic
singular:	NA	*om*	*am*	*on*	*um*	*am*	Ø
plural:	NA	*ā*	*ā(ni)*	*a*	*a*	*ō > a*	**a**

The neuter forms of the demonstrative:

		IE	Skr	Gr	Lat	PG	Gothic
singular:	NA	*tod*	*tad*	τό	--	*þat + a*	**þata**
plural:	NA	*tā*	*tā(ni)*	τά	--	*þō*	**þo**

Remarks:

The development from IE is straightforward with the exception of the singular neuter form **þata** in PG and Gothic. The added **-a** is probably an extension from the personal pronoun **ita** (it), a parallel to the development of the masculine **þana** (see Lesson I), but the **-a** of **ita** and **þana** is itself obscure.

The difference between the nominal plural *-a* and pronominal *-ō* in PG is regular: plain long terminal vowels were shortened unless stressed. In PG stressed terminal vowels would have occurred only on monosyllabic words like *þō* and a few special uninflected items.

The numbers.

	*IE	Skr	Gk	Lat	*PG	Gothic
four	*k^{w}etwōr*	*catur*	τέτταρ-	*quattuor*	*feđwōr*	**fidwor**
five	*penk^{w}e*	*panca*	πέντε	*quinque*	*fimf*	**fimf**
six	*s(w)eks*	*ṣaṣ*	ἕξ	*sex*	*sehs*	**saihs**
seven	*septm̥*	*sapta*	ἑπτά	*septem*	*seb̲un*	**sibun**
eight	*ok̂tō(w)*	*aṣṭa*	ὀκτώ	*octo*	*ahtōw*	**ahtau**
nine	*newn̥*	*nava*	ἐννέα	*novem*	*newn*	**niun**
ten	*dekm̥t*	*daça*	δέκα	*decem*	*tehun*	**taihun**

As can be seen from the above table, the IE numbers show a remarkable coherence in their development, and the PG forms call for little comment. The change of IE *k^w* > PG *f* is not normal, but is accepted by many scholars as occurring exceptionally in a small group of words of which **wulfs** (Lesson I), **fidwor**, and **fimf** are among the most certain examples. In the case of the initial *f* of PG *feđwōr* there is also the possibility of contiguous numbers affecting each other in counting; Latin *quattuor - quinque* instead of expected *quattuor - *pinque* is a relevant example of this.

Some etymologies:

dags < PG **daγa-* < IE **dhogh^{w}o-* < *√dhegh^w* (to burn). Presumed semantics: burn > be bright (in contrast to night). Cf. ON *dag-*, Ger *Tag*, Eng *day*. For the root cf. Skr *√dah* (to burn), Russ *жечь, жгу*. For a completely different etymology relating **dags** to Skr *ahar* (G *ahnas*) day, see Pokorny p.7.

dius < PG **dewza-* (Verner)< IE **dhewso-* (breathing creature) < *√dhew* (breath, smoke) + *-s-*. Cf ON *dýr*, Ger *Tier*, Eng *deer*. For root meaning *breath* cf. Russ *дух* (breath, spirit); for *smoke* cf. Lat *fumus* (< **dhū-mo-s*).

land < PG **landa-* < IE **londho-*. Cf. ON *land*, Ger *Land*, Eng *land*. IE cognates very obscure.

guþ < PG **guda-* < IE **ghudho-* or **ghuto-*. Cf. ON *goð, guð*, Ger *Gott*, Eng *god*. IE cognates very obscure.

skip < PG **skipa-* < IE **skibo-*. Cf. ON *skip*, Ger *Schiff*, Eng *ship*. IE cognates very obscure.

jer < PG **yǣra-* < IE **yēro-* < *√ey* [*√*h_1*ey*] (to go, pass) + *-er/or-*. Cf. ON *ár*, Ger *Jahr*, Eng *year*. o-grade in Gk ὥρα (< **yōra*) season, hour, OCSl *jara* spring, Av *yār*.

witod- < (w. dissimilation) PG **witōþa-* < IE *√weyd* (to see, know)) + *-āto-*. Cf OHG *wizzod*. For the suffix, cf. Lat *-ās, -ātis*. The Gothic word is probably more immediately a derivative from the verb **witan** from this same root, which is widespread in IE, e. g. Skr *√vid*, Gk οἶδα (< **woyd-*), Lat *videre*.

waurd < PG **wurda-* < IE **wr̥dho-* < *√wer* [*werH*] (to speak) + *-dho-*. Cf. ON *orð*, Ger *Wort*, Eng *word*; Lat *verbum* (< **wer-dhom*), Gk ῥῆμα (word, < **wrē-mn̥t-*).

agis < PG **agisa-* < IE **agheso-* < *√agh* [*√*h_2*egh*](to fear) + *-eso-*. Cf. ON *agi*, OHG *egiso;* Gk ἄχος pain, grief.

barn < PG **barna-* < IE **bhorno-* < *√bher* (to bear) + *-no-*. Cf. ON *barn*, Scottish Eng *bairn*. The verb *√bher* occurs in virtually every branch of IE (cf. **bairan**, Lesson 13).

akran < PG **akrana(n)*. The PG word seems to be a straightforward derivative from **akra-* (field): **akra-na-(n)*, continuing an IE **agro-no-m*. To what extent the Germanic words for *acorn*, e. g. ON *akran*, are related to our word is difficult to determine, since popular etymology has linked these words with *oak* on the one hand and *corn* on the other, not to mention some connection with words for *squirrel*.

mikil- < PG **mikila-* < IE **meĝelo-* < *√meĝ* (great) + *-lo-*. Cf. ON *mikil-*, Eng *much*, Lat *magnus*, Gk μεγ(αλ)-, Skr *maha* (< IE variant **meĝh*).

leitil- < PG **lītila-* < IE **leydelo-* < *√ley* (lacking, diminished) + (extension) *-de-* + *-lo-*. Cf. ON *lítil-*, Eng *little*. The IE root has various extensions, e. g. *leys-, loys-* as in PG **laisiz-* > Eng *less*.

god- < PG **gōđa-* (fit, suitable) < IE **ghōdh-* (good, fitting), ō-grade of IE *√ghedh* (fit together, join). Cf. ON *goð-*, Eng *good*, Ger *gut;* Slavic *√god* as in Russ *годиться* (be fitting, suitable).

hail- < PG **hayla-* < IE **kaylo-* (whole, sound). Cf. ON *heil-*, Ger *heil*, Eng *whole, hale;* OCSl *cělŭ*, Russ *целый*.

inwind- < PG **inwinda-* < IE **inwendho-* < **in-* + *√wendh* (turn). The root is found primarily in Germanic; cf. Gothic **gawandjan** (Lesson 7), **windan**, Eng *wend, wind*. Semantics: turned inward > not straight > crooked, unjust.

garaiht- < PG **garihta-* (straightened) < IE **kom-* (prefix) + **reĝto-* < ** √reĝ* (straighten, stretch) + *-to-*. Cf. Ger *gerecht.* For the prefix see Lesson 13. For the unprefixed form, Gothic **raiht**- (straight), cf. ON *rétt-*, Ger *recht*, Eng *right.* Derivatives of the IE root are found throughout most of the IE languages; the closest parallel is Lat *regere* (rule, straighten), past pass. partic. *rectus* (< **regto-*).

ubil- < PG **ub̯ila-*< (Verner) IE ** u̯pélo-* < *√wep* (up, upward from under) + *-lo-*. Cf. Ger *übel*, Eng *evil.* For more on the root see **ufar** (Lesson 3), **uf** (Lesson 9). The semantic development is obscure.

siuk- < PG **sewka-* < IE **sewgo-* (sad, sick). Cf. ON *sjúk-*, MHG *siech*, Eng *sick.* The IE root is poorly attested outside of Germanic.

and < PG **and(a)* < IE **anta* (out toward, facing). Cf. as verbal prefix ON *and-* (against, opposite), Ger *ant-* and *ent-*. The IE base **ant-* (face, front) has given rise to a large number of derivatives. Cf. Gk ἀντάω (meet, confront), ἀντί (against), Lat *ante*, Hitt *hanti* (before).

inu(h) < PG ?. The other Germanic languages have forms reflecting PG **ōnu* or **ēnu*, which are lengthened grades of some more primitive form. The absence of clear cognates other than Greek ἄνευ (without) prevents us from making any kind of accurate reconstruction.

nehwa < PG **nǣhwa*, thought to be from a reduced form of the prefix **an(a)* (cf. Lesson 1) and IE *√okʷ* (to see), i. e. within sight, near. Cf. ON *ná-*, Ger *nahe*, Eng *nigh.* Other etymologies have been suggested and the origin of the word remains obscure.

jainar < PG **yaynar* < IE **yonyo-* + *-r.* **yonyo-* is a compound of two IE pronominal/demonstrative stems **yo-* and *onyo- <**eno-*. The immediate cognates in Germanic are Eng *yon*, Ger *jen(er)* (that one), and the suffixed definite article *-inn* of ON. The change **yonyo-* > **yayna-* is said to be under the influence of the similar word **oyno-* > PG **ayna-* (one). The final *-r* is an adverbial suffix; cf. Gothic **hwar** *where*, **her** *here*, **aljar** *elsewhere.*

her < PG **hēr* < IE **k̂ēyr* < **k̂o(y)-, k̂e(y)-* (this here) + *-r* (see just above). Cf. ON *hér*, Ger *hier*, Eng *here.*

ni < PG **ni, ne* < IE **ne, nei, nē* (not). Cf. OHG *ni, ne*, AS *ni, ne.* Derivatives, with or without various extensions, exist in nearly all branches of IE; cf. Skr *na*, Lat *ne(que)*, Hitt *na(tt).* Eng *not, naught* and Ger *nicht(s)* contain the PG word for *thing*, ** wihti-*, thus **niwihti- nothing.* Cf. Goth **ni waiht** in Lesson 5.

Lesson 3

Feminine a/o-stem (IE *ā*-stem) nouns.

Feminine nouns of the type **giba** are descended from IE ā-stem (earlier *-aH-stem) nouns, also the ancestors of the Latin and Greek First Declensions, *rosa* (rose) and χώρα (country), and the Sanskrit ā-declension *sēnā* (army):

Singular	*IE	Skr	Greek	Latin	*PG	Gothic
N,V	*ā*	*ā*	*ā*	*a*	*ō*	**a**
G	*ās*	*āyās*	*ās*	*ae*	*ōz*	**os**
D	*ây*	*āyāi*	*āi*	*ae*	*ōy*	**ai**
A	*ām*	*ām*	*ān*	*am*	*ōn > ō*	**a**
Abl	*ās*	*āyās*	--	*ā*	--	--
Instr		*ayā*	--	--	--	--
Loc		*āyām*	--	--	--	--

In discussing the IE origin of the masculine o-stem *Ds* in Gothic, i. e. **-a**, we noted that IE long diphthongs in final position were shortened in PG. The development of the dative in the paradigm given above, namely IE **âi* > PG **ōi,* contradicts this statement. The contradiction can be resolved by assuming that different types of long diphthongs were involved in IE, e.g. *ōi* versus *ôi,* where *ō* represents a plain long vowel and *ô* an extra-long vowel. The difference is sometimes expressed as bimoric versus trimoric or plain (or acute) long versus circumflexed long. Most general works on IE allude to this difference and then quickly pass on to other things; it is difficult to find a coherent account of exactly where these trimoric vowels occur in the various paradigms and a consistent theory to account for them. They are, however, part and parcel of standard IE reconstructions and should be accepted as such. The trimoric vowels are apparently the result of contractions, but the deeper reconstructions necessary to explain the origins of the uncontracted forms lie beyond our brief discussions here. It should be noted, however, that original differences in accentuation as well as paradigmatic analogies could also account for some of the disparities. We will be satisfied to give the most general rules as commonly accepted and to point out the exceptions as we proceed.

Plural	*IE	Skr	Greek	Latin	*PG	Gothic
N	*ās*	*ās*	*ai*	*ae*	*ōz*	**os**
G	*âm*	*ānām*	*ōn*	*ārum*	*ôn>ô*	**o**
D	*āmes, ābhyes*	*ābhyas*	*ais*	*īs*	*ōmiz*	**om**
A	*ās*	*ās*	*ās*	*ās*	*ōz*	**os**

Allowing for the already mentioned variation of *-mes, -bhyes* in the *Dpl,* the PG and Gothic development from IE is without complications. The Latin and Greek paradigms have undergone considerable analogical re-formation, which is not our concern here.

The feminine form of the demonstrative **sa**:

Singular	*IE	Skr	Greek	Latin	*PG	Gothic
N	*sā*	*sā*	ἡ	--	*sō*	**so**
G	*tās*	*tasyās*	τῆς	--	*þezōz*	**þizos**
D	*tây*	*tasyāi*	τῇ	--	*þezôy*	**þizai**
A	*tām*	*tām*	τήν	--	*þōn*	**þo**

Plural							
	N	*tās*	*tās*	αἱ	--	*þōz*	**þos**
	G	*tâm*	*tāsām*	τῶν	--	*þezôn*	**þizo**
	D	*tāmes, tābhyes*	*tābhyas*	ταῖς	--	*þaimiz*	**þaim**
	A	*tās*	*tās*	τάς	--	*þōz*	**þos**

As mentioned in connection with the *Gpl* **þize** in Lesson I, PG already exhibits a secondary stem **þez-*, probably extended from the *Gsg þeza.* This same stem appears in the *Gs, Gpl,* and *Ds* of the feminine paradigm, remarkably parallel to the secondary stem *tasy-* in the corresponding Sanskrit singular forms, where an extension from the masc. Gs *tasya* also seems indicated. Once introduced, forms like *tasy-ās* were misdivided into *tas-yās* and the endings with initial *-y-* were introduced into the nominal paradigm cited above: *sēnāyās* replacing **sēnās, sēnāyāi* replacing **sēnāi* etc. The PG and Gothic *Dpl* is borrowed from the masculine and neuter paradigms (Lesson I).

Masculine and Neuter -jo- stem nouns.

Only the masculine singular *N* and *G* and neuter singular *N* and *A* call for comment. According to rule, the PG masc. nom. **haryaz* should have become **haris* in Gothic, but **haris* was replaced at some period with **harjis**, where the **-j-** was extended analogically from the remaining forms of the paradigm. The forms with long stem-final syllables had a longer form of the suffix in PG: **CvCC-iy-*. The singular forms were as follows:

N	*-iyaz*	>	*-iyz*	>	*Gothic* *-īs* (written **-eis**)
G	*-iyesa*		*-iyis*		*-īs* "
D	*-iyay*				*-ya* (written **-ja**)
A	*-iya(n)*		*-iy*		*-ī* (written **-ei**)

The syllabically conditioned allomorphism in the suffix extends back into the IE parent language: *-y-/*-ey-. We shall encounter it again in several of the verbal paradigms. The neuter nominative and accusative singular forms would normally have developed as IE **CvCyom* > PG **CvCya(n)* > Goth **CvCj** = **CvCi** and IE **CvCCeyom* > PG **CvCCiya(n)* > Goth ***CvCCī*** respectively. As mentioned in the grammar, the distinction between the two types is usually not maintained in Gothic.

Feminine -jā-stem nouns.

The situation with the feminine -jā-stem nouns, while similar in Gothic to the preceding, is more complicated in regard to the underlying IE forms. The type **wasti**, from PG **wastī* < IE **wostī* is taken to be the more original nominative form for feminine nouns containing the suffix *-y-* (Gothic -j-) before the inflectional endings. The remainder of the paradigm is exactly the same as that given for **giba** above, on the stem PG **wasty-* < IE **wosty-*. The *Ns* type **sunja**, according to this view, would have arisen from an analogical source.

Some Etymologies:

harjis < PG **harya-* < IE **koryos-* (army, warfare). Cf. Gk κοίρανος (commander, from **koryo-no-s*), Lith *karias* (army); ON *her-*, Ger *Heer.*

siponeis < ? Origin unknown. Cf. AS *sēpan* (to instruct).

gawi < PG **gawya-* < IE **ĝhəwyo-*, perhaps < *√ĝhəw* (gape, yawn) + *-yo-*. Semantics: gape > be empty > empty region. Cf. Gk χάος (empty space), χαῦνος (gaping); Ger *Gau.*

waldufni < PG **wald-* (might, strength) + *-ufni* (see Lesson 22) < IE **waldhm̥nyo-* < *√wal [welH]* (be strong) + extension *-dh-* + suffix *-m̥nyo-*. Cf. Lat *valeo* (be strong), OCSl *vlastĭ* < **vladti* (might); ON *vald,* Ger *Gewalt.*

sunja < PG **sunyō* < **sundyō* (Verner) < IE **sn̥tī, sn̥tyā-* < *√es* (to be) + participial *-n̥t-* + *-ī/yā.* Semantics: that which is > reality, truth. Cf. Skr *satyam* (truth, < **sn̥tyom*), Eng *sooth* (< PG **sanþaz* < IE **sontos*), Eng *sin,* Ger *Sünde,* both from the same PG form as Gothic **sunja**.

þiudangardi < **þiudan**- (see Lesson 1) + **-gardi** < PG **gardī, gardyā-* < IE **ĝhordhī, -dhyā-* < *√ĝherdh* (enclose, fence in). This is a by-form of the more common **gards** (house, enclosure), for which see Lesson 7.

þiwi < PG **þewī, -wyōz* (Verner) < IE **tekʷī, tekʷyā* < *√tekʷ* (run, flow). Semantics: runner > messenger > servant. This is a secondary form on the masc. **þius** < IE **tekʷos.* Cf. ON *þý* (bondwoman), OHG *diu.* The root is widespread in IE; cf. Russ *течь* (to flow), *ток* (current), Skr *√tak* (to hasten).

laisareis < PG **laysāriyaz* < *√lays* + *-āriyaz* (see Lesson 21) < IE **loys-* < *√leys* (to learn). The verbal root is limited to Germanic, for which see **laisjan** in Lesson 5.

fairguni < PG **ferɣunya-*. Cf. ON *fjörgyn* (mother-earth) and AS *firgen-* (mountain). Generally regarded as a borrowing from Celtic **pergunia* and ultimately related to the IE ancestor of Latin *quercus* (oak), assuming a semantic development *oak forest > forest > mountain.* I would suggest an alternate derivation from IE *√perk̂* , combining Pokorny's *√perk* I and 3 (rib, furrow); thus, **perk̂n̥tyom* (a furrowing, rippling); cf. OCSl *prŭsi* (breast) Latin *porca* (the ridge between two furrows), Eng *furrow,* Ger *Furche.*

mawi < PG **mawī, mawyō-* < IE **maghwī, maghwyā-* < *√maghu* + fem. *-ī-/-yā.* Cf. ON *mær.* The extended form **magh-oti-*, originally an abstract noun, underlies Gothic **magaþs** (maiden), Eng *maid,* Ger *Magd.* For the masc. form **magus** (boy) see Lesson 9. Outside of Germanic the root is best attested in Celtic, cf. Irish *mac* (son).

airþa < PG **erþō* < IE ** ertā.* Cf. ON *jörð,* Ger *Erde,* Eng *earth.* The IE base is **er-* (cf. Gk *ἔρα in ἔραζε to the ground); the PG form is based on the extension **er-t-*.

stibna < PG **stiƀnō* < ? Cf. Swedish *stämma,* Ger *Stimme.* The IE origin of the word is obscure.

wasti < PG **wastī, wastyō-* < IE **wostī, wostyā-* < *√wes* to clothe. Cf. Lat *vestis;* for the root cf. Skr *√vas* (to dress), Gk ἕννυμι < **wes-nu-*, Goth **wasjan**.

giba < PG **geƀō* < ? Cf. ON *gjöf,* Ger *Gabe.* The Germanic root *√geb* (to give) is well attested, but the IE cognates are obscure; it is usually assigned to the IE root **ghabh-* (to seize, take), but difficulties with vocalization and meaning make this less than appealing.

gaur- < PG **gawra-* < IE **ghowro-* (fearsome). Cf. Skr *goras* (fearsome), Russ *журить* (to rebuke, scold); ON *gaur-* (disorderly person).

hauh- < PG **hauha-* < IE **kowko-* (arched, high) < *√kew* (bend) + extension *-k-*. Cf. Skr *kucas* (breast), Russ *куча* (heap); ON *hó-* (high), Ger *hoch,* Eng *high.*

jugg- < PG **yunga-< *yuwunga-* (Verner) < IE *yuwn̥ḱó-* < √*yew* (youthful vigor) + *-Hen-* + *-ko-*. Cf. Lat *juvencus* (calf), Skr *juvaças* (young); ON *ung-*, Ger *jung*, Eng *young*. For the IE stem without the suffix *-ko-* cf. Skr *yuvan-* (young), Lat *juvenis*, Russ *юный*.

niuj- < PG **newya-* < IE **newyo-* (new). Cf. Skr *nava-*, Gk νέος, Lat *novus*, Russ *новый*; ON *ný-*, Ger *neu*, Eng *new*.

gredag- < PG **grǣđaɣa-* < IE **ghrēdhako-* < √*gher* (to desire, want) + extension *-ēdh-* + *-ako-*. The adjective is based on a noun, PG **grǣđu-* (greed, hunger). Cf. ON *gráð-*, Eng *greed*, *greedy*. The root without the extension is widespread, e. g. Skr √*har* (to desire), Gk χαίρω (rejoice in). Cf. also Gothic **gairnjan** (to desire) in Lesson 5.

sineig- < PG **senīɣa-* (Verner) < IE ***√*sen* + *-īko-*. Cf. Skr *sanaka-* (old), Lat *senex* (old man). For the IE base **sen-* cf. Gk ἕνος (old, former), Lat *senātus*, *senectus*, *seneo*, etc. , OIr *sen* (old). The suffix **-īko-* > **-eig**- is well represented in Gothic; see Lesson 22.

fairnj- < PG **fernya-* < IE **pernyo-* < √*per²* (pass over) + extension *-n-* + *-yo-*. Cf. ON *fyrnd* (old age), OHG *firni* (old). The IE root *per²* has many extended forms (Pokorny, pp. 810-818!) and will be met with again below.

wilþj- < PG **welþya-* < IE **weltyo-* (wild, uncultivated). The IE root is connected basically with words for *wool, hair, grass*; semantics possibly of the "wild and wooly" type. Cf. ON *vill-*, Ger *wild*, Eng *wild*.

miþ < PG **međ* < IE **medhi* (amid, with). Cf. ON *með*, Ger *mit*. IE **medhi* is the base of the wide-spread adjective **medhyo-* (middle); see **midj**- in Lesson 17.

ufar < PG **ufer*, (Verner) *ub̄er* < IE *uper* (over, above). Cf. ON *yfir*, Ger *über*, Eng *over*; Skr *upari*, Gk ὑπέρ, Lat *(s)uper*.

Lesson 4

The strong adjective inflection.

Sanskrit, Latin, and Greek preserve the original IE system wherein nouns and adjectives were inflected alike according to the nature of their stems. In the strong adjectival inflection of Germanic, however, there has been considerable contamination by the pronominal inflection as represented by the demonstrative **sa**. Since we have already discussed all the forms of **sa**, it should not be difficult for the reader to analyze the paradigms given in §4. I from the historical point of view: the masculine paradigm is a mixture of **dags** and **sa**; the feminine, of **giba** and **so**, the neuter, of **waurd** and **þata**.

The correspondence of the forms with **-aiz-** to the forms of the demonstrative based on **þiz-** is clear enough, but the source of the vowel **-ai-** requires comment. As we noted in our discussion of the feminine demonstrative in Lesson 3, there is a noteworthy parallelism between Gothic and Sanskrit in regard to the distribution of the secondary stem *tasy-:þiz-*, pointing to the genitive singular masculine *tasya:þis* as the generating source. The **-ai-** of **blindaize** etc., however, can only be derived from the masculine nominative plural **toy* > **þai**. The secondary extension of **toy-* in the Sanskrit pronominal paradigm, as the "new" base for *tēṣam, tēbhyas,* and *tēṣu,* lends support to this analogy. Somewhere along the line in the development of PG the two analogical forces merged to produce the deviant forms of our paradigms.

The historical background of the personal pronouns (§4. 3) will be given in Lesson 7.

Some Etymologies:

ahwa < PG **ahʷa* < IE **akʷā*. Cf. Lat *aqua.*

saiwala < PG **saywala* < ?. Cf. Ger *Seele,* Eng *soul.* No IE source is known.

haiþi < PG **hayþī* < IE **kaytī.* Cf. ON *heiðr,* Eng *heath,* Ger *Heide.* The IE word is attested only in Germanic and Celtic.

asneis < PG **azniya-* (harvest worker), a derivative from PG **asan-* (summer, harvest time) < IE **osen-*. Semantics: harvest worker > hired worker. Cf. Eng *esne* (domestic slave). For basic word cf. Goth **asans** (harvest), ON *önn* (hay-making season); Russ *осень* (autumn). The derived verb PG **aznon* (do harvest work) is the source of Eng *earn.*

motareis < **mota** (tax, customs house) + **-arj-** (see Lesson 21). Supposedly from the IE root *med* (to measure).

weihs < PG **wīhs-* < IE *weyḱ-* (house, settlement). Cf. Lat *vicus,* Gk οἶκος (< **woyḱos*), OCSl *vĭsĭ.* Eng *-wick* in *bailiwick* is a borrowing from Latin.

hrot < PG **hrōt-* < IE **krōd-* < √*kred* (framework). Cf. ON *hrót* (roof), AS *hrost* (rafters), Eng *roost.* Probably the source for BSl words for armchair, e. g. Russ *кресло* < **kred-slo-*.

andeis < PG **andiya-* < IE **anteyo-* (lying ahead). Cf. ON *endir,* Ger *Ende,* Eng *end.* A derivative from the prolific IE root **ant-* (face, front).

andbahts < Celtic _*amb(i)-aktos_ (one sent about) < IE _*ambhi-_ (around) + _*aĝtos_ (driven, sent) < √_aĝ_ (drive). The Celtic word _ambactus_ is given in Latin sources as the Gallic word for servant. Cf. also ON _ambátt_ (bondwoman), OHG _ambaht_, and AS _ambiht_.

frod- < PG _*frōđ-_ (Verner) < IE _*prōt-_ (wise). Cf. ON _fróð-_, OHG _fruot;_ Ir _rathaigh_ (to understand), Lith _prõtas_ (understanding).

lagg- < PG _*lang-_ < IE _*(d)longh-_ < √_del_ + _-n-_ + extension _-gh-_. Cf. Ger _lang_, Eng _long;_ Lat _longus_. For the stem without the nasal infix cf. Gk δολιχός (long), OCSl _dlŭgŭ_, Russ _долгий_.

manag- < PG _*manag-_ < IE _*mon(o)gh-_ (abundant). Cf. OHG _manag_, Eng _many;_ OCSl _mŭnogŭ_, Skr _maghavan-_ (generous, < _*mn̥gh-_).

blind- < PG _*blend-_ < IE _*bhlendh-_ (pale, murky, hazy). Cf. ON _blind-_, Ger _blind_, Eng _blind;_ OCSl _(za)blęd-_ (get lost, err), Russ _(за)блудиться_.

anþar- < PG _*anþer-_ < IE _*anter-_ (other) < √_an_ (demonstrative base: there) + _-ter-_. Cf. ON _annar-_, Ger _ander-_, Eng _other;_ Lith _antaras_.

liub- < PG _*lewb-_ < IE _*lewbh-_ (to desire, love). Cf. ON _ljúf-_ (beloved), Ger _lieb_. The IE verbal root is widespread: Ger _lieben_, Eng _love;_ Lat _libet_, _lubet_ (is fitting, desirable), _libens_ (willing), Skr √_lubh_ (long for), Russ _любить_. See also **galaubjan** in Lesson 13.

diup- < PG _*dewp-_ < IE _*dhewb-_ (deep, hollow). Cf. ON _djúp-_, Ger _tief_, Eng _deep;_ Lith _dubùs_ (deep), Ir _domhain_ (deep), Russ _дно_ (bottom, < _*dubnó_).

faw- < PG _*faw-_ < IE _*paw-_ (small, few). Cf. ON _fá-_, Eng _few_. The IE root has several extensions: _-ko-_ in Lat _paucus_; _-ro-_ in Lat _parvus_ (with metathesis from _*paurus_), etc.

halt- < PG _*halt-_ < IE _*kold-_ (broken) < √_kel_ (to break) + _*-tó-_. Cf. ON _halt-_, Eng _halt_ (lame). The IE root is prolific, but the meaning _lame_ seems to be a specifically Germanic development other than Russ _калека_ (a cripple). Note also Lat _in-col-umis_ (unharmed).

jain- < PG _*yayn-_ < IE _*yoyn-_. See **jainar** in Lesson 2.

und < PG _*und-_ (Verner) < IE _*n̥ti_ < √_anti_ (face, facing). Cf. the first element of ON _unz_ (until) and Eng _unto_. There are many derivatives from this IE root; cf. **and** in Lesson 1.

Lesson 5

The conjugation of the present indicative active of all Gothic verbs other than the verb *to be* (**im, is, . . .**) and the preterite-present verbs is derived from that of IE thematic verbs, where the verbal root before the personal endings is augmented with a "thematic" vowel *e* or *o*. It corresponds to the Sanskrit a-conjugation (*vadāmi* speak), Greek ω-verbs (πέμπω send), and the Latin 3rd conjugation (*mittere* send):

	IE	Skr	Gk	Lat	PG	Gothic
1sg	*ō*	*āmi*	*ō*	*ō*	*ō > o > a*	**a**
2sg	*esi*	*asi*	*eis*	*is*	*esi > izi*	**is**
3sg	*eti*	*ati*	*ei*	*it*	*eþi > iđi*	**iþ**
1pl	*ŏ-mes/mos*	*āmas*	*omen*	*imus*	*amez > amiz*	**am**
2pl	*ete, ethe*	*atha*	*ete*	*itis*	*eþe > iđi*	**iþ**
3pl	*onti*	*anti*	*ousi*	*unt*	*anþi > andi*	**and**
1du	*ŏ-wes/wos*	*āvas*	--	--	*owez > ōz*	**os**
2du	*ethes*	*athas*	*eton*	--	*(eþez > iđiz)?*	**ats**
3du	*etes*	*atas*	*eton*	--	--	--

Imperative:

	IE	Skr	Gk	Lat	PG	Gothic
2s	*e*	*a*	*e*	*e*	*e > i*	Ø
2pl	*ete*	*ata*	*ete*	*ite*	*eþe > iđi*	**iþ**
2du	*etom*	*atam*	*eton*	--	*(eþan > iđa)?*	**ats**

The development of the IE forms into PG and Gothic is surprisingly regular, allowing for one or two vagaries of the same sort as were encountered in the nominal inflection, e. g. the complete loss of *-iz* on the lst pers. pl. -**amiz*, a parallel to the dative plural -**amiz* > *-am*. The 2nd pers. dual ending **-ats** is a difficulty. If we reconstruct IE -**ethes* on the basis of Sanskrit *-athas*, we would expect, by conventional phonological theory, PG -**eþes* > -**iđiz* > Goth -***iþs**. Gothic **-ats** is therefore doubly irregular: we must account for the *-a-* instead of *-i-* and the *-t-* instead of *-þ-*. There is no unanimously accepted explanation for either one. The *-a-* can always be blamed on an extension by analogy from elsewhere in the paradigm, but one is hard put to state the exact analogy involved. It is more likely that the basis for the analogy lies in the preterite, as discussed just below.

Weak Verbs: Class I.

The IE verbal suffixes *-y-*, *-ey-* had several functions depending on the stress patterns and the type of base to which they were attached. The suffixes are usually written *-ye-* and *-eye-*, but the final vowel is the thematic vowel discussed in the preceding section and not properly a part of the suffix. Before examining the situation in Gothic, a brief preliminary survey from the IE point of view will be helpful. In IE the suffix had both grammatical and lexical functions:

(a) As a grammatical element marking the present tense system of a certain class of verbal roots. There were three possible constructions:

(I) Zero-grade of the verbal root + suffix + stressed thematic vowel. E.g.

*_k̂l̥yé-_ (conceal) > Gothic **hulji-**
*_tn̥gyé-_ (seem) > Gothic **þugkei-**

(2) Zero-grade of the verbal root + stressed suffix _-éy-_ + thematic vowel. There are no clear Gothic survivors of this type, but contrast the Gothic derivative from the IE root *_wreg_ (pursue, press) with normal thematic present tense inflection and the Latin derivative from the same root with zero-grade plus stressed suffix:

*_wreg-e-ti_ > Gothic **wrikiþ**
*_wr̥g-éye-ti_ > Lat _urget_ (inf. _urgēre_)

(3) Full grade of stressed verbal root + suffix _-y-_ + thematic vowel:

*_gʷhédhye-_ (ask for) > Gothic **bidji-**
*_sédye-_ (sit) > PG *_sityi-_ (cf. ON _sitja_, OHG _sizzen_)
*_léghye-_(lie down) > PG *_ligyi-_ (cf. ON _liggja_, OHG _liggen_)
*_séh_$_1$_ye-_ (sow seed) > *_sḗye-_ > Gothic **saii-** [sēi-]
*_h_$_2$_érh_$_3$_ye-_ (plow) > *_ár̥ye-_ > Gothic **arji-**
*_séh_$_2$_gye-_ (track) > *_sā́gye-_ > Gothic **sokei-**
*_skélh_$_1$_ye-_ (divide) > *_skélye-_ > ON _skilja_ (divide)

(b) As a lexical element producing a causative (factitive) verb. There are at least three distinct formal types:

(1) Full o-grade of the verbal root + stressed suffix _-éy-_ + thematic vowel:

*_bheydh_ (persuade): *_bhoydhéye-_ > Gothic **baidei-**
*_kneygʷh_ (bend): *_knoygʷhéye-_ > **hnaiwei-** (bend, tr.)
*_legh_ (lie): *_loghéye-_ > **lagj-** (lay)
*_sed_ (sit): *_sodéye-_> **satj-** (set)

(2) Lengthened o-grade of stressed verbal root + unstressed suffix _-y-_ + thematic vowel:

*_yes_ (seethe, ferment): *_yṓsye-_ > ON _œ̄s-_

(3) Nominal or adjectival base. The formation of these verbs could have taken place at any time from IE through PG and into Gothic. It is therefore not possible to give an IE formula like the above. Most of the denominatives in Gothic are clearly derived from nouns or adjectives still in the Gothic lexicon. E.g.

andbahtjan (to serve) from **andbaht-** (servant; a loan word from Celtic)
mikiljan (magnify) **mikil-** (great)
namnjan (to name) **namo, namins** (name)
maurþrjan (to murder) **maurþr** (_sn_ murder)

From the above, it is evident that Gothic verbs with infinitives in **-jan** derive from more than one source in the parent language. It should also be noted that with the shift of stress to the root syllable in PG the stress distinctions among the various forms of the suffix were obliterated, and only a careful examination of meaning and phonology will enable the reader to classify the form correctly. In many instances, where etymological correlations from other languages are lacking, such determinations are impossible.

The vast majority of weak verbs, class I, belong to the second major category (b) above, being causative (factitive) verbs based on simple IE roots or denominatives formed on elements within Gothic. There is a significant residue, however, of **-jan** verbs where the suffix is a marker of the present tense system; in addition to **huljan**, and **þugkjan** cited above, there are seven verbs in class 6 of the strong verbs: **fraþjan** (understand), **hafjan** (raise), **hlahjan** (laugh), **-raþjan** (reckon), **-skapjan** (create), **-skaþjan** (injure), **wahsjan** (grow). **Hafjan** (< IE **kh₂pyé-*) and **-skaþjan** (< IE **skh₁thyé-*) conform to original IE types, but the rest do not and are probably secondary denominative formations within PG.

Elsewhere in Germanic the verbs **ligya-* (lie down), **sitya-* (sit), and **swerya-* (swear) show present tense systems with **-ya-* (e.g. ON *liggja, sitja,* and *sverja*), but in Gothic these verbs belong to simple thematic types: **ligan, sitan, swaran.** The class 5 strong verb **bidjan**, probably from the IE root **gʷhedh* (to ask for), also belongs to this group. The possible IE forerunners of these verbs are given in sections (a)(1-3) above.

The Germanic Weak Preterite

The preterite of the weak verb is formally a specific Germanic development, but is related conceptually to similar formations elsewhere in IE, namely the union of a verbal stem with an auxiliary verb of *being* or *doing* to form a periphrastic conjugation. When the verbal element, originally a verbal noun or participle, fuses with the auxiliary, it tends to lose its grammatical identity (i. e. inflectional capabilities) and ultimately becomes a fixed or frozen form. Note, for example, the periphrastic imperfect (*videbam*) and future (*videbo*) of Latin, containing a verbal base no longer grammatically identifiable plus inflected forms of an auxiliary **bam, *bo,* most probably from the IE verb **bhewH* (to be), otherwise represented in Latin by *fui, futurus* etc.

The Germanic weak preterite is basically the same for all classes of weak verbs, the vowel before the endings being properly a part of the verbal stem. The terminal inflected element is usually identified with the IE verb **dhē* [**dheh₁*] (do, make; put, place), the parent of Skr *dadhāmi,* Gk τίθημι, Lat *facio,* OCSl *dějǫ,* Russ *дemь, деnу*; OHG *tōn,* Ger *tun,* Eng *do.* As is clear from the Sanskrit and Greek, the verb **dhē* belonged to the class of IE verbs which formed the stem of their present systems by reduplication, **dhedhē-* (> *dedhē-*), a feature that made the equation attractive for the Gothic plural forms **-dedum, -deduþ, -dedun.** Although there is no reason to reject the identification of the terminal element with IE **dhē,* there are serious morphological problems that cannot be resolved easily with the disparate evidence at our disposal. First, however, a brief table of the endings under discussion:

	Gothic	Old Norse	Old English	Old High German
1sg.	-da	*-ða*	*-de*	*-ta*
2sg.	-dēs	*-ðir*	*-des*	*-tōs*
3sg.	-da	*-ði*	*-de*	*-ta*
1pl.	-dēdum	*-ðum*	*-don*	*-tum, -tōm*
2pl.	-dēduþ	*-ðuþ*	*-don*	*-tut, -tōt*
3pl.	-dēdun	*-ðu*	*-don*	*-tun, -tōn*

The plural endings **-um, -uþ, -un** also occur on the preterites of strong verbs, where they are taken to represent a simplification of the older IE perfect or thematic aorist endings **-me > *-m̥ > -um, *-te > *-þ → -uþ, *-n̥t > *-unþ > un,* the *-u-* of *-uþ* being a result of leveling. The singular forms of the above paradigm, at least, can be identified fairly easily with an IE root aorist inflection of **dhē-*, approximately (without the augment)

1sg.	IE	**dhēm*	>	PG	**dǣm > *dǣ*
2sg		**dhēs*			**dǣs*
3sg		**dhēt*			**dǣþ > *dǣ*

1pl.	IE	**dhēme*	>	PG	**dǣme* > **dǣm*
2pl.		**dhēte*			**dǣþe* > **dǣþ*
3pl.		**dhēnt (?)*			**dǣnþ* > **dǣn*

There is no IE inflection of **dhē* that can produce forms that would develop directly into the plural forms given above for Gothic and West Germanic. The only IE verbal stem where reduplication would produce a long vowel in the reduplicating syllable is the intensive, but undisputed examples of this form (*$C_1éC_2C_1oC_2$-) outside of Indo-Iranian are virtually non-existent.

As stated above, there is no simple way out of this dilemma. The frequent citation of OHG plural forms of the preterite of the verb *tōn* (to do), namely *tātum, tātut, tātun,* as the exact parallels of and therefore a proof for the origin of Gothic -**dedum** etc. is somewhat specious, since the OHG forms, as forms of IE **dhē,* are completely unexplainable, as noted at the end of the preceding paragraph. As a possible solution to the problem I would suggest the following historical process, recognizing its highly speculative nature.

1. The old aorist paradigm given above did not exist in a vacuum. As is clear from the evidence of OHG *tuōn* and AS *dōn* (modern English *do*), it served as the preterite of the PG verb **dō-* < IE **dhō-*, the o-grade ablaut of our root **dhē.* When the forms of this paradigm were suffixed to the present stems of the weak verbs to form the new periphrastic weak preterite, they were placed in an unstressed position, since the primary stress of verbal forms shifted to the root syllable in PG. These unstressed endings were then reduced approximately as follows:

Late PG	sg.	**-dǣm*	*pl.*	**-dǣme*	*>sg.*	**-da(n)*	*pl.*	**-dǣm* →	**-dum*
		**-dǣs*		**-dǣþe*		**-dǣs*		**-dǣþ* →	**-duþ*
		**-dǣþ*		**-dǣnþ*		**-da(þ)*		**-dǣn* →	**-dun*

Subsequently, the isolated and obsolescent plural forms of the aorist paradigm with *-ǣ-* were replaced with the newly developed *-um, -uþ, -un* of the strong preterite, as indicated by the arrows. These forms are the immediate forerunners of the Old Norse, Old English, and Old High German forms given on the preceding page.

2. In late PG the new weak preterite forms were extended to the base **dǣ-* itself, thus forming a new preterite for the verb **dō-*:

Late PG / Pre-Gothic	**dǣđa*	**dǣđum*
	**dǣđēs*	**dǣđuþ*
	**dǣđa*	**dǣđun*

The PG verb **dō-* was lost as an independent verb in Gothic, but prior to its loss the plural forms **dǣđum* etc. replaced the simple *-dum, -duþ, -dun* of the weak preterite paradigm.[1] As can be seen from the forms given on the preceding page, this replacement did not take place elsewhere in Germanic. The verb **dō-* survived, as noted above, in English and High German; the new weak preterite **dǣđa* also survived but underwent further analogical alterations under the influence of the base verb **dhō-* and the subjunctive forms . OHG *tātum, tātut, tātun,* however, preserve the given plural forms exactly.

---

[1] The motivation for such a replacement can only be a matter of even further conjecture but was probably due to complex analogies involving the corresponding subjunctive forms. Although we cannot reconstruct with any certainty the original subjunctive counterparts of the IE aorist paradigm underlying the forms under discussion, we may assume for Pre-Gothic, at least, a base **-dī-* for the weak preterite subjunctive, so that the subjunctive forms corresponding to the newly formed **dǣđa* were **dǣđī, *dǣđīs, *dǣđī; *dǣđīma, *dǣđīþ, *dǣđīna.* Such a pret. subj. paradigm immediately invites an analogy with strong verbs of classes 4 and 5 (e.g. Gothic qemi: qam; beri: bar etc.) and the replacement of the indicative singular with **dađ, *dast, *dađ* or similarly. At the period of Pre-Gothic PG when these forms were still in use they would still be interpreted as the free-standing counterparts of the suffixed (and unstressed) preterite endings, and hence provide the motivation for replacing the plural endings *-dum, -duþ, -dun* with *-dedum, -deduþ, -dedun:* a simple leveling through.

3. The past passive participle of all weak verbs was formed with the suffix **-d-** < PG **-d-* < IE *-tós* (cf. Skr *-tá-*, Gk verbal adjectives in -τός, Lat *-tus*, OCSl *-tŭ*). The accidental coincidence of the stems of the preterite and passive participles in all the weak verb classes is undoubtedly of importance for understanding the further development within PG of certain analogical forms treated in Historical Grammar Lesson 6 below. The use of the passive participle is dealt with in Lesson 9.

Etymologies:

hausjan < PG **hawziyan-* (Verner) < IE **kowseye-* < *√kew* (notice, see) + extension *-s-* + suffix *-eye.* Cf. ON *heyra*, Ger *hören*, Eng *hear;* Gr. (ἀ)κούω (< ** -kowsyō*). From the unextended root cf. Lat *caveo* (beware), Gk. κῦδος (fame, < what is heard).

sokjan < PG **sōkijan-* < IE **sāgeye-* < *√sāg* [*seh_2g-*] (follow a trail) + suffix *-eye-*. Cf. ON *søkja*, Ger *suchen*, Eng *seek;* Gk ἡγέομαι (lead), Lat *sagio* (perceive quickly). Related to **sakan** (Lesson 18).

gairnjan < PG **gerniyan-* < IE **ĝherneye-*, a denom. verb from **ĝherno-* (desirous) < **√ĝher* (to desire) + *-no-*. Cf. ON *girna*, Eng *yearn.* The adjectival base **ĝherno-* is found in ON *gjarn* (desirous of), Ger *gern* (willingly). For related words see **gredag-** (Lesson 3).

matjan < PG **matyan-* < IE **modeye-* < *√med* (be sated, intoxicated) + suff. *-eye-*. Cf. ON *metja* (lap up); Skr *√mad* (be intoxicated, soaked), Lat *madeo* (be soaked, steeped in). Others (cf. LIV 380-I) see **matjan** as a denominative from the noun **mati-** (food, meal) < IE **modi-* (portion) < *√med* (to measure).

hailjan < PG **hayliyan-*< IE **kayleye-* < *√kayl* (whole, sound) + denom. suffix *-eye-*. A denominative verb with factitive force on the adjectival base. Cf. ON *heilan* (n. healing), Ger *heilen* (to heal), Eng *heal.* Cf. **hail-** (Lesson 2)

fraqistjan < PG **fra-kwestiyan-* < a denominative factitive verb based on **fra-kwesti-* (destruction) < IE **g^westi-* < **√g^wes* (blot out, extinguish) + nom. suffix *-ti-*. Cf. OHG *firquisten* (to destroy). For the verbal root cf. Skr *√jas* (to be exhausted), Russ *гасить* (to extinguish, destroy).

laisjan < PG **layziyan-* (Verner) < IE **loyseye-* < *√leys* (follow a track or furrow) + caus. suff. *-eye-*. The base verb occurs in Gothic as PP **lais** (I understand). For the root cf. Lat *lira* (furrow, groove), *deliro* (be crazy < go off the track); Ger *(Ge)leise* (track), Goth **laist** (track, < **lois-ti-*). From PG **layzyan* cf. Ger *lehren* (to teach). The Gothic verb **laistjan** (to follow, Lesson 8) is also from this root, as is Eng *learn* (< PG **liz-nōn-*).

merjan < PG **mǣriyan-* < IE **mēr-/mōr-* (large, significant) + suffix *-eye-*. Semantics: *present as significant* > *preach about.* Cf. ON *mǽra* (tell of), OHG *māren.* Ger *Märchen* (fable), Eng *(night)mare* are related nouns. For root word cf. Ir *mór* (large).

sandjan < PG **sandiyan-* (Verner) < IE **sonteye-* < *√sent* (go) + caus. suffix *-eye-*. Cf. ON *senda*, Ger *senden*, Eng *send.* From the PG noun **senþaz* (journey, way) is derived Goth **ga-sinþa** (traveling companion). There is a second set of derivatives from this same IE root with the general sense of *perceive, sense;* cf. Lat *sentio*, Ger *sinnen*, etc.

mag- < PG **maɣ-* < IE *√magh* (be able). Cf. ON *má*, Ger *mögen*, Eng *may;* Skr *magha-* (might, power), Gk μῆχος (means, remedy < enabler), Russ *мочь, могу* (be able).

huzd < PG **huzda-* < IE **kuzdho-* (treasure, what is hidden) < *√(s)kew* (cover, conceal) + extension *-s-* + suff. *-dho-*. Cf. ON *hodd*, Ger *Hort*, Eng *horde;* Gk κύσθος (female sexual parts), Skr *koṣṭha-* (storeroom, innards). The basic IE root **skew* is very prolific with several extensions (cf. Pokorny pp. 951-3).

swein < PG **swīn-* < IE **suwīno-* < *√su(w)* (sow, pig) + *-īno-*. The IE form with *-īno-* is technically adjectival, as in Lat *suīnus*, Gk ὑηνός, OCSl *svinŭ* (of or pertaining to pigs). The form was substantivized in Germanic and Slavic; cf. ON *svín*, Ger *Schwein*, Eng *swine;* Russ *свинья*. The unsuffixed form is found in Gk ὗς, Eng *sow*, Ger *Sau*.

mel < PG **mǣl-* < IE **mēl-* < *√mē* (to measure) + *-lo-*. Semantics: measure > extent. Cf. ON *mál* (measure, time, mealtime, meal), Ger *Mahl(zeit)*, *mal*, Eng *meal*. The root, with its extensions or suffixes *-t-* and *-r-* is well attested; cf. Gk μέτρον (measure), Lat *mētior* (to measure), Russ *мерить*. For **mela** (scriptures) see **meljan** below in Lesson 9.

haim- < PG **haym(i)-* < IE **koymi-* (home, village) < *√key* (lie, be situated) + *-mo-*. Cf. ON *heim-*, Ger *Heim(at)*, Eng *home;* Gk κώμη (village), Russ *семья* (family). The IE root is prolific, with a number of suffixes. Cf. e. g. . Gk κεῖμαι (be situated), Lat *civis* (citizen; < **keywi-*), Gothic **heiwa-** (house, in cpds.).

stols < PG **stōla-* < IE **stālo-* < *√stā* (to stand, set) + *-lo-*. Cf. ON *stól-* (chair, throne), Ger *Stuhl*, Eng *stool;* OCSl *stolŭ* (throne, seat), but Russ *стол* (table). The IE root *√stā* is one of the most prolific; cf. **standan** (Lesson 18), **staþs** (Lesson 7).

razn < PG **razn-* (Verner) < IE **rosn-* < base **res/ros* (rest, dwell) + *-no-*. Cf. ON *rann* (house). The base **ros-* also occurs in PG **rastya-* (resting place, stopping point), Eng *rest*. The IE root structure is not entirely clear, perhaps **√Hre* + *-s-*, or the like. Pokorny gives the plain root as *erə, rē*. The lengthened o-grade of the root with extension *-w-* is found in PG **rōwā* (rest, repose), from which ON *ró*, Ger *Ruhe*.

munþs < PG **munþa-* < IE **mn̥tho-* < *√menth* (to chew; mouth). Cf. ON *muð-*, *munn-*, Ger *Mund*, Eng *mouth;* Lat *mando* (to chew), Gk μασάομαι (to chew, < **mn̥thyá-*).

un- < PG **un-* < IE **n̥-*, the reduced prefixal form of the general negative **ne, né(i)*. Cf. Skr *a-*, Gk ἀ-, Lat *in-*.

unled- < PG **un-* (see above) + **lǣđ-* (property). Cf. ON *láð-* (landed property), AS *lǣd*. The IE affiliations are murky, but the word is probably related indirectly to the Germanic verbal stem **lǣt-* (leave, let), Gothic **letan** (see Lesson 21), with semantics: *what is left over > accumulated property*. Both PG **lǣt-* and **lǣđ-* would presumably be derived from an IE root **lē(i)* with extensions *-d-* and *-t-* (with Verner) respectively. Cf. Pokorny 665-6, LIV 358.

duhwe < **du-** (see Lesson 1) + **hwe**, the old instrumental of **hwas** (see Lesson 6).

bi < PG **bi-* (especially as verbal prefix). Cf. AS *be-*, *bi-*, Ger *be-*, *bei*. The general meaning *around*, *by*, *near* suggests that this is derived from a reduced form of IE **ambhi* (around), Gk ἀμφί, Lat *ambi-* etc.

waiht- < PG **wihti-* < IE **wekti-* (thing). Cf. ON *vétt* (supernatural creature), AS *wiht* (thing, creature), Ger *Wicht*, Eng *wight;* OCSl *veštĭ*, Russ *вещь* (thing). Very probably a derivative of IE *√wek*^{w} (to speak).

Lesson 6

N-stem nouns:

For reasons that will become clear in the discussion below, it is virtually impossible to reconstruct an IE paradigm of n-stem nouns which takes into account both the case endings and the forms of the suffix at the same time. The inflection of the n-stem nouns, apart from the enigmatic nominative singular, conforms to that of IE nouns with stems ending in a consonant and is basically as follows; the nominative singular endings have been omitted because their inclusion in this table would be misleading.

			*IE	Skr	Gk	Lat	*PG	Gothic
Masculine:								
	Sing.	G	*os, es*	*as*	*os*	*is*	*es > iz*	**s**
		D	*ey, ay*	*e*	*i*	*i*	*i*	∅
		A	*m̥*	*am*	*a*	*em*	*u(n)*	∅
		Abl	*os, es*	*as*	--	*e*	--	--
		Instr	*(bhi, mi, H)*	*ā*	*[phi]*	--	--	--
		L	*i, ∅*	*i*	»D	»D	»D	--
	Plural	N	*es*	*as*	*es*	*es*	*es > iz*	**s**
		G	*ōm*	*ām*	*ōn*	*um*	*ō(n)*	**e**, PWG *ō
		D	*bh(y)os, mes*	*bhyas*	*si*	*ibus*	*miz*	(replaced with **-am**)
		A	*n̥s*	*as*	*as*	*es < ens*	*unz*	(replaced with **-s**)
		Abl	*bh(y)os, mes*	*bhyas*	--	*ibus*	--	--
		Instr	*bhis, mis*	*bhis*	--	--	--	--
		L	*su*	*su*	»D	--	--	--
	Dual	NA	?	*āu*	*e*	--	--	--
Neuter:								
	Sing.	NA	∅	∅	∅	∅	∅	∅
	Plural	NA	*ā*	*(āni)*	*a*	*a*	*ō > a*	**a**

Comments: (1) The ablaut variations in the IE *Gs* and *Abls* were probably due originally to differences in stress. (2) The *Ds* ending of Lat, Gk, and PG is the IE *Ls* ending. (3) The *Gpl* **ō(n)* of PG is continued in PWG **ō*, but was replaced in Gothic with our maverick **e**. (4) The *Dpl* of PG and Gothic is probably an extension from the o-stem nouns and was added directly to the stem without the n-suffix. See below. (5) No single reconstruction is possible for the IE Instrumental singular.

A brief survey of the surviving n-stem nominal types in Greek, Latin, OCSl, and Sanskrit will serve to point up the main problems in the reconstruction of the IE prototypes. In the first three of these languages it is necessary to distinguish only two stem allomorphs: the stem of the nominative singular and the stem before all other cases:

Greek	Ns	ποιμήν	Ἕλλην	ἡγεμών	ἀγών
	Otherwise	ποιμέν-	Ἕλλην-	ἡγεμόν-	ἀγῶν-
		(shepherd)	(Greek)	(leader)	(contest)

Latin	Ns	*praedo*	*cardo*	*sēmen*
	Otherwise	*praedōn-*	*cardin-*	*sēmin-*
		(thief)	(hinge)	(seed)
OCSl	Ns	*kamy*	*sěmę* (neuter)	
	Otherwise	*kamen-*	*sěmen-*	
		(stone)	(seed)	

Apart from the *Ns* forms, Latin, Greek, and OCSl show a single invariant stem before the remaining case endings. Some types exhibit a short vowel (Lat *cardin-, nōmin-*, Gk ποιμεν-, ἡγεμον-, OCSl *kamen-, sěmen-*), others a long vowel (Ἑλλην-, ἀγων-; *praedōn-*). Greek has no neuter nominal forms, these having been re-formed as **-n̥t-*stems: *N *(o)nomn̥* > ὄνομα, *G *(o)nomn̥tos* > ὀνόματος. Neuter forms do occur, however, in n-stem adjectives like σώφρων, *G* σώφρονος, neuter *NA* σῶφρον, *NApl* σώφρονα. Although Latin nouns like *sēmen* are predominantly neuter, there are a few masculines, e.g. *flamen* (a class of priest).

The situation with the n-stem nouns in Sanskrit is more complicated. Masculine nouns of the type *rā́jan-* (king), with stress on the first stem syllable, have five distinct stem allomorphs. For purposes of description, the Sanskrit case endings, excluding the *NVs,* are generally divided into three groups: (1) the strong cases: *As, NA Vd, Npl;* (2) the middle cases: all cases with endings beginning with a consonant; (3) the weak cases: all the rest. Taking as models the masculine nouns *rā́jan-, ātmán-* (soul), *mūrdhán-* (head) and the neuter noun *nā́ma,* we have

Ns	*rā́jā*	*ātmā́*	*mūrdhā́*	*nā́ma*
Vs	*rā́jan*	*ātmán*	*mūrdhán*	*nā́man*
Strong	*rā́jān-*	*ātmā́n-*	*mūrdhā́n-*	*nā́mān-*
Middle	*rā́ja-*	*ātmá-*	*mūrdha-*	*nā́ma-*
Weak	*rā́jñ-*	*ātmán-*	*mūrdhn-́*	*nā́mn-*

The masculine type *ātmán-* has fixed stress on the suffix; *mūrdhán-* has fixed stress on the suffix except in the weak cases, where the stress is shifted to the ending. Neuter nouns like *nā́man-*, having the stress on the first stem syllable, differ from *rā́jan-* only in the *NAs nā́ma* and in the dual cases *NA V,* which are treated as weak cases instead of strong. Cf., for example, neuter *nā́mnī* (two names) with *rā́jānāu* (two kings). There are a number of minor varieties and mixed inflections in Sanskrit, but to note them all would not add materially to our discussion.

The development of this confusing situation is assumed to be approximately as follows:

(1) In earliest IE there was a single -n- derivative suffix **-én/-òn* with typical ablaut patterning, probably dependent on stress. The unstressed suffix **-òn* was used to form neuter abstract nomina actionis from verbal roots, while the stressed form *-én was used to form nomina actoris or agentis.

(2) Both suffixes were subsequently extended to other types of bases, i.e. nominal and adjectival, with the eventual blurring of the original action / actor distinction.

(3) The suffixes **-en* and **-on,* by virtue of step (2), became attached to and associated with other suffixes in addition to maintaining their independent status. Especially noteworthy are **-men/-mon, *-yen/-yon,* and **t-yon-.*

(4) The masculine nominative singular form remains something of a mystery. Three different original forms have been proposed:

(a) lengthening of the vowel of the suffix: thus **-ēn/ōn;*
(b) lengthening of the vowel of the suffix and nasalization of the terminal *-n:* **-ẽ̄/-ȭ;*
(c) an ending *-s*, as elsewhere in the inflection of consonantal stems: **-ens/-ons* or **-ēns/-ōns.*

(c) is phonologically questionable; (a) and (b) are made up for the occasion and cannot be proven or disproven.

(5) The neuter *NAs* was endingless. Thus, IE **sēmn̥* yields Lat *sēmen* and OCSl *sěmę* by regular sound changes for these two languages.

(6) Because of the regular phonological development of IE **a, *o, *e* into Sanskrit *a* and IE **ā, *ō, *ē* into Sanskrit *ā*, all qualitative information has been lost in the Sanskrit paradigms. Some of the Sanskrit forms, however, are the result of regular changes: the reduction of unstressed *-an-* to *-n-* before a vowel and **-n̥-* > *-a-* before a consonant. The lengthening of the vowel in the strong form is not a normal process, however, and must have resulted from a partial leveling through of the long vowel of the nominative, a process carried all the way in Latin *praedo, praedōnis* and Greek ἀγών and Ἕλλην, as well as Gothic **qino, qinons**.

(7) Paradigmatic leveling, or simplification, as in the examples just cited, is a common phenomenon and can easily account also for the leveling through of the short vowel stems in Gk ποιμέν-, ἡγεμόν-, Lat *nōmin-, cardin-*, and the OCSl *kamen-, sěmen-*, erasing all distinctions between strong, middle, and weak forms of the suffix. There is no way to know why short vowels prevailed in one paradigm and long vowels in another.

(8) Prior to any extensive leveling the IE paradigm must have exhibited approximately the following stem allomorphs:

Nominative:	*-ẽ̄, -ēn*	*-ȭ, -ōn*	Neuter: *-n̥, -én, -ón*
Strong:	*-en-*	*-on-*	
Middle:	*-n̥-*	*-n̥-*	
Weak:	*-n-*	*-n-*	

(9) One further point to note before turning to the Gothic forms: the Latin type *cardo* and the Slavic type *kamy (< *kamons* or **kamū)* show a mixing of the *-en* and *-on* types. This could easily have come about by various analogies based on the coincident middle and weak forms of the two types. Because of the differences from one language family to another, this probably took place individually in each language family rather than in IE itself.

(10) It is fairly simple to align the allomorphs of the suffix in the Gothic inflections with the scheme presented in (8) above:

Gothic	**-a**	corresponds to IE	*-ēn* or *-ōn*
	-o		*-ȭ*
	-in-		*-en-*
	-an-		*-on-*
	-on-		*-ōn-* by leveling of *-ȭ* or *-ōn*

The *Dpl* forms with no vestige of the suffix, i.e. **attam**, **qinom**, and **hairtam**, are secondary, based on the corresponding forms of the vocalic declensions **dagam**, **gibom**, and **waurdam**. One would have expected something like IE ** -n̥mes* > PG *-*unmiz* > Goth ***-um** (?). When and by what precise analogy this replacement came about is anybody's guess, but it does parallel *Dpl* replacements elsewhere, e.g. the strong adjectival *Dpl* in **-aim** from the demonstrative **þaim**. It is likely that the masc. *Gpl* and *Apl* forms are also analogical re-formations, replacing expected **attnō* and **attnuns* respectively.

It was noted above in (3) that IE **-en-/-on-* became associated and compounded with other suffixes. For **-men-/-mon-* note Gk ποιμήν and ἡγεμών, the many Sanskrit nouns in *-man-*, and Latin neuters like *agmen* and *regimen.* The **-yon-* suffix is legion in Latin, especially in the further combination **-t-yon-* of the nomina actionis or verbi in *-tio, G -tiōnis.* In Gothic the **-yon-* > **-ja(n)-** suffix is used to denote a person associated with the nominal base to which it is attached, as in **gauja** *countryman* (**gawi**), **fiskja** *fisherman* (**fisks**), **baurgja** *citizen* (**baurgs**), **bandja** *prisoner* (**bandi**), **gudja** *priest* (**gud-**), **kasja** *potter* (**kas**) etc. etc. This suffix was obviously productive and freely applied at the time of our texts. While not specifically Gothic, it is not nearly as frequent or as consistently applied elsewhere in Germanic.

Weak verbs of class I with t-preterites.

In discussing the IE background of the Gothic verbs in **-jan**, it was pointed out that a number of these verbs are IE *(e)ye-*presents, i.e. the formative suffix belongs only to the present system, unlike causatives and denominatives, where the suffix occurs throughout the full inflection of the verb. The past passive (or stative) participles of *(e)ye-* presents were formed in PG and Gothic in one of three ways:[1]

(1) As regular strong verb types, with past passive participles in **-ana-** < PG **-ana-* < IE **-ono-*. These include the seven verbs of strong verbs class 6 given on p. 16 and **bidjan**: **bidan-**, **fraþan-**, **hafan-** etc.

(2) As regular weak verbs class I, e.g. **huljan** (conceal), p.p. **hulid-**, **sokjan**, p.p. **sokid-**. This represents an early extension of the present stem to the full paradigm of these verbs.

(3) As irregular verbs with past passive (stative) participles in **-t/-d/-þ**, similar to the weak verbs, but with the suffix added directly to the verbal base. E.g.

PG	**wurhta-*	Gothic	**waurht-**	wrought
	**buγta-*		**bauht-**	bought
	**þāhta-*		**þaht-**	thought
	**þūhta-*		**þuht-**	deemed, seeming

Also belonging to this type are the past passive (stative) participles of the preterite-present verbs:

IE	**mn̥tós*	PG **mundaz*	Gothic	**mund-**	thought
	**gn̥tós*	**kunþaz*		**kunþ-**	known
	**skl̥tós*	**skuldaz*		**skuld-**	obligated
	**tr̥ptós*	**þurftaz*		**þaurft-**	needed
	**maghtós*	**mahtaz*		**maht-**	able
	**ōghtós*	**ōhtaz*		***oht-**	feared
	**oiktós (?)*	**aihtaz*		***aiht-**	owned

Regardless of whether these forms in **-to-* were originally adjectives or true participles, they gravitated to the participial slot in PG. Once this happened, the analogical force of the coincidental identity of past participle and preterite stems in all regular classes of weak verbs led to the formation of new preterite forms for these verbs, e.g.

PG p.p. **nasid-* : pret. stem **nasid-* : : p.p. **wurht-* : pret. stem **wurht-*.

[1] It will be helpful at this point to refer to the section on the past passive participle in Historical Grammar Lesson 9 below.

The Interrogative Pronoun **hwas.**

The reconstruction of the original forms of the simple interrogative pronoun is complicated by the various analogical alterations that have taken place in the individual languages, especially under the influence of the demonstrative adjectives **so-, *to-*. For purposes of comparison, the masculine singular forms are as follows:

	IE	Skr	Gk	Lat	PG	Gothic
N	*k^wis, q^wos*	*kas*	τίς	*quis*	*hwas*	**hwas**
G	*k^weso*	*kasya*	τινός, H τέο	*cuius*	*h^wesa*	**hwis**
D	*k^wosmōy*	*kasmāi*	τινί, H τέῳ	*cui*	*h^wammǣ*	**hwamma**
A	*k^wom*	*kam*	τίνα	*quem*	*h^wan + a*	**hwana**

At least five different stem forms can be singled out:

(1) **k^wi-* as in Gk τίς, Lat *quis*
(2) **k^we-* as in Homeric τέο, PG **h^wesa*
(3) **k^wo-* as in PG **h^wammǣ, *h^wana*, the neuter **h^waþ* (Gothic **hwa**) (cf. Lat *quod*)
(4) **k^wā-* as in the PG feminine *NA *h^wā(n)*
(5) **k^wu-* as in various adverbs like Skr *ku(tra)* where?, Lat *ubi* (if from **k^wudhi;* cf. Oscan *puf*)

The problems associated with the various case forms are so similar to those of the corresponding forms of the demonstrative adjective **so-, *to-* that they hardly bear repeating here. It should be noted that in Sanskrit the assimilation of the two paradigms is virtually complete, with a difference only in the neuter *NAs kim* instead of **kat* (if it had followed *tat*).

The copula (verb: to be), IE **es-*.

		IE	Skr	OCSl	Gk	Lat	PG	Goth	ON
Singular	1st pers.	*esmi*	*asmi*	*jesmĭ*	εἰμί	*sum*	*ezmi > immi*	**im**	*em*
	2nd pers.	*essi*	*asi*	*jesi*	εἶ	*es*	*essi > issi*	**is**	*ert*
	3rd pers.	*esti*	*asti*	*jestŭ*	ἐστί	*est*	*esti > isti*	**ist**	*er*
Dual	1st pers.	*swes*	*svas*	*jesvě*	ἐστόν	--	?	**siju**	--
	2nd pers.	*stes*	*sthas*	*jesta*	ἐστόν	--	?	**sijuts**	--
Plural	1st pers.	*smes*	*smas*	*jesmŭ*	ἐσμέν	*sumus*	?	**sijum**	*erum*
	2nd pers.	*ste*	*stha*	*jeste*	ἐστέ	*estis*	?	**sijuþ**	*eruþ*
	3rd pers.	*senti,sonti*	*santi*	*sǫtŭ*	εἰσί	*sunt*	*senþi > sinþi*	**sind**	*eru*

Gothic **im, is, ist,** and **sind** are directly descended from the parent IE forms. The dual **siju, sijuts** and plural **sijum, sijuþ** have been re-formed on the stem **sij-** with what appear to be the preterite endings of the strong verb (e.g. **wesu, wesuts, wesum, wesuþ**). This description, however, does not account for their existence, which remains unexplained. The Gk, Lat, and OCSl forms show a partial re-formation in which the stem-stressed singular forms have influenced the original ending-stressed plural and dual forms. The ON plural forms also show this same re-forming, suggesting that it may go back to PG or earlier, and that we may conjecture an alternate PG plural paradigm something like **ezmíz > *ézm̥(z) > *ezum, *esté > *est > *ézuþ, *ezénþi > *ézn̥(t) > *ezun*, the *-u-* of the first and third person forms being extended to the second person. This would account, at least, for the endings **-um, -uþ,** and **-un** appearing in this paradigm. The origin of the stem **sij-**, which is otherwise the stem of the subjunctive, remains obscure; it may somehow have resulted from a re-analysis of the normal 3rd pers. pl. **sinþi* as **si-* + **-inþi.*

Etymologies:

waurkjan < PG **wurkiyan-* < IE **wr̥ĝyé-* < *√werĝ* (work, do) + pres. suffix *-yé-*. Cf. ON *yrkja,* Ger *wirken,* Eng *work;* Av *varəz-,* Gk ἔρδω (< **werĝyō*), fut. ἔρξω, ἔργον (noun: work).

bugjan < PG **buγyan-* < IE **bhwghyé-* < (?) *√bhewgh 2* (to bend) + pres. suffix *-yé-*. Cf. ON *byggja* (acquire a wife), Eng *buy.* Semantics obscure but not unreasonable, depending on early Germanic bargaining practices. I think that a derivation from *√bhewgh 3* (enjoy) is equally likely, however, especially in view of Skr *√bhuj* in the meaning to *acquire and enjoy the use of, own, possess.*

anakumbjan < prefix **ana-** (see Lesson 1) + **-kumbjan** < Lat *accumbere.* The alteration of the word is a little odd, suggesting some sort of popular etymology. Cf. also **kubitus** (table company) < Lat *cubitus.*

daupjan < PG **dawpiyan-* < IE **dhowbye-* < IE **dhowb-* (deep) + denom. suffix *-(e)ye-*. Cf. ON *deypa,* Ger *taufen,* Eng *dip.* The IE base **dhewb-/dhowb-* is adjectival and not verbal; cf. Gothic **diup-** (Lesson 4).

gaumjan < PG **gawmiyan-* < PG **gawm-* (attention, notice)< [IE *√ghow* (heed, observe) + extension *-m-*] + denom. suffix **-ya-* < IE **-(e)ye-*. Cf. ON *geyma,* OSax *gōmian,* OHG *goumen.* For the unextended root cf. OCSl *gověti* (to honor), Russ *говеть* (fast, to receive sacrament), Lat *faveo* (regard with favor). Note also ON *gá* (< PG **gaw-*)(to heed). The religious connotations of the Latin and Slavic, missing in Germanic, are probably of IE date.

timrjan < PG **timriyan-* < IE **demro-* (timber) [< *√dem* (to build) + suff. *-ro-*] + denom. suffix *-(e)ye-*. Cf. ON *timbra,* Ger *zimmern.* For IE **demro-* cf. ON *timbr,* Ger *Zimmer(mann),* Eng *timber.* For *√dem* cf. Gk δέμω (to build) and the words for *house* in many IE languages.

managei < PG **managī(n)-* < IE **monogh-* (see **manag-** Lesson 4) + suffix *-īn-* (Lesson 21).

aiþei < ? A Germanic word, but difficult to reconstruct. Cf. ON *eiða* (mother [poetic]), OHG *eidī;* perhaps also ON *edda* (grandmother). Finnish *aiti* (mother) may be relevant as a contact source. Such words (cf. **atta** below) are usually classified as nursery words (Ger *Lallwort*), of the *mamma* and *pappa* variety, and show coincidental correspondences across a host of unrelated languages. They are not, however, without some historical linguistic interest.

atta < ? Like the preceding. Cf. ON *atti,* Gk ἄττα; Turkish *atta.*

aba < ? probably Germanic, but otherwise etymologically obscure. Cf. ON *afi* man (kinship term).

wato < PG **watō(r), G *watiniz* < IE **wodō(r), woden-* (water). Cf. ON *vatn, vatr,* Ger *Wasser,* Eng *water;* Skr *udā* (*G udnás*), Gk ὕδωρ, Hitt *wātar* (G *wetenas*).

kas < PG **kaza-* < ? No known IE source. Cf. ON *kér,* Swed *kar* (tub).

kasja < PG **kazjan-*, a derivative from **kaz-* with the nominal suffix *-yan-*.

waurstw < PG **wurhstwa-* < IE **wr̥ĝstwo-* < *√werĝ* (work, do) + suffix *-stwo-*. See **waurkjan** above.

namo < PG **namō, naminiz* < IE **nomn̥, nomen-* or **nōmn̥*. Cf. ON *nafn*, Ger *Name*, Eng *name*; Gk ὄνομα, Lat *nōmen*, Hitt *lāman*.

frauja < PG **frawyan-* < IE **prowyon-* (one in charge, in front) < *√pro* (forward) + suffix *-wo-* + suffix *-yon-*. Cf. OHG *frō*, OSax, AS *frēa*, ON *freyr* (also name of a god). One of the many forms of the prolific IE root *√per*.

hairto < PG **hertô, -ten-* < IE **k̂erd( )n* (heart). Cf. ON *hjarta*, Ger *Herz*, Eng *heart*, Gk καρδία (< *k̂r̥dyā*), Lat *cor* (< **k̂ord-*), Russ *сердце*; Hitt *karaz (G kardias)*.

qino < PG **kwenô, -nôn-* < IE **gʷen( )n-*. Cf. ON *kona* (*Gpl kvenna*); Skr *gnā*, Gk γυνή, Russ *жена*. Cf. also **qens** (Lesson 7).

ahma < PG **ahman-* < IE **okm( )n-* < *√ok* (to think sthg over) + suffix *-mon-/-men-*. The root is found in Gk ὀκνέω (to hesitate), Gothic **aha** (mind, understanding), and the PG noun **aht-* from which are derived Ger *acht(geben), Achtung, achten*, and ON *ætla* (to think, suppose, < **ahtil-*).

skatts < PG **skatta-* < ? Cf. ON *skattr*, AS *scéatt*, OSax *scatt*. The range of meaning in Germanic is *property, cattle, money*, very much like Gothic **faihu**, ON *fé*, Lat *pecus*. Russ *скот* (cattle) is said to be a loan word from Germanic. There are no cognates elsewhere in IE.

manna < PG **mannan-* < IE **monw( )n* < **mon(u)-* + suffix *-on/-en*. Cf. ON *maðr* (< **mannr*), Ger *Mann*, Eng *man*; Skr *manus*, Russ *муж* (<**man-gya-*). The variation in the suffixes is not entirely clear; the IE base is probably **mon-*.

kald- < PG **kald-* < IE **goltó-* or **goldho-* < *√gel* (be cold) + suffix *-to-* or *-dho-*. Cf. Ger *kalt*, ON *kald-*, Eng *cold*; Lat *gelidus*, perhaps also Russ *холодн-* (cold), although the initial correspondence is not normal. The verbal root is found in Lat *gelare* (to freeze), ON *kala* (be cold).

weih- < PG **wīc-* < IE **weyk-* < *√weyk* (to single out for sacred purpose). Cf. OHG *wīh* (holy), Ger *Weihe* (consecration); Skr *√vik*, Lat *victima* (offering victim, < **wyk-ti-mā)*. Cf. Gothic **weihan** (to consecrate) Lesson 11.

frawaurht- < PG **frawurht-* < **fra-* (see Lesson 12) + **wurht-* < IE **wr̥ĝt-* < *√werĝ* (work, do). Cf. OSax *farwarht* (sinful). See also Goth **waurkjan** and **waurstw** above.

iþ < PG **eþ* < IE **eti* (further on, moreover). Cf. Skr *ati*, Gk ἔτι, Lat *et*.

unte = **und** (Lesson 4) + **tē* (to, until). PG **tē* and **tō* are derived from IE **dē, *dō* (to here, from here). Cf. OSax *tō*, Eng *to*, Ger *zu*; Russ *до*, Lat *dō(nec)* until. Cf. our remarks on Goth **du** (Lesson 1).

Lesson 7

I-stem nouns.

In IE there was no distinction between masculine and feminine nouns of this type; there were i-stem neuters, surviving, for example, in Latin *mare* and Sanskrit *vāri* (water), but none of these is found in Gothic. The neuter forms of *NA* **þrija** (three), however, do represent this type. The following table presents the inflection of Skr *agnis* (fire), Gk πόλις (city), Lat *hostis* (enemy), and Gothic **taikns** (sign). In Gothic the regular development of the nominative and accusative into forms that were identical to those of of a-stem nouns (e.g. **dags**) led to the complete assimilation of the singular inflection of masculine i-stems to that paradigm. The singular forms of the feminine noun **taikns** represent the original IE inflection.

In IE the formative suffix on i-stem nouns had ablaut gradations similar to those discussed with the n-stem nouns of the preceding lesson, but with a difference in distribution. The full grade **-ey-* occurred in the *Gs, Ds, Ls* (*eyi*), and *Npl;* the weak grade **-y = *-i,* elsewhere.

		IE	Skr	Gk	Lat	PG	Gothic
Sing.	N	*is*	*is*	*is*	*is*	*iz*	**s**
	G	*eys, oys*	*es*	*eōs < ēos*	*is*	*aiz*	**ais**
	D	*eyei*	*aye*	*ei («L)*	*ī*	*ǣi («L)*	**ai**
	A	*im*	*im*	*in*	*im → em*	*i(n)*	Ø
	L	*ēi, eyi*	*āu*	*»D*	--	*»D*	
	V	*i, ey*	*e*	*i*	*is*		
Plural	N	*eyes*	*ayas*	*eis*	*ēs*	*īz*	**eis**
	G	*yōm*	*īnām*	*eōn*	*ium*	*iō(n)*	**e**
	D	*imes*	*ibhyas*	*esi («L)*	*ibus*	*imiz*	**im**
	A	*ins*	*īn*	*eis*	*īs → ēs*	*inz*	**ins**

The development of the PG and Gothic forms is relatively uncomplicated. The *Ds* is probably a continuation of the IE *Ls -*ēi* rather than the IE *Ds *-eyei,* which would theoretically have yielded PG **-î* > Gothic **-ī.* The *Gpl* in **-e** has been discussed; PG *Gpl *-yōn* is regularly continued in OHG *-(e)o.*

r-stem nouns.

The inflection and subsequent development of IE nouns with the suffix **-er/-or* closely parallel that of the n-stem nouns discussed in Lesson 6. In Sanskrit there are two slightly different inflections. The first is represented by *kartar-* (doer), a frequent agent noun type, and the second by *pitar-* (father), which includes only the nouns of relationship (*mātar* mother, *bhrātar-* brother, *duhitar-* daughter, *jāmātar-* son-in-law). The five basic stem forms corresponding to those of the n-stem nouns (Lesson 6) are as follows:

Ns	*kartā*	*pitā*
Vs	*kartar*	*pitar*
Strong	*kartār-, -tṝ-*	*pitar-, -tṝ-*
Middle	*kartṛ-*	*pitṛ-*
Weak	*kartr-*	*pitr-*

The only difference is in the strong form, where the type *kartar-* has leveled through the long *-ā-* of the nominative, while *pitar-* retained the original short vowel. The relationship nouns *swisar-* (sister) and *naptar-* (grandson) have the stem forms of *kartar-*, not of *pitar-*. A difference in gender is reflected only in the *Apl,* where masculine nouns have *-n* and feminine nouns *-s.*

Greek πατήρ (*G* πατρός), ῥήτωρ (speaker, *G* ῥήτορος) and Latin *pater (G patris), victor (G victoris)* preserve the distinction between the IE ablaut variants **-er/-or* (cf. **-en/-on*), a distinction lost in Sanskrit and not apparent in Gothic.

Prior to any leveling, the IE stem variation must have been approximately as follows:

Ns	*-ēr*	*-ōr*	>	PG	*-ǣr, -ōr*	Gothic	**-ar**
Strong	*-er-*	*-or-*			*-er-, -or-*		**-ar**
Middle	*-r̥-*	*-r̥-*			*-ru-*		**-ru-**
Weak	*-r-*	*-r-*			*-r-*		**-r-**

The inflection of these nouns followed the general paradigm given in Lesson 6 for IE nouns with stems ending in a consonant. The PG antecedents of the Gothic inflection were approximately

Singular	PG	N	*-ǣr, -ōr* > *-er, -or*	Gothic	**-ar**
		G	*-riz*		**-rs**
		D	*-ri*		**-r**
		A	*-erun, -arun* > *-er, -ar*		**-ar**
		V	*-er, -or*		**-ar**
Plural	PG	N	*-iriz, -ariz*		(→ **-r-jus**)
		G	*-rō(n)*		(→ **-r-ē**)
		D	*-rumiz*		**-rum**
		A	*-runz*		**-runs**

The Gothic *Npl* has been re-formed on the basis of **sunus** (See Lesson 9); the *Gpl* is our familiar maverick. *Ns* **-ar** in Gothic is usually assumed to have resulted from a shortening within PG of **-ǣr/-ōr* to **-er/-or,* as indicated above, or else represents a leveling through of the short vowel of the *Vs* and *As.* There is a possibility, however, that unstressed PG **ǣ* before **r* appears regularly as *ā* in Gothic. Such a development would also allow for the derivation of the agent suffix **-areis** (cf. **laisareis**) from PG **-ǣriyiz* < IE *-ēreyos* instead of being taken as a loan form from Latin *-arius* (cf. p. xv, fn. 5, and p. 309 below).

The Personal Pronouns of the Third Person.

The IE pronouns of the 3rd person exhibit considerable variation in both stem and inflection as one moves from one subfamily to another. A complete reconstruction of the likely IE forerunners of the Gothic forms is for the most part impossible owing to the absence of precise cognates elsewhere. Sanskrit and Latin offer the best parallel to the masculine and neuter singular forms:

		IE	Skr	Lat	PG	Gothic
masc. sing.	N	*is*	*(ayam)*	*is*	*iz*	**is**
	G	*eso, esyo*	*asya*		*is*	**is**
	D	*esmōy*	*asmāi*		*emmōi* > *emmai*	**imma**
	A	*im*	*im(am)*	(archaic) *im*	*in + a*	**ina**
neuter sing.	N,A	*id*	*id(am)*	*id*	*it + a*	**ita**

The variation in the *Gs eso, esyo* of IE was encountered previously (see Lesson I). The *-am* of Skr *imam* and *idam* is suffixal, appearing elsewhere in the pronominal inflection. As noted above (p. 238), the *-a* suffixed in PG to the *As* forms is presumed to be cognate with the Sanskrit particle *ā* < IE **ō*. The *Gs* and *Ds* of the neuter **id* were presumably the same as the masculine forms.

The Gothic masc. pl., with the exception of the secondary *Gpl*, presupposes an IE *N *eyes, D *imes, A *ins*, parallelling exactly the plural of i-stem nouns (cf. **gasteis** above).

The feminine *Ns* **si** may be compared to OIr *sí* and OCSl *si* (this one, f.). The endings of the feminine forms otherwise follow that of the ā-stem nouns (**giba**, Lesson 3), with stems **es-* and **ey-*: *Gs *esās, Ds esāi, As *eyām; Npl *eyās, Gpl *esām, Apl *eyās.* Whether these are genuine IE forms or secondary formations within Germanic is difficult to determine; it is likely that the forms with base **es-* are not IE, but rather extensions from the demonstrative **sa** within PG.

The preterite form **maht-**: see the comments on weak preterites in **-t-** in Lesson 6 above.

The preterite form **iddja.**

Iddja is universally regarded as a derivative of the IE verbal root *√ey- [$h_1$ey-]* (to go) and thus cognate with Lat *eo, ire,* Gk εἶμι, Skr *√i.* There is no firm agreement, however, on which IE form from this root is the actual forerunner of **iddja**, nor on the exact details of its development. The phonological problem surrounding the graphs **-ddj-** has been discussed in the introductory portion of these historical comments. A reconstruction PG **eyy(a)* from IE **eyH-* seems indicated; under current theory, the only form from the root **$h_1$ey-* having the required collocation of consonants would be the first person perfect form **h_1e$h_1$oyh_2a*, where the *-h_2a* is the lst pers. ending. The subsequent loss of the reduplicating syllable would be normal, but **$h_1$oyh_2a* should yield PG **ayya* > Gothic ***addja**, not **iddja**. This explanation would also require the Ist person form to be the base of a new perfect paradigm, possible, but not especially compelling.

In the light of the adjective/participle origin of the stem of the *-t-* preterites proposed in Lesson 6, it is perhaps at least possible that **iddja** has a similar origin. If there existed in PG an adjective **iþyaz* > (Verner) **iđyaz* from IE **ityós* (gone, past), it, like the adjectival forms in *-t-* cited in Lesson 6, could have served as the base of a secondary preterite. That there was such an adjective in PG is suggested by OSax *frēthi,* OHG *freidi* < PG **fra-iþya-* (past, gone, transitory). This explanation would better account for the inflection of **iddja** as a weak preterite. Needless to say, phonological problems still exist, but no more so than in the derivation given above.

Determination of the IE origin of **iddja** is hampered by two factors: (I) our ignorance of exactly what phonetic reality underlies Wulfila's trigraph **-ddj-**, and (2) the absence of any other finite verbal forms from the IE root *√ey* in Germanic other than Old English *ēode* (preterite of *gān* to go), which is inflected like a regular weak preterite. Is *ēode* the exact cognate of Gothic **iddja** or is it a newly formed weak preterite on the base *ēo-*, which could then itself be either the exact cognate of **iddja** or completely unrelated formally. Without further data speculation seems idle.

Etymologies.

andhafjan < **and-** (Lesson I) + **hafjan** < PG **hafyan-* < IE **kapyé-* < *√kap* [*keh_2p*] (to seize, hold) + pres. suffix *-yé-*. Cf. ON *hefja,* Ger *heben,* Eng *heave;* Lat *capio* (seize), Gk κάπτω (< **kapyō*) (to gulp down). See also **haban** (Lesson II) from this same root. For the semantics compare Gk ὑπολαμβάνω to take up (a discourse), respond, answer.

gaggan < PG **gangan-* < IE **ĝhong-* < *√ĝheng* (stride, walk). Cf. ON *ganga,* OSax *gangan,* Ger *gehen, ging, gegangen.* The Germanic verb is probably a re-formation from a denominative **gangyan;* otherwise the derivation from the IE o-grade of the root is unexplained. In fact, the imperfect of just such a verb is attested once in Gothic **gaggida** (Luke 19:12), but the context is difficult.

galeiþan < **ga-** (Lesson 5) + **-leiþan** < PG ** līþan-* < IE **leyt-* (go, proceed; die). Cf. ON *līða,* AS *līþan* (go, travel), OHG *līdan* (go, perish; go through, experience, suffer), Ger *leiden* (suffer, endure).

gawandjan < **ga-** (Lesson 5) + **wandjan** < PG **wandiyan-* < IE **wondheye-* < *√wendh* (turn) + caus. suffix *-eye-.* Cf. ON *venda* (wend, turn), Ger *wenden,* Eng *wend.* For the simple verb PG **windan-* < IE **wendh-,* cf. Goth *windan,* Eng *to wind.* Cognates in Skr and Gk have to do with *braiding, twisting,* a meaning found in Goth **wandus,** ON *vönr* (bundle of twigs, switch), *vandahús* (wicker-house).

niman < PG **neman-* < IE **√nem* (apportion; take). Cf. ON *nema,* Ger *nehmen;* Gk νέμω (apportion, etc.), νέμεσις (fate, one's portion).

bigitan < **bi-** (Lesson 5) + **-gitan** < PG **getan-* < IE **√ghed* (seize). Cf. AS *begietan* (get, beget); the simple verb is found in ON *geta* (get, beget, guess, mention), Eng *get, (for)get, (be)get.* The IE root with nasal infix, **ghend-,* is found in Lat *(prae)hendo* (seize), Gk χανδάνω (seize).

wairpan < PG **werpan-* < IE **√werb* (bend, turn, twist). Cf. ON *verpa* (throw), Ger *werfen,* AS *weorpan,* Eng *warp* (i.e. twist). The various derivatives of the IE root have to do also with flexible plant parts, sticks, switches, and plant names themselves, ranging from Lat *verbena* to Russ *верба* (willow). The Germanic verb was also applied to weaving, hence the Eng noun *warp* (opp. *woof*).

saihwan < PG **sehʷan-* < IE **√sekʷ* (to notice and follow). Cf. ON *sjá,* Ger *sehen,* Eng *see;* Skr *√sac* (follow, accompany), Gk ἕπομαι (follow), Lat *sequor.* Cf. also **siun** *sn* sight (Lesson 13).

sitan < PG **sityan-* < IE **sédye-* < *√sed* (sit) + pres. suffix *-ye-.* Cf. ON *sitja,* Ger *sitzen,* Eng *sit;* Skr *√sad,* Gk ἵζω, ἕζομαι, Lat *sedeo* (an essive form, < **s$_e$dh$_1$yé*), Russ *сидеть.* On the PG > Gothic development, cf. the comments in Lesson 5.

gards < PG **garđi-* < IE **ghordh-* (enclosure) < *√gherdh.* Cf. ON *garðr* (enclosure), OHG *(mittil)gart* (the world), Ger *Gart(en),* Eng *yard;* Skr *gṛhas* (house), Russ *город, -град* (town etc.). The IE root is an extension in *-dh-* of *√gher* (to enclose) from which Lat *hortus* (<**ghor-to-,* orchard, garden) is derived. Cf. also **þiudangardi** (Lesson 3).

staþs < PG **stađi-* (Verner) < IE **stati-* < *√stā* [*steh$_2$*] (to stand) + *-ti-.* Cf. ON *staðr,* Ger *Stadt,* Eng *stead;* Lat *stati(o),* Gk στάσις (**staty-*). The IE root is one of the most prolific, with numerous suffixes and extensions (Pokorny pp. 1004-1010!).

taikns < PG **taykni-* < IE **doyĝni-* < **doyĝ-,* apparently a by-form of **doyḱ-* < *√deyḱ* (to show). Cf. Ger *Zeichen,* Eng *token.* Also from IE **doyĝ-* is the PG verb **taykyan-* > Eng *teach.* For derivatives in Gothic from the root form **deyḱ* see **gatiehan** (Lesson 14).

qens < PG **kwǣni-* < IE **gʷēni-* (wife, woman). Cf. ON *kvǽn, kván,* AS *cwēn,* Eng *queen.* From the same root as **qino** (Lesson 6).

fiskja < **fisk-** (Lesson 1) + **-jan-,** derivative suffix. See Lesson 6.

nati < PG **natya-* < IE **nodyo-* < √*ned* (to tie) + suffix *-yo-*. Cf. ON *net*, Ger *Netz*, Eng *net;* apart from Lat *nodus* (knot), the derivatives elsewhere are complicated by phonetic and semantic factors. See Pokorny pp. 758-9.

broþar < PG **brōþer-* < IE **bhrāter-* (brother). Cf. ON *bróðir*, Ger *Bruder*, Eng *brother;* Skr *bhrātar-*, Gk φράτηρ (member of a brotherhood), Lat *frater*, OCSl *bratrŭ*, Russ *брат*.

swistar < PG **swester-* < IE **swesor-*. Cf. ON *syster*, Ger *Schwester*, Eng *sister;* Skr *svasar*, Lat *soror*, Russ *сестра*. The intrusive *-t-* of Germanic and Slavic probably resulted from the *-sr-* of the inflected forms with the zero grade of the suffix, e.g. *Gs* **swesros* > **swestros*.

dauhtar < PG **duhter-* < IE **dhug(h)əter-*. Cf. ON *dóttir*, Ger *Tochter*, Eng *daughter;* Skr *duhitar-*, Gk θυγάτηρ, OCSl *dŭšti*, Russ *дочь*.

marei < PG **marīn-* < IE **mori-* (sea) + suffix *-īn-*. Cf. OHG *marī(n)*, and without *-īn-*: ON *marr*, Ger *Meer*, Eng *mere;* Lat *mare*, OCSl *morje*, Russ *море*, Ir *muir*.

auþida < (dissimilation) PG **awþiþō* < **awþi-* (< IE **awti-* deserted, waste-) + suffix *-þō* (< IE **-tā)*. The stem is attested in Gothic **auþi-** (adj., deserted, desert), ON *auðr*, Ger *öde*. There are no clear cognates outside of Germanic.

un- < PG **un-* < IE **n̥-*, reduced form of the negative particle **ne*, **nei*. Cf. **ni** (Lesson 1).

unhulþo < **un-** (neg. particle; see preceding entry) + **hulþ-** (gracious) + suffix **-ōn-*. **hulþ-** < PG **hulþ-* < IE **kl̥t-* (inclined) < √*kel* (to incline). Semantics: *inclined to* > *favorable*. Cf. ON *holl-* (gracious), Ger *hold;* OHG *unholda* (witch).

-a (suffix on various prepositions and adverbs indicating static location, e.g. **dalaþa** down below, but **dalaþ** downward) < PG **-ō* < IE **-ā* (< **-aH*), originally an instrumental ending.

dalaþ < PG **dalaþi* < IE **dhol-* (hollow, valley) [base form **dhel-*] + suffix **-te* (motion toward). Cf. Goth **dals** (valley, pit), Ger *Tal* (valley), Eng *dale;* Gk θόλος (domed roof), θαλάμη (animal's lair), Russ *дол* (valley, dale). For the suffix **-te* cf. Gk ἄλλο-σε (to elsewhere). For the **-a** of **dalaþa** see just above.

faur < PG **fur* < IE **pr̥H* (before). Cf. ON *for* (before), Ger *vor*, Eng *(be)fore*. An extended form from the ubiquitous IE base **per* (Pokorny 810ff.). For the **-a** of **faura** see just above.

ut < PG **ūt-* < IE **ūd-* (out, up). Cf. ON *út(i)*, Ger *aus*, Eng *out;* Skr *ud-*, Lat *usque* (< **ud-s-*), OCSl *vŭz-*.

skuld- < PG **skuld-* < IE **skl̥dho-* or **skl̥tó-* < √*skel* (be obligated). Cf. ON *skuld* (debt), Ger *Schuld* (debt). The Gothic form is an adjective/participle of the verb PP **skul-** (Lesson 14).

wiþra < PG **wiþrō* < IE **witero-* (further apart). Cf. ON *við(r)* (against), Ger *wider* (against), Eng *with;* Skr *vitara-* (further). An IE comparative in *-tero-* on the base **wi-* (apart, asunder). For **-a**, see above.

Lesson 8

The weak inflection of adjectives.

In our discussion of the **-en-/-on-* suffix in IE it was noted that the stressed form of the suffix probably designated originally an agent or actor associated with the verbal root to which it was attached. In time the semantic differentiation between **-en-* and **-on-* was obscured, and both forms came to be used, *inter alia*, in this agent/actor function. The suffix was extended to nominal and adjectival bases and gradually acquired, especially in Proto-Germanic, the added notion of specificity, i.e. *anyone who is or does → someone who is or does.* Latin names like *Cato(n-)*, the sly one, from *catus* (sly), and *Silo*, the pug-nosed one, from *silus* (pug-nosed), are cited in this regard (so Wright, p. 104), but the full development of this suffix as marking *specific member of a class* took place in Germanic, and especially in Gothic, where n-stem nouns of the type **blinda** *a blind man* (someone blind) and **weiha** *a priest* (someone holy) are quite frequent. We have already singled out the large number of nouns in **-ja(n)** designating *someone who is associated with.* To some extent, the use of the demonstrative **sa** with these n-stem nouns involves a redundancy, but **sa** is primarily a mark of reference (something already mentioned), a category similar to, but not at all identical with, specificity. Once the collocation of **sa** and the lexically specific n-stem nouns derived from adjectives became fixed, all adjectives used attributively or substantively with **sa** were brought into this syntactic pattern and the so-called weak inflection of the adjective ensued. It would be more to the point in Germanic grammar to designate strong adjectives as indefinite attributives and weak adjectives as definite attributives. When weak adjectives are used predicatively, they are indistinguishable from weak nouns and may be quite properly lexicalized as such.

The active participle.

The active participle in IE was formed by the addition of the suffix **-nt-*, with consonant inflection, to the present stem of the verb. The alternation between *-e-* and *-o-* that characterizes the thematic inflection in IE carried over for some reason into the form of the active participle; **-ent-* was generalized in Latin (cf. 3rd conjugation verbs, e.g. *mittens, G mittentis*), while **-ont-* dominates in Greek, e.g. *παύων, G παύοντος*. Skr *-ant-* may reflect either form.

Gothic **-and-** is derived from IE **-ont-*. Because the active participle is the actor/agent form *par excellence* of the verb, the incorporation of this form into the weak adjective category characterized above follows quite naturally. A few of the original forms of the consonant inflection survive in nouns of the type **frijonds** (friend) (see §10.2).

For the feminine form of the participle in **-ei(n)** see the discussion of the suffix **-ei(n)** in Lesson 21.

Etymologies

af, af- < PG **af* (prep. and verbal prefix) < IE **ap(o)* (away from). Cf. ON *af*, Ger *ab*, Eng *of;* Skr *apa*, Gk ἀπό, Lat *ab*.

afletan < **af-** + **letan** < PG **lǣta-* < IE **lēd-* < √leh_1d (leave, abandon; be weary). Cf. ON *láta*, Ger *lassen*, Eng *let;* Lith *lẽid-* (to leave, let). In the meaning *weary* cf. Goth lat- (lazy), ON *latr*, Ger *lässig*, etc.; Lat *lassus* (tired, < *lh_1dto-), Gk ληδεῖν (be tired, lazy).

laistjan < PG **laystiyan-*, a denominative verb in *-ya-* from **laysti-* (track, trace) < IE **loysti-* < **loys-* + suffix *-ti-*. For the verb cf. Ger *leisten* (do, perform), AS *lǣstan* (follow, perform), Eng *last.* See also **laisjan** (Lesson 5).

rodjan < PG _*rōđiyan-_ < IE _*rōdh_ (bring about, put right [by speaking]) + suffix _-(e)ye-_. Cf. ON _rœða_ (to speak); Skr _√rādh_ (bring about, succeed), OIr _(no-)rāidi_ (say). IE _*rōdh_ is given in Pokorny p. 59ff. as an extension in _-dh-_ of a prolific root _√ar_, but listed as an independent root _√reh_$_1$_dh_ in LIV, where PG _*rōdya-_ < IE _*roh_$_1$_déye-_, a causative base.

sildaleikjan, a denominative verb from the adjective **sildaleik-** (marvelous, wondrous), a compound of (1) **silda-** < PG _*selda-_ (seldom, rare) < IE _*seldho-_ or _*seltó-_ < _*s(w)e_ (self) + suffixes _-lo-dho-/to-_; cf. Ger _selten, seltsam_, Eng _seldom_. (2) **leik-** (form, likeness, body) < PG _*līk-_ < IE _*līg-_; cf. ON _lík_, Ger _Leiche_. The IE element _*sel-_ is also present in **silba** (Lesson 11).

wairþan < PG _*werþan-_ < IE _√wert_ (to turn). Cf. ON _verða_, Ger _werden;_ Skr _√vṛt_, Lat _verto_, Russ _вертеть, вернуть_.

frawaurhts: see **frawaurht-** and **waurstw** in Lesson 6. The only difference between the PG noun _*wurhti-_ and the adjective _*wurhta-_ is in the stem-final vowel. The noun **waurstwja** (worker) below is a derivative in **-ja(n)** from **waurstw**.

mahts < PG _*mahti-_ < IE _*magti-_ <_√magh_ (be able) + suffix _-ti-_. Cf. ON _máttr_, Ger _Macht_, Eng _might;_ Russ _мочь_ (might, power). See also **mag-** (Lesson 5).

mizdo < PG _*mizdōn-_ < IE _*mizdhon-_ (salary, reward). Cf. Skr _mīḍham_ (prize), Gk μισθός (salary), AS _meord_, Ger _Miete;_ Russ _(воз)мездие_.

bloma < PG _*blōman-_ < IE _*bhlōmon-_ (bloom) < _√bhel_ (to bloom) + extension _-ō-_ + suffix _-mon-_. Cf. ON _blóm_, Ger _Blume_, Eng _bloom;_ without the _-mon-_ suffix cf. Gk φύλλον (< _*bhḷyo-_), Lat _folium_, Ir _bláth_ (<_*bhlō-t_).

gahugds < PG _ga-_ (see Lesson 5) + _*hugdi-_ < PG _√hug_. Cf. the verb **hugjan** (to think), ON _hyggja_, OSax _huggean_, and the noun **hugs** _sm_ (thought), ON _hugr_, OSax _hugi_. No IE source is given in Pokorny, but it seems reasonable to derive the Germanic root _*hug_ from IE _*kwgh-_ or _*kwk-_, an extension in _-gh-_ or _-k-_ of the IE root _√kew_ (feel, sense). **hugjan** would therefore be related to **hausjan** (Lesson 5), which is from an _-s-_ extension of this same root, and formally of the same pattern as _bugjan_ (see Lesson 6). The semantics are similar to that of IE _√weyd_ (see **witan**, Lesson 16). For a particular extension of an IE root to be attested in only one subfamily is not unusual.

ansts < PG _*ansti-_ < IE _*ans-_ (gracious) + suffix _-ti_. Cf. ON _ást_ (love), Ger _Gunst_ (< _*ge-unst_). The base _an(s)-_, _un(s)-_ is well attested in Germanic, but the only possible cognate elsewhere is the -ην- of Gk προσηνής (friendly).

andwairþi < PG _*and-_ (see Lesson 2) + _*wirþya-_ < IE _*wertyo-_ < _√wert_ (to turn) + suffix _-yo-_ See **wairþan** above.

triggw- < PG _*trewwa-_ < IE _*drewwo-_ < _√deru, drew_ (be solid, firm) + suffix _-wo-_; cf. ON _trygg-_, Ger _treu_, Eng _true_. From this same root in Gothic are **trauan** (to trust) (see Lesson 11) and **triu** (tree, wood). On the problem of Gothic **-ggw-** see p. 231. Derivatives from this root with meanings related to _tree_ and _wood_ are common throughout IE, but those with meanings related to _firm, solid_ are very rare outside of Germanic and Balto-Slavic. Cf. Russ _здоровый_ (healthy).

swikunþ- < PG **swekunþa-* < **swe-* [< IE **swe-* self] + **kunþa-* (known) < IE **ĝn̥tó-* < √*ĝen* (to know) + suffix **-to-*. For **swe* cf. Skr *sva-* (self), HomGk ἑέ (self), Lat *suus*, Russ *свой* (of oneself). For ***kunþ-** see Gothic **kunnan** etc. in Lesson 16.

swinþ- < PG **swenþa-* < IE **swent-* (healthy). Cf. ON *svinn-*, Ger *(ge)sund*, Eng *sound*. There are no certain cognates outside of Germanic.

mahteig- < PG **mahtīγa-* (Verner) < IE **maghtīko-* < **maghti-* (might, strength) [< √*magh* + suffix *-ti-*] + suffix *-īko-*. Cf. ON *máttig-*, Ger *mächtig*, Eng *mighty*. See **mahts** above and **mag-** in Lesson 5.

dauþ- < PG **dawþa-* < IE **dhowto-* (dead) < √*dhew* (die) + suffix *-to-*. Cf. ON *dauð-*, Ger *tot*, Eng *dead*. From the root without the suffix cf. Goth **diwan-** (mortal, < **dhew-ono-*), Ir *duine* (man, person < a mortal; < **dhw̥nyo-*), and the verbs ON *deyja* (to die), Eng *die*.

sad- < PG **sad-* (Verner) < IE **sato-* (satisfied, sated) < √*sa* [*seh₂*] (be sated) + suffix *-to-*. Cf. ON *sað-*, Ger *satt*, Eng *sad* (!); Lat *satis*, Russ *сытый*.

fulgin- < PG **fulγena-* (Verner) < IE **pl̥keno-* (hidden) < √*pel* (to conceal) + extension *-k-* + suffix *-(e)no-*. Cf. ON *folgen-*. From this same extended root we have the verbs Gothic **filhan** (hide, conceal; with **ana-**: hand down, entrust), ON *fela* (idem), Ger *(be)fehlen* (reflex.: commend or commit oneself). Cognates of the root, with or without other extensions than *-k-* denote *covering, skin, hide, leather*, and the like. Cf. **anafilhan** (Lesson 17).

hweit- < PG **hweyta-* < IE **k̂weyd-* < √*k̂wey* (be bright, white) + extension *-d-*. Cf. ON *hvít-*, Ger *weiss*, Eng *white;* Skr √*śvid* (to shine), Russ *свет* (light, < **swey-t-*).

wairþ- < PG **werþa-* < IE **wert-*. Probably from the same root as **wairþan** (see above), but the semantics are very obscure. There are thirteen roots √*wer* in IE, most of them with numerous extensions, covering practically the full range of human experience and expression. Take your pick. See Pokorny pp. 1150-1166.

all- < PG **alla-* < IE **alno-* or **olno-* <√*al, ol* (to the other side, other) + suffix *-no-*. Cf. ON *all-*, Ger *all*, Eng *all*. Cognates with meaning related to *other, the other side, beyond* (cf. Lat *ulter, alius*, etc.) abound, but the meaning *all* seems limited to Germanic.

afar < PG **afar-* < IE **apero-* < √*ap* (off, away) + comparative suffix *-ero-*. Cf. Skr *apara-* (following, later; extraordinary), ON *afar* (exceedingly). The IE comparative form in *-tero-*, **ap(o)tero-*, underlies Goth **aftra** (Lesson 15), ON *eptir*, Eng *after*. Cf. **af** above.

Lesson 9

u-stem nouns

In IE there was no difference in the inflections of masculine and feminine u-stem nouns; neuter u-stem nouns differed only in the *NAs, NApl.* The forms given in the following table should be compared with those of the i-stem nouns of Lesson 7. The endings and the ablaut gradations are the same: the full grade *-ew-* in the *Gs, Ds, Ls,* and *Npl,* the weak grade *-w-* elsewhere. The endings given are those of Skr *bhānus* (sun), Gk πῆχυς (forearm), Lat *manus* (hand), *NA* neuter of Skr *madhu* (honey), Gk ἄστυ (town), Lat *genu* (knee).

		IE	Skr	Gk	Lat	PG	Gothic
Sing.	N	*us*	*us*	*us*	*us*	*uz*	**us**
	G	*ews, ows*	*os*	*eos*	*ūs*	*awz*	**aus**
	D	*ewei*	*ave*	*ei (≪L)*	*uī*	*ēw (≪L)*	**au**
	A	*um*	*um*	*un*	*um*	*un > u*	**u**
Plural	N	*ewes*	*avas*	*eis*	*ūs*	*iwiz*	**jus**
	G	*wōm*	*ūnām*	*eōn*	*uum*	*iwôn > iwō*	**iwe**
	D	*umes*	*ubhyas*	*esi (≪L)*	*ubus*	*umiz > um*	**um**
	A	*uns*	*ūn < uns*	*eis*	*ūs*	*unz*	**uns**
Neuter	NAs	*u*	*u*	*u*	*u*	*u*	**u**
	NApl	*ua*	*ūni*	*ua*	*ua*	--	--

The cardinal numbers **ains, twai, treis.**

The masculine *Ns* forms of the numbers from *one* to *three* are as follows:

IE	Skr	Gk	Lat	PG	Gothic
oynos	*ekas*	εἷς (<**sems*)	*ūnus*	*ainaz*	**ains**
dwō, dwoi	*dvāu*	δύω, δύο	*duo*	*twai*	**twai**
treyes	*trayas*	τρεῖς	*trēs*	*þrīz*	**þreis**

The inflections and the forms are somewhat variable. The following comments will illustrate the complexity in reconstructing any one IE paradigm for these words.

One. In Sanskrit, *eka-* (< **oiko-*) follows the inflection of the demonstrative *sa-* (see Lessons 1-3), which is essentially the same as that of the a-stem masculines and neuters and the ā-stem feminines. This is formally quite parallel to the Gothic inflection, since the strong adjective follows precisely those paradigms. The IE base **oi-* that underlies both **oiko-* and **oino-* is a demonstrative/pronominal base with numerous extensions throughout the IE subfamilies. Greek εἷς is not cognate with this series. Latin *ūnus* follows a mixed adjectival/pronominal inflection: *N unus, -a, -um, G unius, D uni, A unum, -am, -um.*

Two. Skr *dva-* follows the dual inflection of the demonstrative *sa,* namely masc. *NA dvāu, G dvayos, D dvābhyām,* neuter and fem. *NA dve.* Gk δύο is either uninflected or has *GD* δυοῖν. Latin has masc. and neuter *duo, G duorum, D duobus, A duo(s);* fem. *duae, duarum, duabus, duas.* Gothic **twai** follows the inflection of the plural of the strong adjective (see Lesson 4), a secondary development replacing the original dual inflection of IE. For the

-ddj- of the Gpl **twaddje** (< PG **twayy-* + - *ē*) see §III.4 of the Intro. The Sanskrit forms are presumed to be closest to the original IE inflection.

Three. Skr *tray-* is inflected in the masc. as *N trayas, G trayānām, D tribhyas, A trīn* (<**trins*); neuter likewise except *NA trīṇi.* The feminine is based on a different stem: *tisṛ-*. The Greek masc. and fem. τρεῖς has *G* τριῶν, *D* τρισί neuter *NA* τρία. Latin masc. and fem. *trēs* has *G trium, D tribus, A trēs;* neuter *NA tria.* All of these, together with the Gothic forms, suggest that the original inflection of IE **tri-* followed that of the i-stem nouns quite regularly.

The past passive participle.

The past passive (or stative) participle in Germanic corresponds formally to one of the several verbal adjectives formed in IE with the suffix **-no-* or **-to-*. In Sanskrit, for example, most verbs form this participle by suffixing *-tá-* directly to the reduced form of the verbal root; a restricted group of roots have *-ná-* instead of *-tá-*. Latin has generalized the **-to-* suffix (e.g. *amātus, missus* < **mit-tus, scriptus* < **scrib-tus* etc.), while in Greek the corresponding form is called a verbal adjective, not a participle, e.g. γραπτός (written, < **graf-tós*). The **-no-* suffix is the more frequent one in Balto-Slavic, however, while **-to-* has become restricted.

The **-no-* suffix was generalized in PG for all strong verbs, but a vowel intervenes between the root and the suffix: **-ena-*, **-ana-*. The stress was originally on the suffix, as is evidenced by the reduced form of the verbal root as well as the action of Verner's Law. In PG and Gothic the reduced form of the verbal root underlies the stem of the preterite plural in strong verbs, classes 1-3, with the result that that stem is identical with that of the past passive participle. In classes 4-6, however, the past passive participle preserves the original reduced form of the root, but the stem of the preterite plural must be explained otherwise (see Lessons 12 and 18).

The weak verbs in PG have uniformly **-đa-* < IE **-tó-*, added to the verbal stem with its characteristic suffix, e.g. **-i-* < **-ey-* for class 1, **-ō-* < **-ā-* for class 2, *-ai-* < **-ēye-* for class 3, and **-nō-* < **-nā-* for class 4. On the important coincidence of this stem with that of the weak preterite, see the discussion of the weak preterite in Lessons 5 and 6. The participial adjective of the preterite-present verbs show the suffix **-to-* added directly to the verbal root, as in Sanskrit and some Latin forms (see Lesson 16).

Etymologies

manwjan, a denominative verb based on the adj. **manwu-** (ready, prepared), possibly, through the meaning *at hand,* to be derived from the IE base **manwu-* < **manu-* (hand) + suffix *-u-*. IE **manu-*, whence Lat *manus,* is a late IE formation based on the earlier heteroclitic *r/n*-stem **mar-/man- (or *mər-/mən-).* Gothic **manwu-** is isolated within Germanic.

taujan < PG **tawyan-* < IE ? Cf. ON *tœja* (help, avail), AS *tāwian* (prepare), Eng *taw* (prepare hides).

þiuþjan, a denominative verb from the noun **þiuþ** (blessing) < PG **þewþa-* < IE **tewto-* < *√tew* (to be favorably inclined) + suffix *-to-*. Cf. ON *þýð-* (friendly), AS *geđīede* (good, virtuous); Lat *tueor* (protect).

lagjan < PG **laɣyan-* < IE **logheye-* (to lay) < *√legh* (to lie) + caus. suffix *-éye-*. Cf. ON *leggja,* Ger *legen,* Eng *lay;* Russ *ложить*. For cognates from the non-causative stem see **ligan** (Lesson 18).

meljan < PG **mǣliyan-*, a denominative verb from **mæla* (written signs; Goth **mela**) < IE **mēl-*, lengthened grade of *√mel*, a root found in words denoting ***black, dark-colored.*** Cf. ON *mæla* (to paint, color), Ger *malen* (to paint); Skr *malina-* (black, dirty), Gk *μελαν-* (black), Russ *малина* (raspberry).

sunus < PG **sunu-* < IE **sūnus* (son) < *√sewH* (to bear a child) + suffix *-nu-*. Cf. ON *sunr, sonr,* Ger *Sohn,* Eng *son;* Skr *sūnus,* Gk υἱός (< *υἱύς < **su-y-us*); Russ *сын.*

magus < PG **maγu-* < IE **maghu-* (boy). Cf. ON *mögr,* OSax *magu;* Ir *mac* (son). See also **mawi** (Lesson 3).

faihu < PG **fehu* < IE **peḱu-*(cattle). Cf. ON *fé,* AS *feoh,* Ger *Vieh;* Skr *paśu-,* Lat *pecu.* The IE root here is *√peḱ* (to shear), found in Gk πέκω, Lat *pecto.*

taihswo < PG **tehswōn-* < IE **deks-* (right side) + suffix *-*won-*. Cf. Skr *dakṣina-* (right, south), Gk δεξιός, Lat *dexter.*

hleidumei < PG **hlīdum-* < IE **ḱlītm̥-* (slanting, not straight) [< *√ḱley* (to lean)] + superlative suffix *-tm̥-* (see Lesson 20). Cf. ON *hlíð* (slope); Ir *clé* (left side), Skr *śrita-* (leaning), Gk κλιτός (leaning). The root is well attested throughout IE (see Pokorny pp. 601-2). Semantics: the association of *left* and *off-center* with *unlucky* and *inauspicious* belongs to the IE institution of augury; cf. Lat *clivius* (inauspicious) from this same root, and the Greek euphemism for the left side, εὐώνυμος, literally *of good name, propitious.*

boka < PG **bōkō* < IE **bhāgā* (beech tree). Cf. ON *bók* (beech; book), Ger *Buch* (book), *Buche* (beech), Eng *book, beech;* Gk φηγός (oak), Lat *fagus* (beech). Apparently beech bark was used for the inscribing of runes.

hairdeis < PG **herdhiya-*, a derivative in *-ya-* from **herdhō* (herd, Goth **hairda**) < IE **ḱerdhā.* Cf. ON *hirðir* (herdsman), Eng *-herd,* Ger *Hirt;* Skr *śardha-* (herd), OCSl *črěda.* Also related are several words denoting *row, sequence,* such as Russ *череда.*

dauþus < PG **dawþu-* < IE **dhowtu-* < **dhowt-* (dead) [see **dauþ-** in Lesson 8] + suffix *-u-*. Cf. ON *dauði,* Ger *Tot,* Eng *death.*

wulþus < PG **wulþu-* < IE **wl̥tu-* (aspect, respect). Cf. AS *wuldor* (glory); Lat *vultus* (face, appearance). The poorly attested IE root *√wel* (to see?), extended as **wleyd-/*wloyd-*, is attested in the Gothic verb **wlaiton** (to look about) and the noun **andawleizn** (face), Ger *Antlitz.*

handus < PG **handu-* < IE ? Cf. ON *hönd,* Ger *Hand,* Eng *hand.* The verbs **frahinþan** and **ushinþan** (to capture, take prisoner) suggest the existence of a root *√kent* (to seize); the noun **kontus* would have meant *seizer* or *thing held.* Possible cognates are Skr *kunta* (spear) and Gk κοντός (shaft, sounding-pole), although the latter is usually assigned to the root *√ḱent* (see **handug-**, Lesson 15).

bida < PG **beđō* < IE **bhedhā* (entreaty? < *√bhedh* (bend, bow the knee). Outside of Germanic the cognates listed for this root (Pokorny p. 114) have to do with *bending, bowing* or *shunning, avoiding,* making the derivation a little uncertain. A semantically more satisfactory etymology has been proposed by Seebold, *Zeitschrift für vergleichende Sprachforschung auf dem Gebiete der indogermanischen Sprachen* 81 (1967), 104-33, and elsewhere, deriving the related verb *bidjan* from IE **ghʷedh* (beg, ask for), but the phonological change of IE **ghʷ* > PG **b* poses serious difficulties. This etymology is assumed in the discussion of **bidjan** in connection with the suffix *-eye-* in Lesson 5, q.v. See also **bidjan** (Lesson 12) for further remarks.

uf < PG **uf-* < IE **upo* (under, up from under). Cf. ON *of,* Ger *auf,* Eng *up;* Skr *upo,* Gk ὑπό, Lat *(s)ub.*

ufta < PG **ufta* < IE ? Cf. ON *opt,* Ger *oft,* Eng *oft(en).* Apparently a Germanic development from the root **uf* of the preceding entry. For the meaning, compare the further derivative **ufjo** (superfluity).

samaleiko < PG **samalīkô* < **saman-* (same; see Lesson 11) + **līka-* (body, form; see Lesson 11) + the adverbial suffix *-ô.*

sums < PG **suma-* < IE **sm̥o-* (some) < √*sem* (one, same, together). Cf. ON *sum-,* OHG *sum,* Eng *some;* Skr *sama-,* Gk ἁμο- (base of ἁμοῦ *somewhere,* ἁμόθεν *from somewhere or other*). The IE root appears in several base forms and extensions; see Pokorny pp. 902-5.

Lesson 10

Weak verbs: class 3.

The verbs of this class are characterized in IE by a suffix **-ē*, earlier **-h$_1$yé-*, added to the zero grade of the root. The suffix is termed *essive* and generally forms verbal stems denoting duration in a state or condition; the term *stative* could also be used. The closest parallel to this class is the Latin second conjugation, where such pairs of verbs as *pendēre* (to be suspended) *vs* third conjugation *pendere* (to hang sthg up) and *jacēre* (to lie, be situated) *vs* third conjugation *jacere* (to throw) nicely illustrate the semantic distinction between the simple transitive verb (third conjugation) and the suffixed essive (or stative) verb.

The gradual phonological merging of the various IE verbal suffixes containing *-y-* (see the types listed in Lesson 5 above, in addition to the essive suffix of the present lesson) led to the extension of the function of the *-ē-* suffix to the closely related iterative and denominative functions, making an exact classification of these verbs virtually impossible. It is unlikely, for example, that genuine essive verbs possessed a preterite passive (perfective) participle, since being intransitive and imperfective by definition would preclude the existence of such a form. The participle in -**aid**- characteristic of these verbs results from the generalization of the -**d**- participle throughout the weak verbal system.

Of the verbs belonging to this class only the following could have originated in true essive types in IE, i.e. zero grade of the root + formative suffix **-h$_1$yé-*:

bauan	< **bhū'ē-* < **bhẉh$_2$h$_1$yé-*	**bhewh$_2$* (to be, dwell)
haban	< **kapē-* < **kh$_2$ph$_1$yé-*	**keh$_2$p* (to seize, hold)
liban	< **libē-* < **lỵbhh$_1$yé-*	**leybh* (to live)
-silan	< **silē-* < **sỵlh$_1$yé-*	**seyl* (to be still, secondary to **sey*)
þahan	< **tahē-* < **th$_2$kh$_1$yé-*	**teh$_2$k* (to be silent)
þulan	< **tḷ'ē-* < **tḷh$_1$h$_1$yé-*	**telh$_1$* (to bear, tolerate)
trauan	< **drū'ē-* < **drẉHh$_1$yé-*	**drewH* (to be firm like a tree)
witan (observe)	< **widē-* < **wỵdh$_1$yé-*	**weyd* (to know)

The two verbs **faian** (to find fault with) and **fijan** (to hate) are both derived from the same IE root **pē, *pi-*, earlier **peh$_1$y-* or the like. The combination of two laryngeals and two *y*'s in **ph$_1$yh$_1$yē-* makes reconstruction sheer guesswork. **Bauan** and **trauan** are usually treated as denominatives based on IE **bhōw-* and **drōw-* respectively (see under etymologies in Lesson 11), but the derivations given above suit the Germanic evidence better.

The PG forms transitional to Gothic and the rest of Germanic are generally reconstructed with the stem **-ǣy-* (i.e. with an additional **-y-*), followed by the regular thematic inflection in the present indicative: **-ǣya, *-ǣyizi, *-ǣyiþi*, etc. Because the contractions assumed for producing the subsequent forms are difficult to parallel elsewhere, the possibility should be allowed that the PG stem form was simply **-ǣ-*, inflected athematically, i.e. **-ǣmi, *-ǣsi, *-ǣþi* in the present, and that the digraph -**ai**- in the Gothic paradigm results from simple unstressed **ǣ* and was never diphthongal. The extreme contractions represented by **haba, habam, haband**, the infinitive **haban**, and the active participle **haband**- would be a result of a simple sound change: unstressed PG **-ǣ-* before a nasal > Gothic **-a-*.

The Personal Pronouns of the First and Second Person

		IE	PG	Gothic	Old Norse	Anglo-Saxon
1st sing.	N	**eĝ(ō)*	**ik, ek*	*ik*	*ek*	*ic*
	G	*(*mey-no-)*	**mīn-*	*meina*	*mín*	*mīn*
	D	**mĕy*	**mĕ(z)*	*mis*	*mér*	*mĕ*
	A	**mĕ*	**mĕk, *mik*	*mik*	*mik*	*mek, me*
2nd sing.	N	**tŭ*	**þŭ*	*þu*	*þú*	*þŭ*
	G	*(*tey-no-)*	**þīn-*	*þeina*	*þín*	*þīn*
	D	**tĕy*	**þĕ(z)*	*þus*	*þér*	*þĕ*
	A	**tĕ*	**þĕk, *þik*	*þik*	*þik*	*þĕ(k)*
1st plural	N	**wey(s)*	**wēz, *wiz*	*weis*	*vér*	*wĕ*
	G	*(*n̥s-er-)*	**unsar-*	*unsara*	*vár*	*ūser*
	D	**n̥s-?*	**uns(iz)*	*uns(is)*	*oss*	*ūs*
	A	**n̥s-?*	**uns(iz)*	*uns(is)*	*oss*	*ūs(ik)*
2nd plural	N	**yu(s)*	**yuz*	*jus*	*(þ)ér*	*gĕ*
	G	*(*esw-er-)*	**ezwar-*	*izwara*	*yðar*	*ēowar*
	D	**esw-?*	**ezwiz*	*izwis*	*yðr*	*ēow*
	A	**eswe*	**ezwiz*	*izwis*	*yðr*	*ēow(ic)*
1st dual	N	**we-dwō*	**wit*	*wit*	*vit*	*wit*
	G	*(*n̥g-er-)*	**unkar-*	**ugkara*	*okkar*	*uncer*
	D	**n̥g-?*	**unkiz*	*ugkis*	*okkr*	*unc*
	A	**n̥ge*	**unkiz*	*ugkis*	*okkr*	*unc(it)*
2nd dual	N	**yu-dwō*	**yut*	**jut*	*þit*	*git*
	G	*(*ingw-er-)*	**inkwar-*	*igqara*	*ykkar*	*incer*
	D	**ingw-?*	**inkwiz*	*igqis*	*ykkr*	*inc*
	A	**inge*	**inkwiz*	*igqis*	*ykkr*	*inc(it)*

(1)The anceps vowels in IE and PG arose from the fact that the pronouns occurred in both stressed and unstressed positions; the long vowel represents the stressed form and the short vowel the unstressed. This same feature also accounts for the variation between stressed **e* versus unstressed **i* in PG.

(2) Each of the pronouns had two distinct bases in IE, one for the nominative and another for the oblique cases. The latter form was inflected for case, as illustrated by the dative and accusative forms given above.

(3) The original genitive forms are not given since they were replaced in the IE dialect leading to PG by a form of the possessive adjective in **-no-* or **-ero-*: **meyno-, *teyno-, *n̥sero-, *eswero-, *n̥gero-, *ingwero-*. The final **-a** of all the Gothic forms may have originated in the IE Gpl ending **-ōn* and have been extended from the plural forms to those of the singular.

(4) The source of the final **-z* of PG **mĕz* and the final **-iz* of the plural dative and accusative pronouns is problematic. There are various possible sources in the locative and instrumental forms of the IE nominal and

pronominal inflections, but the analogies necessary for the extension of the ending to these pronominal bases are completely unconvincing.

(5) The final **-k* of the accusatives **mĕk, *mik, *þĕk, *þik* is generally regarded as a reflex of the IE particle **-ge,* also found on Greek pronominal forms like ἔγωγε, ἐμέγε.

(6) The final **-z* of the PG nominative forms **wēz* and **yuz* is probably IE in origin since it is also found in Hittite *wēs* (we), Tocharian *wes* (we), and Lithuanian *mes* (we) and *jus* (you).

(7) The lst pl. oblique stem **n̥s-* is the reduced form of IE **nĕs, *nŏs,* familiar from Latin *nōs* (we, us).

(8) The 2nd pl. oblique stem **esw-* is an alternate IE oblique stem to **wĕs, *wŏs* (cf. Latin *vōs*), also found in Proto-Celtic and perhaps underlying the Greek dual form σφώ.

(9) The final *-t* of PG **wit* and **yut* is of disputed origin. In view of the Lithuanian dual pronouns *vedu* < **wedwō* (we-two) and *judu* < **yudwō* (you-two) it is difficult not to see **wit* and **yut* originating in the same way, with an early shortening of the final element: PG **witwa* > **wit,* PG **yutwa* > **yut.*

(10) The lst dual oblique stem probably originated in the accusative form **n̥ge* < **n̥* (reduced form of **ne-*) + the particle **-ge* already mentioned above in connection with **mik**. The oblique dual stem **ne-* is well attested in its ablaut variant **nō-* in Skr *nā-u,* Gk νώ.

(11) If a similar origin be posited for the 2nd person accusative **inge,* it would require a base **yen-* + **-ge* > **ingé.* The *-w-* of PG **inkwiz-* and **inkwar-* would be extended from the 2nd person plural forms **izwiz* and **izwar-.* There is, however, no evidence for an IE base **yen* unless it be an assimilated form of **yem-* (twin, duality), i.e. **yemgé* > **yengé.* An IE compound expression such as accusative **ves-yengé* (you the pair, the pair of you), a forerunner of the similar pairing underlying **wit* and **yut* discussed just above, could have been reduced subsequently to simple **yengé* > **ingé.*

Etymologies:

haban < PG **haƀǣn* < IE **kapē-* < *√kap* [*keh₂p*] + essive suffix *-h₁yé-*. Cf. ON *hafa,* Ger *haben,* Eng *have;* Lat *capio,* Gk κάπτω (to gulp down). The IE root is well attested in various words for utensils and devices for holding and gripping; it also underlies Gothic **haftjan** (to join), **hafjan** (to raise up), and the adjective **haft-** (joined).

fijan < PG **fiyǣn-* < IE **piyē-* < *√pēy* [*peh₁y*] (to harm, cause distress to) + essive suffix *-h₁yé-*. Cf. ON *fjá* (to hate); Skr *√pīy* (to abuse). Cf. also the active participle PG **fiyand-,* Gothic **fijands** (enemy), ON *fjándi,* Ger *Feind,* Eng *fiend.*

þahan < PG **þahǣn-* < IE **takē-* < *√tak* [*teh₂k*] + essive suffix *-h₁yé.* Cf. ON *þagnan* (remain silent), OHG *dagēn,* OldSax *thagōn;* Lat *taceo.*

witan, witaida < PG **witǣn-* < IE **vidē-* < *√weyd* (to see) + essive suffix *-h₁yé-*. Cf. Lat *video,* OCSl *viděti,* Russ *видеть.* This is one of the many derived verbs of seeing and knowing from this IE root; note also Gothic **-weitan** in **fraweitan** and **inweitan** (Lesson 14) and the preterite-present verb **wait** (Lesson 16).

fastan < PG **fastǣn-* < IE **pastē-* < adj. base **pasto-* (firm, fast) + denom. suffix *-ē-*. Cf. ON *fasta* (to fast), Ger *fasten* (to fast), Eng *to fast.* From a second denominative PG **fastyan-* we have ON *festa,* OHG *festen,*

AS *fæstan,* all meaning *to fasten, make secure.* Other denominatives occur: Eng *fasten,* Ger *(be)festigen.* The Gothic verb appears to have combined the semantic functions of both PG verbs. Apparently, the only non-Germanic cognate is Skr *pastyam* (dwelling place; cf. Eng *fastness*).

liban < PG **libǣn-* < IE **libhē-* < √*leybh* (to live) + essive suffix *-ē* < *-h₁ye-*. Cf. ON *lifa,* Ger *leben,* Eng *live.* Other than the possible Latin cognate *-lebs* in *caelebs* (one who lives alone), the root is confined to Germanic. If one accepts the possibility that IE labio-velars like g^w and k^w might sporadically produce labial reflexes in Germanic (see HG Intro., §II), a connection with the IE root **leyk*^{w} (leave behind, remain) would appear promising, especially since this would very well suit the meaning of the non-suffixed verb (**bi**)**leiban** (remain), assigned somewhat unsatisfactorily by Pokorny to the root **leyp* (to smear, dirty). It may not be possible in the long run to maintain **leybh,* **leyk*^{w}, and *leyp* as independent roots. LIV, on the other hand, regards **liban** as the essive of √*leyp* (thus **lyph₁yé-*) and **bilaif** (the only attested form of **bileiban**) as a perfect of the root verb; LIV assigns the meaning *kleben bleiben* to the root.

nasjan < PG **nasyan-* < IE **noséye-* < √*nes* (regain one's original state) + caus. suffix **-éye-*. Cf. Ger *nähren* (to nourish, < OHG *nerian* < **nezyan*). The non-causative verb is attested in Gothic (**ga**)**nisan** *to recover, be saved.* Cf. Skr √*nas* (join, embrace), Gk νέομαι (to return home).

nehwjan, a denominative verb in **-jan** formed from the base **nehw-**. As indicated in Lesson 2 above, the etymology of **nehwa** remains uncertain.

giban < PG **geḇan-* < IE **ghebh-*. The root is attested only in Germanic: ON *gefa,* Ger *geben,* Eng *give.* The derivation (so Pokorny, p. 408) from IE **ghabh-* (to seize, hold) is phonologically and semantically difficult.

frijonds < PG **friyond-*, the nominalized participle of the verb **frijon** (to love) < IE √*prī* (to love). Cf. ON *frændi* (friend, kinsman), Ger *Freund,* Eng *friend;* Skr √*pri* (be pleased with), Russ *приятель* (friend).

baurgs < PG **burg-* < IE **bhr̥gh-* < √*bhergh* (to be high, elevated). Cf. ON *borg,* Ger *Burg,* Eng *borough, -bury, -burg;* Skr √*br̥h* (make big or strong), Lat *fortis* (strong, < **forktis* < IE **bhr̥ghtós*), OCSl *brěgŭ* (cliff, shore), Russ *берег.*

bokareis < **boka** (Lesson 9) + suffix **-areis** (see Lesson 21).

kunþi < PG **kunþya-* < IE **ĝn̥tyo-* < √*ĝen* (to know) + suffix *-tyo-*. Cf. Ger *Kunst* (knowledge, art). This is one of the many nominal derivatives from the IE root √*ĝen* (to know). See **kunnan** (Lesson 16) for further information.

laun < PG **lawna-* < IE **lawno-* < √*lāw* (to win, gain) + suffix *-no-*. Cf. ON *laun,* Ger *Lohn,* Eng *loan.* The IE root, with different suffixes, is attested in Gk ληστής (robber), Lat *lucrum* (gain, < **lutlom*), Russ *лов* (catch, in hunting or fishing).

alhs < PG **alh-* < IE **alk-* (to set aside for sacred use, or sim.). Cf. AS *ealh;* Skr √*rakṣ* (to protect), Gk ἀλέξω (to ward off, < **alek-s-*).

fon < PG *fōn-* < IE **pwōn- (G *punés, L *puwéni).* Cf. ON *funi,* Ger *Fun(ke)* (spark). The IE noun was of the alternating r/n-stem type, with an original nominative **pūr or *pewōr,* the forerunner of Ger *Feuer,* Eng *fire,* Gk πῦρ, etc.

armaio < PG **armǣ(y)ōn-*, a noun in **-ōn-* derived from the verbal stem **armǣ-* (to pity, have mercy on), Gothic **arman,** AS *earmian,* Ger *-(b)arm-* in *erbarmen.* The PG verb **armǣ-* is apparently a denominative from the adjectival base **arm-* (poor, needy), ON *arm-*, Ger *arm-*, which is itself etymologically obscure, but probably related to IE **orbho-* (orphaned, unprotected). The shift in semantics belongs to the class of causatives sometimes termed *estimative*, where *to cause to be needy* shifts to *to regard as needy*, hence *to pity*. This is a fairly common phenomenon with causative/factitive derived verbs.

idreiga: there is no clear etymology. The first element **id-** may be a prefix from IE **eti* (away, across, back); the second element is probably related to IE *√re(y)k*, a motion verb of *extending upward, erecting*, well attested in Germanic, e.g. Ger *regen* (arouse, move), *rücken* (to back up), Eng to *rock*, etc. The semantic result *turn away/back > to repent* is appealing.

bandi < PG *bandyō* < IE **bhondhyā-* < *√bhendh* (to bind) + suffix **-yā-*. Cf. ON *bant*, Ger *band*, Eng *band;* Skr *bandha-*. For further derivatives see the verb **bindan** in Lesson 17.

þatei, a compound of **þata** (Lesson 2) and **ei**, a relative particle occurring both alone (see Lesson 15) and in various compounds, e.g. the relative pronouns **saei** etc. (Lesson 11). It is ultimately derived from the locative form **ei* of the IE pronominal base **i-* or **e-*, which in one form or another is represented throughout the IE family.

aiþþau is a compound form of obscure origin, but probably related to ON *eða* (or) and AS *eđđa* (or).

-eins (verbal noun termination): see Lesson 22.

at < PG **at* < IE **ad* (to, at). Cf. ON *at*, OHG *az*, Eng *at;* Lat *ad.*

Lesson 11

Etymologies:

sama < PG **saman-* < IE **somen-, somon-* < *√sem* (one, same, together) + suffix **-on/en-*. Cf. ON *samr*, Ger *sam(t)*, Eng *same*. For *√sem* alone cf. Gk εἷς (< **sems* one), Russ *сам*, and with suffixed **-el-*, Lat *similis, semel*.

silba < PG **selban-* < IE **selbhon-, selbhen-* < *√se* (self) + suffixes *-l-bh-on/en-*. Cf. ON *sjálf*, Ger *selbe*, Eng *self*. For **sel-* cf. **sildaleikjan** (Lesson 8). IE *√se* provides the base for many reflexive pronouns, e.g. Gk σφε, Lat *se, suus*, Russ *-ся, свой*. See also **swes-** (Lesson 15), **swe, swa** (Lesson 13).

wiljan < PG **welyan-* < IE *√wel* (to want, wish) + pres.(?) suffix *-ye-*. Cf. ON *vilja*, Ger *wollen* (*ich will*), Eng *will*; Skr *√vṛ* (to choose), Lat *velle, volo*. The present tense of this verb is properly the preterite subjunctive, for which see HG Lesson 15.

arman < PG **armǣ-* < ? See **armaio** (Lesson 10).

bauan < PG **bōwǣ-*, usually assumed to be derived from the lengthened o-grade of *√bhewH* (to be, live, dwell). Cf. ON *búa*, Ger *bauen*. The IE root is well attested in many derived forms throughout IE, e.g., Skr *√bhū* Gk φύω, Lat *fui, fio*, Russ *быть*. The exact reconstruction of the underlying PG and IE forms for the verbs **bauan** and **trauan** is uncertain. I have given here the generally accepted version, but as indicated in Lesson 10 above, both of these verbs may also be regarded as proper essive forms in IE, i.e. zero-grade of root + essive suffix: PG **būwǣ-* < IE **bhūwē-* < **bhwHh$_1$yé-* and PG **trūwǣ-* < IE **drūwē-* < **drwHh$_1$yé-*.

leikan < PG **līkǣ-* < IE **līgē-* < *√leyg* (to be like) + denom. suffix *-ē-*. Cf. ON *líka*, Eng *like*, Ger *(g)leichen*. The IE root is well developed in Germanic (cf. the nouns **leik** and **leikeis** below, as well as the adjective **galeik-** in Lesson 15). Elsewhere, however, it is found only in Lithuanian. The semantics are approximately *to be like > to conform to expectations > to please*.

liugan < PG **lewɣǣ-* < IE **lewghē-* < *√lewgh* (an oath) + denom. suffix **-ē*. The root is found in Celtic with the meaning *oath* and in Germanic with meanings ranging from Gothic *marriage* to OHG *warfare* in the compound *urliugi* < PG **uslewɣɣa-*, presumably as treatied and non-treatied situations respectively.

trauan < PG **trōwǣ-* (or **trūwǣ-*) < IE **drōwē-* (or **drūwē-*) < **drōw-*, the lengthened o-grade of a secondary root **drew-*, the source of both *tree* and *true* in English. No IE verbal root is reconstructed for the innumerable derivatives in this word family, the assumption being that from the basic meaning of *tree* one can derive all of the associated adjectival meanings like *strong, lasting, true, trustworthy*, as well as the nominal series of *posts, poles, weapons*, and *tools*. See the remarks under **bauan** above.

þulan < PG **þulǣ-* < IE **tḷē-* < *√telh$_1$* (to raise up, bear) + essive suffix **-h$_1$yé-*. Cf. ON *thola*, Ger *dulden*, AS *þolian*, Scotch Eng *thole*; Skr *tula-* (a weight), Gr τέλλω (raise and load on), Lat *tollo*.

weihan < PG **wīhǣ-* < IE **weykē-* < *√weyk* (to set aside for sacred purposes) + suffix **-ē-*. Cf. ON *vígja* (to hallow, consecrate), Ger *weihen*; Skr *√vik*. Note also the adjective **weih-** in Lesson 6.

winnan < PG **wennǣ-* < IE **wenwē-* < *√wen* (strive for) + suffixes *-*w-ē-*. Cf. ON *vinna*, Eng *win*. The source of the *-w-* suffix producing the doubled *-nn-* of the PG form is not entirely clear, but is probably nominal in origin since the resultant doubling shows up in the nouns Gothic **winno**, **winna** (suffering), ON _vinna_ (labor), OHG _winna_ (strife).

wasjan < PG _*wazyan-_ < IE _*woséye-_ < √_wes_ (to clothe) + caus. suffix _*-éye-_. Cf. ON _verja_, AS _werian_ in this sense. Other derivative from IE √_wes_ include Skr √_vas_, Gr ἕννυμι (< _*wes-nu-mi_), Lat _vestis_. Cf. **wasti** (Lesson 3).

gamotjan < PG _*ga-_ + _*mōtiyan-_ < IE _*mōd(e)ye-_ (?). Cf. ON _møta_, Eng meet. The IE form is obscure, since the only cognates outside of Germanic are in Armenian. In PG, the base varies between _*mōt-_, as here and in the noun PG _*mōta-_ (meeting), and _*mat-_, as in _*matl-_ (place for conducting public business, forum; cf. Gothic **maþl**, ON _mál_, AS _mæđel_).

waila < PG _*wela_ < IE √_wel_ (to want, wish). Cf. ON _vel_, Ger _wohl_, Eng _well_. Semantics: adverbial, _according to one's wishes_. For the root see **wiljan** above.

waja < PG _*way-_ < IE _*way_. One of several derivatives in Germanic, including Gothic **wai** (woe!), ON _vei_, Eng _woe!;_ Gothic **wainei** (would that!), ON _veina_ (to complain), Ger _weinen_ (weep). Outside of Germanic cf. Gk οὐαί, Lat _vae!_

leik < PG _*līka-_ < IE _*līgo-_ (form, likeness). Cf. ON _lík_, Ger _Leiche_. See **leikan** just above.

lekeis < PG _*lēkiya-_ < IE _*lēĝeyo-_ < √_leĝ_ (to gather, count, speak) + deriv. suffix _*-eyo-_. Cf. ON _lǽknir_, Eng _leech_ (archaic: physician). The spelling **leikeis**, if not simply representing the frequent interchange of **e** and **ei**, may point to a popular assimilation to the noun **leik** above. Presumably, the IE noun meant _speaker_ in the special sense of _sorcerer, enchanter_, but since the meaning _physician_ is found only in Germanic, an actual derivation from PG _*līkan_ (body) cannot be ruled out completely. The root √_leĝ_ in its other meanings is well attested; cf. Gk λέγω (to speak), Lat _lego_ (pick, pluck, select, read), both with numerous derivatives.

fairhwus < PG _*ferh_^{w}_u_ < ? Possibly from the same root as **fairguni** (Lesson 3), if I read the complicated entry in Pokorny (p. 822) correctly. It is difficult to believe, however, that the Gothic words for _mountain_ and _world_ are borrowed from Celtic. Clear cognates within Germanic are ON _fjörgyn_ (mother earth) and probably ON _fjör_ (life, spirit; dative _fjörvi_), AS _feorh_, OHG _ferah_.

unhulþa < PG _*unhulþan-_ < _*unhulþ-_ (Lesson 7) + suffix _*-an-_.

wraka < PG _*wrakō-_ < IE _*wrogā-_ < √_wreg_ (to pursue, persecute) + suffix _*-ā-_. Cf. ON _rák_, Ger _Rache_ (revenge), AS _wracu_ (revenge), _wræc_ (banishment), Eng _wrack_ (and _ruin_). The root is well attested throughout Germanic, with the verbs _*wrekan-_ and _*wrakyan-_ and the nouns _*wrakaz_ (pursuer) and _*wrakyan-_ (pursuer or pursued), the former underlying Eng _wreak_, the latter, Eng _wretch_. Cf. also Russ _враг_ (enemy).

skadus < PG _*skađuz_ < IE _*skotu-_ < √_skot_ (darkness, shadow). Cf. Ger _Schatten_, Eng _shade, shadow;_ Gk σκότος (darkness).

widuwo < PG _*wiđuwōn-_, new form in _*-ōn-_ < _*wiđuwō_ < IE _*widhewā-_ (f. separated, bereft) < √_weydh_ (to divide) + suffix _*-ewā-_ (f. of _*-ewo-_). Cf. Ger _Witwe_, Eng _widow;_ Skr _vidhāva-_, Lat _vidua_, Russ _вдова_.

Lesson 12

Strong verbs: classes 1-5.

All strong verbs are inflected according to the model of **niman** (§7.4) in the present indicative active; the historical antecedents of this inflection were discussed in Historical Grammar Lesson 5, and there is no need to repeat that material here. It should be noted, however, that the IE counterparts of the strong verbs of classes 1-5 had the endings of the thematic inflection attached directly to the normal e-grade of the root, with no intervening formative suffix and with no vowel gradations in the root; thus: IE **némō, *némesi, *németi,* etc. The present (active) participle and the infinitive were likewise formed from the e-grade of the verbal root: IE **némont-, *némono-* > PG **nemand-, *nemana-*.

The preterite of strong verbs in Gothic is formally a continuation of the IE perfect, which, in the case of the idealized verbal root discussed in the introduction, was based on the o-grade of the root. In the large area of IE that included the forerunners of Greek, Indic, Italic, Celtic, and Germanic the stem of the perfect for a majority of verbs was further characterized by partial reduplication, though this feature is already on the wane in the earliest attested stages of the latter three language families. The extent to which this reduplication was an essential feature is unknown, but there were exceptions: the perfect of IE **weyd-* (to see, know), for example, is found everywhere without reduplication in the perfect. The original inflection of this verb in the perfect was approximately as follows (*V́* represents **é, *ó,* or **á*; the exact vowel cannot be determined):

	IE	Skr	Gk	Gothic
Singular	*wóyda*	*véda*	οἶδα	**wait**
	wóydtha	*véttha*	οἶσθα	**waist**
	wóyde	*véda*	οἶδε	**wait**
Dual	*wydwé*	*vidvá*	---	**witu**
	wydV́thus	*vidáthus*	(ἴστον)	**wituts**
	wydV́tus	*vidátus*	(ἴστον)	---
Plural	*wydmé*	*vidmá*	ἴσμεν	**witum**
	wydé, wydté	*vidá*	ἴστε	**witub**
	wyd- (?)	*vidúr*	ἴσασι	**witun**

Two essential features of this inflections should be noted:

(a) The endings, apart from the 1st person dual and plural, are quite distinct from those of the present active verb discussed above. The 3rd person plural forms of Sanskrit, Greek, and Gothic are so much at variance that no sure IE reconstruction can be made. The plural endings are discussed in Lesson 5. The dual 1st person **-u** follows easily from IE **-we* > PG **-u* after the shift of stress to the stem. The *-ts* of the 2nd person is presumably a continuation of the IE form, which is otherwise based only on Sanskrit, but the **-u-** must be seen as extended by analogy from the rest of the PG dual and plural paradigm.

(b) The stress was on the final stem syllable in the singular, but on the ending in the dual and plural, causing a reduction of the final stem syllable to the zero or reduced grade. Clear evidence of this original feature is preserved in both Greek and Gothic even though the stress has been shifted to the root syllable; Sanskrit preserves the original stress pattern.

The preterites of strong classes 1-3 follow the pattern of **weyd-* exactly. The question of whether these verbs originally had reduplicated stems in the perfect (e.g. **bebhóndha...*, **bebhn̥dhmé...*) is immaterial. The differentiation into three separate classes in Germanic arose solely from the differences in the phonetic development of the zero-grade of the root in the preterite plural and dual and in the past passive participle: **CoyC-* reduces to **CyC-* > PG **CiC-*; **CowC-* reduces to **Cw̥C-* > PG **CuC-*; **CoRC-* reduces to **CR̥C-* > PG **CuRC-*, where *R* = **l*, **m*, **n*, or **r*.

Class	Present Stem	Preterite Singular Stem	Pret. Plural/P. Part. Stem
1	**steygh-* > PG **stīg-*	**stoygh-* > PG **stayg-*	**stygh-* > PG **stig-*
2	**dewk-* > PG **tewh-*	**dowk-* > PG **tawh-*	**dw̥k-* > PG **tuh-*
3	**bhendh-* > PG **bend-* **wert-* > PG **werþ-*	**bhondh-* > PG **band-* **wort-* > PG **warþ-*	**bhn̥dh-* > PG **bund-* **wr̥t-* > PG **wurþ-*

Except for the stem of the preterite plural, the forms of classes 4 and 5 also conform to this model:

Class	Present Stem	Preterite Singular Stem	P. Part. Stem
4	**nem-* > PG **nem-*	**nom-* > PG **nam-*	**nm̥-* > PG **num-*
5	**g^{w}et-* > PG **kweþ-*	**g^{w}ot-* > PG **kwaþ-*	**g$^w{}_e$t-* > PG **kweþ-*

Prior to the general acceptance of the laryngeal theory the plural stem in *-ē-* was explained in two ways:

(a) *-ē-* < IE **-ē-* was spoken of as the *ē* -grade of the *e*-series, with no further explanation of how this particular lengthened grade of this particular series found its way into the stem of these preterite plural forms. Parallels in Latin were cited: *sēdi* (I sat), *vēni* (I came), etc.

(b) A comparison, but not an equation, was made with the Sanskrit perfect stems of the type *sēd-* from the root *sad* < IE **sed-* (to sit). Because this form probably had its origin in the reduplication mentioned above, we must now consider this phenomenon in some detail.

In classes 4 and 5 we are dealing primarily with the Germanic verbs derived from the IE simple root type ***C_1eC_2, which formed the reduplicated perfect stems ***$C_1eC_1\acute{o}C_2$- in the singular and ***$C_1eC_1C_2$*´*- in the plural. These patterns are preserved in Sanskrit, although the merging of IE **a*, **e*, and **o* to *a* has completely obscured the original vocalism of the form. E.g.

IE √*ĝen* (give birth) > Skr √*jan:* Perf. sing. IE **ĝeĝón-* > Skr *jaján-*
pl. IE **ĝeĝn-´* > Skr *jajñ-´*

The Greek verbal system has lost the original IE stress differences and has been standardized with a simple regressive system of accentuation. As a result of this systematic change, or perhaps simply in conjunction with it, the differentiation between the two perfect stems has been lost and only the singular stem is preserved for the root types under consideration: from this same root the single perfect stem is γεγον-.

In Sanskrit, however, there were secondary developments. The reduced form of the reduplicated perfect stems that contained no significant secondary phonetic differentiation of the reduplicated consonant C_1 (as is the case, for example, with the stems of √*han* (to kill) < IE **ghen: jaghán-, jaghn-´*) was replaced, more often than not, with a stem of the form $C_1\bar{e}C_2$. E.g.

√*pat* (to fall, fly)	Perf. singular	*papát-*	plural	*pēt-́* (for *papt-*)
√*bhaj* (to divide)		*babháj-*		*bhēj-́* (for **babhj-*)

Because Sanskrit **ē* can only represent an earlier diphthong **ay* (< IE **ay*, **oy*, **ey*), it is assumed that these secondary forms were extended by analogy from parallel forms of similar verbs where such a form could have developed by a regular phonetic process. The verb √*sad* (to sit): *sasád-*, **sasd-́* is usually singled out, with the assumption that an original **sasd* > **sazd-* > **sayd-* >*sēd*. Although this change is spoken of as "regular", it is not what would be expected within the regular combinatory processes of Sanskrit phonology. It is preferable, therefore, to seek the origin of the change in the perfect stem of roots with initial *y-*, where the development is quite regular, even if there are only two verbs attested that qualify: √*yat* (to stretch): perf. pl. *yēt-́* and √*yam* (to reach): perf. pl. *yēm-* from **yayt-* and **yaym-* respectively.

While there is certainly no reason to reject the comparison of Gothic **brekum**, **setum** etc. with Latin *frēgī*, *sēdī* etc., it must be admitted that a comparison is not an explanation of their origin. The development of the Sanskrit *sēd*-type stem through a combination of phonological and analogical processes suggests a similar solution for our problem, but at a much earlier stage of IE. The *ē* of the Gothic 4th and 5th classes continues PG **ǣ*, as is shown by OHG and AS cognates, and is therefore a continuation of IE **ē*. One source, if not the sole original source, of IE **ē* is in the cluster **-eh₁C-*, which evolved into **-ēC-* with the early loss of the laryngeals. The stem of the perfect plural of roots of the type **h₁eC* provided this configuration exactly, and a few frequent verbs of this shape could very well account for the creation of the plural stems in **-ē-*, which was then extended by analogy to the plural stems of other verbs of the **CeC* type. In Latin no distinction between singular and plural stems is preserved, the stem in **ē*, if retained at all, being used throughout the perfect. In PG, however, the preterite singular maintains its original shape and with the loss of the reduplication, no doubt hasten by its apparent loss in the plural, the existing contrast **nam:*nēm-* came into being. The following table should make this clear:

(a) Examples of the original generating type **h₁eC:*

Root	Early IE		Late IE		
	Perfect Singular	Perfect Plural	Perfect Singular	Perfect Plural	
**h₁ed* (eat)	**h₁eh₁ód-*	**h₁eh₁d-́*	**(e)ód-*	**ēd-́*	cf. Lat *ēdī*
**h₁em* (take)	**h₁eh₁óm-*	**h₁eh₁m-́*	**(e)óm-*	**ēm-́*	Lat *ēmī*
**h₁es* (be)	**h₁eh₁ós-*	**h₁eh₁s-́*	**(e)ós-*	**ēs-́*	Skr *ās-*, Gk ἦ-

(b) Examples of analogically altered types **CeC:*

Root	Late IE		Latin	Gothic	
**sed* (sit)	**(se)sód-*	**sēd-́*	*sēd-ī*	**sat**	**set-um**
**gʷem*	**(gʷe)gwóm-*	**gʷēm-́*	*vēn-ī*	**qam**	**qem-um**
**bhregh* (break)	**(be)bhrógh-*	**bhrēgh-́*	*frēg-ī*	**brak**	**brek-um**
**seqʷ* (follow, see)	**(se)sóqʷ-*	**sēqw-́*	*sĕqu-ī*	**sahw**	**sehw-um.**

Etymologies:

qiman < PG **kʷeman-* < IE **√gʷem-* (to come). Cf. ON *koma*, Ger *kommen*, Eng *come;* Skr √*gam*, Gk βαίνω (< IE **gʷm̥ye-*), Lat *venio* (idem).

brikan < PG _*brekan-_ < IE _√bhreĝ_ (to break). Cf. Ger _brechen,_ Eng _break;_ Lat _frango_ (with _-n-_ infix in present stem; perfect _frēgi_).

fulljan < PG _*fulliyan-_ < IE _*pḷno-_ (full) [< _√pleh_$_1$ + adj. suffix _*-no-_] + denom. suffix _*-eye-_. Cf. ON _fylla,_ Ger _füllen,_ Eng _fill._ For the underlying adjective cf. ON _full-,_ Ger _voll,_ Eng _full._ The IE verbal root is well attested throughout the family with a wide range of meanings; in the meaning _to fill_ cf. Skr _√pṛ,_ Gk πίμπλημι, Lat _compleo._

bidjan < PG _*beđyan-_ < IE _*g_^{w}_hedhye-_ < _√g_^{w}_hedh_ (to ask, pray) + present suffix _*-ye-_. Cf. ON _biðja,_ Ger _bitten,_ Eng _bid._ The IE root _√g_^{w}_hedh_ is also attested in this meaning in Celtic and Balto-Slavic (cf. OCSl _žęždǫ_ thirst for), but the phonological development of IE _*g_^{w}_h_ > PG _*b_ is highly questionable. Pokorny takes **bidjan** to the IE root _√bhedh_ (bow or kneel in supplication), with cognates in Sanskrit, Albanian, and Lithuanian.

fraihnan < PG _*frehnan_ < IE _√preḱ_ (to ask) + present suffix _*-ne-_. Cf. ON _fregna,_ Ger _fragen,_ AS _frignan;_ Skr _√prac,_ Lat _posco_ (< _*perḱ-ske-_), Russ _просить._

gatairan < PG _*ga-_ + _*teran-_ < IE _√der_ (to split, tear, flay). Cf. Ger _(ver)zehren,_ Eng _to tear;_ Skr _√dṛ,_ Gk δέρω (to flay), Russ _драть_ (to tear).

qiþan < PG _*kweþan-_ < IE _√g_^{w}_et-_ (to speak). Cf. ON _kveða,_ AS _cweðan,_ Eng _(be)queathe,_ archaic _quoth;_ Skr _√gad._ The root is well developed only in Germanic.

itan < PG _*etan-_ < IE _√ed_ [_h_$_1$_ed_] (to eat). Cf. ON _eta,_ Ger _essen,_ Eng _eat;_ Skr _√ad,_ Gk ἔδω, Lat _edo,_ Russ _есть_ (<_*едmu_).

gabruka < PG _*gabrukō_ < _*ga-_ + _*brukō_ < IE _*bhṛĝā-_ < _√bhreĝ_ (to break) + nominal suffix _*-ā-_. See **brikan** above.

mats < PG _*mati-_ < IE _*mod-i-_ (portion, measure) < _√med_ (to measure); or < _*mad-i-_ < _√mad_ (to sate, satisfy). Cf. ON _matr;_ Eng _meat._ See **matjan** in Lesson 5. The IE root _√mad_ is well attested throughout most of the IE family, but the simple meaning _food, to eat_ seems limited to Germanic.

waihts: see Lesson 5.

tainjo < PG _*taynyōn-_. Cf. ON _teina_ (twig basket), OHG _zeinna_ (basket). The word is an obvious derivative in _*-yōn-_ from PG _*taynaz,_ Goth **tains** (twig), ON _teinn_ (twig), Eng (mistle)toe, but has no cognates outside of Germanic.

fralet < PG _*fralǣtan_ < _*fra-_ (see above) + _*lǣtan_ < IE _*lēd-o-_ < _√lēd_ (to be lax, weary). Cf. the verb **letan** (Lesson 21) and the adjective **lats** (lazy), ON _latr,_ Eng _late._ The semantic development of the Germanic meaning _let, leave, allow_ from the IE root, well known from Gk ληδεῖν (to be tired, lazy) and Lat _lassus_ (tired; < _*lədtos_), is somewhat obscure, but presumable along the lines of _lax_ > _permissive_ and _lax_ > _negligent._

faheþs < PG _fahǣđiz_ < IE _*poḱēdhi-_ < _√peḱ_ (be glad, gladden, make pleasant) + suffix _*-ēdhi-_. The verbal root is found in Gothic **faginon** (to rejoice), **-fahjan** in **fullafahjan** (to please, satisfy), **fagrs** (suitable), all with cognates elsewhere in Germanic. The only cognates outside of Germanic are in Baltic.

wein < PG _*wīnan_ < Lat _vīnum_ (wine). Cf. ON _vín,_ Ger _Wein,_ Eng _wine;_ Gk οἶνος, Russ _вино._ The word may ultimately be Semitic in origin (cf. Arabic _wayn-,_ Hebrew _yáyin_), but more likely it is an indigenous word taken into both IE and Semitic languages from a third source. The Germanic and Slavic forms are a direct borrowing from Latin.

aiwein- < PG *aywīn- < IE *ayw- (vital force, life, eternity) + adj. suffix *-īn-. The base Germanic noun *aywi- (Gothic **aiws**) is found used adverbially in Gothic **aiw** (ever), **ni aiw** (never), ON *ey* (ever, forever), OHG *n-eo* (never), Ger *nie*, Eng *no*. Cf. Gk ἀεί (always), Lat *aevus* (lifetime, age).

naqad- < PG *nak^{w}ađ- < IE *nog^{w}odh- (naked). Cf. ON *nøkt-*, *nøkviđ-*, Ger *nakt*, Eng *naked;* Lat *nūdus*, Ir *nocht*, Russ *нагой* (< IE *nog^{w}-), Skr *nagna-* (< IE *nog^{w}-no-).

bai- < PG *bay-. Cf. ON *báð-*, Ger *beide*, Eng *both*. An exact reconstruction of the PG and IE forms is impossible because of the variety of cognate forms; cf. Skr *ubhāu*, Gk ἄμφω, Lat *ambo*, Russ *оба*, all of which have a prefixed element. The basic IE forms were probably parallel to those of the number *two* (see Lesson 9), with the base *bhōw, *bhoy. The ON, Ger, and Eng cognates are derived somewhat irregularly from a PG pronominal form *bayōþ-, with the nominal suffix *-ōþ- < IE *-āt-; this word survives intact in Gothic **bajoþs**.

ak < PG *ak < IE *age (?). Cf. AS *ac*, OHG *oh* (but, however). It is speculated that this is really the imperative singular form of the PG verb *akan- (to drive) < IE *ag- (to drive). The exclamatory use of Lat *age* and Gk ἄγε would support this view, since conjunctions and adverbial particles may indeed result from weakened or frozen nominal and verbal forms.

hwe < PG *h^{w}ǣ < IE *k^{w}ē, the instrumental neuter of the interrogative pronoun *k^{w}os (see Lesson 6). A similar form in *-ō underlies Eng *how*.

fairra < PG *ferr- < *ferer- (comparative form) < IE adverbial base *per (out over, across) + suffix *-ero-. Cf. ON *fjar*, Ger *fer(n)*, Eng *far;* Skr *pari*, Gk περί, Lat *per*. The **-a** of the Gothic form is the adverbial ending already encountered in **faura**, **dalaþa**, **uta**, etc.

hwaþ < PG *h^{w}aþ < IE *k^{w}ote < interrogative base *k^{w}o- + adv. suffix *-te (toward; see Lesson 23).

Lesson 13

Etymologies:

ga- < PG **ga-* < IE **kom, ko* (at, near, with). Cf. ON *g-*, AS *ġe-*, Eng *e-* (as in *enough*); Gk κοινός (in common, shared; < **komyós*), Lat *cum, con-, co-*.

wisan < PG **wesan-* < IE *√wes* (to dwell, live, be). Cf. ON *vera* < *vesa*, OHG wesan, Ger *wesen*, Eng *was;* Skr *√vas* (to dwell). The Germanic root *√wes* (to feast, revel) is probably from a separate IE root *√wes* having to do with feeding animals or the like; cf. Skr *vās(tar-)* (shepherd), Hittite **weštara-* (idem).

wrikan < PG **wrekan-* < IE *√wreg* (to pursue, persecute). Cf. ON *reka*, Ger *rächen* (avenge), Eng *wreak, wreck;* Lat *urgeo.*

lisan < PG **lesan-* < IE *√les* (pluck, gather). Cf. ON *lesa*, Ger *lesen;* Lith *lèsti* (pick at grain etc.).

bairan < PG **beran-* < IE *√bher* (carry, bear). Cf. ON *bera*, Ger *gebären*, Eng *bear;* Skr *√bhṛ*, Gk φέρω, Lat *fero*, Russ *брать*.

galaubjan < **galaub-** (dear, valuable) + denom. suffix **-jan. galaub-** < PG **ga-* + **lawb-* < IE **lowbh-* < *√lewbh* (to love, desire). Cf. Ger *(g)lauben* (to believe), Eng *(be)lieve;* ON *liúfr* (dear), Ger *lieb, lieben*, Eng *love;* Skr *√lubh* (desire), Lat *lubet* (is pleasing), Russ *любить*.

drigkan < PG **drenkan-* < IE **dhrenĝ-* < *√dhreĝ* (to pull, draw) with *n-* infix. Cf. ON *drekka*, Ger *trinken*, Eng *drink.* It is difficult to distinguish among the many derivatives from the three partially synonymous IE roots *√dherāgh, √dhreĝ(h),* and *√trag;* see Pokorny *sub radicibus.*

bloþs < PG **blōþ-* < IE **bhlōt-* < *√bhel* (to swell, blossom) + extension **-ō-* + suffix **-to-*. Cf. ON *blóð*, Ger *Blut*, Eng *blood.* The semantics are obscure, but that is true for many of the cognates listed by Pokorny under *√bhel*[3] and *√bhel*[4], which should probably be conflated into a single root.

smakka < PG ? The only cognates are in Slavic: OCSl *smoky*, originally a feminine *ū-* stem noun, and Russ *смоква*. An early borrowing from a single source with the shape **smokkō* would conform to the nominative singular of both Gothic and OCSl.

aurtja = **aurti-** + the actor suffix **-jan-**; **aurti-** is a borrowing from Latin *hortus* (orchard).

hlaiw < PG **hlayw-* < IE **kloyw-* (a shelter, lean-to) < *√kley* (to lean) + suffix **-wo-*. Cf. ON *hlé* (shelter), Eng *lee(ward);* Lat *clivus* (hill, slope). The *n* -extension of the root is widely attested: Gk κλίνω, Lat *clīno*, PG **hlīn-*, Ger *lehnen*, Eng *to lean.*

siuns < PG **seɣwní-* < IE **sekʷní-* < *√sekʷ* (to follow, see) + nom. suffix **-ni-*. Cf. ON *sýn*, AS *sīen.* For more on the root *√sekʷ* see **saihwan** in Lesson 7.

missadeþs = **missa-** + **-deþs. missa-** < PG **missa-* < IE **mitto-* (exchanged, wrong) < *√meyt* (to exchange) + part. adj. suffix **-to-*. Cf. ON *mis-*, Ger *miss-*, Eng *miss-*. **-deþs** < PG **dǣđi-* < IE **dhētí-* (deed) < *√dheh₁* + nominal suffix **-ti-*. Cf. ON *dáð*, Eng *deed;* OCSl *-dětĭ.* On the root *√dheh₁* see the discussion of the weak preterite in Lesson 5.

misso < PG _*missô_ < IE _*mittô_ (wrongly, reversely, mutually), an adverbial form of the adjective _*mitto-_ underlying **missa-** in the preceding entry, q. v.

jabai is a compound of **ja-** and **-bai.** The former is presumably derived from the IE pronominal base _*i, *ei;_ the latter, from IE _*bhē, *bhō,_ an indefinable particle that also underlies OCSl _bo_ (for, since, because). It seems probable that _*bhō_ is a fixed or frozen form of the injunctive of the verb _*bhew-_ (to be), with the semantic development _let it be that ..._ > _if._ Cf. **bauan** (HG Lesson 11).

swe, swa, swaswe < PG _*swō, *swē_ < IE _*swō, *swē_ (so, thus), adverbial forms (Locative, Instrumental) of the reflexive pronominal base _*swe-._ Cf. ON _svá,_ Ger _so,_ Eng _so;_ Gk ὥς (so, thus), OLat _sōc,_ Lat _sic._ Note also the first element of Goth **swaleik-** (such), ON _slíkr,_ Ger _solch-,_ Eng _such._

þau. Origin uncertain; probably from the IE pronominal stem _*to-._

þan < PG _*þan_ < IE _*tom,_ the adverbially used masc. acc. sing. of the demonstrative stem _*to-_ (Lesson I). Cf. Ger _dann,_ Eng _then;_ Skr _tadā_ (neuter _tad_ + adv. _-ā_), Lat _tum, tunc._

Lesson 14

Etymologies:

beidan < PG **bīđan-* < IE *√bheydh* (to convince, trust). Cf. ON *bíða*, Eng *bide;* Gk πείθω (to persuade), Lat *fīdō* (trust). Note also the PG causative **bayđiyan-* (to force, compel), Gothic **baidjan**, ON *beiða.* In addition to some fuzzy semantics there is disagreement on the matter of voice. The Latin and Germanic point to an original simple verb with stative or mediopassive meaning (to trust, wait trustingly) in contrast to the Greek verb πείθω. It is likely that πείθω as an active, quasi-causative verb is a back-formation from the middle πείθομαι.

gateihan < **ga-** + **-teihan** < PG *tīhan-* < IE *√deyk̂* (to point out, show, tell). Cf. ON *téa, tjá,* Ger *zeihen, zeigen;* Skr *√diç*, Gk δείκνυμι, Lat *dīcō.* The PG causative **tayhyan-* underlies Eng *teach.*

urreisan < **us-** + **-reisan** < PG **rīs-* (rise, flow) < IE *√er* [*h₃er*] + extensions **y* and **s.* Cf. ON *rísa* (rise), Ger *reisen* (travel), Eng *rise.* The IE forms derived from the root **h₃er* are numerous and phonologically complex; they include Skr *√ri* (to flow), Gk ὄρνυμι, Lat *orior.* The *s-* extension appears only in Germanic.

inweitan = **in-** + **-weitan** < PG **wītan-* < IE *√weyd* (to know, see). See **witan** (Lesson 10) for further comments.

usleiþan, afleiþan: see **galeiþan** (Lesson 7).

afgaggan: see **gaggan** (Lesson 7).

afniman: see **niman** (Lesson 7)

hund < PG **hunda-* < IE **k̂m̥tó-* (hundred). Cf. ON *hund(rað),* Ger *hund(ert),* Eng *hund(red);* Skr *çatam,* Gk -κατον, Lat *centum.* Russ *-cmo.* The second element of the ON, Ger and Eng words is PG **raþ-* (count).

reiks < PG **rīk-* ← IE **rēĝ-* (king, ruler) < *√reĝ* (straighten, put in order, extend). Cf. ON *ríkr* (adj., mighty), Ger *reich* (rich), Eng *rich;* Skr *rāja-* (king), Lat *rex.* PG **rīk-* is assumed to be a borrowing from Celtic **rīk-*, where the **ī* is regular. IE **rēĝ-* would ordinarily end up as **rǣk-* in PG.

þrutsfill- < PG **þrūtes-* + **fell.* PG **þrūtes-* < IE **trūdes-* (leprosy). Cf. OIr *trosc* (< **trudsko-*), AS *đrustfell.* PG **fell-* (skin, hide) < IE **pelno-* < *√pel* (to cover) + suffix **-no-*. Cf. Gothic **fill**, Ger *Fell,* AS *fell;* Lat *pellis.*

baud-: etymology unknown.

hwaiwa < PG **hwaywa* < IE **kʷoywō,* an adverbial form of the adjective **kʷoywo-* (of what sort?), ultimately from the interrogative base **kʷo-*. See also **hwas, hwa, hwo** (Lesson 6), **hwe** (Lesson 12), and

hwan < PG **hwan* < IE **kʷom* < **kʷo-* (interrogative base) + adverbial suffix (or masc. *As* ending) **-m.* Cf. Ger *wann,* Eng *when;* Lat *cum* (older *quom*), Russ *ко(гда).*

biþe < **bi** (Lesson 5) + **-þe** < PG **þǣ* < IE **tē*, an adverbial form of the pronominal base **to-* (see Lessons I-3).

miþþanei < **miþ** (Lesson 3) + **þan** (Lesson 13) + **-ei** (relative particle; see Grammar Lesson 11]).

sundro < PG **sundrō* < IE **sn̥terṓ* (separate, apart) < **seni-*, **senu-* + comp. suffix **-ter-* + adverbial suffix **-ṓ*. Cf. ON *sundr-*, Ger *sonder* (apart, without), Eng *(a)sunder;* Skr *sanutár* (separated, far from), Lat *sine* (without).

þairh < PG **þerh-* < IE **terḱwe* (through, across) < *√ter* (rub, bore through) + suffix **-ḱwe*. Cf. Ger *durch*, Eng *through;* Skr *tiraçca* (through, across). Sorting out the seven roots *√ter*, most of which have numerous "extensions", as well as the "related" roots *√terd* and *√terk*, is one of the most bewildering problems in IE root assignment; see Pokorny pp. 1070-77.

inn, as an adverb and verbal prefix, is assumed to be from an extended form **enin-* of the base IE **en-* (see Lesson 1). Gothic **inna** (cf. **ut: uta, dalaþ: dalaþa**) and **innana** (cf. **hind-ar: hindana**) are from this same extension, which seems to be attested only in these Germanic forms.

Lesson 15

The subjunctive

The Gothic present subjunctive has its origin in the IE optative inflection of the thematic verbs, which consisted of the verbal base + the thematic vowel **-o-* + the weak form of the optative suffix **-yē-*, i.e. **-ī-* + the secondary personal endings. The reduction of the sequence **-oī-* to the simple diphthong **-oy-* took place within IE, resulting in the following paradigm:

	IE	Sanskrit	Greek	Gothic
singular	**nemoym̥*	*namēyam*	νέμοιμι	**nimau**
	**nemoys*	*namēs*	νέμοις	**nimais**
	**nemoyt*	*namēt*	νέμοι	**nimai**
dual	**nemoywe*	*namēva*	---	**nimaiwa**
	**nemoytom*	*namētam*	νέμοιτον	**nimaits**
	**nemoytām*	*namētām*	νεμοίτην	---
plural	**nemoyme*	*namēma*	νέμοιμεν	**nimaima**
	**nemoyte*	*namēta*	νέμοιτε	**nimaiþ**
	**nemoyn (?)*	*namēyur*	νέμοιεν	**nimaina**

Remarks:

(1) The final **-a** of Gothic **-aima**, **-aiwa**, **-aina** points to a long vowel in PG and in IE, but there is no evidence elsewhere to support such a reconstruction. The IE form of the 3rd pers. plural secondary ending is not at all certain; there is no way to reconcile the Greek, Sanskrit, and Gothic forms.

(2) The source of 1st pers. sing. **-au** remains obscure, but note that both Greek and Sanskrit have similar problems in this form: Sanskrit *-am* is apparently clipped from the thematic secondary inflection, as in the imperfect *anam-am*, for example, while Greek -μι is a primary ending borrowed from the indicative of the athematic verbs, e.g. δείκνυμι. Thus Gothic **-au** may represent an earlier **-ayō*, where the primary thematic ending **-ō* is added directly to the optative base in **ay-*, or it may be derived directly from IE **-oym̥* > PG **-ayum* > **-ayu* > Gothic **-au**. Neither contraction has a clear phonological parallel elsewhere in the language, but both are certainly possible.

The Gothic preterite subjunctive reflects basically this same inflection, but with the optative suffix (stressed **yē*, unstressed **ī*) and the secondary personal endings attached directly to the verbal base without an intervening thematic vowel. The original paradigm seems to have been characterized by ultimate stress and, if the Gothic forms are a direct inheritance, was properly the optative active of the present perfect, which, for the perfect base **woyd-* (to know), was approximately as follows:

sing.	**wy̥dyēm*	dual	**wy̥dīwé*	plural	**wy̥dīmé*
	**wy̥dyēs*		**wy̥dītom*		**wy̥dīté*
	**wy̥dyēt*		**wy̥dītām*		**wy̥dīn(t)* (?)

In the pre-PG phase of IE the **ī* of the dual and plural forms was extended to the singular; the 1st person singular **-m* was at some point replaced with the present ending leading to **-au** discussed above; and the 3rd person plural form was reshaped on the basis of the other dual and plural forms. Since the reduced (zero) grade of the verbal base was the same as that of the preterite plural, it is only natural that when the inflection was extended to the newly formed weak preterites of Germanic the preterite plural form was taken as the base for the inflection., e.g.

drus- : drusjau :: nasided- : nasidedjau

In Sanskrit, however, the **yē* > **yā* of the singular was extended throughout the active paradigm and the contrast **yē/ī* was lost.

In Greek the thematic forms -οιμι, -οις ... given above were extended to most of the optative paradigms, but the contrast between stressed **yē* and unstressed **ī* was preserved in the optative present of athematic verbs, although it was partially obscured by subsequent contractions and shifts of stress. For example, from the present stem ἱστα- (to stand) we have sing. ἱσταίην..., pl. ἱσταῖμεν... from original **sisth₂yēm* and **sisth₂īmés* respectively. This type of inflection has been extended to various types of contract verbs, e.g. τιμῴην, φιλοίην, δηλοίην, φανοίην.

The present subjunctive of Early Latin *esse* is frequently cited as an example of this inflection (*s-* is the zero grade of **es-*, to be): *siem, sies, siet, simus, sitis, sint.* The undifferentiated **ī* is found throughout the perfect subjunctive (e.g. *viderim, videris* ...), but the secondary extension of the perfect stem with **-er-* < **-es-* prevents a direct comparison with the Gothic forms.

On the cohortative and jussive.

The Gothic cohortative form that is identical to the indicative has no counterpart elsewhere in IE and must be assumed to be an actual indicative form pressed into service for that function. The rare 3rd person imperative (jussive) in **-adau**, pl. **-andau**, is derived from IE **-etōd* and **-ontōd* respectively. An *-u* was added to the PG forms **-eþa-* and **-anþa-*. Clear cognates are found in Sanskrit *-atu*, pl. *-antu;* Gk -έτω, pl. -όντω; Lat *esto(d).* The Sanskrit forms are suggestive: they seem to be derived from the secondary endings *-at* and *-ant* with the addition of a particle *-u*, like the Germanic; the IE **-ō* reflected in the Latin and Greek would have yielded *-ā* in Sanskrit.

Etymologies:

anabiudan < **ana-** (Lesson I) + **-biudan** < PG **bewđan-* < IE *√bhewdh* (be awake, attentive; awaken, make attentive). Cf. ON *bjóða* (bid, offer, order), Ger *bieten* (bid, offer), Eng *bid;* Skr *√budh* (awake), Gk πεύθομαι (become aware of), Russ *будить* (awaken). The semantic shift to *ordering, commanding* is also found in Baltic.

faurbiudan < **faur-** (Lesson 7) + **-biudan** (see just above). Cf. ON *forboða, fyrirbjóða,* Ger *verbieten,* Eng *forbid.* For the sense of **faur-** here note the uses of the preposition **faur** given in Voc. 7; hence : *to make someone beware of* > *to tell someone not to do.*

driusan < PG **drewsan-* < IE **dhrews-*, an extension in -s- of the root *√dhrew* (to crumble and fall, drop). Cf. AS *drēosan* (to fall); Gk θραύω (crush, crumble). Note also Gothic **drau(h)snos** *fpl* crumbs. The long *ū* of the related verb PG **drūsyan* > AS *drūsian* (be sluggish) > Eng *drowse* and of the **b*-extended root in PG **drūpyan* > ON *drúpa* (hang down over, hover), Eng *droop,* suggest a more complex form of the root, like **dhrewH.* See Pokorny p. 274 for further possible cognates and extensions of this phonologically and semantically troubled root.

tiuhan < PG **tewhan-* < IE *√dewk* (to draw, pull, lead). Cf. Ger *ziehen,* Eng *tow;* Lat *dūcō.*

gahrainjan < PG **ga-* + **-hrayniyan-*, a denom. verb on the adjectival base **hrayni-* (clean, pure) < IE **kroyni-* < *√krey* (to cut fine, separate, sift out) + extension **-n-* + formant **-i-*. Cf. ON *hrein-*, Ger *rein.* The root is well attested, e.g. Gk κρίνω (< **krinyō*), Lat *cernō* (< **krinō*), Russ *кроить* (esp. to cut out a pattern). The meaning *clean, pure* is specifically a Germanic development.

hropjan < PG **hrōpiyan-*, a denominative verb on the noun **hrōp-* (a shout). Cf. AS *hrōpan*, Ger *rufen.* The IE etymology is uncertain, but the word is undoubtedly related to the IE root *√ker*, which, with a dozen or more extensions, is the putative source of hundreds of words denoting various sounds and the things or animals that produce them. See Pokorny 567-71.

þliuhan < PG **flewhan-* < IE **plewk-* < *√plew* (to flow, etc.) + the extension **-k-*. Cf. ON *flýja*, Ger *fliehen*, Eng *flee.* The PG **flewgan-* (to fly), ON *fljúga*, Ger *fliegen*, Eng *fly*, is apparently derived from the same IE base **plewk-*, the *-g-* resulting perhaps from contamination with the PG noun **flugla-* (bird; see HG Lesson I), where the *-g-* may be accounted for by Verner's Law. The simple root *√plew* is well attested, e.g. Skr *√plu*, Gk πλέω (< **pléwō*, to swim, sail), Lat *pluere* (to rain), Russ *плыть,плавать* (to swim, float).

gajuko < PG **gayukōn-* < **ga-* + **-yuk-* + suffix **-ōn-*. The underlying IE root is either the noun **yugom* (yoke) > PG **yuka(n)* > Goth **juk**, Ger *Joch*, Eng *yoke*, or the related verbal root *√yewg* (to join together), found in Skr *√yuj*, Gk ζεύγνυμι, Lat *jungo* (< **yu̯-n-g-*). Gothic **gajuko** is literally *a joining together > comparison, likening, similitude.* The exact process by which the word came into being is indeterminate.

malma < PG **malman-* < IE **molmon-* < *√mel* (to grind fine) + suffix **-men-/-mon-*. Cf. OSax *melm* (sand), Ger *Mulm* (powdery decay), *mulmen* (to turn to dust). The IE verbal root is widely attested, e.g. Skr *√mr̥*, Lat *molō*, Russ *молоть*.

fotus < PG **fōtu-* < IE **pŏd- *pĕd-* (foot) + nom. formative **-u-*. Cf. ON *fótr*, Ger *Fuss*, Eng *foot;* Skr *pad-*, Gk πούς, ποδός, Lat *pēs, pedis*, Russ *под* (bottom).

gadrauhts < PG **gadruhti-*, originally an abstract noun in PG **-ti-* < IE **-ti-* based on the stem of the past passive (resultative) participle **gadrug-* of the verb **drewgan-*, Gothic **driugan** (to serve as a soldier), AS *drēogan* (to hold out, endure). From the same stem without the prefix *ga-* are Gothic **drauhti-** (the military), OHG *truht* (troop, company), OSax *druht-*, ON *drótt* (the king's personal guard). Note also the PG adjective **drewg-*, ON *drjúg-* (strong, enduring). Pokorny pp. 252-5 assigns these words to the extension in **-ewgh* of the root 2 *√dher* (hold firm, support), which, although well attested, has a bewilderingly wide range of secondary meanings.

rign < PG **regna-* < IE **rekno-* (rain) < *√rek* + suffix **-no-*. Cf. ON *regn*, Ger *Regen*, Eng *rain;* Lithuanian **rõkti* (to rain fine, mist). A variant IE root *√reg* underlies Lat *rigare* (to water).

hweila < PG **hwīlō* < IE **kwīlā* < *√kweyH* (to rest comfortably) + suffix **-l-* + nom. formative **-ā*. Cf. ON *hvíla*, Eng *while;* Lat *quie(s), (tran)quīlus*, Russ *(по)чить*.

gudja < PG **guđyan-*, an agent noun in *-yan-* on the base **guđ-* (deity), for which see Lesson 2. Cf. ON *goði.*

haubiþ < PG **hawƀiþ-* < IE **kawput-*, **kawpit-*. Cf. ON *höfuð*, Ger *Haupt*, Eng *head.* This form of the IE word is found only in Germanic; a by-form **kaput-* without *-w-* is evidenced by Latin *caput.*

ustauhts, an abstract noun in **-ti-* < IE **-ti-* on the base of the passive participle **ustauh-** of **ustiuhan** (see **tiuhan** above).

galeik- < PG **galīk-* < **ga-* + **līk-*, originally meaning *having the same form*. Cf. ON *(g)lík-*, Ger *gleich*, Eng *like*. For further information see **leikan** and **leik** in Lesson 11.

dwal- < PG **dwal-* < IE **dhwol-* < *√dhwel* (be disturbed, impeded, handicapped). Cf. ON *dœlsk-* (foolish, < PG **dwōlisk-*), Ger *toll*, Eng *dull*. The root is well developed in Germanic; note PG **dwel(y)an-* (be impeded > delay, tarry) underlying ON *dvelja*, Eng *dwell*, and PG **dwalmōn-* (be foolish) with its various cognates. The IE root *√dhwel* is an extension in **-el-* of the zero grade of the more primitive root *√dhew* with innumerable cognates throughout IE (see Pokorny pp. 261-7!).

handug- < PG **handuɣ-*, **handaɣ-* < IE **ḱontakó-* (sharp, pointed) < *√ḱent* (be pointed) + adjectival suffix **-kó-*. Cf. OHG *hantag* (pointed); Gk κεντέω (to stick, stab). For the adjectival suffix **-ag-** in Gothic see Lesson 22.

swes- < PG **swǣs-* < IE **swēs-* (one's property) < **swe-* (reflexive pronominal base) + extension **-s-*. Cf. ON *svás-* (dear, beloved), OHG *swās*. Because this particular IE form is not attested outside of Germanic, it has been suggested that the Germanic words are derived from the better attested extension **swēdh- + *-so-*, but this is phonologically incompatible with the Germanic form. The IE reflexive base **se*, **swew*, **swe* is, of course, widely attested; see **sein-** in Lesson 4.

suns, suns-(aiw) is generally considered etymologically obscure, but Eng *soon* and OHG *sān(o)* are considered to be cognates within Germanic. A connection with IE **sm̥-* , the zero grade of **sem-* (together with, the same), seems likely, however. The zero grade leading to PG *sum-z- > **sunz-* would accord well with its prefixal use in Gothic **sunsaiw** (originally: at the same time > immediately). If Eng *soon* and OHG *sān*(o) are really cognate, they must go back to a non-prefixed form because of the long vowel, PG **sōn* or **sǣn*.

niund- < PG **ne(w)und-* < IE **newn̥to-* (ninth) < **newn* (nine) + suffix **-to-*. Cf. ON *níundi*, Ger *neunte*, Eng *ninth;* Gk εἵνατος (< **enwn̥to-*). See also **niun** in Lesson 2.

utana = **ut** (Lesson 7) + the suffix **-ana** (see Lesson 23). Cf. Ger *aussen*.

ei < PG **ī* < IE **ei*, originally the Locative case of the demonstrative stem **e-*, the source of innumerable conjunctive particles and adverbs throughout the IE family. Gk εἰ (if) is directly comparable. See Pokorny 281-6.

aftra < PG **aftr-* < IE **apoter-* < **apo* (from, away, back) + comparative suffix **-ter-*. Cf. ON *eftir*, Eng *after*. For IE **apo* see also **af** in Lesson 9.

Lesson 16

Because the infinitives of the PP verbs **witan**, **kunnan**, and **munan** are secondary forms in Germanic, based on the reduced form of the new present (= old preterite) stem, the etymologies of these three words are best stated in terms of the stem corresponding to the IE perfect.

wait, witum < PG **wayt, *witum* < **wayta, *witm̥* < IE **wóyda, *widmé* < *√weyd* (to see, know). Cf. ON *vita*, Ger *wissen;* Skr *√vid*, Gr οἶδα, Lat *videre*, Russ *ведать, видеть*.

kann, kunnum < PG **kann, kunnum* < **kánna, *kn̥nm̥*. Cf. ON *kunna*, Ger *kennen*, Eng *ken*. Only the PG plural forms **kn̥nm̥* etc. correspond to a viable IE prototype, namely the infixed **-né-/-n-* present tense forms of the root *√ĝneh*$_3$ (to know): **ĝn̥-n-h*$_3$*-mé* etc., which, with the shift of stress to the root syllable in early PG and subsequent vowel reductions, produced **kunnum* etc. PG **kann* was generated as a new singular base by the analogy with strong verbs, class 3, e.g. *runnum*: *rann* :: *kunnum* : *kann*. The IE root *√ĝneh*$_3$, usually represented as *√ĝen* or *√ĝenə* in post-laryngeal IE, is widely attested in a variety of forms, e.g. Skr *√jñā*, Grk γιγνώσκω (cf. noun γνῶσις), Lat *(g)nosco*, Russ *знать*.

man, munum < PG **man, *munun* < **mana, *mn̥m̥* < IE **móna, *mn̥mé* < *√men* (to think, be aware of). Cf. ON *muna*, Ger *meinen;* Skr *√man*, Gk μιμνήσκω (perf. μέμονα), Lat *memini* (remember), Russ *(по)мнить* (remember).

hugjan < PG **huɣyan-* < IE **kw̥ghyé-* or **kw̥kyé-* < *√kew* (to note, sense, hear) + extension **-gh-* or **-k-* + present suffix **-yé-*. Cf. ON *hyggja*, OSax *huggean*, OHG *huggen*. The IE root, plain and with the extensions **-s-* and **-d-*, is widely attested: Gk κοέω, Lat *caveo*, Russ *чуять*; for the **-s-* extension see **hausjan** in Lesson 5. The association of PG **huɣyan-* with a **-gh-* or **-k-* extension of this root is a conjecture on my part and is not found in Pokorny.

wenjan < PG **wǣniyan-* < IE **wēneye-* < **wēni-* (noun: hope) [< IE *√wen* (to strive for, desire)] + denom. suffix **-eye-*. Cf. ON *væna*, AS *wēnan*. For the noun PG **wǣni-* cf. Gothic **wens** (hope), ON *ván*, AS *wēn*, Ger *Wahn*. For the IE root *√wen* cf. Skr *√van*, Lat *venus* (love), *venustus* (charming).

þugkjan < PG **þunkiyan-* < IE **tn̥gyé-* < *√teng* (to think, know) + present suffix **-ye-*. Cf. ON *þykkja*, Ger *dünken*; Lat *tongeo* (a very rare dialectal word: to know). Note also Gothic **þagkjan** < PG **þankyan-* < IE **tongéye-* (with causative suffix): ON *þekkja*, Ger *denken*, Eng *think*.

steigan < PG **stīɣan-* < IE *√steygh-* (to stride, step up). Cf. Skr *√stigh*, Gk στείχω, Russ *(до)стигать* (reach, attain).

kindins < PG **kindena-* < **kendina-* < IE **ĝentino-* < **ĝenti-* (race, people) [< *√ĝen* (to beget) + nominal suffix **-ti-*] + suffix **-no-*. The word probably originally designated the head of a **ĝenti-*, perhaps with the more restricted sense of sub-tribe or clan. The IE root *√ĝen* is well attested in virtually all members of the IE family; cf. Skr *√jan*, Gk γίγνομαι, Lat *gigno, (g)natus*.

hundafaþs < **hunda**- hundred (Lesson 14) + -**faþs** < PG **faþiz* < IE **poti-* (lord, head of house). Cf. Skr *pati-*, Gk πόσις, Lat *potis* (powerful), Lith *pàts* (husband), Russ *господь* (the Lord, < **ghosti-poti-* lit. guest-master, host, = Lat *hospes, hospitis*).

auso < PG **auz-ōn-/-en-* < IE **ows-ōn-/-en-*. Cf. ON *eyra*, Ger *Ohr*, Eng *ear;* Gk οὖς (< **ows-os*), Lat *auris* (< **ows-is*), Russ *ухо*.

augo < PG **awɣ-ōn-/-en-* , apparently a modified form of **aɣw-ōn-/-en-*, altered to bring it closer in form to PG **awz-ōn-/-en-* (ear) just above. PG **aɣw-ōn-/-en-* < IE **okwen-*. Cf. ON *auga*, Ger *Auge*, Eng *eye;* Skr *akṣi-*, Gk ὄμμα (< **okʷmn̥-*), Lat *ocu(lus)*, Russ *око*.

anabusns < PG **anabūsniz* < *ana- (Lesson I) + **būsnis* < IE **bhūdhsni-* < *√bhewdh* (be awake, attentive) + suffix **-sni-*. Cf. ON *býsn* (warning, omen, wonder). For further comment see **anabiudan** (Lesson 15).

frijaþwa < PG **frijaþwō* < IE **priyotwā* < *√prī* (to love, like) + suffix **-tw-*. Cf. Skr *priyatva*, Russ *приятель* (friend). The root *√prī* is phonologically complex; as a verbal root it appears in Skr *√prī* (to please), Gothic **frijon** (Lesson 19) and **frijonds** (Lesson 10).

ju < PG ** yu* < IE **yu*, an adverb based on an inflected form of the ubiquitous demonstrative base **i-*, **ei-*, **e-*. Cf. AS *iū*, *gēo* OHG *ju*. See Pokorny pp. 281-6.

-u: no clear etymology.

aufto: no clear etymology.

duþe < **du** (Lesson I) + **-þe** < IE **tē*, an instrumental form of the demonstrative pronoun **to-* (see **sa** in Lesson I). A variant **tō* underlies OSax *thō*, OHG *duo*, and Lith *tuõ*, all meaning approximately *then, thereupon, at that*. Cf. also Gk τῇ and τῷ, Skr *tā* in the same meaning. Gothic **-þe** is also found in **biþe** (Lesson 14) and **jaþþe** (< **jah-þe**), a correlative conjunction: **jaþþe X jaþþe Y** either X or Y.

bisunjane, the *Gpl* of ***bisunja** environ, lit. that which is around, < **bi-** (Lesson 5) + ***sunja** < PG **sundyan-* < IE **sn̥tyon-* < **sont-* (participle of *√es* to be) + suffix **-ey-/-y-* + **-on-/-en-*. Cf. **sunja** in Lesson 3.

Lesson 17

For the IE antecedents of Strong verbs, class 3, see Historical Lesson 12.

Prior to their assimilation to ya-stem types (Historical Lesson 4), i-stem adjectives followed the inflection of i-stem nouns treated in Historical Lesson 7.

Etymologies:

bindan < PG **bindan-* < IE **bhendh-* (to bind). Cf. ON *binda*, Ger *binden*, Eng *bind;* Skr *√bandh*. See also **bandi** (Lesson 10).

finþan < PG **finþan-* < IE **pent-* (to step, find). Cf. ON *finna*, Ger *finden*, Eng *find;* cognates elsewhere are primarily nominal: Skr *panthā* (path), Gk πάτος (path), πατέω (to walk), Lat *pons, pontis* (bridge), Russ *путь* (path).

duginnan = **du-** (Hist. Less. 1) + **-ginnan** < PG **ginnan-* , with no certain IE etymology. Cf. OHG *(bi)ginnan*, Eng *(be)gin*. Probably from IE *√ghend*, var. *√ghed* (to seize, grasp) and cognate with **bigitan** (Lesson 7), but the phonological development is not at all clear. But compare the following entry.

rinnan < PG **rinnan-* < IE **rinwe-* < **h₃rynH-*, the infixed n-present of **√h₃reyH* (to well up, flow, run). Cf. ON *rinna*, Ger *rennen*, Eng *run;* Gk ὀρίνω, Skr **√ri*, Russ *ринуть* (to flow). The IE root is obviously phonologically complex and is represented (post-laryngeally) by Pokorny p. 328 as *√er, or, r*. The derivation given here is that of LIV p. 271. The reconstruction of the root and form seems sound enough, but the phonological development into PG remains tentative. The strong preterite forms PG **rann-*, **runn-* are necessarily an internal PG analogical development.

filhan < PG **felhan-* < IE **pelk-* < *√pel* (to hide, cover over) + extension **-k-*. Cf. ON *fela*, Ger *(be)fehlen* (entrust > charge, order); cognates outside of Germanic are mainly nominal: Gk πέλας (skin, hide), Lat *pellis* (< **pel-n-*), Russ *плёнка* (film, chaff). Cf. **þrutsfill** (Lesson 14).

swiltan < PG **sweltan-* < IE *√swel* (to burn, smoulder) + extension **-d-*. Cf. ON *svelta* (to starve, die), AS *sweltan* (to die). Semantics: burn, smoulder > die out > die. From the plain root *√swel* are Skr *√svar* (to shine), Gk εἵλη (sunlight), Lith *svelti* (to smoulder), Ger *schwelen* (to smoulder).

uslaubjan: see **galaubjan** (Lesson 13).

ganisan: see **nasjan** (Lesson 10).

ataugjan = **at-** (Lesson 10) + **augjan** (to show) < PG **awɣiyan-*, a denominative verb from **awɣ-* (eye), Lesson 16. Cf. ON *éygja*, Eng *to eye*, Ger *äugen*, all of which, however, mean *to look at* rather than *to show*.

hazjan < PG **hazyan-* < IE **kosyé-*, probably from *√kes* (to comb) + denominative suffix **-ye-*. Cf. AS *herian*. Although this etymology is not given in Pokorny, the transfer of meaning to that of *touch, caress, coddle* well attested in Slavic for this root could easily have been carried a step further in PG: *to caress > encourage > praise*. Cf. especially Czech *kochati, kosnąti*. An equally plausible derivation from IE *√k̑ens* (Skr *√çaṅs* to praise; Lat *censeo* to think, deem) has also been proposed.

ufkunþi: see **kunþi** (Lesson 10).

fraiw < PG **frayw-*. Cf. ON *fræ, frjó*. No known etymology. The word is probably derived from an extended form of IE *√per²* (D) (to give birth, bring forth); cf. Lat *pario* (give birth), Lith *perė́ti* (to breed). For the semantics compare Egyptian *prt* (seed, fruit, offspring) from the root *pry* (to go forth) and Hebrew *pərî* (fruit, progeny) < *√pry* (to put forth fruit).

þiuda < PG **þewđō* < IE **tewtā́* (nation, people). Cf. ON *þjóð*, AS *đēod*, OHG *diot*, adj. *diutisc* (> Ger *deutsch*); OIr *tūath*, Lith *tautà*. See also **þiudans** (Lesson 1).

daur < PG **dur-* < IE **dhwṛó-* (door). Cf. ON *dyrr, dura-*, Ger *Tür*, AS *duru*, Eng *door;* Skr *dur-, dvar-*, Gk θύρα, Lat *forēs* (pl.), OCSl *dvŭri* (pl.).

hraini-: see **gahrainjan** (Lesson 15).

auþi-: see **auþida** (Lesson 7).

andanemi- < PG **anda-* (Lesson 2) + **nǣmi-* < IE **nēmi-* (taking, receiving) < *√nem* (to take, receive). Cf. ON *nám* (noun: seizure), OHG *nāmi* (agreeable), Ger *(ge)nehm*. See **niman** (Lesson 7)

eisarnein- < PG **īsarnīn-* < IE **eisornīn-* < **eisorn-* (iron) + adj. suffix **-īn-*. The IE word **eisorn-* is posited on the basis of the Germanic and Celtic cognates: ON *ísarn*, Ger *Eisen*, Eng *iron;* OIr *īārn*. Beyond that, however, there is no concensus; Pokorny takes it to the root *√eis* (to move swiftly or violently), but the wide semantic range of the possible cognates makes for little certainty. There is a possible connection with meteors and meteoric iron, a known source of iron for early societies. Cf., for example, the New Egyptian word for iron, *biꜣ-n-pt* (Coptic ⲃⲉⲛⲓⲡⲉ), lit., the metal from the sky.

midj- < PG **medy-* < IE **medhyo-* (middle). Cf. ON *miðr*, Ger *mitte(n)*, Eng *mid;* Skr *madhya-*, Gk μέσος, Lat *medius*, Russ *между* (between).

maht-: see **mahts** (Lesson 8), **magan** (Lesson 5).

frumist-, superlative of **fruma** (first, prior) < PG **frum-* < IE **pṛmó-* < *√per* (forward, out across) + suffix **-mo-*. Cf. MHG *frum* (brave, virtuous), Ger *fromm*, AS *forma, fyrmest*, reshaped in modern English to *foremost*. For further cognates of IE *√per*, with its numerous extensions and suffixes, see Pokorny pp. 810-819.

samaþ < PG **sama(n)-* (see **sama**, Lesson 11) + adv. suffix **-þ* < IE **-te* (motion toward). Cf. **dalaþ** (Lesson 7).

Lesson 18

Strong Verbs: Class 6.

The present/preterite ablaut **a/o** (PG **a/ō*) can be accounted for by assuming that we are dealing with verbs derived from IE roots which, prior to the loss of laryngeals, had the forms $C_1eh_2C_2$ or $C_1eh_3C_2$. The present stem would then exhibit the zero-grade of the root before a stressed thematic vowel or the present suffix **-yé-*: $C_1h_2C_2(y)\acute{e}$- > $C_1aC_2(y)\acute{e}$- or $C_1h_3C_2(y)\acute{e}$- > $C_1oC_2(y)\acute{e}$-. The stem of the perfect singular, namely $C_1eC_1oh_2C_2$- > $C_1eC_1\bar{o}C_2$- or $C_1eC_1oh_3C_2$- > $C_1eC_1\bar{o}C_2$-, was apparently leveled through the full perfect inflection, but the reduced form was retained in the stem of the past passive participle.

The following roots fit this pattern and, along with others now lost, may account for the creation of this ablaut class in Germanic:

Root	Present stem (zero-grade)	Perfect stem (o-grade)	Gothic
*keh$_2$p	*kh$_2$pyé- > *kapyé-	*kekoh$_2$p- > *(ke)kōp-	**hafjan, hof**
*kleh$_2$t	*klh$_2$tyé- > *klatyé-	*kekloh$_2$t- > *(ke)klōt-	**-hlaþ(j)an, *-hloþ**
*seh$_2$g	*sh$_2$gé- > *sagé-	*sesoh$_2$g- > *(se)sōg-	**sakan, sok**
*steh$_2$t	*sth$_2$nté- > *stanté-	*sestoh$_2$t- > *(se)stōt-	**standan, stoþ**

Note here that *kleh$_2$t is a t-extension of the root √kleh$_2$ (to lay out, place) and that *steh$_2$t- is a similar extension of √steh$_2$ (to stand). The present stem *sth$_2$nt- is the zero-grade of the infixed n-present of the extended root.

Most of the remaining verbs probably entered this class by various analogies. For example, IE roots of the form Ceh_1C would also have generated perfects with stem vowel *ō* (*$C_1eC_1oh_1C_2$ > *$C_1eC_1\bar{o}C_2$-); the present stems with *a* would have to be analogical. Other examples from Strong Verbs: Class 7 are discussed in Lesson 21; cf. especially the verbs **tekan, taitok** (to touch) and **garedan, garairod** (to consider, attend to) from the IE roots *teh$_1$g and *reh$_1$dh respectively. Note also the etymology suggested for the PP verb **og** in Lesson 20

Etymologies:

fraþjan < PG **fraþyan-* < IE **protye-* (to understand) < *√pret* + suffix **-ye-*. Cf. Lith *(su)prat-* and Gothic **frod-** in Lesson 4. The IE cognates are too few to support an exact reconstruction. If, for example, the IE root were originally a t-extension of a more primitive *preh$_2$, namely *preh$_2$t-, this would comport better with the Germanic evidence. See our discussion of these verbs above.

andhafjan, ushafjan: see **andhafjan** (Lesson 7).

sakan < PG **sakan-* < IE **sagé-* < *sh$_2$gé- < √seh$_2$g (to follow a trail, track) + stressed thematic vowel. For a different formation from this same root see **sokjan** in Lesson 5. The semantics are a bit obscure, but the Germanic cognates seem to have a legal setting, hence: *pursuit at law > judgement, rebuke*, etc. Cf. Gothic **sokns** (an inquiry), AS *sōcn*, ON *sōk* (legal complaint). The legal connotations of the cognate Gk ἐξηγέομαι are noteworthy in this regard.

standan < PG **standan-* < IE **stanté-* < *sth$_2$nté-, the infixed *n* present of the secondary root **stat-*, which is an extension in **-t-* of the primitive root *√sta* < *steh$_2$ (to stand). Cf. ON *standa*, Eng *stand.* From the primitive root cf. Skr *√sthā*, Gk ἵστημι, Lat *sto, sisto*, Russ *стоить*, Ger *stehen.*

ligan < PG **leγan-* < IE **legh-* (to lie, be situated). Cf. ON *liggja*, Ger *liegen*, Eng *lie;* Gk λέχεται (dialectal), Russ *лежать*. See also **lagjan** in Lesson 9. Gothic **ligan** stands apart from the other Germanic verbal cognates, which presuppose PG **leγγan-* < IE **leghyé-*, a present stem in **-yé-*.

satjan < PG **satyan-* < IE **sodéye-* < *√sed* (to sit) + caus. suffix **-éye-*. Cf. ON *setja*, Ger *setzen*, Eng *set;* Skr *sādáya-*, Russ *садить*. See also **sitan** in Lesson 7 and the discussion in §18.5.

urraisjan < **us-** (LessonI) + **raisjan** < PG **raysiyan-* < IE **royséye-* < *√reys* (to rise) + caus. suffix **-éye-*. The root *√reys* is a secondary form consisting of the primitive root *√h₃er* + the extensions *-y-* and *-s-*. Cf. ON *reisa*, Eng *raise*. For further cognates see **urreisan** (Lesson 14), where it was noted that this particular development of the IE root occurs only in Germanic. See also §18.5.

sigqan < PG **senkʷan-* < IE **sengʷ-* (to sink). Cf. ON *sökkva*, Ger *sinken*, Eng *sink*. Rare outside of Germanic: Armenian *ankan-* and Gk ἐάφθη (he sank, < **éśŋgʷ-*).

sweran < PG **swǣran-* < IE **swēr-* (adj. heavy; secondarily a verbal root) < *√swer* (to weigh, be heavy). Cf. Gothic **swer-** (honored), Ger *schwer* (heavy), Lith *svarùs* (heavy).

sunno < PG **sunnōn-*, **sunnin-* < IE **sunwon-*, *sunwen-* < *√swel, swen* + suffix **-won-/-wen-*. Cf. ON *suðr* (south < sunward), Ger *Sonne*, Eng *sun*. The IE cognates are difficult to reconcile systematically with any one primitive form. Compare, for example, Skr *suvar, sūra* (< **suwer-*), Gk ἥλιος (< **sāwel-yo-*), Lat *sol* (< **sāwel-*); Gothic **sauil** (< **sāwel-*), ON *sól;* Russ *солнце*.

sinista < PG **senistan-* < IE **sen-* (old) + superlative suffix **-ist-* + **-on-/-en-*. See **sineig-** (Lesson 3).

sauil: see **sunno** just above.

liuhaþ < PG **lewhaþ-* < IE **lewkat-* < *√lewk* (to shine) + suffix **-at-*. Cf. Ger *Licht*, Eng *light;* Skr *√ruc* (to shine), Gk λευκός (white, shining), Lat *lux*, Russ *луч* (ray, beam).

asans < PG **asan-* < IE **oson-* (harvest time). Cf. ON *önn*, Ger *Ern(te)*, Russ *осень*. See also **asneis** (Lesson 4).

þiumagus = **þiw-** (see **þiwi**, Lesson 3) + **magus** (Lesson 9).

usliþa < PG **usliþan-*, based on the stem of the pp. of **usleiþan** (Lesson 14). The probable semantics are *one whose strength is gone;* cf. Eng *goner*.

weinagards = **wein** (Lesson 12) + **gards** (Lesson 7).

spedist- is the superlative of ***sped-** (late) < PG **spǣd-*. Cf. Ger *spät*. This word is assigned by Pokorny to *√sp(h)ē(y)* [*speh₁*] (to grow stout, succeed, go forward). The formal and semantic relationships are less than satisfactory; the word is best left without an etymology beyond PG.

juþan: see Lesson 23.

jainþro = **jain-** (Lesson 4) + **-þro** (Lesson 23).

usdaudo, an adverb in **-o** (Lesson 23) from the adjective **usdaud-** (eager, assiduous) < **us-** (Lesson I) + **-daud-** < PG **dawd-* < IE **dhowto-* (dead) < *√dhew* (to die) + suffix **-to-*. This etymology assumes that the prefix **us-** has a negative force (rare, but possible) and that **daud-**, in addition to its normal meaning of *dead*

(Lesson 8) also meant *listless, spiritless,* for which there is some support in Germanic. I would suggest as an alternate derivation *swift* > *assiduous, eager,* taking it to the IE base **dhowt-* < *√dhew* (to flow, run) + suffix **-to-*. Cf. Skr *√dhav* (to run), Gk θόος (swift). Cf. the semantics of **þiwi** (Lesson 3).

fairraþro = **fairra** (Lesson 12) + **-þro** (Lesson 23).

þande = **þan** (Lesson 13) + **-de** (Lesson 23).

Lesson 19

Weak verbs: class 2.

This class of verbs can be compared directly to the Latin First Conjugation and to Greek contract verbs in -άω. It originated in IE as a denominative class based on nominal stems in *-ā- plus the denominative suffix *-ye-/-yo-; these verbs were presumably inflected as ordinary thematic verbs in the present system (*-āyō, -āyesi, -āyeti* etc.). The contractions attested in Latin, PG, and partially in Greek may well have begun in IE itself. Because of the *-i-* in the Old English verbs of this class, as represented by the infinitive *sealfian* (Gothic **salbon**), to anoint, Ist pers. sing. pres. *sealfie*, pl. *sealfiaþ*, a more conservative reconstruction is required in PG, where the uncontracted stem in *-ōy- is retained in these three forms at least, for which there is no convincing alternate (i.e. analogical) source.

		Greek	Latin	OHG	Old English	Gothic
Indicative	Is	-άω, -ῶ	*-ō*	*-ōm*	*-ie*	*-o*
Active	2s	-άεις -ᾷς	*-ās*	*-ōs(t)*	*-as(t)*	*-os*
	3s	-άει, -ᾷ	*-at*	*-ōþ*	*-aþ*	*-oþ*

The OHG Ist pers. sing. in *-m* further suggests an original thematic (IE *-āmi, -āsi, -āti* etc.) rather than a thematic inflection. One is apparently forced to reconstruct both paradigms for the parent language. Note the similar situation with weak verbs, class 3, discussed on p. 275 above.

The PG passive participle in *-ōđ- is probably inherited (e.g. from IE *-āyetó-; cf. Lat *-ātus*) and, as with the secondary preterites of preterite-present verbs, could have provided the analogical base for the extension of the weak preterite to this class. It is equally probable, however, that these verbs developed these preterite forms along with all of the other derived (i.e. weak) verbs by periphrasis.

[For the IE origin of the dual pronouns see Historical Grammar Lesson 10. The dual forms of the verb have already been introduced with the historical discussion of the various verbal inflections.]

Etymologies:

aihtron: denom. from ***aihtr**- < PG **ayhtr-* < IE **oyktr-* < √*eyg* (cry out in need) + *-tro-*. Cf. Gk οἰκτρός (piteous, wretched), Ir *iacht* (to groan, lament).

awiliudon: denom. from **awiliud**- (praise) < ***awi**- + ***liud**-. ***awi**- < PG **awi-* < IE **awi-* (what is desired) < √*aw-* (to desire, long for). Cf. Skr √*av* (to favor), Lat *aveo* (long for). ***liud**- < PG **lewđ-* < IE **lewt-* < √*lew,law* (to praise) + extension *-t-*. Cf. Lat *laud-* (< IE **law-* + extension *-d-*); ON *ljóð* (verse, song), Ger *Lied* (song), AS *lēoþ*.

faginon: denom. from ***fagin**- (happy) < PG **faɣ( )n-* < IE **pok̂n-́* < √*pek̂* (be happy, glad; make pleasant). Cf. ON *fegin-* (glad, joyful), AS *fægnian* (to rejoice). The root is well developed within Germanic. See **faheþs** (Lesson 12) for further information.

hwarbon: denom. from ***hwarb**- < PG **hwarƀ-* < IE **kworp-́* (turning, returning) < √*kwerp* (to turn, return). The root is well developed in Germanic; cf. Gothic **hweilahwairb**- *adj* transitory, **gahwairb**- *adj* obedient, **hwairban** *sv 3* to wander (< PG *hwerbǣ́n-*), ON *hverfa* (turn, circulate, disappear), Ger *werben*, etc. Note also Toch B *karp-* (return, go).

idreigon: denom. from **idreiga** (see Lesson 10).

wopjan < PG **wōpiyan-* < IE **wāb-* (to cry out) + suffix *-eye-*. Cf. ON *œpa*, OSax *wōpian*, Eng *weep;* OCSl *vabiti* (call to, lure).

hweilan < PG **hwīlǣn-* < IE **hwīlē-* < **hwīl-* (see **hweila**, Lesson 15) + essive suffix *-ē-*.

frijon: denom from ***frija** (love) < PG **friyō* < IE **priyā* (love; wife). Cf. ON *frjá* (to love), MHG *vrīen.* See **frijonds** (Lesson 10) and **frijaþwa** (Lesson 16) for further cognates.

staiga < PG **staygō* < IE **stoyghā* < *√steygh* (to step, climb). Cf. ON *stígr*, Ger *Steig;* Gk στοῖχος (line, row). The root also occurs in Gothic **steigan** *sv 1* to climb.

barnilo < **barn** (Lesson 2) + diminutive suffix -(**i**)**lo**- < PG **-lōn-* < IE **-lōn-*. Cf. the masculine form of the suffix on **magula** (little boy, **magus**) and the feminine (?) on **mawilo** (little girl, **mawi**). IE suffixes in **-l-* have a wide range of forms and meanings; as a parallel to the diminutive use cf. Latin *filiolus* (small son; *filius*), *agellus* (little field; *ager*).

nahts < PG **naht-* < IE **nok^wt-* (night). Cf. ON *nátt*, Ger *Nacht*, Eng *night;* Skr *nakt-*, Gk νύξ, νυκτός, Lat *nox, noctis*, OCSl *noštĭ.*

gabaurþs < PG **ga-* + **burþ-* < IE **bhr̥ti-* (bearing, burden, birth) < *√bher* (bear, esp. a child) + suffix *-ti-*. Cf. ON *byrð* (birth), Ger *Geburt*, Eng *birth.* See also Gothic **bairan** (Lesson 13), **barn** (Lesson 3), **baurþei** (burden), **barms** (bosom, lap), and **berusjos** (parents) from this same root.

sinþs < PG **sinþ-* < IE **sent-* (a going, journey, path) < *√sent* (to go, proceed). Cf. ON *sinn* (time, instance), OHG *sind* (way, journey). For the verbal root see **sandjan** (Lesson 5).

ainaha- < **ain**- (Lesson 9) + suffix -**aha**- (Lesson 22).

auhumist- < **auh**- + superlative suffixes -**um**- and -**ist**- (see Lesson 20). The source of the basic adjective **auh**- is unclear. A derivation from IE *√ok̂* = *√ak̂* (be sharp, pointed) is certainly possible; for the meaning cf. Gk ἀκμή (highest point), ἄκρος (uppermost), OIr *ēr* (high; < **akros*) from this root.

Lesson 20

The comparative and superlative degrees of adjectives.

Two suffixes were used in IE to form the comparative degree of adjectives:

(1) **-yes-*, with the ablaut gradations **-yos-*, **-yōs-*, and **-is-*, added directly to the adjectival base without its formative suffix, e.g. **swādi-* (or **swādu-*) sweet, comparative **swādis-*;

(2) **-tero-*, added to the adjectival stem with its formative suffix. Because this suffix is also employed to form contrastive spatial and temporal adjectives, its use to form simple comparatives is possibly secondary.

The subsequent development of these two suffixes varied considerably from language to language. While a detailed discussion of their occurrence in the individual IE subfamilies would be out of place here, the following brief comments on these suffixes in Sanskrit, Greek, Latin, and Gothic should be helpful.

In Sanskrit the ending **-yes-* appears as *-yas-* or, much more frequently, *-īyas-*; the exact source of the vowel lengthening in the latter is unknown, but compare the Greek parallel below and note the variation between *-ĭš-* (< **-yes-*) and *-ěiš-* (< **-ēyes-*) in OCSl. The distribution of this suffix in Sanskrit provides a clue to the curious fact that it is added, e.g. in Greek and Germanic, to the adjectival base without its formative suffix: it seems originally to have been used to produce comparative adjectives from verbal bases directly, and not through the intermediary of the simple adjective. Such is the case with the majority of its occurrences, where it could be categorized almost as an intensive stative participle. The form was, however, sometimes associated with a simple adjective and was eventually extended to ordinary adjectival bases. The suffix **-tero-* > *-tara-*, on the other hand, functions freely as a comparative suffix and was added to adjectival stems of every sort.

In Greek, as in Germanic below, the suffix **-is-* was compounded with the suffix **-en-/-on-*. With the regular loss of the intervocalic *-s-* in Greek, the resulting form is - ίων, G -ίονος. The length of the -ι- varies from dialect to dialect: in Attic it is long; in Epic and Doric it is more frequently short. Assimilations are also regular and frequent, e.g. ταχύς (swift), θάσσων (swifter, < *θαχιων). The direct association with a verbal base found in Sanskrit is not present in Greek. The comparative suffix -τερο-, is much more frequent and is added freely to adjectives of every stem type.

In Latin, the ablaut variant **-yōs-* underlies the suffixes *-ior* (neuter *-ius*) of the comparative. Here again there is no trace of a formative suffix before this ending; cf. *altus, altior; tristis, tristior.* The suffix *-ter* is limited to a small number of non-comparative contrastive adjectives like *dexter* (right), *sinister* (left), *alter* (the other), *uter* (which of the two?), etc.

In Germanic, the comparative suffix **-is-* dominates completely, compounded, as in Greek, with the suffix **-en-/-on-*. Since this latter suffix is also the source of the so-called weak adjectival inflection, it would appear that the rule stating that comparative adjectives are always inflected as weak adjectives is a reversal of the true historical situation: the n-inflection of the comparative adjective is probably inherited from a late phase of IE, while the n-inflection of simple adjectives is an extension within Germanic. The influence of the comparative adjectives on the development of the weak adjectival inflection should not be underrated, especially in view of their frequent epithetic usage. The etymologies of the irregular comparative adjectives like **batiz-**, **minniz-** etc. are given below. The suffix **-tero-* (Gothic **-þar**), as in Latin, survives only on a few contrastive adjectives, i.e. **anþar** (other) and **hwaþar** (which of the two?), and a few isolated items such as **aftaro** (behind).

The superlative degree of adjectives in IE was formed in one of several ways:

(1) by the addition of the suffix **-to-* (or **-tho-*) to the reduced grade of the comparative suffix **-is-*, producing **-isto-*. This form has approximately the same distribution in Sanskrit (*-iṣthas*) and Greek (-ιστος) as the corresponding comparatives in *-(ī)yas-* and -ιων respectively. It is the normal superlative suffix in Germanic.

(2) by the addition of the suffix **-tm̥o-*. In Sanskrit, *-tama-* (< **-tm̥o-*) is the regular superlative suffix for those adjectives that form their comparatives in *-tara-*. In Greek, the superlative suffix corresponding to the comparative -τερο- is -τατο-, formed by the addition of the suffix **-to-* to **-tm̥-*: **-tm̥to-* > *-tato-* or else, at a later period in Pre-Greek, by the simple replacement of **-mo-* in **-tamo-* (< **-tm̥o-*) with **-to-*.

The plain suffix **-tm̥o-* underlies the -**um**- of Gothic **aftum**- etc. (see the Grammar Lesson) and of Latin *-imus*, e.g. in *intimus, optimus*. Since most of the words with these suffixes have contrastive spatial or directional meanings, it is apparent that the use of the suffix **-tm̥o-* closely parallelled that of **-tero-* in both Latin and Germanic.

The Germanic comparative and superlative forms in **-ōz-* and **-ōst-* pose a problem. Wright (p. 112-3) and others see the origin of these suffixes in analogically formed comparatives from adverbs ending in **-ô* in PG with the subsequent extension of the form (at random?) to various simple adjectives. This new formation was facilitated by the fact that the unaugmented comparative suffix PG **-iz* was regularly used to form the comparative of adverbs (cf. Gothic *hauhis* higher, *mais* more, etc.). The formation of the superlative in **-ōst-* would have involved just one more simple analogical step. Although the exact analogy that produced the original PG **-ōz* is difficult to reconstruct, there seems to be no other likely source for these endings.

Etymologies:

þarf, þaurbum < PG **þarf-, *þurb-́* < IE **(te)torp-, (te)tr̥p-́* < *√terp* (satisfy; require for satisfaction). Cf. ON *þarf, þurfum*, Ger *darf, durfen;* Skr *√tr̥p* (be satisfied), Gk τέρπω (satisfy, delight), Toch *tsārw-* (rejoice).

gadars, gadaursum < PG **ga- + *dars-, *durz-́* < IE **(de)dhors-, *(de)dhr̥s-́* < *√dhers* (be bold, dare). Cf. Eng *dare;* Skr *√dhr̥ṣ*, Gk θαρσέω.

og < PG **ōɣ, *oɣum* < IE **āgh-, *āgh-́* < **$h_2ch_2$ógh-, *h_2eh_2gh-́* < *√agh [h_2egh]* (to fear). Cf. ON *óa(sk)* (be afraid); Gk ἄχομαι (be troubled), OIr *(ad)-ágathar* (to fear).

aih, aigum < PG **ayh-, *ayg-́* < IE **oyk-, *ayk-́* < **HeHóyk-, *HeHyk-́* [*√Heyk*]. Cf. ON *á, eigum*, OHG *eigan* (to own); from PG **ayɣinōn-* are derived ON *eigna*, Ger *(an)eignen*, Eng *to own*. The only cognates outside Germanic are Skr *√iç* (to possess) and its derivatives.

ushramjan < **us**- (Lesson 1) + **hramjan** < PG **hramyan-* < IE **kromeye-* < **krom-* (wooden framework) + denom. suffix **-eye*. Cf. ON *hremma* (to clutch < to enclose), AS *hremman* (to narrow, hinder). I have not been able to verify Russ *кромы* (loom) and *закромить* (to board up) as given by Pokorny.

haitan < PG **haytan-* < IE **koyd-* < ? Cf. ON *heita*, Ger *heissen*, AS *hātan*. No clear cognates exist outside Germanic. The root is taken by Pokorny as possibly a d-extension of the root *√k̑ēy* (to set into motion), but is defined as a separate entry **k̑eyd* (to call) in LIV. See also the discussion of strong verbs, class 7, in Lesson 21 below.

fraliusan < **fra**- (Lesson 12) + **-liusan** < PG **lewsan-* < IE **lews-* < *√lew* (to release, let loose) + extension *-s-*. Cf. ON *losa*, Eng *lose*. Note also Gothic **lausjan** (release, set loose), Ger *lösen* < PG **lawsyan-*, and the adjective **laus-** (empty). For the plain root √*lew* cf. Skr √*lū*, Gk λύω, Lat *solvo* (< **se-luo*), loosen, dissolve.

laþon: a denominative from ***laþa** (invitation) < PG **laþō* < IE **latā* < √*la* + suffix *-t-*. Cf. ON *lǫð* (invitation), *laða* (to invite), Ger *laden*. The root √*la* (Pokorny's **lēi*, *ləi*, to want, wish) is otherwise attested only in Greek.

garazna < **ga-** (Lesson 12) + **razn** (Lesson 5). See also §21.4.2.

nehwundja < PG **nǣhw-* (Lesson 2) + **-undyan-* < IE **-n̥tyon-* < **-n̥t-* (part. adj. suffix) + **-yen-/-yon-* (see Lesson 6). This combination of suffixes is not found elsewhere in Gothic.

manaseþs < **mana-** (stem of **manna** Lesson 6) + **-seþs** (seed) < PG **sǣđ-* < IE **sēto-* (seed) < √*sēi* [*seh₁y*] (to sow) + suffix *-to-*. Cf. ON *sáð*, Ger *Saat*, Eng *seed*. See the verb **saian** *sv 7* to sow (Lesson 22) for further information.

aftumist-: secondary superlative in **-ist-** on **aftum-** (see above) < PG **aftum-* < IE **aptm̥-* < **ap* (see **af**, Lesson 9) + superlative suffix **-tm̥-*. Cf. AS *æftemest*. See also **aftra** (Lesson 15) and **aftaro** (Lesson 21).

frum- < PG **fruman-* < IE **pr̥mon-* (first, foremost) < **pro* [extended form of √*per* (out across, forward)] + suffix *-mon-/-men-*. Cf. AS *frum*, MHG *vrum*, Ger *fromm;* Gk πρόμος (leader).

wairsiz- < PG **wirsizan-*, comparative of **wirs-* < IE **wers-* (elevated, high). Cf. ON *verri*, OHG *wirsiro*, Eng *worse;* Skr *varṣīyas-* (higher), Russ *верх* (top, summit). Semantics: higher > more extreme > worse.

juhiz- < PG **yūhizan-* < **yunhizan-* < earlier **yúnhisan-*, comparative of PG **yungaz* < earlier **yuwungáz* (note stress). See **jugg-** (Lesson 3) for further details. The Gothic pair *jugg-/juhiz-* is an excellent example of Verner's Law.

alþiz- < PG **alþizan-*, comparative of PG **alþy-* (old) < IE **altyo-* < √*al* (grow, nourish) + suffix *-tyo-*. Cf. ON *ellri* (elder, < PG **alþizan-*), Eng *elder;* Ger *alt*, Eng *old*. For the root cf. especially Latin *alo* (to nourish) with its numerous derivatives, including *altus* (high < full-grown), and Gothic **alan** *sv 6* to grow (intrans.), ON *ala* (to nourish).

maiz- < PG **mayzan-* < IE **mayson-*, comparative in **-ison-* of **ma-* (large). Cf. ON *meir*, Ger *mehr*, Eng *more*. IE **ma-* is a reduced grade of **mē-/mō-*, which, with the extension *-r-*, underlies Gothic **merjan** (Lesson 5).

hardu- < PG **harđu-* < IE **kartu-* < **kart-* (strong) + suffix *-u-*. Cf. ON *harð-*, Ger *hart*, Eng *hard;* Gk (Homer) κρατύς (strong). Pokorny assigns IE **kart-* to the root **kar 3*, with suffixed *-t-*, but the derivatives are too varied formally and semantically to allow the formulation of a proper verbal root.

batiz- < PG **batizan-* < IE **bhadison-*, comparative of **bhad-* (good). Cf. ON *betri*, Ger *besser*, Eng *better*, Skr *bhadra-* (good, fortunate, < **bhad-ro-*).

Lesson 21

Strong verbs: class 7.

The verbs in the second group, as represented by **tekan**, **taitok**, conform quite well to the models presented in the discussions of the strong preterite in Lessons 12 and 18, which should be reviewed at this point. Of the seven Gothic verbs in this group, only **tekan** is without convincing cognates outside Germanic (see Etymologies below); for the remainder the original present and preterite stems were approximately as follows:

	Root (LIV)	Present Stem (e-grade)	Perfect Stem (o-grade)
gretan	*ghreh$_1$d	*ghreh$_1$d- > *ghrēd-	*gheghroh$_1$d- > *gheghrōd-
letan	*leh$_1$d	*leh$_1$d- > *lēd-	*leloh$_1$d- > *lelōd-
-redan	*reh$_1$dh	*reh$_1$dh- > *rēdh-	*reroh$_1$dh- > *rerōdh-
saian	*seh$_1$	*seh$_1$- > *sē-	*sesoh$_1$- > *sesō-
waian	*h$_2$weh$_1$	*h$_2$weh$_1$- > *(a)wē-	*h$_2$weh$_2$woh$_1$- > *(a)wāwō-
***laian**	*leh$_1$	*leh$_1$ > *lē-	*leloh$_1$ > *lelō-

Remarks:

(1) The perfect of *h$_2$weh$_1$ was apparently simplified to *wewō- in PG by analogy with *sesō- and *lelō-.

(2) The stem of the perfect singular was extended to the dual and plural at some stage. There is no trace of the original reduced grade plural stems in Germanic.

(3) On the basis of the foregoing, the antecedent forms of **tekan** can be assumed to have been

*deh$_1$g   *deh$_1$g- > *dēg-   *dedoh$_1$g- > *dedōg-.

The main problem with the verbs of the first group of class 7 verbs, as represented e.g. by **maitan, maimait,** lies in the fact that the stem vowels of the present and preterite are the same, reflecting PG *a and IE *a or *o. None of the models proposed thus far would yield this result. Before considering the solutions that have been proposed, it will be helpful to list the preterite (IE perfect) singular stems of the verbs belonging to this group.

	Root (LIV)	Root (Pokorny)	IE Perfect singular
falþan, faifalþ	---	*pel(+t)	*pepolt-
haldan, haihalþ	*keldh	*kel(+dh)	*kekoldh-
-staldan, staistalþ	*steldh	*stel(+dh)	*stestoldh-
fahan, faifah	*paḱ	*păḱ	*pepōḱ-
hahan, haihah	*kenḱ	*kenḱ	*kekonḱ-
-aikan, -aiaik	---	---	**eoyg-
fraisan, faifrais	---	---	**peproys
haitan, haihait	*ḱeyd	*ḱēi(+d)	*ḱeḱoyd-
laikan, lailaik	*leyg	*leig	*leloyg-
maitan, maimait	*meyH	*mai(+d)	*memoyd-
skaidan, skaiskaiþ	*sḱheyd	*sḱĕi(+d)	*sḱhesḱhoyd-
slepan, saislep	*sleh$_1$b	*(s)lĕb	??
hwopan, hwaihwop	---	---	??

aukan, aiauk	**h₂ewg*	**aweg, *aug*	**h₂eh₂owg-*

Although at least half of these roots are composite, with dental extensions in particular, the forms presupposed for the stage of IE leading into PG are essentially the same as those of strong verbs of classes 1-6, so that the perfect forms suggested above, if shorn of their reduplicating syllables, would conform to the prototypes of the strong preterites of these six classes. How, then, can we account for the prevailing *-a-* of the present tense form? Two solutions underlie the presentation of these verbs in LIV, reflecting the prevailing scholarly view; neither solution is quite convincing.

(1) One can simply say that the vowel of the perfect was extended to the present stem in PG. This is the solution offered for **haldan** (LIV p. 311, note 4) and reluctantly suggested, as an alternative, for **hahan** (LIV p. 290). This type of solution is unsatisfactory because the transfer of the vowel from the perfect to the present is completely unmotivated. It seems to state, in essence, that we can account for the a-vowel of the present stem in these verbs by not accounting for it!

(2) The present stems of these verbs can be assigned to a completely different pattern having an o-grade in IE. The only present type that qualifies is the pattern **C₁éC₁oC₂-* (type 1g in LIV); the reduplicated perfect of this type differed from the present only in stress: **C₁eC₁óC₂-*. This solution assumes the loss of reduplication in the PG present. LIV explicitly favors this etymology for **-staldan** (p. 541), **hahan** (p. 290, note 2), **haitan** (p. 285), **laikan** (p. 363), and **skaidan** (p. 496). There are two objections to this solution. The loss of the reduplication in the present but not in the perfect (preterite) is very strange and appears to be contrary to the vast majority of strong verbs in PG with non-reduplicated preterites. The more serious objection, however, is that not one of the roots involved in this entire first group of class 7 verbs exhibits this type of present stem in any other IE subfamily, i.e. the descendants of these particular reduplicated presents occur only in Germanic. It is obvious that the origin of this verbal class remains an open question.

Noun formation: the suffixes *-ei*, *-nds*, *-areis*, and *-assus*.

(1) The suffix **-ei** (*G* **-eins**) used to form abstract feminine nouns from adjectival bases has no exact counterpart elsewhere in IE, and its origin, therefore, is a matter for conjecture rather than reconstruction by direct comparisons. In addition to this derivational function, the suffix has a second use, namely, to form the weak feminine inflection of (a) active participles (in **-andei**, *G* **-andeins**) and (b) comparative adjectives (in **-izei**, *G* **-izeins**). The use of the suffix to form feminine adjectives does have striking partial parallels elsewhere in IE and these may throw some light on its development as a nominal suffix.

In Sanskrit the suffix *-ī* (*G -yās;* see *ā-* and *yā*-stem nouns in Lesson 3) is used regularly to form the feminine of active participles in *-ant-* (thus *-antī, G -antyās*), in *-vāṅs* (thus *-uṣī, G -uṣyās; -us-* is the weak form of *-vas-*), of the comparatives in *-īyas* (thus *-īyasī, G -īyasyās*), and of adjectives formed with various suffixes, including adjectives in *-u-* (*N* masc. *-us*, fem. *-vī*). These can be parallelled for the most part in Greek; note especially the present active participle in -οντ- with feminine -ουσα, *G* -ούσης (< **-ontya, G *-ontyās*), the perfect active participle in masc. -ως, *G* -οτος (< **-wōs, G *-wotos*), fem. -υια, *G* -υιης (< **-usya, G *-usyās*). Parallels in Baltic make it clear that we are dealing with an IE phenomenon here, but the suffix in all these languages is that of the IE **-yā*-stem inflection, while Gothic **-ei**, *G* **-eins** has been modified to that of an n-stem inflection. This metamorphosis of the ending was probably a result of various analogies during the evolution of the so-called weak adjective in Proto-Germanic (see Lessons 7 and 8). To judge from the evidence of Sanskrit and Greek, the number of IE adjectival types forming feminines in **-ī*, G **-yās* must have been quite extensive. We have no way of knowing how many of these found their way into early PG, but the absorption of the form into the weak adjectival system automatically involved nominalization, and its subsequent independent use as an abstract noun would have required only a simple step.

(2) The substantivized active participles like **frijonds** (see Lesson 10 for inflection) preserve the original IE consonantal inflection (Lesson 6) of the participial stem in **-ont-* (Lesson 8). The feminine ***friyondi** (*Apl* **friyondyos**) would seem to be the sole survivor in Gothic of the IE *-ī, G -yās* adjectival suffix discussed in the preceding paragraph.

(3) The agential suffix **-areis** (-ārj-) is assumed to be a direct borrowing from Latin *-ārius*, as on *notarius* (secretary), *sicarius* (assassin) etc. The fact, however, that none of the words containing this suffix in Gothic is itself a borrowing from Latin, together with the high frequency of the suffix in Old High German (*-āri*) and Anglo-Saxon (*-ere*), suggest that a native Germanic source should be considered. The phonetic problems, however, are formidable, since there is no recognized source for Gothic *-ā-* in this environment. But cf. p. 264 above.

(4) The suffix **-assus** is generally regarded as derived from IE **-attu-* < **-adtu-*, analyzed as an abstract noun in **-tu-* on stems ending in **-ad-*. The nominal formation was presumably originally associated, as a kind of verbal noun, with denominative verbs in **-eye-* based on nominal stems ending in **-ad-*, thus **-adye-*, the ancestor of the prolific denominative verbal class in -άζω in Greek. The three verbs of this type in Gothic are **kaupatjan** (to strike), **lauhatjan** (to lightning), and **swogatjan** (to sigh), generally classified as intensives or iteratives.

Etymologies

letan: see **aftletan** (Lesson 8)

gretan < PG **grǣtan-* < IE **ghrēd- [ghreh₁d]* (to weep), attested only in Germanic. Cf. ON *gráta*, AS *grǣtan*. This is listed as a separate root in LIV, but assigned by Pokorny to *√gher 1*, albeit with hesitation. The causative verb IE **ghrōdeye-* >PG **grōtyan-* (cause to weep) underlies ON *grœta* (cause to weep), but Ger *grüssen* (to greet), Eng *greet*. The semantics remain a bit obscure.

tekan < PG **tǣkan-* < IE **dēg- [?deh₁g]* (seize, touch). Cf. ON *taka* (take, touch), Eng *take;* Tocharian A *tek-*, *tak-* (touch). It is difficult not to make a connection with Lat *tango, tetigi, tactus*, but this requires an IE root **teh₂g* or the like. Because even within Germanic the stem vowels of ON *taka* and Eng *take* are not the expected reflexes of PG *ǣ*, all reconstructions remain quite tentative.

maitan < PG **maytan-* < IE **mayd-* < *√may* (hack, hew) + extension *-d-*. Cf. ON *meita*, OHG *meizzan*. From IE **mayt-* (with extension *-t-*) we have Goth **gamaiþ-** (crippled), ON *meiða* (to maim, wound), OldSax *mǣded* (crazy), Eng *mad*. LIV (sub *1.mei̯H*) tentatively follows Pokorny on this, but assigns the meaning *gering werden, schwinden* to the root.

slepan < PG **slǣpan-* < IE **slēb- [*sleh₁b]* (to sleep). Cf. Ger *schlafen*, Eng *sleep*. The IE root in this form is attested only in Germanic. Pokorny regards it as a prefixed-s form of the broader root *√lĕb, lŏb, lab, ləb* (to hang down loosely) and cites a number of cognates including Lat *labor, lapsus* (to slip, glide) and a variety of Germanic words for *lip, tip, rabbit-ears, louts*, etc. A related (?) root *√(s)lĕp...*, with final **-p*, underlies another long series of cognates. All in all, it is probably preferable to follow the example of LIV, which lists a single doubtful root *?*sleh₁b* (schlaff sein) for Gothic **slepan**, Ger *schlafen*, and Eng *sleep*, together with BSl cognates meaning *weak*.

gakunnan < PG **ga-* + **kunnǣ-*, a secondary verb based on the stem of the preterite-present verb **kunnan** (Lesson 16), q.v. for further etymological information. Since the origin of **kann, kunnum** is itself rather complex, there can be little certainty on the exact sequence of development of the secondary weak verb except to note that it already existed in PG (cf. OHG *kunnēn* to know).

horinon: a denominative verb from **hors** (adulterer, whore-monger) < PG **hōr-* < IE **kāro-* (dear, desirable) < *√kā [*keh₂]* (to desire) + suffix *-ro-*. Cf. ON *hórr*, Ger *Hurer*, Eng *whore;* Lat *cārus* (dear); Skr *kāma-* (love, < **kā-mo-*).

andbahtjan: a denominative verb based on **andbahts** (Lesson 4).

marzjan < PG **marziyan-* < IE **morseye-* < √*mers* (to disturb, annoy, neglect) + caus./denom. suffix *-eye-*. Cf. AS *mierran,* OHG *marren;* Skr √*mṛṣ* (to neglect, fail to heed), Lith *miršti̇̀* (forget).

ufrakjan < PG **uf-* + **rakjan-* < IE **roĝéye-* (to extend) < √*reĝ* (straight, straighten, put right) + caus. suffix *-éye-*. Cf. ON *rekja,* Ger *recken,* Eng *reach.* Note also **garaiht-** (Lesson 2) and **reiks** (Lesson 14) from this same root.

bandja < PG **bandyan-* < IE **bhondhyon-* < √*bhendh* (to bind) + suffix **-yen-/-yon-*. For further information see **bindan** (Lesson 17).

brinno < PG **brennō(n)-* < IE **bhrenwon-* < **bhrenu-* (to burn) [< √*bhrew* (to well up, seethe) + nasal infix] + suffix **-on-/-en-*. Cf. AS *bryne* (burning). The basic Germanic verb here is PG **brennan-* (to burn), Goth *brinnan,* ON *brinna,* Ger *brennen,* Eng *burn.* The derivation from IE √*bhrew* is that of Pokorny; others, assuming that PG **b-* may represent IE **ĝhʷ-*, take it to the root √*ĝhʷer* (hot, warm), which underlies, inter alia, PG **warm-* (warm). LIV includes Goth *brinnan* under both *b^hre̯iH* (to cut) and *g^{uh}er,* but queries each entry.

heito < PG **hītō(n)-* < IE **kīdon-* < √*kī,kai* [*keh$_2$y-*] (heat) + extension *-d-* + suff. *-en-/-on-*. Cf. ON *hiti,* AS *hǣte* (< PG **haytya-*), Eng. heat. The IE root is perhaps a y-extension of a more primitive **keh$_2$*, which, with a w- extension **keh$_2$w-*, underlies Greek καίω.

skaut < PG **skawt* < IE **skowd-* < √*skewd* (throw, shoot, hasten). Cf. ON *skaut,* Ger *Schoss;* from the same root is derived the PG verb **skewtan-* (to shoot, dash), ON *skjóta,* Ger *schiessen,* Eng *shoot.*

swaihro < PG **swehrō(n)-* < IE **swek(u)ron-* < **swekrū-* (mother-in-law) + suffix **-on-/-en-*. Cf. ON *svǣra,* Ger *Schwieger(mutter);* Skr *çvaçrū-,* Arm *skesur,* Lat *socrus,* OCSl *svekry.*

wens: see **wenjan** (Lesson 16).

unweis- < **un-** (Lesson 5) + **-weis-** < PG **wīss-* < IE **weyd-so-* < √*weyd* (to know) + suffix **-(e)s-o-*. Cf. ON *vīss* (wise), Ger *weise,* Eng *wise.*

hwileik- < PG **hwīlīk-* < IE **kwey-* (interrog. stem) + **līg-* (see **leikan** and **leik** in Lesson 11). **swaleik-**: cf. **swe, swa** (Lesson 13)

þaursu- < PG **þursu-* < IE **tṛsu-* < √*ters* (be dry) + suffix **-u-*. Cf. ON *þurr,* Ger *dürr;* Skr *tṛṣu-* (thirsty), Gk τέρσομαι (be dry), Lat *torreo* (roast etc.), *terra* (the earth, < **tersa-*). Note also PG **þursyan-* (to thirst), Gothic **þaursjan**, ON *þyrst-* (< **þyrsiþ-*), Ger *dürsten,* Eng *thirst.*

baitraba: adverb in **-aba** (Lesson 23) on the adjective **baitr-** < PG **baytr-* < IE *bhoydro-* (biting) < √*bheyd* (to split) + suffix **-ro-*. Cf., from **bhidro-*, ON *bitr,* Ger *bitter,* Eng *bitter;* Skr √*bhid* (to split), Lat *findo.* Note also PG **bītan* (to bite), Gothic **beitan**, ON *bíta,* Ger *beissen,* Eng *bite* from this same root.

ja, jai < PG **ya(y)* < IE **yāy*, the fem. locative sing. of the pronominal base **i-*. Cf. ON *já,* Ger *ja,* Eng *yea.* This is one of the innumerable particles and adverbs derived from the pronominal base **e-*, **ei-*, **i-*.

hwarjis < PG **hwaryiz* < IE **kworyis* < **kwo-* (interrog. base) + adv. suffix *-r* + the pronominal element **is* from the base **e-*, **ei-*, **i-*. Cf. ON *hverr* (which?). The base **kwor* occurs in PG **hwar* (where), Goth **hwar**, ON *hvar,* Eng *where.* **hwaþar** < PG **hwaþer-* < IE **kwo-* (interrog. base) + suffix **-tero-* (see the discussion of the comparative in Lesson 20).

aftaro: adverb in **-o** (Lesson 23) on stem **aftar-**. See **aftra** (Lesson 15), **afar** (Lesson 8), **af** (Lesson 9).

Lesson 22

The Passive.

The inflection of the Germanic present passive is closely parallelled in Sanskrit and Greek. The relevant forms are as follows:

	*IE	Sanskrit	Greek	PG	Gothic
1s	*-omay, -ay*	*-e*	-ομαι	---	**(-ada)**
2s	*-esay*	*-ase*	*-εσαι	*-ezay*	**-aza**
3s	*-etay*	*-ate*	-εται	*-eþay*	**-ada**
3pl	*-ontay*	*-ante*	-ονται	*-anday*	**-anda**

Remarks:

(1) There is no trace of the original 1st person singular form in Germanic. In Gothic the third person form is also used for the first person.

(2) The exact vocalization of the PG forms cannot be reconstructed. On the fate of final unstressed IE **-ay* in Germanic, see our comments in the discussion of the dative singular ending **-a** in Lesson 1.

(3) The **-a-** of the Gothic singular forms is apparently a result of the leveling through of the **-a-** of the plural **-anda**. Note that in Gothic this 3rd person plural form is used for 1st and 2nd person plurals as well.

(4) The loss of the class marker **-ai-** < PG **-ǣ-* in the indicative passive of weak verbs, class 3, i.e. **haban**, should be noted; we have already seen this truncation in the infinitive, present participle, and present active subjunctive of this class of verbs (see Lesson 10).

The present passive subjunctive in Gothic consists of the above endings added to the subjunctive verbal base in **-ai-** (IE optative **-oy-*). To these has been added a particle **-u**; whence and why are a matter of conjecture.

Noun Formation.

-iþa, -ida. The suffix proper is **-þa** < IE **-tā*, the *-t-* suffix of numerous adjectives and passive participles + the formative suffix of the *ā*-declension. Cognate formations occur frequently throughout IE, e.g. Skr *kṛṣnatā* (blackness, < *kṛṣna-* black), Gk ἀρετή (virtue, < √*ar* to fit, suit), Lat *senecta* (old age, < *senec-* old), Russ *доброта* (goodness, < *добрый*). The vowel *-i-* preceding the suffix in Gothic has been clipped from *i*-stem or *ja*-stem bases and made part of the suffix.

-eins, -ains, -ons. The mixed inflection of these suffixes suggests a mixing of verbal nouns in PG **-ni-* and **-nō-* < IE **-ni-* and **-nā-* added to the verbal stem with its characteristic suffix: **eyni-* > PG **-īni-* > Goth *-ein-*, PG **-ǣyni-* > Goth *-aini-*, PG **-ōni-* > Goth *-oni-*, etc. Precise parallels are hard to find. There are verbal nouns in *-ni-* in Sanskrit, e.g. *hāni-* (abandonment, √*hā*), *glāni-* (weariness, √*glā*), but these are quite rare and are limited to the small subset of verbs having passive participles in *-na-*.

-oþus, -odus. Formed by the addition of the nominal suffix **-þu-** < IE **-tu-* to verbal bases of weak verbs, class 2. Close parallels are found in Latin *-ātus,* which forms the regular supine of all first conjugation verbs and abstract nouns denoting various offices, e.g. *consulatus* (the consulship). The use of the IE suffix **-tu-* for the formation of verbal nouns is widespread, e.g. the post-Vedic Sanskrit infinitive in *-tu-* and the OCSl supine in *-tŭ.*

-ufni, -ubni. From PG **-ubnya-* < **-umnya-* < IE **-m̥nyo-*, the reduced form of the suffix **-men-/-mon-* + the suffix **-yo-*.

-duþs. PG **-dūþi-* < IE **-tūti-*. Exactly parallelled by Lat *-tūs, G -tūtis,* e.g. *senectūs* (old age), *virtūs* (manliness, virtue).

Adjective formation.

The IE suffix **-ko-* was a fundamental one for the formation of adjectives, combining with various thematic vowels and other suffixes to produce, inter alia, **-oko-, *-iko-, *-īko-, and *-isko-*. The Gothic suffixes **-aga-**, **-aha-**, **-eiga-** and **-iska-** are derived from this group of IE suffixes, the variation between **-h-** and **-g-** being a regular result of Verner's Law as determined by the original IE stress patterns.

In Sanskrit the use of *-( )ka* to form adjectives gradually increased in frequency from the earliest period of the language to the point that in the latest stages the suffix could be added to virtually any noun or adjective to make an equivalent word. It was also especially useful in providing a conveniently inflectable termination to sometimes cumbersome *bahuvrihi* compounds. In Greek the suffix in the form -ικός became the most productive adjectival suffix in Attic Greek. The suffix is less frequent in Latin, but nevertheless well attested in a wide variety of combinations, e.g. *-cus, -icus, -īcus, -icius, -aceus.*

The derivatives of IE **-isko-* are less frequent and more specialized in meaning. In Greek, for example, -ισκος is used to form diminutive nouns, e.g. παιδίσκος (little boy, < παῖς). The source of the **-is-* is uncertain, but is probably the reduced form of IE **-yes-* which we have already met in its comparative function.

The Gothic adjectival suffix **-eina-** < PG **-īna-* < IE **-īno-* has its clearest cognate in Latin *-īnus,* e.g. *marīnus* (of the sea, < *mare*), *Latīnus* (of Latium). The corresponding suffix in Greek is with a short vowel, from IE **-ino-*, e.g. ἀνθρώπινος (human, < ἄνθρωπος), and likewise in Sanskrit, where the very frequent adjectival suffix *-in-* belongs to the consonantal inflection, reflecting IE **-in-* without the added thematic vowel of **-ino-* and **-īno-*.

Etymologies:

bisaihwan: bi- (Lesson 5) + **saihwan** (Lesson 7)

mitan < PG **metan-* < IE *√med* (to measure). Cf. ON *meta* (to assess), Ger *messen,* Eng *mete;* Gk μέδομαι, Lat *medeor* (look after, cure), *modus* (measure).

galukan: ga- (Lesson 5) + **-lukan** < PG **lūkan-* < ? *√lewg* (to bend, twist). Cf. ON *lúka,* Eng *lock;* Gk λυγίζω (to wind, twist). The source of the long *-ū-* in the PG form remains obscure.

fraisan < PG **fraysan-* < ?? Cf. AS *frāsian* (ask, investigate). There are no known cognates outside Germanic.

slahan < PG **slahan-* < IE *√slak* (to hammer, strike). Cf. ON *slá,* Ger *schlagen,* Eng *slay, slaughter.* Derivatives of this root are found only in Germanic and Celtic.

saian < PG **sǣan-* < IE *√sē(y)* [**seh*$_1$] (to sow). Cf. ON *sá*, Ger *säen*, Eng *sow;* Lat *sero (*siso), serere, sevi, satus*; OCSl *sějati.*

sneiþan < PG **snīþan-* < IE *√sneyt* (to cut). Cf. ON *sníða*, Ger *schneiden*, AS *snīđan.* Cognates outside Germanic are rare.

lewjan < PG **lǣwiyan-* < IE *√lēw* (leave, abandon) + denom. suffix *-eye-*. Cf. AS *lǣwan* (betray), OHG *(gi)lāen* (betray). All cognates outside Germanic are in BSl, e.g. OPrussian *aulaūt* (to die), Czech *leviti* (soothe, alleviate).

andanahti: anda- (Lesson 16) + **naht-** (Lesson 19).

maurgins < PG **muryen-* < IE **mr̥kén-* < *√merk* (flicker, grow dark, twilight). Cf. ON *morginn*, Ger *Morgen*, Eng *morning;* OCSl *mrŭknoti* (grow dark), Ir *breachtach* (variegated, < **mr̥kto-*). *√merk* is an extended form of *√mer* (flicker).

waurts < PG **wurt-* < IE **wr̥d-*. Cf. ON *rót*, Ger *Wurz(el)*, Eng *root;* Lat *rad(ix)*, Ir *fréamh.* Pokorny gives the root as variable: *u̯(e)rád-, u̯ₑrəd-, u̯rəd;* it is possibly an extension in **-H-d-* of one of the thirteen roots *√wer* presented there.

gamunds < PG **gamundi-* < **ga- + -mundi-* < IE **mn̥tí-* < *√men* (to think) + suffix **-ti-*. Cf. AS *gemynd*, OHG *gimunt.* See **gamunan** (Lesson 16).

sarwa < PG **sarwa* < IE **sorwo-* < *√ser* (to string together) + suffix **-wo-*. Cf. ON *sørvi* (necklace), OHG *saro* (armor); Gk εἴρω (string together, < **seryō*), Lat *sero* (idem).

hairus < PG **heru-* < IE **keru-* < *√(s)ker* (to cut) + formative **-u-*. Cf. ON *hjörr*, AS *heoru.* The root is widely attested in the IE languages in a bewildering variety of forms and meanings. See Pokorny pp. 938-46.

raiht- < PG **reht-* < IE **reĝto-* < *√reĝ* (to set straight) + suffix **-to-*. Cf. ON *rétt-*, Ger *recht*, Eng *right;* Gk ὀρεκτός (extended), Lat *rectus.* Note also **garaiht-** (Lesson 2) and **reiks** (Lesson 14).

briggan < PG **bringan-* < IE **bhrenk-*, probably a cpd. of *√bher* (to carry) (cf. **bairan**, Lesson 13) and *√enek* (to reach, attain). The root *√enek* is the source of Goth PP **ganoh** (it suffices) and related words, AS *genōh*, Eng *enough*, Ger *genug*, etc. The preterite base **braht-** results by regular phonetic development from PG **branht-*, a secondary *-t-* (weak) preterite on the old strong preterite (IE perfect) base **branh-* < IE **bhronk-*.

Lesson 23

Weak verbs, class 4.

This class of verbs is formally derived from the late IE present formation consisting of the reduced grade of the verbal root + the suffix **-nā-/-nə- [neh₂-/nh₂-].* In the singular the stress was originally on the suffix, but in the plural and dual the stress was on the endings, with the consequent reduction of the suffix to **-nə-*. E.g.

1st pers. sing.	IE *bhn̥dhnāmi*	Skr *badhnāmi*	Early PG **bundnōmi*	Gothic -**bundna**
1st pers. pl.	*bhn̥dhnəmés*	*badhnīmas*	**bundnamés*	-**bundnam**

With the retraction of the stress to the root syllable by Late PG, the inflection of the verb was assimilated to that of the regular strong verb except for the preterite -**bundnoda** etc., where the -**no**- is a retention of the original **-nā-* and not an unmotivated imitation of the type **salboda**. The inflection of the preterite as a weak verb is, of course, secondary in Germanic.

This present tense class in Late IE originated from a misdivision of earlier infixed nasal presents from triconsonantal roots whose third consonant was h_2. Thus, for example, from the early IE root *√meth₂* (snatch away) was formed the present stem **metnéh₂-* > **metnā-*, re-analyzed as *√met* + a formative **-nā-*. The suffix was then generalized and extended to other types of roots.

What is not clear, however, is the process whereby this old present tense formative came to be identified universally with the inchoative function we find in Germanic, especially in Gothic and Scandinavian. Perhaps what seems obvious synchronically should also be taken into account diachronically: some of these verbs look like verbally inflected perfective (passive or stative) participles in **-(a)n-*. It certainly seems possible that somewhere along the line in pre-PG the *-n-* of the inherited forms, by now completely non-functional and hence unidentifiable, was re-interpreted as the *-n-* of the passive participle, leading ultimately to the creation of a new large class of inchoative verbs by extension to any other adjectival base. This reinterpretation would have been facilitated by the fact that the reduced form of the verbal root was characteristic of both the passive participle and the inherited *-nā*-forms. This suggestion assumes that at least some of the inherited verbs had an inchoative semantic component.

Adverbs.

Adverbs in IE were formed from nominal, pronominal, adjectival, and prepositional bases in various ways, sometimes employing suffixes that seem to have been specifically adverbial, like **-te*, indicating motion toward, as in Gk ἄλλοσε (to elsewhere), and sometimes employing case forms in an adverbial function, especially the accusative, ablative, and instrumental. Each IE language subsequently developed its own adverbial "system" by various analogical extensions with the result that while it is relatively simple to identify the bits and pieces of individual sets like Gr πόθι (where at?), πόθεν (where from?), πόσε (where to?), or Skr *atra* (here), *tatra* (there), *kutra* (where) or Eng *where, whither, whence, there, thither, thence,* exact parallels of whole sets are hard to find.

Gothic -**þ** (motion toward) is derived from IE **-te* illustrated above. -**þro** (motion from) < IE **-trōd* and -**dre** (motion toward) < IE **-trēd* are ablative case forms of a base formed with the suffix **-tr-*, probably the reduced form of **-ter-*, whose functions were discussed in Lesson 20 in connection with the comparative. Latin provides good evidence for the adverbial use of **-ter* in such words as *breviter, leniter,* etc. The Gothic suffix -**na** (motion from) also finds its closest parallel in Latin, i.e. *-nē* in *supernē* (from above).

The origin of Gothic **-ba** is uncertain. It may well be an altered form of the IE instrumental/adverbial suffix **-bhi*, the source of Greek -φι that exercises instrumental, locative, and ablative functions in Homer, e.g. δακρυόφι(ν) (tearfully), ὄρεσφι (on the mountains).

The suffix **-r** (at rest in a place) is derived from IE **-r*. Cf. Lat *cur* < older *quōr* (why), Skr *antar* (inside), *punar* (again), etc.

The higher numbers.

The **-lif** (**-lib-**) of ***ainlif** (eleven) and **twalif** (twelve) is derived from IE **likʷ-*, the reduced form of the root *√leykʷ* (to leave, abandon, let remain). The words originally meant something like *one-left, two-left*, i.e. left over after counting to ten. They are parallelled exactly in the Lithuanian teens, all of which are formed with the same suffix in its Baltic form *-lika: vienúolika* (eleven), *dvýlika* (twelve), *trýlika* (thirteen), etc. For the root *√leykʷ* cf. Grk λείπω (to leave), Lat *linquo;* Gothic **leihwan** (to lend), ON *ljá*. See also **liban** (Lesson 10). For the equation of IE **kʷ* and PG **ḇ* see p. 230, if **ḇ* < **f* as a result of Verner's Law; otherwise the equation is unexplained.

The **-tigjus** of 20 to 60 and the **-tehund** of 70 to 100 are both derived from IE **dekm̥t-* (a decade, ten). **-tehund**, an uninflected form, presupposes the stress **dékm̥t-*; **-tigjus**, on the other hand, presupposed either no stress, i.e. enclitic to the initial cardinal, or **dekḿ̥t* > PG **teɣund*. This form of the noun was somehow assimilated to the u-stem inflection: sing. ***tigus**, pl. **tigjus**.

For **hunda** see Lesson 14.

þusundi *sf* < PG **þūsundī (G -*dyōs)* < IE **tūsn̥tī (G -*tyās)* < **tūs-* (multitude) + suffixes *-n̥t-ī/-yā*. The word may have been reanalyzed in PG as **þūs-hund-* (many hundred). Cf. OCSl *tysęšta* (<**tūsentyā*). The element IE **tūs-* has well-attested cognates in Germanic, Celtic, and BSl, and is an extension in *-s-* of the more primitive root *√tēw* [*tewh₂*] (to swell up).

For **frum-** see Lesson 20; for **anþar-** see Lesson 4.

The ordinals from **þridj-** to **taihund-** are derived from IE forms with the suffix **-to-*. Neither Grimm's Law nor Verner's Law affects the **-t-** of **fimft-** and **saihst-**, but the **-d-** of the remaining forms results from IE **-t-* > PG **-þ-* > (by Verner) **-đ-*. The source of the **-u-** in **ahtud-** is unknown.

Etymologies:

anastodjan < **ana-** (Lesson 1) + **-stodjan** < PG **stōđiyan-* (to station, place), a denom./caus. verb in **-yan-* on the nominal base **stōđ(w)-* (stand, station) < IE **stādh(w)-* < *√stā* [*steh₂*] + the extension **-dh-*. Cf. ON *stóð* (G *-var;* landing-place, abode), *stöðva* (to stop, halt), *stóð* (a stud of horses), Eng *stud*. See also **standan** (Lesson 18) and **staþs** (Lesson 7).

usluknan: inchoative corresponding to **uslukan** (Lesson 22).

usfullnan: inchoative corresponding to **usfulljan** (Lesson 12).

bandwjan < PG **bandwiyan-*, a denom./caus. verb in **-yan-* on the noun **bandwa* (sign, gesture) < IE **bhondhwā-* < *√bhendh* (to bend) + suffix **-wā-*. Cf. ON *benda* (to bend; to beckon), Eng *bend*. Apparently two different PG verbs, **bandyan-* (to bend, < **bandya-* a band, as sthg bent around sthg) and **bandwyan-* (to make a **bandwa*, i. e. a nod or hand-sign), have merged in ON *benda*. The nouns **bandwa** *sf* and **bandwo** *wf* occur in Gothic. Pokorny lists Gothic *bandwjan* under the root *√bhā* (to shine), but labels it as questionable. The reasoning here, perfectly plausible, is that *bandwjan* is derived from IE **bhānteye-* (approx.: to produce a manifestation). Without further close cognates, however, the etymology remains open. The derivation from *√bhendh* is my suggestion and seems to be the more plausible, especially in the light of the Old Norse forms.

laugnjan < PG **lawyniyan-*, a denom./caus. verb in *-*yan-* from **lawyn-* (hidden, denied) < IE **lowghno-* < *√lewgh* (to tell a lie) + suffix *-*no-*. Cf. ON *leyna* (hide, conceal), Ger *leugnen* (disavow). From the root *√lewgh* we have Gothic **liugan** *sv 2* (to lie), ON *ljúga*, Ger *lügen*, Eng *lie;* OCSl *lŭgati*, Russ *лгать*.

hauhjan < PG **hawhiyan-*, a denom./caus. verb in *-*yan-* from the adjective **hawh-* (high), Lesson 3.

andhausjan < **and-** (Lesson 2) + **hausjan** (Lesson 5).

goljan < PG **gōliyan-* < IE **ghōleye-* < *√ghel* (to cry out) + denom./caus. suffix *-*eye-*. Cf. ON *gœla* (to soothe, calm), OSax *gōlian* (gladden). From the basic root are ON *gjalla* (to scream), Ger *gellen*, Eng *yell;* Russ *галиться* (to mock).

infeinan < PG **in-* + *-*fīnan*, for which I suggest the following etymology: an inchoative verb formed on the participial adjective **fiyan-* < IE *√pey* (be fat; fatten, nourish). The form would be an exact parallel to **keinan** discussed in Grammar Lesson 14 under strong verbs, class I. Neither Pokorny nor Holthausen gives an etymology for this word. I take the Gothic meaning of *showing mercy* from the notions of *nourishing, sustaining*, and the like.

fraqistnan: see **fraqistjan** (Lesson 5).

talzjan < PG **talziyan-*, a denominative verb in *-*yan-* from **talz-* < IE **dolos-* (narrative, account?) < *√del* (to count, recount) + suffix *-*os-*. Cognates with this meaning occur only in Germanic; note especially ON *tala* (to talk), Ger *erzählen* (tell), Eng *tell, talk* (< IE *√del* + extension *-g-*).

gadauþjan, afdauþjan: a causative/denominative verb based on **dauþ-** (dead) Lesson 8. **gadauþnan** is the corresponding inchoative.

usgeisnan < **us-** (Lesson I) + **geisnan**, an inchoative verb in **-na-** based on PG **gīs-* < IE **gheys-* (be frightened, dismayed). Cf. Avestan *zaēša-* (frightful); ON *geiski* (fear, terror). The causative transitive verb **usgaisjan** also occurs in Gothic. From this same root is PG **gayst-* > Ger *Geist*, Eng *ghost.*

garaihtei: see **garaiht-** (Lesson2).

hiuhma < PG **hewhman-* < IE **kewkmon-* (heap, throng) < *√kew* (to bend, arch) + extension *-k-* + suffix *-*men-/-mon-*. The IE root has extensions in *d, g, k, b, bh, p*, and *mb(h)*, with a wide variety of often discordant meanings. The *k*-extension is also attested in Indic, Celtic, and BSl, and underlies the adjective *hauh-* (Lesson 3).

gawairþi: presumably from the same root as **wairþan** (Lesson 8), but the semantics are far from clear.

andbahti: see **andbahts** (Lesson 4).

armahairtei: an abstract noun in **-ei(n)** based on the adjective **armahairt-** (merciful) < PG **armahert-* < **arma-* (see **arman**, Lesson II) + **hert-* (see **hairto**, Lesson 6).

audag- < PG **awdaya-* < IE **awdhoko-* < **awdh-* (good fortune, wealth) + suffix **-oko-*. Cf. ON *auðin-* (granted by fate), *auðr* (wealth), OHG *ōtac* (rich, fortunate). Pokorny takes **awdh-* as an extension in *-dh-* of the root √*aw* (to weave, spin) and says that the meanings listed here are based "auf die Vorstellung der webenden oder spinnenden Schicksalgöttin und des von ihr Zugeteilten."

þadei: The relative adverbs **þarei** (where), **þadei** (to where), and **þaþroei** (from where) are formed by suffixing the relative particle **ei** (cf. pp. 45, 54) to the simple adverbs **þar** (there), ***þaþ** (thither), and **þaþro** (thence). ***þaþ** (thither) is derived from IE **tote* < **to-* (pronominal base) + **-te* (adverbial suffix: toward). To the series **þar**, ***þaþ**, **þaþro** compare the interrogatives **hwar** (where?), **hwaþ** (whither?), **hwaþro** (whence?).

nauh < PG **nuh* < IE **nuk^we* < **nu* (now) + the conjunctive suffix **-k^we* (> Gothic **-uh**). Cf. Ger *noch.* From **nu* we have Gothic **nu**, ON *nu*, Ger *nu(n)*, Eng *now.*

Glossary

The following glossary contains the full extant vocabulary of the Gothic Bible with the exception of the proper names and a few of the transcribed Greek words. In regard to order, **hw** follows **h**, and **þ** follows **t**. Compound words are listed alphabetically, e.g. **gahuljan** is found under G. The existence of compound verbs, however, is indicated under each root verb; thus, e.g., the entry

> **huljan** *wv 1* hide, conceal, disguise (cf. **and-**, **dis-**, **ga-**)

refers to the existence of **andhuljan**, **dishuljan**, and **gahuljan**. A hyphenated entry indicates that the root verb itself is not attested, e.g.

> **-hamon: afhamon, anahamon, andhamon, gahamon, ufarhamon.**

An asterisk marks unattested entry forms about which there could be some dispute because of grammatical ambiguity, e.g.

> **staþs*** (G **staþis***) *sm* shore

where only the dative **staþa** is attested, but cognates elsewhere in Germanic make the reconstructed N and G virtually certain.

A

aba *wm* man, husband (§6.1)
abr- *adj* strong, violent, mighty
abraba *adv* strongly, very much
-abrjan: biabrjan
abu = **af** + **-u**
af *prep D* of, from, by, away from, out of
afagjan *wv 1* frighten, make anxious
afaikan *sv 7* (P **afaiaik**) deny (strongly)
afairzjan *wv 1* deceive, lead astray
afar *prep A* after (temporal); *D* following, according to
afardags *sm* the next day
afargaggan *sv 7* follow, follow after
afarlaistjan *wv 1* follow, follow after
afarsabbatus* *sm* day after the Sabbath; **þis dagis afarsabbate** on the first day of the week
afaruh = **afar** + **-uh**
afblindnan *wv 4* become blind
afdailjan *wv 1* divide up, apportion
afdaubnan *wv 4* become deaf
afdauid- *part adj* tired (<**afdojan***)
afdauþjan *wv 1* kill, put to death
afdobnan *wv 4* be silent
afdojan* *wv 1* to tire; conjectured for **afdawid-** *qv*
afdomeins *sf vn* damnation
afdomjan *wv 1* to judge, condemn
afdrausjan *wv 1* cast down
afdrugkja *wm* drunkard
afdumbnan *wv 4* hold one's peace, remain silent
afetja *wm* glutton
affilhan *sv 3* hide (sthg: *A*; from: **faura** *D*)
afgaggan *sv 7 irreg* go away, depart (from: **af** *D*).
afgiban sik *sv 5* depart, separate oneself
afgrundiþa *sf* abyss
afgud- *adj* godless, impious
afgudei *wf* ungodliness
afhaban sik *wv 3* refrain (from: **af**)
afhaimjai *Npl adj* far from home
afhamon *wv 2* doff, take off (clothing)
afhlaþan- *part adj* burdened (< **afhlaþan*** *sv 7*)
afholon *wv 2* defraud
afhrainjan *wv 1* cleanse, purify
afhrisjan *wv 1* shake off
afhugjan *wv 1* bewitch
afhwapjan *wv 1* choke, quench
afhwapnan *wv 4* be choked, quenched; to drown
aflageins *sf vn* remission, laying aside
aflagjan *wv 1* lay aside
afleiþan *sv 1* go away, depart (from: **af** *D*).
aflet* *sn* forgiveness, pardon
afletan *sv 7* leave, forsake; forgive (sthg: *A*); put away, put aside, divorce
aflets *sm* forgiveness, forgiving
aflifnan *wv 4* remain, be left
aflinnan *sv 3* depart
afmaitan *sv 7* (P **-maimait**) cut off; to behead (smn: *D* + **haubiþ**)
afmarzeins *sf vn* deceitfulness, guile
afmarzjan *wv 1 passive* be discouraged, fall away from the faith
afmawid- *part adj* weary (<**afmojan***)
afniman *sv 4* take away, remove (*A*; from: **af** *D*)
afqiþan *sv 5* renounce, forsake
afhrainjan *wv 1* cleanse, purify
afsateins *sf vn* divorce

afsatjan *wv 1* to divorce, remove
afskaidan *sv* 7 (P **-skaiskaiþ**) separate, divide
afskiuban *sv 2* push aside
afslahan *sv 6* kill, slay
afslaupjan *wv 1* doff, take off
afslauþjan *wv 1* frighten, make anxious
afslauþnan *wv 4* be beside oneself with fear or anxiety
afsneiþan *sv 1* cut off, kill
afstandan *sv 6* stand off, depart; abandon (*D*)
afstass *sf* (*G* **afstassais**) rebellion; divorce
afswaggwjan *wv 1* shake one's resolve
afswairban *sv 3* wipe out
afta *adv* behind, backwards
aftana *adv* from behind
aftaro *adv* behind, from behind; **du aftaro** up from behind
aftaurnan *wv 4* be torn away
aftiuhan *sv 2* draw away, push off or away, to take aside
aftra *adv* back, backwards; once again; back to a former state
aftraanastodeins *sf vn* recommencement, new beginning
aftum- *adj* the following, next, last
aftumist- *superl adj* last, final; **aftumist haban** be at the point of death
afþaursjan *wv 1* be (or make?) thirsty
afþliuhan *sv 2* flee
afþwahan *sv 6* wash (oneself)
afwairpan *sv* 3 throw (sthg: *D*) away, put away
afwalwjan *wv 1* roll (sthg) away
afwandjan *wv 1* turn (self) away
aggilus *sm* angel (pl. variable: -i- or -u-stem) <Lat *angelus* <Gk ἄγγελος
aggwiþa *sf* anguish, distress
-aggwjan: gaaggwjan
aggwu- *adj* narrow
agis (*G* **agisis**) *sn* fear, respect
-agjan: afagjan, inagjan, usagjan
agl- *adj* shameful
aglaitei *wf*, **aglaiti*** *sn* lewdness, lasciviousness
aglaitgastald- *adj* shamefully acquisitive
aglaitiwaurdei *wf* indecent language
agliþa *sf* anguish, distress
-agljan: usagljan
aglo *wf* anguish, distress
agluba *adv* with difficulty, hard
aglu- *adj* hard, difficult
aha *wm* mind, understanding
ahaks *sf (?)* dove
ahana *sf* chaff
ahjan *wv 1* think, suppose
ahma *wm* spirit; the Holy Spirit; **ahma weihs** *idem*; **ahmin seinamma** to one's self
ahmein- *adj* spiritual
ahmateins *sf vn* inspiration
ahs *sn* ear of grain
ahtau *num* eight
ahtaudog- *adj* eight days old
ahtautehund *num* eighty
ahtud- *ord num adj* eighth
ahwa *sf* river, water
aibr usually corrected to **tibr*** (offering) on the basis of AS and OHG cognates.
aigan* *v* see **aihan***
aigin *sn* property, inheritance
-aiginon: gaaiginon
aihan *PP* (§20.1) own, have, possess (cf. **fair-**)
aihtron *wv 2* beg for; pray (on behalf of: **faur** *D*)
aihtrons *sf* begging, request, prayer
aihts *sf* property
aihwatundi *sf* thornbush, lit. horsetooth
-aikan: afaikan
aikklesjo *wf* (the) church, congregation< Gk ἐκκλησία
ain- *adj* see **ains**
ainabaur *sm(i)* an only-born child
ainah- *adj* only
ainakl- *adj* alone, isolated
ainamundiþa *sf* unanimity
-ainan: gaainan
ainfalþ- *adj* single, simple, onefold
ainfalþei *wf* simple goodness of disposition, candor
ainhwaþaruh *pron* either of two
ainhwarjizuh *indef pron* everyone, each singly
ainlif* *num* (D **ainlibim**) eleven
ains *num* one (§9.2); *adj* alone, only (§4,2c); *indef pron* a certain one; **ains... jah ains** the one ... the other
ainshun *indef pron* with neg.: no one; *adj* no, none (§22.2)
aipiskaupei *wf* bishopric
aipiskaupus *sm* bishop
aipistaule (*D* **-lein**, *A* **-lein**; *Apl* **-lans**) letter, epistle < Gk ἐπιστολή
air *adv* soon, early
airinon *wv* 2 be a messenger
airis *adv* earlier
airizans *pl comp adj* used as noun: ancestors, forefathers
airkniþa *sf* purity, genuineness
airþa *sf* earth, land, region
airþakund- *adj* earthly, of the earth
airþein- *adj* of the earth
airus *sm* messenger
airzei *wf* heresy, false doctrine

airzj- *adj* astray, erring, deceived

airziþa *sf* heresy, false doctrine

airzjan *wv 1* deceive, lead astray (cf. **af-**)

aistan *wv 3* revere, honor (cf. **ga-**)

aiþei *wf* mother

aiþs *sm* oath

aiþþau *conj* or, or else; then (marking apodosis) (§19.2); **aiþþau jah** truly

aiw *adv* with neg.: never

aiwaggeli *sn* gospel < Gk εὐαγγέλιον

aiwaggelista *wm* evangelist < L *evangelista* <Gk εὐαγγελιστής

aiwaggeljan *wv 1* preach the gospel

aiwaggeljo *wf* gospel <Gk εὐαγγέλιον

aiwein- *adj* eternal (Voc. 12)

aiwiski *sn* shame, disgrace

aiwiskon *wv 2* act shamefully (cf. **ga-**)

-aiwjan: usaiwjan

aiws *sm* time, lifetime, age, world, eternity; **in aiwins, du aiwa** forever; **aiwa dage** (w. neg.) never

aiz *sn* brass, money, coin

aizasmiþa *wm* coppersmith

ajukduþs* *sf* eternity

ak *conj* but, however (follows neg. phrase or statement)

akei *conj* but, nevertheless (§14.2)

aket*, **akeit*** *sn* (?) vinegar; Lat *acetum*

akran *sn* fruit

akranalaus- *adj* barren, unfruitful

akrs *sm* (cultivated) field

alabrunsts *sf* holocaust, burnt offering

alakjo *adv* collectively, together

alamans* *pron* everyone

alan *sv 6* grow, be nourished

alaþarb- *adj* very poor, destitute

aldoma* *wm(?)* old age

alds *sf* life, generation; **ald bauan** lead one's life

aleina *sf* cubit

alew* *sn* olive oil

alewj- *adj* olive-; **Fairguni Alewjo** the Mount of Olives

alewabagms *sm* olive tree

alhs *f* temple

alja *conj* except, unless; *prep D* except

aljakun- *adj* foreign, strange

aljakunja *wm* stranger, outsider

aljaleikaid- *adj* allegorical

aljaleiko(s) *adv* otherwise

aljan *sn* zeal, jealousy; **in aljana briggan** to make jealous

aljan *wv 1* rear, nourish, fatten

aljanon *wv 2* to love jealously (cf. **in-**)

aljar *adv* elsewhere

aljaþ *adv* elsewhere, in another direction

aljaþro *adv* from elsewhere

alj- *adj* other, another

all- *adj* all, every (§8.4)

allandjo *adv* fully

allaþro *adv* from all sides, from everywhere

allawaurstw- *adj* perfect, whole, complete

allawerei *wf* uprightness, honesty

allis *adv* in general, wholly; **ni allis** not at all; *conj* for, because; **nih allis** because ... not; **allis ... iþ** it is true that ... but (§14.2)

allwaldands *m* the Almighty

-alþan: usalþan

alþj- *adj* old; **þo alþjona** olden times

alþiz- *comp adj* elder

amen *adv* truly, indeed, Amen <Gk ἀμήν < Heb *ʾāmēn*

ams or **amsa** *m* shoulder (declension uncertain)

an *interrog particle* and then?

ana *prep A,D* in, into; on, onto, upon; to, against; *adv* thereon, thereupon (§1.4)

anaaukan *sv 7* add to; continue to do, do again (w. inf.)

anabiudan *sv 2* bid, command, order (smn: *D*; to do sthg: inf., **du** inf., **ei** subj.)

anabusns *sf* order, command(ment)

anadrigkan sik *sv 3* become intoxicated (with: *D*)

anafilh *sn* tradition, thing committed; (re)commendation

anafilhan *sv 3* commit, entrust, hand down as tradition (*A*; to: *D*).

anafulhano *pp wn* used as noun: tradition

anagaggan *sv 7 irreg* (pret. **-iddja**) come

anahaban *wv 3* take hold of; passive: be gripped (by fever)

anahaitan *sv 7* to call on (*A*); to rebuke, scold (*D*)

anahamon *wv 2* don, put on (clothing)

anahaimj- *adj* in one's native land (form uncertain; attested in pl. only)

anahnaiwjan *wv 1* put, place, lay down

anahneiwan *sv 1* stoop down

anahweilan *wv 3* to rest, refresh

anainsakan *sv 6* place before, present to (*D*)

anakaurjan *wv 1* importune, bother

anaks *adv* immediately, at once

anakumbjan *wv 1* lie down, sit down; recline at table (an adaptation in Gothic of Lat *accumbere*)

anakunnains *sf vn* reading, recognition

anakunnan *wv 3* read, recognize

analageins *sf vn* a laying on

analagjan *wv 1* lay on

analatjan *wv 1* hinder, thwart

analaugni- *adj* hidden, secret

analaugnei *wf* secrecy, concealment
analaugniba *adv* secretly
analeiko *adv* in the same way
anamahtjan *wv 1* injure, damage, do harm or damage to
anamahts *sf* abuse, ill-treatment; tyranny
anameljan *wv 1* enroll
anaminds *sf* supposition
-anan: uzanan
anananþjan *wv 1* dare, have courage to
ananauþjan *wv 1* force, compel
ananiujan *wv 1* renew
ananiujiþa *sf* renewal
anapraggan *sv 7* oppress
anaqal *Asg* tranquillity
anaqiman *sv 4* approach
anaqiss *sf* blasphemy
anaqiþan *sv 5* blaspheme, slander
anaqiujan *wv 1* arouse, bring to life
anasilan *wv 3* be or become silent, still
anasiuni- *adj* visible
anaslawan *wv 3* die down
anaslepan *sv 7* (pret. **-saislep**) fall asleep, (fig.) die
anastodeins *sf vn* beginning; a new beginning, first fruits of a new undertaking
anastodjan *wv 1* begin, commence (intrans.)
anatrimpan *sv 3* tread upon, tramp on
anaþaima anathema < Gk ἀνάθεμα
anaþiwan *wv 3* to subject, reduce to servitude
anaþrafstjan *wv 1* comfort, console
anawairþ- *adj* future, about to happen, coming
anawiljei *wf* honesty, fairness; due respect
and *prep A* along, throughout; in, on, among
andabauhts *sf* ransom
andabeit *sn* reproach
andahafts *sf* answer; judgement, sentence
andahait *sn* confession, creed
andalauni *sn* recompense
andalaus- *adj* endless
andanahti *sn* evening
andaneiþ- *adj* contrary, hostile
andanem *sn* acceptance, reception
andanemeig- *adj* holding fast to
andanemi- *adj* pleasant, agreeable
andanumts *sf* acceptance; assumption
andasetj- *adj* abominable
andastaþjis *sm* adversary, enemy
andastaua *wm* adversary at law
andaþaht- *adj* circumspect, reasonable
andaugi *sn* face
andaugiba *adv* openly, publicly
andaugjo *adv* openly, publicly
andawairþi *sn* price, value
andawaurdi *sn* answer, reply
andawizns *sf* salary, sustenance
andawleizn *sm* or *sn* face
andbahti *sn* (*G* **-teis** or **-tjis**) service, ministry; liturgy
andbahtjan *wv 1* serve, minister to (*D*)
andbahts *sm* servant
andbeitan *sv 1* reproach, threaten, charge (not to do)
andbindan *sv 3* unbind, untie, release (from: **af** *D*), explain
andbundnan *wv 4* become unbound
andeis *sm irreg* (*Apl* **-ins**) end; aim, goal
andhafjan *sv 6* answer, respond to (smn: *D*, **wiþra** *A*); say (sthg: *A*) in reply.
andhaitan *sv 7* acknowledge, confess (sth: *D*); call upon (smn: *D*) in thanksgiving or prayer; to declare
andhamon *wv 2* put away from oneself, doff
andhausjan *wv 1* obey, listen to (smn: *D*)
andhruskan *v* to question, inquire into
andhuleins *sf vn* revelation, uncovering
andhuljan *wv 1* uncover, reveal, disclose
andilaus- *adj* endless
andiz-uh ... **aiþþau** *conj* either ... or
andletnan *wv 4* depart, die
andniman *sv 4* accept, receive, take
andqiþan *sv 5* speak with (*D*); take leave of (*D*)
andrinnan *sv 3* compete in running; strive, dispute
andsaihwan *sv 5* take into consideration
andsakan *sv 6* dispute, contest, contend against
andsaljan *wv 1* to offer, present
andsitan *sv 5* take into consideration
andspeiwan *sv 1* despise
andstald* *sn* support
andstaldan *sv 7* furnish, provide (with: *D*)
andstandan *sv 6* withstand, resist
andstaurran *wv 3* murmur against, reproach
andtilon *wv 2* be devoted to (*D*), take an interest in (*D*)
andþagkjan (± **sik**) *wv 1* become aware of, recall, be mindful of, realize (*G*)
andwairþ- *adj* present
andwairþi *sn* presence, face, person; **in andwairþja** in the presence of (cf. **andawairþi***)
andwairþis *prep G,D* opposite, facing
andwasjan *wv 1* undress
andwaurdjan *wv 1* to answer; dispute, contradict
andweihan *sv 1* fight (against: *D*)
anno* *wf(?)* wages (Lat. *annona* provisions)
ans* *sm(?)* (*D* **anza**) log, beam
ansteig- *adj* gracious, favorable
ansts *sf* favor, grace

anþar- *adj* other, second (§4.2c); *pl* the others, the rest; **anþar ... anþar** the one ... the other
anþarleikei *wf* difference
anþarleiko *adv* otherwise, differently
apaustaulei *wf* apostleship
apaustaulus, apaustulus *sm* apostle; pl. *N* **-eis**, *G* **-e**, *A* **-uns, -ans** <Gr ἀπόστολος
aqizi *sf* axe
ara *wm* eagle
arbaidjan *wv 1* work, toil, suffer (cf. **bi-**, **miþ-**, **þairh-**)
arbaiþs *sf* (*G* **-aidais**) work, toil, labor
arbi *sn* inheritance
arbinumja *wm* heir
arbja *wm* heir
arbjo *wf* heiress
arhwazna *sf* arrow
arjan *wv 1(?)* plow
arka *sf* coffer, money-box < Lat *arca*
arkaggilus *sm* archangel < Gk ἀρχάγγελος
arm- *adj* poor; *superl* **armost-**
armahairt- *adj* merciful
armahairtei *wf* mercy
armahairtiþa *sf* mercy, charity, pity
armaio *wf* mercy, pity, alms
arman *wv* 3 pity, have pity on (cf. **ga-**)
arms *sm(i)* arm
arniba *adv* safely, surely
aromata *pl* spices < Gk ἀρώματα
arwjo *adv* in vain
asans *sf* harvest, harvest season
asiluqairnus *sf (?)* mill-stone
asilus *sm* ass, donkey
asilus *sf* jenny-ass
asneis *sm* servant, hireling
assarjus* *sm* penny < Lat *assarius*
astaþ *Asg* certainty (but see note to Lk I:4)
asts *sm* branch, twig
at *prep A, D* at, by, to, with, of (§10.4)
ataþni* *sn* year
ataugjan *wv 1* show (sthg: *A*; to: *D*); passive or + **sik** appear
atbairan *sv 4* bring, take, carry, offer
atdriusan *sv 2* fall at, into
atfarjan *wv 1* arrive at, land
atgagg *sn* access, approach
atgaggan *sv* 7 (pret. **atiddja**) come or go up (to: **du** *D*); enter (**in** *A*); ± **dalaþ** descend, go or come down (to, onto: **ana** *A*; from, off of: **af** *D*)
atgaraihtjan *wv 1* put into good order
atgiban *sv 5* give up, deliver up, imprison
athaban sik *wv 3* come towards
athafjan *sv 6* take down
athahan *wv 3* hang (trans.), let down (nets)
athaitan *sv 7* call to oneself
atisk *sn(?)* grain, grain field
-atjan: fraatjan
atkunnan *wv 3* award, confer on
atlagjan *wv 1* lay, lay on; put on clothes
atligan *sv 5* lie in, be within
atnehwjan sik *wv 1* draw near, be at hand
atniman *sv 4* receive, accept
atrinnan *sv 3* run up to
atsaihwan *sv 5* beware (of: **faura** *D*); take care (not to do: **ni** + inf.); busy self with, give attention to (*G*, **du** *D*)
atsatjan *wv 1* present, offer
atsnarpjan *wv 1* to touch, handle
atstandan *sv 6* stand near
atsteigan *sv 1* ± **dalaþ** descend, come down (from: **af** *D*; out of: **us** *D*; into: *A*)
atta *wm* father, forefather
attekan *sv* 7 touch
attiuhan *sv 2* pull towards, bring
atþinsan *sv 3* attract
atwairpan *sv 3* cast down
atwalwjan *wv 1* roll sthg to
atwisan *sv 5* be at hand
atwitains *sf vn* observation, scrutiny
atwopjan *wv 1* call to, summon (*A*)
aþnam *Dpl* years; cf. **ataþni**
aþþan *conj* however, but, still
audag- *adj* blessed
audagei *wf* blessedness
audagjan *wv 1* consider blessed or happy
audahaft- *adj* blessed
aufto *adv* perhaps, indeed, probably
augadauro *wn* window
augjan *wv 1* show (cf. **at-**)
augo *wn* eye
auhjodus *sm* tumult
auhjon *wv 2* cry out, make a noise
auhns* *sm* oven
auhsa* *wm* (*Gpl* **auhsne**) ox (§6.1)
auhsus *sm* ox
auhum- *adj* high, higher
auhumist- *superl adj* highest, chief
auk *conj* because, for; but; also (§14.2)
aukan *sv* 7 (P **aiauk**) add, increase (cf. **ana-**, **bi-**, **ga-**)
auknan *wv 4* increase (intr.) (cf. **bi-**)
aurahi* *sf* or **aurahjo*** *wf* tomb, grave
aurali* *sn* napkin < Lat *orarium*
aurkeis* *sm* jug, cup (<Lat. *urceus*)

aurtigards *sm(i)* garden <Lat *hortus* + Goth **gards**
aurtja *wm* farmer, vintner (based on Lat *hortus*)
auso *wn* ear
auþi- *adj* desert, waste; childless
auþida *sf* wilderness, desert
aweþi *sn* flock
awiliudon *wv 2* thank, give thanks (to: *D*; for: **faur** *A*, **fram** *D*, **in** *G*)
awiliuþ (*G* **-dis**) *sn* thanks
awistr *sn* sheepfold
awo *wf* grandmother
azet- *adj* easy; *comp* **azetiz-**
azetaba *adv* easily, willingly
azeti* *sn* ease, comfort
azgo *wf* ashes
azymus *sm* unleavened bread (*Gpl* **-e**) < Gk τὰ ἄζυμα

B

-ba *encl particle* if
badi *sn* bed
bagms *sm* tree
bai (*A* **bans**, *D* **baim**; *neuter NA* **ba**) *num* both
baidjan *wv 1* force, compel (cf. **ga-**)
bairabagms *sm* mulberry tree
bairan *sv 4* bear, carry; produce (cf. **at-**, **fra-**, **ga-**, **innat-**, **þairh-**, **us-**, **ut-**)
bairgahei *wf* hill-country
bairgan *sv 3* hide; keep, preserve (*D*) (cf. **ga-**)
bairht- *adj* bright, clear, manifest
bairhtaba *adv* brightly, clearly
bairhtei *wf* brightness; **in bairhtein** openly
bairhtjan *wv 1* reveal, make manifest (cf. **ga-**)
baitr- *adj* bitter; **baitraba** *adv* bitterly
baitrei *wf* bitterness
bajoþs *num* both
balgs *sm(i)* wine-skin, leather bag or bottle
balsan *sn* balsam <Lat. *balsamum* < Gk βάλσαμον
balsagga usually taken as error for **halsagga*** *qv*
balþaba *adv* boldly
balþei *wf* boldness
balþjan *wv 1* make a decision, dare, venture
balwawesei *wf* evil
balweins *sf vn* torment, pain
balwjan *wv 1* torment, plague (*D*)
bandi *sf* bond, fetter
bandja *wm* prisoner
bandwa *sf* sign, token
bandwo *wf* sign, token
bandwjan *wv 1* give a sign, signal, nod (cf. **ga-**)
banja* *sf* blow, wound
bansts *sm(i)* barn, granary
barbarus *sm(?)* a non-Greek person < Gk βάρβαρος
barizein- *adj* barley
barms *sm(i)* bosom, lap
barn *sn* child
barnilo *wn* little child, son; general affectionate address
barnisk- *adj* childish
barniskei *wf* childish ways
barniski *sn* childhood
barusnjan *wv 1* treat with honor and respect
batist- *superl adj* best
batiz- *comp adj* better
-batnan: gabatnan
bauains *sf vn* abode, dwelling
bauan *wv 3 irreg* (§10.1) inhabit, dwell (cf. **ga-**)
baud- *adj* deaf, dumb; insipid, tasteless
-baugjan: usbaugjan
bauhta *P* of **bugja**
-bauljan: ufbauljan
baur *sm(i)* son, child
baurgja *wm* citizen
baurgs *f* city, town (§10.2)
baurgswaddjus *sf* city-wall
baurþei *wf* burden
beidan *sv 1* await, expect (*G*) (cf. **ga-**, **us-**)
beist *sn* leaven, yeast
-beistjan: gabeistjan
beitan *sv 1* bite (cf. **and-**)
berusjos *sm pl* parents
bi *prep A, D* by, around; at, by, near; concerning, on account of, according to (Voc. 5)
biabrjan ana *wv 1* be overcome with amazement at
biarbaidjan *wv 1* aspire to
biaukan *sv 7* increase, add to
bibaurgeins *sf* encampment
bibindan *sv 3* bind, wrap (with: *D*)
biauknan *wv 4* become greater
bida *sf* prayer, request
bidagwa *wm* beggar
bidan *var* of **bidjan** *qv*
bidjan *sv 5 irreg* ask, beg, pray (cf. **ga-**, **usbidan**)
bidomjan *wv 1* to judge, pass sentence on
bifaih *sn* covetousness, cupidity (?)
bifaiho *wf* covetousness (?)
bifaihon *wv 2* exploit, deceive, outwit
bigairdan *sv 3* gird on
bigitan *sv 5* find, meet with
bigraban *sv 6* surround with an embankment or palisade

bihait *sn* strife, malicious gossip
bihaitja *wm* boaster
bihlahjan *sv 6* laugh at, deride, mock
bihwe *interrog adv* why?
bihwairban *sv 3* press, crowd around
bikukjan *wv 1* cover with kisses
bilaibjan *wv 1* have left over, leave over
bilaigon *wv 2* to lick
bilaikan *sv 7* mock
bileiban *sv 1* remain
bileiþan *sv 1* leave, forsake, abandon (smn: *D* or *A*); leave behind at one's death
bimait *sn* circumcision
bimaitan *sv 7* circumcise
bimampjan *wv 1* deride
binah *PP* it is permitted, it is lawful (§20.1)
binauht- *part adj* sufficient
bindan *sv 3* bind; tie up, tether (*A*; with: *D*) (cf. **and-**, **bi-**, **ga-**)
biniman *sv 4* take away, steal
biqiman *sv 4* befall, come upon (*A*)
biraubon *wv 2* rob, strip
bireikei *wf* danger
bireikj- *adj* endangered, in danger
birinnan *sv 3* run about
birodeins *sf vn* murmuring, muttering
birodjan *wv 1* murmur; mutter (sthg: *A*) in disapproval
birunains *sf vn* pursuit, persecution
birusjos *var* of **berusjos** *qv*
bisaihwan *sv 5* see, look, look around at (A); look after (*G*)
bisatjan *wv 1* beset, set around
bisauleins *sf vn* defilement
bisaulnan *wv 4* become dirty, unclean, defiled
bisitan *sv 5* sit with, sit near, sit about
bisitands *m* neighbor
biskaban *sv 6* shave
biskeinan *sv 1* shine
bismeitan *sv 1* smear, anoint
bisniwan *sv 5* precede, take precedence over (**faur**)
bispeiwan *sv 1* spit upon
bistandan *sv 6* surround
bistigqan *sv 3* stumble; strike (against: *A*, **du** *D*, **bi** *D*)
bistugq *sn* stumbling
bisunjane *adv* round about, nearby
biswairban *sv 3* wipe, wipe dry
biswaran *sv 6* swear, adjure
bitiuhan *sv 2* go about, visit
biþagkjan *wv 1 irreg* think, believe
biþe *conj* when, while, as soon as; *adv* thereupon, then, afterward
biþeh *adv* after that, then
biþwahan *sv 6* wash (oneself)
-biudan: anabiudan, faurbiudan
biugan *sv 2* bend (cf. **ga-**)
biuht- *adj* accustomed, wont to
biuhti *sn* custom
biuþs* *sm* or **biuþ*** *sn* (*G* **-dis**) table
biwaibjan *wv 1* wind around, encompass, clothe
biwandjan *wv 1* shun
biwindan *sv 3* wrap around, swaddle
biwisan *sv 5* have a good time
blandan sik *sv 7* mix (with: *D* or **miþ**)
blauþjan *wv 1* abolish, annul, abrogate (cf. **ga-**)
bleiþ- *adj* merciful
bleiþei *wf* mercy
bleiþjan *wv 1* have pity on (cf. **ga-**)
-blesan: ufblesan
bliggwan *sv 3* beat, strike, scourge, whip (cf. **us-**)
blind- *adj* blind
blinda *wm* blind man
-blindjan: gablindjan
-blindnan: afblindnan
bloma *wm* flower
blotan *sv 7* revere, worship, honor
blotinassus *sm* worship, service
bloþ (*G* **-þis**) *sn* blood
bloþarinnand- *part adj* hemorrhaging
bnauan *sv 7(?)* to rub
boka *sf* letter of alphabet; pl. book, scripture, epistle; **bokos afsateinais** or **afstassais** a bill of divorcement
bokareis *sm* scribe, scholar
bota *sf* advantage
botjan *wv 1* avail, be of use, help; improve, make better (cf. **ga-**)
brahta *P* of **briggan**
brahwa *Ds* in the phrase **in brahwa augins** in an instant
braidei *wf* breadth
braid- *adj* broad
-braidjan: usbraidjan
brakja *sf* strife
-brannjan: gabrannjan, inbrannjan
briggan (**bringan**) *sv 3 irreg* (*P* **brahta**) bring, lead
brikan *sv 4* break; quarrel, fight (cf. **ga-**, **uf-**)
brinnan *sv 3* burn (intr.) (cf. **uf-**)
brinno *wf* fever
broþar *m* brother (§7.2)
broþrahans *mpl* brethren
broþrulubo, broþralubo *wf* brotherly love
bruk- *adj* useful

brukjan *wv irreg* (*P* **bruhta** §6.2) use, partake of; treat, deal with (all with *G*, rarely *D*) (cf. **us-**)
brunjo *wf* breastplate
brunna *wm* well, spring; flow, issue
brusts *f* breast
bruþfaþs (*G* **-fadis**) *sm(i)* bridegroom
bruþs *sf* bride; daughter-in-law
bugjan *wv irreg* (*P* **bauhta** §6.2) buy (*A*; for a price: *D*, **us** *D*; to redeem (smn: *A*) (cf. **fra-**, **us-**)
-bundnan: andbundnan
byssaun *As* = Gk βύσσον (*A*) fine linen

D

-daban: gadaban
daddjan *wv 1* suckle, nurse (a child)
dags *sm* day; **daga hwammeh, dagis hwizuh** day by day; **himma daga** today
daigs *sm* dough, paste
daila *sf* (1) partnership; (2) mina (coin)
dailjan *wv 1* deal out, divide up (cf. **af-**, **dis-**, **fra-**, **ga-**)
dails *sf* portion, share; **us dailai** partly
daimonareis *sm* demoniac; < Gk δαίμων with Gothic ending **-areis**
dal *sn* valley, dale, ditch
dalaþ *adv* downward; **und dalaþ** to the bottom; **dalaþa** below; **dalaþro** from below
-dammjan: faurdammjan
daub- *adj* deaf; obdurate, hardened
daubei *wf* deafness; obduracy
daubiþa *sf* deafness; obduracy
-daubjan: gadaubjan
-daubnan: afdaubnan
-daudjan: usdaudjan
daug *PP* it is good for, benefits (§20.1)
dauhtar *f* daughter (§7.2)
dauhts *sf* feast
dauns *sf* smell, odor, savour
daupeins *sf vn* baptism; washing
daupjan *wv 1* baptize, wash self (cf. **uf-**)
daupjands (*G* **-ndins**, *D* **-ndin**, *A* **-nd**) *m* baptizer
daur *sn* door
daurawarda *wm*, **daurawardo** *wf*, **daurawards** *sm* door-keeper, porter
dauro* *wf* door; pl. doorway, portal
-daursan: gadaursan
dauþ- *adj* dead
dauþeins *sf vn* peril of death
dauþjan *wv 1* put to death (cf. **af-**, **ga-**)
-dauþnan: gadauþnan, miþgadauþnan
dauþublj- *adj* sentenced to death
dauþus *sm* death
diabaulus *sm* devil <Gk διάβολος
diabula *sf* slanderer (f.) < Gk διάβολος
diakaunus *sm* deacon < Gk διάκονος
digan *sv 1 (irreg)* fashion (from clay) (cf. **ga-**)
digan- *part adj* made of earth
digrei *wf* abundance
disdailjan *wv 1* share, divide up
disdriusan *sv 2* fall upon
dishaban *wv 3* seize, hold fast
dishniupan *sv 2* tear apart, break (trans.)
dishnupnan *wv 4* break, tear (intrans.), be torn
disniman *sv 4* possess
dissigqan *sv 3* to set (of the sun)
dissitan *sv 5* settle upon, seize upon
disskaidan *sv 7* divide up
disskreitan *sv 1* rend, tear
disskritnan *wv 4* be torn, rent asunder
distaheins *sf vn* dispersion
distahjan *wv 1* destroy, waste
distairan *sv 4* tear to pieces
distaurnan *wv 4* tear, rip (intrans.)
diswilwan *sv 3* plunder
diswinþjan *wv 1* crush
diswiss *sf* dissolution
diup- *adj* deep
diupei *wf* depth
diupiþa *sf* depth
-diupjan: gadiupjan
dius (G **diuzis**) *sn* wild beast
diwan *sv 5* die; **þata diwano** mortality
-dobnan: af-
-dojan*: afdawid-
domjan *wv 1* to judge (cf. **af-**, **bi-**, **ga-**)
doms *sm* judgement
-draban: gadraban
dragan *sv 6* drag, carry (cf. **ga-**)
dragk *sn* a drink
dragkjan *wv 1* give to to drink (cf. **ga-**)
draibjan *wv 1* drive, trouble, vex; + **sik** be troubled
drakma *wm* < Lat *drachma* < Gk δραχμή
drauhsna *sf* crumb, fragment
drauhtinassus *sm* warfare
drauhtinon *wv 2* wage war
drauhtiwitoþ *sn* military campaign
-drausjan: afdrausjan, gadrausjan
dreiban *sv 1* drive (cf. **us-**)

drigkan *sv 3* drink (cf. **ana-**, **ga-**)
driugan *sv 2* serve as a soldier
driusan *sv 2* fall down, fall (upon: **ana** *D*; into: **in** *A*), crowd against (cf. **at-**, **dis-**. **ga-**, **us-**)
driuso *wf* slope
drobjan *wv 1* cause trouble, stir up
drobna *wm* trouble, disturbance
drobnan *wv 4* become anxious, troubled (cf. **ga-**, **in-**)
drugkanei *wf* drunkenness
drunjus *sm* music, sound, voice
drus *sm* fall
du *prep D* (§1.4) to, towards, against; **du þammei** to the end that, because
duatgaggan *sv* 7 go to, come to (smn: *D*)
duatrinnan *sv 3* run to
duatsniwan *sv 5* hurry towards
dugan* *PP* be good for, avail, profit (§20.1)
dugawindan *sv 3* entangle
duginnan *sv 3* begin (to do: inf.)
duhwe *interrog adv* why? wherefore?
dulgahaitja *wm* money-lender, creditor
dulgis *Gs* debt
dulþjan *wv 1* celebrate a festival
dulþs *sf* feast, festival
dumb- *adj* dumb, unable to speak
-dumbnan: afdumbnan
durinnan *sv 3* run to
dustodjan *wv 1* begin
duþe, duþþe for that reason, therefore, because; **duþe ei** to the end that, because
dwal- *adj* foolish
dwalawaurdei *wf* foolish talk
dwaliþa *sf* foolishness
dwalmon *wv 2* be foolish, rave

EI

ei *conj* so that; *interrog particle* whether; *rel particle* used suffixally or alone (§§16.2, 19.5)
eis *pron* they (§7.3)
eisarn *sn* iron; pl. fetters, irons
eisarnabandi *sf* chain, iron fetters
eisarnein- *adj* iron
eiþan *conj* therefore

F

fadar *m* father
fadrein *sn* paternity, lineage; with masc. pl. modifiers: parents, grandparents, forefathers
fadreins *sf* family, lineage
faginon *wv 2* rejoice, be glad (at: *D*, **in** *G*) (cf. **miþ-**)
fagr- *adj* beautiful; fit, suitable
fahan *sv* 7 (P **faifah**) catch, seize, lay hands on (cf. **ga-**)
faheþs *sf* (*D* **fahedai**) joy
-fahjan: fullafahjan
-fahrjan: gafahrjan
faian *wv 3* find fault with
-faihon: bifaihon, gafaihon
faihu *sn* cattle, property; money
faihufrik- *adj* greedy, covetous
faihufrikei *wf* covetousness, greed
faihugairn- *adj* covetous, greedy
faihugairnei *wf* covetousness, greed
faihugawaurki *sn* means of livelihood
faihugeigan *wv 3* be greedy, covetous
faihugeigo *wf* greed
faihuskula *wm* debtor
faihuþraihns* *sm(?)* wealth
fairaihan *PP* partake of
fairgreipan *sv 1* seize, catch hold of
fairguni *sn* mountain
fairhaitan *sv* 7 in **þank fairhaitan** to thank
-fairhwjan: waifairhwjan
fairhwus *sm* world
fairina *sf* accusation, charge
fairinon *wv* 2 accuse, charge
fairn- *adj* last, most recent (error for **fairnj-** ?)
fairnj- *adj* old
fairniþa *sf* oldness, staleness
fairra *adv* far, far off; **fairra** *D* far from; as *prep* w. verbs of motion: from
fairraþro *adv* from afar
fairrinnan *sv 3* extend, reach to
fairweitjan *wv 1* look around
fairweitl *sn* spectacle
fairzna *sf* heel
falþan *sv* 7 (P **faifalþ**) fold, close
-falþs *adj* -fold (onefold etc.) (§23.7)
fana *wm* piece of cloth, patch
fani *sn* mud, mire, soft clay
faran *sv* 6 go, fare (cf. **at-**)
farjan *wv 1* travel, go (cf. **at-**)
faskjam *Dpl* with bands (Lat. *fascia*)
fastan *wv 3* fast; keep, observe (cf. **ga-**)

fastubni *sn* fasting; observance (of law)
faþa *sf* hedge
-**faþs** *sm(i)* (G **fadis**) master, leader, chief
fauho *wf* fox
faur, faura *prep A* along; to, at, or along the front or side of; (of time) before; for, on behalf of (Voc. 7)
faura *prep D* same as **faur** above; *adv* before, previously
fauradauri *sn* street, space before a door
faurafilli *sn* foreskin
fauragagga *wm* governor, steward
fauragaggan *sv 7* go before; precede (**faura** *D*); take charge of, manage (*D*)
fauragaggi *sn* administration, stewardship
fauragaggja *wm* governor, administrator, chief steward
fauragahaitan *sv 7* foretell
fauragahugjan *wv 1* make up one's mind
fauragaleikan *wv 3* set forth, present
fauragamanwjan *wv 1* prepare in advance
fauragameljan *wv 1* write previously
fauragaredan *sv 7* destine, determine beforehand
fauragasatjan *wv 1* to offer, present
fauragateihan *sv 1* foretell, inform beforehand
faurahah *sn* curtain, veil
fauramanwjan *wv 1* prepare in advance
fauramaþleis *sm* ruler, prince; chief, head
fauramaþli *sn* administration, governance
faurameljan *wv 1* portray, present
fauraqiman *sv 4* appear, come
fauraqiþan *sv 5* foretell, prophesy
faurarahnjan *wv 1* outdo
faurasandjan *wv 1* send on ahead
faurasatjan *wv 1* to present, set before
faurastandan *sv 6* rule, govern; stand before or near
fauratani *sn* sign, portent, wonder
faurbauhts *sf* redemption
faurbigaggan *sv 7* go before, precede
faurbisniwan *sv 5* precede
faurbiudan *sv 2* forbid, order (smn: *D*; not to do: **ei** + subj.)
faurdammjan *wv 1* dam up
faurdomeins *sf vn* prejudice, partiality
faurgaggan *sv 7* (pret. -**iddja**) pass by
faurhah *var of* **faurahah** *qv*
faurht- *adj* fearful, afraid
faurhtei *wf* fear, astonishment
faurhtjan *wv 1* be afraid, fear (± **sis**)
faurlageins *sf vn* exhibiting; **hlaibos faurlageinais** Temple "Shew-bread"
faurlagjan *wv 1* lay before
faurqiþan *sv 5* make excuses, excuse
faurrinnan *sv 3* precede, go before
faursigljan *wv 1* to seal
faursniwan *sv 5* hurry before, anticipate; to have occurred previously
faurstasseis *sm* chief, ruler
faurþis *adv* formerly, beforehand
faurþizei *conj* before (requires subj.)
faurwaipjan *wv 1* muzzle, restrain
faurwalwjan *wv 1* to roll sthg (*D*) in front of (*A*)
faw- *adj* few (*Mpl* **fawai**); *comp* **fawiz**-
-**feinan: infeinan**
fera *sf* region, district
ferja* *wm* spy
fetjan *wv 1* adorn
fidurdog- *adj* of four days
fidurfalþ- *num adj* fourfold
fidurragini *sn* tetrarchate
fidwor *num* (*D* -**im**) four
fidwortaihun *num* fourteen
fidwor tigjus *num* forty
figgragulþ *sn* finger-ring
figgrs *sm* finger
fijan *wv 3* to hate
fijands, fiands *m* enemy
fijaþwa, fiaþwa *sf* hatred, enmity
filaus *adv* much (more, less)
filhan *sv 3* hide, conceal (*A*; from: **faura** *D*); bury (cf. **af-, ana-, ga-, us-**)
filigri *sn* den, cave, hiding-place
fillein- *adj* of skin, leather-
filu *neuter adj* used adverbially: much, very, a lot, greatly
filudeisei *wf* cunning, guile
filufaih- *adj* manifold, varied
filugalaub- *adj* very precious, costly
filusna *sf* multitude
filuwaurdei *wf* verbosity
filuwaurdjan *wv 1* talk a lot, be verbose
fimf *num* five
fimft- *ord num adj* fifth
fimftaihun *num* fifteen
fimftataihund- *ord num adj* fifteenth
fimf tigjus *num* fifty
finþan *sv 3* find (out about), learn of (from: **at** *D*), hear
fiskja *wm* fisherman
fiskon *wv 2* to fish
fisks *sm* fish
fitan *sv 5* to labor in childbirth
flahtom *Dpl* braids
flaut- *adj* boastful
flautjan *wv 1* to boast
flodus *sf* flood, stream

flokan* *sv 7* (*P* **faiflok**) bewail, lament
fodeins *sf vn* food
fodjan *wv 1* feed, nourish, rear
fodr *sn* sheath, scabbard
fon *n* (*G* **funins**) fire (§10.2)
fotubandi *sf* foot-irons
fotubaurd *sn* footstool
fotus *sm* foot; **du fotum** *G* at the feet of
fraatjan *wv 1* dole out (to the poor)? fritter away (?)
frabairan *sv 4* bear, endure
frabauhtaboka *sf* bill of sale
frabugjan *wv 1* (P **-bauhta**) sell (*A*; for a price: **in** *A*)
fradailjan *wv 1* divide, distribute
fragan *sv(?)* to ask, question
fragiban *sv 5* give graciously, grant; pardon, forgive
fragibts, fragifts *sf* in *pl* betrothal, giving in marriage
fragildan *sv 3* pay back, restore
frahinþan *sv 3* capture, imprison
fraihnan *sv 5* (*P* **frah**) ask, interrogate (cf. **ga-**)
fraisan *sv 7* (*P* **faifrais**) to tempt, test, try (cf. **us-**)
fraistubni *sf* temptation
fra-itan *sv 5 irreg* (P **fret**) consume, devour
fraiw *sn* seed; offspring
frakunnan *PP* despise (*D*) (§16.3)
frakunþ- *part adj* despised
fraletan *sv 7* liberate, set free; permit (smn: *A*; to do: inf.); lower, let down; forgive (smn: *D*; sthg: *A*); leave, withdraw (from: *A*).
fralet *sn(?)* forgiveness, remission (of sin)
fralets *(s)m* freedman
fralewjan *wv 1* betray
fraliusan *sv 2* lose (sthg: *D*)
fralusnan *wv 4* be lost, perish, go astray
fralusts *sf* loss, perdition
fram *prep D* (§1.4) from, since; by, through the agency of; **fram himma nu** henceforth; *adv* further on
framaldr- *adj* of great age, very old; *comp* **framaldroz-**
framaþj- *adj* strange, foreign, of someone else
framaþjan *wv 1* alienate
framgahts* *sf* progress
framis *adv* further, onward
framwairþis *adv* henceforth
framwigis *adv* always, continually
franiman *sv 4* receive, take
frarinnan *sv 3* encounter, chance to meet
fraqiman *sv 4* spend, expend, use up, destroy (*D*)
fraqisteins *sf vn* waste, destruction
fraqistjan *wv 1* destroy (*A*, less commonly *D*)
fraqistnan *wv 4* be destroyed, perish
fraqiþan *sv 5* curse, disparage, reject as unsuitable
fraslindan *sv 3* swallow up, devour
frastisibja *sf* adoption
frasts* *sm(i)* child
-fratwjan: usfratwjan
fraþi *sn* understanding
fraþjamarzeins *sf vn* deception, illusion
fraþjan *sv 6* understand, perceive (sthg: *D*); think, know, suppose; **samo fraþjan in** *D* live in harmony with (cf. **fulla-**)
frauja *wm* lord, master; the Lord
fraujinassus *sm* lordship
fraujinon *wv 2* rule, be lord (cf. **ga-**)
fraujinonds *m* ruler
frawairpan *sv 3* throw away
frawairþan *sv 3* become corrupt
frawardeins* *sf vn* destruction, ruin
frawardjan *wv 1* destroy, ruin, corrupt, disfigure
frawaurht- *adj* sinful; as noun: sinner
frawaurhts *sf* sin, evil-doing
frawaurkjan *wv 1* to sin (± **sis**)
fraweit *sn* revenge, vengeance; justice
fraweitan *sv 1* to avenge
fraweitands *m* avenger
frawilwan *sv 3* rob, plunder, seize
frawisan *sv 5* spend, use up
frawrikan *sv 5* persecute
frawrohjan *wv 1* denounce, accuse
freidjan *wv 1* spare, save; refrain from
freihals *sm* freedom
frei-, fri- *adj* free; **frijana briggan** to set smn (*A*) free (from: *G*)
friaþwamildj- *adj* tender-loving
frijaþwa, friaþwa *sf* love; **frijaþ haban miþ** to love
frijei *wf* freedom
frijon *wv 2* to love; enjoy (doing sthg)
frijondi *sf* friend (f.)
frijonds *m* friend (§10.2)
frijons *sf* kiss
-frik- *adj* greedy
-frisahtjan: gafrisahtjan
-frisahtnan: gafrisahtnan
frisahts *sf* example; image, picture; riddle, enigma
-friþon: gafriþon
friusa *Ds* cold, frost
frod- *adj* wise; *comp* **frodoz-**
frodaba *adv* wisely, with understanding
frodei *wf* understanding, wisdom
frum- *comp adj* former, prior, first (§23.7); **fram fruma** from the very first; **fruma Sabbato** the day before the Sabbath *or* the first day of the week
frumabaur *sm(i)* first-born son
frumadei *wf* precedence, pre-eminence

frumist- *superl adj* first, foremost; best, chief; *adv* firstly
frumisti *sn* beginning
frums* *sm* beginning
fugls *sm* bird, fowl
fula *wm* foal
fulgin- *adj* hidden
fulhsni *sn* secret, hidden thing
full- *adj* full (§4.2c)
fullafahjan *wv 1* satisfy, serve
fullafraþjan *wv 1* be fully in command of one's senses
fullatoji- *adj* perfect
fullaweis- *adj* complete, perfect (in wisdom)
fullaweisjan *wv 1* persuade (cf. **ga-**)
fullawit- *adj* complete, perfect (in wisdom)
fulleiþs *sf* or **fulleiþ** *sn* fullness
fulljan *wv 1* fill *A* (with: *G*), fulfill (cf. **ga-**, **ufar-**, **us-**)
fullnan, fulnan *wv 4* become full (of: *A* or *G*) (cf. **ga-**, **us-**)
fullo *wf* fullness
ful- *adj* foul
funisk- *adj* fiery

G

ga- verbal prefix; see §§5.3;13.2
gaaggwei *wf* constraint, limitation
gaaggwjan *wv 1* constrain, make anxious
gaaiginon *wv 2* take possession of; get the advantage of
gaainan *wv 3* separate, isolate
gaaistan *wv 3* revere, show reverence toward
gaaiwiskon *wv 2* abuse, mistreat; make ashamed
gaarbja *wm* fellow-heir
gaarman *wv 3* have pity on
gaaukan *sv 7* increase
gabaidjan *wv 1* force, constrain
gabairan *sv 4* bring forth; compare
gabairgan *sv 3* keep, preserve
gabairhteins *sf vn* appearance, manifestation
gabairhtjan *wv 1* reveal, manifest, declare
gabandwjan *wv 1* beckon, give a signal
gabatnan *wv 4* to profit, gain, benefit
gabauan *wv 3* dwell
gabaur *sn* collection (of money), taxes
gabaur *sm* carousing, revelry
gabaurgja *wm* fellow-citizen
gabaurjaba *adv* willingly, gladly
gabaurjoþus *sm* pleasure
gabaurþiwaurda *sn pl* genealogy
gabaurþs *sf* birth; birthplace; generation; **mel gabaurþais** birthday; **us gabaurþai** by nature, natural
gabei *wf* riches
gabeidan *sv 1* abide, dwell
gabeig, gabig- *adj* rich
gabeistjan *wv 1* to leaven
gabidjan *sv 5* pray for, ask for
gabigjan *wv 1* make rich
gabignan *wv 4* become rich
gabinda *sf* bond, ligament
gabindan *sv 3* bind, tie up, tether (*A*; with: *D*)
gabiugan *sv 2* bend
gablauþjan *wv 1* cancel, annul
gableiþeins *sf vn* mercy, pity
gableiþjan *wv 1* to pity
gablindjan *wv 1* to blind
gablindnan *wv 4* to become blind
gabotjan *wv 1* make useful; **aftra gabotjan** restore
gabrannjan *wv 1* burn (trans.)
gabrikan *sv 4* break
gabruka *sf* fragment, crumb
gabundi *sf* bond
gadaban *sv 6* happen, befall, be fitting
gadaila *wm* sharer, partner
gadailjan *wv 1* divide
gadars *PP* I dare
gadaubjan *wv 1* make deaf, harden
gadauka* *wm* member of household
gadaursan *PP* (§20.1) to dare (to do: inf.)
gadauþjan *wv 1* kill, put to death, execute
gadauþnan *wv 4* die, perish
gadeþs* (*D* **-dedai**) *sf* deed
gadigan *sv 1 irreg* to fashion (from clay)
gadigis* (conjecture for **gadikis**) *sn* clay vessel, fashioned object
gadiliggs *sm(?)* cousin
gadiupjan *wv 1* deepen, dig deep
gadob- *adj* becoming, fit
gadomjan *wv 1* judge, pass judgement, condemn
gadraban *sv 6* hew out
gadragan *sv 6* pile up, pile together
gadragkjan *wv 1* give to drink
gadrauhts *sm(i)* soldier
gadrausjan *wv 1* throw down, fell
gadrigkan *sv 3* to drink
gadriusan *sv 2* fall, be cast
gadrobnan *wv 4* become anxious, be troubled
gafahan *sv 7* catch, take, seize, overtake; apprehend as a criminal
gafahrjan *wv 1* prepare, make ready
gafah *sn* or **gafahs** *sm* a catch, haul
gafaihon *wv 2* take advantage of, outwit, defraud
gafastan *wv 3* keep, observe, hold fast

gafaurds *sf* chief council
gafauri- *adj* well-behaved, dignified
gafehaba *adv* decently, properly
gafeteins *sf vn* clothing
gafilh *sn* burial
gafilhan *sv 3* hide, conceal, bury
gafraihnan *sv 5* ask; learn by inquiry
gafraþjei *wf* cleverness, good sense
gafraujinon *wv 2* rule, be lord over
gafreideins *sf vn* keeping, preserving
gafrijons *sf vn* kiss
gafrisahtjan *wv 1* to copy, portray
gafrisahtnan *wv 4* be copied, imitated
gafriþon *wv 2* reconcile
gafriþons *sf vn* reconciliation
gafulgin- *adj* hidden
gafullaweisjan *wv 1* persuade, bring into common agreement
gafulljan *wv 1* fill
gafullnan *wv 4* become full
gagaggan *sv 7* (± **sik**) collect, assemble (intr.); come to pass
gagahaftjan *wv 1* join together
gagaleikon sik *wv 2* be transformed
gagamainjan *wv 1* to defile
gagatilon *wv 2* fit or join together (trans.)
gagawairþnan *wv 4* become reconciled
gageigan *wv 3* gain, acquire
gagg *sn* road, way, wayside
gaggan *sv 7* (P **iddja**) go (cf. **af-**, **afar-**, **ana-**, **at-**, **duat-**, **innat-**, **faur-**, **faura-**, **faurbi-**, **ga-**, **inn-**, **miþ-**, **þairh-**, **ufar-**, **us-**, **ut-**, **wiþra-**)
gagrefts *sf* order, decree
gagud- *adj* godly, pious
gagudaba *adv* piously
gagudei *wf* piety, goodness
gahaban *wv 3* take hold of, hold fast to; seize, take prisoner; + **sik** to refrain (from: **af** *D*)
gahaftjan sik *wv 1* join (self to)
gahaftnan *wv 4* be joined to
gahahjo *adv* in sequence, coherently
gahail- *adj* whole, sound, unharmed
gahailjan *wv 1* to heal
gahailnan *wv 4* be healed, become whole
gahait *sn* promise
gahaitan *sv 7* call together; to promise
gahamon *wv 2* put on, don
gahardjan *wv 1* harden
gahaunjan *wv 1* make humble
gahauseins *sf vn* hearing; what is heard, sermon, message
gahausjan *wv 1* hear
gahilpan *sv 3* to help (*G*)
gahlaiba *wm* comrade, companion
gahlaifs* *sm* companion, comrade
gahnaiwjan *wv 1* to humble, abase
gahobains *sf vn* self-control
gahorinon *wv 2* commit adultery
gahraineins *sf vn* cleansing, purification
gahrainjan *wv 1* cleanse, purify (*A*; of: *G*)
gahugds *sf* thought, mind, conscience
gahuljan *wv 1* cover, conceal
gahwairb- *adj* obedient
gahwatjan *wv 1* sharpen; entice, induce
gahweilains *sf vn* stopping, resting
gahweilan *wv 3* to stop, cease, rest; + **sik ana** rest upon
gahweitjan *wv 1* to whiten
gahwotjan *wv 1* rebuke, charge strictly (not to do sthg)
Gaiainna *wm* Gehenna, Hell < Gk Γέεννα < Heb *Gêhinnôm*
gaibnjan *wv 1* make like, made equal
gaidreigon *wv 2* repent, regret
gaidw* *sn* want, lack
gailjan *wv 1* gladden, cheer up
gairda *sf* girdle, belt
-gairdan: bigairdan, ufgairdan
gairnei *wf* desire, longing
gairnjan *wv 1* to desire, wish for, long for, aspire to (*G* or inf.)
gairu *sn* goad, sting
gairuni *sn* passion, suffering
-gaisjan: usgaisjan
gaitein- *adj* goat-, belonging to a goat
gaitein *sn* a kid
gaits *sf* goat
gajiukan *wv 3* conquer, be victorious
gajuk *sn* pair
gajuka *wm* companion
gajuko *wf* parable, comparison, similitude
gakannjan *wv 1* make known
gakaron *wv 2* to care for
gakausjan *wv 1* to test, try
gakiusan *sv 2* test, try; approve of
gakroton *wv 2* break, smash
gakunnan *wv 3* recognize, observe, read, learn of
gakunds, gakunþs *sf* persuasion; the use of this word in Lk 3:23 is obscure.
gakusts *sf* test
galagjan *wv 1* lay, set, place; bury
galaisjan *wv 1* teach
galaista *wm* follower; **galaista wisan** *D* to follow smn
galaistjan *wv 1* follow
galatjan *wv 1* hinder

galaþon *wv 2* invite, call together
galaub- *adj* precious, valuable
galaubein- *adj* believing, faithful
galaubeins *sf vn* faith, belief
galaubjan *wv 1* believe (smn: *D*), entrust (sthg *A*; to: *D*)
galaugnjan *wv 1* hide; *pass inf* remain hidden; + **sik** hide oneself, withdraw into seclusion
galausjan *wv 1* loosen, undo
galeik- *adj* similar, like
galeika* *wm* sharer of the same body
galeikan *wv 3* please (smn: *D*); take pleasure in (*D*)
galeiki* *sn* likeness, image
galeikinon *wv 2* cure, heal
galeiko *adv* in like manner, likewise
galeikon *wv 2* liken, compare (sthg: *A*; to sthg: *D*); resemble, be like (sthg: *D*)
galeiþan *sv 1* go, travel, come
galewjan *wv 1* betray, hand over
galga *wm* gallows, cross
galigri *sn* spouse(?), intercourse(?)
galisan sik *sv 5* gather, assemble
galiug *sn* lie; heathen idol; as *adv* falsely; **galiug taujan** to falsify
galiugaapaustaulus *sm* false apostle
galiugabroþar *m* false brother
galiugaguþ *sn* heathen idol, false god
galiugan *wv 3* to marry
galiugapraufetus *sm* false prophet
galiugaweitwoþs (*G* **-odis**) *sm* false witness
galiugaxristus *sm* false Christ
galiuhtjan *wv 1* illumine, bring to light
galukan *sv 2* shut, close, lock; shut (smn: *A*) in; net, catch (fish); consign (smn: *A*; to: **in** *D*)
galuknan *wv 4* be shut up
gamagan* *PP* be of significance, matter
gamaid- *adj* weak, feeble, bruised
gamaini- *adj* (in) common; unclean, defiled; **gamainiwairþan** to participate in
gamainduþs (*G* **-þais**) *sf* community
gamainei *wf* community
gamainja *wm* participant, sharer
gamainjan *wv 1* defile, pollute
gamaitan *sv 7* mutilate, scarify
gamainþs *sf* congregation, assembly
gamalwjan *wv 1* to bruise
gamalteins *sf vn* dissolution, departure
gaman *sn* companion, fellow-man
gamanwjan *wv 1* prepare, make ready
gamarzeins *sf vn* obstacle, hindrance
gamarzjan *wv 1* offend
gamatjan *wv 1* eat
gamaudeins *sf vn* remembrance
gamaudjan *wv 1* remember; remind
gamaurgjan *wv 1* curtail, cut short
gameleins *sf vn* writing
gameljan *wv 1* write, record, enroll; **þata gamelido** writing, scripture
gamikiljan *wv 1* praise, magnify
gaminþi *sn* remembrance
gamitan *sv 5* measure (*A*) out to (*D*), apportion to
gamitons *sf vn* thought
gamot *PP* find room, fit in (§20.1)
gamotjan* *wv 1* meet
gamunan *PP* (§16.3) remember, recall (sthg: *G*; that...: **þatei** + indic.)
gamunds *sf* remembrance, memory; **du gamundai** *G* in remembrance of
ganagljan *wv 1* nail on
ganah *PP* it suffices (§20.1)
ganaitjan *wv 1* treat shamefully
ganamnjan *wv 1* to name
gananþjan *wv 1* cease, stop
ganasjan *wv 1* save, rescue, redeem; heal
ganatjan *wv 1* moisten
ganauha *wm* sufficiency
ganawistron *wv 2* bury, inter
ganiman *sv 4* take to or with oneself; to conceive (a child)
ganipnan *wv 4* mourn, be sorrowful
ganisan *sv 5* become whole, be saved, recover (in both physical and spiritual senses)
ganists *sf* salvation; well-being, health
ganiþjis *sm* kinsman
ganiutan *sv 2* to catch
ganoh- *adj* enough, numerous (§4.2c)
ganohjan *wv 1* bestow lavishly, satisfy
ganohnan *wv 4* be satisfied, richly supplied (with: *D*)
gansjan *wv 1* cause, produce
gapaidon *wv 2* clothe (with: *D*)
gaqiman *sv 4* assemble, come together
gaqiss- *adj* consenting
gaqiss (*G* **-issais**) *sf* consent
gaqiþan sis *sv 5* w. 3pl. subj.: agree among themselves
gaqiujan *wv 1* give life to, make live
gaqiunan *wv 4* be brought to life
gaqumþs *sf* assembly, synagogue
garaginon *wv 2* advise, give counsel
garahnjan *wv 1* assess
garaid- *adj* fixed, appointed, due
garaideins *sf vn* readying, preparing; rule, regulation
garaidjan *wv 1* prepare, establish
garaiht- *adj* righteous, just; *comp* **garaihtoz-**

garaihtaba *adv* justly
garaihtei *wf* righteousness
garaihteins *sf vn* righteousness
garaihtiþa *sf* justice
garaihtjan *wv 1* deem just; direct, guide aright
garaþjan *sv 6* (P **garoþ**) to count
garazna *wm* neighbor
garazno *wf* female neighbor
garda *wm* fold, pen, yard
gardawaldands *m* master of the house
gards *sm(i)* house, household, court; in cpds: enclosed area
garedaba *adv* decently, properly
garedan *sv* 7 (P **garairoþ**) reflect on, consider
garehsns *sf* plan; appointed time
garinnan *sv 3* come together quickly
gariud- *adj* honorable, dignified
gariudei *wf* modesty
gariudi *sn* dignity, probity
garuni *sn* consultation, counsel
garunjo *wf* flood, high water
garuns *sf* market-place, street
gasahts *sf* reproof
gasaihwan *sv 5* see, perceive
gasakan *sv 6* rebuke, reprove (*D*)
gasalbon *wv 2* anoint
gasaljan *wv 1* offer, sacrifice
gasandjan *wv 1* see off
gasateins *sf vn* foundation
gasatjan *wv 1* set, place, lay; add; appoint; **namo gasatjan** to name; **aftra gasatjan** to restore
gasibjan *wv 1* become reconciled
gasigljan *wv 1* to seal, confirm
gasigqan *sv 3* sink
gasinþja, gasinþa *wm* companion
gasitan *sv 5* sit, sit down
gaskadweins *sf vn* clothing, covering
gaskafts *sf* creation; creature
gaskaidan sik *sv* 7 draw away from, separate oneself from (**af**)
gaskaideins *sf vn* difference
gaskaidnan *wv 4* be severed, parted
gaskalki *sn* fellow-servant
gaskaman sik *wv 3* be ashamed
gaskapjan *sv 6* (P **gaskop**) create, make
gaskaþjan *wv 1* injure
gaskeirjan *wv 1* translate, interpret
gaskoh- *adj* shod
gaskohi *sn* pair of shoes
gaslawan *wv 3* become silent
gasleiþjan *wv 1* injure; +**sik** to suffer loss of
gaslepan *sv* 7 (P **gasaislep**) fall asleep, (fig.) die
gasmeitan *sv 1* smear
gasmiþon *wv 2* produce, bring about
gasniumjan *wv 1* hurry, hasten, come
gasniwan *sv 5* achieve, attain (**du**)
gasokjan *wv 1* seek, search for
gasoþjan *wv 1* satisfy, fill
gaspillon *wv 2* announce
gastagqjan *wv 1* dash against, cause to stumble
gastaldan *sv* 7 (P **gastaistald**) possess
gastandan *sv 6* stand fast, stand still, remain; (± **aftra**) be restored
gastaurknan *wv 4* become rigid
gasteigan *sv 1* climb, ascend, descend (into: **in** *D*)
gastigod- *adj* hospitable
gastigodei *wf* hospitality
gastojan *wv 1* to judge, sentence
gastoþan* conjectured form (infinitive) for **gastoþanan** in Rom 14:4: to keep standing, make stand
gastraujan *wv 1* strew; furnish
gasts *sm(i)* guest
gasulid- *part adj* (firmly) founded
gasuljan* *wv 1* to found, lay a foundation for (conjectured for the preceding entry)
gasunjon *wv 2* justify, declare just
gasupon *wv 2* to season
gasweran *wv 3* glorify, make known
gaswikunþjan *wv 1* make known, proclaim
gaswiltan *sv 3* die
gaswinþjan *wv 1* strengthen
gaswogjan *wv 1* sigh
gataiknjan *wv 1* warn, give a sign
gatairan *sv 4* tear to pieces, destroy; relax, fail to maintain
gatalzjan *wv 1* teach, instruct
gatamjan *wv 1* to tame
gatandjan *wv 1* sear, brand
gatarhjan *wv 1* characterize, mark; **gatarhid-** notorious
gatarnjan *wv 1* deprive of
gataujan *wv 1* do, make, perform
gataura *wm* tear, rent
gataurnan *wv 4* be torn; cease, perish, come to an end
gataurnand- *part adj* perishable
gataurþs *sf* destruction
gateihan *sv 1* tell, relate, make known
gatemiba *adv* suitably, fitly
gatewjan *wv 1* appoint, designate
gatil- *adj* fit, convenient
gatilaba *adv* conveniently
gatilon *wv 2* attain, obtain
gatiman *sv 4* to suit

gatimreins *sf vn* construction, edification
gatimrjan *wv 1* build
gatimrjo *wf* building
gatiuhan *sv 2* lead, draw, bring, take
gatrauan *wv 3* trust, entrust; be persuaded
gatrudan *sv 4 irreg* trample, tread under foot
gatulgjan *wv 1* strengthen; fix, set; + **sik** persist;
gatulgid- *part adj* firm, lasting
gatwo *wf* street
gaþagki *sn* attention, concern; **us gaþagkja** sparingly
gaþahan *wv 3* fall silent
gaþairsan *sv 3* wither, dry up
gaþarban *wv 3* abstain from; exercise self-control
gaþaurb- *adj* restrained, self-controlled
gaþaursnan *wv 4* dry up, wither
gaþeihan *sv 1* grow, advance, progress
gaþiuþjan *wv 1* bless
gaþiwan *wv 3* to subject, reduce to servitude
gaþlahsnan *wv 4* be startled, frightened
gaþlaihan *sv 7* comfort, console; take into one's arms, caress; admonish, exhort (all with *D* object)
gaþlaihts *sf* consolation, comfort
gaþliuhan *sv 2* flee
gaþrafsteins *sf vn* comfort
gaþrafstjan *wv 1* comfort, console
gaþrask *sn* threshing-floor
gaþreihan *sv 1* afflict
gaþulan *wv 3* suffer, bear, endure
gaþwastjan *wv 1* strengthen, fortify
gauja *wm* countryman; pl. surrounding region
gaumjan *wv 1* see, perceive, heed (*D*)
gaunon *wv 2* lament, mourn
gaunoþa *As* mourning, lamentation
gaur- *adj* sad, sorrowful
gaurei *wf* sorrow, trouble
gauriþa *sf* sorrow
gaurjan *wv 1* to trouble, distress, grieve
gawadjon *wv 2* pledge, betroth
gawagjan *wv 1* shake, stir
gawairpan *sv 3* throw, throw down
gawairþeig- *adj* peaceful, at peace
gawairþi *sn* peace
gawaknan *wv 4* wake up, awaken (intr.)
gawaldan *sv 7* rule, hold sway over
gawaleins *sf vn* choice, election
gawaljan *wv 1* choose, select
gawamm- *adj* impure, unclean
gawandjan *wv 1* turn (tr. or intr.), turn (sthg: *A*) around, bring (sthg: *A*) back; + **sik** to turn around, return; be converted
gawargeins *sf vn* condemnation
gawargjan *wv 1* condemn
gawaseins *sf vn* clothing
gawasjan *wv 1* to clothe; + **sik** to clothe oneself, dress
gawaurdi *sn* conversation, intercourse
gawaurki *sn* business; profit, gain
gawaurkjan *wv 1* make, prepare, appoint
gawaurstwa *wm* fellow-worker
gaweihan *wv 3* sanctify, consecrate
gaweison *wv 2* visit, take care of (*G*)
gawenjan *wv 1* suppose, believe, think
gawi *sn* region, district, neighborhood
gawidan *sv 5* bind, join together
gawigan *sv 5* shake down
gawilj- *adj* willing
gawinnan *sv 3* suffer
gawiss *sf* (*Apl* **gawissins**) ligament, connection
gawizneig- *adj* sharing joy (in: *D*)
gawrikan *sv 5* avenge, vindicate
gawrisqan *sv 3* bear fruit
gawundon *wv 2* to wound
gazaufylakio *Ds* = Gk γαζοφυλακίῳ treasury
gazds *sm* sting
-geigan: gageigan
-geisnan: usgeisnan
giba *sf* gift, offering
giban *sv 5* give; **giban matjan** to feed (*D*); **giban wulþu** to glorify (*D*) (cf. **af-**, **at-**, **fra-**, **us-**)
gibands *m* giver
gibla *wm* pinnacle, gable
gild *sn* tax
-gildan: fragildan, usgildan
gilstr *sn* tribute, tax
gilstrameleins *sf vn* tax registration
gilþa *sf* sickle
-ginnan: duginnan
gistradagis *adv* tomorrow
-gitan: bigitan
giutan *sv 2* pour (cf. **ufar-**)
glaggwo *adv* accurately
glaggwuba, glaggwaba *adv* accurately, diligently
glitmunjan *wv 1* shine, glitter
god- *adj* good
godakund- *adj* of noble birth
godei *wf* goodness, virtue
goleins *sf vn* greeting
goljan *wv 1* to greet, salute (smn: *A*)
graba *sf* ditch, embankment
graban *sv 6* dig, till (cf. **bi-**, **uf-**, **us-**)
gramjan *wv 1* enrage (cf. **in-**)
gramsta *Ds* splinter
gras *sn* grass, blade of grass; vegetables

gredag- *adj* hungry, greedy
gredon *wv 2* be hungry, be greedy; used impersonally with the accusative, e.g. **gredoþ mik** I am hungry
gredus *sm* hunger
greipan *sv 1* seize, take hold of, capture (cf. **fair-**, **und-**)
gretan, greitan *sv* 7 (*P* **gaigrot**) weep, lament (over: **bi** *A*)
grets *sm* weeping
grindafraþj- *adj* despondent
griþs* *sf* (*A* **grid**) step, pace; status
groba *sf* den, lair, cave
grunduwaddjus *sm* and *sf* foundation
gudafaurht- *adj* god-fearing, devout
gudalaus- *adj* godless
gudaskaunei *wf* form of God
gudblostreis or **guþblostreis** *sm* worshiper of God
gudhus *sn* temple
gudisk- *adj* divine
gudja *wm* priest; **(sa) auhumista/maista/reikista gudja** the high-priest
gudjinassus *sm* office of a priest
gudjinon *wv 2* be a priest
gulþ *sn* gold
gulþein- *adj* of gold, golden
guma *wm* man
gumakund- *adj* male
gumein- *adj* male, manlike
gund *sn* cancer, canker
-gutnan: usgutnan
Gutþiuda *sf* the Goths
guþ *sn* (*pl* **guda**) god; **Guþ** (*G* **Gudis**) God (takes masc. modifiers); see §2.7 for details on the writing of this word
guþblostreis: see **gudblostreis**

H

haban *wv 3* have, hold, possess; hold, consider, reckon (to be); keep, observe; to be, be about to, destined to; **ubil, ubilaba haban** to be ill; **wairs haban** to be worse; **gafahana haban** hold captive; **haban gadaban** to be in store for (*A*); **aftumist haban** be at point of death; **habaiþ wisan at** be held ready for (cf. **af-**, **ana-**, **at-**, **dis-**, **ga-**, **uf-**)
hafjan *sv 6* raise, lift, carry (cf. **and-**, **at-**, **ufar-**, **us-**)
-hafnan: ufarhafnan
haft- *adj* burdened (with: *D*), having
haftjan *wv 1* join, cling to (cf. **ga-**, **gaga-**)
-haftnan: gahaftnan
hahan *sv* 7 (P **haihah**) to hang (cf. **at-**, **us-**)
hahan *wv 3* hang, be suspended
haidus *sm* way, manner
haifstjan *wv 1* strive, fight
haifsts *sf* fight, strife
haih- *adj* one-eyed, half blind
hail- *adj* whole, sound; safe
hailag- *adj* holy
hailjan *wv 1* heal, cure (smn or sthg: *A*) (cf. **ga-**)
-hailnan: gahailnan
hails *interj* hail!
haimoþli *sn* home territory, homestead
haims *sf(i)* in *sing.*, *sf* in *pl.* village, town; country estate
hairaiseis *Npl* = Gk αἱρέσεις sects, factions
hairda *sf* herd, flock
hairdeis *sm* shepherd, herdsman
hairto *wn* heart
hairus *sm* sword
hairþram *Dpl* innards (as seat of affections)
haitan *sv* 7 (*P* **haihait**) call, name; order, command; invite (cf. **ana-**, **and-**, **at-**, **fair-**, **ga-**, **fauraga-**, **us-**)
haiti *sf* order, command
haiþi *sf* field, heath
haiþiwisk- *adj* wild
haiþno *wf* heathen (i.e. non-Jewish) woman
haizam *Dpl* torches
hakuls *sm* cloak
halb- *adj* half (§4.2c)
halba *sf* half; **in þizai halbai** in this regard
haldan *sv* 7 (P **haihald**) hold; take care of, tend
haldis *adv* more, rather; **niþe haldis** by no means
halisaiw *adv* hardly
halja *sf* Hell
halk- *adj* empty, needy
hallus *sm* stone, slab
hals *sm* neck
halt- *adj* lame
hamf- *adj* one-handed, maimed
-hamon: afhamon, anahamon, andhamon, gahamon, ufarhamon
hana *wm* rooster, cock
handug- *adj* wise, clever; *comp* **handugoz-**
handugei *wf* wisdom, cleverness
handus *sf* hand
handuwaurht- *adj* hand-made
hansa *sf* company, group, crowd
hardiz- *comp adj* harder etc.
-hardjan: gahardjan

hardu- *adj* hard, strict, severe; difficult to understand; *comp* **hardiz-**
harduba *adv* severely, grievously
harduhairtei *wf* hardheartedness
harjis *sm* army, host
hatan *wv 3* to hate
hatis *sn* (*D* **hatiza**) hatred, anger
hatizon *wv 2* to be angry
hatjan *wv 1* to hate
haubiþ *sn* (G **haubidis**) head
hauh- *adj* high; *superl* **hauhist-**
hauhaba *adv* highly
hauhei *wf* height(s)
hauheins *sf vn* praise
hauhhairt- *adj* arrogant, proud
hauhhairtei *wf* pride, arrogance
hauhis *adv* higher
hauhisti* *sn* the highest point, the heights, Highest Heaven
hauhiþa *sf* height; elevation, glory
hauhjan *wv 1* glorify, praise, exalt; raise, elevate (cf. **ufarhauhid-**, **ushauhjan**); see Voc. 23.
-hauhnan: ushauhnan
hauhþuht- *adj* having high thoughts, proud, haughty
haun- *adj* humble, modest
hauneins *sf vn* humility
hauniþa *sf* humbleness, humble bearing
haunjan *wv 1* to humble (cf. **ga-**)
haurds *sf* door
hauri *sn* coal, carbon; pl. brazier
haurn *sn* horn; skin, husk
haurnja *wm* horn-blower
haurnjan *wv 1* to blow a horn
hauseins *sf vn* sense of hearing; report, word, preaching
hausjan *wv 1* to hear, listen to (smn: *D*; sthg: *A*); to hear about (smn: **bi** *A*, **fram** *D*); to heed (sthg: *G*) (cf. **and-**, **ga-**, **uf-**)
hausjon *wv 2* to hear
hawi *sn* hay, grass
hazeins *sf vn* praise
hazjan *wv 1* to praise (smn: *A*; for: **in** *G*)
heito *wf* fever
heiwafrauja *wm* master of a household
her *adv* here, hither
heþjo *wf* chamber, room
hidre *adv* hither
hilms *sm* helmet
hilpan *sv 3* to help, assist (smn: *G*) (cf. **ga-**)
himinakund- *adj* heavenly, from heaven
himins *sm* Heaven, sky, the heavens
himma, hina: see **his***
hindana *prep G* behind, beyond, on yonder side of
hindar *prep A, D* behind, beyond, over, among
hindarleiþan *sv 1* go behind; perish
hindarweis- *adj* deceitful
hindarweisei *wf* deceitfulness
hindumist- *adj* hindmost, outermost
-hinþan: frahinþan, miþfrahinþan, ushinþan
hiri *interj* Come here! dual **hirjats**, pl. **hirjiþ**
his* *dem pron/adj* preserved in certain phrases: **himma daga** on this day, today; **und hina dag** to this day; **und hita, und hita nu** until now; **fram himma** henceforth
hita: see ***his**
hiufan *sv 2* mourn, weep, lament
hiuhma *wm* crowd, multitude
hiwi *sn* appearance, form
hlahjan *sv 6* to laugh (cf. **bi-**)
hlaifs *sm* (*G* **hlaibis**) loaf, bread
hlaine *Gpl* hills
hlaiw *sn* grave, tomb
hlaiwasnos *sf pl* tombs, graves
hlamma *sf* trap, snare
hlas- *adj* cheerful, glad; *comp* **hlasoz-**
hlasei *wf* gladness
-hlaþjan: see **afhlaþjan**
-hlaupan: ushlaupan
hlauts *sm* lot; **hlauts imma urrann** it fell to his lot
hleibjan *wv 1* take care of (*D*)
hleidum- *adj* left (not right)
hleidumei *wf* left hand, left side; **af/in hleidumein** on the left (of: *G*)
hleiþra *sf* tent, booth
Hleþrastakeins *sf* Feast of the Tabernacles (John 7:2)
hlifan *sv 5* steal
hliftus *sm* thief
hlijans *Apl* booths, tents
hliuma *wm* hearing, ability to hear
-hlohjan: ufhlohjan
hlutr- *adj* pure
hlutrei *wf* purity
hlutriþa *sf* purity
hnaiw- *adj* humble, lowly
hnaiweins *sf vn* humility, abasement
hnaiwjan *wv 1* abase, lower (cf. **ana-**, **ga-**, **uf-**)
hnasqjaim *Dpl adj* soft, tender
hneiwan *sv 1* bend down, bow (cf. **ana-**)
-hniupan: dishniupan
-hnupnan: dishnupnan
hnuþo *wf* thorn, splinter
hoha *wm* plow
holon *wv 2* injure, treat with violence, deceive (cf. **af-**)

horinassus *sm* whoredom, adultery
horinon *wv 2* commit adultery, be promiscuous (cf. **ga-**)
horinondei *pres part* as *wf noun* adulteress
hors *sm* adulterer
hrainei *wf* purity
hraineins *sf vn* purification
hraini- *adj* clean, pure
hrainjahairt- *adj* pure of heart
hrainjan *wv 1* cleanse (cf. **af-**, **ga-**, **us-**)
hraiwadubo *wf* turtledove
hramjan *wv 1* crucify (cf. **us-**)
-hrisjan: afhrisjan, ushrisjan
hropjan *wv 1* cry out, call out (cf. **uf-**)
hrops *sm* a cry
hrot *sn* roof
hroþeig- *adj* victorious
hrugga *sf* staff
hruk *As* crowing
hrukjan *wv 1* to crow
-hruskan: andhruskan
huggrjan *wv 1* be hungry, used impersonally with *A:* **huggreiþ mik** I am hungry
hugjan *wv 1* think, suppose, believe (that...: inf. or **ei** + subj.) (cf. **af-**, **and-**, **fauraga-**, **ufar-**)
hugs *sm* mind, understanding
huhjan *wv 1* store up
huhrus *sm* hunger
hulistr *sn* covering, veil
huljan *wv 1* hide, conceal, disguise (cf. **and-**, **dis-**, **ga-**)
-hulon: ushulon
hulþ-*adj* gracious
hulundi *sf* cave
-hun *suffixed particle* (§22.2)
hund* *sn* (*pl* **hunda**) hundred
hundafaþs *sm(i)* (*G* **-fadis**) centurion
hunds *sm* dog
hunsl *sn* sacrifice, offering
hunslastaþs *sm(i)* (*G* **-stadis**) altar
hunsljan *wv 1* to sacrifice
hunþs* *sm* booty
hups *sm(i)* hip, loins
huzd *sn* treasure
huzdjan *wv 1* store up, hoard treasures

HW

hwa *interrog pron* what (§6.3); *adv* why; **hwa þatei** why
hwadre *interrog adv* whither
hwairban *sv 3* to walk (cf. **bi-**)
hwairnei *wf* skull
hwaiteis *sm* wheat, grain
hwaiwa *conj, interrog adv* how, in what way
hwan *interrog adv* when, whenever; (before *adj* or *adv*) how; (before comparatives) how much; **hwan lagg mel** for how long a time; **nibai hwan** lest at any time; **hwan filu** how much
hwanhun *adv* in **ni hwanhun** at no time, never
-hwapjan: afhwapjan
-hwapnan: afhwapnan
hwar *interrog adv* where
hwarbon *wv 2* walk about, wander
hwarjis *interrog pron* who, which (of many), which one (§21.3)
hwarjizuh *indef pron.* each, every, each one, everyone
hwas, hwa, hwo *interrog pron* who, what (§6.3); *indef pron* anyone, anything (§17.3)
hwashun *indef pron* with neg. **ni hwashun** no one (§22.2)
hwassaba *adv* sharply
hwassei *wf* sharpness, severity
hwaþ *interrog adv* whither
hwaþar *interrog pron* which of two; *conj.* whether (§21.3)
hwaþaruh *indef pron* each of two
hwaþjan *wv 1* to foam
hwaþo *wf* foam
hwaþro *interrog adv* whence, from where
hwazuh *indef pron* each, every, each one, everyone (§21.3)
hwazuh saei *indef pron* whosoever (§22.2)
hwe *interrog adv* with what, wherewith, how; **hwe galeiks** like what? **hwe galeikon** to liken to what?
hweh *adv* at any rate
hweila *sf* time, hour, season, while
hweilahwairb-*adj* of short duration, transitory
hweilan *wv 3* cease (doing: participle) (cf. **ana, ga-)**
hweilohun *adv* in **ni hweilohun** not even for a moment
hweit- *adj* white
-hweitjan: gahweitjan
hwelauþ- *interrog adj* how great
hwileik- *interrog adj* what sort of
hwilftrom *Dpl* coffin
hwo *interrog pron* feminine of **hwas** (§6.3)
hwoftuli *sf* glory, source of pride
hwopan *sv 7* (*P* **hwaihwop**) boast, be proud of
hwota *sf* threat, abuse
hwotjan *wv 1* to rebuke, charge (not to) (cf. **ga-**)

I

ibai *interrog particle* expecting yes-or-no answer(§20.6); **iba, ibai** *conj* lest, that ... not
ibdaljin *Ds* descent, slope
ibn- *adj* even, level; equal, like
ibnaleik- *adj* equal
ibnaskaunj- *adj* equally beautiful
ibnassus *sm* evenness
-ibnjan: gaibnjan *wv 1* make like, make equal
ibuk- *adj* turned back
iddja *P* of **gaggan** (§7.4b)
idreiga *sf* repentance; **inu idreiga** irrevocable
idreigon *wv 2* (± **sik**) to repent (of: **ana** *D*) (cf. **ga-**)
idweit *sn* reproach, shame
idweitjan *wv 1* to reproach, blame, revile (*D*)
Iesus: spelling and inflection §11.5
iftum- *adj* the next, the following
igqara *pron G* of you two (dual); **iggqar-** *poss adj* idem
igqis *pron DA* you two (dual)
ija her (*As*); they, them (neuter pl.) (§7.3)
ik *pron* I (§10.5); **ikei** I who (§12.3c)
im *copula* (§6.4) I am
in *prep D* in, on, among; at, during; ; *A* into, toward; *G* on account of, about, concerning (§1.6)
inahei *wf* soberness, self-control
inagjan *wv 1* rebuke, threaten
inah- *adj* wise; smug, conceited (Rom. 12:16)
inaljanon *wv 2* to make angry
inbrannjan *wv 1* put into the fire, burn
indrobnan *wv 4* become sad, troubled
infeinan *wv 4* have pity on, be moved to pity for (smn: **du** *D*)
ingardj- *adj* of the same household
ingramjan *wv 1* provoke
inilo *wf* excuse, pretext
inkilþo *adj f* pregnant
inkunja *wm* fellow-countryman
inliuhtjan *wv 1* enlighten
inmaideins *sf vn* change, exchange
inmaidjan *wv 1* change, exchange, transfigure
inn *adv* in, within
inna *adv* within
innakund- *adj* of the same household
innana *adv* within; *prep G* within, inside
innatbairan *sv 4* carry in
innatgaggan *sv 7 irreg* (P **-iddja**) enter (into: **in** *A*)
innatgahts *sf* approach, entry
innattiuhan *sv 2* lead in, bring in
innaþro *adv* from within
inngaggan *sv 7 irreg* (P **-iddja**) enter, proceed
inngaleiþan *sv 1* go in, enter
inniman *sv 4* take in, receive
Inniujiþa *sf* renewal; Feast of the Dedication (John 10:22)
innum- *adj* innermost
inrauhtjan *wv 1* become agitated, deeply moved
inreiran *wv 3* shake, quake
insahts *sf* narrative, statement
insaian *sv 7* sow in, implant
insaihwan *sv 5* look at; look around at (*D*); give heed to, pay attention to (*D*)
insailjan *wv 1* tie ropes to
insakan *sv 6* set before, present (sthg: *A*; to: *D*)
insandjan *wv 1* send, send forth
instandan *sv 6* persist, be at hand
inswinþjan *wv 1* strengthen; + **sik** to be strong
intandjan *wv 1* burn up
intrusgjan *wv 1* graft; *pp* **intrusgan-** or **intrusgid-**
intundnan *wv 4* burn (intrans., fig.)
inu, inuh *prep A* without, except
inuh (1) = **inu**; (2) = **in** *prep* + **-uh**
inwagjan *wv 1* stir up
inweitan *sv 1* worship; greet respectfully, salute (*A*)
inwidan *sv 5* reject, repudiate, refuse
inwind- *adj* unjust, perverse
inwindiþa *sf* injustice, crime
inwisan *sv 5* be present, near at hand
is *pron NG* he, his, its (§7.3)
is *copula 2nd pers sg* thou art, you are (§6.4)
ist *copula 3rd pers sg* he (she, it) is, there is (§6.4)
ita *pron NA* it (§7.3)
itan *sv 5* (*P* **-et**) eat (cf. **fra-**)
iþ *conj* but, however, if (§13.1)
iudaiwisko *adv* living in accord with Jewish law and custom (cf. **judaiwisk-** *adj*)
iudaiwiskon *wv 2* to live in accord with Jewish law
iumjo *wf* multitude
iup *adv* upwards, up; **iupa** above; upward
iupana *adv* from above
iupaþro *adv* from above
iusila *sf* easement
iusiz- *comp adj* better
ize *pers pron Gpl* of them (m., n. §7.3); also = **izei**
izei, ize *rel pron* who, which (§19.5)
izwar- *poss adj* your (pl.) (§4.2c)
izwara *pron 2nd pers pl G* of you (§10.5)
izwis *pron 2nd pers pl DA* (to) you (§10.5)
izwizei *rel pron 2nd pers pl DA* (to) you who (§12.3)

J

ja. jai *adv* yes, truly, indeed

jabai *conj* if, even if, although; equivalent to a strong negation in Mk 8:12 in imitation of a Hebrew oath formula; **jabai** ... **aiþþau**... either ... or; **jabai nu** if then (§19.2)

jah *conj* and, also; *particle* even; **jah** ... **jah**... both ... and ...; **ni þatainei** ... **ak jah** not only ... but also ... (§13.1)

jai *adv* yes, truly, indeed

jain- *adj* that, yon

jainar *adv* there, in that place

jaind, jaindre *adv* thither, to that place

jaindwairþ- *adj* lying in that direction

jainþro *adv* thence, from there

jaþþe *conj* and if; **jaþþe** ... **jaþþe**...whether ... or ...

jau *conj* whether; if so, so then

jer *sn* year

jiuka *sf* anger

jiukan *wv 3* contend (cf. **ga-**)

jota *wm* iota (letter of Gk alphabet: ἰῶτα)

ju *adv* already, still, yet; w. neg.: not yet, no longer

judaiwisk- *adj* Jewish

juggalauþs (*G* **-dis**) *sm(i)* young man

jugg- *adj* young, fresh, new

juhiz- *comp adj* younger

juk *sn* yoke

jukuzi* *sf* yoke

junda *sf* youth

jus *pron 2nd pers pl N* you (§10.5)

juþan *adv* already; **juþan ni** no longer

juzei *rel pron 2nd pers pl* you who (§12.3c)

K

kaisar, Kaisar *sm* emperor, the Caesar

kaisaragild *sn* tribute money

kalbo *wf* calf, heifer

kald- *adj* cold

kalkinassus *sm* adultery, fornication

kalkjo *wf(?)* harlot

kann *PP* I know (**kunnan**) (§16.3)

kannjan *wv* I to make known (cf. **ga-**, **us-**)

kapillon *wv 2* cut off the hair (< Lat *capillus*)

kara *sf* care, anxiety, concern; **ni kar(a) ist** *A G: A* does not care about *G*

karkara *sf* prison, jail < Lat *carcer*

karon *wv 2* care for, be concerned about (cf. **ga-**)

kas *sn* vessel, pot; property

kasja *wm* potter

katils *sm* kettle, water-jar (< Lat *catillus*)

kaupatjan *wv 1 irreg* (P **kaupasta** §6.2) strike with palm of hand

kaupon *wv 2* to traffic, trade

kaurban special type of gift <Gk κορβᾶν < Aram *qorbān* an offering

kaurei *wf* burden, weight

kauriþa *sf* weight, burden

kaurjan *wv 1* to burden, weigh down; importune, bother (cf. **ana-, miþ-**)

kaurn *sn* grain, wheat

kaurno *wn* grain, a grain

kauru- *adj* heavy

kausjan *wv 1* taste, test, try (cf. **ga-**)

keinan *sv 1* (irreg. P **-keinoda**) bud, sprout (cf. **us-**, **miþus-**)

kelikn *sn* (watch-)tower, upper room

kilþei *wf* womb

kindins *sm* ruler, governor

kinnus *sf* cheek

kintus *sm* cent < Lat **centus* = *centenionalis*

kiusan *sv 2* choose, test (cf. **ga-**, **us-**)

klismjan *wv 1* to make a lot of noise

klismo *wf* cymbal

kniu *sn* knee

knoþs* *sf* (*D* **-dai**) race, people

knussjan *wv 1* kneel (± **kniwam**)

Kreks *sm* a Greek

kriustan *sv 2* gnash one's teeth

-kroton: gakroton

krusts *sf* gnashing of teeth

kubitus *sm* company at a meal (< Lat *cubitus*)

kukjan *wv 1* to kiss, embrace *D* (cf. **bi-**)

kumei *imper* Arise! <Gk κουμει < Aram *qûmî*

kunawida* *sf* chain, fetter

-kund- *part adj* born

kuni *sn* race, tribe, generation

kunnan *PP* (§16.3) to know (smn, sthg: *A*; that ... **þatei** + indic.) (cf. **fra-**, **ga-**)

-kunnan (*wv 3*): **anakunnan, atkunnan, gakunnan, ufkunnan**

kunþ- *part adj* known

kunþa *P* of **kunnan** I knew (§16.3)

kunþi *sn* knowledge, recognition

kunþs *sm* an acquaintance

kustus *sm* test, trial, proof

L

lagg- *adj* long
laggamodei *wf* long-suffering, patience
laggei *wf* length
lagjan *wv 1* lay, lay down, set, place; **kniwa lagjan** bend one's knees (cf. **af-**, **ana-**, **at-**, **faur-**, **ga- ufar-**, **us-**)
laian* see **lauan***
laiba *sf* remnant
-laibjan: bilaibjan
laigaion legion < Gk λεγεών <Lat *legio*
-laigon: bilaigon
laikan *sv* 7 (P **lailaik**) leap for joy, play (cf. **bi-**)
laiks *sm(i)* leaping, dancing
lais *PP* I know
laisareis *sm* teacher, master
laiseig- *adj* good at teaching
laiseins *sf vn* doctrine, teaching
laisjan *wv 1* teach (smn: *A*; sthg:*A*; smn to do sthg: *A* + inf.); + **sik** learn (cf. **ga-**, **us-**)
laistjan *wv 1* follow (smn: *A*, **afar** *D*); follow after, pursue (sthg: *A*) (cf. **afar-**, **ga-**)
laists *sm(i)* track, step
lamb *sn* lamb, sheep
land *sn* land, country
landis *adv* over the land, far away
lasiw- *adj* lazy, weak; *superl* **lasiwost-**
lat- *adj* lazy, lax
latei *wf* laziness
latjan *wv 1* delay, detain (cf. **ana-**, **ga-**)
laþaleiko *adv* willingly
laþon *wv 2* invite, call (cf. **at-**, **ga-**)
laþons *sf vn* invitation; redemption; consolation
lauan* *sv* 7 (P **lailo**) revile
-laubjan: galaubjan, uslaubjan
laudi *sf* form, likeness
laufs (*G* **-bis**) *sm* leaf, foliage
laugnjan *wv 1* deny, lie (cf. **ga-**)
lauhatjan *wv 1* to lightning
lauhmuni*, **lauhmoni*** *sf* lightning, flash
laun *sn* reward, pay
launawargs *sm* an ungrateful person
laus- *adj* empty
lausawaurd- *adj* speaking empty words, speaking vainly
lausawaurdei *wf* empty words, vain discourses
lausawaurdi *sn* idem
laushandj- *adj* empty-handed
lausjan *wv 1* set free, deliver, loosen; reclaim; collect (taxes) (cf. **ga-**, **us-**)
lausqiþr- *adj* fasting
lausqiþrei *wf* fasting
-leiban: bileiban
leiht- *adj* light, slight
leihwan *sv 1* lend; + **sis** borrow
leik *sn* body, flesh, corpse; **bi leika** by race, according to the flesh
leikains *sf vn* liking, pleasure
leikan *wv 3* to please (cf. **ga-**, **fauraga-**)
leikein- *adj* corporeal, of the flesh
leikinon *wv 2* to heal (cf. **ga-**)
-leikon: galeikon, gagaleikon, ingaleikon, miþgaleikon, þairhgaleikon
lein *sn* linen
leitil- *adj* little, small, unimportant; *adv* a little, a while
-leiþan: afleiþan, bileiþan, galeiþan, ingaleiþan, miþinngaleiþan, hindarleiþan, þairhleiþan, ufarleiþan, usleiþan
leiþu *sn* strong drink
lekeis *sm* physician
lekinassus *sm* healing
lekinon see **leikinon**
letan *sv* 7 (P **lailot**) let, allow; let remain, leave behind; utter (cf. **af-**, **fra-**, **us-**)
-letnan: andletnan
lew *sn(?)* occasion, opportunity
lewjan *wv 1* betray, hand over; to turn (the other cheek) (cf. **fra-**, **ga-**)
libains *sf vn* life
liban *wv 3* be alive; to live (on: **bi** *A*) (cf. **miþ-**)
-lifnan: aflifnan
ligan *sv 5* lie down, lie (cf. **at-**, **uf-**)
ligrs *sm* bed, couch
-linnan: aflinnan
lisan *sv 5* to gather, collect (cf. **ga-**)
listeig- *adj* cunning
lists *sf* cunning, craftiness
litai *Ds* hypocrisy
liteins *sf vn* prayer, petition
-litjan: miþlitjan
liþus *sm* limb of body
liub- *adj* dear, beloved
liubaleik- *adj* amiable, pleasing
liudan *sv 2* spring up, grow up
liuga *sf* marriage
liugan *wv 3* to marry (subject man, object woman; *passive* to marry (subject woman) (cf. **ga-**)
liugan *sv 2* to tell a lie, lie
liugn *sn(?)* a lie

liugnapraufetus* *sm* false prophet
liugnawaurd- *adj* lying, deceitful
liugnja *wm* liar
liuhadei *wf* light
liuhadein- *adj* bright, shining
liuhadeins *sf vn* light
liuhaþ *sn* (G **liuhadis**) light, fire
liuhtjan *wv 1* give light, illumine (cf. **ga-**, **in-**)
-**liusan: fraliusan**
liuta *wm* hypocrite
liutei *wf* hypocrisy
liut- *adj* hypocritical
liuþareis *sm* singer
liuþon *wv 2* sing
lofa *wm* palm of hand
lubains *sf vn* hope
lubjaleis- *adj* skilled in magic and potions
lubjaleisei *wf* skill in magic and potions
ludja *sf* face
luftus *sf(?)* air
-**lukan: galukan, uslukan**
lukarn *sn* light, candle < Lat *lucerna*
lukarnastaþa *wm* candlestick; lampstand
-**luknan: galuknan, usluknan**
lun *sn* ransom
-**lusnan: fralusnan**
luston *wv 2* to desire, covet
lustus *sm* desire, lust
lustusam- *adj* longed-for, desired
luton *wv 2* deceive, mislead (cf. **us-**)

M

magan* *PP* (§§5.6, 15.2) to be able, can (cf. **ga-**)
magaþei *wf* maidenhood, virginity
magaþs *sf* maiden
magula *wm* little boy
magus *sm* boy, servant
maht- *adj* possible; able, capable (Voc. 17)
mahta *P of* **magan** I might (§7.4a)
mahteig- *adj* mighty; possible; able, strong enough (to do: inf.)
-**mahtjan: anamahtjan**
mahts *sf* might, power, strength; virtue; miracle, marvel
maidjan *wv* I falsify (cf. **in-**)
maihstus *sm* dunghill
maile *Gpl* wrinkles
maimbrana *wm* parchment < Lat *membrana*
-**mainjan: gamainjan, gagamainjan**
mais *adv* more, rather; **mais þau** more than, rather than; **filu mais** much more; **und filu mais** so much the more; **hwan filu ... mais þamma** the more ... so much the more
maist *adv* at most
maist- *superl adj* greatest, chief; *pl* used as noun: dignitaries, important people
maitan *sv* 7 (P **maimait**) cut, hew, hack (cf. **af-**, **bi-**, **ga-**, **us-**)
maiþms *sm* gift
maiz- *comp adj* more, greater, elder
malan *sv 6* grind
malma *wm* sand
malo *wf(?)* moth
-**malwjan: gamalwjan**
mammo *wf* flesh
mammona *wm* mammon, wealth < Gk μαμωνᾶς < Aram *māmôn*
-**mampjan: bimampjan**
man *PP* I think (**munan**) (§16.3)
manag- *adj* much, many, great; *comp* **managiz-**; *superl* **managist-** (cf. **maiz-**, **maist-**)
managduþs *sf* abundance
managei *wf* crowd, throng; the people, the masses; a people, a nation; **managei filu** a lot (of sthg); **manageins filu** many people, dense crowds
managfalþ- *adj* manifold
managiz- *comp adj* more, greater
managjan *wv 1* increase (trans.)
managnan *wv 4* become numerous, increase (cf. **us-**)
manamaurþrja *wm* murderer
manaseþs *sf* (G **-sedais**) mankind; the world (usually with **so**); multitude
manaulja *Ds* form, appearance
manleika *wm* image, picture
manna = Gk μάννα = Heb *mān* manna
manna *wm irreg* (§6.1) man; **ni manna** no one
mannahun *indef pron* w. neg.: no one (§22.2)
manniskodus *sm* humanity
mannisk- *adj* human, of man
manwiþa *sf* preparation; means, wherewithal
manwjan *wv 1* prepare (cf. **faura-**, **ga-**, **fauraga-**)
manwu- *adj* ready, prepared
manwuba *adv* in readiness
maran aþa = Gk μαρὰν ἀθά = Aram *māran ʾăṯā* our Lord has come
marei *wf* sea, lake
marikreitum *Dpl* pearl < Gk μαργαρίτης
marisaiws *sm* sea

marka *sf* boundary, coast, border land
marzeins *sf vn* offense, hindrance
marzjan *wv 1* offend, hinder, cause trouble for, lead astray (*A*) (cf. **ga-**)
matibalgs *sm(i)* food bag
matjan *wv 1* eat; feed (cf. **ga-**)
mats *sm(i)* food
maþa *wm* worm
maþl *sn* market-place
maþleins *sf vn* manner of speaking, speech
maþljan *wv 1* speak
maudjan *wv 1* remind (*D*) of (*G*) (cf. **ga-**)
maurgins *sm* morning, morrow; **in maurgin** on the next morning; **du maurgina** tomorrow; **at maurgin waurþanana** when it was morning
-maurgjan: gamaurgjan
maurnan *wv 3* mourn, be anxious or concerned (for: *D*)
maurþr *sn* murder
maurþrjan *wv 1* to murder
mawi (G **maujos**) *sf* maiden, young girl
mawilo *wf* maiden, young girl
megs *sm* son-in-law
mein- *poss adj* my (§4.2c)
meina *pers pron 1st pers sg* of me (*G* of **ik**) (§10.5)
mekia *As* sword
mel *sn* time, hour, season; pl. **mela** writings, scripture; **mel gabaurþais** birthday; **mela lagga** for a long time; **manag mel** many a time; **us þamma mela** from that time on
mela *wm* grain-measure, bushel
meljan *wv 1* write, set forth in writing (cf. **ana-**, **faura-**, **ga-**, **fauraga-**, **uf-**, **ufar-**)
mena *wm* moon
menoþs *m* month
mereins *sf vn* preaching, proclaiming
meriþa *sf* rumor, report, fame
merjan *wv 1* preach, proclaim, make known (cf. **us-**)
merjands *m* preacher, proclaimer
-mernan: usmernan
mes *sn* table, platter; prob. from Lat *mensa*
midgardiwaddjus *sm(?)* dividing wall
midjasweipains *sf* the Deluge
midj- *adj* middle, mid (§4.2c; Voc. I7)
midjungards *sm(i)* earth, world
miduma *sf* middle, midst; **in midumai** in the middle of the group
midumonds *m* mediator
mik *pron A 1st pers sg* me (*A* of **ik**) (§10.5)
mikil- *adj* great, large, important
mikilaba *adv* greatly
mikilduþs *sf* greatness
mikilei *wf* greatness
mikiljan *wv 1* magnify, praise, exalt (cf. **ga-**)
mikilnan *wv 4* be magnified
mikilþuht- *adj* high-minded; proud
mildiþa *sf* mildness, kindness
milhma *wm* cloud
militon *wv 2* be a soldier < Lat *militare*
miliþ *sn* honey
miluks *f* milk
mims, mimz *sn* flesh, meat
minnist- *adj* least, smallest
minniz- *comp adj* less, smaller
mins *adv* less
minznan *wv 4* lessen
missadeds, missadeþs (*G* **-dedais***) *sf* misdeed, sin
missaleik- *adj* various, different
missaqiss *sf* discord
missataujanda *wm* evil-doer
misso *adv* each other, reciprocally (Voc. I3)
mitadjo *wf* measure
mitan *sv 5* to measure (cf. **ga-**, **us-**)
mitaþs *f* (G **mitads**) measure, grain-measure
miton *wv 2* consider, ponder
mitons *sf vn* thought, considering
miþ *prep D* with, among, together with; through, by, near; *adv* along with
miþarbaidjan *wv 1* to work with (*D*)
miþfaginon *wv 2* rejoice with (*D*)
miþfrahinþan *sv 3* take (*A*) captive along with (*D*)
miþgaggan *sv 7* accompany (*D*)
miþgaleikon *wv 2* jointly imitate
miþgaqiujan *wv 1* make alive along with (*D*)
miþgardiwaddjus: see **midgardiwaddjus**
miþgasinþa *wm* traveling companion
miþgatimrjan *wv 1* build jointly
miþgatiuhan *sv 2* bring or take along
miþinngaleiþan *sv 1* enter along with (*D*)
miþkaurjan *wv 1* to burden in addition
miþliban *wv 3* live together
miþlitjan *wv 1* be jointly hypocritical
miþniman *sv 4* receive, accept
miþqiman *sv 4* come with, accompany (*D*)
miþsatjan *wv 1* transport, shift
miþskalkinon *wv 2* serve together
miþsokjan *wv 1* dispute with (*D*); discuss together
miþstandan *sv 6* stand together (with: *D*)
miþswiltan *sv 3* die together
miþþan *adv* then, while
miþþanei *conj* while, during
miþþiudanon *wv 2* rule together with (*D*)
miþuskeinan *sv 1* (*irreg*) spring up together

miþwissei *wf* conscience
mizdo *wf* reward, compensation, pay
modag- *adj* angry
mota *sf* customs-house
-motan: gamotan
motareis *sm* tax-collector, publican
motastaþs *sm* (*D* **-da**) tollhouse
-motjan: gamotjan, wiþramotjan
moþs* (G **modis**) *sm* anger
mukamodei *wf* moderation, good-naturedness
mulda *sf* dust
muldein- *adj* of dust, of earth
-muljan: faurmuljan
munan *wv 3* think, consider, intend
munan *PP* (§16.3) think, believe, suppose (that...: inf. or **ei** + subj.) (cf. **ga-**)
mundon *wv 2* note, mark
mundrei* *wf* aim, goal
-munnon: ufarmunnon
muns *sm(i)* thought, intention
munþs *sm* mouth

N

nadrs* *sm* adder, viper
-nagljan: ganagljan
-nah: binah, ganah
nahtamats *sm(i)* supper, evening meal
nahts *f* night
naiteins *sf vn* blasphemy
-naitjan: ganaitjan
namnjan *wv 1* to name (cf. **ga-**)
namo *wn irreg* name (§6.1)
-nanþjan: anananþjan, gananþjan
naqad- *adj* naked
naqadei *wf* nakedness
nardus *sm* nard
naseins *sf vn* salvation
nasjan *wv 1* to save (cf. **ga-**)
nasjands *m* saviour
nati *sn* net
natjan *wv 1* to make wet, moisten (cf. **ga-**)
naudibandi *sf* chain, fetter
naudiþaurft- *adj* necessary
nauh *adv* still, yet; **ni nauh** not yet
nauhþan, nauhþanuh *adv* still, yet
nauhuþþan *adv* and also, and yet
naus *sm(i)* corpse
nauþjan *wv 1* to force, compel (cf. **ana-**)
nauþs *sf* need, constraint
nawi- *adj* dead
-nawistron: ganawistron, miþganawistron
ne *adv* nay, no
nehw *adv* nearby, close by
nehwa *prep D* near; *adv* near
nehwis *comp adv* nearer
nehwjan sik *wv 1* approach, draw near (cf. **at-**)
nehwundja *wm* neighbor
nei *adv* not
neiþ *sn* envy, hatred, rancor
neiwan* *sv 1* be angry (at: *D*), rancorous
neþla *sf* needle
ni *adv* not; **ni ... ak...** not ... but ...; **ni alja ...alja** no(t) other... than; **ni ... ni** (or **nih**) neither ... nor; see also under **þanamais, þanaseiþs, þatanei, ainshun, aiw, allis, waihts.**
nibai, niba *conj* unless, except that, if ... not
nidwa *sf(?)* rust
nih *conj* and not, not even; **nih ... nih** neither ... nor; in contrary-to-fact protases: if not (§19.2)
niman *sv 4* take, take away; receive, accept (cf. **af-, and-, at-, bi-, dis-, fra-, ga-, in-, miþ-, us-**)
-nisan: ganisan
nist = **ni ist** is not
niþan *sv 5* to help
niþjis *sm* kinsman
niþjo *wf* female kinsman
niu *interrog particle* Is it not so (that)... (= Lat *nonne*) (§20.6); **niu aiw** never
niuhseins *sf vn* visitation, coming to assist
-niuhsjan: biniuhsjan
-niujan: ananiujan
niujasatiþs *sm* (*G* **-dis**) novice
niuj- *adj* new, young
niujiþa *sf* newness
niuklahei *wf* despondency
niuklah- *adj* young, childish, under-age
niun *num* nine
niund- *ord adj* ninth
niuntehund *num* ninety
niutan *sv 2* attain, enjoy the use of (cf. **ga-**)
-nohjan: ganohjan
-nohnan: ganohnan
nota* *wm* stern of a ship
nu *adv* now, so, consequently; therefore; also used as uninflected adjective: present, existing; or noun: the present (time); see also **jabai, sai, þan, þannu** (§13.1)
nuh *adv* or *conj* therefore
nunu *adv* or *conj* therefore

nuta *wm* fisherman

O

o *interj.* O! Oh!
ogan* *PP* (± **sis**) to fear
ogjan *wv 1* terrify
ohteigo: see **uhteigo**
osanna *exclam* Hosanna < Gk ὡσαννά < Aram *hôša*ʿ *nā*

P

paida *sf* tunic, shirt, undergarment
-paidon: gapaidon
Paintekuste = Πεντηκοστή Pentecost
parakletus *sm* comforter <Gk παράκλητος
Paraskaiwe <Gk παρασκευή day of preparation before the Sabbath
Paska, Pasxa *indecl* the Passover <Gk πάσχα < Aram *pasḥā*
paurpura *sf* purple <Gk πορφύρα, Lat *purpura*
paurpurod- *part adj* (dyed) purple
peikabagms *sm* palm-tree
pistikein- *adj* genuine, pure < Gk πιστικός w. Gothic suff. **-ein-**
plapja *sf* street (hapax; possibly error for **platja*** < Lat *platea*)
plats* *sm* patch of cloth; **lagjan** (*A*) **du plata** apply sthg as a patch
plinsjan *wv 1* to dance
-praggan: anapraggan
praitoriaun Pretorium < Gk πραιτώριον < Lat *praetorium*
praizbytairei *wf* college of elders < Gk πρεσβυτερεῖον
praufeteis *f* prophetess < Gk προφῆτις
praufetja *NApl* prophecy
praufetjan *wv 1* prophesy
praufetus, praufetes *m* prophet < Gk προφητής
psalmon *As*, **psalmo** *Gpl*, **psalmom** *Dpl* < Gk ψαλμός psalm
pugg *As* **purse**
pund *sn* pound

Q

qainon *wv 2* weep, mourn, lament
qairrei *wf* meekness
qairru- *adj* meek, gentle
qairu *sn* splinter
qens, qeins *sf* wife, woman
qiman *sv 4* come, arrive (cf. **ana-, bi-, faura-, fra-, ga-, miþ-, us-**)
qinakund- *adj* female
qinein- *adj* female; as noun *npl* foolish women
qino *wf* woman, wife
qisteins *sf vn* destruction
qistjan *wv 1* destroy (cf. **fra-, us-**)
-qistnan: fraqistnan
qiþan *sv 5* say, speak, tell, name ; **ubil qiþan** speak evil of, curse; **waila qiþan** speak well of, praise (cf. **af-, ana-, and-, faur-, faura-, fra-, ga-, us-**)
qiþuhaft- *adj* pregnant
qiþuhafto *f adj noun* pregnant woman
qiþus *sm* body, womb
qiu- *adj* alive, living
-qiujan: anaqiujan, gaqiujan, miþgaqiujan
-qiunan: gaqiunan
qrammiþa *sf* dampness
qums *sm* advent, arrival

R

rabbaunei master, teacher < Gk ῥαββονεί < Aram *rabbûnî*
rabbei master, teacher < Gk ῥαββί <Aram *rabbî*
ragin *sn* opinion, judgement, decree
ragineis *sm* counselor, governor
raginon *wv 2* rule, be ruler (cf. **ga-**)
rahnjan *wv 1* count, reckon, number (cf. **faura-, ga-**)
rahton *wv 2* offer, present
raidjan *wv 1* determine, fix, appoint (cf. **ga-**)
raiht- *adj* right, straight
raihtaba *adv* rightly; straightway
raihtis *conj* for, because; *adv* still, then, however (§14.2)
-raihtjan: garaihtjan, atgaraihtjan
raka term of abuse < Gk ῥακά < Aram (form uncertain)
-raisjan: urraisjan
-rakjan: ufrakjan
-rannjan: urrannjan
rasta *sf* mile

-raþjan: garaþjan
raþiz- *comp adj* easier
raþjo *wf* number, account
-raubon: biraubon
raud- *adj* red
-rauhtjan: inrauhtjan
raupjan *wv 1* pluck, pick off
raus *sn* reed
razda *sf* language, speech
razn *sn* house
-redan: garedan, fauragaredan, undredan, urredan
reikj- *adj* powerful, mighty; **reikist-** as noun: the mightiest, the chief
reiki *sn* power; rule; kingdom
reikinon *wv 2* to rule, govern
reiks *m* ruler, prince; prominent citizen, community leader (§10.2)
reiran *wv 3* tremble (cf. **in-**)
reiro *wf* trembling
-reisan: urreisan
rign *sn* rain
rignjan *wv 1* to rain
rikan *sv 5* heap up
rimis *sn* rest, repose
rinnan *sv 3* run, hasten (cf. **and-**, **at-**, **duat-**, **bi-**, **du-**, **fair-**, **faur-**, **fra-**, **ga-**, **und-**, **ur-**)
rinno *wf* torrent
riqis, riqiz *(G* **-zis***)* *sn* darkness
riqizein- *adj* dark
riqizjan *wv 1* become dark
riurei *wf* destruction, perishing
riurj- *adj* mortal, perishable
riurjan *wv 1* destroy
rodjan *wv 1* speak; say (sthg: *A*; to smn: *D*, **du** *D*) (cf. **bi-**, **miþ-**)
rohsns *sf* hall, courtyard
rum- *adj* spacious, roomy
-rumnan: urrumnan
rums* *sm* or *sn* room, space
runa *sf* secret, mystery; counsel, consultation
runs *sm* running; flow, issue; **run gawaurkjan sis** to rush violently

S

sa, so, þata *dem adj and pron* this, that; used as *pers pron* he, she, it; used also as definite article (§§1.4, 2.2, 3.3, 8.2)
sabana *Ds* fine linen < Lat *sabanum*
Sabbato *indecl* the Sabbath; **Sabbato daga** on the Sabbath
Sabbatus *sm* the Sabbath, a week < G σάββατον < Aram *šabbāṯ*
sad- *adj* full, satisfied; **sad itan** satisfy one's hunger, eat one's fill
saei *rel pron* he who, that which (§§11.1, 12.3)
saggqjan, sagqjan *wv 1* cause to sink, sink (trans.) (cf. **uf-**)
saggqs *sm* sinking, setting (of sun), the West
saggws *sm(i)* song, music
sah, soh, þatuh *dem pron* this, that (§18.4)
sahwazuh saei/izei *indef pron* whosoever (§22.2)
sai *interj* see! look! behold! **sai nu** note then, behold then
saian, saijan *sv 7* (*P* **saiso**) to sow (seed: *D*) (cf. **in-**)
saiands *pres part as noun* sower
saihs *num* six
saihst- *ord num adj* sixth
saihs tigjus *num* sixty
saihwan *sv 5* to see, notice, take heed (cf. **and-**, **at-**, **bi-**, **ga-**, **in-**, **þairh-**, **us-**)
-sailjan: insailjan
sainjan *wv 1* be late, delayed
sair *sn* sorrow
saiwala *sf* soul, spirit, life
saiws *sm* sea, lake
sakan *sv 6* dispute (with: *D*); rebuke, reproach (*D*) (cf. **and-**, **ga-**, **in-**, **anain-**, **us-**)
sakjo *wf* strife
sakkus *sm* sackcloth
sakul- *adj* quarrelsome
salbon *wv 2* anoint (cf. **ga-**)
salbons *sf* ointment
saldra *sf* coarse jesting
saliþwos *sf pl* dwelling, mansion; guest-chamber
saljan[1] *wv 1* reside, dwell, remain (cf. **us-**)
saljan[2] *wv 1* sacrifice, bring an offering (cf. **and-**, **ga-**)
salt *sn* salt
saltan *sv 7* to salt
sam- *adj* same (§11.2)
samafraþj- *adj* being of the same mind
samakunj- *adj* of the same race
samalaud- *adj* equally great
samaleiko *adv* likewise, in the same way
samaleik- *adj* alike, of the same sort
samana *adv* together, in the same place, with one another
samaqiss *sf* agreement, accord
samasaiwal- *adj* unanimous
samaþ *adv* together, in/to the same place
samjan *wv 1* seek to please

sandjan *wv 1* send (smn: *A;* to: **du** *D;* to do sthg: inf.) (cf. **ga-**, **faura-**, **in-**, **miþin-**, **gamiþ-**, **us-**)
sarwa *sn(?) pl* weapons, armour
satjan *wv 1* set, place, put; to plant (cf. **af-**, **at-**, **bi-**, **ga-**, **fauraga-**, **miþ-**, **us-**)
sauhts *sf* sickness, disease, illness
sauil *sn* sun
-sauljan: bisauljan
-saulnan: bisaulnan
sauls *sf* pillar
saurga *sf* sorrow, grief
saurgan *wv 3* to sorrow, grieve; be troubled
sauþa *sf* grounds, basis
sauþs (G **saudis**) *sm(i)* sacrifice, burnt-offering
sei *rel pron f* who, which (§19.5)
sein- *poss pron adj* his/her/its/their own (always refers to the subject of the clause) (§4.3)
seinagairn- *adj* selfish
seitein- *adj* daily
seiþu- *adj* late; as noun: evening
seli- *adj* good, kind
selei *wf* goodness, kindness
si *pers pron* she (§7.3)
sibja *sf* relationship
-sibjon: gasibjon
sibun *num* seven
sibuntehund *num* seventy
sidon *wv 2* (+ **sis**) to practice, do habitually
sidus *sm* custom, habit
sifan *wv 3* rejoice
siggwan *sv 3* sing, chant, recite, read (cf. **us-**)
sigis *sn* victory
sigislaun *sn* victory reward, prize
sigljan *wv 1* to seal < Lat *sigillare* (cf. **faur-**, **ga-**)
sigljo *wn* a seal < Lat *sigillum*
sigqan *sv 3* sink, go down (of sun) (cf. **dis-**, **ga-**)
sij- present indicative plural and present subjunctive stem of the copula
sik *refl pron* (*G* **seina**, *D* **sis**) oneself; **sis misso** (to) one another
-silan: anasilan
silba *pron* self (§11.2)
silbasiuneis* *sm* eyewitness
silbawilj- *adj* willed by oneself, voluntary
sildaleik *sn* wonder, astonishment
sildaleik- *adj* wonderful, marvelous
sildaleikjan *wv 1* to marvel, be astonished (at: **ana** *D*, **bi** *A*, **in** *G*); to astonish
sildaleiknan *wv 4* be marveled at
silubr *sn* silver
silubrein- *adj* silver, of silver
simle *adv* once, at one time formerly
sinaps *sm* or **sinap** *sn* mustard
sind *3rd pers pl copula* they are, there are
sineig- *adj* old
sinist- *superl adj* oldest; used nominally: an elder
sintein- *adj* daily
sinteino *adv* always, continually
sinþs* *sm* time, occasion (used in expressing cardinal adverbs: **ainamma sinþa, twaim sinþam** once, twice, etc.)
siponeis *sm* pupil, disciple
siponjan *wv 1* to be a disciple
sis *D* of **sik** *qv*
sitan *sv 5* sit, be sitting (cf. **and-**, **bi-**, **dis-**, **ga-**, **us-**)
sitls *sm* seat, chair, nest, stall
siujan *wv 1* sew
siuk- *adj* sick, ill, diseased
siukan *sv 2* be sick
siukei *wf* sickness, infirmity
siuns *sf* sight, appearance
skaban *sv 6* to shave (cf. **bi-**)
skadus *sm* shade, shadow
-skadwjan: ufarskadwjan
skaftjan sik *wv 1* prepare oneself, make ready (for: **du**)
skaidan *sv 7* (P **skaiskaiþ**) divide, separate (trans. and intrans.) (cf. **af-**, **dis-**, **ga-**)
-skaidnan: gaskaidnan
skal *PP* I shall (**skulan***) (§§14.3, 15.2)
skalja* *sf* tile, brick
skalkinassus *sm* service
skalkinon *wv 2* to serve (cf. **miþ-**)
skalks *sm* servant, slave (= Gk δοῦλος)
skaman sik *wv 3* to be ashamed (of: *G*); despair of (cf. **ga-**)
skanda *sf* shame
-skapjan: gaskapjan
-skarjan: usskarjan
skattja *wm* money-changer
skatts *sm* money, coin
skaþis *sn* harm, injustice
skaþjan *sv 6* injure (cf. **ga-**)
skaþul- *adj* harmful
skaudaraip *sn(?)* leather thong, shoe-lace
skauni- *adj* beautiful
skaurpjo* *wf* scorpion < Lat *scorpio*
skaut *sn(?)* hem of a garment
skeima* *wm(?)* lantern
skeinan *sv 1* to shine (cf. **bi-**)
skeiri- *adj* clear
skeireins *sf vn* commentary, interpretation
-skeirjan: gaskeirjan

skewjan *wv 1* walk, go, stroll
skildus* *sm* shield
skilja *wm* butcher, butcher's shop
skilliggs *sm* coin (acc. to Mossé p. 254 a calque on Lat *clipeus* shield > engraved metal disk > coin; thus Goth **skildu-** + **-igg-**)
skip *sn* ship
-skiuban: afskiuban
skohs *sm* shoe
skohsl *sn* demon, evil spirit
-skreitan: disskreitan
-skritnan: disskritnan
skuft* *sn* hair (of the head)
skuggwa *wm* mirror
skul- *adj* guilty, in debt, liable (for *A*)
skula *wm* debtor, one who owes (to: *D*); one who is guilty (of: *G*), subject (to: *D*)
skuld- *part adj* lawful; **skuld ist** it is lawful, right, proper (for smn: *D*; to do sthg: inf.)
skulan* *PP* to owe, be obliged; to be about to, shall, will
skura *sf* shower; **skura windis** a storm
slahals *sm* bully, rowdy
slahan *sv 6* strike, hit, beat (cf. **af-**)
slahs *sm(i)* stroke; plague, illness
slaiht- *adj* smooth
slauhts *sf* slaughter
-slaupjan: afslaupjan
-slauþjan: afslauþjan
-slauþnan: afslauþnan
slawan *wv 3* be silent, remain silent (cf. **ana-**, **ga-**)
sleidj- *adj* fierce; dangerous
sleiþa *sf* harm, damage
sleiþei *wf* danger
-sleiþjan: gasleiþjan
slepan sv 7 (P **saislep**) sleep, fall asleep (cf. **ana-**, **ga-**)
sleps *sm* sleep
-slindan: fraslindan
sliupan *sv 2* slip (cf. **uf-**)
smairþr *sn* fat; sap, vitality
smakka *wm* fig
smakkabagms *sm* fig-tree
smal- *adj* small; *superl* **smalist-**
smarna *sf* refuse, dung
-smeitan: bismeitan, gasmeitan
-smiþon: gasmiþon
smyrn *sn* myrrh < Gk σμύρνα
snaga *wm* garment
snaiws *sm* snow
-snarpjan: atsnarpjan
sneiþan *sv 1* cut, reap (cf. **af-**, **uf-**)
sniumjan *wv 1* hurry, hasten (cf. **ga-**)
sniumundo *adv* with haste, quickly; **sniumundos** *comp adv* quicker, with greater haste
sniwan *sv 5* to hasten, hurry (cf. **duat-**, **bi-**, **faurbi-**, **faur-**, **ga-**)
snorjo *wf* basket
snutr- *adj* wise
snutrei *wf* wisdom
soei *rel pron f* (§§11.1, 12.3)
sokareis *sm* one who disputes or inquires
sokeins *sf vn* search, inquiry; point at issue
sokjan *wv 1* seek, desire, look for (*A*); dispute (with smn: **miþ** *D*), question; **sokjan samana** to reason together, discuss (cf. **ga-**, **miþ-**, **us-**)
sokns *sf* search, inquiry, speculation
soþa *Ds* filling, satisfying
-soþjan: gasoþjan
spaikulatur *m* spy, executioner < Lat *speculator*
spaiskuldra *Ds* spit, saliva
sparwa *wm* sparrow
spaurds *f* measure of length, race-course
spediz- *comp adj* later, last; *superl* **spedist-** last, latest, most recent
spedumist- *superl adj* last
speiwan *sv 1* spit (cf. **and-**, **bi-**)
spilda *sf* board, plaque; writing tablet
spill *sn* fable, story, legend
spilla *wm* narrator, one who tells
spillon *wv 2* tell, narrate, spread news of (cf. **ga-**, **þiuþ-**, **us-**, **waila-**)
spinnan *sv 3* to spin
sprauto *adv* quickly, soon
spyreida *wm* large basket < Gk σπυρίδ-
stafs* (*G* ***stabis**) *sm(i)* basic element
-stagqjan: gastagqjan
staiga *sf* path, way, road
stainah- *adj* stony
stainein- *adj* of stone
stainjan *wv 1* to stone
stains *sm* stone, rock; **stainam wairpan** to stone
stairno *wf* star
stairo *wf* barren woman
staks *sm(i)* mark, scar
-staldan: andstaldan, gastaldan
stamm- *adj* having a speech impediment
standan *sv 6* stand, stand firm (cf. **af-**, **and-**, **at-**, **bi-**, **faura-**, **ga-**, **in-**, **miþ-**, **twis-**, **us-**)
staþs (G **stadis**) *sm(i)* place; **jainis stadis** over to the other side
staþs* (G **staþis***) *sm* shore
staua *wm* judge
staua *sf* judgement

stauastols *sm* the judgement-seat
-staurknan: gastaurknan
-staurran: andstaurran
stautan *sv 7* strike, push
steigan *sv 1* go up, ascend, climb (cf. **at-**, **ga-**, **ufar-**, **us-**)
stibna *sf* voice
stigqan *sv 3* thrust, push; make war (cf. **bi-**, **ga-**)
stikls *sm* cup
stiks *sm* point, moment
stilan *sv 4* steal
stiur *sm* calf
stiurjan *wv 1* establish; assert, maintain
stiwiti* *sn* patience, tolerance
-stodjan: anastodjan, dustodjan
stojan *wv 1 (P* **stauida**) to judge (cf. **ga-**)
stols *sm* throne
stoma *wm(?)* substantial nature, essence
-stoþan: gastoþan*
straujan *wv 1* strew *D* (on: **ana** *D*) (cf. **ga-**,**uf-**)
striks *sm(i)* stroke
stubjus *sm* dust
-suljan: gasuljan*
suljom *Dpl* sandals
suman *adv* once in the past, already; partially, partly
sums *indef pron* some one, some of, a part of; **sums** ... **sums**... the one... the other; **sumai** ... **sumai** ... some ... others...; **bi sumata** in part (§9.3)
sundro *adv* apart, alone, privately
sunja *sf* truth; **bi sunjai** truly, verily
sunj- *adj* true
sunjaba *adv* truly
sunjein- *adj* true
sunjon *wv 2* justify, declare true (cf. **ga-**)
sunjons *sf vn* verifying, defending
sunno *wf* or *wn irreg* (See Voc. 18) sun
suns *adv* immediately, at once, straightway
sunsaiw *adv* immediately, straightway
sunsei *conj* as soon as
sunus *sm* son
supon *wv 2* to season (cf. **ga-**)
suqnis *Gs* belly, womb
suti- *adj* sweet, patient, peaceable; *comp* **sutiz-**
suþjan *wv 1* to itch, tickle
suþjon *wv 2* to itch, tickle
swa, swah *adv* so, thus, just so; **swa filu** (**swe**) as much (as)
swaei *conj* so that, so as (to); in as much as; *adv* thus, so
-swaggwjan: afswaggwjan
swaihra *wm* father-in-law
swaihro *wf* mother-in-law

-swairban: afswairban, biswairban
swalaud- *adj* so great
swaleik- *adj* such, of this sort
swamms *sm(?)* sponge
swaran *sv 6* to swear an oath (cf. **bi-**, **ufar-**)
sware *adv* in vain, without good reason
swart- *adj* black;
swartiza *Ds* ink
swaswe *rel adv* even as, just as; *conj* so that
swe *adv conj* like, as, just as, so that; about, approximately **swe...swa...** as..., so...; **swe ... jah** (**swa jah, swah**) like ... so too ...
swegniþa *sf* joy
swegnjan *wv 1* rejoice
sweiban *sv 1 (P* **swaif**) cease
swein *sn* swine, pig
swer- *adj* honored, highly esteemed
sweran *wv 3* to honor, esteem, respect (cf. **ga-**, **un-**)
swerei *wf* honor
sweriþa *sf* honor
swes- *adj* of one's own; as noun *sn* one's property, possessions
sweþauh *adv* yet, indeed, however
swibla *Ds* sulfur, brimstone
swiglja *wm* piper
swiglon *wv 2* to play the pipes or flute
swikn- *adj* pure
swiknei *wf* purity
swikneins *sf vn* purification
swikniþa *sf* purity
swikunþ- *adj* evident, open, manifest, known
swikunþaba *adv* openly, manifestly
-swikunþjan: gaswikunþjan
swiltan *sv 3* to be dying (cf. **ga-**, **miþga-**)
swinþ- *adj* strong, sound, healthy; *comp* **swinþoz-**
swinþei *wf* power, might, strength
-swinþjan: gaswinþjan, inswinþjan
swinþnan *wv 4* grow strong (cf. **ga-**)
swistar *f* sister (§7.2)
swogatjan *wv 1* sigh
-swogjan: gaswogjan, ufswogjan
swultawairþja *wm* one near death
swumfsl, swumsl *sn* pool
synagogafaþs (*G* **-fadis**) *sm* leader of the synagogue
synagoge f synagogue < Gk συναγωγή

T

tagl *sn* hair
tagr *sn* tear (lacrima)

tagrjan *wv 1* weep
tahjan *wv 1* to tear, rend (cf. **dis-**)
taihsw- *adj* right (not left)
taihswa *sf* the right hand or side
taihswo *adj noun wf* the right hand; **af** or **in taihswon** on the right
taihun *num* ten
taihund- *ord num adj* tenth; **taihundo dails** a tenth
taihuntaihundfalþ- *num adj* hundredfold
taihuntehund, taihuntaihund *num indecl* hundred
taiknjan *wv 1* point out, show, indicate (cf. **ga-**, **us-**)
taikns *sf* token, sign, wonder
tainjo *wf* basket
tains *sm* twig, branch
-tairan: distairan, gatairan
taitrarkes = Gk τετράρχης tetrarch
taleiþa young girl < Gk ταλιθά < Aram *ṭalyəṯā*
talzeins *sf vn* instruction
talzjan *wv 1* teach, instruct (smn: *A*) (cf. **ga-**)
talzjands* *m* teacher
-tamjan: gatamjan
tandjan *wv 1* ignite, kindle. light (cf. **ga-**, **in-**)
-tarhjan: gatarhjan
tarmjan *wv 1* shout for joy
-tarnjan: gatarnjan
taui (*G* **tojis**) *sn* deed, work
taujan *wv 1* do, act, behave (toward: *D*); make, produce; cause (to do: inf.) (cf. **ga-**, **missa-**)
-taurnan: aftaurnan, distaurnan, gataurnan
-tehund *num sn* decade (occurs only as second element in **sibuntehund** seventy etc. §23.7)
-teihan: gateihan, fauragateihan
tekan *sv 7* (*P* **taitok**) to touch (cf. **at-**)
tewa* *sf* order, arrangement
-tewjan: gatewjan
tigus* *sm* decade (only in the plural for forming the tens from 20 to 60, e.g. **twai tigjus** 20; §23.7)
til *sn* grounds, cause
-tilon: andtilon, gatilon, gagatilon
-timan: gatiman
timbrjan: see **timrjan**
timreins *sf vn* building, constructing; discipline, training
timrja *wm* carpenter, builder
timrjan, timbrjan *wv 1* to build, construct (often fig.) (cf. **ana-**, **ga-**, **miþga-**)
tiuhan *sv 2* to lead, guide, draw (*A*; to smn: *D*, **du** *D*) (cf. **af-**, **at-**, **innat-**, **bi-**, **ga-**, **miþga-**, **us-**)

tojis, toja: see **taui**
trauains *sf vn* trust
trauan *wv 3* to trust (cf. **ga-**)
trausti *sn* covenant
triggwa *sf* covenant
triggwaba *adv 1* truly, assuredly
triggw- *adj* faithful, true, reliable
trigo *wf* grief, sorrow
triu *sn* tree, wood, staff
triwein- *adj* wooden, of wood
trudan *sv 4 irreg* to tread (cf. **ga-**)
-trusgjan: intrusgjan
-trusnjan: ufartrusnjan
tugglam *Dpl* gloss to **stabim** *Dpl* basic elements of the universe, probably a reference to the constellations and astrology (cf. AS *tungal*)
tuggo *wf* tongue
tulgiþa *sf* fortress, stronghold; sureness, certainty
tulgjan *wv 1* strengthen, fortify (cf. **ga-**)
tulgu- *adj* firm, fast
tundnan *wv 4* catch fire, be ignited (cf. **in-**)
tunþus *sm* tooth
tuzwerjan *wv 1* to doubt
twai *num m* (*f* **twos**, *n* **twa**) two (§9.2)
twai tigjus *num* twenty
twalibwintru- *adj* twelve winters old
twalif (*G* **-libe**)*num* twelve
tweifl *A sg* doubt
tweifleins *sf vn* doubt
tweihnai *num adj* two each (§23.7)
twis(s)tandan *sv 6* take leave of (*D*)
twisstass *sf* dissension

Þ

þadei *rel adv* where, wheresoever, whither
þagkjan *wv 1* (*P* **þahta** §6.2) think, ponder, consider (cf. **and-**, **bi-**)
þahains *sf vn* silence
þahan *wv 3* be silent, remain silent (cf. **ga-**)
þaho *wf* clay
þahta *P* of **þagkjan**
þairh *prep A* through; by, by means of; on account of; according to (a source); through the agency of
þairharbaidjan *wv 1* to work through (e.g. the night)
þairhbairan *sv 4* carry through
þairhgaggan *sv 7* go, come, or walk through (**þairh** *A*); to pierce (A)
þairhgaleikon *wv 2* assimilate
þairhleiþan *sv 1* go through
þairhsaihwan *wv 5* see through
þairhwakan *sv 6* keep watch

þairko *wn* hole; **þairko neþlos** eye of a needle
-þairsan: gaþairsan
þan *conj* when; (postpositive) then, therefore; *adv* then, at that time; **þan nu** when then, so when
þanamais *adv* still, further, furthermore; w. neg.: no more, no longer
þanaseiþs *adv* further, more, still; w. neg.: no more, no longer
þande *conj* if, when; as long as, until; because, since
þanei *rel adv* when; to whatever extent
-þanjan: ufþanjan
þank *As* thanks
þannu, þanuh *conj* then, therefore, so; **þannu nu** so therefore, but then indeed (§13.1)
þar *adv* there
þarb- *adj* needy, lacking (*G*)
þarba *wm* beggar
þarba *sf* poverty
-þarban: gaþarban
þarei *rel adv* where
þarf *PP* I need (**þaurban**)
þarih- *adj* unshrunken (of cloth)
þaruh *conj* therefore, but, and; *adv* there, now (§13.1)
þata *dem pron and adj n sg* that, this, it (§2.2)
þatahwah þei *indef pron n sg* whatsoever (§22.2)
þatain, þatainei *adv* only; **ni þatainei ... ak** not only ... but also
þatei *conj* because, that, if; often introduces a direct quotation
þatei *rel pron n sg* (§§11.1, 12.3)
þaþro *adv* from there, thence
þaþroei *rel adv* from where, whence
þaþroh *adv* from then on, afterwards; from there
þau *conj* (1) after comparative: than; (2) introducing second part of a disjunctive interrogation: or; **þau ni** or not; (3) in apodosis of unreal conditions: then (§19.2). *adv* but just, only just; after an *interrog pron*: then, in that case, perhaps.
þauh jabai *conj* even though
þaurban* *PP* (§20.1) to need, lack (sthg: *G*), be in want; to require (that: **ei** + subj.)
þaurft- *adj* needy, necessary; *comp* **þaurftoz-**
þaurfts *sf* need, necessity
þaurnein- *adj* thorny, made of thorns
þaurnus *sm* thorn
þaurp *sn(?)* field
þaursjan *wv 1* to thirst (personal subject or impersonal w. *A*: **þaurseiþ mik** I am thirsty) (cf. **af-**)
-þaursnan: gaþaursnan
þaurstei *wf* thirst
þaursu- *adj* dry, withered
þeei *conj* in **ni þeei** not that, not because
þei *conj* that, so that (§16.2); *rel particle* that (§§19.5, 22.2)
þeihan *sv 1* thrive, prosper, progress (cf. **ga-**, **ufar-**)
þeihs *sn* time
þeihwo *wf* thunder
þein- *poss pron adj 2nd pers sg* your, thy (§4.2)
þeina of you (*G* of **þu**)
þewis *sn* slave, servant
-þinsan: atþinsan
þishun *adv* chiefly, especially, even
þishwaduh þadei *adv* whithersoever (§22.2)
þishwah *indef pron* whatsoever
þishwaruh þei *rel adv* wheresoever (§22.2)
þishwazuh (**ei, þei, saei**) *indef pron* whosoever
þiubi *sn* theft
þiubjo *adv* secretly
þiuda *sf* people, nation; pl. the Gentiles, the heathens, the non-Jews
þiudangardi *sf* kingdom; palace, court
þiudanon *wv 2* to rule (cf. **miþ-**)
þiudans *sm* king
þiudinassus *sm* kingdom
þiudisko *adv* after the manner of the non-Jewish people
þiufs, þiubs *sm* (*G* **-bis**) thief
þiumagus *sm* servant
þius* *sm* (*G* **þiwis***) servant
þiuþ *sn* good, what is good, blessedness
þiuþeig- *adj* good, blessed
þiuþeins *sf vn* goodness, blessing
þiuþiqiss *sf* blessing
þiuþjan *wv 1* bless, praise (smn: *A* or *D*) (cf. **ga-**, **un-**)
þiuþspillon *wv 2* bring or tell as good news
þiwadw *As* servitude
-þiwan: anaþiwan, gaþiwan
þiwi (G **þiujos**) *sf* maidservant
þlahsjan *wv 1* frighten (cf. **ga-**)
-þlahsnan: gaþlahsnan
-þlaihan: gaþlaihan
þlaqu- *adj* tender, soft
þlauhs *sm(i)* flight
þliuhan *sv 2* flee (from: **af, faura** *D*); to shun, turn aside from (*A*) (cf. **af-**, **ga-**, **unþa-**)
þrafsteins *sf vn* consolation
þrafstjan *wv 1* console, comfort; w. **sik**: take courage, be cheerful (cf. **ana-**, **ga-**)
þragjan *wv 1* to run
þramstei *wf* locust
þreihan *sv 1* to press, crowd, throng (cf. **ga-**)
þreihsl *sn* anguish, distress
þreis* (*n* **þrija**) *num* three (§9.2)

þridj- *ord num adj* third
þridjo *adv* for the third time
þriskan *sv 3* thresh
-þriutan: usþriutan
þroþjan *wv 1* exercise (cf. **us-**)
þrutsfill *sn* leprosy; **þrutsfill habands** a leper
þrutsfill- *adj* leprous, having leprosy
þu *pers pron 2nd pers sg N* thou (§10.5)
þuei *rel pron 2nd pers sg* thou who (§12.3c)
þugkjan *wv 1* (P **þuhta** §6.2) seem to be, turn out to be; serve as, be in role of; think, believe (that...: inf. or **ei** + subj.); also impers. with *D*
þuhta *P* of **þugkjan**
þuhtus *sm* conscience
þuk thee, you (sg.) (*A* of **þu**)
þulains *sf vn* patience, sufferance
þulan *wv 3* tolerate, endure, put up with, thole (cf. **ga-**, **us-**)
þus to thee, to you (sg.) (*D* of **þu**)
þusundi *sf* thousand (§23.7)
þusundifaþs (*G* **-dis**) *sm(i)* chilarch, leader of a thousand
þuthaurn *sn* trumpet
þuthaurnjan *wv 1* sound the trumpet
þuthaurnjando *n part noun* trumpeting, "sounding brass"
þwahan *sv 6* to wash (**af-**, **bi-**, **us-**)
þwahl *sn* baptism
þwairh- *adj* angry
þwairhei *wf* dispute, quarrel; **in þwairhein briggan** enrage, make angry
þwastiþa *sf* certainty, sureness
-þwastjan: gaþwastjan
þymiama *wm* incense < Gk θυμίαμα

U

-u *encl interrog particle* (attached to the first word of its clause) (§20.6)
ubilaba *adv* badly, evilly
ubil- *adj* bad, evil; *n* used as noun: **þata ubil(o)** evil; **ubil haban** to be ill; **ubil qiþan** *D* to speak evil of, to curse
ubiltoj- *adj* evil-doing; as noun: an evil-doer
ubilwaurd- *adj* evil-speaking
ubilwaurdjan *wv 1* to speak evil of
ubizwa *sf* portico
ubuh = **uf** + **-uh**
uf *prep A* (motion implied, e.g. to put, lay, set sthg) under, into subjection under; *D* (static, e.g. situated) under, subject to, during the reign of
ufaiþj- *adj* under oath
ufar *prep A, D* over, above, beyond
ufarassjan *wv 1* increase, make abundant; become abundant
ufarassus *sm* abundance; high office; **ufarassau** *adv* in abundance, excessively, especially
ufarfull- *adj* abundant, overfull
ufarfullei *wf* overfullness, abundance
ufarfulljan *wv 1* fill to overflowing
ufargaggan *sv 7* go too far, transgress
ufargiutan *sv 2* to overflow
ufargudja *wm* chief-priest
ufarhafjan sik *sv 6* raise oneself (over: **ufar**)
ufarhafnan *wv 4* be exalted
ufarhamon *wv 2* clothe in (*D*)
ufarhauhid- *part adj* puffed up, conceited
ufarhauseins *sf vn* disobedience
ufarhiminakund- *adj* belonging to highest heaven
ufarhleiþrjan *wv 1* spread a tent (over: **ana**)
ufarhugjan *wv 1* be proud, pride self on
ufarjaina *adv* throughout
ufarlagjan *wv 1* lay over, cover
ufarleiþan *sv 1* go across, cross over
ufarmaudei *wf* forgetfulness
ufarmeleins *sf vn* inscription, superscription
ufarmeli *sn* inscription, superscription
ufarmeljan *wv 1* inscribe, superscribe
ufarmunnon *wv 2* forget (*D*)
ufaro *adv* above; *prep G, D* over, above, upon
ufarranneins *sf vn* sprinkling
ufarskadwjan *wv 1* to overshadow
ufarskafts *sf* first-fruits
ufarsteigan *sv 1* spring up, mount up, surpass
ufarswara* *wm* perjurer
ufarswaran *sv 6* commit perjury
ufartrusnjan *wv 1* strew over
ufarþeihan *sv 1* excel, surpass
ufarwisan *sv 5* be in excess, dominate, prevail
ufbauljan *wv 1* puff up
ufblesan *sv 7* inflate, puff up
ufbloteins *sf vn* entreaty
ufbrikan *sv 4* reject, despise
ufbrinnan *sv 3* burn up, scorch
ufdaupjan *wv 1* baptize, submerge, wash
ufgairdan *sv 3* gird up
ufgraban *sv 6* dig up
ufhaban *wv 3* hold up, bear up
ufhauseins *sf vn* obedience, regard

ufhauseins *sf vn* obedience, regard
ufhausjan *wv 1* submit to (*D*), obey (*D*), listen to (*D*)
ufhlohjan *wv 1* cause to laugh
ufhnaiweins *sf vn* submission, obedience
ufhnaiwjan *wv 1* make subject to (**uf** *A*)
ufhropjan *wv 1* cry out
ufjo in **ufjo mis ist** it is superfluous for me ...
ufkunnan *wv 3* (*irreg pret* **ufkunþa** §16.3) recognize, acknowledge; sense, realize (sthg: *A*; that ... **þatei** + indic.)
ufkunþi *sn* knowledge, perception, realization
ufligan *sv 5* lie under; to faint, fail, succumb
ufmeljan *wv 1* to sign
ufrakjan *wv 1* stretch forth, stretch out, lift up (usually with **handu**)
ufsagqjan *wv 1* to sink (trans.)
ufsliupan *sv 2* move surreptitiously, slip in or out
ufsneiþan *sv 1* slay, slaughter
ufstraujan *wv 1* strew *D* (on: **ana** *D*)
ufswalleins *sf vn* insolence
ufswogjan *wv 1* to sigh deeply
ufta *adv* often
ufþanjan *wv 1* stretch, extend; + **sik** stretch oneself
ufto *adv* perhaps
ufwair- *adj* married (of a woman)
ufwopjan *wv 1* cry out (to: *D*, **du** *D*)
ugkis *pron D,A dual* us two
-uh, -h *encl particle* with force of a conjunction: but, and, now, therefore (§15.2); **-uh þan** (§13.1)
uhteig- *adj* having leisure time for
uhteigo *adv* opportunely
uhtiug- *adj* convenient, opportune
uhtwo *wf* early morning
ulbandus *sm* camel
unagand- *adj* fearless
unagei* *wf* fearlessness; *D* as *adv* fearlessly
unairkn-*adj* unholy, godless
unaiwisk- *adj* having no reason to be ashamed
unanasiuniba *adv* invisibly
unandhullid- *part adj* undisclosed, hidden
unandsakan- *part adj* uncontested
unandsokj- *adj* incontestable
unatgaht- *adj* inaccessible
unbairand- *part adj* sterile, barren
unbarnah- *adj* childless
unbauran- *part adj* unborn
unbeistei* *wf* unleavened bread
unbeistjod- *part adj* unleavened
unbiari* *sn* wild beast
unbilaistid- *part adj* inscrutable, unfathomable
unbimait *sn* lack of circumcision
unbimaitan- *part adj* uncircumcised
unbruki- *adj* useless
und *prep A* unto, until, up to ; *D* for; **und þatei** *conj* until, while; **und hwa** how long? **und hina daga, und hita** until now; **und filu mais** all the more
undar *prep A* under
undaraist- error for **undarist-** *adj superl* lowest, innermost
undarleij- *adj* the least
undaro *prep D* under
undaurnimats *sm* breakfast, noonday meal
undgreipan *sv 1* seize, take hold of
undiwanei *wf* immortality
undredan *sv 7* furnish, provide, grant
undrinnan *sv 3* fall to one's share
unfagr- *adj* unfit, unsuitable; ungrateful
unfairin- *adj* blameless
unfairinodaba *adv* blamelessly
unfairlaistid- *adj* inscrutable, incomprehensible
unfaurj- *adj* gossipy
unfaurweis- *adj* unintentional
unfraþjand- *part adj* not understanding
unfreideins *sf vn* severe treatment
unfrod- *adj* lacking understanding
unfrodei *wf* folly, lack of understanding; frustration, rage
ungafairinod-, ungafairinond- *part adj* blameless
ungahaband- sik *part adj* lacking self-control
ungahobains *sf vn* self-indulgence, lack of self-control
ungahwairb- *adj* unruly, disobedient
ungakusan- *part adj* unqualified, unfit
ungalaub- *adj* without value
ungalaubeins *sf vn* unbelief, disbelief
ungalaubjand- *part adj* unbelieving
ungaraihtei *wf* lawlessness
ungasaihwan- *part adj* unseen, unseeable
ungastod- *adj* lacking a firm basis
ungatass- *adj* insubordinate, idle
ungatewid- *part adj* idle, undisciplined
ungawagid- *part adj* immovable
unhaband- *part adj* not having
unhail- *adj* sick
unhaili *sn* sickness, illness, disease
unhanduwaurht- *adj* not made by hand, i.e. spiritual, not physical
unhindarweis- *adj* without hypocrisy
unhraini- *adj* unclean, impure
unhrainei *wf* impurity
unhrainiþa *sf* impurity
unhulþa *wm* unclean spirit, demon; the Devil
unhulþo *wf* unclean spirit, demon

unhwapnand- *part adj* unquenchable
unhweil- *adj* unceasing, continual
unkarj- *adj* careless, neglectful
unkaureins *sf vn* not being a burden
unkja *wm* measure of length < Lat *uncia*
unkunnand- *part adj* not knowing
unkunþi *sn* ignorance
unkunþ- *adj* unknown
unled- *adj* poor, indigent
unledi *sn* poverty
unliub- *adj* unloved
unliugaid- *part adj* unmarried
unliugand- *part adj* not lying
unliut- *adj* unfeigned
unlustus *sm* discouragement, indifference
unmahteig- *adj* weak; impossible
unmahts *sf* weakness, infirmity
unmanariggw- *adj* inhuman, savage
unmanwu- *adj* unprepared
unmildj- *adj* without natural affection, unloving
unnutj- *adj* foolish, useless
unqenid- *adj* unmarried (of a man)
unqeþj- *adj* that cannot be spoken, ineffable
unriurei *wf* immortality, incorruptibility
unriurj- *adj* immortal, indestructible
unrodjand- *part adj* not speaking, dumb
unsahþaba *adv* incontestably
unsaihwand- *part adj* not seeing
unsaltan- *part adj* unsalted
unsara *pron* of us; **unsar**- *poss pron adj* our (§4.2c)
unseli- *adj* unholy, wicked, evil
unselei *wf* wickedness, craftiness; injustice, unrighteousness
unsibj- *adj* lawless, impious; **insibjis** as noun: transgressor, criminal
unskaw- *adj* sober
unsuti *sn* disorder, insurrection
unsweiband- *part adj* unceasing
unswer- *adj* without honor, shameful
unsweran *wv 3* dishonor, treat shamefully
unswerei *wf* shame, disgrace, dishonor
unsweriþa *sf* disgrace, dishonor
unswikunþoz- *comp adj* less known, more unknown
untal- *adj* uneducated, foolish; disobedient
unte *conj* because, since, until; that (§14.2)
untilamalsk- *adj* rash, arrogant
untriggw- *adj* unfaithful, unreliable
unþaþliuhan *sv 2* escape
unþiuda *sf* a non-people (cf. Deut. 32:21)
unþiuþ *sn* evil, wickedness
unþiuþjan *wv 1* to curse
unþwahan- *part adj* unwashed
unufbrikand- *part adj* giving no offense
unuhteigo *adv* inopportunely
unuslaisid- *part adj* uneducated
unusspillod- *part adj* unexpoundable, beyond understanding
unwah- *adj* blameless
unwairþaba *adv* in an unworthy manner
unwamm- *adj* pure, blameless
unwammei *wf* purity
unwaurstwo *wf* idler
unweis- *adj* ignorant (of: **bi** *A*), unlearned
unweniggo *adv* unexpectedly
unwerein *As* indignation
unwerjan *wv 1* be unable to tolerate, be displeased with
unwis- *adj* uncertain
unwita *wm* a senseless person
unwitand- *part adj* ignorant
unwiti *sn* ignorance, folly
unwunand- *part adj* anxious, troubled
urraisjan *wv 1* raise, rouse, awaken
urrannjan *wv 1* cause to come forth, cause to rise
urreisan *sv 1* arise
urrinnan *sv 3* go forth, go out from, proceed; spring up (of seed); rise (of sun)
urrists *sf* resurrection
urrugk- *adj* (meaning uncertain: depraved?)
urrumnan *wv 4* spread, expand (intrans.)
urruns *sf* departure
urruns *sm* evacuation (fecal); the East, sunrise
us *prep D* out, out of, from (§1.4)
usagjan *wv 1* frighten badly, terrify
usaiwjan *wv 1* exert oneself
usalþan *sv 7* grow old
usanan *sv 6* die, expire
usbairan *sv 4* carry out; bear, endure, suffer
usbalþei *wf* constant irritation
usbaugjan *wv 1* sweep out
usbeidan *sv 1* await, look for; be patient with (**ana** *D*)
usbeisnei *wf* patience, long-suffering
usbeisneig- *adj* patient, long-suffering
usbeisns *sf* patience, long-suffering
usbidjan *sv 5* obtain through prayer
usbliggwan *sv 3* beat severely, scourge
usbloteins *sf vn* entreaty
usbraidjan *wv 1* extend, reach out
usbruknan *wv 4* be broken
usbugjan *wv 1* buy
usdaud- *adj* zealous; comp **usdaudoz**-
usdaudei *wf* zeal, perseverance
usdaudjan *wv 1* strive, endeavor, try hard

usdaudo *adv* zealously
usdreiban *sv 1* drive out, send away (*D* or *A*)
usdriusan *sv 2* go back on a promise
usdrusts *sf* a falling away, rough road
usfairin- *adj* blameless
usfarþo *wf* in **usfarþon gataujan us skipa** be shipwrecked
usfilh *sn* burial
usfilhan *sv 3* bury
usfilm- *adj* amazed, astonished
usfilmei *wf* astonishment
usfodeins *sf vn* food, nourishment
usfraisan *sv 7* tempt
usfratwjan *wv 1* make wise
usfulleins *sf vn* fullness, fulfillment
usfulljan *wv 1* fulfill, complete
usfullnan *wv 4* be fulfilled, be brought to completion, come to pass
usgaggan *sv 7* go out, go forth, go away (out of: **ut us** *D*)
usgaisjan *wv 1* astound, make aghast; passive: be beside oneself
usgeisnan *wv 4* be amazed, astonished, dismayed, aghast
usgiban *sv 5* give out, reward, pay; restore, show
usgildan *sv 3* repay, reward (smn: *D*)
usgraban *sv 6* dig out, dig through, pluck out
usgrudj- *adj* lazy, listless
usgutnan *wv 4* flow out, gush out, be poured out
ushafjan *sv 6* take up, lift up; w. **sik**: depart
ushahan sik *wv 3* hang oneself
ushaist- *adj* poor, needy
ushaitan *sv 7* provoke
ushauhjan *wv 1* exalt
ushauhnan *wv 4* be exalted
ushinþan *sv 3* take away as captive
ushlaupan *sv 7* leap up, rise quickly
ushrainjan *wv 1* clean out, sweep out
ushramjan *wv 1* crucify, hang
ushrisjan *wv 1* shake off
ushulon *wv 2* hollow out
uskannjan *wv 1* make known
uskeinan (P **-keinoda**) *sv 1 irreg* spring up, grow; put forth, produce
uskiusan *sv 2* single out, test (*A*); cast out, reject (*D*)
uskunþ- *adj* evident, manifest, well-known
uslagjan *wv 1* lay out, stretch out; + **handuns** place one's hands (on: **ana** *A*)
uslaisjan *wv 1* instruct
uslaubjan *wv 1* allow, permit (smn: *D;* to do: inf.); tolerate
uslauseins *sf vn* redemption
uslausjan *wv 1* redeem, set free
usleiþan *sv 1* go away, go or come out (from: *A*, **us** *D*); pass out (through: **þairh** *A*); set out (across: **hindar** *A*)
usletan *sv 7* exclude, shut out
usliþa *wm* a paralyzed person
usluk *sn* opening
uslukan *sv 2 irreg* open, draw (sword)
usluknan *wv 4* be opened, unlocked
usluneins *sf vn* redemption
usluton *wv 2* lead into error
usmaitan *sv* 7 (P **usmaimait**) cut down, off
usmanagnan *wv 4* increase (intrans.)
usmernan *wv 4* be preached, proclaimed
usmet *sn* behavior, lifestyle
usmitan *sv 5* behave, conduct oneself; **uswiss usmitan** be in error
usniman *sv 4* take out, away, down
usqiman *sv 4* destroy, kill (*A* or *D*)
usqiss (*D* **-ssai**) *sf* accusation
usqistjan *wv 1* to kill (*A* or *D*)
usqiþan *sv 5* proclaim, bruit about
ussaihwan *sv 5* look up, observe; to receive one's sight
ussakan *sv 6* lay before, present (in arguing)
ussaljan *wv 1* stay over night with
ussandjan *wv 1* send out, forth, away
ussateins *sf vn* (meaning uncertain: origin, birth?)
ussatjan *wv 1* set, place; plant, lay out; beget
ussiggwan *sv 3* recite, read
ussindo *adv* especially
ussitan *sv 5* sit up
usskarjan *wv 1* in passive: recover oneself
ussokjan *wv 1* investigate
usspillon *wv 2* tell, inform; expound fully
usstaggan *sv (?)* pluck out, tear out
usstandan *sv 6* stand up, rise up, come out or from (a place: **us** *D*); to rise from the dead
usstass (*G* **-ssais**) *sf* resurrection
ussteigan *sv 1* go up, ascend (into: **in** *A*; onto: **ana** *A*)
usstiurei *wf* excess; riot
usstiuriba *adv* licentiously, riotously
ustaikneins *sf vn* demonstration, proof; manifestation; singling out, designation
ustaiknjan *wv 1* show, demonstrate; single out
ustauhts *sf* end, completion, fulfillment
ustiuhan *sv 2* lead out, up; take up; drive forth; finish, perfect
usþriutan *sv 2* threaten, trouble
usþroþeins *sf vn* exercise, training
usþroþjan *wv 1* exercise, train
usþulains *sf vn* patience

usþulan *wv 3* endure, put up with
usþwahan *sv 6* wash out
uswahsan- *part adj* full-grown
uswahsts *sf* growth, increase
uswairpan *sv 3* cast out, drive out, overthrow
uswakjan *wv 1* wake up (intrans.)
uswalteins *sf vn* overthrow, subverting
uswaltjan *wv 1* overthrow, overturn
uswandi *sf* scheming, craftiness
uswandjan sis *wv 1* turn oneself away from *(D)*
uswaurht- *adj* just, righteous, right
uswaurhts *sf* justice
uswaurpa *sf* rejection
usweih- *adj* unholy, profane
uswen- *adj* having no hope (of: *G*)
uswindan *sv 3* to plait, braid
uswiss- *adj* dissolute, vain
uswissi *sn* vanity
ut *adv* out, forth
uta *adv* outside
utana *prep G* from outside (of); *adv* outside
utaþro *prep G* from outside (of)
utbairan *sv 4* carry out, convey out
utgaggan *sv 7* go out
uzeta *wm* manger
uzon *pret* of **usanan**
uzu = **us** + **-u**
uzuh = **us** + **-uh**

W

waddjus* *sf* wall
wadi *sn* pledge, security deposit
wadjaboka* *sf* promissory note
-wadjon: gawadjon
waggari* *sn* pillow
waggs *sm* paradise
wagjan *wv 1* shake, move (cf. **af-**, **ga-**, **in-**, **us-**)
wahsjan *sv 6* grow, increase (cf. **ufar-**, **us-**)
wahstus *sm* growth, stature
wahtwo *wf* watch
wai *interj* woe! **wai nei** ...! if only ...! would that ...!
waian *sv* 7 (P **waiwo**) to blow
-waibjan: biwaibjan
waidedja *wm* criminal, evil-doer
waifairhwjan *wv 1* wail, lament loudly
waihjo *wf* battle, struggle
waihsta *wm* corner
waihstastains *sm* cornerstone
waiht *sn*, **waihts** *sf* thing, affair; usually with neg. **ni: ni waiht** (*A*) nothing; **ni waihtai** in nothing at all, not at all
waila *adv* well, rightly
wailadeþs (*G* **-dedais**) *sf* benefit
wailamereins *sf vn* (good) news; good repute
wailamerj- *adj* praiseworthy
wailamerjan *wv 1* preach (as) good tidings
wailaqiss *sf* blessing
wailawisan *sv 5* to feast, carouse
wailawizns *sf* nourishment, well-being
wainah- *adj* needy (reading not certain)
wainei *interj* would that...!
-waipjan: faurwaipjan
waips *sm(?)* crown, wreath
wair *sm* man
wairaleiko *adv* in a manly fashion
wairdus *sm* host
wairilo *wf(?)* lip
wairpan *sv 3* throw, cast (sthg: *D* or *A*); **stainam wairpan** to stone (smn: *A*) (cf. **af-**, **at-**, **fra-**, **ga-**, **inn-**, **us**)
wairs *adv* worse
wairsiz- *comp adj* worse
wairþ *sn(?)* price, value
wairþ- *adj* worthy (of: *G*; to do: inf.); *A* **wairþana briggan** make smn (*A*) worthy (of: *G*)
wairþan *sv 3* become, happen, be, take place; to take up with, reside with (*D*) (cf. **fra-**)
wairþida *sf* worthiness, dignity
-wairþjan: gagawairþjan
-wairþnan: gagawairþnan
wairþon *wv 2* to treasure, value
wait *PP* I know (**witan**)
waitei *adv* perhaps
wajamereins *sf vn* blasphemy; ill repute
wajamerjan *wv 1* slander, blaspheme, speak ill of
wakan *sv 6* wake up, be watchful (cf. **þairh-**)
-wakjan: uswakjan
-waknan: gawaknan
waldan *sv 7* to rule, govern (cf. **ga-**)
waldufni *sn* power, dominion; authority
walis- *adj* genuine, legitimate
waljan *wv 1* choose (cf. **ga-**)
waltjan *wv 1* roll, beat or dash against (cf. **us-**)
-walugjan: uswalugjan (reading uncertain)
walus *sm* staff
walwison *wv 2* to wallow
-walwjan: afwalwjan, atwalwjan, faurwalwjan
wamba *sf* belly, womb
wamme *Gpl* spot, stain

-**wammjan: anawammjan**
wan *sn* want, lack; **wan wisan** *D* to be lacking to
wan- *adj* lacking, wanting
wanains *sf vn* lack, failure
wandjan *wv 1* turn, turn around (cf. **af-**, **at-**, **bi-**, **ga-**, **in-**, **us-**)
wandus *sm* staff
waninassus *sm* want, need, lack
war- *adj* sober, attentive
wardja *wm* guard
-**wardjan: frawardjan**
warei *wf* caution, cunning
wargiþa *sf* condemnation
-**wargjan: gawargjan**
warjan *wv 1* forbid
warmjan *wv 1* to warm; to cherish
wasjan *wv 1* to clothe (cf. **and-**, **ga-**)
wasti *sf* clothing
wato *wn* water (§6.1)
waurd *sn* word
waurdah- *adj* verbal, having the ability to speak
waurdajiuka *sf* strife about words
-**waurdjan: andwaurdjan, filuwaurdjan, ubilwaurdjan**
waurkjan *wv 1* (*P* **waurhta** §6.2) to work, do, perform; fashion, create; cause (*A*; to do: inf.; to be: adj.) (cf. **fair-**, **fra-**, **ga-**, **us-**)
waurms *sm* snake
waurstw *sn* work, deed
waurstwa *wm* worker
waurstwei *wf* work, activity
waurstweig- *adj* effective; real, actual
waurstwja *wm* worker, laborer
waurts *sf* root
wegs (*irreg Dpl* **wegim**) *sm* wave; storm
weih- *adj* holy
weiha *sm* priest
weihan *wv 3* sanctify, make holy (cf. **ga-**)
weihan *sv 1* to fight, strive (cf. **and-**)
weihiþa *sf* holiness
weihnan *wv 4* become holy, be hallowed
weihs (*G* **weihsis**) *sn* town, village
wein *sn* wine
weinabasi *sn* grape
weinagards *sm(i)* vineyard
weinatains *sm* vine-branch
weinatriu *sn* vine
weindrugkja *wm* wine-drinker
weipan *sv 1* to crown
weis *pers pron* we (§10.5)
-**weisjan: fullaweisjan, gafullaweisjan**
-**weison: gaweison**
-**weitan: fraweitan, inweitan**
-**weitjan: fairweitjan, idweitjan**
weitwodei *wf* witness, testimony
weitwodi *sn* testimony
weitwodiþa *sf* testimony, witness
weitwodjan *wv 1* bear witness; **galiug weitwodjan** bear false witness (cf. **miþ-**)
weitwoþs *sm* (*Gpl* -**de**) witness (§10.2)
wenjan *wv 1* to hope, expect (that...: inf. or **ei** + subj.); to set one's hopes (on: **du** *D*) (cf. **faura-**, **ga-**)
wens *sf* hope, expectation
wepn* *sn* weapon
-**werjan: tuzwerjan, unwerjan**
-**widan: gawidan, inwidan**
widuwairn- *adj* orphaned; comfortless
widuwairna *wm* orphan
widuwo *wf* widow
wigadeinom *Dpl* thornbushes
-**wigan: gawigan**
wigans *sm* war ? (Luke 14:31)
wigs *sm* road, way, journey
wiko *wf* cyclical time period
wilja *wm* will, wish
wiljahalþei *wf* respect of person, partiality
wiljan *v* be willing, will, wish (§§11.3, 15.2)
wilþj- *adj* wild; not cultivated
wilwa *wm* robber
wilwan *sv 3* rob, take by force (cf. **dis-**, **fra-**)
-**windan** *sv 3* to wind (cf. **bi-**, **duga-**, **us-**)
winds *sm* wind
winja *sf* pasture
winna *sf* sorrow, suffering
winnan *sv 3* suffer, sorrow (cf. **ga-**)
winno *wf* sorrow, suffering
wintrus *sm* winter
winþiskauro *wf* winnowing-fan
-**winþjan: diswinþjan**
wipja *sf* crown
wis *sn* calm sea
wisan[1] *sv 5* be (cf. **at-**, **faura-**, **fra-**, **in-**, **miþ-**, **ufar**) (§§6.4, 15.2)
wisan[2] *sv 5* to feast, carouse (cf. **waila-**)
wisan[3] *sv 5* remain, dwell (cf. **ga-**, **miþga-**, **þairh-**); but see p. 62, note 4.
wists *sf* being, existence; **wistai, us wistai** by nature
wit *pers pron dual N* we two
witan* *PP* (§16.3) know (sthg: *A*; that...: **þatei** or **ei** + indic.)
witan *wv 3* guard, keep an eye on (*D*); observe, keep (laws etc.: *D*)

witodafasteis *sm* expert in the law
witodalaisareis *sm* teacher of the law
witodalaus- *adj* lawless
witodeigo *adv* lawfully
witoþ *sn (G* **witodis**) law; the Law of Moses
witubni *sn* knowledge
wiþon *wv 2* shake, wag
wiþra *prep A* against, over against; by, near; to, in reply to, in return for; on account of
wiþragaggan *sv 7* go to meet
wiþragamotjan *wv 1* go to meet
wiþrawairþ- *adj* situated opposite
wiþrus *sm* lamb
wizon *wv 2* revel, indulge oneself
wlaiton *wv 2* to look around
wlits *sm* face, countenance
wlizjan *wv 1* strike in the face
wod- *adj* mad, possessed by demons
wokains *sf vn* vigil, watch by night
wokra *Ds* interest (on money)
wopjan *wv 1* cry out (to: *D*, **du** *D*); crow (cf. **at-**, **uf-**)
woþj- *adj* sweet
wraiq- *adj* crooked
wraka, wrakja *sf* persecution
wrakjan *wv 1* persecute
wraks *sm* persecutor
wratodus *sm* journey
wraton *wv 2* to travel
wrekei *wf* persecution
wrikan *sv 5* persecute (cf. **fra-**, **ga-**)
-wrisqan: gawrisqan
writ *sm(i)* stroke, point (in written text)
wriþus *sm* herd
wrohjan *wv 1* accuse, bring charges against (cf. **fra-**)
wrohs *sf* accusation
wruggo *wf* snare
wulan *sv 4* seethe, rage
wulfs *sm* wolf
wulla *sf* wool
wullareis *sm* wool-washer, fuller
wulþag- *adj* glorious
wulþriz- *adj comp* worthier
wulþrs *sf* value, worth
wulþus *sm* glory, splendor
wulwa *sf* robbery
wund- *adj* wounded; **haubiþ wundan briggan** to wound in the head
-wundon: gawundon
wundufni *sf* wound, affliction
wunns *sf* suffering, affliction

X

Xristus *proper name* Christ (Voc. 13)

Selected Bibliography

The Goths

Hodgkin, T. *Italy and her Invaders*, 3 vols., 2nd ed., 1892-6 (reprinted New York, 1967).

Thompson, E. A. *The Goths in Spain*, Oxford, 1969.

Schütte, G. *Our Forefathers, the Gothonic Nations*, Cambridge, vol. 1, 1929; vol. 2, 1933.

Schmidt, L. *Geschichte der deutschen Stämme bis zum Ausgange der Völkerwanderung.* I. Abt. *Die Geschichte der Ostgermanen*, 2nd ed., Munich, 1934.

The Gothic Language

Wright, Joseph. *Grammar of the Gothic Language.* Second edition with a supplement to the grammar by O. L. Sayce, Oxford, 1954.

Streitberg, W. *Gotisches Elementarbuch.* 6th ed., Heidelberg, 1920.

Mossé, F. *Manuel de la langue gothique*, Paris, 1942.

Bennett, W. H. *An Introduction to the Gothic Language.* New York, 1980.

The Gothic Bible, the Skeireins, and Other Texts

Bennett, W. H. *The Gothic Commentary on the Gospel of John: Skeireins aiwaggeljons þairh Iohannen.* New York, 1966.

Dietrich, E. *Die Bruchstücke der Skeireins. (Texte und Untersuchungen zur altgermanischen Religionsgeschichte. Texte:* II. Band) Strasbourg, 1903.

Streitberg, W. *Die Gotische Bibel.* I. Teil. *Der gotische Text und seine griechische Vorlage mit Einleitung, Lesearten und Quellennachweisen, so wie den kleineren Denkmälern als Anhang*; II. Teil. *Gotisch-griechisch-deutsches Wörterbuch*, 7th ed., with a supplement by P. Scardigli, Heidelberg, 2000.

The Germanic Languages

Hirt, H. *Handbuch des Urgermanischen*, Heidelberg. Teil I. *Laut- und Akzentlehre*, 1931; Teil II. *Stammbildungs- und Flexionslehre*, 1932; Teil III. *Abriss der Syntax*, 1934.

Prokosch, E. *A Comparative Germanic Grammar*, Philadelphia, 1939.

Etymological Dictionaries: Gothic and IE

Feist, S. *Vergleichendes Wörterbuch der gotischen Sprache mit Einschluss des Krimgotischen und sonstiger zerstreuter Überreste des Gotischen*, 3rd ed., revised and corrected. Leiden, 1939.

Holthausen, F. *Gotisches etymologisches Wörterbuch. Mit Einschluss der Eigennamen und der gotischen Lehnwörter im Romanischen*, Heidelberg, 1934.

Lehmann, W. P. *A Gothic Etymological Dictionary.* Leiden, 1986.

LIV: Rix, Helmut, ed. *Lexikon der indogermanischen Verben; die Wurzeln und ihre Primärstammbildungen*, Wiesbaden, 1998.

Pokorny, J. *Indogermanisches etymologisches Wörterbuch*, 3rd ed., Tübingen and Basel, 1994.

Bibliography

Mossé, F. *Bibliographia Gothica. A Bibliography of Writings on the Gothic Language to the End of 1949. Toronto Medieval Studies* XII (1950).

Index of Etymologies (Gothic)

References are to the etymological sections of the Historical Grammar lessons.

References are to the relevant paragraphs in the grammatical Lessons.

Corrections and Emendations

Page	Line	For	Read
26	10	follow	follows
33	A24	**þo**	**þos**
54	8	εἶς	εἱς
56	C6	**þata is**	**þata ist**
63	B8	**du**	**þu**
68	9	**eis skulum**	**eis skulun**
71	C1 line 3	**ist**	**is**
76	14	τῇ	τῇ
78	16	**gadrauhts** *wm(i)*	**gadrauhts** *sm(i)*
83	2	leprousy	leprosy
93	36	**seinam**	**seinaim**
101	8	come	comes
105	C18	**is**	**ist**
111	15	elipsis	ellipsis
113	#29 line 3	manaseþs.	manaseþs."
228	10	*iu au au*	*iu eu au*
229	20	*r, l, m, n, w, y*	*ṛ, ḷ, ṃ, ṇ, ẉ, ỵ*
		y and w	*ỵ and ẉ*
234	11	**-ōi...*-oi, *-ei*	**-ōy...*-oy, *-ey*
236	34	*-ōi*	*-ōy*
242	22	**agro-n-om*	**aĝro-no-m*
259	21	**buɣta*	**buhta*
260	6	*q^wos*	*k^wos*
		hwas	*h^was*
284	31	**(g^we)gwóm-*	**(g^we)g^wóm-*
	32	**bhregh*	**bhreĝ*
		**(be)bhrógh-*	**(be)bhróĝ-*
		**bhrēgh-́*	**bhrēĝ-́*
302	15	original thematic	original athematic
310	19	IE **swek(u)ron*	IE **swekr(u)on*
	34	**kworyis < *kwo*	**k^woryis < *k^wo*
	35	**kwor*	**k^wor*
	36	**kwo-*	**k^wo-*
312	31	*?√lewg*	*IE ?√lewg*
355	37	**weiha** *sm*	**weiha** *wm*

In the Texts (pp. 141-226) read **ist** for **is** in the following verses:

150	Lk 6:4	178	Mk 12:7
156	Lk 9:9	180	Mk 15:34
158	Lk 10:7	186	Mt 10:26
165	Lk 20:14	190	Jn 7:6
166	Lk 20:22	205	Rom 9:5
170	Mk 4:26	208	Rom 10:12
172	Mk 6:18	226	1Tim 6:10

p. 103, line 22: Delete the entire sentence beginning "Contrast, for example, ..." The citation is not correct.

p. 118, line 10: Replace the first sentence "Most of the unprefixed nouns ..." with the following: "Most of the derivational processes which produced the various inflectional categories of nouns in IE (*o*-stems, *ā*-stems, *i*-stems etc.) are no longer productive in PG and Gothic."

p. 239, line 5: The IE forms should properly have a palatal *k̂*, i.e. **k̂emen-*, **ak̂men-*, and *√ak̂*, on the basis of the sibilant reflexes in the satem-languages, e.g. Skr. *açman* (stone, sky) < **ak̂-men-*. But several non-sibilant reflexes in BSl, including Russ *камень* cited here, point to a variant root with velar *k*. Pokorny (p. 18, note 1), however, attributes these phonological exceptions in BSl to a Veneto-Illyrian substratum. On p. 22 he suggests ("wahrscheinlich") that **k̂emen-* contains the zero grade of the root *√ak̂*, but on p. 557 (sub radice 3. *k̂em*) he calls this attribution to the root *√ak̂* on his own p. 22 "kaum richtig."

p. 240, line 11: Since the etymology of Gothic **ga-** from IE **kom* (see p. 287) is widely accepted in spite of the fact that the initial consonant is not the *h-* one would expect from Grimm's Law (p. 232), we should probably allow for a similar deviation with Gothic **du** < IE **dō*. In both cases we are probably dealing with a sporadic irregular voicing of PG voiceless consonants in unstressed positions (**du** is a prefix as well as a preposition) akin to the process known as Verner's Law (p. 232). Thus the equation of Gothic **du** with Eng *to*, Ger *zu*, would be valid.

p. 282: The dual and plural forms in the IE paradigm of **wóyda* should have *ỵ* for *y*; thus, *wỵdwé* etc.

p. 284, line 6. Delete the last half of the first paragraph beginning with the sentence "Although this change..." and replace it with the following: "The sound change involved here belongs to the earlier Proto-Indo-Iranian stage and can be substantiated by parallels in Avestan and Old Persian. The inherited perfect plural stem *sēd-* < **sayd-* in Sanskrit was reinforced by an identical type which developed from verbs whose initial consonant was *y-*, e.g. the perf. pl. stems *yēt-* < **yayt-* (root *yat* to stretch) and *yēm-* < **yaym-* (root *yam* to reach). These forms then provided the basis for the analogical extension of *-ē-* to the perf. pl. stems of other verbs."

p. 284, line 33: Delete Latin *sĕqu-ī*. Although a cognate of Gothic **saihwan**, the infinitive form *sequī* is not relevant to the discussion here. No active perfect form of Latin *sequī*, a deponent verb, is attested.

Passim: Because the spirantization of intervocalic voiced stops is posited as a change within PG (see p. 233, Remark 2), the PG forms given in the etymologies sometime have this spirantization indicated and sometimes not.

www.ingramcontent.com/pod-product-compliance
Lightning Source LLC
LaVergne TN
LVHW061236100826
845148LV00008B/969

* 9 7 8 1 5 9 7 5 2 3 9 4 3 *